MW01621075

FRA ANGELICO

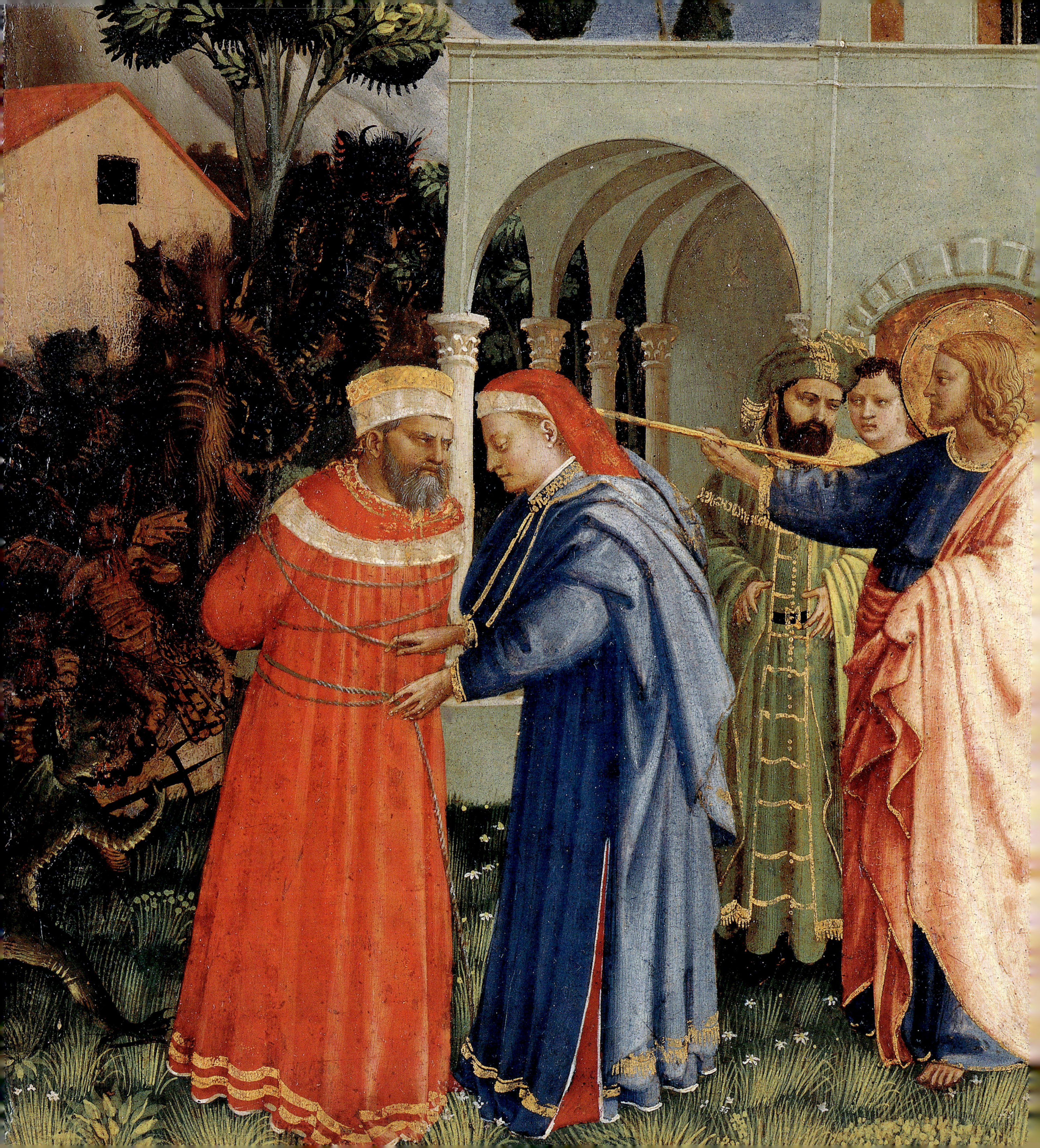

FRA ANGELICO

by Laurence Kanter and Pia Palladino

with contributions by Magnolia Scudieri, Carl Brandon Strehlke, Victor M. Schmidt, and Anneke de Vries

THE METROPOLITAN MUSEUM OF ART, NEW YORK

YALE UNIVERSITY PRESS, NEW HAVEN AND LONDON

This volume has been published in conjunction with the exhibition "Fra Angelico" held at The Metropolitan Museum of Art, New York, October 26, 2005–January 29, 2006.

The exhibition is made possible by the Homeland Foundation, Inc.

The exhibition catalogue is made possible in part by the Roswell L. Gilpatric Publications Fund.

The exhibition is supported by an indemnity from the Federal Council on the Arts and the Humanities.

Published by The Metropolitan Museum of Art, New York

John P. O'Neill, Editor in Chief
Gwen Roginsky, Associate General Manager of Publications
Ellen Shultz, Editor
Bruce Campbell, Designer
Margaret Rennolds Chace, Managing Editor
Paula Torres, Production Manager
Robert Weisberg, Assistant Managing Editor
Jayne Kuchna and Jean Wagner, Bibliographers

Translation of essay VI from the Italian by Pia Palladino

Cataloging-in-Publication Data
Kanter, Laurence B.
Fra Angelico / by Laurence Kanter and Pia Palladino ; with contributions by Magnolia Scudieri ... [et al.].
p. cm.
"This volume has been published in conjunction with the exhibition "Fra Angelico" held at The Metropolitan Museum of Art, New York, October 26, 2005–January 29, 2006."
Includes bibliographical references and index.
ISBN 1-58839-174-4 (hardcover) — ISBN 1-58839-175-2 (pbk.) — ISBN 0-300-11140-1 (Yale University Press)
1. Angelico, fra, ca. 1400–1455—Exhibitions. I. Palladino, Pia. II. Angelico, fra, ca. 1400–1455. III. Metropolitan Museum of Art (New York, N.Y.) IV. Title.
ND623.F5A4 2005
759.5–dc22 2005023349

Cover/jacket: Fra Angelico. *Paradise* (detail), left panel of *The Last Judgment* (see cat. 32)

Frontispiece: Fra Angelico. *The Apostle Saint James the Greater Freeing the Magician Hermogenes* (detail of cat. 25 A)

Printed and bound in Spain

CONTENTS

SPONSOR'S STATEMENT

The Homeland Foundation is honored to sponsor the "Fra Angelico" exhibition at The Metropolitan Museum of Art. As the Homeland Foundation supports a wide range of cultural, charitable, and religious programs and organizations, it is most fitting that it join with The Metropolitan Museum of Art in presenting the first comprehensive exhibition of the works of the great Italian Renaissance religious artist Fra Angelico, the "angelic friar," ever assembled on our shores.

The Homeland Foundation was founded in 1938 by financier and philanthropist Chauncey D. Stillman. Since Mr. Stillman's death in 1989, the Foundation has continued to honor his memory through its generosity in funding religious, intellectual, and cultural enterprises, and in its aid to the poorer citizens of the world.

The Homeland Foundation's sponsorship of projects in the art world—particularly those involving religious art—is longstanding and extensive. Its interest in the "Fra Angelico" exhibition stems from its participation in renovating the "Fra Angelico" chapel, also known as the Cappella Niccolina, at the Vatican. Recently, Homeland restored the Casina of Pius IV, the Papal Academy of Science, near Saint Peter's Basilica, which was built in 1560 and contains many striking examples of mosaics, frescoes, and stucco art.

Homeland has also made possible the restoration of Raphael's tapestry of *The Healing of the Lame Man* located in the Raphael Tapestry Room in the Pinacoteca Vaticana, and has helped to restore a fresco by Perugino and one by Cosimo Rosselli on the walls of the Sistine Chapel. In 1986, the Foundation hosted a discussion held in New York by those engaged in the complex task of cleaning and restoring the Sistine Chapel.

Homeland has seized the opportunity to lend its assistance in enabling the public to view at firsthand Fra Angelico's lavish, vibrantly colored works, with their monumental figures of the Holy Family, beautiful angels, glorious saints, and stately martyrs. They are a testament both to his consummate skill as an artist and to his sincere religious devotion. Fra Angelico was beatified by the Vatican in 1984.

The Homeland Foundation would like to thank Philippe de Montebello, Director of The Metropolitan Museum of Art, and the Museum's staff for their efforts in organizing this celebration of religious art in a magnificent exhibition for all to enjoy.

E. Lisk Wyckoff, Jr.
President
Homeland Foundation, Inc.

DIRECTOR'S FOREWORD

It is a commonplace, but nonetheless true, that the best-known artists are often the least understood. Generations of admirers cultivate an impression of the artist and his works that is frequently anecdotal and rarely revised or questioned, even though it may have been formulated in a period in which the biases and preferences were different from our own. So it has long been with Fra Angelico, who was among the earliest—if not the very first—Italian Renaissance painters to be restored to the canon of greatness after centuries of neglect in the English-, French-, and German-speaking world. Much of the nineteenth-century revival of interest in the *Pictor Angelicus* was founded upon the very evident and very powerful spiritual content of his paintings: legend described him as a humble and saintly friar who never picked up his brushes without praying first, and who shed tears whenever he painted a crucifix. This is the image of Fra Angelico that reigned in the popular imagination up through the time of the last (and only) monographic exhibition dedicated to the artist—held in Florence in 1955, to commemorate the fifth centennial of his death in 1455—and that may still be found in textbooks and studies published more recently. Indeed, although he had long been known as the Blessed Angelico—Beato Angelico, in Italian—his official beatification by Pope John Paul II in 1984 was the climax of a movement that began almost immediately after the artist's death and that could be said to have gathered nothing if not momentum over the succeeding five hundred years.

To be sure, cracks had already appeared in the façade of accepted wisdom before 1955, but it was only as a consequence of the exhibition that year that serious archival research into Angelico's life was undertaken, with surprising results. Almost overnight, it seemed, Angelico became a younger and more worldly man, whose career had begun well before his fortieth year as had previously been believed. From a modest, reclusive, and self-sufficient spiritualist, borrowing what he wished from the pictorial experiments of artists more innovative than himself, Angelico evolved into a competitive intellect and an active participant in the cultural revolution of early-fifteenth-century Florence. He also acquired a notably expanded corpus of works accepted as his, which, in turn, has greatly enhanced our appreciation of his artistic genius. It is in an effort to synthesize this newly mined information, to test new theories of interpretation, to scrutinize the new—and many old—attributions scattered through numerous specialized publications, and, of course, to stimulate even more critical reappraisal of Angelico's towering accomplishments that The Metropolitan Museum of Art takes great pride in presenting this exhibition, the most comprehensive since the centenary celebration of 1955 and the first ever outside of Italy.

It is increasingly difficult today to organize a monographic exhibition devoted to a Renaissance artist, the majority of whose works are painted either on wood panels, making them extremely fragile, or else in fresco, making them utterly immovable. Such an undertaking is all the more difficult for an artist so important and highly esteemed that even well-disposed individuals and institutions are chary of parting with the treasures by him jealously guarded in their collections. It is only through the exceptional generosity of private collectors and professional colleagues in museums around the globe—over fifty of whom have contributed to the success of this enterprise—that such a feat could now be realized. Although they are too numerous to thank individually, our gratitude to these lenders is limitless, both for the priceless works of art they have entrusted to our care and for this expression of their belief in our mission.

I am certain that the confidence and support of the lenders are due in no small measure to their respect for our curatorial and conservation staff, especially Laurence Kanter, Pia Palladino, George Bisacca, Charlotte Hale, and Dorothy Mahon: their original insights, careful research, and patient attention to details have made possible the unforgettably pleasurable communion with one of the greatest artistic minds of the Western tradition, whose masterpieces are presented on the walls of our galleries and in the pages of this catalogue. Seventy-five works by Fra Angelico—some of them new attributions, many never seen publicly before, and several cleaned for this occasion, revealing them to be of unexpected quality—are arranged alongside forty-five works by his assistants and closest followers, to create an entirely new impression of the development of Florentine painting in the early years of the fifteenth century. For the first time ever, Fra Angelico may be seen to have enjoyed a flourishing career between 1410 and 1420, before his great contemporary Masaccio had even turned seventeen years old: something long known from documents to have been true, but not previously demonstrable on the basis of surviving works of art. Techniques of physical examination and analysis not available to earlier generations of scholars now permit a more accurate assessment of Angelico's style as a draftsman, making visible the preparatory underdrawings preserved beneath layers of pigment on his panel paintings and thus providing a new standard for attributions of his surviving works on paper, all but one of which are included in this exhibition. Technical examination, often allied with clever intuition, has also made possible the recognition of many paintings, once thought to be entirely independent of one another, as fragments of a single altarpiece or tabernacle, radically altering our vision of the artist's working method and his chronology. Very few of these advances would have been feasible without the opportunity for close and extended study provided by this exhibition.

No amount of planning, research, or diplomacy will result in a great exhibition without the generous support of enlightened patronage, and we have been unusually fortunate in this instance to have discovered the perfect patron in the Homeland Foundation, Inc., whose long-standing involvement in cultural and religious projects is well known. Their sponsorship of the cleaning of Angelico's frescoes in the Cappella Niccolina at the Vatican, as well as their interest in the fifteenth-century decoration of the Sistine Chapel, prepared them for the complexities of an enterprise such as this, and their enthusiastic commitment has made possible much that would otherwise have been scarcely imaginable. The exhibition catalogue is made possible in part by the Roswell L. Gilpatric Publications Fund. As always, we are grateful to the Robert Lehman Foundation for their generous contribution not only of the galleries in which this exhibition is mounted, but also of the time dedicated to this project by the curators of their Collection—Laurence Kanter and Pia Palladino—who have worked unremittingly for nearly three years to bring about its realization.

Philippe de Montebello
Director, The Metropolitan Museum of Art

ACKNOWLEDGMENTS

The idea of mounting a monographic exhibition of the work of Fra Angelico was first floated, timidly, in April 2002, but was quickly shelved as hopelessly unrealistic. A short time later, acting on the encouragement of numerous friends, a sketchy and cautious outline was presented to Philippe de Montebello, who immediately lent his enthusiastic support to a proposal that must have seemed to him unlikely ever to come to fruition. To Philippe, therefore, we owe our first debt of gratitude, although our deepest obligation is to the many lenders—their number far exceeded our most optimistic expectations—who approved our importunate requests, and to the Homeland Foundation, Inc., whose generous sponsorship enabled this project to become a reality. Without the combined good will of all these individuals and institutions, our acknowledgments would be entirely academic.

Four colleagues and friends—Magnolia Scudieri, Carl Strehlke, Victor Schmidt, and Anneke de Vries—are credited on the title page for their contributions to this book and to the exhibition, and we would like to emphasize here how much poorer both would have been without their participation. All four of them not only put aside other projects to find time to write about Fra Angelico but were unstintingly generous with ideas and advice, as well as diplomatic with criticisms, in our many conversations. Less obvious, because their names are not recorded on the title page of this volume, yet equally consequential has been the input of two colleagues in the Department of Paintings Conservation at The Metropolitan Museum of Art: George Bisacca and Charlotte Hale. Their assistance with the technical analysis of works by Fra Angelico has led to important new insights into the artist's working method, and Charlotte's cleaning and restoration of Angelico's Rotterdam *Madonna* (cat. 6), unfortunately begun too late to be fully documented here, has been nothing less than a revelation. It is impossible to imagine that this painting could ever have been doubted as a masterpiece by Fra Angelico had it always been known in its cleaned state, free of the coarse overpaints that encrusted its surface and obscured its original qualities for perhaps as many as four centuries. At least three more paintings—the *Saint Peter Preaching* (cat. 29) from the Museo di San Marco, *Saint Francis's Trial by Fire before the Sultan* (cat. 24 A) from the Lindenau-Museum, Altenburg, Germany, and the *Scenes from the* Ninfale Fiesolano (cat. 2) from the Bowdoin College Museum of Art—were cleaned for this exhibition with exciting results, and many others were treated, to varying degrees, in preparation for their journey to New York. We are grateful to all the superintendencies, museums, and conservation facilities that authorized or undertook this work, especially to Jeroen Giltaij in Rotterdam, Jutta Penndorf in Altenburg, Katy Kline at Bowdoin, Holger Manzke in Berlin, Dianne Dwyer Modestini in New York, and the entire staff at the Museo di San Marco and at the Opificio delle Pietre Dure in Florence.

Research for this exhibition was facilitated by the collegiality and generosity of countless individuals, among whom we would particularly like to thank Mark Aronson, Carmen Bambach, Roberta Bartoli, Roberto Bellucci, Giorgio Bonsanti, Miklós Boskovits, Alessandro Cecchi, Giampaolo Chinellato, Keith Christiansen, Marco Ciatti, Roberto Contini, Andrea Di Lorenzo, Consuelo Dutschke, Albert Elen, Everett Fahy, Ross Finocchio, Gaudenz Freuler, Cecilia Frosinini, Patricia Garland, Dillian Gordon, Stratton Green, Nica Gutman, Sandra Hindman, Erica Holmquist-Wall, Steven Kornhauser, Michel Laclotte, Margaret Lawson, Anne Leader, Mark Leonard, Jeanne McKee-Rothe, Anastasia Mikliaeva, Norman Muller, Andrea Rothe, Elliot Rowlands, Dora Sallay, Laurent Sozzani, Serena Urry, Elizabeth Walmsley, Tim Warner-Johnson, Catherine Whistler, and Amee Yunn. Additionally, for their help not only in securing priceless information but also in pursuing many delicate loans (some of which did not materialize, almost as much to the regret of the would-be lenders as to our own), we would like to thank Rita Albertson, Sivigliano Alloisi, Rafael Alonso, Joseph Baillio, Sergio Benedetti, Duncan Bull, Robert Burke, Peter Cannon-Brookes, Matteo Ceriana, Hugo Chapman, Alan Chong, Anthony Crichton-Stuart, Elizabeth Easton, Anne Eschapasse, Richard Feigen, Larry Feinberg, Lucia Fornari Scanchi, Francesca Giampaolo, Marco Grassi, Nicholas Hall, Derek Johns, Raymond Keaveney, George Keyes, Christopher Lloyd, Archbishop Celestino

Migliore, Esther Moench, Arnold Nesselrath, Lynne Orr, Giuseppe Pavanello, Beata Piasecka, Luciana Prati, Jock Reynolds, Betsy Rosasco, Paola Rosina, Francis Russell, His Excellency the Duque de San Carlos, Elena Sharnova, Hannah Singer, William P. Stoneman, Cornelia Syre, Luke Syson, Jacqueline Thalman, Dominique Thiebaut, Ernst Vegelin van Claerbergen, Stefan Weppelman, Stefan Wolohojian, Eric Zaffran, and all the owners and museum directors who allowed us access to their files and to their works of art.

Every exhibition—and exhibition catalogue—is a product of collaboration among highly talented professionals, very few of whom are mentioned on a title page or even singled out for special thanks in acknowledgments. It is impossible to redress this oversight here, except to express our sincere gratitude to everyone at The Metropolitan Museum of Art involved in the editing, design, and production of this catalogue; in the preliminary and the final stages of the organization, transport, installation, labeling, and lighting of this exhibition; in the financing; in the publicity and the educational programs; and in every aspect of the thousands of miscellaneous but critical chores that contribute to the success of any undertaking on this scale. Special thanks are due to Dan Kershaw, Sophia Geronimus, Herb Moskowitz, and Egle Žygas, and to our indefatigable editor, Ellen Shultz. Above all, however, we are indebted to Lesley Schorpp in the Robert Lehman Collection, whose patience, organizational skills, and good humor ensured that no details were overlooked and no problems grew too large to be resolved. As always, we are indebted to the directors of the Robert Lehman Foundation for their support of our work and for their committed belief in the value and importance of scholarship in museums. Finally, we would like to offer a word of thanks, for all their help over the years, to two individuals who unfortunately cannot be here to share our pleasure in this exhibition: Hubert von Sonnenberg, who took a great interest in this project almost from its inception; and John Pope-Hennessy, who loved Fra Angelico and who almost certainly would have disagreed with at the very least half (or perhaps more) of the contentions advanced in the following pages.

Laurence Kanter and Pia Palladino

LENDERS TO THE EXHIBITION

AUSTRIA
Vienna, Graphische Sammlung Albertina: 22

DENMARK
Copenhagen, Statens Museum for Kunst: 1 A, 1 C

FRANCE
Paris, Musée du Louvre: 30 C, 34 I, 42 B
Strasbourg, Musée des Beaux-Arts: 54 B

GERMANY
Altenburg, Lindenau-Museum: 24 A, 34 D, 34 E, 34 F
Berlin, Gemäldegalerie, Staatliche Museen Preussischer Kulturbesitz: 32
Munich, Alte Pinakothek, Bayerische Staatsgemäldesammlungen: 21 C, 21 D
Stuttgart, Staatsgalerie: 37 C

IRELAND
Dublin, National Gallery of Ireland: 34 H

ITALY
Florence, Museo di San Marco: 25 B, 29
Forlì, Pinacoteca Civica: 27 A, 27 B
Livorno, Parrocchia di Santa Maria del Soccorso: 33
Parma, Galleria Nazionale: 21 A
Perugia, Galleria Nazionale dell' Umbria: 30 B
Turin, Galleria Sabauda: 25 I
Vatican City, Vatican Museums: 24 B, 30 A
Venice, Fondazione Giorgio Cini: 34 B, 46 B, 49

THE NETHERLANDS
Amsterdam, Rijksmuseum: 31 B
Rotterdam, Museum Boijmans Van Beuningen: 6, 47 A, 47 B, 47 C, 47 D, 47 E, 47 F, 47 I

SPAIN
Barcelona, Museu Nacional d'Art de Catalunya: 18

SWITZERLAND
Bern, Kunstmuseum: 7, 35

UNITED KINGDOM
London
British Museum: 26
Courtauld Institute of Art Gallery: 13 A, 13 B, 13 C
National Gallery: 10 B, 10 C, 21 B, 44 D
H.M. Queen Elizabeth II: 25 H
Oxford, Christ Church Picture Gallery: 42 A

UNITED STATES
California
Los Angeles, J. Paul Getty Museum: 16 A, 16 B, 41
San Francisco, The Fine Arts Museums of San Francisco: 25 E, 52
Connecticut
Hartford, The Wadsworth Atheneum Museum of Art: 31 A
New Haven, Yale University Art Gallery: 16 C, 16 D, 37 A, 44 B
Washington, D.C.
National Gallery of Art: 34 G
Illinois
Chicago, The Art Institute of Chicago: 34 C
Maine
Brunswick, Bowdoin College Museum of Art: 2
Massachusetts
Boston
Isabella Stewart Gardner Museum: 28
Museum of Fine Arts: 36 A, 57
Cambridge
Fogg Art Museum, Harvard University Art Museums: 14, 39, 47 G, 47 H
Houghton Library, Harvard University: 5 A, 5 B, 5 C
Williamstown, The Sterling and Francine Clark Art Institute: 54 A
Worcester, Worcester Art Museum: 48, 55

Michigan
Detroit, The Detroit Institute of Arts: 20, 25 F, 25 G, 60
Minnesota
Minneapolis, The Minneapolis Institute of Arts: 17, 34 A
New Jersey
Princeton, The Art Museum, Princeton University: 9
New York
Brooklyn, Brooklyn Museum: 50
Buffalo, Albright-Knox Art Gallery: 5 D
Glens Falls, The Hyde Collection: 44 A
New York
Collection Richard L. Feigen: 4, 25 D, 43, 58, 59, 61
The Metropolitan Museum of Art: 1 B, 5 E, 8, 10 A, 17, 23, 37 B, 44 C, 46 A, 51, 53, 56
Ohio
Cleveland, The Cleveland Museum of Art: 15, 40 A
Pennsylvania
Philadelphia, Philadelphia Museum of Art: 25 C
Texas
Fort Worth, Kimbell Art Museum: 25 A

Private collection(s): 3 A, 3 B, 12 A, 12 B, 36 B, 38, 40 B, 45

Collection T. Robert and Katherine States Burke: 19

The Barbara Piasecka Johnson Collection Foundation: 11

FRA ANGELICO

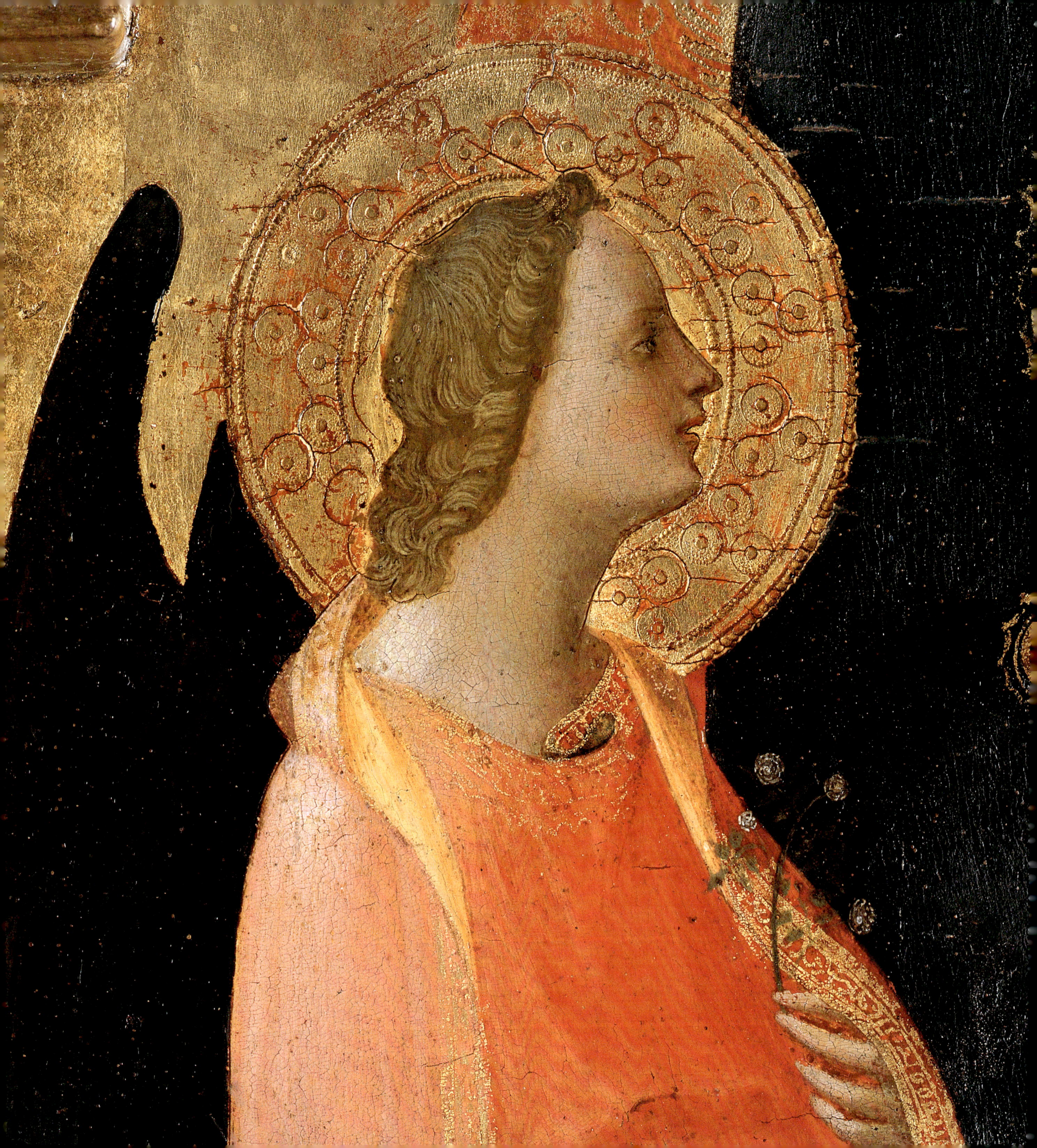

Chapter I
Fra Angelico: The Early Works (about 1410–21)

LAURENCE KANTER

Opposite:
Fra Angelico. *Virgin and Child Enthroned, with Two Angels* (detail of cat. 6, during treatment)

The early career of the artist who would come to be known as Fra Angelico has always been a subject of speculation—one that, until relatively recently, has been based on misleading popular tradition and a paucity of documentary evidence. As with so many Renaissance painters, in the case of Fra Angelico popular tradition derived from the biography of him included in Giorgio Vasari's *Lives of the Painters*, first published in 1550, revised in 1568, and relied upon uncritically for nearly four centuries afterward as an unimpeachable source for "historical" information about the painter.[1] According to Vasari, Angelico was born in 1387 and entered the Dominican order at the age of twenty in 1407, taking up residence in the Observant community at Foligno prior to the establishment of the new convent at San Domenico in Fiesole. For generations of admirers who had embraced Angelico as the embodiment of spiritual values in Renaissance painting, these "facts" were adequate to establish the artist's origins and his unique merits: it was his vocation as a Dominican, and, even more, his adherence to the strict observance of the Rule of that order, which both distinguished him from other painters and explained the distinctive qualities of his style. In keeping with the image of the artist as the devout and contemplative soul portrayed by Vasari, it was more appropriate to emphasize his resistance to the secular, humanistic influences converging around him in early-fifteenth-century Florence than to assess his possible role in advancing their progress.

As the maturing discipline of art history shifted its focus from Romantic biography to historical documentation and more penetrating deduction from visual evidence, it became increasingly apparent that this profile of the artist was not entirely satisfactory. The earliest known document referring to a surviving painting by Fra Angelico concerned a small payment, registered in 1429, for the high altarpiece of the Dominican convent of San Pier Martire in Florence (see cat. 13).[2] Notwithstanding the fact that he would have been over forty years old at the time, it was difficult for scholars to agree on identifying more than a handful of works by Angelico that might have been painted earlier than this one. Acknowledging that all, or nearly all, of Angelico's conventionally recognized masterpieces were painted after 1429, furthermore, entailed acceptance of the implication that his considerable accomplishments as a painter were all derivative of trends explored and perfected by other masters—a conclusion both based on and tending to perpetuate his reputation as an artist relatively isolated from the mainstream in the artistic world of his time.

The first substantial challenge to this notion of Angelico's beginnings and of his overall significance came from the preeminent Italian art historian, Roberto Longhi, in his seminal essay of 1940, "Fatti di Masolino e di Masaccio."[3] Longhi's thesis proceeded from the observation that among the first generation of Florentine masters exposed to the towering achievement of Masaccio in the Brancacci Chapel frescoes, only Angelico demonstrated a level of understanding and an ability to adopt the lessons of this revolution in visual thinking that was at all comparable to the original accomplishments of Masaccio himself. Adding this considerable intellectual achievement to the traditional outlines of the artist's biography, it became essential for Longhi to identify a pre-history, so to speak, for the painter: to find the raw material on which the fertilizing catalyst of Masaccio's genius operated, producing the works for which Fra Angelico is more familiarly known. Longhi advanced a radical proposal attributing to the young Angelico the celebrated *Thebaid* in the Uffizi (fig. 19)—until then generally associated with the semi-mythical name of Gherardo Starnina—as well as two of the scattered drawings from a *rotulus* illustrating the account of a journey to the Holy Land made by the Dominican lay brother Petrus de Cruce in 1417 (see pp. 27–39, and cat. 5). The seeds of Longhi's ideas were quick to bear fruit: in the first instance, in the form of soft-spoken critical response from his arch-rival, Mario Salmi,[4] and in a series of articles by Licia Collobi-Ragghianti.[5] Both authors used Longhi's suggestions as a springboard in an effort to identify some of Angelico's closest followers and to separate their work from the master's autograph production, attempting to restore a relatively pure sampling of material on which to base an evaluation of his accomplishment. Although neither of these exercises was entirely successful, they led to two fundamental advances in scholarship in the early 1950s that form the basis of all subsequent research into Angelico's life and career. The first of these was a full-length monograph by John Pope-Hennessy, which attempted for the first time to treat Angelico as a rational, highly intellectual painter and, as Longhi had, to situate him positively within the context of his contemporaries and peers.[6] Not all of Pope-Hennessy's contentions, even as revised in a second edition of his book issued in 1972, have stood the test of time, but his vision of Fra Angelico's personality has not been challenged in the fifty years since it was first formulated, and his list of autograph works, as well as his outline of the artist's development, remains central to nearly all English-language summaries of Angelico's career.

Longhi, in 1940, did not have the means at hand to challenge the material data in Vasari's biography, according to which Angelico would still have been thirty years old when he painted his very first work. This situation changed with the archival research of Stefano Orlandi, O.P., and of Werner Cohn, which was prepared for publication concurrently with the exhibition in Florence in 1955, commemorating the cinquecentenary of Angelico's death.[7] Easily the most important of these archival discoveries was the notice of Fra Angelico's admission to membership in the Confraternity of San Nicola da Bari at the Carmine in 1417, at which time he was still known by his secular name, Guido di Pietro, and, therefore, had not yet entered the Dominican order. This discovery permitted the wholesale rejection of Vasari's chronology and led to the suggestion, now generally acknowledged, of advancing Angelico's birth date to the second half of the 1390s, if not all the way up to the year 1400. Subsequent research has revealed that Angelico was still referred to as Guido di Pietro as late as 1418, and, indeed, is first called by his religious name, Fra Giovanni, only in 1423.[8] This establishes a window of opportunity for his entry into the Dominican order between 1419 and 1422, and suggests that rather than professing his vows with the Observant Dominicans in exile in Foligno, he may have entered the convent of San Domenico in Fiesole directly, which was newly built in 1419. Unfortunately, as the records of that convent for these years are not preserved, it cannot be positively ascertained exactly when he took his vows and whether he was a very young man at the time, as was typical in that period, or whether entering the order was the result of a mature and considered deliberation.[9]

The significance of this unresolved question lies in determining how long Angelico—that is, Guido di Pietro—had been a practicing artist before he became a Dominican. The 1417 document recording his entry into the Confraternity of San Nicola da Bari qualifies him as a painter, and his sponsor for admission was the painter and miniaturist Battista di Biagio Sanguigni (1393–1451). The document of 1418 also refers to Guido di Pietro as a painter and as it records the payment to him for production of an altarpiece for the church of Santo Stefano al Ponte, he probably was neither a neophyte nor a junior assistant in another master's shop. Such vague intimations cannot lead to a reliable determination of the artist's date of birth, but it is perhaps possible to infer from them that he is likely to have been born about 1395, so that he would have been roughly twenty-three years old in 1418, and thus his artistic apprenticeship, wherever it occurred, may have begun about 1410.

Identifying the shop in which Guido di Pietro might have served his apprenticeship is considerably less difficult than specifying the moment, and represents a necessary first step in any hypothetical reconstruction of his early career. The accumulated circumstantial evidence alone would suggest a connection between Fra Angelico and the studio of Lorenzo Monaco prior to that artist's death in 1423 or 1424. Guido di Pietro in 1417 was living in the same parish in which Lorenzo Monaco's studio was situated, and his friend and sponsor for admission to the Confraternity of San Nicola da Bari, Battista Sanguigni, had been trained in that studio. It was Angelico who was chosen to complete (or repaint) Lorenzo Monaco's monumental altarpiece of the *Deposition* for Palla Strozzi's chapel in the sacristy at Santa Trinita; it was Angelico who was commissioned to paint a *Last Judgment* for Santa Maria degli Angeli, which—as will be seen—was possibly another assignment to complete a work left unfinished by Lorenzo Monaco at his death; and it is the decorative style of Lorenzo Monaco and his assistants that fills the borders and defines the initial letters in the first illuminated manuscript confidently attributable to Fra Angelico: a gradual painted for the convent of San Domenico, Fiesole (now in the library at San Marco, Ms. 558). Some of the technical peculiarities of Angelico's painting style also point to a period of training in the workshop of Lorenzo Monaco, or at the very least to some years of service as an assistant there. Among these are the very similar palette employed by the two artists and their nearly identical manner of filling the corners of irregularly shaped picture fields with summary indications of dense forests. More significant still is the unusual technique employed by Guido di Pietro in the Uffizi *Thebaid,* to render trees as small circular reserves of black underpaint highlighted with a few symbolic leaves of yellow or light green—a technique otherwise encountered in Late Trecento and Early Quattrocento Florentine painting only in predella panels by Lorenzo Monaco.

An attempt to pinpoint the period of time that Guido di Pietro might have spent in Lorenzo Monaco's studio—either as an apprentice or, more likely, as a journeyman assistant previously trained in the workshop of another master—may be

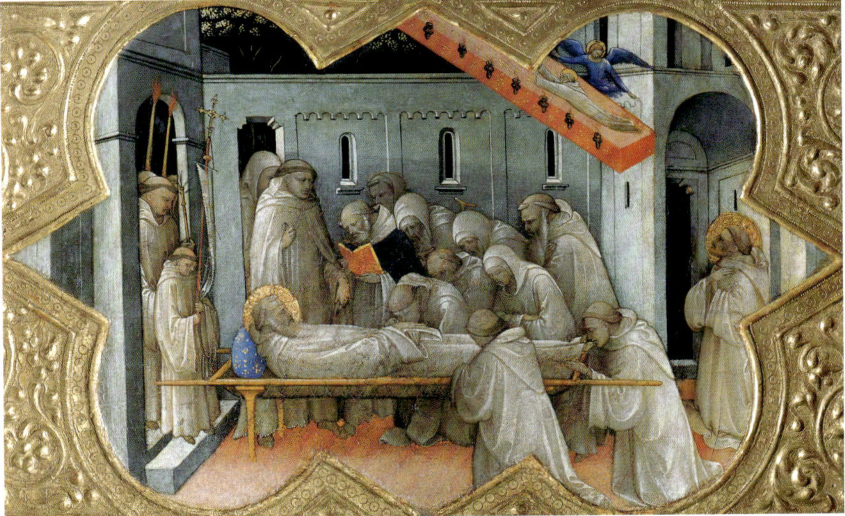

Figure 1. Lorenzo Monaco. *The Death of Saint Benedict*. About 1411–13. Galleria degli Uffizi, Florence

restricted to the years between 1404, when Lorenzo Monaco moved away from the angular Gothicism of his own early style toward the rounder, more graciously proportioned, and lyrical forms that would most influence later generations of painters, and 1417, by which time Guido di Pietro was an independent master. This period of little more than a decade was the most prolific of Lorenzo Monaco's career, during which a number of his most memorable images were created. However, only a few of them bear more than a tangential relationship to Fra Angelico's later interests as a painter, and all are clustered within a narrow time frame bracketed by the San Procolo *Annunciation* (1409) and the Monte Oliveto (1410) altarpiece on the one hand, and the great Uffizi *Coronation of the Virgin* altarpiece from Santa Maria degli Angeli (1413) on the other.

The predella to the *Coronation of the Virgin* altarpiece, painted for the high altar of Santa Maria degli Angeli and dated February 1414,[10] comprises six panels: four recount episodes from the life of Saint Benedict and the other two, events from the infancy of Christ. The first three panels, reading from left to right, are typical of the works by Lorenzo Monaco painted up to then. Executed in his characteristic light-on-dark technique, with swirling highlights following the sinuous Gothic lines of the drapery folds or the contours of the figures, they reflect no special care in integrating narrative and setting: their compositions are organized in relation to the decorative form of the picture surround rather than to support the dramatic demands of their subjects, and their architectural settings are only suggestively convincing. Behind the scene of the death of Saint Benedict (fig. 1), for example, is a wall pierced by three windows. The aperture on the right is seen, appropriately, from the left and the middle aperture is centralized, but the opening on the left incorrectly is also viewed from the left. Twelve mourning monks cluster in an implausibly tight group around the bier of the saint, those further in the background inexplicably larger than those closer to the foreground, while a procession of acolytes entering from the left includes two notional figures holding long tapers, the relationship of which to the doorway through which they are passing is impossible to determine. Comparison of this or of either of the other two scenes on the left half of the predella—showing *Saint Benedict in the Sacro Speco* (fig. 2) and the *Nativity* (fig. 3)—with similar subjects painted earlier (or later) in Lorenzo Monaco's career reveals that such casual oversights as these are typical in the Camaldolese master's work. His narrative preoccupations were evocative rather than descriptive, and

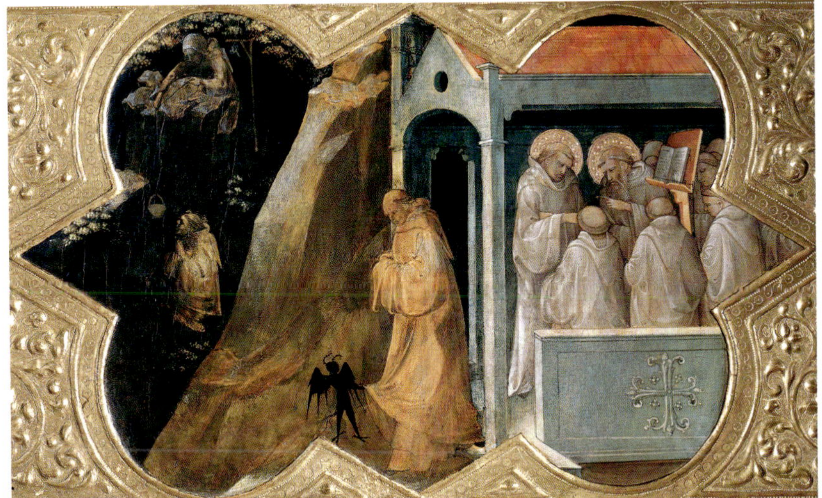

Figure 2. Lorenzo Monaco. *Saint Benedict in the Sacro Speco*. About 1411–13. Galleria degli Uffizi, Florence

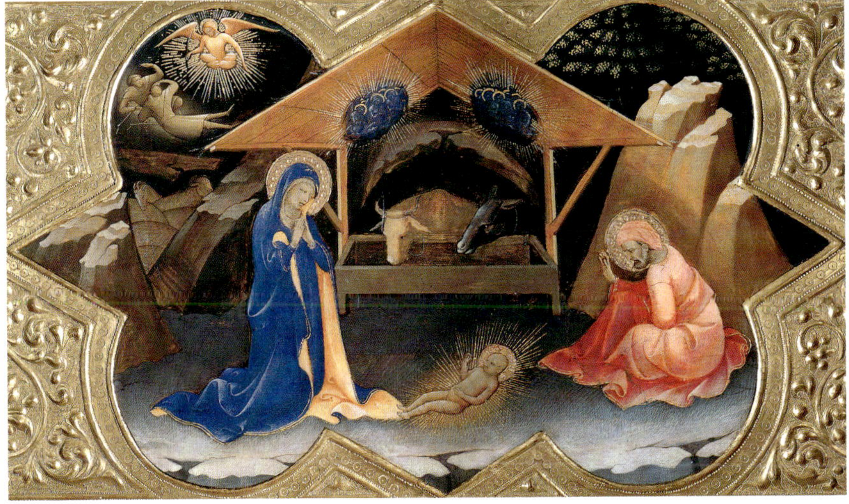

Figure 3. Lorenzo Monaco. *The Nativity*. About 1411–13. Galleria degli Uffizi, Florence

Figure 4. Fra Angelico (?). *The Adoration of the Magi*. About 1411–13. Galleria degli Uffizi, Florence

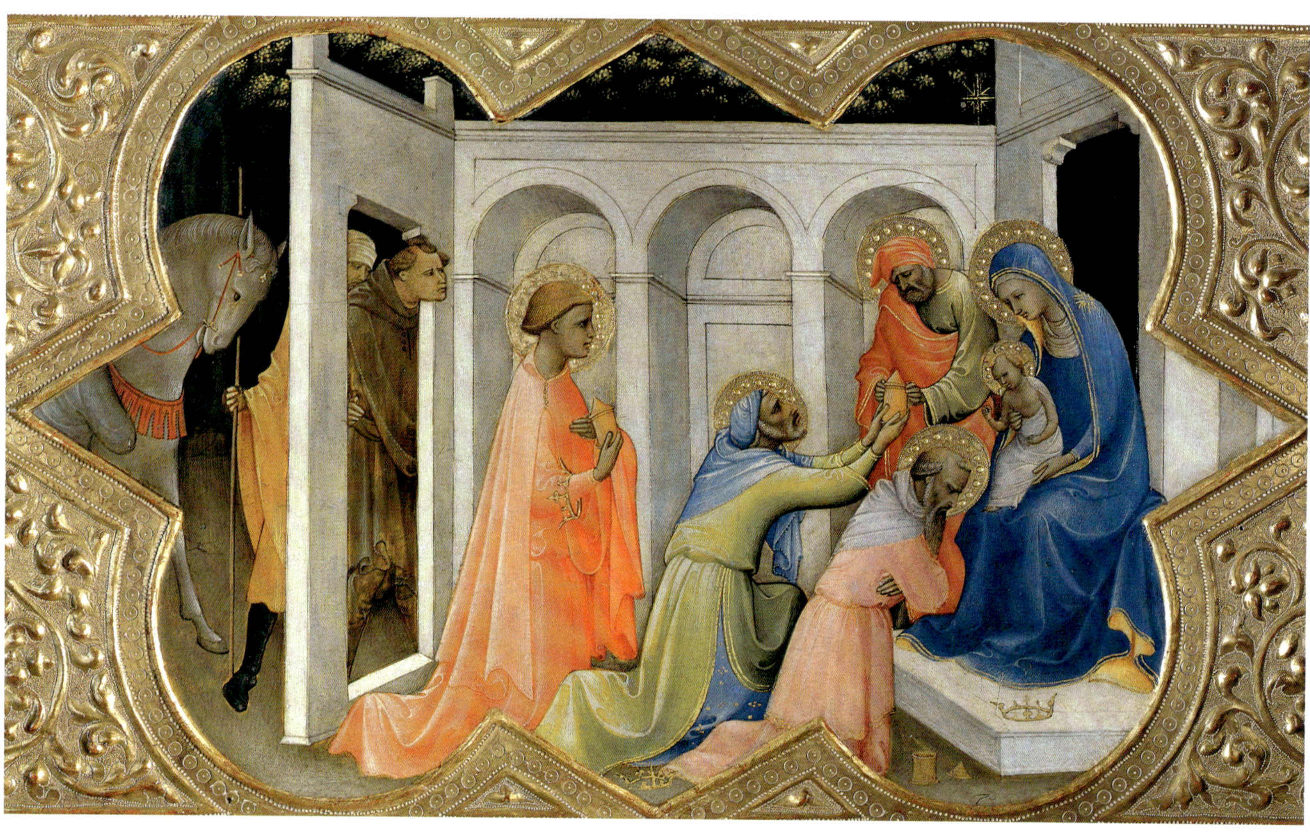

Figure 5. Fra Angelico (?). *The Rescue of Saint Placidus, and the Meeting of Saints Benedict and Scholastica*. About 1411–13. Galleria degli Uffizi, Florence

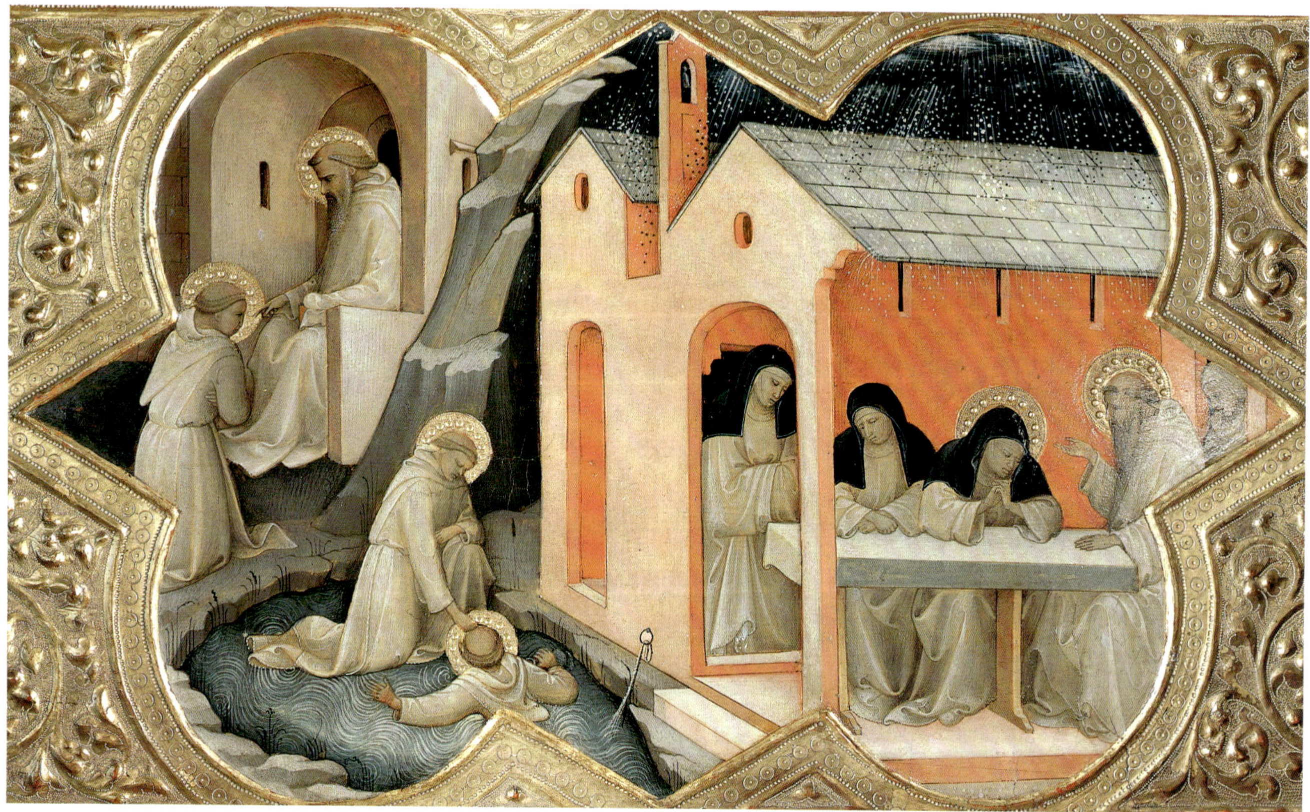

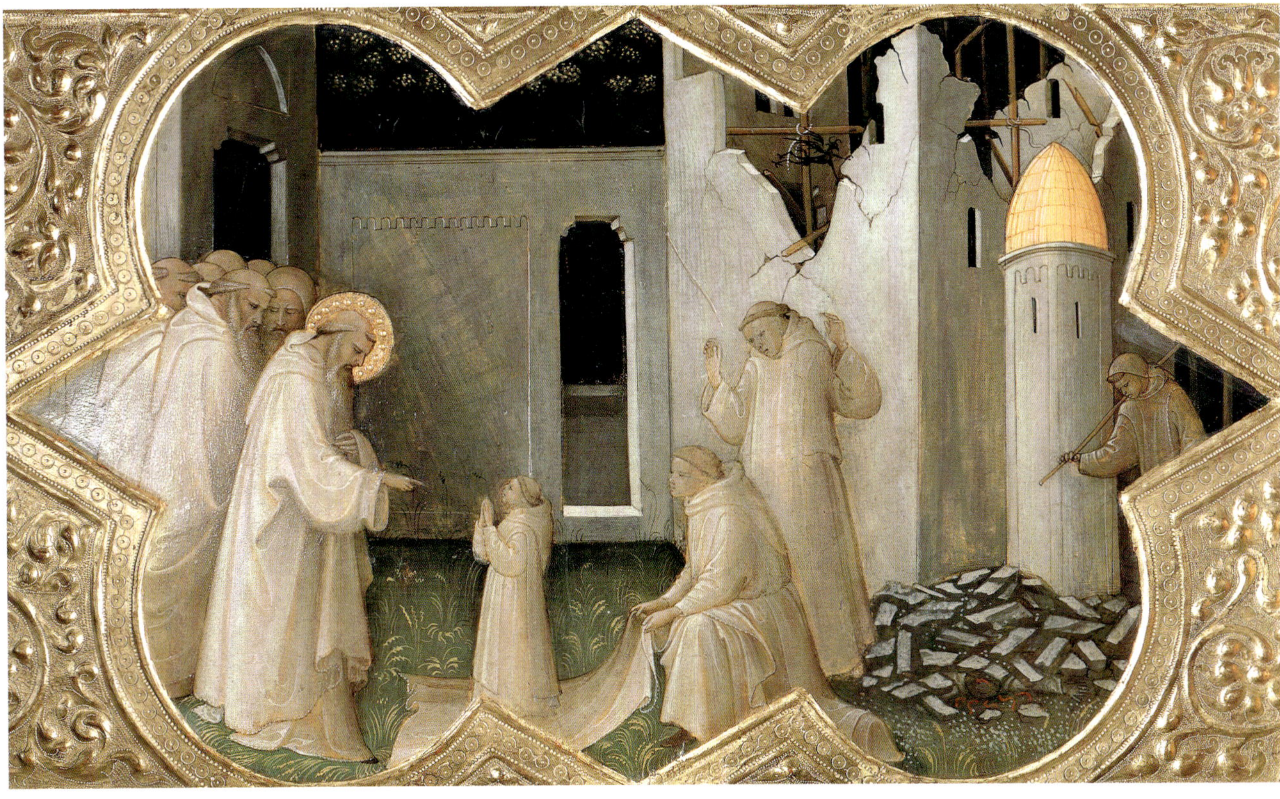

Figure 6. Fra Angelico (?). *Saint Benedict Resuscitating a Young Monk*. About 1411–13. Galleria degli Uffizi, Florence

realistic visual detail rarely held more than a passing fascination for him.

By contrast, the three scenes in the right part of the predella of the Santa Maria degli Angeli *Coronation*—the *Adoration of the Magi* (fig. 4), the rescue of Saint Placidus with the meeting of Saints Benedict and Scholastica (fig. 5), and Saint Benedict raising a young monk (fig. 6)—reveal a painstaking attention to realistic detail. All of the architectural forms in these scenes are carefully ruled, arches are inscribed with a compass rather than drawn freehand as on the left half of the predella, and foreshortening is meticulously accurate in every instance. Lorenzo Monaco's usual rocky landscapes are softened with grasses—a detail rarely encountered elsewhere in his work—and where there are standing figures, they bend the grasses realistically beneath their feet. All of the fissures, fallen bricks, and fractured tie rods in the building that collapsed on a hapless monk in the third scene are entirely persuasive and carefully visualized from a single viewing point. Hail is shown bouncing off the roof tiles above Saint Scholastica's head in the second scene, as it would in real life, and the artist has scrupulously included a fishing net tied to a ring at the side of the monastery to explain the proximity of the body of water from which Placidus was saved from drowning. This device, a remarkable intellectual conceit for that date, is conspicuously absent from the same scene (fig. 7) incorporated below Lorenzo Monaco's altarpiece of the *Coronation of the Virgin* (1407; National Gallery, London) from San Benedetto fuori della Porta a Pinti. Similarly, in the scene of the *Adoration of the Magi,* the youngest king slips his crown over his arm while reverently waiting his turn to pay homage to the Christ Child as a curious retainer thrusts his head through the open doorway

Figure 7. Lorenzo Monaco. *The Rescue of Saint Placidus, and the Meeting of Saints Benedict and Scholastica*. About 1407. National Gallery, London

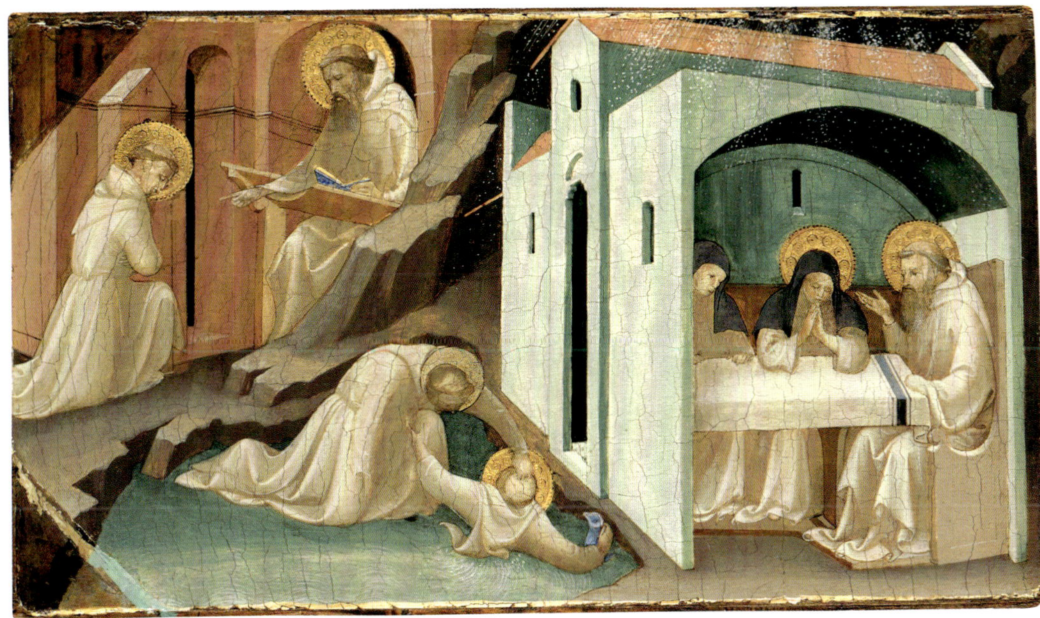

at the left. Once again, the earlier *Adoration of the Magi* from the predella of the San Benedetto *Coronation* altarpiece omits both these gratuitous naturalistic details, as does the same scene below Lorenzo Monaco's later altarpiece of the *Annunciation* from the Salimbeni Chapel in Santa Trinita, probably painted about 1417.

The figure types and proportions in these three scenes on the right of the Uffizi predella are also subtly different from those found in the three companion panels on the left side of the predella, or usually encountered in Lorenzo Monaco's work. The figures are less attenuated and their stances not as sinuous. Their expressions are more equable, and even the range of colors with which they are rendered is less exaggerated in its contrasts and closer to the earth tones and soft pastels that would later characterize Angelico's signature painting style. Perhaps most significant, however, is the different system of highlights used to model the forms in the left and right halves of the predella. On the left, Lorenzo Monaco's standard practice of reinforcing the dynamism of curved forms with strokes applied parallel to their profiles is fully in evidence. On the right, highlights are designated with cross-hatching—again, a practice conspicuously absent in other paintings by Lorenzo Monaco but typical of Fra Angelico's mature works.

Three additional panel paintings are known that exhibit many of the same qualities as those on the right half of the *Coronation of the Virgin* predella and probably should be considered the products of the same precocious mind at work at approximately the same moment. Two of these might have belonged to the predella of an as yet unidentified altarpiece from Lorenzo Monaco's workshop: today they are divided between the Musée des Beaux-Arts, Nice, and the Pinacoteca Vaticana. The first panel, portraying the funeral of a bishop saint (fig. 8), is, like the Uffizi predella, remarkable for the attention paid to the details of its setting and narrative. The saint's bier, convincingly foreshortened, rests behind two slender colonnettes on the floor of a sanctuary, surrounded by mourning figures in various attitudes of grief. Compared to the funeral of Saint Benedict at the left on the Uffizi predella, however, the cluster of mourners forms a spatially lucid and coherent knot. One young monk at the left bears a processional cross that is cropped at the lintel supporting the barrel vault above him, establishing its exact measure in relation to the height of the building and its exact position in space behind the picture plane. Another young mourner, at the right, stands in an antechamber of the sanctuary. Both the figure and a window that pierces the wall above his head are cropped, almost casually but highly realistically, by the frame of the doorway through which he peers—a gratuitous detail that lends the scene the effect of portraying a specific moment in time. Yet, most surprising of all is the view of the colonnade of

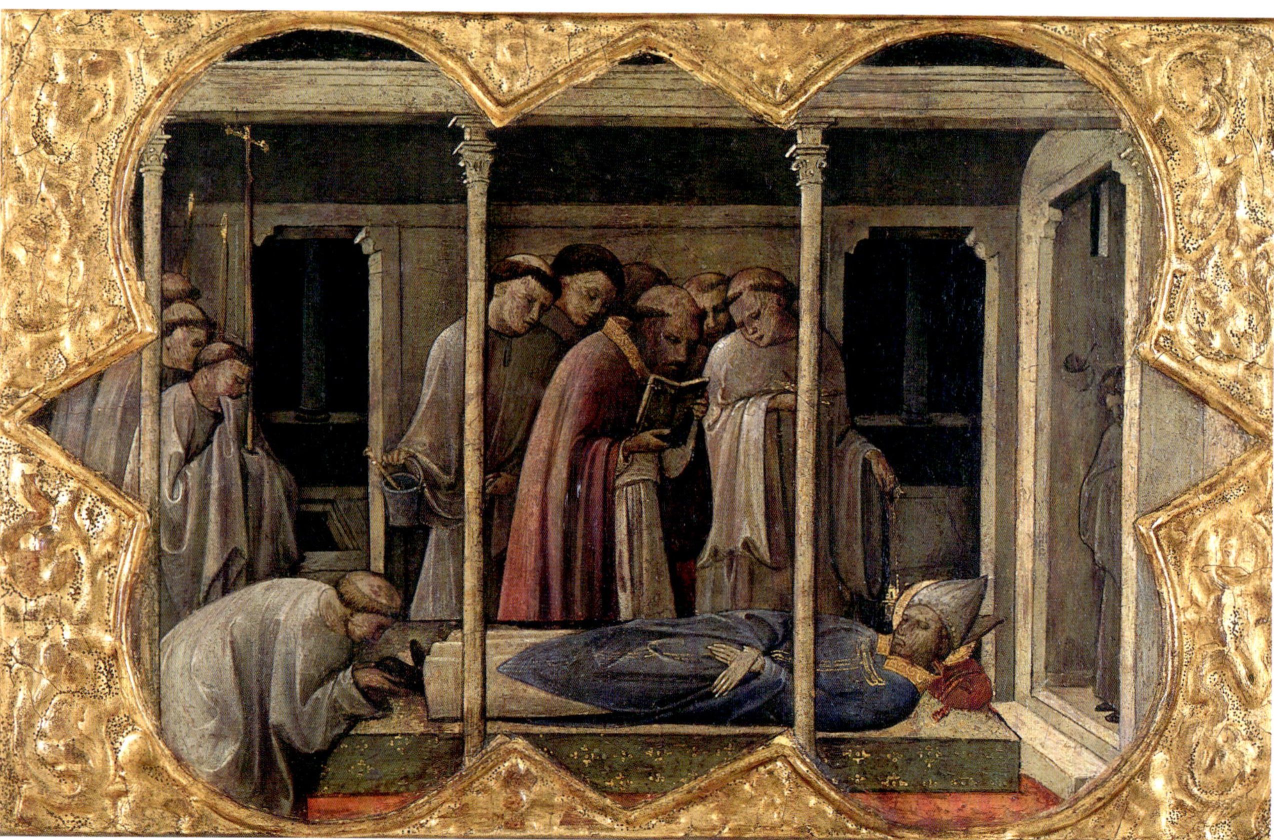

Figure 8. Fra Angelico (?). *The Funeral of a Bishop Saint*. About 1411. Musée des Beaux-Arts, Nice

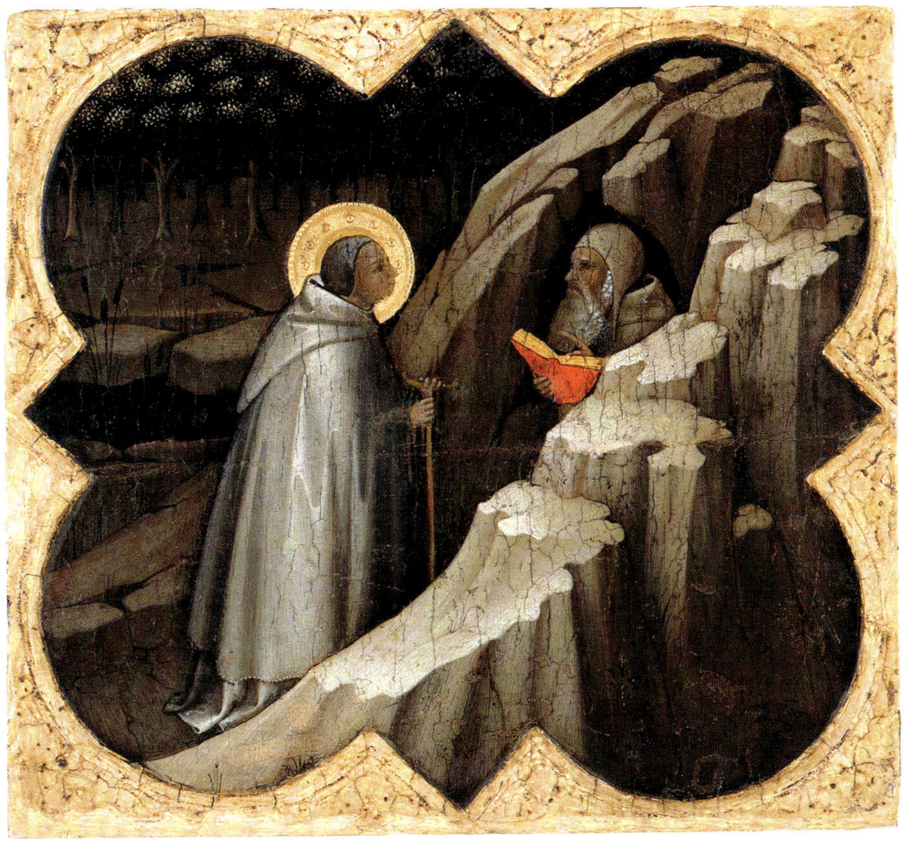

Figure 9. Fra Angelico (?). *Saint Benedict Meeting Saint Paul the Hermit in the Wilderness.* About 1411. Vatican Museums, Vatican City

a monastic cloister seen through two doorways cut into the rear wall of the sanctuary: not only is this an astonishingly advanced perspectival device for so early a date but it also is an amazingly refined addition to the narrative content of the scene. Through the left portal one can see a paving slab from the floor of the cloister that has been lifted and set ajar, revealing below it the tomb prepared to receive the mortal remains of the bishop saint.

It is difficult to judge the figure style of the Nice *Funeral of a Bishop Saint,* as so many of the heads in the painting have been damaged and restored. The bishop, himself, and the priest above him reading from the Office of the Dead remain the most reliable figures, and the half-visible mourner at the right also is fairly well preserved. These figures bear a suggestive similarity to those on the right half of the Uffizi predella, although all that may be said of the others is that their poses are less exaggeratedly Gothic, and more supple and naturalistic, than those typically depicted by Lorenzo Monaco. By contrast, the scene of *Saint Benedict Meeting Saint Paul the Hermit in the Wilderness* (fig. 9) in the Pinacoteca Vaticana, which relates to the Nice panel in the form, although not the size, of its quatrefoil surround and in the *pastiglia* decoration of its outer margins, is in an excellent state of preservation. Its composition is extremely simple, affording few opportunities for the displays of naturalistic finesse evident in the other panels discussed so far. The figure of Saint Benedict is painted with brilliantly confident assurance in a technique unmistakably related to that of the right half of the Uffizi predella, with the draperies carefully modeled with crosshatched highlights, their folds accurately measuring the precise volume of the space occupied by the figure.

The compact proportions and softly rounded features of the figures in the Uffizi and Vatican panels establish a link with the final painting in this group, a *Virgin and Child Enthroned, with Saints Peter, Paul, John the Baptist, and Anthony Abbot* (fig. 10), now in the San Diego Museum of Art. Somewhat conventional in its composition, although progressive in its orientation of the bodies of the four saints to define a semi-circle of space around the Virgin, it does introduce one particular novelty worthy of the inventive talents of our still unnamed master. Setting off the principal scene from the three smaller figures of the dead Christ and the mourning Virgin and Saint John the Evangelist in the pinnacle above is a decorative motif intended to recall the tracery that might fill half of a lancet window in a Gothic church. In this case, however, it is not painted as a simple ornamental element but rather as a fully three-dimensional pierced arch of cut stone—an invention entirely unique in paintings from this period.

The author of these delicate fancies was an artist of a caliber superior to that of any of his contemporaries in the early

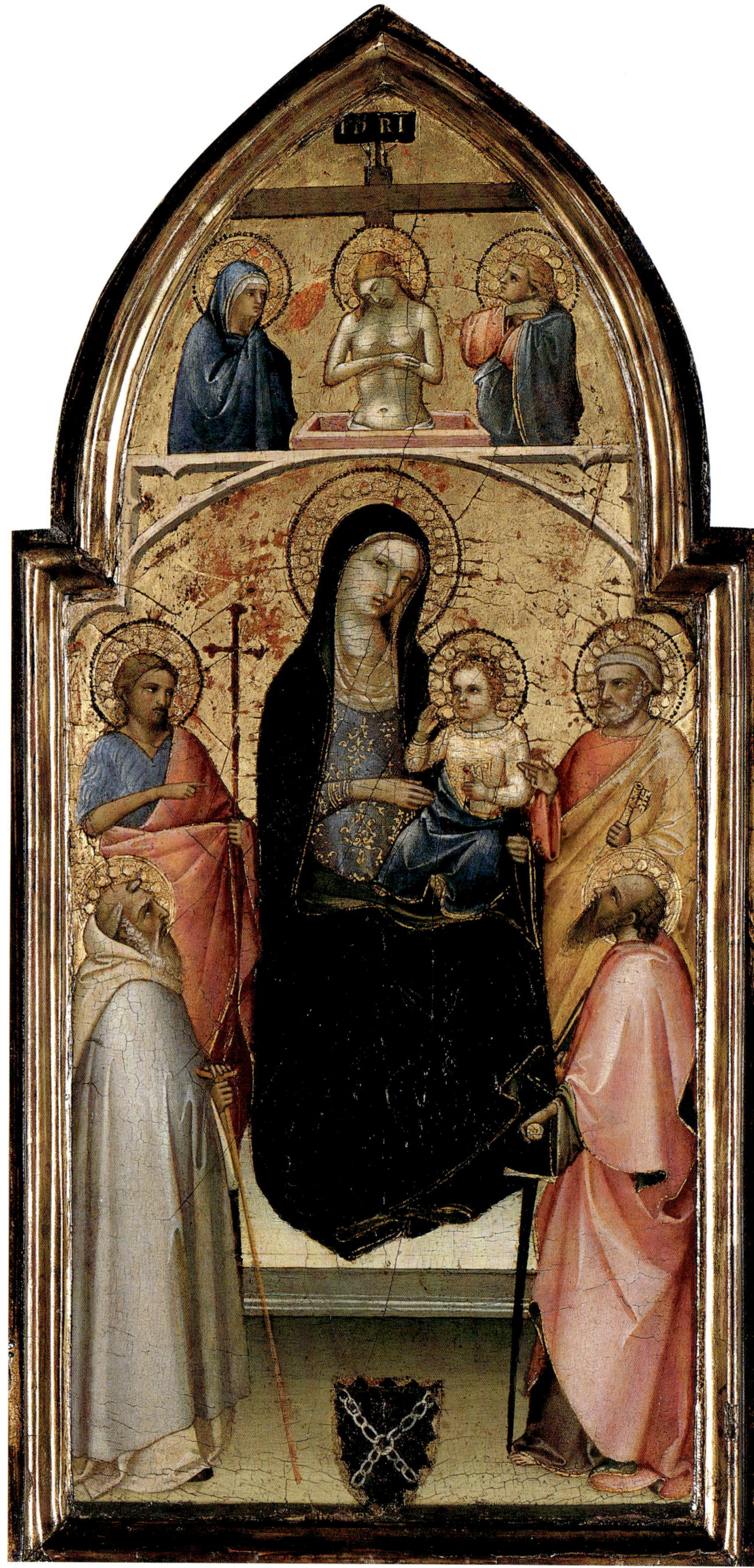

Figure 10. Fra Angelico (?). *Virgin and Child Enthroned, with Saints Peter, Paul, John the Baptist, and Anthony Abbot.* About 1411. San Diego Museum of Art

or middle years of the second decade of the fifteenth century, and of a temperament that was essentially different from that of Lorenzo Monaco, in whose shadow he was working. Could this artist have been the young Guido di Pietro? Not only do the facts inferred from his biography allow for such a possibility but everything about his later painting style suggests that he was an artist fully capable of so progressive a leap in pictorial thinking. Still lacking, however, is a positive and tangible link between this style of painting and Fra Angelico's earliest, universally recognized works. Such a link might be supplied, if only tenuously, by a set of drawings included in this exhibition (see cat. 1), prepared for an illuminated gradual commissioned from Lorenzo Monaco sometime shortly after 1410 but never actually painted. It is not the approach to narrative or the complexity of the spatial settings that distinguish the compositions of these drawings but the astonishing accuracy of botanical observation evident in the articulation of their foliated initials. Well beyond the means of Lorenzo Monaco, himself, talented as he was in this area, some of the forms employed in these initials do not recur exactly as they appear here in any fifteenth-century Florentine manuscripts, but they can be found as details in slightly later panel paintings by Fra Angelico. The sgraffito decoration of carpets and cloths of honor, and even the engraved decoration of halos in the paintings of the Virgin in Saint Petersburg (fig. 11), Pisa (fig. 12), and Rotterdam (cat. 6), for example, include herons and twisting stems of flowers, with buds seen alternately from above and below, which compare closely to these.

The earliest paintings arguably executed by Guido di Pietro as an independent master—free, that is, from any supposed obligation to mimic the characteristics of another artist—are the three tabernacles just mentioned, in Saint Petersburg, Pisa, and Rotterdam, all portraying the Virgin and Child. Chronologically, the first was probably the Saint Petersburg painting, representing the Madonna of Humility with four angels (fig. 11), the most Gothic of the three paintings in the exaggerated tilt of the richly embroidered carpet, the curling folds of the hems of the draperies, and the delicate proportions of the figures. All of these features are conscious imitations of the style of Lorenzo Monaco's paintings of the same subject and a further indication of the tabernacle's early date. No painting by Lorenzo Monaco ever established nearly as effective a sense of spatial recession as does the Saint Petersburg *Virgin and Child,* however, with the music-making angels in the lower corners kneeling in lost profile, one wing of each angel projecting straight back to the viewer and their draperies pooling on the carpet in a completely persuasive yet very precocious exercise of perspectival foreshortening. These same qualities characterize the two panels (cat. 3) portraying the

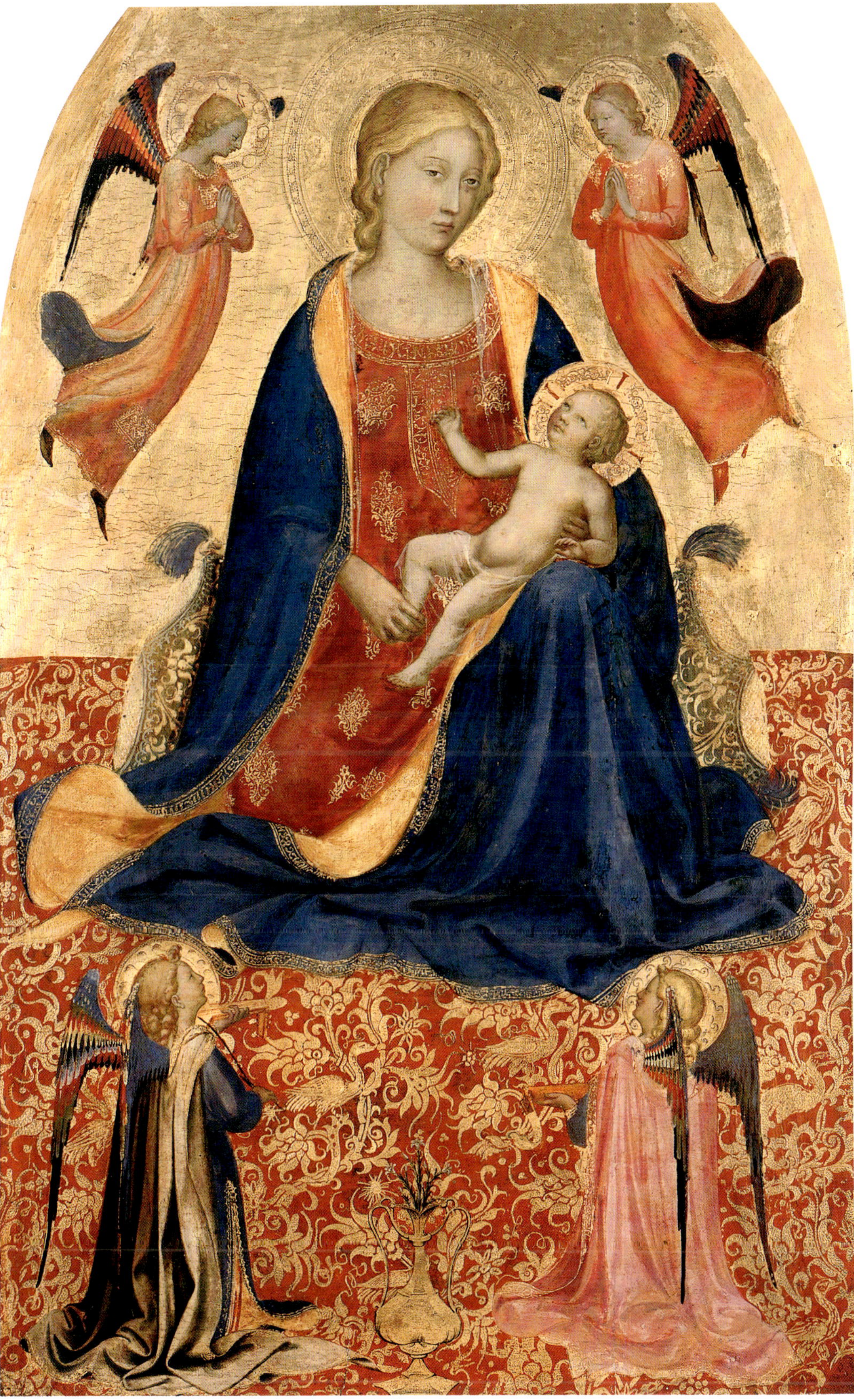

Figure 11. Fra Angelico. *Virgin and Child, with Four Angels* (*Madonna of Humility*). About 1415. State Hermitage Museum, Saint Petersburg

Annunciation, recently discovered in a private collection, which, together with the Saint Petersburg tabernacle, constitute the most substantial link between the paintings from the studio of Lorenzo Monaco discussed above—especially the San Diego *Madonna*—and the more easily recognized mature works of Fra Angelico. A date for the *Annunciation* panels and the Saint Petersburg tabernacle of about 1415, shortly after Guido di Pietro left Don Lorenzo's studio, is reasonable although not absolutely demonstrable.

The Pisa tabernacle, also a Madonna of Humility (fig. 12), is simpler and more severe in composition than the Saint Petersburg *Virgin*. It includes no ancillary figures of angels and is slightly larger than the Saint Petersburg painting, conveying a sense of monumentality that contrasts with the Gothic playfulness of the latter, and suggests that it is more advanced in date. The Pisa *Madonna* has been described as dependent on the influence of Masaccio, presumably in recognition of the tactility and monumentality of the figures and the ambitious spatial effects created by the Child's restless, forward-leaning pose and foreshortened halo. To ascribe these accomplishments to the influence of Masaccio, however, is to misunderstand and seriously underestimate the nature of Angelico's own precocious interest in these same problems, which, as has been seen, may date back to 1413 or possibly earlier. The Rotterdam *Madonna* (cat. 6), the most accomplished and "mature" of these three images, already recalls Angelico's work of the 1420s, yet it is doubtful that even it was painted much later than 1417.

Unfortunately, the altarpiece from Santo Stefano al Ponte completed by Guido di Pietro before 1418 is not known to have survived, and the establishment of a precise chronology for Angelico's work in this period must remain inferential and, for the moment at least, hypothetical. One of the difficulties posed by the few paintings by Angelico reasonably assigned to this decade is that they vary so widely in type, as though the artist were consciously experimenting with different affectations to satisfy different classes of patrons. Nowhere is this problem more acutely obvious than with the largest painting attributed to the young Angelico—the so-called *Thebaid,* or scenes from the lives of the Desert Fathers, in the Galleria degli Uffizi in Florence (fig. 19): it is a short step from the oddly caricatural figures scattered throughout this masterpiece to the foreground figures in the Griggs *Crucifixion* (cat. 8) or to some of the saints in the predella of the high altarpiece from San Domenico, Fiesole (cat. 10), and it is reasonable to assume that this great painting was executed about or only slightly earlier than 1420. It is not clear, however, that it represents a dependable indicator of Angelico's style at that moment, or whether the nature of its subject elicited an intentionally coarse response from the artist, in the same way that *bas-de-page*

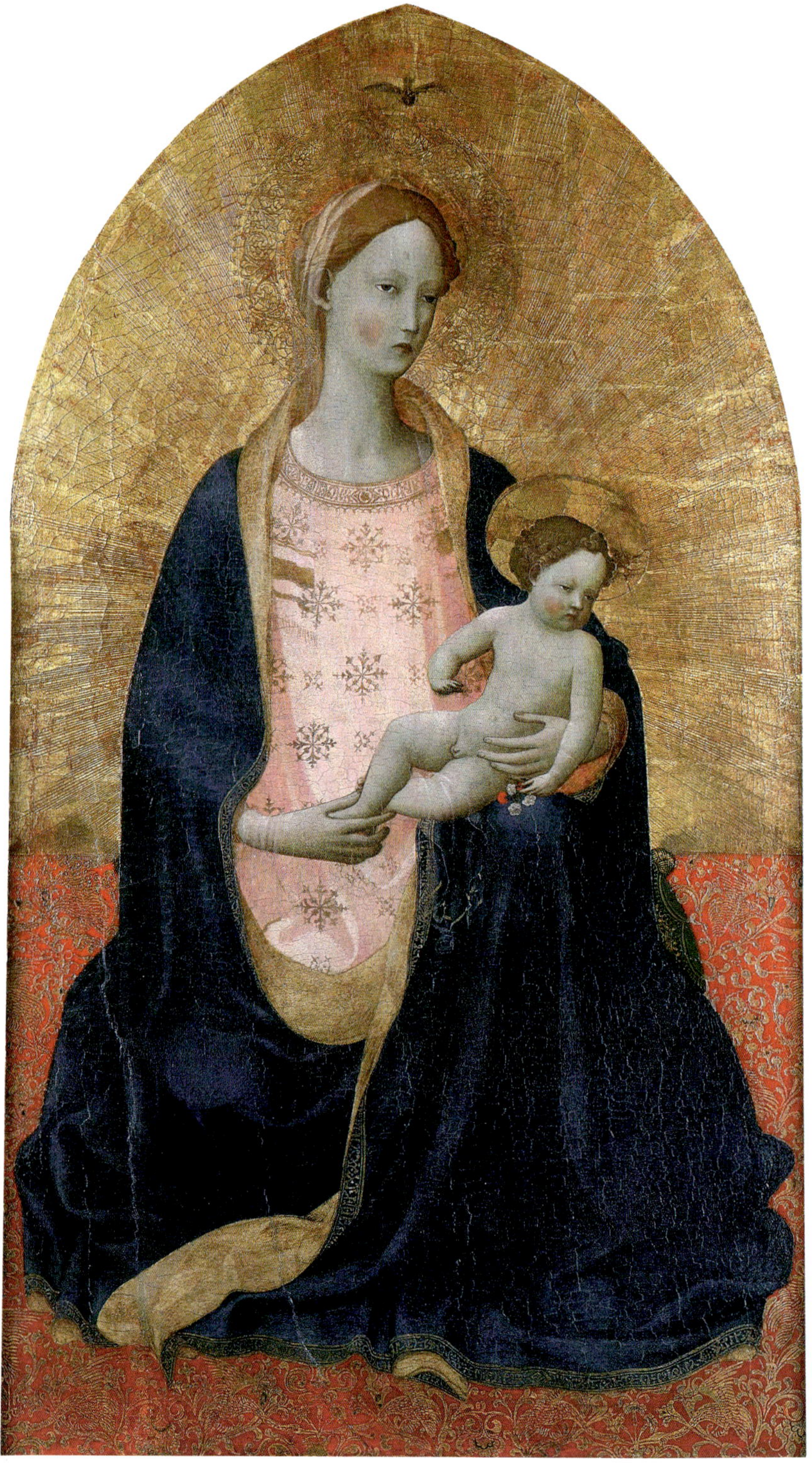

Figure 12. Fra Angelico. *Virgin and Child (Madonna di Cedri)*. About 1415–17. Museo Nazionale di San Matteo, Pisa

drolleries in illuminated manuscripts are deliberately rendered with less delicacy than are the principal subjects in the historiated initials. Such a dichotomy in Angelico's approach has been observed elsewhere—notably, in the San Domenico predella panels and in the Griggs *Crucifixion*—and continues into his mature career with increasingly emphatic, and transparent, results: as, for example, in the distinction between painting styles that characterizes the blessed and the damned in his visions of the Last Judgment.

Even more problematic, however, is the nature of the commission of the Uffizi *Thebaid* as a faithful copy of another work of art, described more fully in Pia Palladino's essay in this catalogue (see pp. 33–37). Thus, the exaggerated postures of the figures, their proportions, and their disposition in space do not result from a natural tendency in Angelico's stylistic development; they represent his attempts to update and at the same time remain faithful to the Trecento prototype he was asked to replicate. Only in the painting's details is it possible to recognize Angelico's particular genius for naturalistic observation: all these details point to a date for the work approximately contemporary with that of the Griggs *Crucifixion* or of the predella to the San Domenico high altarpiece. Shortly afterward, the young painter's attention would be drawn irresistibly to the innovations in pictorial realism brought to Florence by Gentile da Fabriano and then quickly supplanted by those of a younger Tuscan master, Masaccio. However, the interaction of Angelico with Gentile and with Masaccio is properly the subject of the next chapter in his career, comprising the decade between 1422 and 1432, a decade of rapid change in the development of Florentine painting in which this prodigiously talented artist was once thought to have played a negligible or even non-existent part.

1. Vasari (Milanesi ed.) 1878–85, vol. II, pp. 505–34.
2. The document was first published by Orlandi 1954 a, p. 180.
3. Longhi 1940, pp. 145–91 (reprinted in Longhi 1975).
4. Salmi 1950, pp. 75–81, 146–56.
5. Collobi-Ragghianti 1950 a, pp. 363–78; Collobi-Ragghianti 1950 b, parts 1–2; Collobi-Ragghianti 1955 b, pp. 22–47.
6. Pope-Hennessy 1952.
7. Orlandi 1954 a, pp. 161–97; Orlandi 1955 b, vol. II; Orlandi 1964; Cohn 1955, pp. 207–16; Cohn 1956 a, pp. 218–20; Florence 1955; Baldini 1956, pp. 78–85; Baldini 1977, pp. 236–46.
8. Orlandi 1964, p. 173; for the document of 1418, see p. 169.
9. Gilbert 1984, pp. 281–87.
10. Bent 2000, pp. 348–54; see Frosinini 1998, pp. 15–20, for a discussion of the interpretation of the date in the inscription accompanying this altarpiece. Kanter (forthcoming) will present evidence suggesting that the commission awarded to Lorenzo Monaco for the high altarpiece for Santa Maria degli Angeli may date to 1411.

1.

A.

The Miracle of the Loaves and Fishes in an Initial L

Pen and ink on parchment, 31.6 x 23.1 cm (12⁷⁄₁₆ x 9⅛ in.)
Statens Museum for Kunst, Copenhagen (KKSgb4652)

The miracle of the loaves and fishes is recounted in the Gospel of John (6: 5–13): "When Jesus therefore had lifted up his eyes, and seen that a very great multitude cometh to him, he said to Philip: Whence shall we buy bread, that these may eat? . . . One of his disciples, Andrew, the brother of Simon Peter, saith to him: There is a boy here that hath five barley loaves, and two fishes; but what are these among so many? Then Jesus said: Make the men sit down. . . . The men therefore sat down, in number about five thousand. And Jesus took the loaves: and when he had given thanks, he distributed to them that were set down. In like manner also of the fishes, as much as they would. And when they were filled, he said to the disciples: Gather up the fragments that remain, lest they be lost. They gathered up therefore, and filled twelve baskets with the fragments of the five barley loaves, which remained over and above to them that had eaten."

The initial *L* begins the Introit to the Mass for the fourth Sunday in Lent: *Laetare Jerusalem* ("Rejoice, O Jerusalem"); the Miracle of the Loaves and Fishes illustrates the Gospel lesson for that day. The fragmentary text visible above the initial, *ia*[*m*] *a*[*m*]*plius,* concludes the Communion hymn from the Mass for the preceding Saturday: [*Nec ego te condemnabo*], *iam amplius* [*noli peccare*] ("Neither will I condemn thee, but do not sin again").

B.

Christ and the Apostles Entering the Temple in Jerusalem in an Initial D

Pen and ink on parchment, 30.5 x 24.1 cm (12 x 9 ½ in.)
The Metropolitan Museum of Art, New York. Purchase, Lila Acheson Wallace Gift, 1999 (1999.391)

Entering the city of Jerusalem, Jesus went first to the temple, where he drove out the money changers and healed the blind and lame: "And the chief priests and scribes, seeing the wonderful things that he did, and the children crying in the temple, and saying: *Hosanna to the Son of David*; were moved with indignation" (Matthew 21: 15). The children crying "Hosanna" fill the first bay of the Temple directly in front of Christ, while several indistinct forms lightly sketched in the second bay of the temple, at the right, may have been intended to indicate the fleeing sellers or money changers. The scene illustrates the continuation of the Gospel lesson (Matthew 21: 1–9) read at the blessing, distribution, and procession of the palms before Mass on Palm Sunday. The partial syllable, "*cel,*" visible at the top of the cutting concludes most of the antiphons ([*Hosanna in ex*]*cel*[*sis*]) recited at the blessing and procession of the palms, and the initial *D* begins the Introit to the Mass for Palm Sunday: *Domine ne longe facias auxilium tuum a me* ("O Lord, be not far from me with your aid").

C.

Christ Washing the Feet of the Apostles in an Initial D

Pen and ink on parchment, 29.6 x 23.5 cm (11 ⅝ x 9 ¼ in.)
Statens Museum for Kunst, Copenhagen (KKSgb4654)

The story of Jesus washing the feet of his disciples is recounted in the Gospel of John (13: 4–9): "He riseth from supper, and layeth aside his garments, and having taken a towel, girded himself. After that, he putteth water into a basin, and began to wash the feet of the disciples, and to wipe them with the towel wherewith he was girded. He cometh therefore to Simon Peter. And Peter saith to him: Lord, dost thou wash my feet? Jesus answered, and said to him: What I do thou knowest not now; but thou shalt know hereafter. Peter saith to him: Thou shalt never wash my feet. Jesus answered him: If I wash thee not, thou shalt have no part with me. Simon Peter saith to him: Lord, not only my feet, but also my hands and my head."

The initial *D* begins the Communion hymn at the conclusion of the Mass for Maundy Thursday: *Dominus Jesus, postquam cenavit cum discipulis suis, lavit pedes eorum* ("The Lord Jesus, after he had eaten the supper with his disciples, washed their feet"). Above the initial is a fragment of the preceding offertory hymn from the same Mass: [. . . *non moriar, sed vivam, et narrabo*] *opera Do*[*mini*] ("I shall not die, but live, and shall declare the works of the Lord").

The two Copenhagen initials were previously identified as part of a group of six unfinished illuminations cut from a missing volume of the gradual from the famous series of choir books written for the Camaldolese monastery of Santa Maria degli Angeli in Florence.[1] The other four—all *bas-de-page* illuminations rather than initials—illustrate the Entry into Jerusalem (Biblioteca Apostolica Vaticana, Cod. Rossiano 1192.34), for Palm Sunday (fig. 13); Christ in the House of Mary and Martha (Biblioteca Apostolica Vaticana, Cod. Rossiano 1192.37), for Monday in Holy Week (fig. 14); Judas

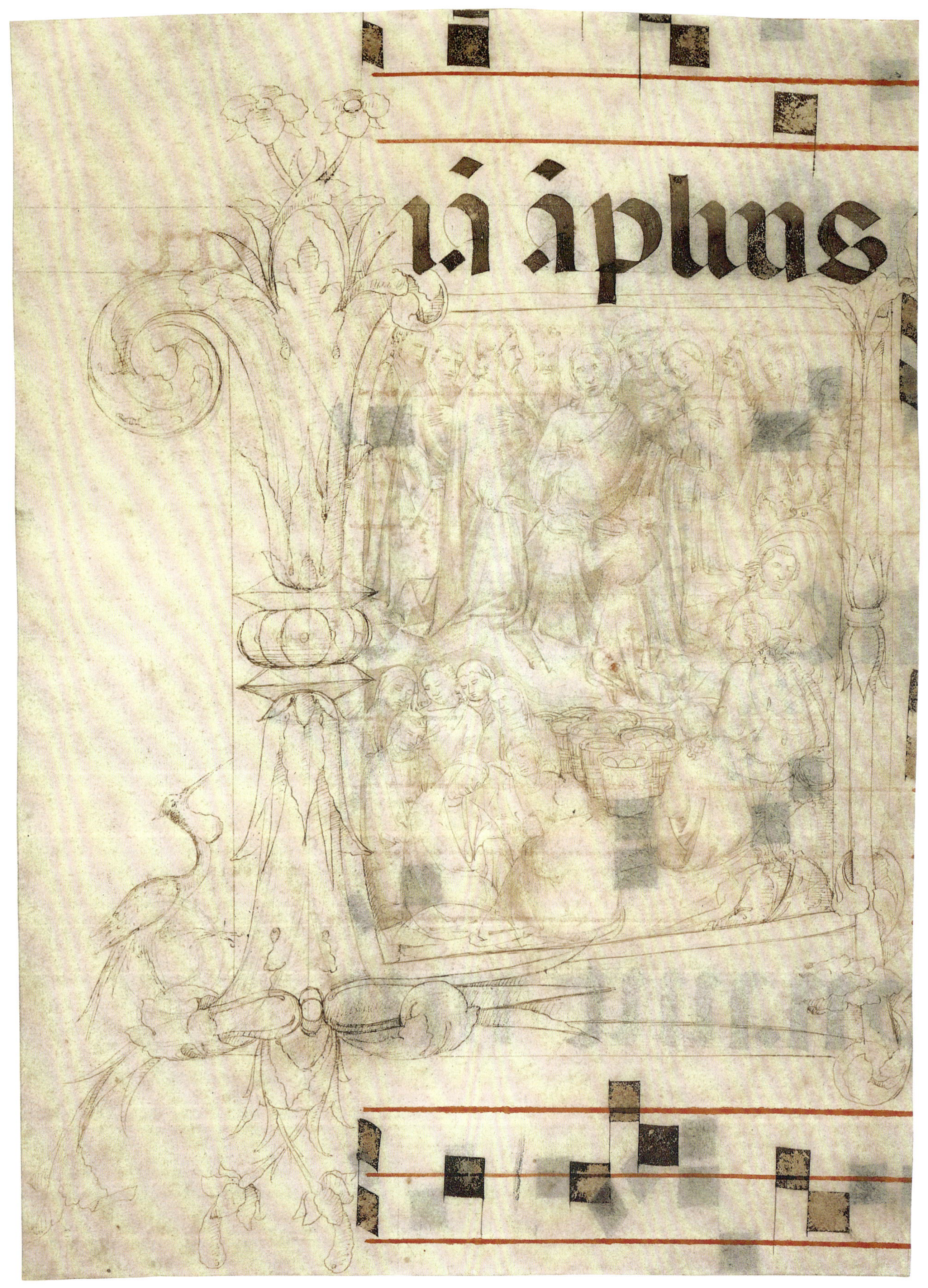

1: A

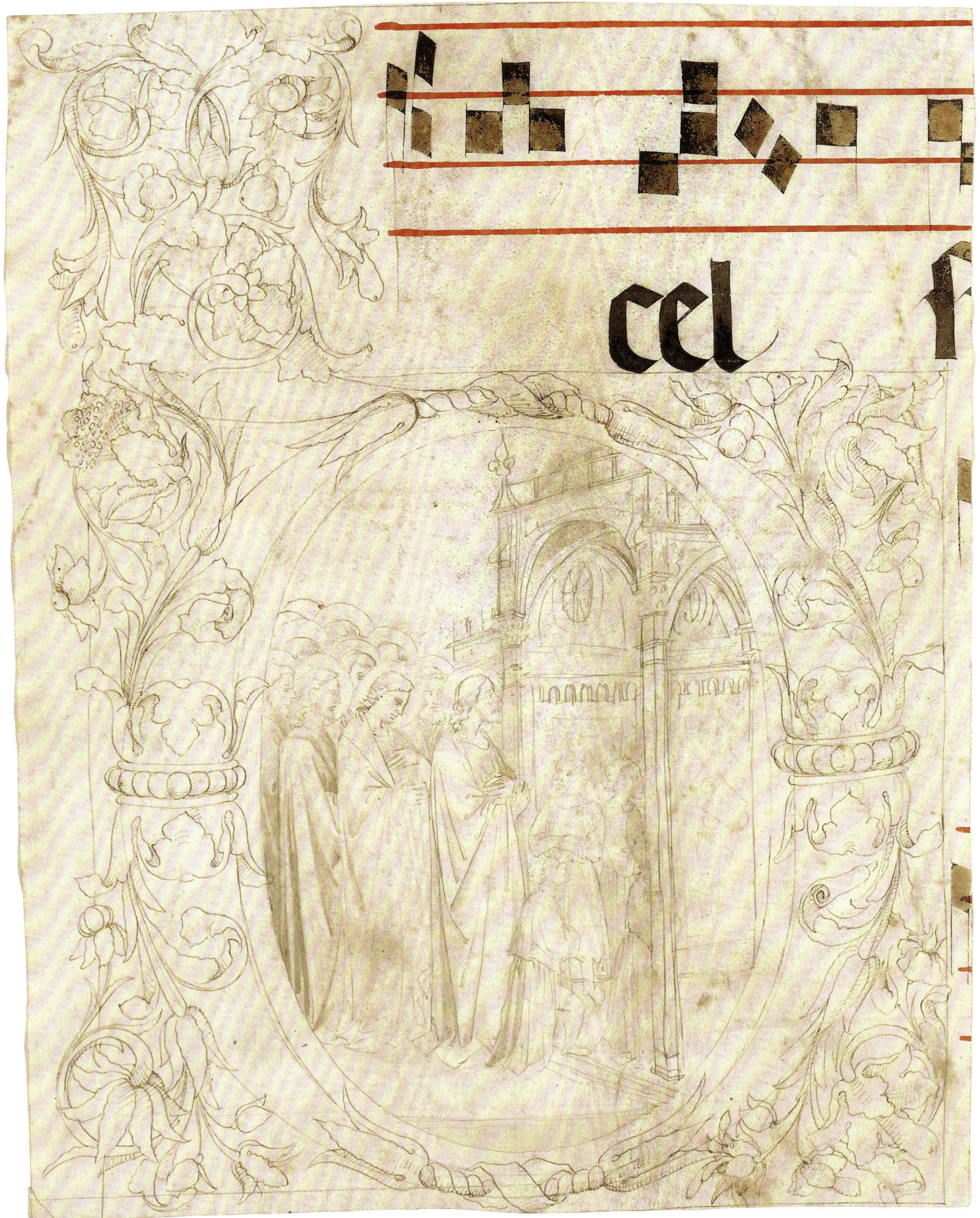

1: B

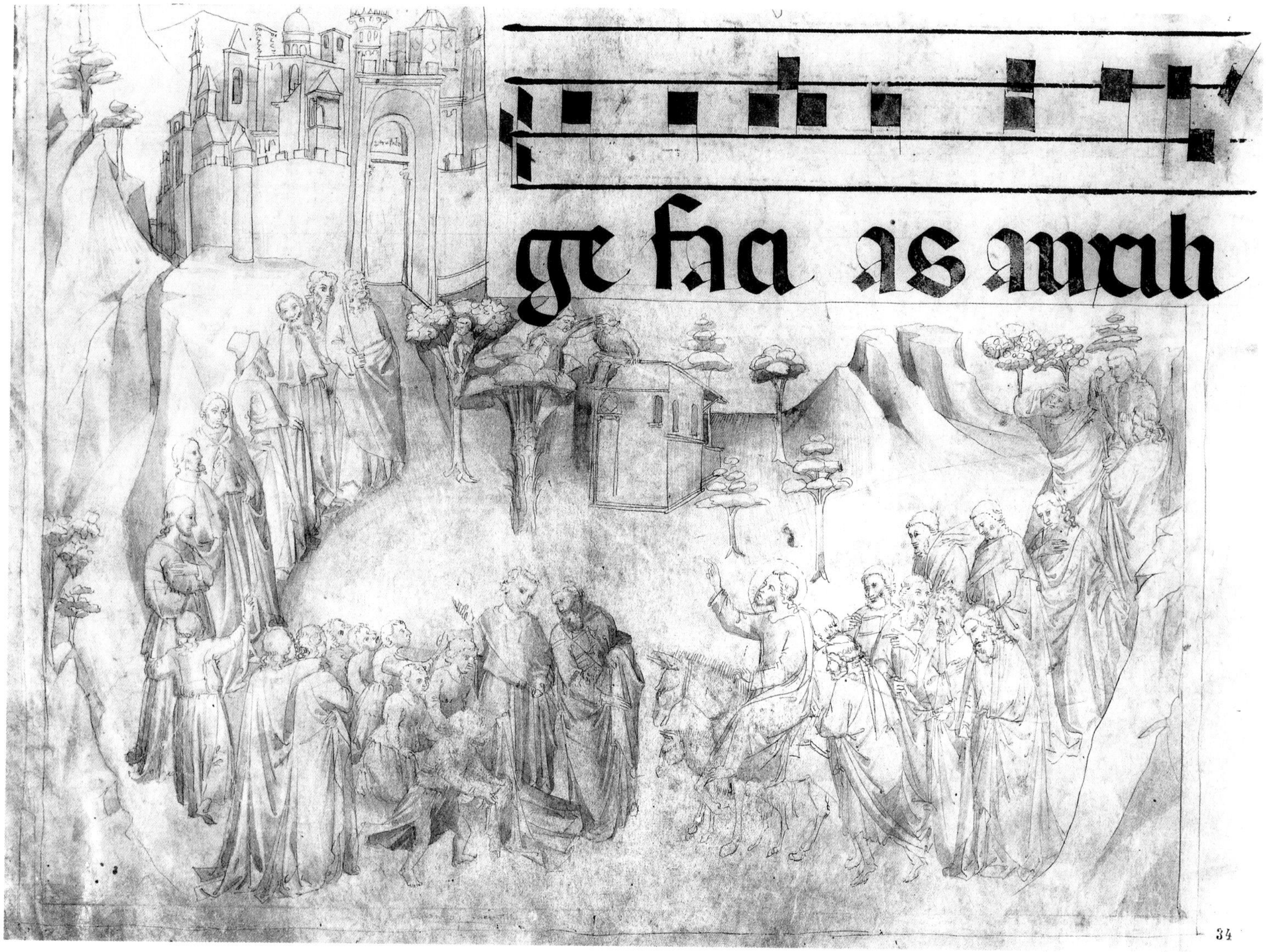

Figure 13. Lorenzo Monaco. *The Entry into Jerusalem.* About 1410. Biblioteca Apostolica Vaticana, Vatican City (Cod. Rossiano 1192.34)

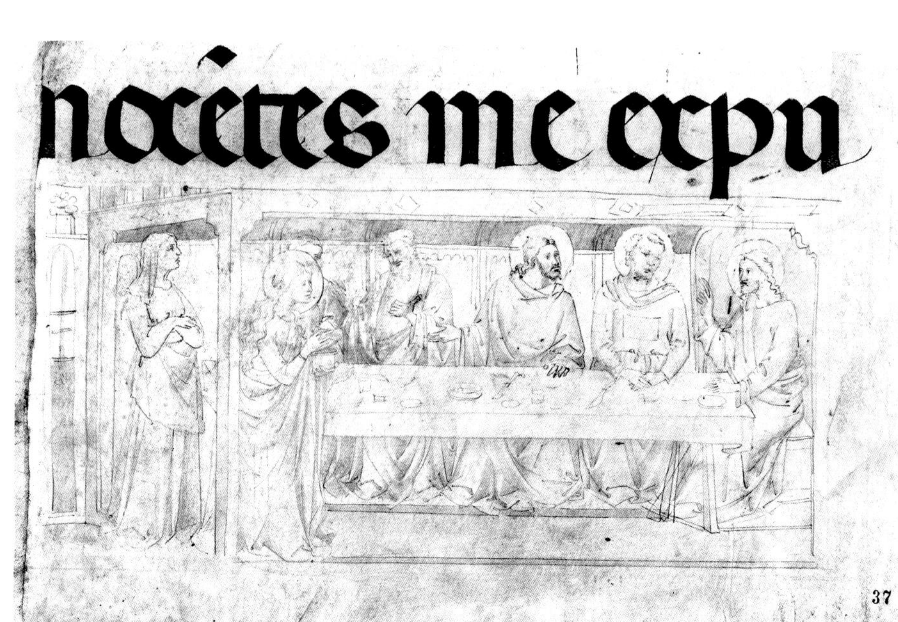

Figure 14. Lorenzo Monaco. *Christ in the House of Mary and Martha.* About 1410. Biblioteca Apostolica Vaticana, Vatican City (Cod. Rossiano 1192.37)

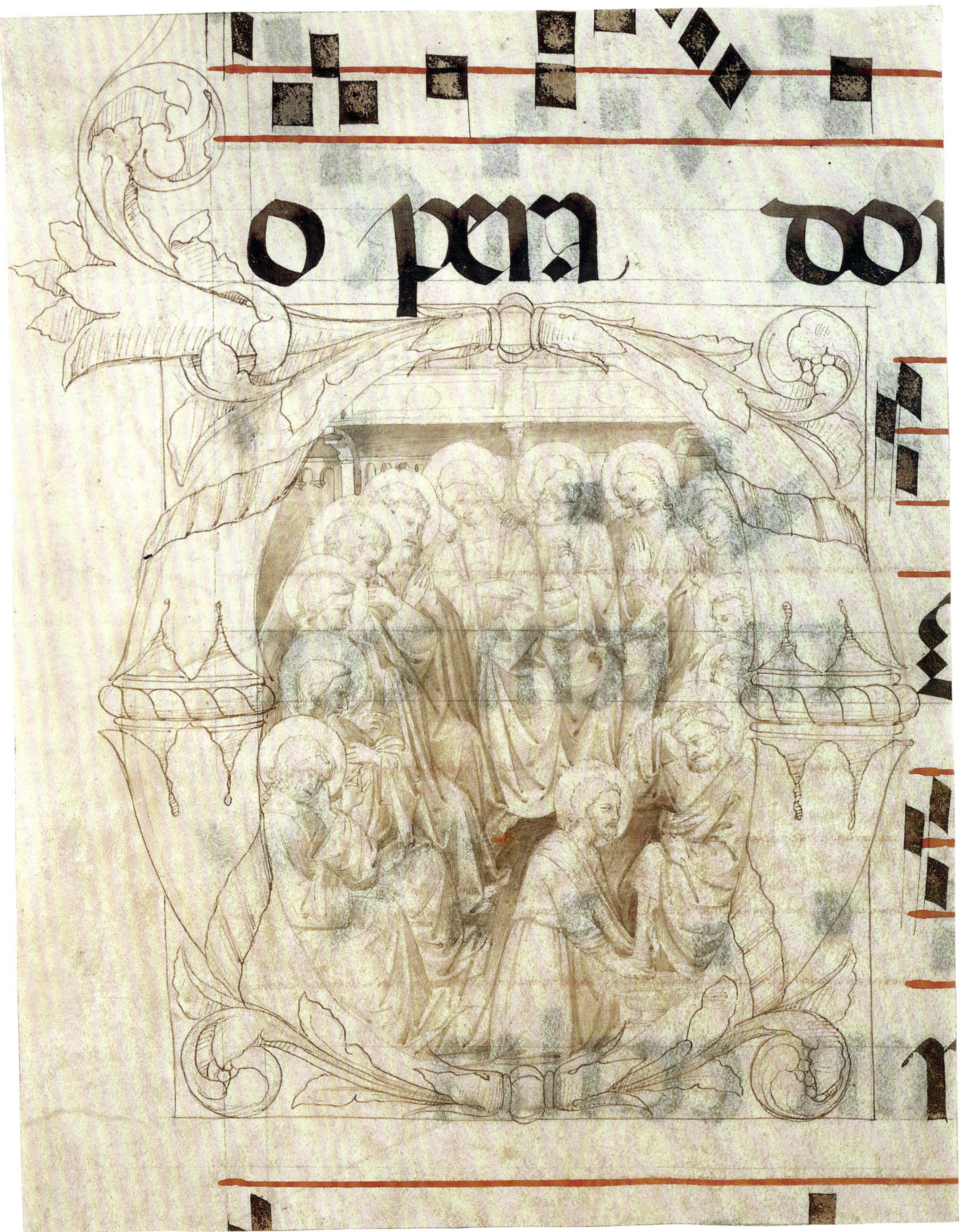

I: C

receiving thirty pieces of silver (Statens Museum for Kunst, Copenhagen, TU 3, 54), for Wednesday in Holy Week; and the Last Supper (Biblioteca Apostolica Vaticana, Cod. Rossiano 1192.35), for Maundy Thursday. The Metropolitan Museum of Art's recently discovered initial *D* can be shown to have been removed from the same folio as the *bas-de-page* Entry into Jerusalem. That fragment includes one musical staff and line of text "*. . . ge facias auxili . . .*," continuing the Introit to the Mass for Palm Sunday. Thus, the New York and Vatican fragments were immediately contiguous, with nothing between them: the indications of two musical staves cropped at the right of the New York initial provide adequate space for the missing text of the Introit, "*Domine ne lon. . . .*"

These seven initials and *bas-de-pages* all illustrate texts for feast days in the fourth week of Lent and Holy Week—precisely the period missing from the three known volumes of a four-volume gradual included among the famous choir books of Santa Maria degli Angeli in Florence. The first volume of this gradual (Biblioteca Medicea Laurenziana, Florence, Cor. 18) covers the period from the first Sunday of Advent to the second week in Lent, and is dated 1410 in a colophon (fol. 140*v.*), which refers to the completion of its text and pen-work initials only. This volume contained four illuminated pages,[2] two of which were left unfinished as pen-and-ink drawings like the present initials. The third part of the gradual, so described in its incipit and dated 1409 in a colophon (Biblioteca Medicea Laurenziana, Florence, Cor. 3; see cat. 41), begins with the Mass for Easter Sunday and was similarly left incomplete. In this last case, however, eight initials were fully drawn and painted by Lorenzo Monaco, probably before 1413,[3] while twelve additional ones were completed later by two or perhaps three other artists, some of them possibly painted over unfinished drawings such as those discussed here. The fourth volume of the gradual (Biblioteca Medicea Laurenziana, Florence, Cor. 4), like the first, is dated 1410 in a colophon, but it was left unilluminated and was not painted until much later, between 1505 and 1506, by Attavante.[4]

Previous discussions of the drawings removed from the first two volumes of this gradual have focused primarily on their relationship to Lorenzo Monaco—an attribution, together with a date of about 1410–13, that was only firmly established when their provenance was recognized in 1994. Indeed, there is little doubt that Lorenzo Monaco was responsible for the historiated *bas-de-page* drawings and the centers of the initials, but too little attention has been paid to the structure and foliate decoration of the initials themselves on the folios in Copenhagen and in the Metropolitan Museum. These are rendered with a botanical naturalism and a graphic precision wholly foreign to Lorenzo Monaco's interests or accomplishments. A comparison with the drawn initial (British Museum, 1860-6-16-42) removed from folio 1*v.* in Cor. 18, part of the same commission and presumably coeval with the Copenhagen and New York drawings, underscores the radical difference in approach adopted in the last three works. Rather than employing the generic beads or gems; fantastic birds; ribbons; and flatly drawn, schematic curls of the acanthus fronds typical of the style of border and initial decoration practiced in the workshop of such illuminators as Don Simone Camaldolese, the artist of the Copenhagen and New York initials took great pains to foreshorten all his forms to create a notional three-dimensionality, and shaded them carefully to heighten their tactility. He also introduced some forms not otherwise seen in the borders of Florentine (or any other) manuscripts up to this date, such as seedpods accurately studied from nature, or open flowers drawn alternately from above and below.

That Lorenzo Monaco enjoyed the assistance of an unusually talented collaborator or pupil in planning the initials in this volume of the Santa Maria degli Angeli gradual is clear. That this pupil or collaborator might have been the young Guido di Pietro (Fra Angelico) is suggested by the proposal, outlined above, to identify Angelico as the author of the three final scenes of the predella to Lorenzo Monaco's *Coronation of the Virgin* altarpiece from the high altar of Santa Maria degli Angeli (Galleria degli Uffizi, Florence), begun probably in 1411 and completed and installed in 1413. These scenes are characterized by the same insistent naturalism in representation and the same structural precision found in the Copenhagen and New York initials, and to a degree not encountered in the work of any other painter or illuminator active at this early date. Some related floral and vegetal motifs occur in one other Florentine manuscript of this period: Cor. 43, in the Biblioteca Medicea Laurenziana, Florence, now widely recognized as the masterpiece of Angelico's mature career as an illuminator,[5] although these motifs are not organized according to the same decorative principles as in the Copenhagen and New York initials. Perhaps more revealing is the appearance of many of the motifs and devices found in the drawings—especially, the alternating views from above and below of flower petals and the particular form of the acanthus *rinceaux*—in the engraved halos of Angelico's early images of the Madonna (in Pisa, Saint Petersburg, Rotterdam [cat. 6], and in the Johnson Collection [cat. 11]), as well as in the patterned brocades of the draperies in these paintings. While it cannot be claimed with absolute certainty, then, that these drawings represent the first task assigned to the young Guido di Pietro as a (hypothetical) journeyman in Lorenzo Monaco's studio, there is a strong possibility that such was, indeed, the case. LK

1. L. Kanter, in Kanter et al. 1994, pp. 274–83. For the choir books from Santa Maria degli Angeli, see Levi D'Ancona 1993–94; L. Kanter, in Kanter et al. 1994, pp. 229–48, 262–67, 272–87.
2. Folios 1*v.*, 52*r.*, 56*v.*, and 118*r.* Folio 1 was removed from the volume and is now in the British Museum, London (1860-6-16-42). The drawn *bas-de-page* from folio 118 was also removed from the volume and is now in Paris (Musée du Louvre, Département des Arts Graphiques, R.F. 28970). Folio 52*r.*, the only illuminated page still in the volume, was provided with a fully painted initial, the center of which was left blank. Folio 56, now in the British Library, London (Add. Ms. 35,254G), was treated similarly except that its historiated center was completed later (about 1505–6) by Attavante. See L. Kanter, in Kanter et al. 1994, pp. 272–74, for the identification of these illuminations.
3. See L. Kanter, in Kanter et al. 1994, pp. 282–87, and catalogue 41, for a listing and a discussion of the dating of these initials, as well as of the other illuminations added to this volume.
4. Levi D'Ancona 1978, pp. 213–35; Levi D'Ancona 1995, p. 73.
5. A. Dillon Bussi, in Di Lorenzo 2001, pp. 30–35; A. Dillon Bussi, in Scudieri and Rasario 2003, pp. 160–61.

FRA ANGELICO (?)

2. *Scenes from the "Ninfale Fiesolano"*

Tempera on panel: overall, 44.5 x 142 cm (17 ½ x 55 ⅞ in.); picture surface, 28.9 x 126.3 cm (11 ⅜ x 49 ¾ in.)
Bowdoin College Museum of Art, Brunswick, Maine. Gift of the Samuel H. Kress Foundation (1961.100.001)

The story of the *Ninfale Fiesolano* is recounted in five episodes drawn from Boccaccio's epic poem. At the left, Diana, seated before a rocky cave, admonishes her nymphs to observe her laws of chastity while the young Africo, hiding in the woods behind her, listens and espies the nymph Mensola. As described by Boccaccio, Diana is radiant with a "light so like a flame one could not fix his gaze on her,"[1] although neither she nor her nymphs wear the nearly transparent linen garments described in the poem; they are clad instead in fashionable robes of costly fabric, with high collars and long sleeves. Mensola is at the far right, in the group of nymphs, "perhaps fifteen years of age. Her hair was golden blond and curled; her garments were of purest linen. She had such sparkling eyes that no one beholding them could be unhappy and an angelic face and nimble movements. In her hand she bore her keen-edged dart."[2]

Africo is seen at the center of the panel, asleep on his cot, and his mother, Alimena, is seated on the ground outside holding a spindle and a distaff. Faithful to the poem, Africo's home is depicted as a simple hut, "erected without mortar. They built their homes of stones and wood alone, and some walled theirs with nothing more than earth and wattles."[3] One night, in his sleep, Africo had a vision of Venus "encircled in resplendent light,"[4] which enflamed his love for Mensola; Venus urged him not to fear Diana and to pursue the nymph. Africo did so but could not find her, and when he returned home later on, he was greeted by his parents, Girafone and Alimena, who warned him against Diana and her nymphs. Respectful of his parents' concern but undeterred, Africo resumed his search the next day and came across Mensola in a ravine. The nymph ran off as he protested his love. "She kept her javelin in her hand and, after having fled some distance, glanced behind her sternly. Then growing bold through fear, she launched the spear with keen and accurate arm, intending to bestow a mortal wound on Africo. . . . But when she saw the weapon whistling through the air, she looked into her lover's face, which she thought fashioned indeed in paradise. Then keenly she repented having launched the spear and, moved by pity, she gazed at him and cried, 'Lad, alas, watch out, for now I cannot help you!'"[5]

Unable to find Mensola again, Africo pined for her and took sick, praying once more to Venus for aid. The goddess advised him to dress as a woman, join the nymphs, and seduce his beloved. Africo then stole a dress from his mother and went to find the nymphs. He helped them kill a wild boar and was accepted as one of them, befriending Mensola in particular. "Nor had they advanced very far when they came upon two nymphs bathing entirely naked in a pool. . . . Soon they each began undressing, while Africo and Mensola talked on together. 'Sweet friend,' Mensola said to him 'will you bathe here with us?'. . . Before he had fully disrobed, all the nymphs were in the water. Then, stripping bare, he moved toward them . . . rushing to the water [he] seized her alone who pleased him most. And all the other nymphs dashed from the water. . . . They did not stay to dress, however, but straightway fled. . . . Abandoning their bows and arrows, they hurried off in all directions."[6]

The Bowdoin cassone was correctly catalogued by Fern Rusk Shapley as "Circle of the Master of the Griggs Crucifixion," although without naming the authority on which she based this attribution.[7] She identified the subject as "Scenes from a legend," referring to three distinct exempla of the breach of Chastity among the followers of Diana, including the stories of Diana and Callisto and Diana and Endymion. Paul Watson first described the subject of the painting, and of a related panel formerly in the Honolulu Academy of Arts (fig. 15) also cited by Shapley, as scenes from the *Ninfale Fiesolano,* accepting Shapley's attribution for both works to the circle of the Master of the Griggs Crucifixion, alias Giovanni Toscani (d. 1430).[8] The ex-Honolulu cassone, which is a typical work by Giovanni Toscani, follows closely the selection of episodes and the composition of the Bowdoin cassone, adding an unexplained genre detail of two small boys on the roof of

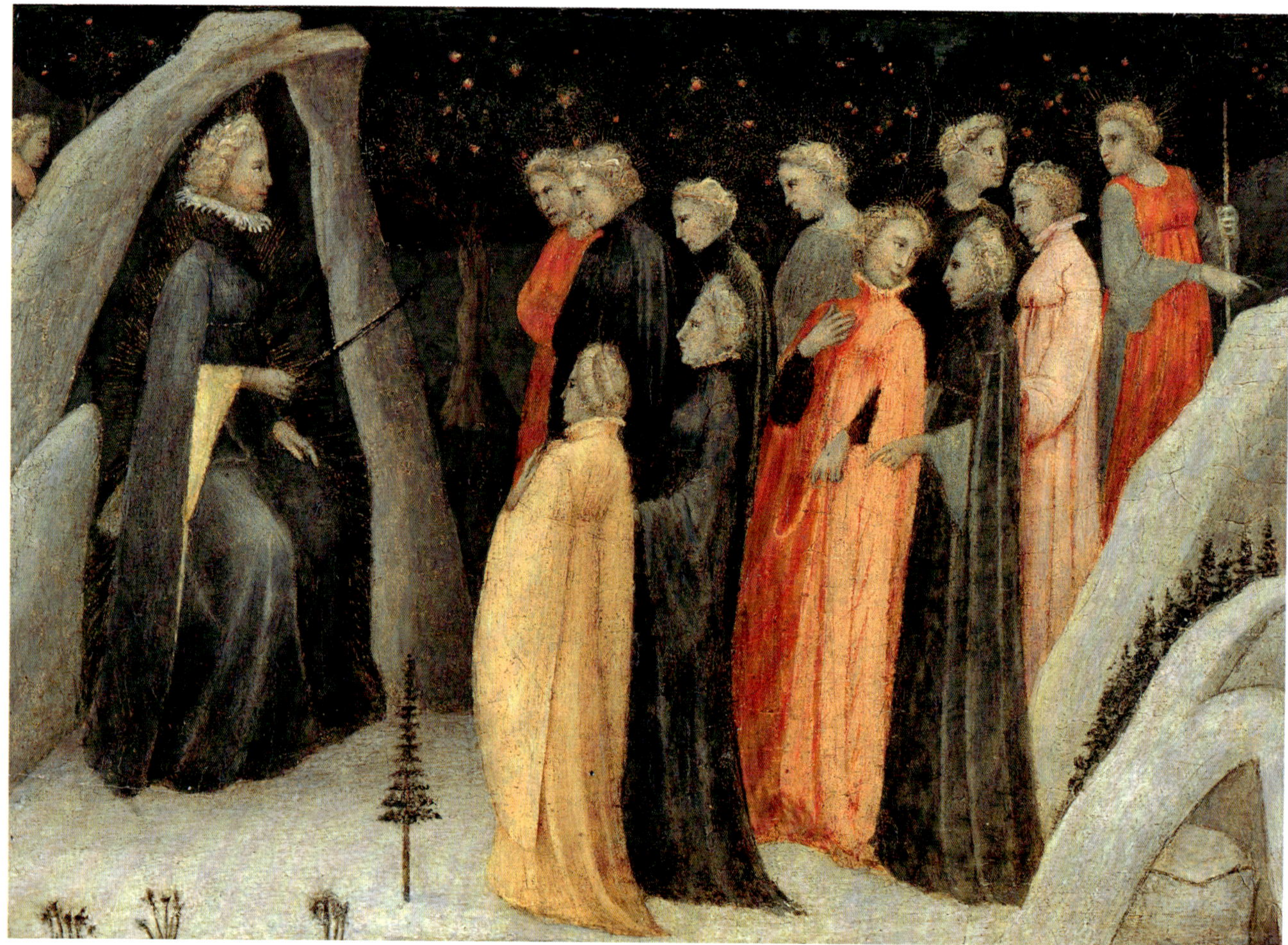

2: detail

Africo's hut at the center of the painting and substituting the scene of the rape of Mensola at the right with a much tamer vignette of Africo approaching three nymphs seated around a fountain to ask how he might find Mensola. A third cassone illustrating Boccaccio's poem, in the Musée Bonnat in Bayonne, repeats the scene of Mensola's rape as seen on the Bowdoin panel almost exactly, but replaces all the preceding episodes with scenes of the hunt.[9]

Despite the obvious similarities in their arrangement and, in some cases, the direct repetition of motifs and gestures, the pronounced differences in conception between the Bowdoin and ex-Honolulu cassoni reveal two clearly distinct artistic personalities at work. Giovanni Toscani's panel, formerly in Honolulu, employs a proportionally taller picture field and larger-scale figures than does the Bowdoin panel, yet it effectively eliminates all sense of spatial recession and continuity of landscape painstakingly maintained in the latter. Diana's nymphs at the left of Giovanni Toscani's panel are disposed in a rigorously isocephalic frieze, pressing closely against the picture plane, while those in the front ranks in the Bowdoin panel form a well-articulated semi-circle around the goddess, the others moving diagonally upward and back in space the farther they are from her. The sleeping Africo in his hut—the most severely damaged and liberally repainted part of the Bowdoin cassone—is situated in the middle ground, which is ringed with hills, trees, and a river in front and closed off at the back by a curiously gratuitous glimpse of a second gabled roof. Africo reclines on a bed covered with fine cloth, which falls in naturalistically rendered pleats at the corners. Giovanni Toscani shows him, instead, sleeping on a rudimentary reed mat (or striped cushion ?), beneath a schematically visualized shed roof placed as far forward as the spindly, hieroglyphic trees in front of it will permit. Even in the lively, engaging scenes at the right, in Toscani's panel, the artist makes little effort to calibrate the relative scale of the figures set at different points in space or to rationalize their placement amid the landscape elements, which, themselves, are of utterly fantastic design. In the Bowdoin panel, on the other hand, the lake in which the nymphs bathe represents a remarkable feat of landscape painting in its own right, considering its probable date—suggested by the costumes of Diana and her nymphs at the left—in the first decade of the fifteenth cen-

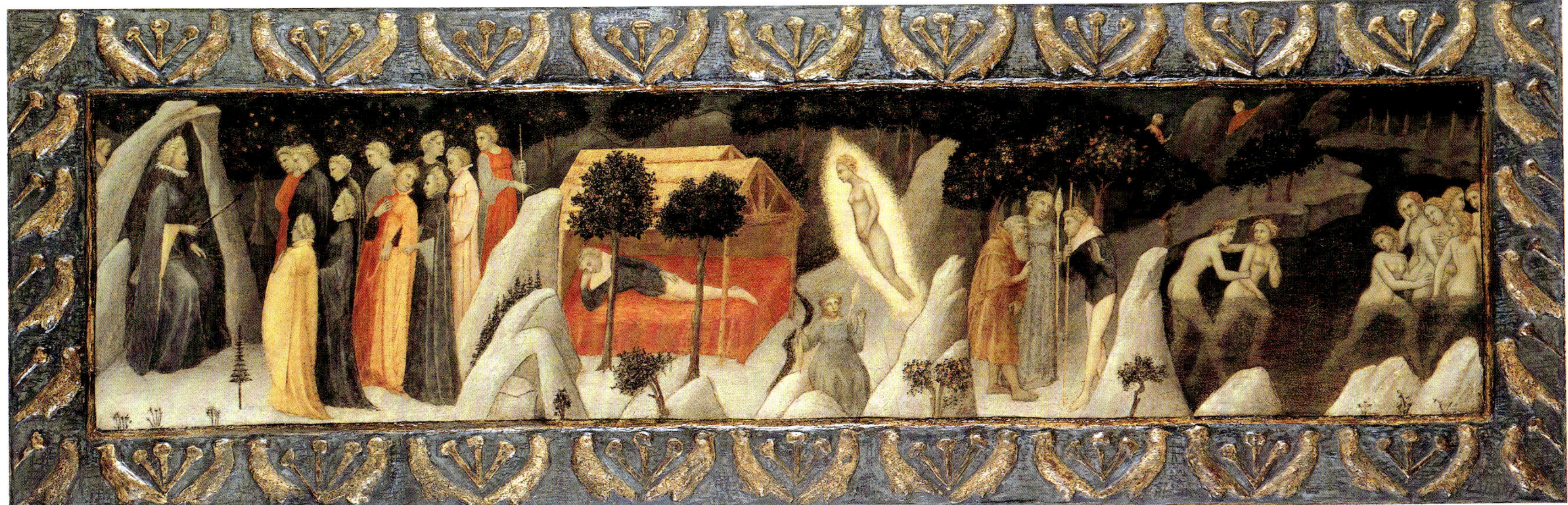

2

tury, while the panic and confusion of the fleeing nymphs, unconventionally cropped at the right edge of the composition, is entirely convincing.

Given the nicked and abraded state of the Bowdoin cassone, a typical result of the rough handling to which such objects were commonly exposed, it would be hazardous to advance a firm attribution for its authorship. While the ex-Honolulu panel conforms in every respect to the other known cassone panels by Giovanni Toscani, no paintings certainly by the same hand as the Bowdoin panel have been discovered. Yet, its ambitious treatment of space and of landscape detail and its sophisticated development of narrative do suggest a strong parallel with the early works of Fra Angelico—an impression reinforced by casual similarities to some of the scenes from the legends of the Desert Fathers in the Uffizi *Thebaid*. A conjectural attribution to Fra Angelico at some date around the time of his appearance in the studio of Lorenzo Monaco (about 1410–14)—presumably, during the earlier part of this span of years—may be proposed, pending the emergence of further material to clarify this virtually unknown moment in his career.

LK

1. Boccaccio 1960 ed., stanza 11.
2. Ibid., stanza 30.
3. Ibid., stanza 40.
4. Ibid., stanza 43.
5. Ibid., stanzas 110–111.
6. Ibid., stanzas 235–241.
7. Shapley 1966, p. 100.
8. Watson 1971, pp. 331–33; Watson 1985–86, p. 152; Callmann 1979, p. 75, fig. 2; Callmann 1995, pp. 46–47 (as Florentine, about 1425). See also Boskovits 1991, pp. 46–48, where an attribution by E. Fahy to the Master of Charles of Durazzo is accepted and extended to the Bayonne cassone (see note 9, below) as well. Fahy (1994, p. 242 n. 26) later withdrew this suggestion in favor of an attribution to Giovanni Toscani. For the identification of the Master of the Griggs Crucifixion with Giovanni Toscani, see catalogue 8.
9. Watson 1985–86, p. 152; Callmann 1995, p. 46, fig. 7.

Figure 15. Giovanni Toscani. *Scenes from the Ninfale Fiesolano*. About 1415–20. Formerly, Honolulu Academy of Arts

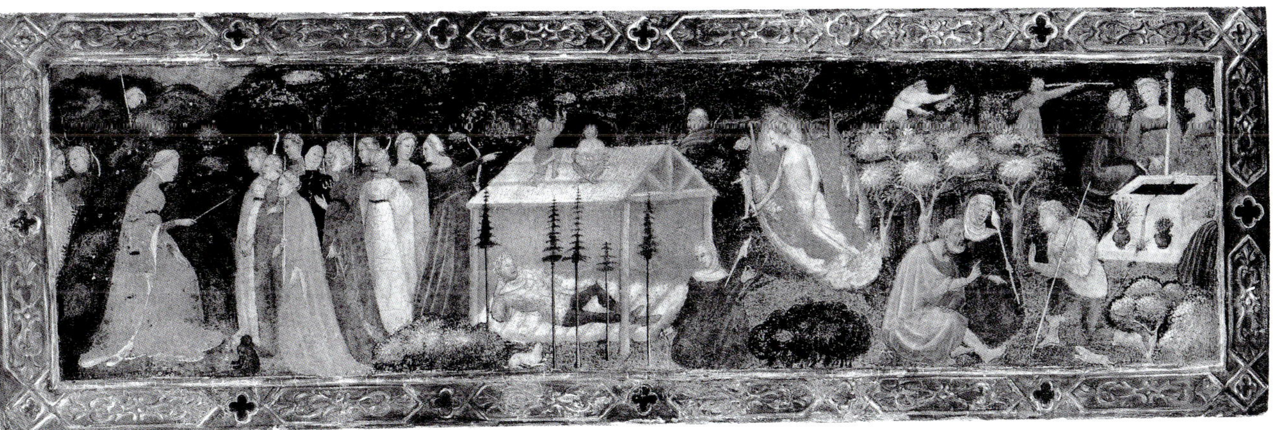

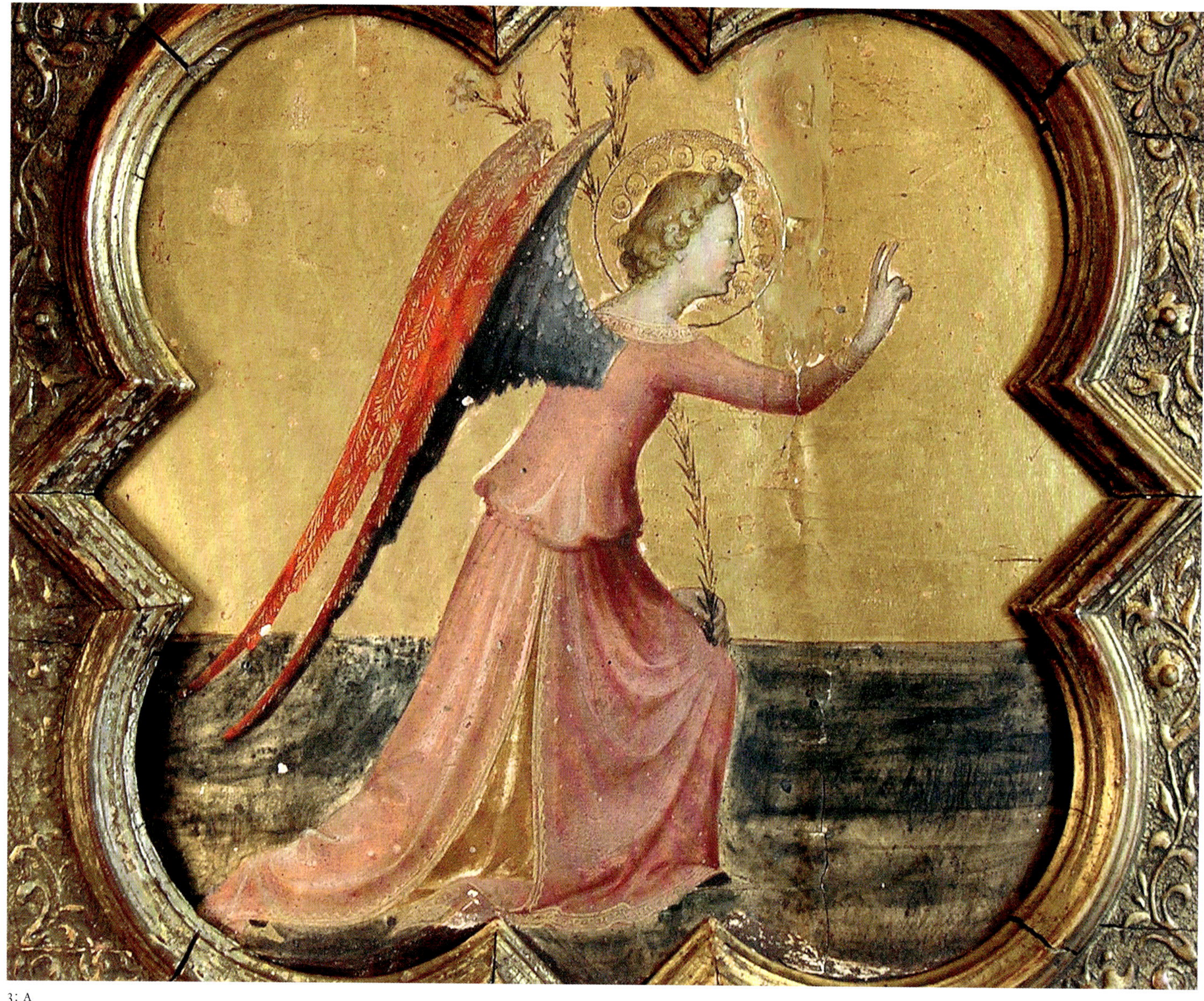

3: A

FRA ANGELICO

3

A.

The Annunciatory Angel

Tempera on panel, 29 x 31.2 cm (11⅜ x 12¼ in.)
Private collection

B.

The Virgin Annunciate

Tempera on panel, 29.8 x 31.5 cm (11¾ x 12⅜ in.)
Private collection

If, as seems likely, the Bowdoin cassone (cat. 2) was painted by Fra Angelico in the workshop of another master, the present panels may enjoy the distinction of being the earliest known independent paintings by the young artist. Previously unpublished,[1] they represent the Annunciation in two quatrefoil medallions—a pictorial equivalent to Ghiberti's bronze reliefs on the north door of the Baptistery in Florence. The Angel Gabriel, on the left, kneels as he rushes forward on what appears to be a thinly painted grassy meadow. He holds an exaggeratedly long lily in his left hand and raises his right hand as he declaims his greeting. His wings—beautifully drawn with a profile identical to those of the angels in the Rotterdam *Madonna* (cat. 6)—are painted red above and blue on their undersides, with each feather carefully highlighted or shaded and picked out in mordant gilt detail. The Virgin, on the right, is seated on a carved stool in a grassy (?), walled courtyard before the half-open door of her bedroom. Her hands are folded modestly in her lap and a book rests on her knee. A small vision of God the Father appears in the upper left lobe of the composition, with a line of mordant gilt rays following his gesture of blessing toward the Virgin, and the dove of the Holy Spirit flies between them. It is especially in this panel that Angelico's penchant for gratuitous naturalism is most in evidence: the beautiful folds of the Virgin's robe as it fans out on the ground around her; the seams and tassels of the cushion, the carved knobs on the back of the chair; the inlaid design on the *cassapanca* in

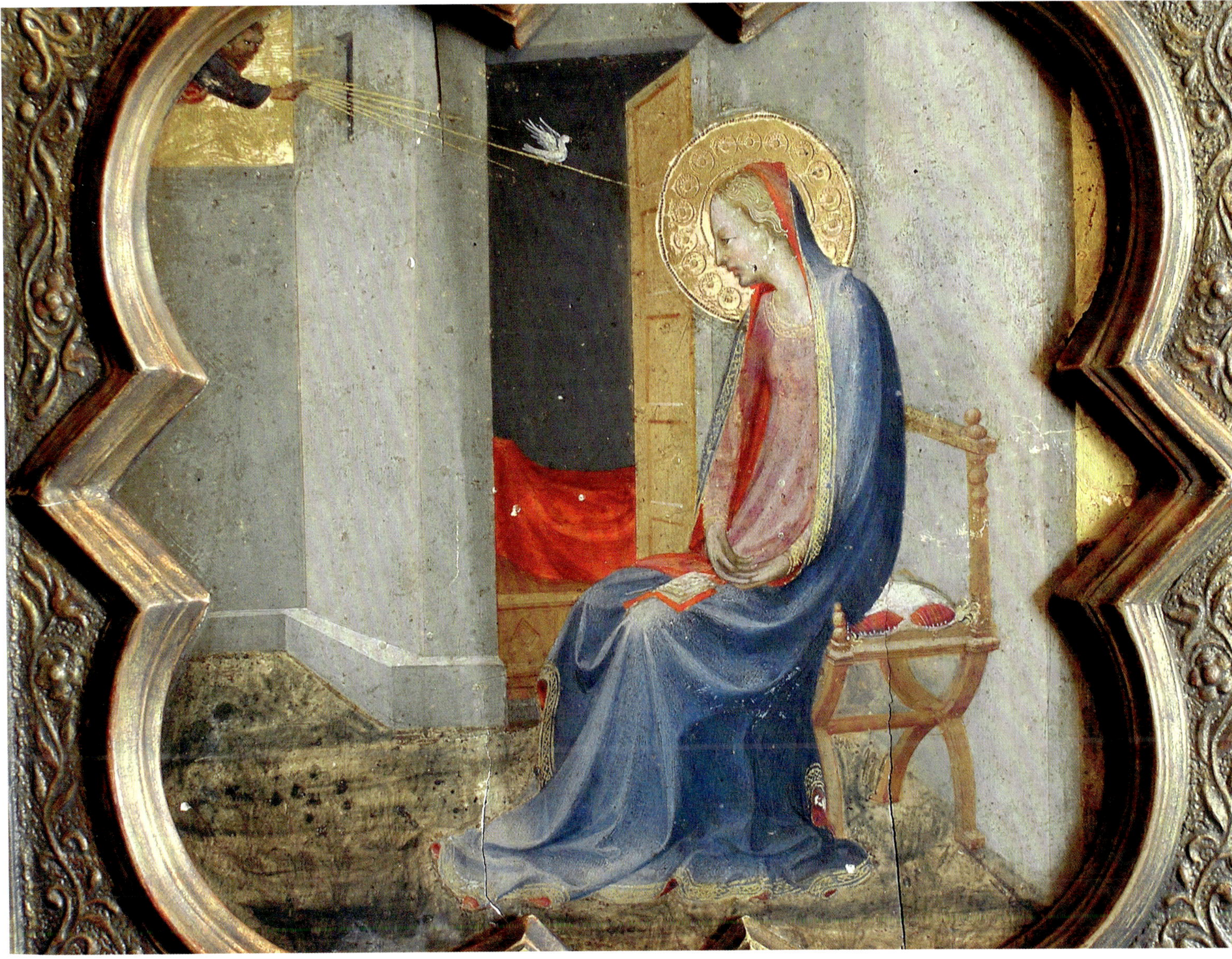

3: B

front of the Virgin's bed; and the aggressive foreshortening of the skirt molding on the wall at the left, the panels of the door behind the Virgin, or the legs of her stool. Details such as these, combined with Angelico's characteristic manner of rendering heads and facial features, and the fact that the figures' halos are treated identically to those of the angels in the Rotterdam picture, leave no doubt as to the attribution of these panels. At the same time, the simplicity and unabashed Gothicism of the two paintings—and their undisguised dependence on Ghiberti's models—argue for a date for them even earlier than such works as the Rotterdam *Madonna* or the *rotulus* drawings of about 1417 (cat. 5): it is probable that they were painted between that year and Angelico's departure from the studio of Lorenzo Monaco in 1413 or 1414.

The original function of these panels is not clear. Both are painted on their reverse sides, which might suggest that they are fragments of tabernacle or reliquary wings, or of *custodia* doors. It has not yet been possible to determine, however, whether this paint is original, and the fact that, despite being modest in scale, both panels are made up of two planks, with seams three or four inches from their right edges, could imply that they are actually fragments of a structure much wider than tabernacle wings. Their shape and size might suggest that they were part of the predella of an altarpiece—perhaps coincidentally, they are exactly the same height as the Nice *Funeral of a Bishop* (fig. 8) discussed above—but it is unusual in such a context to find an Annunciation scene divided over two panels

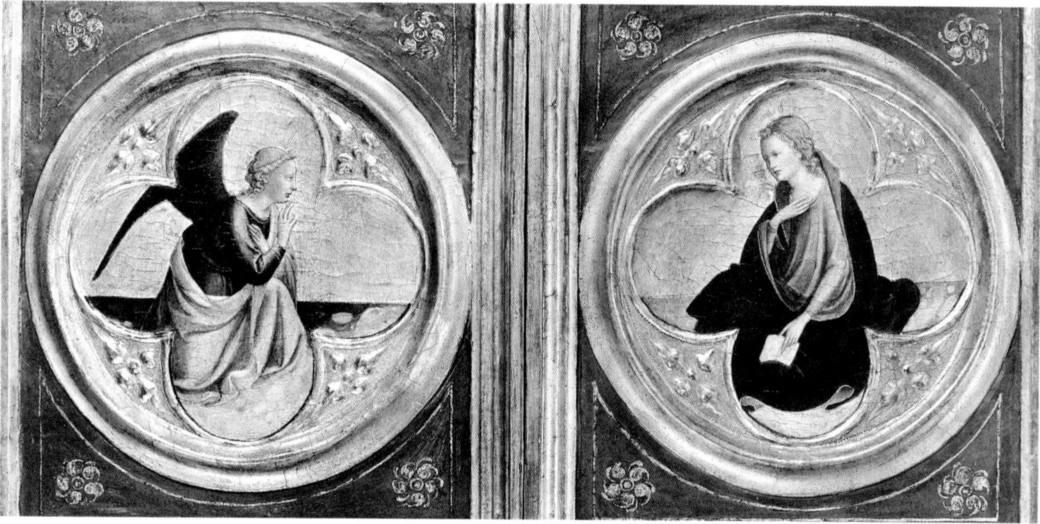

Figure 16. Fra Angelico. *The Annunciation*. About 1420. Formerly, Collection Baron von Tucher, Vienna

and even more unusual to find such panels with a vertical wood grain. The division of the scene into two distinct compositions and the vertically grained panel supports are more typical of the painted decoration on altarpiece spandrels and pinnacles; in fact, loosely related panels by Angelico are incorporated in the lateral pinnacles of the San Pier Martire triptych of about 1422–23 (cat. 13) and also supposedly filled the missing pinnacles of the San Domenico high altarpiece of a year or two earlier (fig. 16; see cat. 10). The possibility must be entertained that these paintings could be surviving fragments of the altarpiece commissioned for the chapel of Giovanni de' Gherardini in Santo Stefano al Ponte in August 1413, for which Guido di Pietro received final payment (often disbursed a year or more after the completion of work) in February 1418.[2] As nothing is known of the subject of that painting, however, such a proposal must remain purely hypothetical.

LK

1. I am grateful to Dr. Elena Sharnova in Moscow and to Dr. Roberta Bartoli in Berlin for calling these panels to my attention.
2. Cohn 1956a, pp. 218–20. The commission of 1413 was awarded to Ambrogio di Baldese, who, however, was subsequently paid—in January 1415 and April 1417—solely for painting frescoes in the chapel. The only other references to the altarpiece are two payments to "*Guidoni petri pictori*" (Fra Angelico) in January and February 1418, the last one specified as "*pro residuo solutionis tabule altaris dicte cappelle quam fecit*."

FRA ANGELICO

4.
Saint Joseph (?)

Tempera on panel, 17.8 x 16.7 cm (7 x 6 ⅝ in.)
Collection Richard L. Feigen, New York

This fragmentary head of a saint looking down toward the right clearly was excised from a larger narrative composition. Judging from the angle of his gaze and his pained or sorrowful expression and furrowed brow, he could portray Joseph of Arimathaea from a scene of the Deposition or Lamentation over the dead Christ. The figure type and the faint indications of background would also be appropriate for a representation of Saint Joseph from a scene of the Nativity or the Adoration of the Magi. As Fra Angelico normally reserves for the Virgin the type of pseudo-Kufic halo decoration visible here, cropped at the lower-left corner of the panel, it is most likely that this fragment once comprised part of a scene of the Adoration, but it should be noted that the artist's compositions of those subjects are usually oriented in the other direction.

Not mentioned in any of the literature concerning Fra Angelico or Early Quattrocento Florentine painting, this panel appeared at a London sale with an attribution to Giovanni Toscani, proposed by Everett Fahy.[1] The figure does, indeed, relate to Toscani's work, but even more specifically to those paintings formerly attributed to Toscani (alias, the Master of the Griggs Crucifixion), which now are widely recognized to be early works by Fra Angelico. The patterns in the engraved halo of the saint, with its twisting floral vine, and the pseudo-Kufic script in the cropped halo in front of him, are also consistent with other examples seen in early panels by Angelico as well as with the engraved decoration of the cloths of honor in the Pisa and Rotterdam (cat. 6) paintings of the Madonna. It is likely that the Feigen *Saint Joseph (?)* should be situated chronologically among these paintings, which date to the latter half of the second decade of the fifteenth century, and that when its composition was complete it was the largest of these works. As such, it may offer an impression of the appearance of the missing altarpiece, its subject unknown, painted by Fra Angelico for the Gherardini Chapel in Santo Stefano al Ponte between 1415 and 1417, which is recorded in two documented residual payments, dated January and February 1418—the earliest preserved notices of a work of art associated with Angelico.[2]

LK

1. Sotheby's, London, October 18, 1995, lot 50.
2. Cohn 1956a, pp. 218–20.

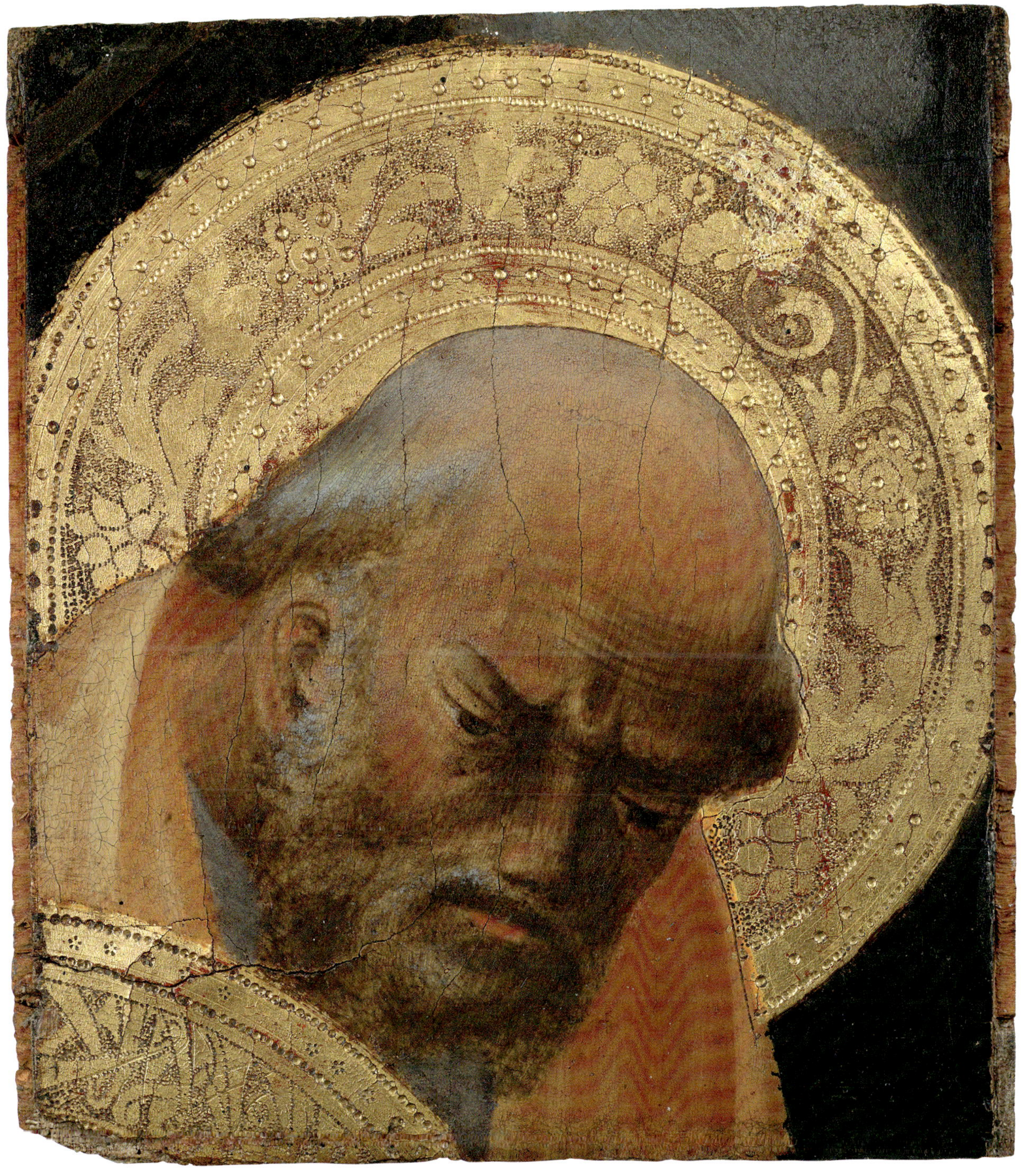

4

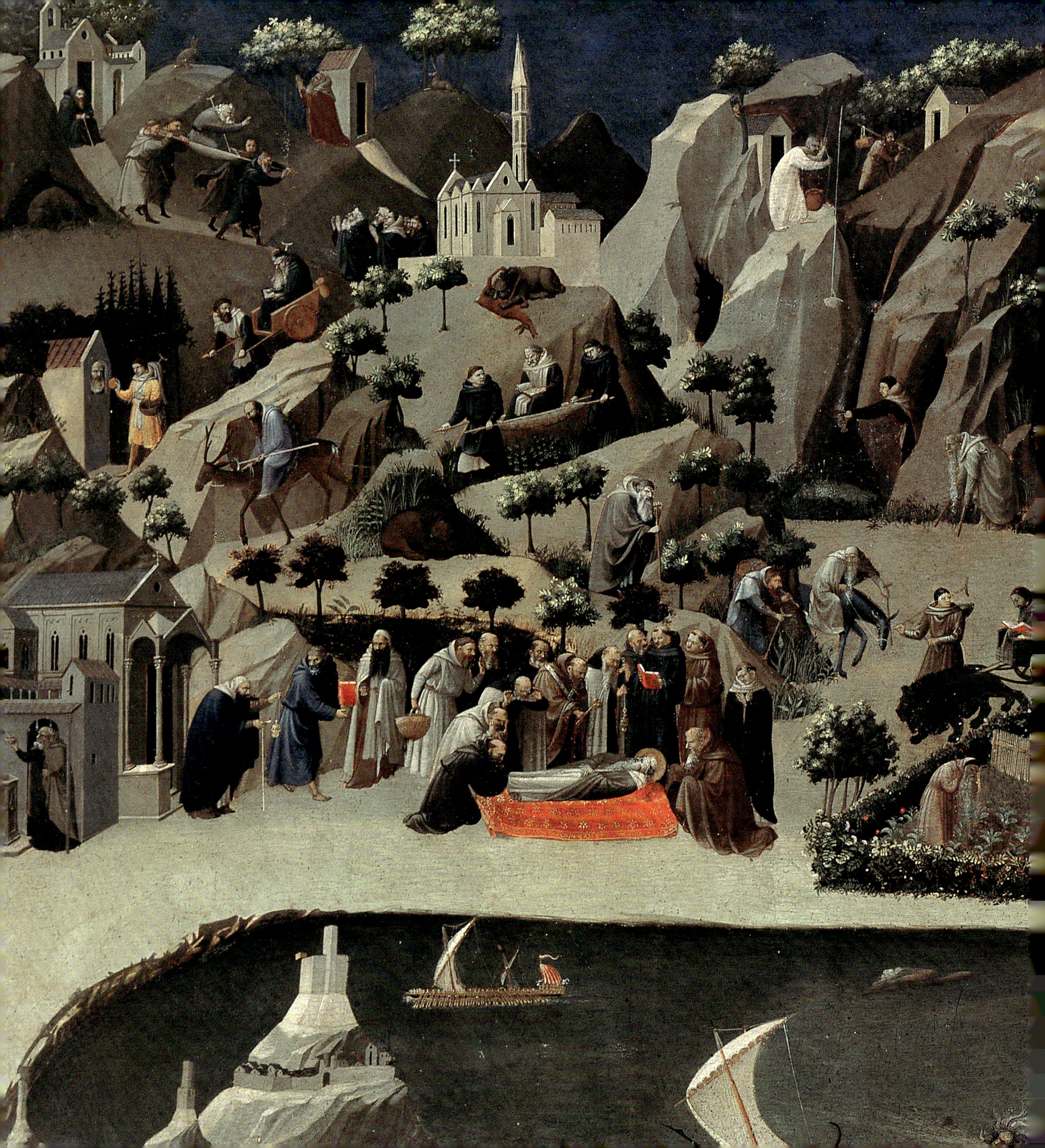

Chapter II
Pilgrims and Desert Fathers: Dominican Spirituality and the Holy Land

PIA PALLADINO

Among the various types of devotional objects created during the Middle Ages and the Renaissance are those associated with the Crusades and the pilgrimage to the Holy Land. A singular example of this kind of production is represented by the seven surviving fragments of an illustrated pilgrimage *rotulus* (roll), five of which are included in the present exhibition (see cat. 5). Written in a Dominican scriptorium in Florence in the early decades of the fifteenth century, and decorated by a team of artists that included the young Fra Angelico, this work casts a revealing light on the religious and intellectual environment that may have shaped the painter's imagination in the earliest and least-documented phase of his career.

Made of separate membranes of papyrus or, later on, parchment glued together, the roll had been the principal vehicle for writing, from antiquity up to the fourth century, when it was replaced by in the bound volume. Despite the dominance of the manuscript codex, the roll continued to be produced well into the Middle Ages, however, to fulfill certain practical or ceremonial functions. Among the most common examples from the fourteenth and early fifteenth centuries are official documents in roll form such as charters and diplomas; obituary rolls, which could extend as much as thirty meters in length, as more strips with new names were added on to the original; genealogies and illustrated chronicles, whose linearity of content lent itself to the format; prayer rolls, carried on the body, which served a meditative or talismanic purpose; and pilgrim guides to the Holy Land and Rome, which could be more easily carried and presented in this shape,[1] and which often included maps or drawings of the holy sites, along with a list of indulgences to be gained at each stop.[2] The five drawings in this exhibition, whose precise purpose, content, and attribution have been a subject of debate among scholars since their first appearance on the art market (see cat. 5), appear to be fragments of a unique type of illustrated pilgrimage roll, both spiritual guide and travel manual, intended for a specifically Dominican audience.

Three of the roll's fragments (cat. 5 A–C) are now in the collection of the Houghton Library in Cambridge, Massachusetts. The first and longest of these, A, consists of three separate pieces of parchment glued together (fig. 18). Taking up most of the length of the roll is a text known as the *Peregrinationes totius terrae sanctae*—one of numerous surviving versions of a popular medieval pilgrim guide to the most venerated places in the Holy Land, citing the indulgences earned by each one of the visits. Immediately following this is a second text enumerating the various stops on the return journey from the Holy Land across the Mediterranean, and the many other pilgrimage destinations throughout Europe (see Appendix). Both texts, as indicated by the explicit that appears in the second fragment, B, were written in 1417 at the behest of the Dominican lay brother Petrus de Cruce, who had visited these sites at various points in his life.

Petrus de Cruce may be identified as the bearded figure—wearing a skullcap and the white habit with black scapular typical of Dominican lay brothers—who appears twice in the drawing located directly above the text of the *Peregrinationes*. At the left, he is shown nearing land in a small vessel, seated in prayer before a large book, possibly a bible. Facing him, with his back to the ship's prow, is a second bearded figure dressed in Oriental costume. Another Oriental-looking figure, with turban and pointed beard—perhaps a sailor—seems to be pointing toward the approaching coastline. At the right, Petrus de Cruce is depicted again, kneeling before an imposing tomb outside the walls of a city. He is identified as a pilgrim by the small red cross painted on his shoulder, by the wooden staff and rosary beads in his left hand, and by the palm in his right hand—an allusion to the palm of Jericho, which pilgrims customarily brought back from Jerusalem.[3] The illustration may be intended to represent Petrus de Cruce's arrival at Jaffa, the port of entry to the Holy Land and the final stop for the boats of pilgrims following the usual sea route from Venice; from there, the travelers would make their way on foot to Jerusalem, the heart of the Holy Land, perhaps symbolized by the walled city in the drawing. The large sarcophagus might refer to Christ's tomb, the Holy Sepulcher, which, according to the Bible, was originally located outside the walls of Jerusalem, near the site of the Crucifixion (Matthew 27: 33; Mark 15: 22; John 19: 17),

Opposite:
Figure 17. Fra Angelico. *Thebaid* (detail of fig. 19). 1420. Galleria degli Uffizi, Florence

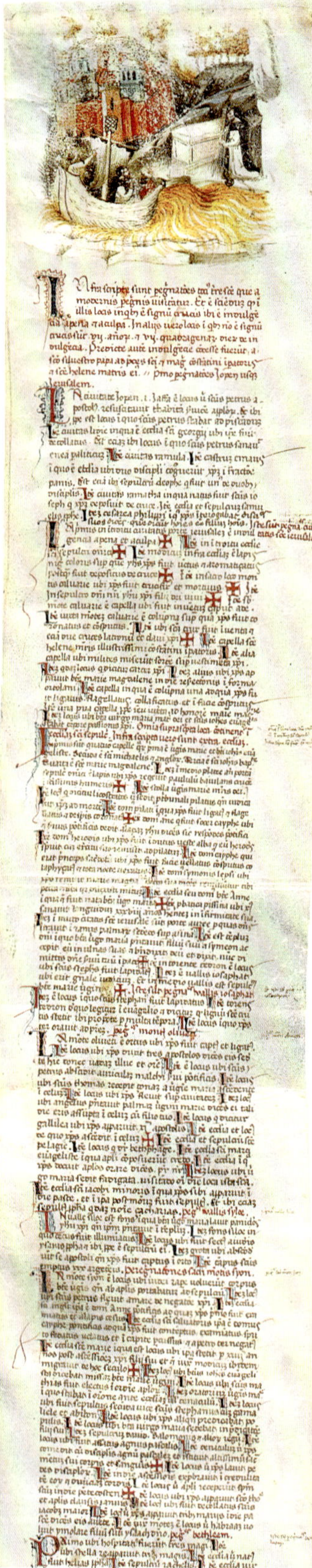

Figure 18. Pilgrimage Roll of Petrus de Cruce (detail; see cat. 5 A). About 1417–20. Houghton Library, Harvard University, Cambridge, Massachusetts (*1990M-16)

until it was incorporated into the city in the fourth century by the emperor Constantine, who built a basilica over it.

The second fragment in the Houghton Library, B, was separated from the first one, prior to 1928 by its owner at the time, the Munich book dealer Jacques Rosenthal.[4] As noted, it contains the explicit to the "Itinerary" of Brother Petrus de Cruce: "*Suprascrita loca et venerationes sanctorum sunt que ego frater Petrus de Cruce conversus ordinis predicatorum non semel set bis terque diversis temporibus vidi et pro devotione mea visitavi ut Deo placuit. Omnia autem hic hoc ordine scribi feci ut aliis sit quondam itinerarium in annis Dominice Incarnationis. M°.ccccxvii°. Indictione .x. die xxvi.a mensis Marcii*" ("Written above are the places of holy worship that I, Brother Petrus de Cruce, a lay brother of the Order of Preachers, have seen and visited for my devotion, not once, but on two and three different occasions. However, I have had everything written down in this order, that it might one day constitute an itinerary for others, in the year 1417 of the Incarnation of the Lord, tenth indiction, on the 26th day of the month of March"). Located immediately under this text is an illustration of two miraculous events that are recorded in the first person in the second part of Petrus de Cruce's itinerary: "*In provincia Regium in civitate Barensi corpus sancti Nicolai, et in reversione in quaedam silva aggressus fui a quinque serpentibus venenonsi et invocato nomine sancti Nicolai recesserunt me dimisso incolume. In Monte Gargano ecclesiam et locum Archangeli Michaelis, et in reverssione similiter tres lupi rapaces aggresi fuerunt me post quos venerunt alii duo et invocatis nominibus sancti Michaelis et Nicholai me dimiserunt in pace*" ("In the province of Reggio in the city of Bari [is] the body of Saint Nicholas, and on returning through a certain wood I was attacked by five poisonous snakes; and having invoked the name of Saint Nicholas they retreated leaving me unharmed. On Mount Gargano [is] the church and sanctuary of the Archangel Michael, and on returning I was similarly attacked by three rapacious wolves, behind which came two others, and upon invoking the names of Saint Michael and Saint Nicholas they left me in peace").

The composition of this drawing is organized in two separate registers: in the upper one is the armor-clad figure of Saint Michael the Archangel, posed on a rocky, wooded mountaintop that is meant to evoke the famous sanctuary dedicated to him on the promontories of the Gargano, along the Adriatic coast of Southern Italy, in the region of Puglia. Founded in the last decade of the fifth century on the site of the saint's first apparition to a herder named Gargano, by the Late Middle Ages this sanctuary had become one of the most venerated sites in the West, and an obligatory stopping place on the major pilgrimage routes of Europe. One such route, still popular in the fifteenth century, was the *iter magnum*, or "great journey," which passed through Rome on the way to its final destination in the Gargano.[5] Included among the stops on this itinerary was the city of Bari, located further south along the Adriatic coast, and home to the tomb of Saint Nicholas, Archbishop of Myra (Turkey), whose relics had been transferred to Bari in the eleventh century.[6] Although Saint Nicholas is invoked twice by Petrus de Cruce, it is Saint Michael alone who is depicted in the drawing, as if presiding over both miraculous events: an indication, perhaps, of the preeminence of one sanctuary over the other. As in drawing A, Petrus de Cruce is clearly identified by his dress and by the pilgrim's attributes of a red cross on his shoulder, a staff, and rosary beads. In close adherence to the text, he is shown first, in the lower half of the composition, being threatened by five hissing snakes, and next, in the upper half, being attacked by five wolves, three facing him and two behind him. In the top right corner is a summarily rendered building complex, perhaps intended to represent Saint Michael's sanctuary in the Gargano.

The third drawing, C, also in the Houghton Library, conforms in technique and dimensions to fragments A and B, and may illustrate various real or imaginary episodes in Petrus de Cruce's journey to the Holy Land. In the upper register of the composition, the friar, identified by the same skullcap and habit as in the first two drawings but this time shown without a beard or pilgrim's attributes, kneels before a Muslim ruler, surrounded by dignitaries and other figures, inside the walls of a city. He is depicted a second time, in the middle register, standing at the seashore and holding a large volume to his chest, as a man in a short costume, perhaps a soldier, forcefully grabs him by the shoulder. His head is turned toward a bearded figure in pilgrim's dress and hat. Standing opposite them, as if presiding over an arrest, is a bearded, turbaned dignitary accompanied by two other figures. Advancing behind them is a hunter with his dead prey strapped to a pole. In the lower register of the composition, more hastily executed and colored in, is a shipwreck scene, possibly the prelude to the events described above. Inside a vessel similar to the one occupied by Petrus de Cruce in the first drawing is a fierce looking figure, maybe the Devil, brandishing a section of the broken mast that he appears to have used to cast the five unfortunate passengers into the sea. One of the figures in the water, in skullcap and religious habit, is perhaps identifiable as Petrus de Cruce, while the bearded pilgrim with a satchel on his back, also emerging from the waves, might be the same individual as the standing figure next to the friar in the middle register.

A fourth fragment from the same roll, D, is now in the Albright-Knox Art Gallery in Buffalo. Clearly unfinished, with unevenly applied washes of color, the drawing depicts several miraculous events on a pilgrimage journey undertaken by a Dominican friar, possibly Petrus de Cruce. In the upper register the friar is shown exchanging greetings with the Devil disguised as a pilgrim; behind them, a lay pilgrim is about to be beaten with a stick by the Devil, here dressed in a monk's habit. In the lower register the same friar, now accompanied by two tonsured friars, is attacked by two snakes, which he appears to be warding off with the sign of the cross.

A fifth fragment, E, also included in this exhibition, now belongs to The Metropolitan Museum of Art in New York. The illustration, with only its most essential elements loosely sketched in, may allude to Petrus de Cruce's real or imaginary visits to two popular holy sites located on the pilgrimage route between Damascus and Beirut: the holy mountain where Noah built his ark and the place outside Beirut where Saint George supposedly slayed the dragon that was devouring the local youth. On a rocky outcropping in the upper left of the composition is a wooden, roofed structure with one window, meant to represent Noah's ark. In the foreground, Petrus de Cruce is shown standing at the foot of a tower, next to an unidentified figure holding a pilgrim's staff and pointing up toward a dragon. The image might refer to the tower where, according to popular belief, the dragon's victims were placed to await their fate.

The same roll also included two more fragments, formerly in the Koenigs Collection in Amsterdam and now temporarily in the State Pushkin Museum, Moscow (Koenigs Inv. no. I.101, I.102). The first Koenigs drawing (fig. 23) shows a beardless friar wearing a skullcap, possibly Petrus de Cruce, being attacked by a large snake in a rocky landscape dotted with trees. He is carrying a pilgrim's staff and beads in one hand, while, with his other hand, he prepares to hurl a stone at the snake. Indistinctly sketched on his left shoulder is a form that might be construed as the cockleshell worn by pilgrims returning from Santiago de Compostela, the famous pilgrimage site in Spain, which is listed at the end of Petrus de Cruce's itinerary.[7] The second drawing (fig. 24) shows the same friar conversing with a bearded monk outside a cave. On top of the mountain rising behind them is the decapitated body of a saint, whose soul is being carried up to Heaven by an angel; on the other side is another rocky outcrop on which Moses is kneeling to receive the Tablets of the Law from God, who emerges from the clouds. The three vignettes presumably illustrate the passage in the *Peregrinationes totius terrae sanctae* dedicated to the holy sites of Mount Sinai: "*Item in monte Synay est monasterium sive ecclesia sancte Marie de Rubo in qua requiescit corpus sancte Katerine virginis. Item post tribunam istius ecclesia est locus ubi Deus appa ruit Moysy in medio rubi. Item in medio montis est locus ubi Helias fecit penitentiam. Item in sumitate montis Deus de dit tabulas legis Moysy. + Item viridarium in quo est locus ubi sanctus Honofrius fecit penitentiam. Item alius mons sancte Katerine in cuius sumitate angeli posuerunt corpus eiusdem virginis . . .*" ("Also on Mount Sinai is the monastery or church of Saint Mary of the [Burning] Bush in which lies the body of the virgin Saint Catherine. Also behind the tribune of this church is the place where God appeared to Moses in the [burning] bush. Also halfway up the mountain is the place where Elijah did penance. Also on top of the mountain [is where] God gave Moses the Tablets of the Law. + Also the garden in which is the place where Saint Onophrius did penance. Also another mountain dedicated to Saint Catherine, on the summit of which angels placed that Virgin's body . . .").

Like the miraculous events illustrated in catalogue 5 B, C, and D, the main subject of Koenigs I.102 would appear to be an imaginary meeting between a Dominican friar, possibly Petrus de Cruce, and the prophet Elijah who, according to the Bible, fled to Mount Sinai after slaying the prophets of Baal, and took refuge in a cave where he heard the voice of God (3 Kings 19: 9–18). Since the Early Christian era, this site was one of several stops for pilgrims visiting the ridge of mountains collectively known as Mount Sinai. Their principal destination was the famous Monastery of Saint Catherine, built in the sixth century by the emperor Justinian, in a gorge below the so-called Mountain of Moses, where the prophet was believed to have received the Tablets of the Law from God. Perhaps reflecting earlier pilgrims' guides, the monastic complex of Saint Catherine is referred to in the text of the *Peregrinationes* as Saint Mary of the Bush, which was the name of the first small chapel erected on this site by the empress Helena, mother of Constantine the Great, in the place where Moses' Burning Bush was presumed to have grown. By the tenth century, however, the monastery had already assumed the dedication to Saint Catherine of Alexandria, the fourth-century Christian martyr who was beheaded for refusing to renounce her faith. According to legend, her body was miraculously transported by angels to the top of the highest peak in the Sinai peninsula, where it was found by monks who provided a proper burial for it inside their monastery. It is this episode that is alluded to in the drawing, in which Petrus de Cruce is shown pointing up to the rocky ridge with the saint's remains.

Some of the doubts concerning the common provenance of these seven fragments have resulted from the mistaken assumption by a number of scholars that catalogue 5 A and B comprised a complete roll between them. Yet, physical evidence confirms that at least one additional fragment was already missing at the time of their first publication in the Rosenthal catalogue of 1928. A narrow strip of old parchment glued along the top edge of A indicates where another section was joined to the roll at that point, in the same manner as the three separate pieces of which it is presently composed. An identical strip of parchment also remains along the top edge of C—the only other fragment that was listed by Bernard Berenson as formerly in the collection of Jacques Rosenthal,[8] although it does not appear in the 1928 catalogue. The location of the other four fragments before 1930 is unknown, but it may be worthwhile speculating whether, like B, they, too, had been detached from the roll by Rosenthal, presumably sometime before 1928, not simply to "protect" the drawings but to sell them as independent works of art. Beyond this, the most compelling evidence for the fragments' association is their common width, parchment preparation, and drawing technique, which conform to those of other illustrated rolls from the same period.[9]

Perhaps the greatest obstacle encountered in the assessment of these works as a unit, however, has been the difficulty, evidenced in the generic titles assigned to them by scholars, in interpreting the drawings' relationship to the text. Beginning with Rosenthal's comments on A and B, it generally has been assumed that the roll contains two separate and independent texts: the *Peregrinationes totius terrae sanctae* and that of Petrus de Cruce, with the explicit on B referring only to the friar's list of pilgrimage destinations in the Mediterranean Sea and across Europe. Such an interpretation has been justified by the contrast between Petrus de Cruce's seemingly unique account, occasionally written in the first person, and the standardized nature of the *Peregrinationes,* an impersonal text that appears in countless manuscript copies from the fourteenth century on, and in printed editions beginning in 1470.[10] Possibly copied from a much older prototype by someone who had never even visited the Holy Land, the text of the *Peregrinationes* is, in fact, more often than not included as an appendage or an introduction to a personal and actual pilgrimage experience, and it is sometimes even incorporated into miscellaneous collections of unrelated material.[11]

Since it is Petrus de Cruce who is clearly the protagonist of the only two scenes unquestionably related to the roll, it has been assumed that other illustrations to the manuscript should also allude to his more personal text. As noted above, however, drawing B alone makes direct reference to one of only two passages written in the first person (the other passage describes the friar's purchase of a relic in the convent of San Domenico in Bologna). The interpretation of A, as well as of the other five fragments related to the roll, has proved elusive, and is complicated by the fact that they all seem to revolve around the figure of a Dominican friar, who would appear to be dressed, although with some minor variances, in the same habit and skullcap as Petrus de Cruce. Degenhart and Schmitt,[12] who first pointed out the relationship between Koenigs I.102 and the text of the *Peregrinationes,* avoided the issue of the friar's identity, focusing only on Moses and Saint Catherine in the background of that composition. Other authors have referred generically to the foreground scene as that of a "hermit receiving a novice,"[13] or as an episode in the life of an unknown saint.[14] The same uncertainty has affected the interpretation of Koenigs I.101 and of C, D, and E, which cannot even be said to illustrate specific passages in the *Peregrinationes.*

A consideration of the relationship of the roll to contemporary pilgrimage literature, and an examination of its unique character as an object, however, offer some insights into the possible nature and significance of the drawings, as well as clues as to their authorship. To begin with, textual and circumstantial evidence suggests that the *Peregrinationes* and Petrus de Cruce's personalized account, despite their different character, were intended to be read as a continuous text: a single itinerary for pilgrims to the Holy Land and Europe, undersigned by Petrus de Cruce. Such an interpretation would account for the placement of the drawing of Petrus's arrival in the Holy Land at the head of the *Peregrinationes,* as an illustration of the author's real or imaginary journey to those sacred places, as well as to the ones listed in the second part of his itinerary. His more personal account begins where the *Peregrinationes* text leaves off, by listing, in successive order, the usual stops on the return journey from the Holy Land across the Mediterranean, from the islands of Cyprus, to Patmos, Rhodes, Crete, Mothone, and Corfu, and up along the Dalmatian coast back into Italy. As the text of the explicit makes apparent, everything written "above it," which clearly was copied down by the same scribe, was arranged by the author in a preset order, so as to serve as an itinerary for others. In the absence of a standardized itinerary on the model of the *Peregrinationes* for all of the pilgrimage routes across Europe, the author must have set out to provide his own, making his personal text conform to its style and tone.

However, the most compelling evidence for reading the roll as a complete itinerary is the existence, unknown to previous scholars, of one other copy of the same text—beginning with the *Peregrinationes* and ending with Petrus de Cruce's explicit—in an eighteenth-century codex in the Biblioteca Nazionale, Florence (Conventi Soppressi da ordinare 67, no. 165). The small volume, from the library of the suppressed Filippine convent of San Firenze in Florence, was first published as one of numerous surviving manuscripts of the *Viaggio in Terrasanta* of Lionardo Frescobaldi: a widely disseminated account, written in Italian as opposed to Latin, of the journey to the Holy Land undertaken by three Florentine citizens in 1384.[15] Immediately following the Frescobaldi text, which takes up folios 1 to 79 of the codex, is the itinerary of Petrus de Cruce (folios 80–95). The introduction to the volume reads as follows: "*Descrizioni d'un viaggio di Terra Santa fatto dal Caval. Lionardo Frescobaldi nel* 1383 [sic] *assieme con altri Fiorentini. / Ed altro fatto da Frà Pietro della Croce Converso Domenicano nel* 1417. */ Copiati da un manoscritto antico poco intelligibile*"

("Descriptions of a journey to the Holy Land made by Caval. Lionardo Frescobaldi in 1383 [*sic*] together with other Florentines. And another made by the Dominican Lay Brother Pietro della Croce in 1417. Both copied from an old, poorly legible manuscript"). The texts, as stated in an anonymous inscription on the volume's last page, below Petrus de Cruce's explicit, were copied on August 26, 1784.

Several important clues may be derived from the Biblioteca Nazionale codex: 1) That the "Itinerary" of Petrus de Cruce is not unique, as is commonly supposed, but existed in more than one copy; 2) That the roll, which is still in excellent condition and clearly legible, is not likely to be the "badly legible" manuscript referred to, but a second copy—a fact that might also account for the minor, although numerous, inconsistencies in the wording of the two texts; 3) That, as a result, the date of 1417 in the explicit should be applied with some caution to the roll as well as to its illustrations; 4) That missing fragments of the roll may have included another pilgrimage text, if not that of Frescobaldi, which may have shed some light on the more obscure subjects of the drawings.

The last observation is particularly relevant in light of the fact that the best clue to the interpretation of the subject of the Metropolitan Museum drawing, E, whose content has puzzled scholars the most, is offered by the separate and equally popular account of the same pilgrimage known as the *Viaggio ai luoghi santi* (*Journey to the Holy Places*), which was written by one of Frescobaldi's two traveling companions, Giorgio Gucci:

> *Per detto cammino, cioè da Damasco a Baruti, nulla cosa notabile si truova da fare menzione se none che, alle due parti del cammino in su, una alta montagna per la quale passiamo, la quale montagna si chiama l'Arca, e così per Arca è segnato in sulla carta de navicanti. E'l nome di questa montagna Arca si è perché dicono, e così di verità pare che fosse, che in su detta montagna fu fatta l'arca di Noè. . . . Fuori di Baruti per ispazio di circa a uno miglio o a uno miglio e quarto, è dove San Giorgio uccise il drago; ed è ogni cosa che si vede in propria forma, come la detta storia per Iscrittura narra. Prima si truova uno pedale di torre, alta circa di braccia VI; e sali su per una scala che è fuori della torre. In sul quale luogo gli uomeni della città mandavano la preda che il drago dovea mangiare; ed è in propria forma come se la città fosse in sul poggio di Sansipolcro e se detta torre fosse in sulla strada della porta a San Friano* [sic] . . . ("Along this way, that is from Damascus to Beirut, there is nothing worthy of mention, except for a tall mountain rising up from both sides of the way, which is called the Ark, and as such it is marked on sailors' maps. And the name of this mountain, Ark, is thus because they say, and in truth it seems so, that on the said mountain Noah's ark was built. . . . Outside of Beirut, about a mile or a mile and a quarter away, is where Saint George killed the dragon; and everything that is visible is just as it is written down in the story. First there is the base of a tower, about six *braccia* high; and you go up a ladder outside the tower. On which place the men of the city would send the prey that was to be eaten by the dragon; and it is just as if the city were on the Poggio of Sansepolcro and the said tower on the road to the gate of San Frediano . . . ").[16]

Like the texts written by his fellow travelers, Lionardo Frescobaldi and Simone Sigoli, Gucci's *Viaggio ai luoghi santi* is characteristic of the more personal, anecdotal type of Holy Land pilgrimage literature, written in the vernacular, which appeared between the fourteenth and the fifteenth century. Based on individual experience but also on previous accounts and hearsay—which explains their sometimes repetitive nature—these writings constitute a literary genre of their own, something between a travel diary and a popular guidebook.[17] While the three Florentine "diaries" have many elements in common, suggesting that they borrowed from one another, they seem to be distinguished by the inclusion of different versions or aspects of local legends. Thus, Gucci's text, which is preserved in nine known manuscripts written between the fourteenth and the sixteenth century,[18] is the only one of the three that includes the mention of a tower in relation to the legend of Saint George, although they all describe the mountain on which Noah's ark was built and the church dedicated to Saint George. Significantly, there is no reference to a dragon's tower in the standard medieval source for the lives of the saints, Jacopo da Varagine's *Golden Legend*; nor is the structure described in the most famous and widely circulated of Italian pilgrimage "diaries," the *Libro d'Oltremare* of the Franciscan friar Niccolò da Poggibonsi, composed between 1346 and 1350 and known from at least fifteen manuscript copies and no less than sixty-two printed editions dating from the sixteenth to the nineteenth century.[19] Therefore, it is possible to speculate that Gucci's text could, indeed, have been the direct source for the scene depicted in drawing E—in which case the figure standing next to Petrus de Cruce and pointing to the dragon's tower, who is generally identified as a monk but whose hat is of a type worn by the early-fifteenth-century Florentine ruling class rather than by any religious order, may allude generically to the kind of lay pilgrim represented by Gucci or his companions.[20] In this sense, the scene may be compared to the one in the Koenigs drawing of the imaginary meeting between Petrus de Cruce and the prophet Elijah. Paralleling the structure of the contemporary pilgrimage account, the drawings situate Petrus de Cruce at the center of actual and imaginary pilgrimage episodes that borrow their inspiration from a multitude of sources. It is worth noting that two out of the nine surviving manuscript copies of Gucci's text are preserved in the Dominican libraries of San Domenico in Fiesole and of San Marco in Florence, where, it has been proposed, they might have inspired the itinerary of another Dominican, Filippo Rinuccini, who traveled to the Holy Land in 1474.[21] A resident in San Marco, Filippo Rinuccini was, coincidentally, a descendant of the Andrea Rinuccini who had accompanied Gucci, Frescobaldi, and Sigoli on their pilgrimage, but who had fallen ill and died in Damascus.[22] The circulation of Gucci's text in Florentine Dominican circles suggests that it could have been one of many sources used for the illustrations of Petrus de Cruce's itinerary, even if it was not actually appended to the roll.

The notion of the drawings as illustrations of an ideal pilgrimage, of which Petrus de Cruce is made the protagonist, is reflected, above all, in the miraculous events portrayed in drawings C, D, and Koenigs I.101. A review of contemporary—or earlier—pilgrimage literature has not turned up a specific incident or description, as in the case of Gucci's text, which might have served as a single source for the unfolding of events described in C, tentatively identified as Petrus de Cruce's shipwreck, arrest, and audience before a sultan. On the other hand, stories of miraculous survivals at sea, whether real or invented, appear as a leitmotif of many pilgrimage accounts, presumably because of the actual possibility of death faced by travelers on the long and treacherous sea voyage to the Holy Land, whether as a result of a shipwreck, pirate attacks, or illness.[23] Once arrived at their destination at the port of Jaffa, or—if they followed the alternate route, as Frescobaldi and his companions did—at the port of Alexandria in Egypt, the pilgrims were met by local customs agents who inspected them and any possessions they might be carrying before sending them to the governor's residence, where they would be interviewed and pay a duty.[24] In Alexandria, we are specifically told, they were brought before the malik, or Muslim governor, for the questioning to which Westerners were subjected in order to obtain information about Christianity.[25] It is this city, described by Niccolò da Poggibonsi as situated directly on the sea and "enclosed all around by very high walls, inside which are beautiful palaces" (*"murata d' intorno d'altissime mura, e dentro belli palagi"*),[26] which should perhaps be identified as the setting for Petrus de Cruce's audience before a Muslim ruler in drawing C.

Beyond recalling contemporary pilgrims' experiences, the scene might also be an attempt on a symbolic level to cast Petrus de Cruce as another Saint Francis, alluding to the famous encounter in 1219 between the saint and al-Malik al-Kamil, Governor of Damietta. According to the account of this event by Jacques de Vitry, then Bishop of Acre, the saint was taken prisoner by the Muslims and preached "for several days" before the ruler who, fascinated with his words, "begged him to pray for him, the king of Egypt, so that God might show him what religion he wished him to embrace."[27] The comparison to Saint Francis might explain why Petrus de Cruce is shown holding a large volume, possibly a Bible, to his chest as if to protect it from possible confiscation. Presumably the same book before which he is shown in prayer in drawing A, it might be intended to present the friar's journey to the Holy Land in missionary terms. It may not be coincidental, in this context, that the scene in A should recall an illustration of Saint Francis's arrival by boat in the Holy Land, depicted in a mid-fifteenth-century illuminated codex of Bonaventure's *Life of Saint Francis* (Museo Francescano dell'Istituto Storico dei Cappuccini, Rome; inv. 1266).

The ultimately didactic or moralizing intent of the drawings is further reflected in the choice of subjects of D and of Koenigs I.101. These scenes depict Petrus de Cruce—identified by the usual dress, pilgrim's staff, and skullcap—at the center of several dramatic events that evoke the various encounters between the Devil and the Desert Fathers described in early patristic literature. According to the Early Church Fathers, in the fourth and fifth centuries, the inhospitable desert regions of the Upper Nile Valley had been settled by monks, living alone or in small communities, whose sanctity and ascetic existence provided the model for the eremitical ideal of Western monasticism. The sites associated with the most famous of these figures, Saint Paul the Hermit and Saint Anthony Abbot, were soon included in the standard repertory of pilgrimage destinations and are, in fact, listed in the *Peregrinationes* (see Appendix). Travelers undoubtedly bore in mind the colorful legends that had grown up around the lives of the desert hermits, which had been compiled by early writers such as Saint Athanasius, Saint Jerome, and Palladius and became known collectively from the Latin edition as the *Vitae patrum*. Dominating such stories are the miraculous accounts of the monks' daily struggles with the Devil, who appeared to them in innumerable shapes and forms, whether in the guise of a fellow monk or priest, or of a ferocious beast or poisonous reptile crossing their path. Athanasius, the fourth-century bishop of Alexandria, wrote in his *Life of Saint Anthony,* "It is very easy for the Enemy to create apparitions and appearances of such a character that they shall be deemed real and actual objects.... One had the form of a lion, and another had the appearance of a wolf, and another was like unto a panther, and all the others were in the forms or similitudes of serpents, and of vipers, and of scorpions. The lion was roaring as a lion roareth when he is about to slay; the bull was ready to gore [him] with his horns . . . and the snakes and the vipers were hissing, and they appeared in the act of hurling themselves upon him."[28]

Set in a rugged landscape perhaps meant to recall the Egyptian desert, and focusing on encounters between pilgrims and the Devil, drawings D and Koenigs I.101, in particular, appear to have been intended to cast the pilgrimage journey in terms of the spiritual, ascetic experience of those early Desert Fathers. A symbol of this analogy is the skullcap worn by Petrus de Cruce—it was not part of the standard dress of Dominican lay brothers but was a specific requirement of a monk's attire as stated in the Rule of Saint Pachomius (about 290–346), the founder of the first eremitic communities in the desert and the father of cenobitic monasticism.[29]

Viewed in this light, the drawings become part of the same spiritual culture that witnessed, in the words of Ellen Callmann,[30] the "sudden and brief appearance" in Tuscany, between the fourteenth and fifteenth centuries, of the Thebaid as a subject of both panel paintings and frescoes. The basis of these images, the most famous examples of which are those in the Camposanto in Pisa and in the Uffizi in Florence (fig. 19), are stories of the Desert Fathers set in a landscape that is meant to evoke the Egyptian desert near Thebes, which was settled by Saint Anthony and his followers. Art historians have analyzed the emergence of this theme in relation to the religious revivals that swept across Europe in the fourteenth century and the reforms undertaken in various monastic communities to reassert the eremitic origins of the monastic experience. For the Dominicans, whose convents were modeled on monastic and, especially, Cistercian custom, the Observant reforms meant a return to the original constitutions and, significantly, to those values embodied in Gérard de Frachet's *Vitae fratrum* (*Lives of the Brethren*), written between 1256 and 1259—a collection of legends of Dominican worthies that consciously imitated the *Vitae patrum*.[31]

Not coincidentally, perhaps, it was a friar in the Dominican scriptorium of Santa Caterina in Pisa, Domenico Cavalca (1270–1342), who, in the fourteenth century, popularized the early patristic sources by translating the *Vitae patrum* into Italian. Written in a Tuscan vernacular directed at the layman as well as the less-educated monk, Cavalca's *Vite de' Santi Padri* became one of the most widely circulated texts of the Late Middle Ages, rivaled in popularity outside monastic confines only by Jacopo da Varagine's *Golden Legend*.[32] Both these works, along with ancient patristic texts, provided the inspiration for most of the identifiable scenes in *Thebaid* paintings, beginning with the Camposanto frescoes in Pisa, generally dated between 1335 and 1340.[33] Part of a larger cycle that has been convincingly analyzed in terms of the tenets of Dominican preaching,[34] the Pisan *Thebaid* is typical of all surviving representations of the theme. The composition is articulated around superimposed mountainous zones sprinkled with churches, hermits' huts, and other architectural details, among which individual or small groups of hermits are shown going about their business or dealing with the Devil's various appearances. Rather than reading as a continuous narrative, the image is a compilation of different episodes or stories all arranged on the same plane and artificially divided from each other by rocky outcrops, trees, or architecture.

While reflecting the content as much as the compositional structure of *Thebaid* images, none of the specific episodes represented in drawing D occurs in the Pisan fresco or in any other, later depictions of the theme. Instead, the scenes would appear to be based on a loose interpretation of a variety of sources from Athanasius to Cavalca, including *The Golden Legend*. The episode of Petrus de Cruce facing the serpent seems to allude generically to the trials faced by Saint Anthony, as recorded by Saint Athanasius, as well as to the particular story narrated by Cavalca in his Life of Saint Macarius, under the heading "How he killed the snake and went into the Thebaid desert."[35] Likewise, the vignette of the pilgrim being chased by the Devil dressed as a monk might illustrate Cavalca's tale of the beating received by a disciple of Saint Macarius, who, having been sent on ahead by his master, collided on the road with "a priest of the idols who was running at great speed holding a huge stick";[36] but it may also refer more broadly to other episodes of monks being attacked by the Devil with sticks, such as the story of Moses the Ethiopian,[37] which is represented in two mid-fifteenth-century versions of the *Thebaid* attributed to the Florentine painter and illuminator Giuliano Amidei (in Christ Church Picture Gallery, Oxford, England, and Private collection, Scotland, respectively). Petrus de Cruce's encounter with the Devil dressed as a pilgrim might, in turn, be based on the same story, derived from Cavalca's Life of Saint John the Hermit, which inspired the scene of the hermit being approached by the Devil as a female pilgrim in the Camposanto *Thebaid*,[38] but, at the same time, it might also allude to other tales of the Devil's appearance as a pilgrim, such as those recounted in *The Golden Legend* and depicted in earlier paintings.[39] Not without relevance to the didactic nature of the drawings is the miniature of Christ's encounter with the Devil dressed as a pilgrim-hermit, in a fourteenth-century moralizing treatise on the Passion of Christ, in the Biblioteca Nazionale, Florence.[40] This array of references suggests, in the final analysis, that drawing D should be viewed in the same light as *Thebaid* images: as a "summa," in the words of Alessandra Malquori,[41] of well-known medieval figurative traditions and familiar patristic literary allusions that offered the viewer a multiplicity of levels of interpretation.

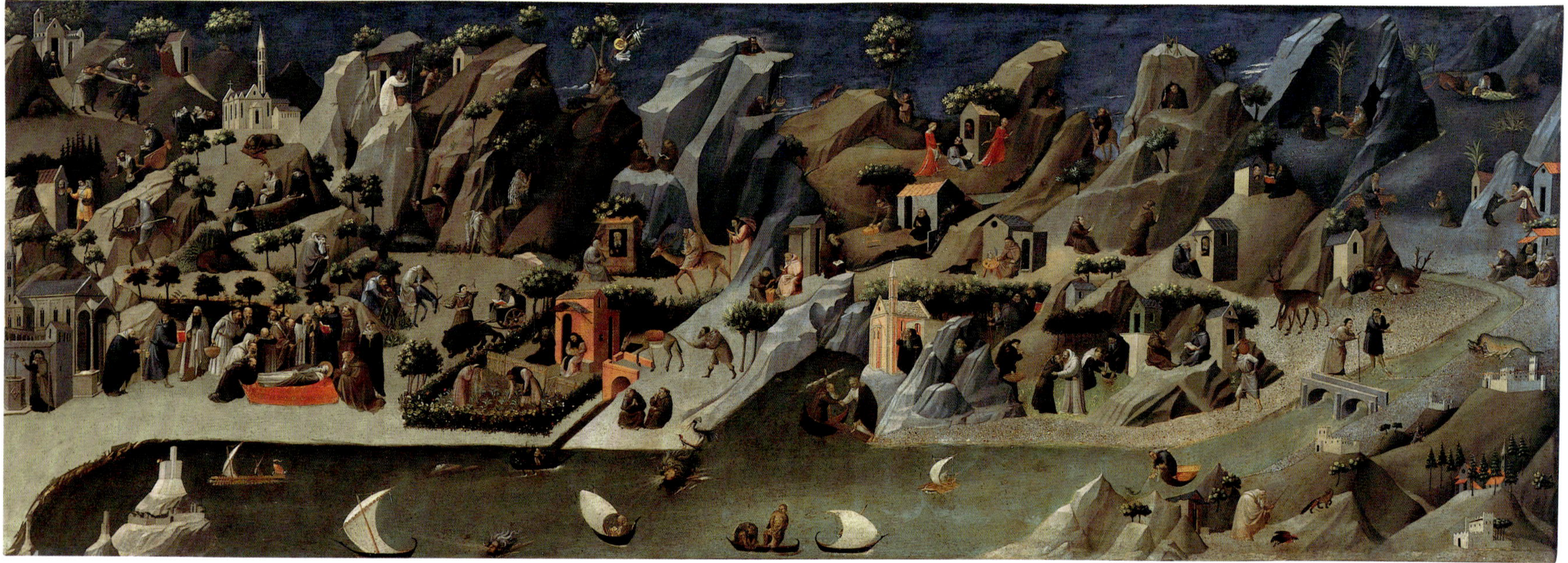

Figure 19. Fra Angelico. *Thebaid*. About 1420. Galleria degli Uffizi, Florence

It may have been the compositional and thematic relationship among *Thebaid* paintings in general and drawing D that prompted Roberto Longhi to compare it, along with B, to the celebrated *Thebaid* panel in the Uffizi, all three of which he considered as the earliest works of Fra Angelico's career. Longhi's proposal of authorship for the Uffizi *Thebaid,* which was previously attributed to the Late Gothic painter Gherardo Starnina, has been accepted by most recent scholars, and crucial analogies for the painting have been singled out in other works now almost unanimously regarded as autograph products of Angelico's early years, such as the Griggs *Crucifixion* in The Metropolitan Museum of Art (cat. 8) and the Princeton *Penitent Saint Jerome* (cat. 9). Ironically, while it is no longer possible to maintain an attribution to Fra Angelico for B and D, the two drawings discussed by Longhi, it can be shown that Angelico was, indeed, involved in the production of the present roll, to which he contributed two other illustrations: E and Koenigs I.102 (see the arguments developed below, on p. 47).

A clue to the circumstances surrounding Fra Angelico's intervention in the decoration of the roll sometime between 1417, the date of Petrus de Cruce's explicit, and about 1420 may be gathered from its undisputed creation in Florentine Dominican circles. Nothing is known of Petrus de Cruce beyond what may be inferred from the explicit, where he states that he is a conversus, or lay brother—that is, a member of the Dominican order who had taken his vows but was not ordained. Situated on the lowest rung of the ecclesiastical ladder, lay brothers were usually the least-educated members of the order, who were expected to honor all the requirements of monastic life but were excluded from holding office or conducting religious services. Contrary to what has generally been assumed, therefore, it is unlikely that Petrus de Cruce himself would have had the financial resources or the knowledge to commission the roll and its elaborate illustrations. We may presume, however, that the friar was responsible for the original manuscript from which the roll was copied. Like all members of a religious order who had undertaken a pilgrimage, he would have dictated his text to a scribe from memory or from notes and then presented it to his Dominican superiors in order to obtain the *approbatio,* or official church approval, without which it could not be made available for copying.[42]

The various levels of interpretation elicited by the drawings would appear to suggest that the roll copy of Petrus de Cruce's text was commissioned by an erudite patron within the Florentine Dominican establishment or by someone closely affiliated with it. The particular choice of a roll, as opposed to a codex, might indicate that it was meant to be carried by its owner on a planned pilgrimage journey. It is equally possible, on the other hand, that the roll format was chosen simply for its archaizing quality, independent of its practical use. Petrus de Cruce's text, enhanced by the accompanying drawings, may have been intended to serve a purely contemplative purpose, like other known copies of pilgrims' diaries that were made to lead the reader on a "spiritual pilgrimage" (*peregrinatio spiritualis*) rather than on an actual one.[43] As the introduction to an anonymous fourteenth-century itinerary states: "These are the journeys which must be undertaken by pilgrims who go overseas in order to save their soul, and which every person in their own home can also make, by reflecting on every place mentioned below, and by reciting at every holy site a God our Father and a Hail Mary."[44] Commenting on the character of pilgrimage literature in general, Jean Richard[45] has aptly stated that whether designed to confirm the reality of the pilgrimage and the sanctuaries visited or to reaffirm the truth of the Catholic faith, through stories of miraculous events, these writings were first and foremost for the "edification" of the faithful.

Beyond this, the roll's illustrations suggest a more specific purpose: to reassert the values of Dominican piety and missionary zeal. The emphasis on the missionary nature of Petrus de Cruce's journey, and the parallels with Saint Francis, as shown in C, may be interpreted in light of the Dominican order's own missionary presence in the Holy Land, which was regulated by the founding of the Societas Fratrum Peregrinatium (Society of Pilgrim Friars) in the early fourteenth century. The notion of the Dominican pilgrim-missionary, which was at the core of this organization, was embodied by one of the most celebrated Florentine members of the order, Fra Ricoldo da Montecroce (1243–1320). In 1288, Fra Ricoldo had left the convent of Santa Maria Novella and embarked on a long missionary journey through the Holy Land and Asia, recording his experiences in a well-known *Itinerarium* that was intended to be, as the author noted in his preface, as much a spiritual guide as a travel account.[46] By the middle of the fourteenth century, Fra Ricoldo's example had nurtured the creation of a legion of missionaries inside the walls of Santa Maria Novella, which, effectively, became the local headquarters of the Society of Pilgrim Friars.[47]

In the first half of the fifteenth century, Fra Lorenzo di Domenico de Cardoni (d. 1438), an esteemed theologian and, between 1422 and 1425, Prior of Santa Maria Novella, became the organization's first Florentine vicar-general.[48] Cardoni's tenure as prior coincided with the declining years of Leonardo Dati, who had entered Santa Maria Novella about 1375 and was Master General of the Dominican Order from 1414 until his death in 1425. One of the principal personalities involved in bringing the newly elected pope Martin V to Florence in 1419, Leonardo Dati was responsible for many of the construction projects undertaken at Santa Maria Novella in preparation for the pope's stay in the convent and the consecration of the church in 1420. Andrea De Marchi has recently postulated that Dati may have been one of Angelico's earliest patrons and that he may have commissioned the (now lost) works for Santa Maria Novella attributed to the artist by Vasari.[49] Dati was an ardent promoter of the Dominican Observant reform movement

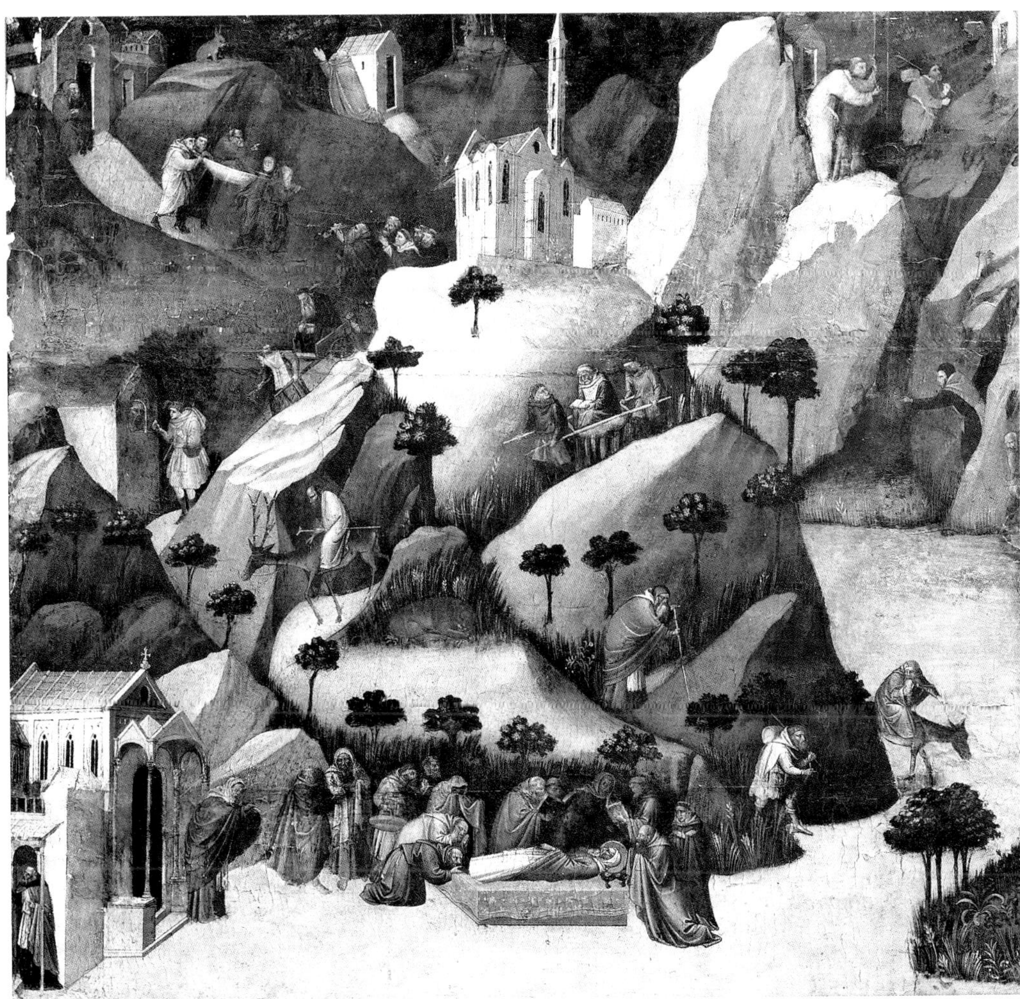

Figure 20. Workshop of Orcagna (?). *Thebaid*. Keresztény Múzeum, Esztergom, Hungary

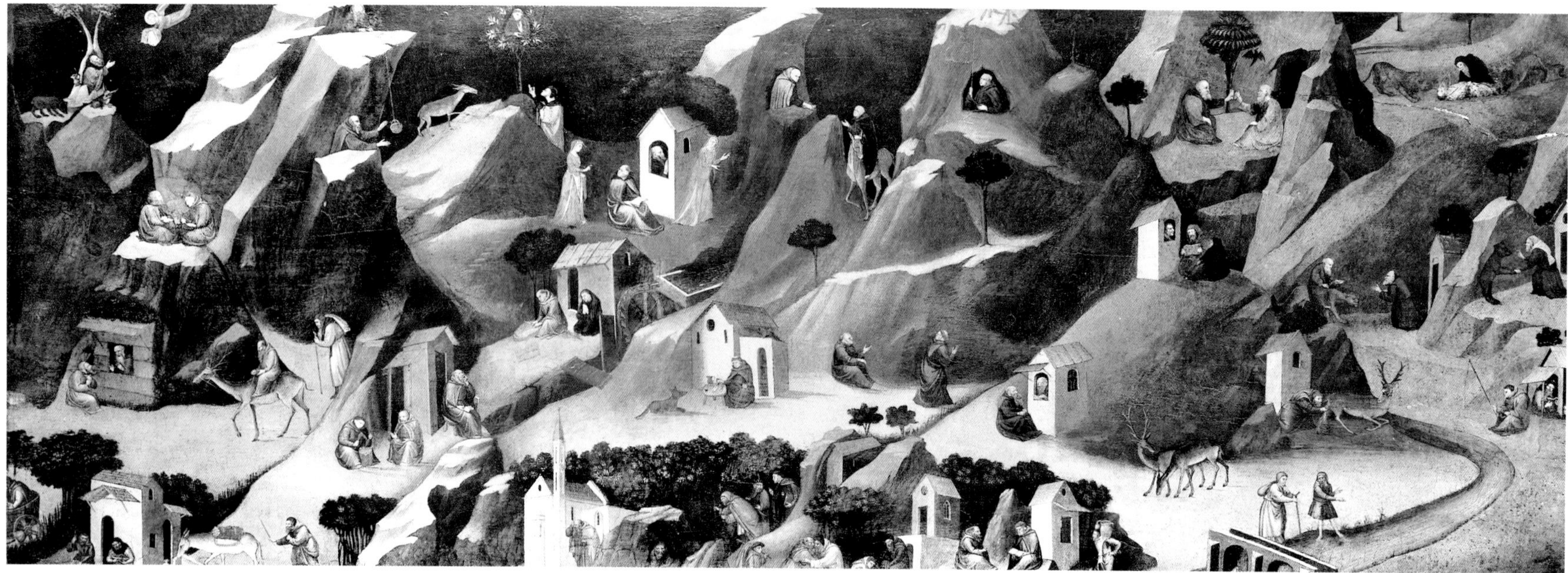

Figure 21. Workshop of Orcagna (?). *Thebaid*. Private collection, England

instigated by his famous contemporary Giovanni Dominici (1356–1420), who had also taken the Dominican habit in Santa Maria Novella. A statesman, writer, and brilliant preacher, Dominici promoted his cause across Italy and went on to found the Observant convents of Corpus Domini in Venice (1391) and of San Domenico in Fiesole (1406).[50] Personalities such as Fra Lorenzo de Cardoni, Leonardo Dati, and Giovanni Dominici, who is reported to have gone on a pilgrimage to Jerusalem in 1401,[51] define the intellectual and spiritual atmosphere centered around the convent of Santa Maria Novella that inspired the production of the roll and that underlies the drawings' multiple points of reference.

In light of the thematic relationship of the drawings to Thebaid imagery, it is worth speculating whether the impetus for the appearance of this theme in Florentine painting should also be sought within the confines of Santa Maria Novella. In her eloquent analysis of the cultural climate that may have led to the commission for the Uffizi *Thebaid,* Alessandra Malquori[52] focused on the Camaldolese convent of Santa Maria degli Angeli and the reform movement inspired by the humanist scholar and prior Ambrogio Traversari (1386–1439), who promoted the study and translation of patristic texts. Yet, in a separate study, the same author highlighted the specifically Dominican interest in the theme, reflected in the Dominican-inspired Pisan cycle, and the inclusion of one of the earliest Florentine representations of the subject on the walls of the convent of Santa Maria Novella.[53] Executed sometime between the last decades of the fourteenth century and the first decade of the fifteenth, and located near the Chiostrino dei Morti, the Santa Maria Novella frescoes are discussed by Malquori, like the Pisan cycle, in direct relationship to the order's self-appointed missionary role in disseminating the values of the eremitical experience. It may be possible to suggest, within this context, that the Dominicans of Santa Maria Novella also had a part in the commission for the earliest known *Thebaid* on panel, now divided between the Keresztény Múzeum in Esztergom, Hungary (fig. 20), and a private collection in Britain (fig. 21). Originally almost three meters long, this *Thebaid* is the largest of the surviving Florentine paintings of the subject and is generally considered the prototype for later versions, beginning with Angelico's panel in the Uffizi.

Following Offner[54] and Boskovits,[55] the Esztergom/Private collection *Thebaid* is generally attributed by scholars to Mariotto di Nardo and dated between 1380 and 1400. However, as Callmann first observed,[56] the panel, which has a "spaciousness" entirely foreign to Mariotto, does not fit easily within the artist's more routinely prosaic production. The sophisticated spatial solutions, most evident in the cogently built architectural structures, the subtleties of modeling, and the expressive facial types that distinguish those parts of the Esztergom panel still in their original condition (fig. 22)[57] betray decidedly Orcagnesque qualities that would seem to situate its execution somewhat earlier than is generally assumed. If so, it is worth speculating whether this *Thebaid,* whose early provenance—before its appearance on the art market in the nineteenth century—is unknown,[58] could, in fact, have been produced in the Orcagna workshop at, or for, Santa Maria Novella, thus providing an obvious model for the young Fra Angelico.

Although commonly associated, like their fresco counterparts, with monastic communities, the exact function of such *Thebaid* panels is not known. Beginning with Longhi, most scholars have connected the Uffizi *Thebaid* with the panel by

Fra Angelico showing "many stories of the Desert Fathers," listed in an inventory of the Medici palace compiled after the death of Lorenzo the Magnificent in 1492.[59] This identification has been questioned most recently by Boskovits,[60] who maintains that the Uffizi *Thebaid* was more likely commissioned for an eremitic order in Florence and perhaps set into a wall or used as a *spalliera* on a bench in a place frequented by the monks outside the areas for common prayer, such as the sacristy. Circumstantial evidence would seem to suggest, however, that the Uffizi *Thebaid* is the painting described in the 1492 inventory as located "*nell'andito che va alla chamera di Piero*" ("in the corridor that goes to the bedroom of Piero [de' Medici]"), but that, originally, it might have been intended to decorate an unidentified Medici family chapel. It is a curious coincidence, in fact, that the same inventory should list a second, unattributed *Thebaid* panel in the chapel of the Medici villa at Careggi, the family's favorite country residence outside Florence.[61] That picture, perhaps identifiable with the fifteenth-century copy of Fra Angelico's painting now divided between the Szépmüvészeti Múzeum in Budapest and (formerly) the Bartolini Salimbeni Collection in Florence, is recorded in the inventory as "a panel 3⅞ br. [*braccia*] long and 1⅓ br. [*braccia*] wide, with a gold frame around it, in which are painted stories of the desert fathers, and also a small tablet with prayers written on it."[62] While its precise location is not mentioned, the picture is listed at the beginning of the inventory of the chapel, after some benches and before the altar table, indicating that it may have been set into the wall not far from the altar.[63] This evidence would seem to point to an alternative function for such images—outside monastic confines—as objects of private devotion, possibly accompanied, as in the present case, by a set litany of prayers to be recited before them. The presence of a fresco cycle of stories of the Desert Fathers, in the palace of the great fifteenth-century Florentine merchant Giovanni Rucellai, would appear to confirm that the theme appealed to the educated, pious lay person perhaps as a source of meditation on the eremitic ideal, comparable, in many ways, to the "inspirational" copies of pilgrimage accounts.[64]

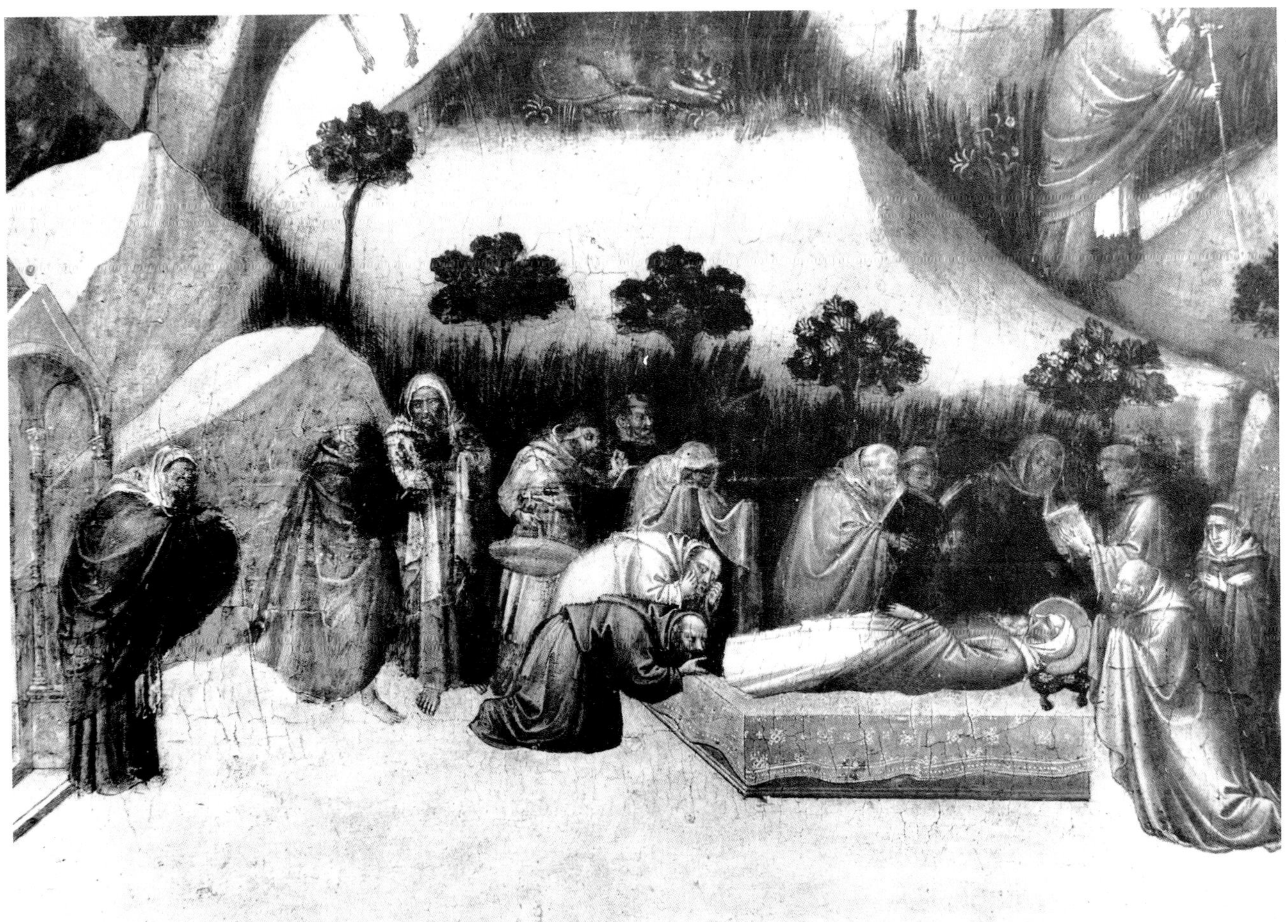

Figure 22. Workshop of Orcagna (?). *Thebaid* (detail of fig. 20)

1. For a general discussion of the medieval roll, see Wattenbach 1958, pp. 150–74, and, more recently, Kelly 1996, pp. 15–20; Agati 2003, pp. 126–34. For an interesting discussion of illustrated medieval amulet rolls, see Skemer 2001, pp. 197–227.
2. W. Wattenbach (1958, p. 167) cites a thirteen-foot roll, from the fourteenth century, in the Library of Saint Gall, Switzerland (inv. 1093), containing a description of the sites to be visited in Rome, accompanied by a list of indulgences and drawings of the principal monuments (*Mirabilia Romae*). See Scherrer 1875, pp. 405–7.
3. These various elements of the pilgrim's attire and their significance are discussed at length in Jonathan Sumption's fundamental study *Pilgrimage: An Image of Mediaeval Religion* (1975, pp. 171–75). See also Cardini 2002, pp. 326, 367–68.
4. Rosenthal 1928, no. 173, pp. 95–97. As stated in this publication (p. 96), the drawing was separated in order to protect it: "*Die erste Zeichnung* [see cat. 5 A] *ist ein wenig beuscheuert, die zweite* [see cat. 5 B] *ist zur Schonung abgetrennt worden und liegt lose unter Passepartout bei.*"
5. Evidence of the presence of medieval pilgrims from France, Germany, and Great Britain remains to this day in the inscriptions they left on the walls of the church of Saint Michael. D'Arienzo 2003, pp. 219–44 (with earlier bibliography); Sensi 2003, vol. I, pp. 194–96, vol. III, pp. 1219–26.
6. For a discussion of the various pilgrimage stops, see Pasculli Ferrara 2000.
7. For the meaning of this symbol, see Sumption 1975, pp. 174–75.
8. Berenson 1938, vol. II, p. 159.
9. Among the most pertinent comparisons, in terms of parchment support and technique, are the Giottesque monochromatic drawings that decorate a fourteenth-century roll of Peter of Poitiers's *Genealogy of Christ*, in the Biblioteca Casanatense, Rome (Ms. 4254); illustrated in Pietrangeli 1993, p. 50, pl. X.
10. Röhricht 1963, pp. 100–101 n. 267.
11. In a fourteenth-century codex in Vienna (Österreichische Nationalbibliothek, cod. 3763), the *Peregrinationes* text appears between a treatise on the Office of the Priest (*De officio sacerdotis*) and a papal bull from Leo VIII, whereas in a fifteenth-century manuscript in London (British Library, codex Harley 3810) it is found among assorted texts of Old English poetry, medicine, and astronomy; see Brefeld 1994, pp. 121–22.
12. Degenhart and Schmitt 1968, pp. 274–76.
13. Berenson 1938, vol. II, p. 18; Berenson 1961.
14. Elen 1989, p. 167 n. 302; M. Maiskaya, in Pushkin State Museum 1995, p. 163 n. 81.
15. Delfiol 1982, pp. 175–76.
16. Gucci 1990 ed., pp. 303–4.
17. Cardini 2002, pp. 176–77.
18. Calzolari et al. 1975, pp. 295–96.
19. Niccolò da Poggibonsi 1945 ed.; Cardini 2002, pp. 233–35.
20. The same kind of hat is worn, for example, by one of the elegantly attired gentlemen in the courtly scene represented on an early-fifteenth-century Florentine cassone panel attributed to the Master of the Griggs Crucifixion, in Madison, Wisconsin (University of Wisconsin, Study Collection, 61.4.3).
21. Calzolari et al. 1975, pp. 296–97.
22. It is not unlikely, given this relationship, that Filippo Rinuccini might even have owned a personal copy of Gucci's "diary."
23. Cardini 2002, pp. 379–82. As noted by the same author (p. 340), between the fourteenth and the fifteenth century, the typical sea journey to the Holy Land, from Venice to Jaffa, undertaken during the favorable summer season might last on average from one month to a month and a half, while the return trip, under less favorable weather conditions, could take more than two months.
24. As evidenced by the account of Niccolò da Poggibonsi (1945 ed., pp. 7–10) and that of Lionardo Frescobaldi (in Lanza and Troncarelli 1990, p. 175), the quality of the reception was greatly dependent on the class and the financial means of the pilgrim, with the poorer ones—including the clergy, who were not allowed to carry vast sums—often risking prison if they could not afford the necessary tribute.
25. Cardini 2002, p. 322.
26. Niccolò da Poggibonsi 1945 ed., p. 99.
27. "Jacques de Vitry's Letter, 1220," in Habig 1979, p. 1609; Cardini 2000, pp. 138–39.
28. Budge 1934, p. 20.
29. The Rule was described by Palladius (365–425) in his history of the holy monks (Budge 1934, pp. 191–92). Pertinently, scholars such as F. Cardini (2002, pp. 198–200) have noted the existence of a strong link, in the medieval imagination, between the notions of pilgrimage and eremitism, pointing specifically to the not-uncommon stories of those pilgrims who, upon their return from the Holy Land, decided to prolong their edifying experience by leading an eremitic life. By extension, it has also been observed that throughout the Middle Ages, but especially in the fourteenth century, hermits were among those most favored to carry out so-called "vicarious" pilgrimages—those journeys undertaken on behalf of unable or unwilling individuals, often as part of testamentary dispositions (Sensi 2003, vol. III, pp. 367–68).
30. Callmann 1975, p. 3.
31. Hood 1993, pp. 18–22.
32. For a detailed discussion of the circulation of this text, repeatedly copied, annotated, and often luxuriously illuminated for a large and devout lay audience, see Delcorno 1998, pp. 14–22.
33. Callmann 1975, pp. 5–6.
34. Frugoni 1988, pp. 1557–1643.
35. Cavalca 1858 ed., p. 83.
36. Ibid., pp. 132–33.
37. Ibid., pp. 86–87.
38. Ibid., p. 52. The tale refers to one of the exempla in Cavalca's Life of Saint John the Hermit: in the story, the hermit lets the Devil into his hut in the guise of a woman who had lost her way. Whereas other versions of the *Thebaid,* referring to this or similar episodes of the Devil's appearance as a woman, show her in contemporary dress, the Camposanto fresco is the only one in which she is distinguished by a pilgrim's hat and staff.
39. F. Cardini (2002, p. 459 n. 5) refers to the story of the Devil dressed as a pilgrim who strangles a child, in the Life of Saint Nicholas of Bari—a subject depicted in a predella by Ambrogio Lorenzetti in the Galleria degli Uffizi, Florence.
40. Melania Ceccanti, who first published this manuscript (2001–2, pp. 171–80), highlighted its pedagogical intent, presenting it as another manifestation of the development, in the fourteenth century, of a religious literature in the vernacular that, like Cavalca's text, was aimed at a cultivated lay audience.
41. Malquori 2001, pp. 121–23.
42. Cardini 2002, pp. 186–87.
43. F. Cardini (ibid., p. 263) cites the example of the illuminated copy of the Paduan nobleman Gabriele Capodilista's *Itinerario,* which he gave to the abbess and nuns of San Bernardino in Padua upon his return from the Holy Land in 1458. Like other examples of illustrated pilgrims' guides, the manuscript's decoration is limited to more or less topographically accurate depictions of the sites visited. See Momigliano Lepschy 1966.
44. "*Questi sono i viaggi che debbono fare li pellegrini che vanno Oltremare per salvare l'anima loro e che può fare ciscuna persona stando nella casa sua, pensando in ciascuno luogo che di sotto è scritto, e in ogni luogo dica uno Paternostro e Avemaria*" (Lanza and Troncarelli 1990, p. 315).
45. Richard 1984, p. 151.
46. Loenertz 1937, pp. 13–15; Orlandi 1955 b, vol. I, pp. 308–19.
47. Papi 1982, p. 98.
48. Orlandi 1955 b, vol. II, p. 195. R. Loenertz (1975, p. 128) suggests that Cardoni may have held the title between 1432 and 1434.
49. De Marchi 1992, pp. 136–38.

50. On Dominici, see Orlandi 1955 b, vol. II, pp. 77–126; Cracco 1963, pp. 657–64. E. Marino, O.P. (2000, pp. 147, 155), has suggested that Fra Angelico took the name "fra Giovanni" in honor of Giovanni Dominici.
51. Orlandi 1955 b, vol. II, p. 93. Dominici's close friend and the founder of the Hieronymite monastery in Fiesole, Carlo Guidi of Montegranelli (see cat. 59), apparently died in 1417 or 1419 in Venice, from where he had intended to set out on a pilgrimage to the Holy Land (see Ridderbos 1984, p. 74). Depending on the actual date of his death, it is tempting to speculate on whether he might have had something to do with this commission.
52. Malquori 2001, pp. 132–35.
53. Malquori 1996, pp. 79–93.
54. Verbal communication, cited in Callmann 1975.
55. Boskovits 1968, pp. 6–7; M. Boskovits, in Bellosi 2002, p. 171.
56. Callmann 1975, p 14.
57. The Esztergom panel underwent a radical restoration in 1991–92, when numerous areas of loss were filled in. The photographs illustrated here predate that intervention.
58. The Esztergom fragment can be traced back to 1878, when it was one of sixty-three Italian paintings acquired by Janos Simor from the collection of Canonico Raffaele Bertinelli in Rome. There is no evidence as to how Canonico Bertinelli formed his collection (see Gardner 1998, p. 108). The Private collection panel, which was sold at Christie's, London, June 28, 1974, was in a Scottish private collection before it was acquired by the Reverend W. Davenport Bromley at the Joly de Bammeville sale in London in 1854. See Brigstocke 1976, pp. 585–89.
59. "*Una Tavoletta di legname di br. 4 incircha, di mano di fra' Giovanni, dipintovi più storie di santi padri*" (Spallanzani and Gaeta Bertelà 1992, p. 80); M. Boskovits, in Bellosi 2002, p. 164 (with earlier bibliography).
60. M. Boskovits, in Bellosi 2002, pp. 164–65.
61. The villa was built between 1417 and 1459 on land acquired by Cosimo de' Medici. Cosimo died at the villa in 1464, as did his sons Piero (in 1469) and Lorenzo the Magnificent (in 1492). See Zangheri 1989, pp. 41–59.
62. "*Una tavola lungha br. 3 7/8, larga br. 1 1/3, con cornicione d'oro atorno, dipintovi drento storie di santi padri e più una tavoletta schrittovi orationi*" (Spallanzani and Gaeta Bertelà 1992, p. 133). M. Boskovits, in Bellosi (2002, p. 164) unconvincingly identifies the Budapest/ Bartolini Salimbeni *Thebaid* as another autograph work by Angelico; A. De Marchi (1992, p. 149 n. 53), followed by C. B. Strehlke (1998, p. 15), tentatively suggested that the latter painting may be a copy by Giovanni Toscani.
63. In an earlier inventory (1482) of the Careggi villa (Contorni 1991–92, p. 14), the painting is listed immediately after the altar with the *Lamentation* altarpiece by Rogier van der Weyden (now in the Galleria degli Uffizi).
64. Malquori 1993. Giovanni Rucellai (1403–1481) is best known as the patron of the great Renaissance architect Leon Battista Alberti, whom he commissioned to build the façade of Santa Maria Novella and his Florentine palace with the nearby Loggia, as well as his private chapel in the church of San Pancrazio, a replica of the Holy Sepulcher of Jerusalem; according to a letter addressed to his mother, Rucellai had sent two envoys to the Holy Land with the specific purpose of taking measurements of the Holy Sepulcher to ensure the accuracy of the replica (Perosa 1960, p. 136; Kent 1981, pp. 58–61).

Five Fragments from a Pilgrimage Roll

5.

A.

Brother Petrus de Cruce Arriving in the Holy Land, and Kneeling before the Holy Sepulcher

Pen and wash on parchment, 141.2 x 13.8 cm (55⅝ x 5⅜ in.)
Harvard University, Cambridge, Massachusetts. The gift of Mr. Arthur Sachs to the Fogg Art Museum (1956.180a), transferred to Houghton Library, Harvard College Library (*1990M-16)

B.

Brother Petrus de Cruce Being Attacked by Wolves on Mount Gargano, and by Snakes near Bari

Pen and wash on parchment, 25.7 x 13.6 cm (10⅛ x 5⅜ in.)
Harvard University, Cambridge, Massachusetts. The gift of the Honorable Mr. and Mrs. Robert Woods Bliss to the Fogg Art Museum (1936.116), transferred to Houghton Library, Harvard College Library (*1990M-16)

C.

The Shipwreck of Brother Petrus de Cruce, His Capture, and His Audience before a Muslim Ruler

Pen and wash on parchment, 30.2 x 13.8 cm (11⅞ x 5⅜ in.)
Harvard University, Cambridge, Massachusetts. The gift of Mr. Arthur Sachs to the Fogg Art Museum (1956.180b), transferred to Houghton Library, Harvard College Library (*1990M-16)

The subjects, attribution, and common origin from a single roll of these five fragments, along with two others formerly in the Koenigs Collection (fig. 23, 24), have been a matter of dispute and speculation since their first appearance on the art market in the late 1920s and early 1930s (for an extended discussion of the content, significance, and reconstruction of the drawings and accompanying texts, see the preceding essay, "Pilgrims and Desert Fathers: Dominican Spirituality and the Holy Land"). Drawings A and B were first published in 1928 by the Munich antiquarian-book dealer Jacques Rosenthal, who pointed out that they were fragments of the same pilgrimage roll, and that B had been separated from the longer fragment A in order to protect the drawing.[1] According to the explicit that appears at the top of B, dated 1417, the roll recorded the various pilgrimage journeys, to the Holy Land and to other sites across Europe, undertaken by the Dominican lay brother Petrus de Cruce at different points during his lifetime.

By 1930, both A and B were in the collection of Henry Oppenheimer in London, together with D. Drawings B and D were lent by Oppenheimer to the 1930 Exhibition of Italian Art at the Royal Academy, where they were catalogued by Arthur Popham as "Tuscan School, 1417."[2] Popham correctly described the subject of B, but identified D generically as "Two Scenes from the Legend of a Holy Hermit," noting that it belonged to a larger series that included "a drawing in the Metropolitan Museum of Art." It is not clear which drawing in the present group he might have been referring to, since E did not enter the Metropolitan Museum's collection until 1972.

The same three fragments—A, B, and D—were given fuller consideration by Kenneth Clark, who, presuming them to have been excised from different rolls, noted, in a review of the Royal Academy exhibition,[3] that they seemed to have been executed by the same hand, although D appeared "more competently drawn." According to Clark, the "free, racy" style of execution, and the use of transparent washes in these works, placed them in the category of "popular" illumination a less expensive alternative to the traditional gold-and-tempera technique of manuscript painting. Describing the scenes as "incidents in the lives of Dominican saints and worthies," the same author went on to suggest that they might have originated in the school of San Marco and concluded with the following, interesting observation regarding their possible authorship: "The only painter with whose style they have anything in common seems to be Fra Angelico. It is impossible to associate them with any of his pupils, as the date—1417—is too early for any of those, Zanobi Strozzi, Domenico di Michelino, and so forth, whose names have come down to us. Possibly, the drawings were done by Father Petrus himself, who had enough sense to use his small talent for such spontaneous work and never attempted a picture."

Clark's comments were not addressed in the next mention of the three fragments, which were sold as "Anonymous, Tuscan School, 1417,"[4] at the auction of the Oppenheimer Collection in 1936. Two years later, however, Bernard Berenson published the three drawings, one of which, B, was by then in the Fogg Art Museum in Cambridge, under the rubric "School of Lorenzo Monaco."[5] Berenson also included C in this group, listing it as formerly in the Rosenthal Collection in Munich and noting that although the four fragments were not all by the same hand, they were probably part of the same roll. Appearing separately in Berenson's volume and not viewed in connection with the roll were the two Koenigs drawings, then still in Haarlem, both of which were assigned to the "School of Fra Angelico," "close to Domenico di Michelino."[6] These attributions remained unchanged in the 1961 Italian edition of the *Drawings of the Florentine Painters,* which also identified E—now in The Metropolitan Museum of Art, but then in the collection of Julius Böhler in Munich—as part of the same series as A–D.[7] At this time, Berenson further refined his attribution of B, which he described as by a "delicate follower of Fra Angelico and Masolino, near Rossello di Jacopo Franchi."

A direct attribution of B and D to Fra Angelico was first advanced by Roberto Longhi, who, without remarking on other fragments in the series, regarded these two works as the earliest products of the artist's career, along with the Uffizi *Thebaid* (fig. 17, 19).[8] Both drawings, however, were rejected from Fra Angelico's corpus by John Pope-Hennessy, who assigned them instead to an anonymous "Master of 1417," and initially suggested that this artist may have been Fra Angelico's teacher in the art of manuscript illumination.[9] Pope-Hennessy's attribution was maintained by Claus Virch in the 1962 catalogue of drawings in the collection of Walter Baker, of New York, which by then included E.[10] In Virch's opinion, this work seemed nearer stylistically to D than to any of the other three drawings then associated with the roll, although, he concluded, "whether all four illustrations actually did once belong to the same scroll is now difficult to decide, especially as the

D.

A Dominican Friar [Petrus de Cruce ?] Encountering the Devil Disguised as a Pilgrim, and Being Attacked by Snakes

Pen and wash on parchment, 24.1 x 13.5 cm (9 1/2 x 5 5/16 in.)
Albright-Knox Art Gallery, Buffalo, New York. Elisabeth H. Gates Fund, 1936 (1936:4)

E.

A Dominican Friar [Petrus de Cruce ?] and a Companion below the Dragon's Tower

Pen and brush, with brown ink, on parchment, 18.3 x 13.7 cm (7 1/4 x 5 3/8 in.)
The Metropolitan Museum of Art, New York. Bequest of Walter C. Baker, 1971 (1972.118.260)

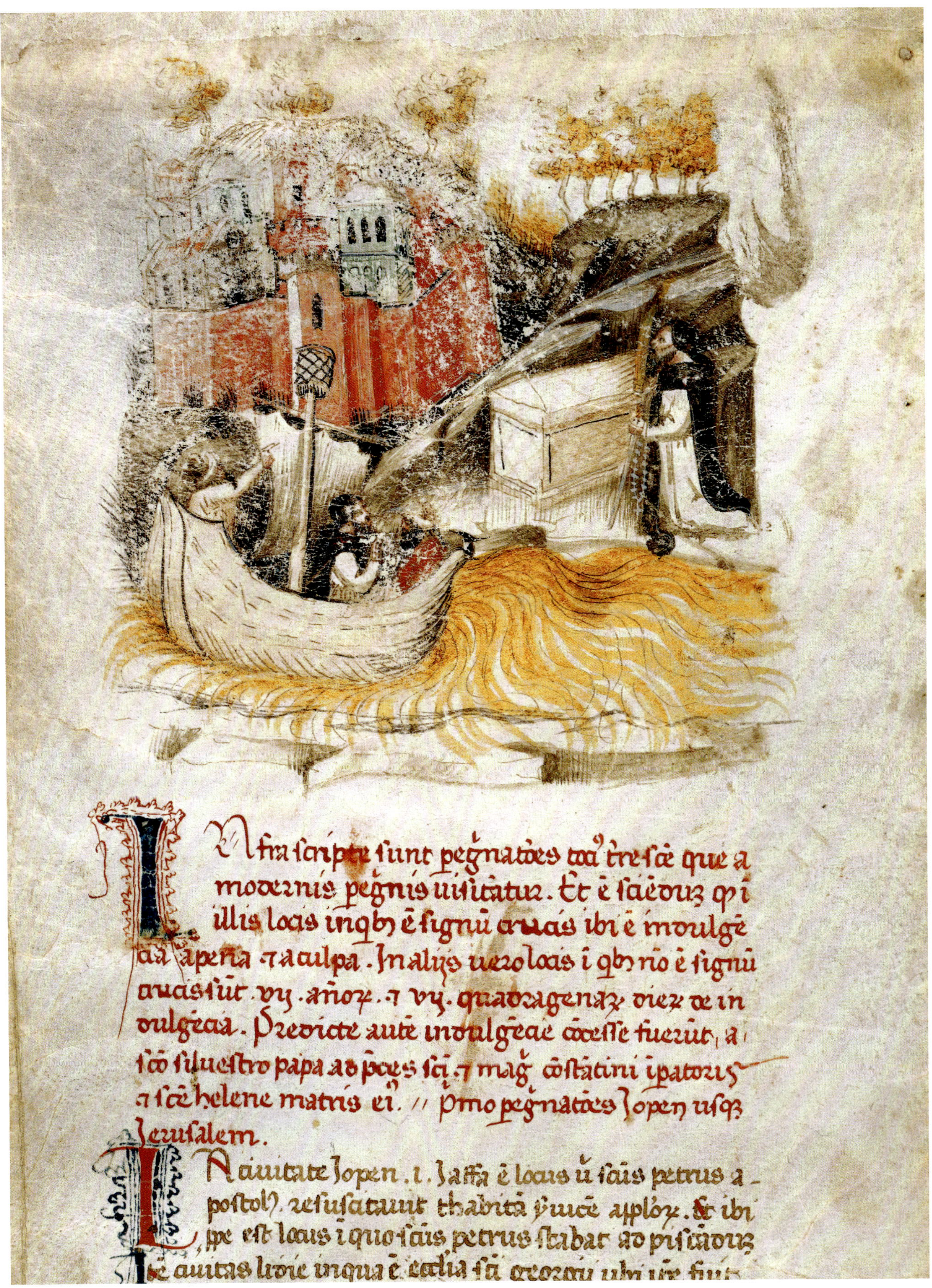

5: A

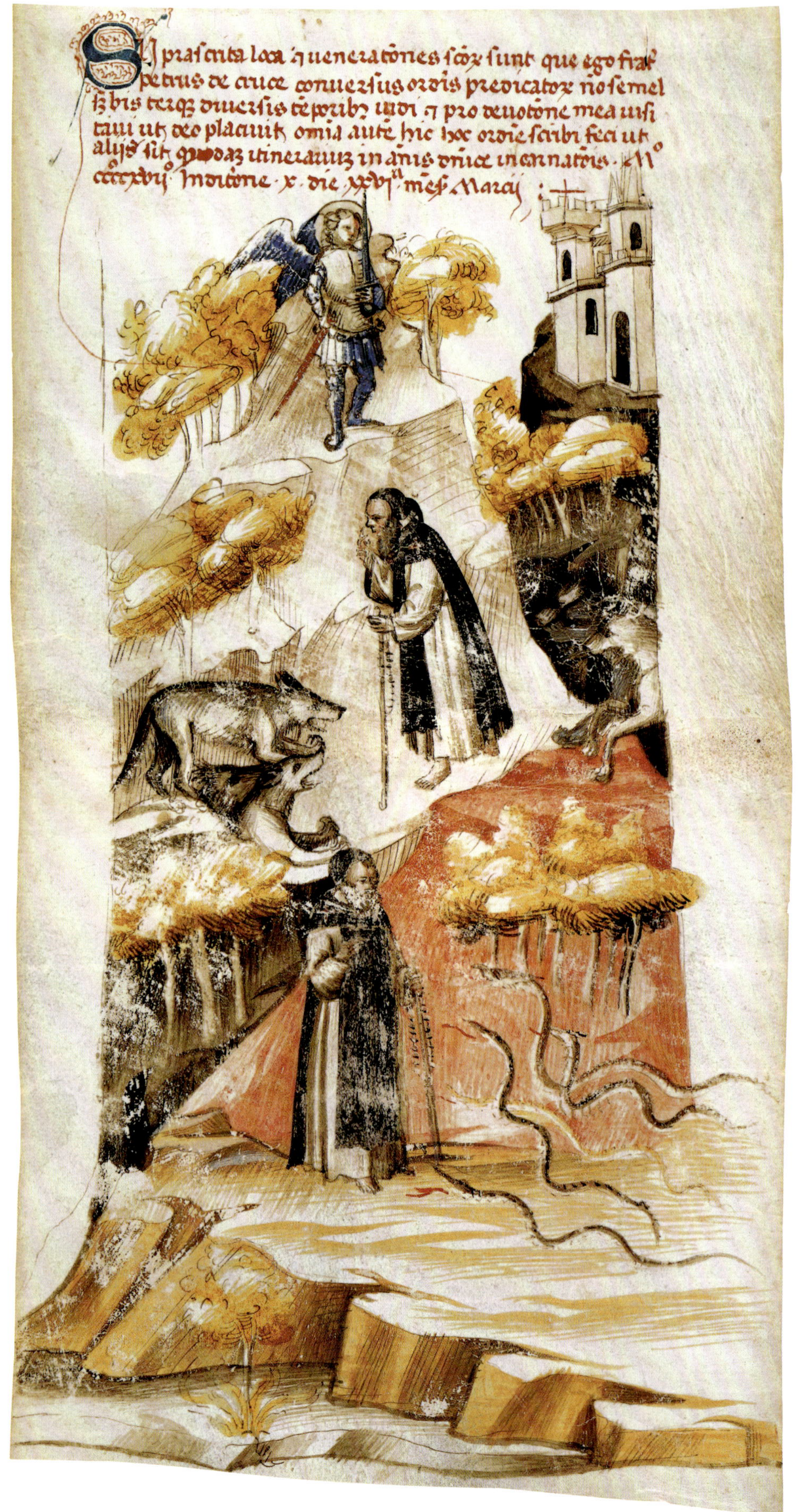

5: B

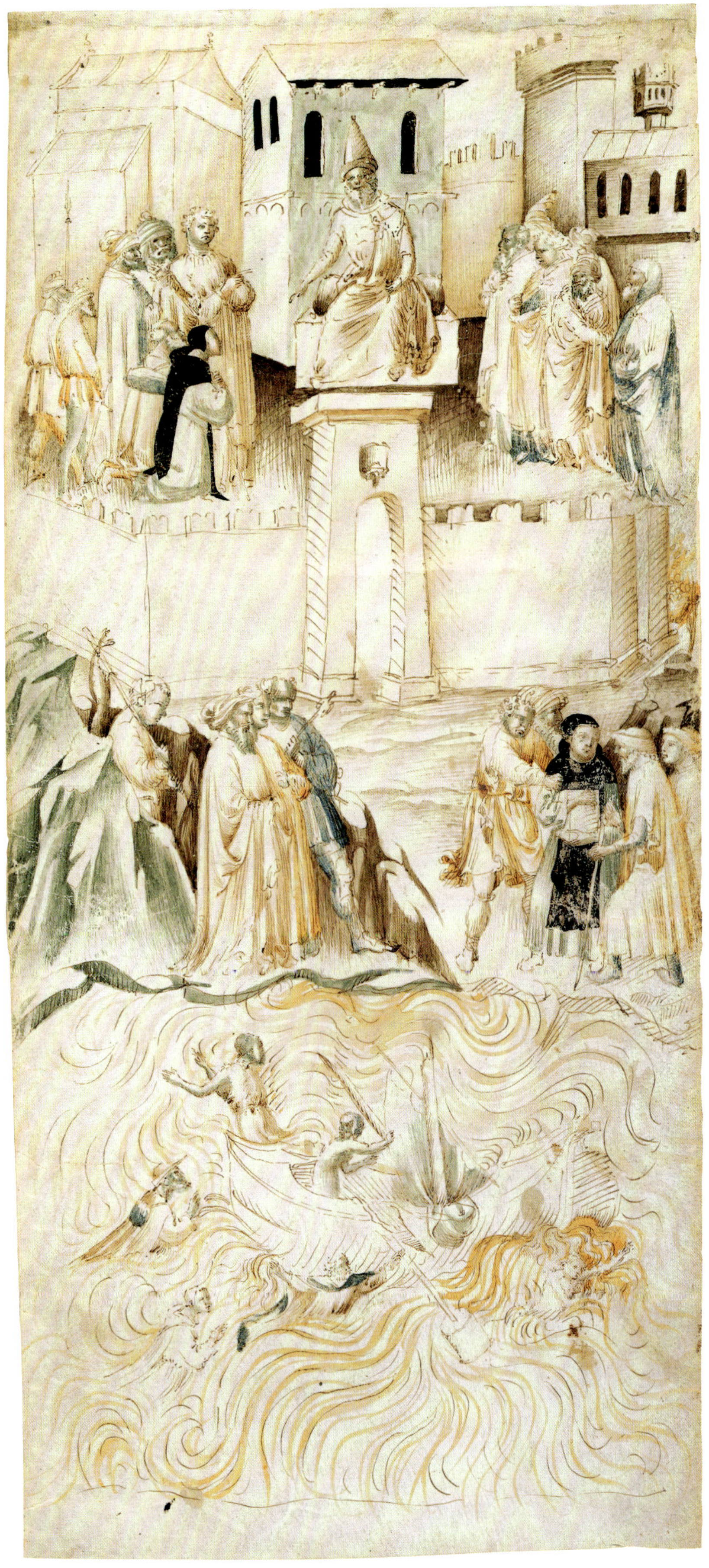

5: C

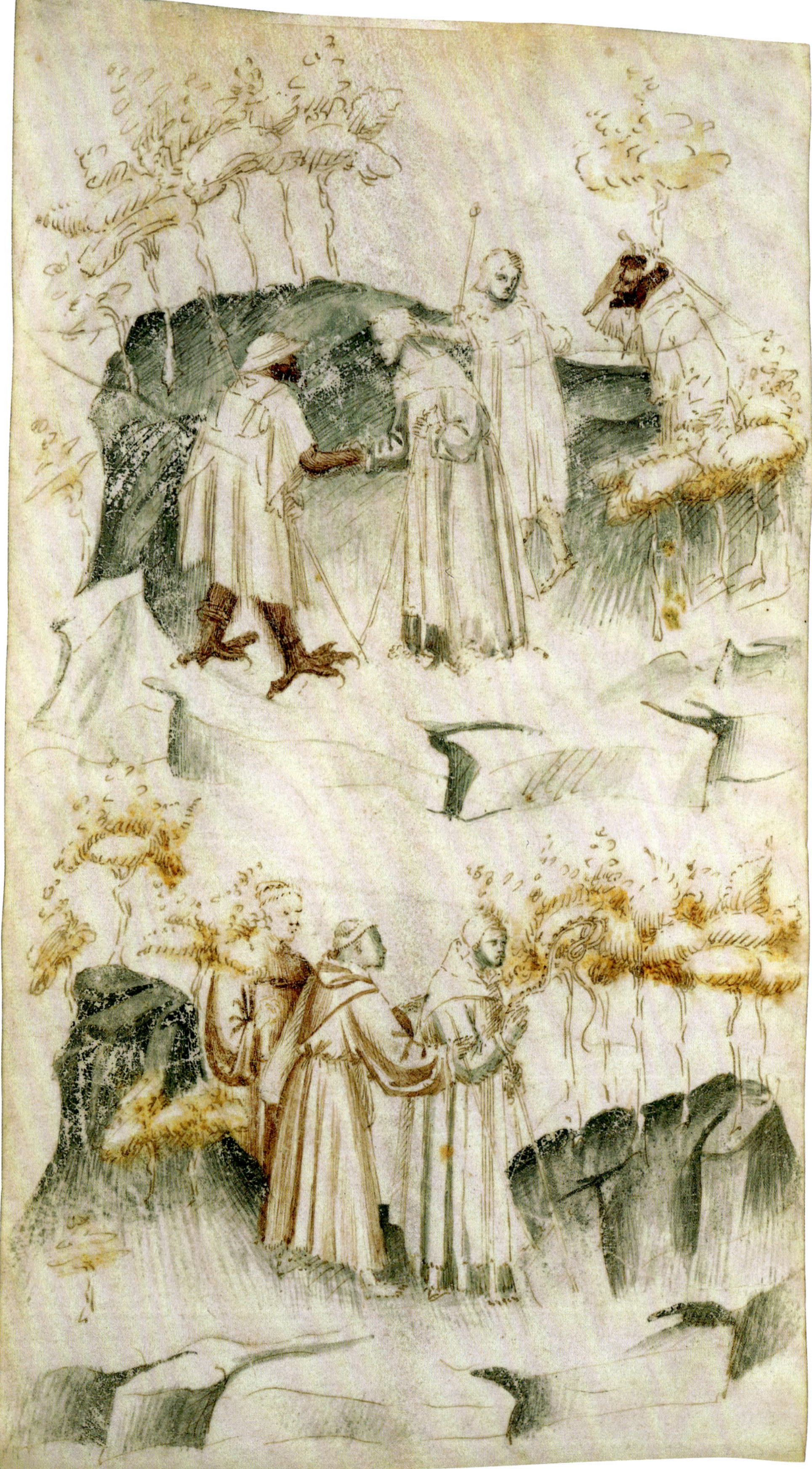

5: D

only description of the scroll [in the 1928 Rosenthal catalogue] seems to speak against this."

In the last and most comprehensive study of the drawings to date, Degenhart and Schmitt first associated the two Koenigs fragments with drawings A through E, cataloguing the entire series as "Tuscan, 1417."[11] According to the authors, whether the seven drawings were intended to illustrate the same roll or were excised from related texts written in the same scriptorium, they were clearly the product of a common artistic and intellectual milieu, most probably located within monastic confines.

Although it can now be demonstrated on the basis of both physical and iconographic evidence (see pp. 27–32) that all seven fragments were removed from a single roll, it is apparent, as most scholars have observed, that more than one artist was involved in their execution. Roberto Longhi's contention that Fra Angelico was one of these artists was based on the relationship he perceived between drawings B and D and Angelico's early *Thebaid* in the Uffizi. These two drawings, however, may not be by a single hand and both are more distinctly Late Gothic in sensibility than the *Thebaid*, lacking the overall spatial clarity, plastic modeling of forms, and luminous quality that distinguish the painting as an Early Renaissance creation, despite its compositional adherence to earlier prototypes. Drawing B, which is certainly by the same hand as A, does recall the Uffizi *Thebaid* in the structure of its landscape and in the short, solidly proportioned figures and animals, but despite these superficial formal similarities, its composition lacks the unity of vision or subtlety of handling that is reflected in the execution of even the smallest parts of Angelico's painting. In contrast to the incipient naturalism and monumental quality that characterize the *Thebaid*, drawings A and B are defined by a charming, decorative sensibility, most evident in B, in the elaborate definition of the archangel's armor and in the elegant artificiality of his pose. While the radical foreshortening of the saint's feet and of those of Petrus de Cruce below him reflects an awareness of Renaissance spatial principles, the application of these principles is confined to details rather than extended throughout the composition, resulting in ambiguities that are incompatible with the coherence of Angelico's vision. Other distinguishing traits of this artist's style are the coarsely drawn facial features, rendered in thick, dark outlines, which fail to define the underlying bone structure, and the simply constructed shapes and architectural forms.

A second hand may have been responsible for the execution of D, which employs a less ambitious compositional structure than B, yet betrays a more sophisticated spatial and narrative sense. Rather than attempting to unify the composition through artificially connected rock formations, the artist focused on each of the two superimposed zones as a separate, independent unit. The result, both times, is a spatially coherent

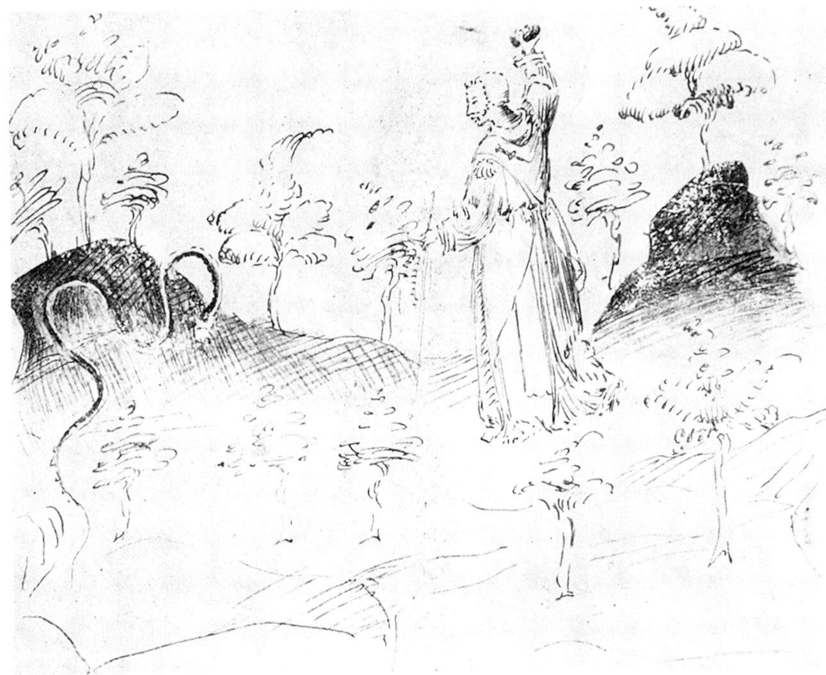

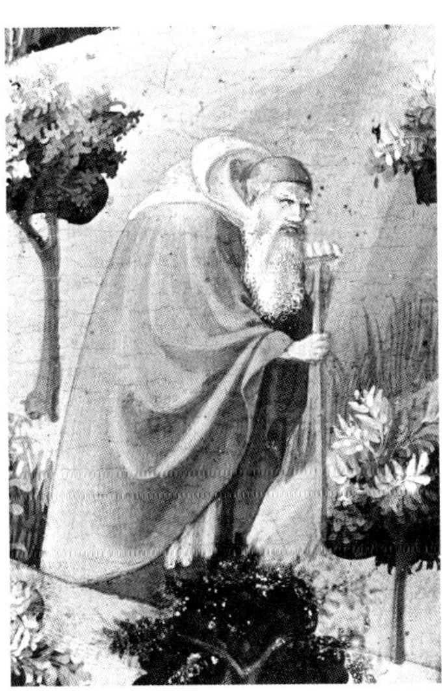

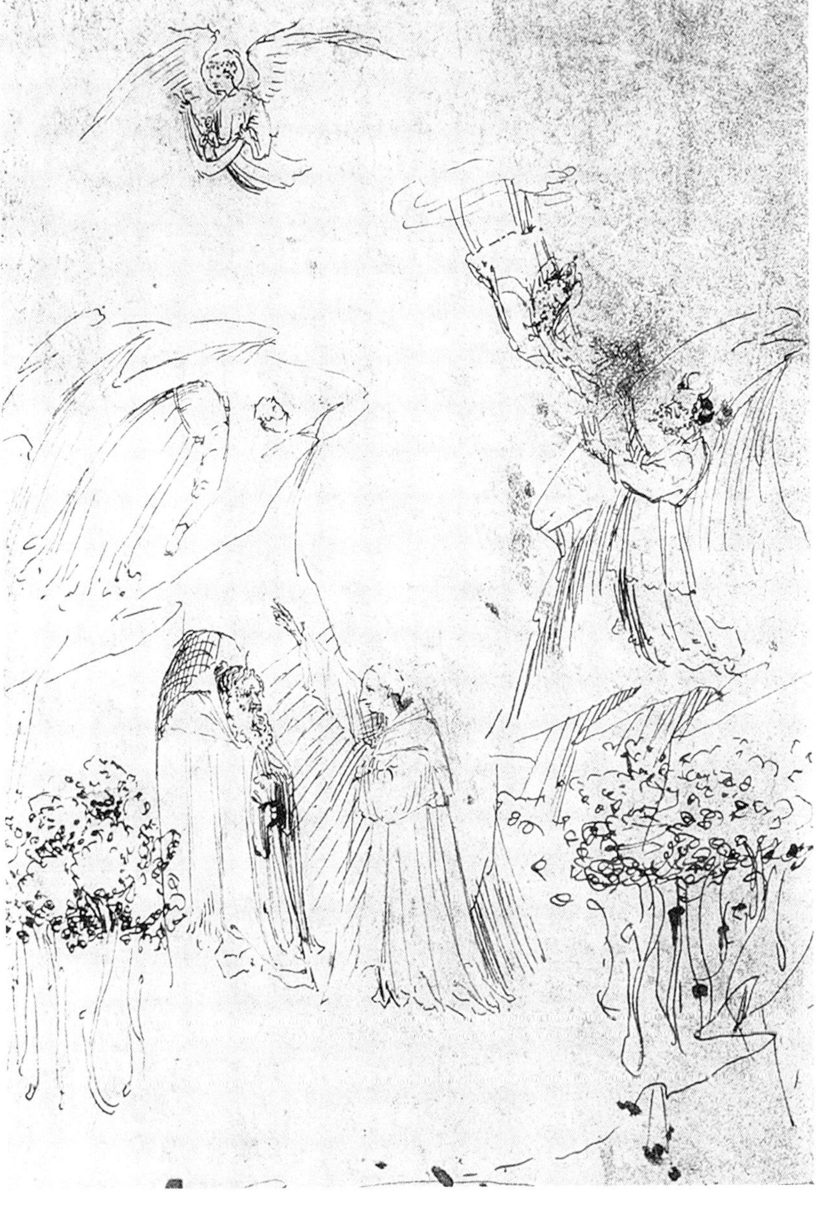

Figure 23 (above). School of Lorenzo Monaco. *Scene from the Pilgrimage of Petrus de Cruce* (?). About 1417–20. State Pushkin Museum of Fine Arts, Moscow (Koenigs I.101)

Figure 24 (far right). Fra Angelico. *Petrus de Cruce* (?) *on Mount Sinai*. About 1417–20. State Pushkin Museum of Fine Arts, Moscow (Koenigs I.102)

Figure 25 (near right). Fra Angelico. *Thebaid* (detail of fig. 19)

setting, with the definition of the rocks and trees similar to that in drawing B, but inhabited by more graceful, expressive figures whose fluid gestures impart greater liveliness to the entire scene. Characteristic of this artist's drawing technique is a delicate, brittle line employed to describe forms and individual features in minute detail, from the Devil's pointed talons to his ferocious profile. The same delicacy of execution affects the application of the green and yellow washes. In contrast to A or B, this drawing is distinguished by a more subtle approach to coloring, with less saturated washes and more studied effects of light and shadow.

The same fussy technique that characterizes D is evident in one of the two Koenigs drawings (I.101; fig. 23), which is possibly by the same hand although not brought to the same degree of finish. Common to both works are similarly proportioned figure types, with elongated necks and minute features, and the same distinctive way of representing trees, with their slender trunks rendered in quick broken pen strokes.

While sharing stylistic and formal elements with D and Koenigs I.101, drawing C shows a higher degree of finish and a more accomplished execution. As in D, the composition is divided into distinct, superimposed zones, each organized in terms of its own internal logic. At the same time, an attempt has been made to give the appearance of a continuous narrative by providing an unbroken, logical transition from one setting to the next. Characteristic of this drawing is the same

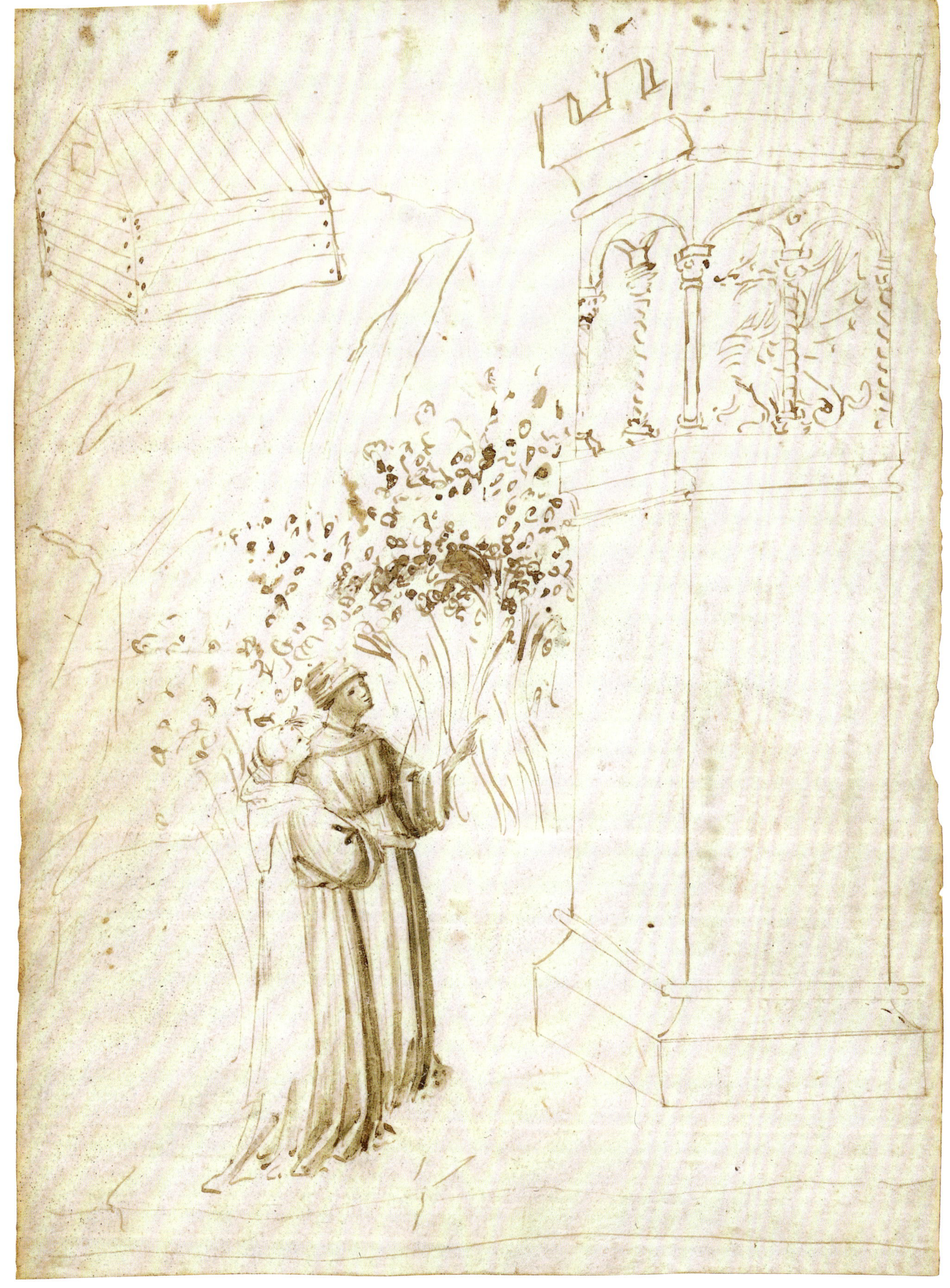

5: E

delicate, precise rendering of the forms that distinguishes D and Koenigs I.101, and the same subtle application of washes. In this case, however, the individual lines are drawn with a new level of energy and descriptive virtuosity, and are combined with dramatic effects of light and shadow, to produce a more immediately powerful composition. From the tumultuous, swirling waves of the sea to the artificially fluttering folds of the soldier's tunic in the middle ground, to the jagged rock formations rising up like flames, individual forms are described in undulating rhythms that, more than in any other drawing in the series, echo the poetic late creations of Lorenzo Monaco. That this work is the product of an artist who had fully absorbed the lessons of Lorenzo Monaco is also reflected in the balance achieved between narrative and decorative concerns. Each separate scene features animated figures engaged in lively interaction, their expressive gestures helping to articulate the sequence of events. Enriching the composition are the carefully rendered if insubstantial architectural structures whose abstracted shapes serve as a theatrical stage set for the scene in the upper register; and a variety of exotic and picturesque characters, some of whom, like the hunter with his prey, are clearly extraneous to the story yet add to its overall charm.

Although the distinctions among these five drawings may indicate the intervention of two or more different hands in their execution, they are unified by their varying degrees of dependence on the Late Gothic idiom of Lorenzo Monaco and by some shared graphic idiosyncrasies, such as the use of hatched outlines and of parallel, diagonal strokes to define trees and foliage. Given the scarcity of surviving drawings from this period and the resulting difficulty in associating most of them with a particular artist or workshop, Berenson's categorization of this group as "School of Lorenzo Monaco" remains a valid indicator of their visual and cultural orientation.

A different spirit, more consistent with Angelico's Early Renaissance vision, animates the last two drawings in the series, E and Koenigs I.102 (fig. 24). That these two fragments are the product of the same hand is reflected in their shared graphic and formal mannerisms, which also set them apart from the other images. The fastidious technique employed in the previous drawings, with their carefully hatched lines, is replaced here by a linear fluidity and confident use of simple, uninterrupted pen strokes to articulate both volume and structure. Peculiar to this artist alone is his method of delineating the foliage of the trees with small circular strokes instead of parallel hatchings,[12] and of rendering the trunks in unbroken serpentine lines. Aside from these technical distinctions, the drawings betray a marked departure from the traditional narrative and compositional formulas employed in A through D by sharing several unrelated episodes in a single, visually coherent spatial setting that closely recalls the model of the Uffizi *Thebaid*.

Confirming the possibility that these two drawings are, in fact, by the author of the Uffizi *Thebaid*—the young Fra Angelico—is the commanding monumentality of some of the figures that inhabit these compositions. In the Koenigs drawing, the massive bulk of the prophet Elijah, whose twin image may be found among the Desert Fathers of the *Thebaid* (fig. 25), appears to carve out the space behind him in the same way that the figure of God the Father, plunging to earth with dramatic force, gives shape to an utterly believable hole in the clouds. The same rational approach is evident in the solidly built architectural forms that distinguish drawing E, sketched out in all their essential components according to logically conceived viewing points. In addition to the *Thebaid,* specific comparisons for both drawings may also be found in other paintings by Angelico datable to the same early phase in his career, such as the Hermitage and the Rotterdam *Madonna* (see cat. 6) or the recently discovered *Annunciation* fragments in a private collection (cat. 3)—possibly the artist's earliest independent work—which are distinguished by identical flowing lines and a slender physiognomic type, with a long neck, small head, and pointy features.

All of the above considerations would appear to indicate a date for Angelico's intervention in the series in close proximity to that of the Rotterdam *Madonna*—sometime between 1417, the date recorded on drawing B, and about 1420. Beyond this, the precise circumstances leading to the artist's involvement in this commission remain mysterious, although a possible clue may yet be discovered in the specifically Dominican context of the roll's production (see essay II, pp. 33–37). PP

1. Rosenthal 1928, no. 173, pp. 95–97.
2. Popham 1930, nos. 418, 420, pp. 231–32; Popham 1931, nos. 11–12, pp. 4–5.
3. Clark 1930, p. 175.
4. Oppenheimer sale, 1936, lots 3–5.
5. Berenson 1938, vol. II, p. 159.
6. Ibid., p. 18.
7. Berenson 1961, pp. 37, 277–78.
8. Longhi 1940 (1975 ed.), pp. 37–38.
9. Pope-Hennessy 1952, pp. 4, 205; Pope-Hennessy 1974, p. 234. This hypothesis was omitted in the second edition of Pope-Hennessy's monograph.
10. Virch 1961, no. 2, pp. 13–14.
11. Degenhart and Schmitt 1968, pp. 274–76.
12. A similar technique is evident in the painted foliage in the backgrounds of the Munich predella panels and in the altarpiece for the high altar of San Marco by Fra Angelico.

6.

Virgin and Child Enthroned, with Two Angels

Tempera on panel: overall, 103.8 x 53.9 cm (40⅞ x 21 3/16); picture surface, 80.5 x 47.2 cm (31 11/16 x 18⅝ in.)
Museum Boijmans Van Beuningen, Rotterdam (Inv. no. 2555)

The physical and aesthetic aspects of the panel have been severely compromised by overpaintings, with the most serious changes in the figure of the Virgin and of the angel to the right. The Virgin's mantle is reduced to a dark, mat blot, and the modeling of the folds, which must have been visible in her lap and at her shoulders, as well as the color of the lining have been obliterated. The lining probably was bright green, as in the *Virgin of Humility* in the Hermitage, Saint Petersburg (fig. 11), or yellow, as in the San Domenico high altarpiece. The angel to the right originally wore a robe of green and red silk. The wings of both angels, too, have been covered by a dense, dark layer of overpainting. These alterations were probably made in the nineteenth century, possibly to cover discolorations.

An unusual feature of the panel's support is the slightly arched insert at the base extending across its full width and up nearly to the full height of the painted marble pavement in the foreground. As the paint covering the insert is consistent with that on the rest of the panel, it reveals the insert to be an original piece, used to complete the support. Such an economical use of wood may seem peculiar but it has parallels in other panel paintings, including a later predella panel from the workshop of Fra Angelico himself.[1] A compound support is, of course, less stable than a single plank, and the join between the two pieces of wood has caused some damage to the paint surface, which was rather coarsely repainted. The oldest photographs show that the marble pavement originally had some dark veins and that the folds in the garment of the angel at the left are a modern addition.

The carpentry is essentially original. The two applied acanthus moldings are absent from the earliest known photograph of the painting; they do not quite fit, and were probably added when the painting was on the German art market after World War I. Traces of capitals and bases on either side of the two angels indicate that spiral colonnettes (now lost) once flanked the picture field. The predella below the panel is original as well, although its inscription, "AVE MARIA GRATIA PLENA," has been renewed. It is, therefore, unnecessary to link the painting with a painted predella now in Bern (see cat. 7), as was recently proposed on account of the assumption that the framing of the Rotterdam painting is not original.[2]

The painting is an example of a type of tabernacle that was very common in Florence during the late fourteenth and early fifteenth centuries. It may have been commissioned on the occasion of a wedding, but the two coats of arms on the predella, presumably those of the husband and his bride, are no longer legible. The one on the right may have contained a lion (or perhaps a griffon) rampant, *or,* facing left. Unfortunately, there are too many Florentine families with this motif in their coats of arms to suggest a plausible identification.

As to its more recent provenance, a note written on the oldest photograph of the painting known today states that it was "bought by Papa from the mayor of Fucecchio, sold to Julius Böhler, c. 1918."[3] The Italian owner of the painting before its sale to the dealer Julius Böhler of Munich could not be ascertained, but the mayor of Fucecchio, a town to the west of Florence, no doubt was Emilio Bassi, who held this position from 1898 until 1919.[4] After Böhler, the painting passed to the dealer Cassirer in Berlin, who sold it to S. von Auspitz in Vienna. In 1932, it was acquired, through K. W. Bachstitz in The Hague, by D. G. Van Beuningen in Vierhouten, and, with the rest of his collection, came to the Boijmans museum in 1958.

When the painting was with Cassirer it was ascribed to Masolino, whose authorship was retained in the 1952 catalogue of the Van Beuningen Collection.[5] However, in the early 1920s, Arduino Colasanti already had proposed an attribution to Arcangelo di Cola da Camerino, which was followed by Berenson, Procacci, Zeri, and, into the 1970s, by *studiosi* from the Marches.[6] When the artistic personality of Arcangelo became defined more accurately, it was found that the quality of the Rotterdam panel was too high for this charming Marchigian painter. Zeri, who in 1950 still supported Colasanti's attribution, changed his mind in 1969 in favor of an anonymous but very gifted Florentine painter active about 1425—an opinion endorsed by John Pope-Hennessy and by several Dutch publications.[7] In the meantime, as early as 1928, Roberto Longhi, in one of his many famous footnotes, had ascribed the painting to the young Angelico, which was supported by a number of Italian critics.[8] Zeri hesitated to sanction this attribution, one reason being that the beginnings of Fra Angelico's career were still not well defined. Miklós Boskovits has done precisely this; in 1976, he argued that the Rotterdam *Virgin and Child,* as well as the versions of the *Virgin of Humility* in the Hermitage and in the Museo Nazionale di San Matteo in Pisa are key works in the reconstruction of the artist's early oeuvre,[9] and the attribution of all three paintings to Fra Angelico has been fully accepted since.[10]

Even in its present state, the Rotterdam picture shows that Fra Angelico was an inquisitive painter who subtly reformulated a traditional theme and elevated it to a high artistic level. The bright colors, particularly noticeable in the angel on the left, as well as the slender proportions of the figures, especially the angels, recall the work of Lorenzo Monaco. The splendor is enhanced by the marble pavement and by the red brocade that completely covers the Virgin's throne and continues onto

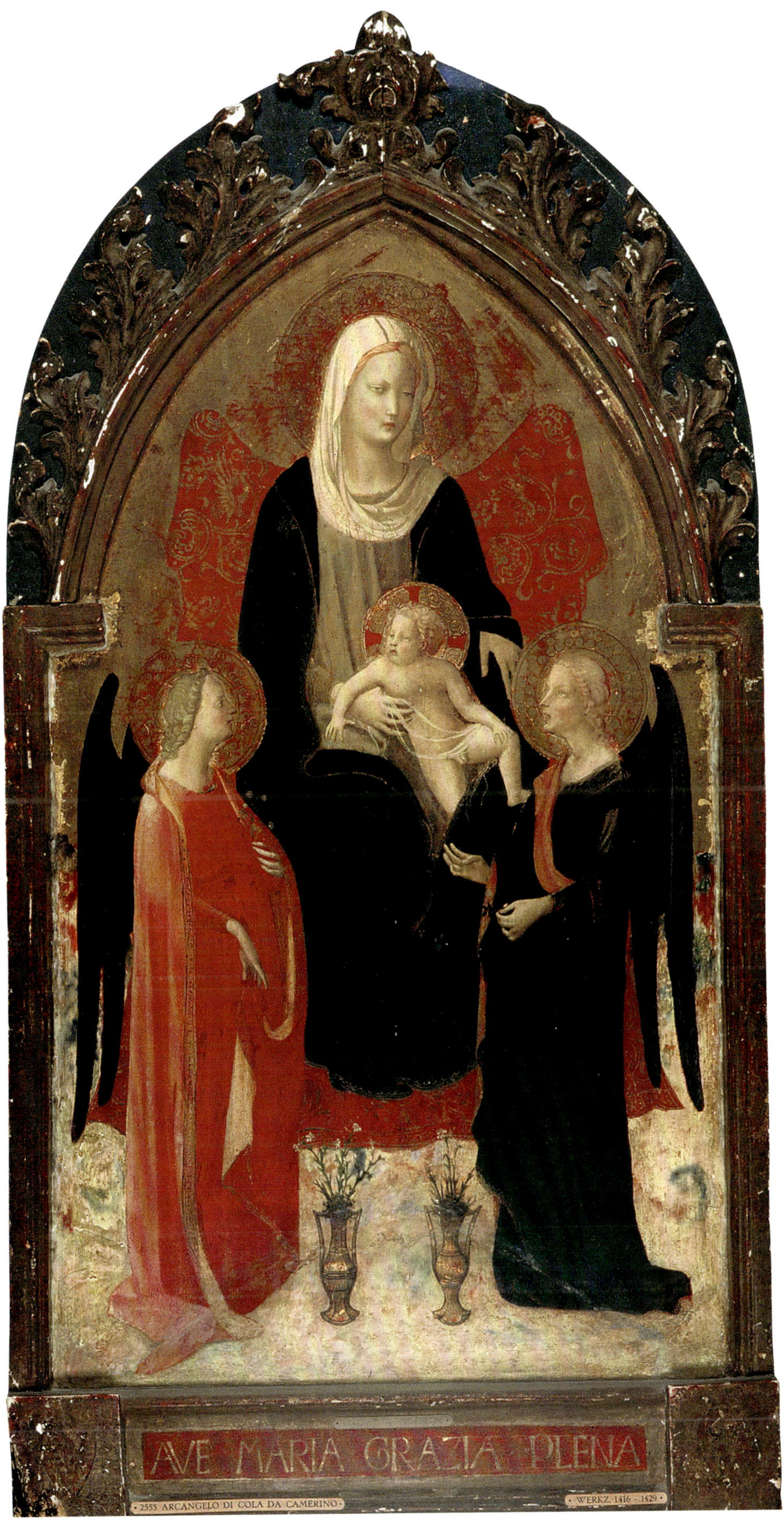

6

the floor. The brilliant hues of the marble pavement represent an early instance of Fra Angelico's predilection for depicting such floors and materials, which manifested itself later on a grander scale in such paintings as the *Annunciation* in the Prado and in the version in Cortona, or in the *Coronation of the Virgin* in the Louvre. An important precedent for the splendidly rendered marble is the throne in Giotto's *Virgin and Child, Enthroned with Angels and Saints,* now in the Uffizi but in Fra Angelico's day still on display in the church of the Ognissanti. Furthermore the vases of lilies and roses being offered by the two angels kneeling in the foreground reappear in the Rotterdam painting and show that also in this respect Fra Angelico followed an age-old Florentine tradition. Although the floor in the Rotterdam picture is somewhat darker in the background, the abstract blotches of color tend to lend it the appearance of an almost-flat screen. Spatial depth is conveyed solely by the attitudes of the figures and their positions in relation to one another. Their three-dimensionality is underscored by the patterns of the folds of their draperies, and by the subtle modeling of their heads and hands. Remarkable in this respect is, as Laurence Kanter pointed out to me, the shadow cast by the Child's right arm as he reaches forward across the Virgin's wrist. The figures are enlivened by the sinuous lines of their garments—as, for example, the Virgin's veil, the hems of the mantles, or the seemingly gratuitous curve of the neckline of the robe worn by the angel at the left. Despite these almost calligraphic lines, the draperies modify traditional Gothic patterns. Although the robe of the angel to the right falls in a series of cascading *V*-shaped folds, the typically Gothic, diagonal drapery patterns, often deliberately enhanced by the action of a figure raising up part of its garments, are completely lacking here. The angel to the left is perhaps more telling still, because the figure does pull on the hem of his garment with an extremely refined gesture of the right hand. Whereas the right part of the mantle simply hangs down from the shoulder, the other part is drawn over the left arm and hand toward the angel's middle, thereby enveloping the figure and indicating its solid three-dimensionality. It is not unlikely that Fra Angelico found his inspiration for such figures in sculpture. By the second decade of the fifteenth century, sculptors like Donatello and Nanni di Banco already were developing alternatives to the traditional Gothic patterning of the folds to stress the physical presence of a figure.

There is another reason to suggest that Fra Angelico was looking at contemporary sculpture. Images of the Virgin in which only a white veil covers her head (instead of the traditional blue mantle) are not that common in painting but are

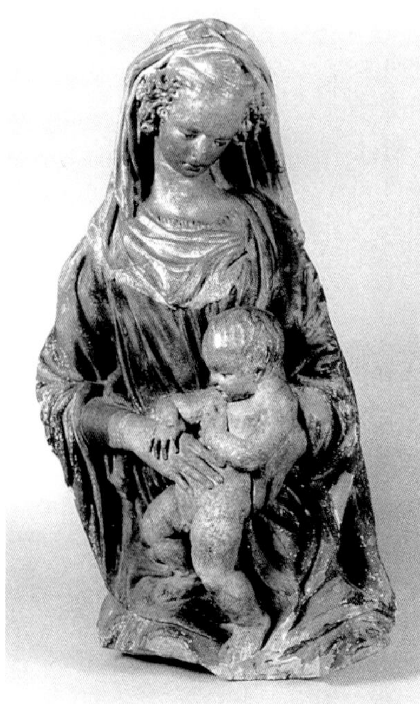

Figure 26. Nanni di Bartolo. *Virgin and Child*. About 1420. Private collection, Turin

found in a number of terracotta half-length figure groups attributed to Donatello and his circle.[11] Also characteristic of these sculptures is the ever-changing attitude of the Child, often shown naked, as a baby Hercules. One such terracotta, attributed to Nanni di Bartolo (fig. 26), comes particularly close in the iconographic type of the Virgin, as well as in the Child's physical appearance and his almost unruly attitude.[12] At the same time, Fra Angelico shows the advantages of painting in the rendering of the diaphanous cloth covering the Child and held by the Virgin—an effect, obviously lacking in the terracotta.

Nanni di Bartolo's terracotta has been dated on stylistic grounds to about 1420, which provides us some idea of the date of the Rotterdam *Virgin and Child* as well. Whether scholars have attributed the picture to Fra Angelico or not, most have noted its similarities to the *Virgin of Humility* in the Hermitage, an observation that is confirmed by such details as the pattern of the brocade.[13] The facial types and the somewhat darker modeling of the figures here, in respect to the *Virgin of Humility*, suggest a date close to the high altarpiece from San Domenico in Fiesole, the main part of which may have been completed as early as 1420 or 1421 (see cat. 10).

VMS

1. The panel in question is *The Dream of Pope Innocent III and Saints Peter and Paul Appearing to Saint Dominic* in the Yale University Art Gallery (cat. 37A); the support consists of two parts joined together. Another, much-earlier example is Ugolino di Nerio's *Daniel* in the Johnson Collection, at the Philadelphia Museum of Art (no. 89), originally a pinnacle of the now-dispersed polyptych for the main altar of Santa Croce, Florence.
2. Freuler 2001, pp. 120–23.
3. "Comprato da Papà dal / Sindaco di Fucecchio / vendito a Julius Böhler c. 1918." Florence, Kunsthistorisches Institut, Photo Library, no. 450045.
4. Information kindly supplied by Professor Alberto Malvolti, Fucecchio.
5. Hannema 1952, no. 18, p. 10.
6. Colasanti 1921–22, pp. 538–45, esp. pp. 539–40; Procacci 1929, pp. 119–27, esp. pp. 119, 127; Berenson 1929–30, pp. 133–42, esp. pp. 136, 140; Serra 1934, p. 287, fig. 365; Zeri 1950, pp. 33–38, esp. p. 33; Vitalini Sacconi 1968, p. 86; Zampetti 1971, p. 76.
7. Zeri 1969, pp. 5–15, esp. p. 13; Pope-Hennessy 1974, p. 232; Van Os and Prakken 1974, pp. 44–45; Vos and Van Os 1989, pp. 182–86; Kleeman and Willner 1993, pp. 53–55.
8. Longhi 1928 a, pp. 154–59, esp. p. 154 n. 5; Longhi 1940, pp. 145–91, esp. p. 174; Salmi 1950, pp. 75–81; Collobi-Ragghianti 1955 b, pp. 22–47, esp. pp. 23, 46 notes 2, 5; Chiarini 1960, pp. 278–81, esp. pp. 279–80; Baldini 1970, p. 86.
9. Boskovits 1976a, pp. 37–39.
10. Baldini 1986, p. 273; Schmidt 1995, pp. 87–91; Spike 1996, no. 99, p. 246; Bonsanti 1998, no. 14, p. 118; Freuler 2001.
11. See Bellosi 1989, pp. 130–35.
12. Galli 2002, pp. 124–26.
13. Klesse 1967, nos. 320, 320 a, p. 366.

GIOVANNI DI FRANCESCO TOSCANI

7. *Saint Nicholas of Bari, Saint Lawrence, and Saint Peter Martyr, with a Donor*

Tempera on panel, 10.5 x 55 cm (4⅛ x 21⅝ in.)
Kunstmuseum, Bern. Bequest of Adolf von Sturler, 1881 (Inv. no. 874)

This predella, painted on one horizontal plank of wood, portrays three saints in half length, each in a gilt roundel framed by a white fictive marble molding projecting forward from a green *faux-marbre* ground. The perspectival projection of these moldings is highly approximate, as though each roundel is to be viewed from the center of the green marble field alongside it. The receding faces of the moldings are shaded uniformly from top to bottom for an alternation of color and pattern rather than to simulate the actual effects of directed lighting. The left roundel shows Saint Nicholas of Bari wearing a red chasuble and holding his crosier and the three golden balls emblematic of his charity in his left hand as he raises his right hand in a gesture of blessing. Saint Lawrence, in the center roundel, clasps a palm in his right hand and supports an iron grille, the symbol of his martyrdom, with his left hand. Saint Peter Martyr, in the right roundel, wearing a Dominican habit and holding a book in his left hand, turns to the left to address a small figure dipicted as though kneeling in front of the painted moldings. The figure, undoubtedly meant to represent the donor of the complex from which this predella derives, wears a white robe with a scapular and may be a Dominican or a Dominican tertiary.

The history of this predella's attributions reflects the many changes of opinion to which all the panels included in the problematic group of works now associated with the early career of Fra Angelico have been subjected. Like the Griggs *Crucifixion* (cat. 8) and the Princeton *Saint Jerome* (cat. 9), the predella once was thought to be by Masolino before it became categorized as the work of an independent Florentine painter of the early fifteenth century.[1] In 1974 the predella was ascribed to Giovanni di Francesco Toscani, following the identification of the Master of the Griggs Crucifixion as that painter,[2] but only shortly afterward—even before the heterogeneity of this group was widely recognized—it was isolated

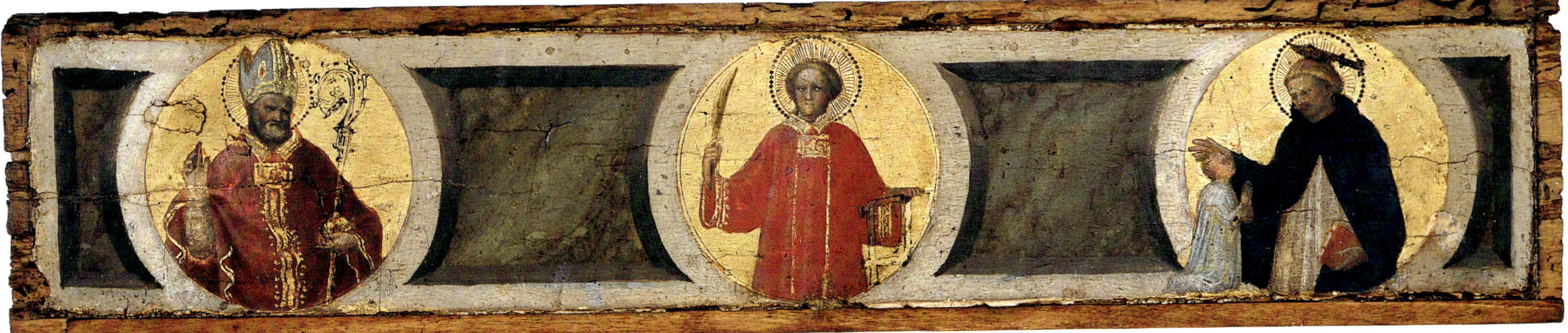

7

from other paintings attributed to Toscani and assigned instead to the young Fra Angelico.[3] Most recently, Gaudenz Freuler has argued at greater length in support of an attribution to Fra Angelico and a date of about 1420, citing figural similarities to the Uffizi *Thebaid* and, in a more general sense, the interplay of influences from Lorenzo Ghiberti, Arcangelo di Cola da Camerino, and Gentile da Fabriano, which seem to characterize much of Angelico's work at the outset of his career.[4] In addition, Freuler proposed a reconstruction situating the Bern predella below Angelico's Rotterdam *Virgin and Child Enthroned, with Two Angels* (cat. 6), as a private devotional tabernacle, possibly commissioned by a member of the lay confraternity of Saint Peter Martyr at Santa Maria Novella.

Freuler's hypothetical reconstruction was based in part on an approximate coincidence of measurements between the Bern predella and the Rotterdam *Virgin and Child,* as well as on the assumption that the present frame of the latter was a modern pastiche.[5] The Rotterdam frame, however, is original and intact, and indicates that the painting was never completed by a predella. Furthermore, stylistic affinities between the paintings in Rotterdam and in Bern are more generic than significant and are, in fact, a result of the influence of the former on the latter rather than evidence of their common authorship. The caricatured expressions of the three saints in the Bern predella and their very particular proportions—small, rounded heads; high foreheads; and tiny eyes, mouths, and chins—are characteristic not of Fra Angelico's early works but rather of the late predella panels by Giovanni Toscani. Similar figures are encountered in the scenes of the predella that once stood below the Ardinghelli altarpiece from Santa Trinita, documented as a work by Toscani from 1423/24,[6] or in the three panels that have recently, and plausibly, been identified as the predella to a documented altarpiece of 1430 from Santa Maria Oltr'Arno.[7] The Bern predella was certainly painted by Giovanni Toscani as well, in all likelihood in about the middle or the second half of the 1420s. It is possible that the tentative perspective of its fictional painted moldings reflects the artist's interest in Masaccio's pictorial experiments with architectural illusionism, particularly in the *Trinity* fresco in Santa Maria Novella—in which case the predella would have to be dated close to the end of Giovanni Toscani's career.

Although Freuler's reconstruction cannot be accepted as proposed, its singular merit lies in calling attention to the category of object from which the Bern predella was removed. It is unquestionably complete in its present format and dimensions and therefore—unlike the Courtauld Institute predella (cat. 13), to which it is superficially related in form—was not once part of an altarpiece. Giovanni Toscani painted a number of devotional tabernacles in the 1420s featuring images of the Virgin and Child but it is not clear with which of these, if any, the Bern predella may be associated. On the other hand, Freuler's suggestion that the patron of this tabernacle may have been a lay brother from the Confraternity of Saint Peter Martyr is highly compelling. Not only does that saint protect the kneeling donor, wearing a Dominican scapular, at the right of the predella but, in addition, the location of the confraternity's chapel in Santa Maria Novella might further explain Toscani's precocious response to Masaccio's *Trinity* fresco in the same church. LK

1. Toesca 1930, p. 15 (as Workshop of Fra Angelico); Bern 1936, p. 16 (as close to Masolino); Collobi-Ragghianti 1950b, part 1, pp. 463, 468 (as by Zanobi Strozzi); Pope-Hennessy 1952, p. 203 (as Style of Fra Angelico), and Pope-Hennessy 1974, pp. 231, 239 (as imitator of Fra Angelico); Micheletti 1959, p. 56 (as by Masolino); Berenson 1963, vol. 1, p. 137 (as mostly by Masolino).
2. Wagner 1974, pp. 91–94; Roberts 1993, p. 215.
3. Boskovits 1976a, pp. 39–40; Boskovits 1976b, pp. 30–54; Strehlke 1994, pp. 25–42.
4. Freuler 2001, pp. 118–23.
5. Van Os and Prakken 1974, p. 44.
6. Philadelphia Museum of Art; Galleria dell'Accademia, Florence; and private collection, Florence; see Strehlke 2004, pp. 420–25.
7. Philadelphia Museum of Art and National Gallery of Victoria, Melbourne; see Strehlke 2004, pp. 426–29.

8.
The Crucifixion

Tempera on panel, 64 x 49 cm (25¼ x 19¼ in.)
The Metropolitan Museum of Art, New York.
Maitland F. Griggs Collection, Bequest of
Maitland F. Griggs, 1943 (43.98.5)

Among the best known but least understood paintings from Early Quattrocento Florence in any public collection is this moving image of the crucified Christ surrounded by a ring of Roman cavalrymen with four holy figures supporting the fainting Virgin at the foot of the cross, in the foreground. Considered to be a work by Masolino when it entered the Griggs Collection in 1925, it was used by Offner as the centerpiece for the creation of a new artistic personality, whom he described as an early Florentine convert to the styles of Gentile da Fabriano and Masaccio.[1] Offner named the artist the Master of the Griggs Crucifixion after this painting but, later, Luciano Bellosi recognized several of the panels singled out by Offner as parts of a documented altarpiece of 1423–24 by Giovanni Toscani (d. 1430).[2] The group of works attributed to the Griggs Master by Offner and to Giovanni Toscani by Bellosi and others is not entirely homogeneous, however, and while it is correct to identify the majority of them as by Giovanni Toscani, several important examples are not by that painter. Chief among these are three paintings included in this exhibition: the *Ninfale Fiesolano* from Bowdoin (cat. 2), the *Penitent Saint Jerome* from Princeton (cat. 9), and, ironically, the present panel—originally, the eponymous work of the group. That the Griggs *Crucifixion* was painted by Fra Angelico early in his career was first proposed by Bellosi himself on the basis of its similarities to the predella of the high altarpiece from San Domenico in Fiesole (now in London; see cat. 10). While this attribution has recently gained wider acceptance especially among Italian critics, it has not been universally embraced;[3] it is, however, correct.

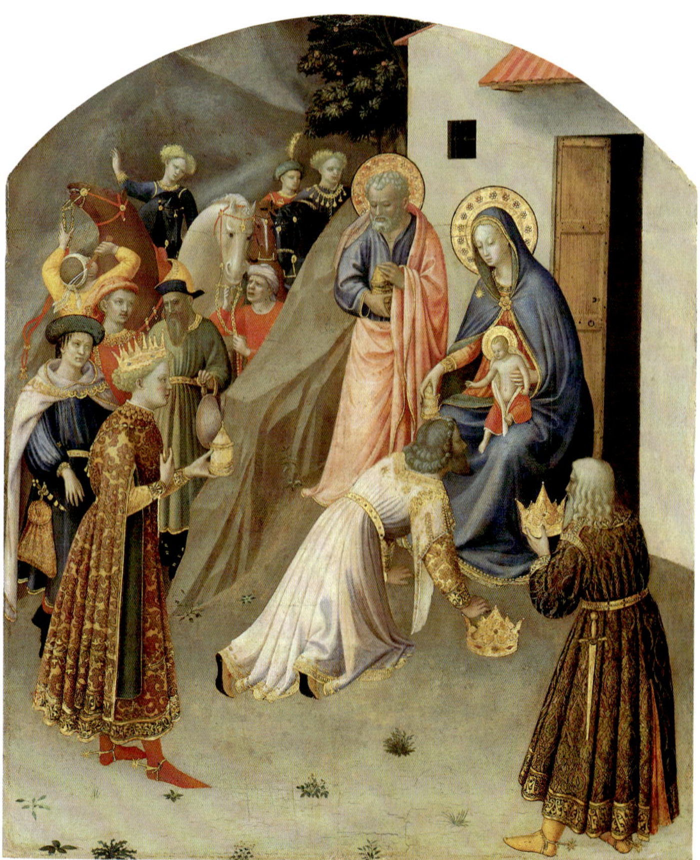

Figure 27. Fra Angelico. *The Adoration of the Magi*. About 1419. Abegg-Stiftung, Riggisberg, Switzerland

The main objection raised by scholars in rejecting the Griggs *Crucifixion* as the work of Fra Angelico depends upon the assumption that the painting must postdate Gentile da Fabriano's *Adoration of the Magi* altarpiece, which was finished in 1423—by which time Angelico's style was decidedly more mature. The basis for this assumption was the belief that the ring of mounted soldiers and the upturned head of the executioner holding the reed and sponge at the left of the cross were inspired by figures in Gentile's altarpiece. These connections, however, are superficial, and none of the spatial effects so brilliantly mastered in this painting is incompatible with Angelico's work prior to 1423. Typical of Fra Angelico's style are such details as the faultless foreshortening of the soldier at the left, portrayed in three-quarter lost profile, and the meticulous rendering of the rings of his belt and the trappings of his horse. Similarly, the gratuitous naturalism of showing the gauntlets of the rightmost soldier hanging from his sword belt or the tensed position of his foot and boot in the stirrup are hallmarks of Angelico's empirical approach to narrative. The composition of the scene is ambitious but, as might be expected from a youthful work, it is not resolved with the same intellectual rigor characteristic of Angelico's later paintings, and, in this respect, resembles the Riggisberg *Adoration of the Magi* (fig. 27) or the even more complex *Thebaid* (fig. 19) in the Uffizi. The ring of horsemen in the *Crucifixion* establishes a measurable circle of space around the cross, which is seen decidedly from the right and very slightly off-center. The carefully calibrated perspectival devices that create this spatial illusion are somewhat compromised by the combination of two different viewing angles: down onto the mourning saints in the foreground, and up toward the soldiers' heads and the muscular but pathetic figure of Christ isolated in the upper half of the panel. Each of these viewpoints is painstakingly consistent in its construction, but the elision from one to the other is not seamless, leading some scholars to suggest that the mourning figures in the foreground either might have been added by a second hand or copied by Angelico from a separate source and inserted uncomfortably in this context.[4]

Dating the Griggs *Crucifixion* depends not on its relationship to Gentile's *Adoration* altarpiece but rather to Angelico's

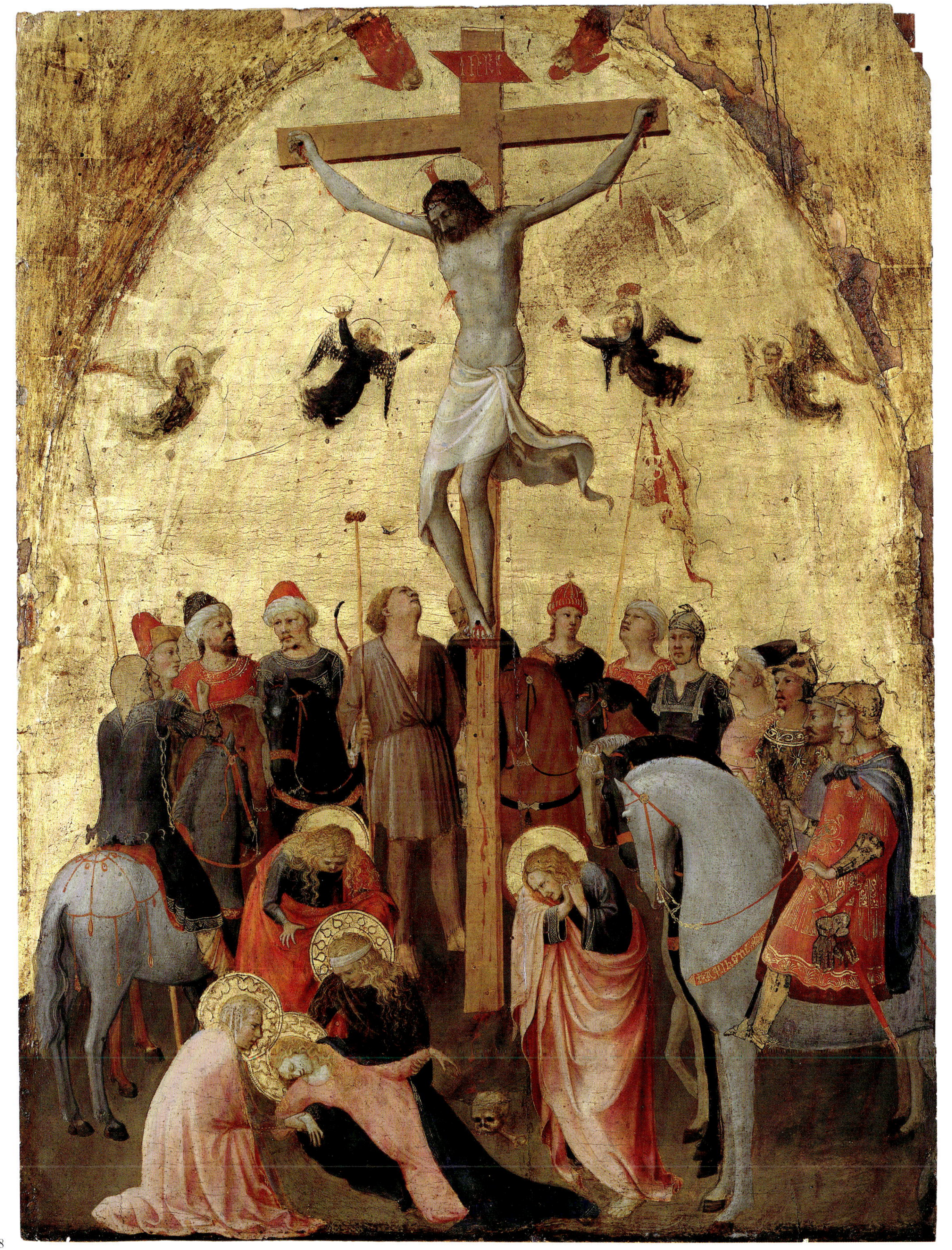

8

San Domenico high altarpiece, to which the figure types in the smaller painting are particularly close. The date of the San Domenico altarpiece is not attested by documents nor has it been the subject of wide-ranging agreement among scholars, although it serves as a crucial point of orientation for most works from the artist's early career. A reasonable terminus post quem is provided by Barnaba degli Agli's donation of funds for the reconstruction of the convent of San Domenico in 1418, as the patron's name saint, Barnabus, appears to the right of the Virgin in Angelico's altarpiece. Traditionally, the San Domenico altarpiece was dated to the late 1420s, if not to the early years of the following decade; yet, there is no reason to suppose that this highly important element of liturgical furnishing could not have been commissioned immediately upon receipt of Barnaba degli Agli's gift, and it is here suggested (see p. 69) that the altarpiece was, indeed, painted, if not installed, as early as 1420 or 1421.

Further complicating the issue is the not unreasonable presumption that Angelico had already professed his vows at San Domenico when he received this commission, but the date at which he may have done so is unknown. The last record in which Fra Angelico is identified by his secular name, Guido di Pietro, dates to 1418, and the first mention of his name in religious orders, Fra Giovanni, dates to 1423. It is sometimes assumed that the young painter began his novitiate in 1419 with the founding of San Domenico in Fiesole, and that after the prescribed year as a novice he took his solemn vows in 1420. This may have been so but it cannot be assumed as fact. Not only is it possible that his novitiate could have begun as late as 1422/23 but it is also equally possible that he may have decided to join the Dominican order in 1418, serving his novitiate at Santa Maria Novella in Florence and joining the community in Fiesole in 1419 as an ordained priest and friar. Carl Strehlke has recently proposed that Angelico's earliest activity was associated with the decorative campaigns undertaken at Santa Maria Novella as early as 1417, in preparation for the arrival of Martin V and the papal court two years later. Furthermore, Eugenio Marino persuasively argued that Angelico joined the newly founded convent of San Domenico in Fiesole rather than the well-established intellectual community and patronage network at Santa Maria Novella primarily because his profession as a painter prevented him from becoming an ordained friar there—as a "manual laborer" he could only have aspired to the status of a lay brother (conversus)—whereas at San Domenico he was not barred from full ordination.[5] The issue is more important than a matter of biographical quibbling, for the Griggs *Crucifixion* alone, of all the works in Angelico's oeuvre, appears to be signed, and the signature, in the form of an inscription in mordant gilt lettering across the bridle of the horse at the far right, reads "*Fr*[*ater*] *Ihones*" (Iohannes), or Fra Giovanni, implying that it was painted only after the artist entered the Dominican order.[6]

In addition to the problems of its attribution and date, the original function of the Griggs *Crucifixion* remains mysterious. Although its subject is commonly encountered on the pinnacles of altarpieces, Strehlke has argued that it is unlikely that this painting was created for that purpose, as the scale of the figures and the abundance and intricacy of its decorative details imply that it was meant to be viewed at or near eye level. Initially, he suggested that it might have formed a diptych with the *Adoration of the Magi* now in Riggisberg, but he later withdrew that proposal in favor of identifying the Riggisberg panel as part of a small altarpiece of a very slightly differing date.[7] In actuality, however, there is no reason that the present painting could not have occupied the pinnacle of an altarpiece, and some evidence for believing that it is unlikely to have been anything else. Its original panel support has been thinned and cropped along all four sides, but X-radiographs reveal that the painted field was never significantly larger nor different in shape from its present form. Traces of the outlines of engaged capitals appear at the left and right approximately halfway up the composition, which results in a picture field of exceptionally squat proportions relative to typical independent tabernacles or triptychs of the period. The extensive spandrels are also atypical of early-fifteenth-century tabernacles, and vague indications at the upper-right and -left corners of the possible removal of angled frame moldings are more commonly encountered in altarpiece fragments than in independent devotional pictures. The sum of this evidence is not absolutely conclusive but tends to underscore the likelihood that this panel originally may have served as the central pinnacle of an altarpiece rather than as part of another type of object. It should be noted as well that compensation for a lower viewing angle could also explain the awkward resolution of the scale of the figures and of the points of view, eliding the foreground and middle ground within the composition itself.

LK

1. Offner 1933, p. 173.
2. Bellosi 1966, pp. 44–58.
3. Boskovits 1994, pp. 365–68; C. B. Strehlke, in Kanter et al. 1994, pp. 324–26: "whether the Griggs *Crucifixion* is by Angelico is still an open question"; Russell 1996, p. 317; Bonsanti 1998, pp. 115–16.
4. C. B. Strehlke, in Kanter et al. 1994, p. 324; Bonsanti 1998, p. 116.
5. Marino 2000, pp. 135–338.
6. Strehlke (2003 b, p. 23) argues that this inscription may refer to the panel's patron rather than to its author, as no other signed works by Angelico are known. The argument is circular and the evidence could be interpreted either way. If, however, "Fra Giovanni" does not in this instance refer to Angelico himself, the *Crucifixion* could be dated even earlier than about 1419/20.
7. C. B. Strehlke, in Kanter et al. 1994, p. 326; Strehlke 2003b, p. 19.

9.
The Penitent Saint Jerome in a Landscape

Tempera on panel: overall, 57 x 41 cm (22½ x 16⅛ in.)
The Art Museum, Princeton University.
Bequest of Frank Jewett Mather, Jr. (63.1)

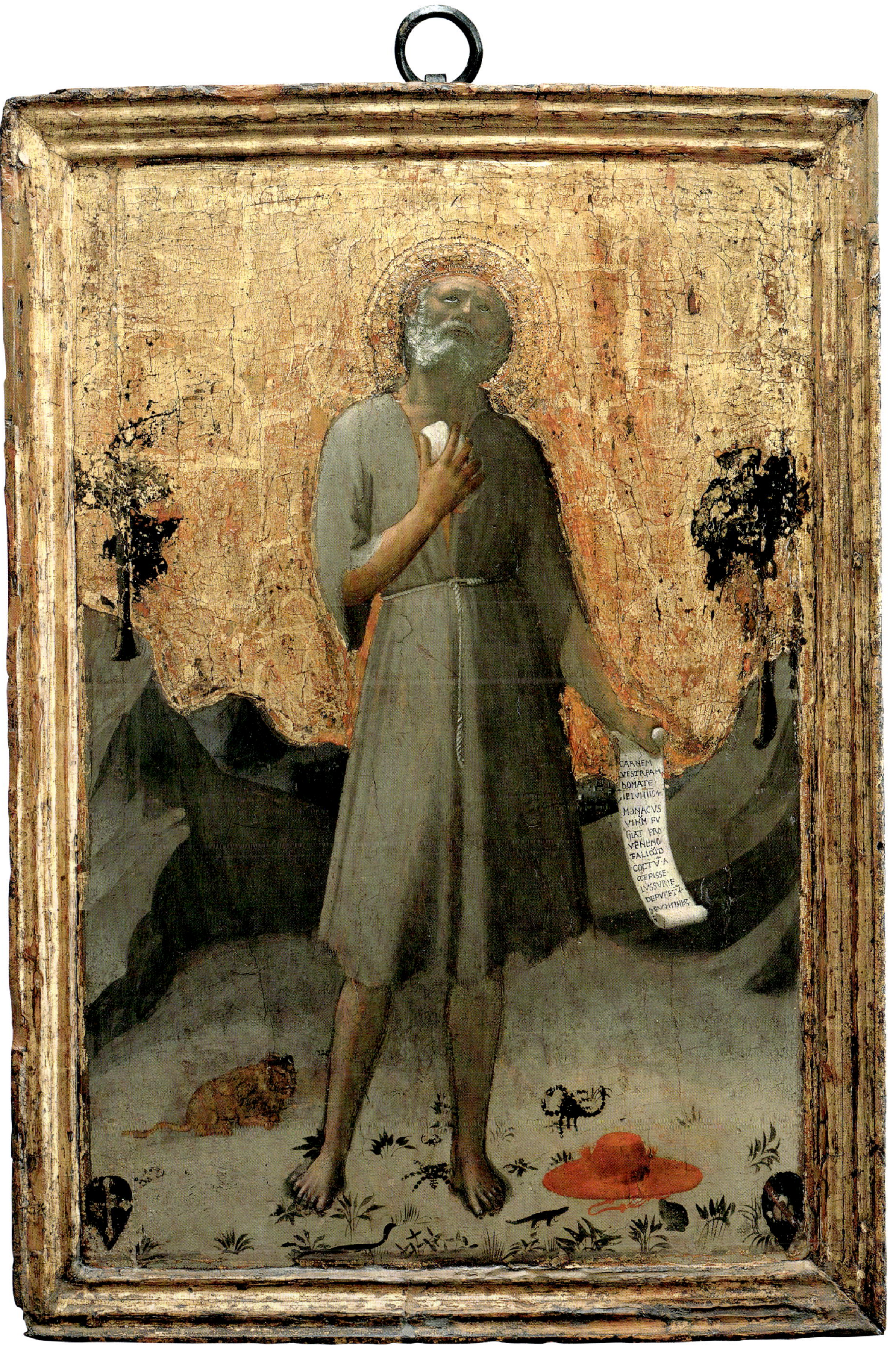

9

Like the Griggs *Crucifixion* in New York (cat. 8), Princeton's *Penitent Saint Jerome* was first published, by Richard Offner, with an attribution to Masolino, which it retained among English-speaking scholars (except for Berenson, who alternatively suggested Sassetta) for over half a century.[1] A majority of Italian art historians instead followed Roberto Longhi in assigning the painting to the young Fra Angelico.[2] It was authoritatively deleted from Masolino's oeuvre only in 1974 by John Pope-Hennessy, who, however, was unable to accept Longhi's attribution to Fra Angelico, astutely pointing out affinities for the pose of the figure in works by the Master of the Griggs Crucifixion, and for the landscape setting in paintings by the Master of the Sherman Predella.[3] A direct attribution to the Master of the Griggs Crucifixion (Giovanni Toscani) was defended by Marvin Eisenberg, largely on the basis of similarities in figure type to that artist's eponymous work in The Metropolitan Museum of Art.[4] As the Griggs *Crucifixion* itself can now be recognized as a work by Fra Angelico, not by Giovanni Toscani, recent scholarship is nearly unanimous in recognizing the Princeton panel as the work of Angelico as well.[5]

Not previously considered in discussions of its authorship, dating, or significance, however, has been the puzzling condition of the Princeton *Saint Jerome,* which, to a great extent, is a Quattrocento restoration of an earlier image, apparently undertaken to mask damages the panel had suffered from exaggerated warping shortly after it was first painted.[6] The panel support is unusually coarse grained and knotty. In typical Tuscan fashion, it comprises three planks: one wide board in the center to which two narrow boards are nailed and glued at the sides. As is often the case, warping caused the top and bottom frame moldings, attached across the wood grain, to disengage at the corners, but it also resulted in the left member of the support pulling away from the main panel; it was reattached and the moldings were repaired by planing the backs to conform to the curvature of the panel, after which they were reapplied, using square linen patches to reinforce the mitered corner joins.[7] Finally, the frame moldings and the background were regilded to hide these restorations, and a gray line was painted around the landscape to cover the repairs to the barb of the frame where it is not gilded. Regilding necessitated repainting the trees, the horizon line, and parts of the figure where its silhouette was compromised by the newly applied gold. Saint Jerome's head, left arm (including the scroll in his left hand), and both legs are entirely repainted: in these areas, two distinct layers of paint and ground are visible. In the top layer, repaints comprise pale flesh tones over a dark terra-verde ground, but largely intact beneath it is the original layer of ruddy flesh tones over a light terra-verde ground. The saint's unrestored right arm is painted in this earlier technique, while his draperies and much of the landscape also reveal only a single layer of paint and are thus presumably part of the original image.

It follows that any attribution of the Princeton *Penitent Saint Jerome* must be qualified by reference to the first or second stage of work on the panel. The invention of the full-length image of the saint, presented in a knee-length gray tunic, standing in a desert landscape in a frontal pose, centered and filling nearly the full height of the picture field, is a product of the first campaign. Naming the artist or dating this facet of the picture's execution is all but impossible on stylistic grounds, although iconographic evidence (see below) may suggest a date about 1400. The restorations to the head, left arm, and legs, as well as the addition of a cardinal's berretta and some of the grasses in the foreground, should be recognized as the work of the young Fra Angelico and must be situated close to the putative date of the Griggs *Crucifixion* and the San Domenico high altarpiece, about 1420. Angelico strove to mitigate the insistent planarity of the earlier image with the dramatic foreshortening of the saint's upturned head, the most remarkable aspect of the painting; the forward-curling sweep of the scroll, and the angle of the saint's hand grasping it; and the classicizing pose and modeling of the legs. It can only be presumed that the legs were repainted to correct or update the figure's original, more Gothic, and less naturalistic appearance since this area of the painting does not overlap the gold ground or any major repairs in the landscape and was not compromised by structural work on the panel support. It is likely that Angelico repaired the trees on either side of Saint Jerome as well, although these areas of the painting have suffered extensive losses from flaking and are difficult to judge in their present state.

Another key factor in assessing the authorship of the Princeton panel has been the issue of its early ownership, as indicated by the coats of arms painted in the lower corners. These coats of arms were identified by Offner as those of the Gaddi and Ridolfi families of Florence, and were associated by him with the marriage of Agnolo di Zanobi Gaddi to Maddalena Ridolfi in 1424. It is unlikely that Angelico could have painted an image in this style, inseparable from that of the Griggs *Crucifixion,* as late as 1424;[8] conversely, acceptance of this date as a terminus a quo for the Griggs *Crucifixion* has made it difficult for many scholars to support the attribution of that painting to Fra Angelico. Both shields, however, seem to be the result of yet another, later intervention on the panel: they are painted in an oily medium over the landscape, and the ground around the left shield is extensively repaired. They may well have been applied to the panel on the occasion of the 1424 wedding or added to it at an even later date, but they have no value as evidence for dating the painting itself. Carl Strehlke has observed, furthermore, that the inscriptions on Saint Jerome's (restored) scroll, which may be translated as "overcome your flesh by fasting; the monk should avoid wine as if it were poison; eating cooked food is considered luxurious," are appropriate to an eremitic or penitential commission, not to a matrimonial context.[9]

Images of the penitent Saint Jerome first appear in Italian painting at the turn of the fifteenth century; a predella panel by Lorenzo Monaco, probably painted in 1395 or 1396, is the earliest known example.[10] The rapidly increasing popularity of this iconography of the saint in Tuscany, replacing more traditional representations of Jerome in cardinal's garb seated in his study or at a scholar's desk, is usually associated with the establishment of a Hieronymite community in Fiesole by Carlo Guidi da Montegranelli (about 1330–1417). Although Carlo Guidi retired to the hills of Fiesole as a hermit about 1360, it was not until much later that his followers were organized into a congregation, whose rule was formally approved by Innocent VII in 1406 and confirmed by Gregory XII in 1415.[11] Concurrently, the crowds of lay people who sought spiritual guidance from Carlo Guidi founded the socially prominent Confraternity of Santa Maria della Pietà, called the Buca di San Girolamo, which first met in 1410; in 1411 this confraternity relocated from Fiesole to Florence, establishing its headquarters at the Ospedale di San Matteo in the Piazza San Marco, and their constitutions (*capitoli*), drafted in 1413, were illuminated, perhaps not coincidentally, by Battista di Biagio Sanguigni.[12]

The great majority of Florentine images of the penitent Saint Jerome, including a figure in Zanobi Strozzi's altarpiece for the Hieronymite monastery in Fiesole and three examples by Fra Angelico from the 1430s or early 1440s (see cat. 37), show him dressed in a Hieronymite habit, a full-length light or dark gray robe with a leather belt. Only the Princeton panel and a polychromed terracotta statue painted by Giuliano Amidei in 1454[13] show him, instead, in a short habit with a Franciscan knotted rope belt. As this statue, which may well have been conceived as a copy of the figure in the Princeton panel, was made for—and is preserved on the premises of—the Buca di San Girolamo, it may be inferred that the Princeton panel was, from an early date, the property of a member of this confraternity, and that it was a well-known and revered object. It is not clear, however, whether, in the first instance, it portrayed Saint Jerome, given the paucity of other images of the saint wearing a similar habit, or whether it might have depicted another hermit, or perhaps Saint John the Baptist, and was converted by Angelico into an image of the Church Father in penance. LK

1. Offner 1920, pp. 68–76; Venturi 1924, pp. 132–34; Berenson 1932a, p. 513; Pope-Hennessy 1939, pp. 183–84.
2. Longhi 1940, p. 174; Salmi 1948, p. 234; Collobi-Ragghianti 1955b, pp. 23–24; Boskovits 1976a, p. 31.
3. Pope-Hennessy 1974, p. 231.
4. Eisenberg 1976, pp. 274–83.
5. Bellosi 1988, p. 196; Strehlke 1994, pp. 31–32; Bonsanti 1998, p. 116; Spike 1996, p. 264; Strehlke 1998, p. 17; G. Bonsanti, in Bellosi 2002, pp. 172–73; Strehlke 2003b, pp. 4–27.
6. I am grateful to Norman Muller for first calling attention to the anomalies in the paint surface of the Princeton *Saint Jerome* and for his very generous assistance in formulating an explanation for them. The conclusions reached here do not necessarily reflect his opinion, however. See Muller 2003, pp. 28–31.
7. The top molding can be seen to bridge a measurable gap between the center and the left side panel that was already present when the molding was applied: gesso drips along the vertical sides are undisturbed, the top edges remain flush, and the corners are not split.
8. Berti (1963, p. 38), and Baldini (1970, p. 86) objected to Longhi's attribution on the grounds that this date seemed too late for the style of the painting.
9. Strehlke 1998, p. 17; Strehlke 2003b.
10. Meiss 1974, pp. 134–40. For the dating of Lorenzo Monaco's *Penitent Saint Jerome,* see L. Kanter, in Kanter et al. 1994, pp. 232–33.
11. Rice 1985, p. 70.
12. Sebregondi 1991, pp. 3, 123–24.
13. Ibid., pp. 125–27.

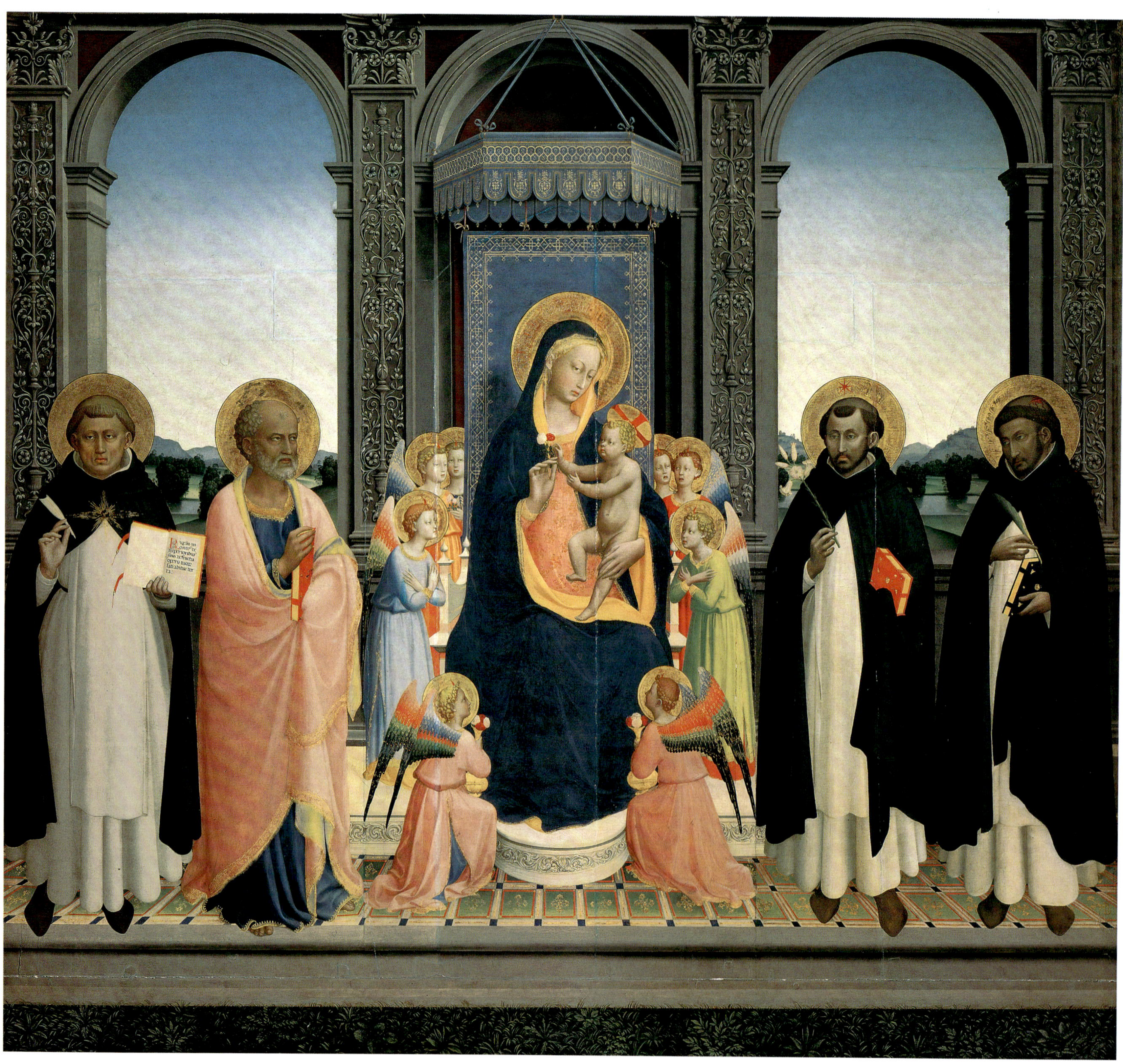

Chapter III
A Velvet Revolution: Fra Angelico's High Altarpiece for San Domenico in Fiesole

ANNEKE DE VRIES

The San Domenico high altarpiece (fig. 28), Fra Angelico's earliest surviving large-scale work, occupies a special position within the context of developments in contemporary painting that become clear when it is compared to a group of similar compositions whose affinity has hitherto remained unnoticed. Also escaping attention until now are some of the compositional problems encountered by Fra Angelico in executing the work for San Domenico's high altar—the consequence of the transition from the polyptych form to that of the Renaissance altarpiece. These oversights undoubtedly are due to the irrevocable alterations to which the San Domenico altarpiece was subjected by Lorenzo di Credi in 1501. The shape of the painted surface was changed, as was the backdrop against which the figures are placed, and, in addition, their costumes were overpainted, including the Virgin's mantle.[1]

However, it is possible to reconstruct at least part of the original appearance of the altarpiece with the aid of X-radiographs of the main panel (fig. 29, 30, 31). These were on view in the exhibition "Firenze restaura" in 1972.[2] Umberto Baldini, the curator of that exhibition, also referred to them in an article on the reconstruction of the altarpiece, but in recent literature on the subject they have been overlooked.[3] Baldini used them mainly to establish the appearance of the Madonna's throne, now hidden from view by a cloth of honor. In the X-radiographs the throne is recognizable as an architectural structure with a curved back topped by a conch, but additional architectural details are revealed that are not recorded by Baldini: under the architrave immediately below the conch is an arched frieze.

In a number of respects, the original composition of Fra Angelico's altarpiece displays analogies with the center panel of an altarpiece (fig. 32) by his older contemporary Bicci di Lorenzo for the chapel of Simone da Spicchio in the Collegiata at Empoli. Not only are the posture and suggestion of movement of the Christ Child in both paintings the same but also the decorative detail of the arched frieze behind the Virgin's similarly inclined head. These resemblances suggest that the two compositions are in some way connected, but the differences between both paintings seem to indicate that Bicci drew inspiration from Fra Angelico, rather than vice versa. Whereas in the San Domenico high altarpiece the Christ Child's attention clearly is drawn toward the roses in the Virgin's right hand, Bicci's Christ Child looks into the void, holding his mother's little finger with one hand and making an unfocused waving motion with the other. While a strong sense of depth and support is conveyed by the Virgin's curving left hand around Christ's fully extended left leg in Fra Angelico's altarpiece, there is no logic in the conventional way Bicci's Christ Child is poised on the Virgin's left hand. What makes this comparison all the more interesting is the fact that we can be certain when exactly Bicci executed the altarpiece: payments disclose that he was at work on the painting from as early as July 1423 until April 1424.[4] This provides a terminus ante quem for the San Domenico high altarpiece, which accords perfectly with the current tendency to date it shortly after the convent was occupied, in 1419.

Bicci's *Madonna* is one of a group of somewhat similar and more or less contemporary compositions first singled out for comparison by James Stubblebine and his students.[5] Apart from the example in Empoli, the group includes images of the Madonna by Arcangelo di Cola da Camerino (in Bibbiena; fig. 33), Giovanni dal Ponte (in Cambridge; fig. 34), the Master of Borgo alla Collina (in Helsinki; fig. 37), and altarpieces by Rossello di Jacopo Franchi (in the Galleria dell'Accademia, Florence) and by Francesco d'Antonio (in Avignon; fig. 35), but, most significantly, Masaccio's San Giovenale altarpiece (fig. 36). The primary element shared by all of these pictures is the curved shape of the back of the Virgin's throne. However, Stubblebine and his students also noted other similarities: the strong and consistent lighting from one side, and the plasticity in the rendering of the Virgin's knees; furthermore, in some instances, the posture of the Christ Child and of the angels surrounding the throne are also alike. The fact that the San Domenico high altarpiece belongs to this group of works as well was overlooked.[6] However, its affinity with the group is not limited to the particular type of the throne and the poses of the accompanying angels; even though the play of light on

Opposite:
Figure 28. Fra Angelico. *Virgin and Child Enthroned, with Eight Angels, and Saints Thomas Aquinas, Barnabas, Dominic, and Peter Martyr* (San Domenico High Altarpiece). About 1419–21. San Domenico, Fiesole

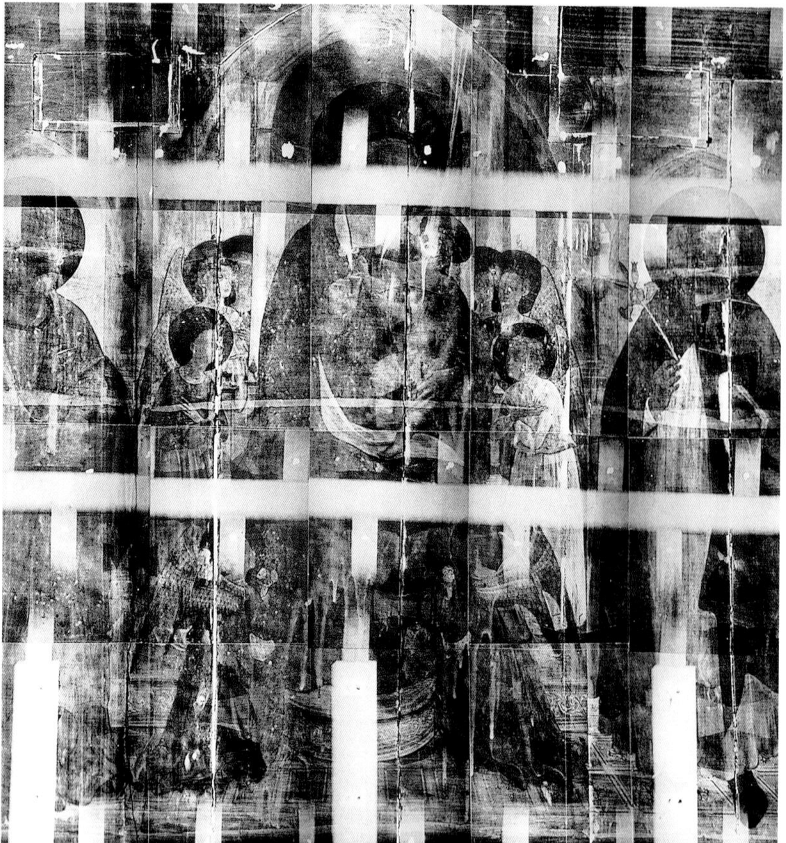

Figure 29

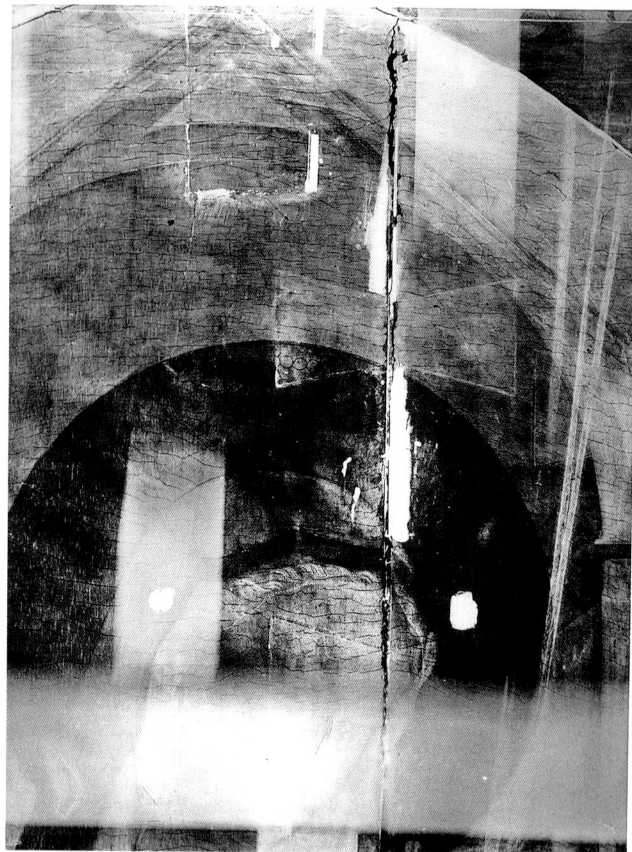

Figure 30

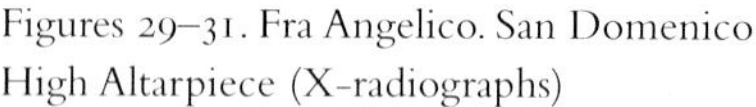

Figures 29–31. Fra Angelico. San Domenico High Altarpiece (X-radiographs)

Figure 31

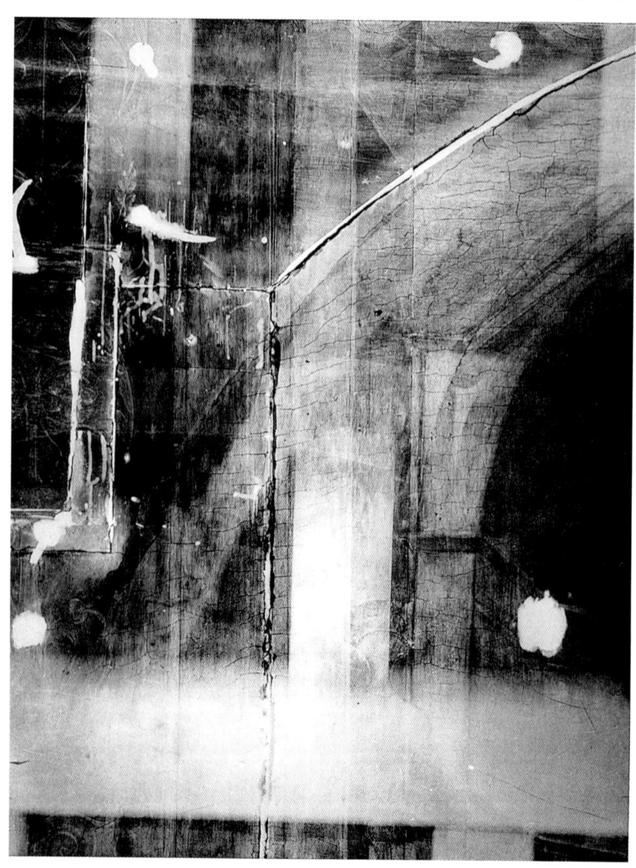

the throne and the sculptural depiction of the Virgin's knees cannot be judged because of Lorenzo di Credi's overpainting, the subtle shading apparent in the bodies of the angels and the Child, and on the armrests of the throne, is the result of a consistency in the rendering of light, which enters the scene from the right.

It is perhaps telling that as recently as about 1980 Stubblebine and his students did not look for signs of these Early Renaissance artistic concerns in Fra Angelico's oeuvre, but, instead, focused on the relationship between the group of paintings under consideration and the innovations Masaccio brought to Florentine painting in the 1420s. They dismissed the possibility that the compositions were directly dependent on the San Giovenale triptych, deeming it of not high enough quality to warrant an attribution to Masaccio himself. It was suggested that the San Giovenale altarpiece and the other paintings of the Madonna were all based on a lost prototype by Masaccio. While a complete rejection of the attribution to Masaccio is no longer tenable, the assumption that this group of paintings of the Madonna was not inspired by the San Giovenale altarpiece is probably correct. That work presents too many problems to be considered a plausible prototype. First and foremost, the triptych was painted for a small church in an out-of-the-way location. Those who wanted to see it required a whole day to travel to Cascia, which does not appear to have been the case even with Masaccio's Pisa altarpiece.[7] The hypotheses of Ivo Becattini and Luciano Berti that the triptych was not moved to its final destination until after 1436, and may have been kept on display in San Lorenzo in Florence for a time after its completion, was convincingly dismissed by Anna Padoa Rizzo.[8]

These practical objections aside, the San Giovenale triptych, dated April 23, 1422, clearly stands apart in a number of respects both from the examples cited by Stubblebine and his students and from the San Domenico high altarpiece. Masaccio's rendering of the curvature of the back of the Virgin's throne, contrary to what one might expect, is the least pronounced, mainly because of the composition's high viewpoint in combination with the picture's soft, overall lighting, which is devoid of any dramatic shading. Furthermore, it is the only instance of a throne with a rather archaic Cosmatesque decoration, in place of the classicizing features found in the work of some of the other painters. Yet, the much clearer affinities that link the rest of the pictures in Stubblebine's group to the center panel of Fra Angelico's altarpiece are interesting, because the San Domenico high altarpiece in all likelihood is the earliest painting among them. Bicci's Empoli altarpiece can be dated to 1423–24, and the altarpiece by Arcangelo di Cola, of which only the *Madonna* in Bibbiena now remains, was probably the one commissioned by the Florentine banker Esaù Martellini before 1427; the earliest date proposed for the latter is 1423–24.[9] The triptych by Giovanni dal Ponte, to which the panel of the *Madonna* in Cambridge belonged, was reconstructed by Curtis Shell and probably correctly dated to about 1427–30.[10] A chronology for Rossello's oeuvre is hard to establish because of a lack of datable works, but there is no reason to date the Accademia triptych before about 1427–30. The *Madonna* by the Master of Borgo alla Collina could also date from about 1425–30. Finally, Francesco d'Antonio's Rinieri altarpiece in Avignon very likely was painted about 1430.[11]

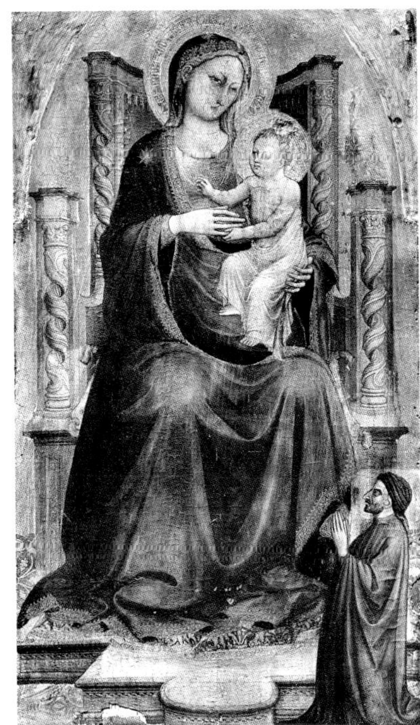

Figure 32. Bicci di Lorenzo. *Virgin and Child Enthroned, with a Kneeling Donor.* 1423–34. Museo della Collegiata di Sant'Andrea, Empoli

It seems clear that Bicci borrowed from the San Domenico high altarpiece shortly after it was finished for his Empoli polyptych. Whether the other painters did the same is hard to ascertain because for the most part they were more subtle and more skilled at absorbing new motifs into their own idiom. This explains the differences between the various groups of the Virgin and Child: only occasionally are compositions copied *ad litteram,* and when this happenend it must have been at the patron's request. Andrea di Giusto's 1435 replica of the Monte Oliveto altarpiece by Lorenzo Monaco, dated 1410, for the Olivetan monastery in Prato is a case in point. For most painters in this period, once they had established a personal style in the early part of their career they were reluctant to

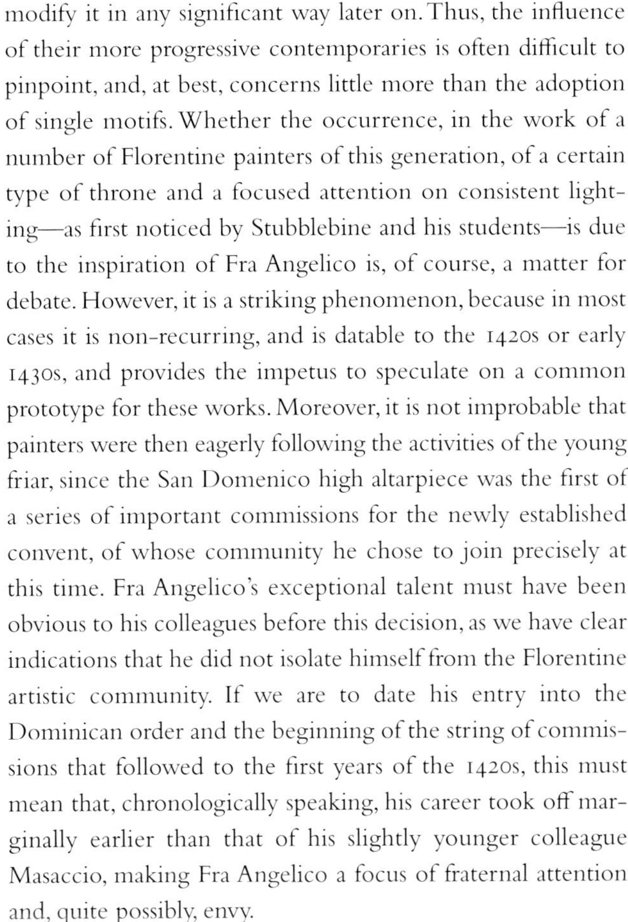

modify it in any significant way later on. Thus, the influence of their more progressive contemporaries is often difficult to pinpoint, and, at best, concerns little more than the adoption of single motifs. Whether the occurrence, in the work of a number of Florentine painters of this generation, of a certain type of throne and a focused attention on consistent lighting—as first noticed by Stubblebine and his students—is due to the inspiration of Fra Angelico is, of course, a matter for debate. However, it is a striking phenomenon, because in most cases it is non-recurring, and is datable to the 1420s or early 1430s, and provides the impetus to speculate on a common prototype for these works. Moreover, it is not improbable that painters were then eagerly following the activities of the young friar, since the San Domenico high altarpiece was the first of a series of important commissions for the newly established convent, of whose community he chose to join precisely at this time. Fra Angelico's exceptional talent must have been obvious to his colleagues before this decision, as we have clear indications that he did not isolate himself from the Florentine artistic community. If we are to date his entry into the Dominican order and the beginning of the string of commissions that followed to the first years of the 1420s, this must mean that, chronologically speaking, his career took off marginally earlier than that of his slightly younger colleague Masaccio, making Fra Angelico a focus of fraternal attention and, quite possibly, envy.

As we have seen, the San Domenico high altarpiece appears to be the earliest surviving example among a group of depictions of the Virgin enthroned on a monumental marble structure with a curved, niche-like back. There are some curved-backed thrones in Florentine Trecento painting, with Giotto's *Madonna* from the Stefaneschi altarpiece and the *Maestà* by the Master of Figline, now in Figline Valdarno, among the most well known. Examples in paintings from the decades around 1400 are difficult to come by, probably because the structure occupied by the seated Madonna often was hidden by a cloth of honor. When Fra Angelico decided to employ this type of throne again, he added a new element, not found in the group of panels by his contemporaries: a canopy. It seems that he had some trouble arriving at a suitable form for the tympanum-like top: the X-radiograph not only shows that the small triangular decoration was moved about slightly but reveals both an inscribed narrow, pointed arch and a wider, rounded arch partly surrounding the Virgin's halo.

Both the revival of the curved-backed throne and the addition of the canopy invite us to seek their source of inspiration. Obviously, because of its material, marble, sculpture is the place to look. Surprisingly, we encounter a similar type of throne in the two smaller stained-glass oculi on the façade of Florence Cathedral representing Saints Lawrence and

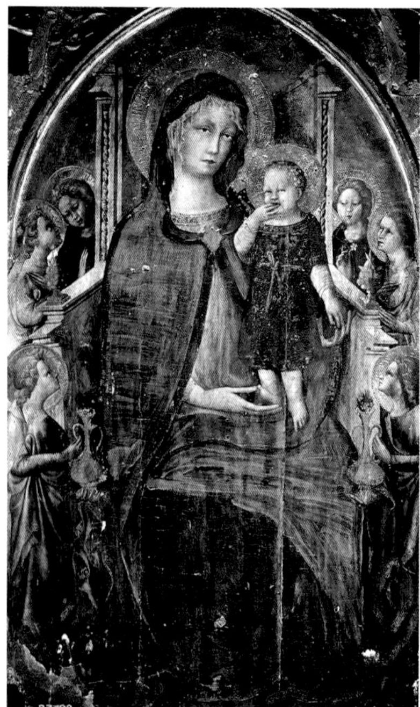

Figure 33. Arcangelo di Cola da Camerino. *Virgin and Child Enthroned, with Six Angels.* About 1423–27. Prepositura dei Santi Ippolito e Donato, Bibbiena

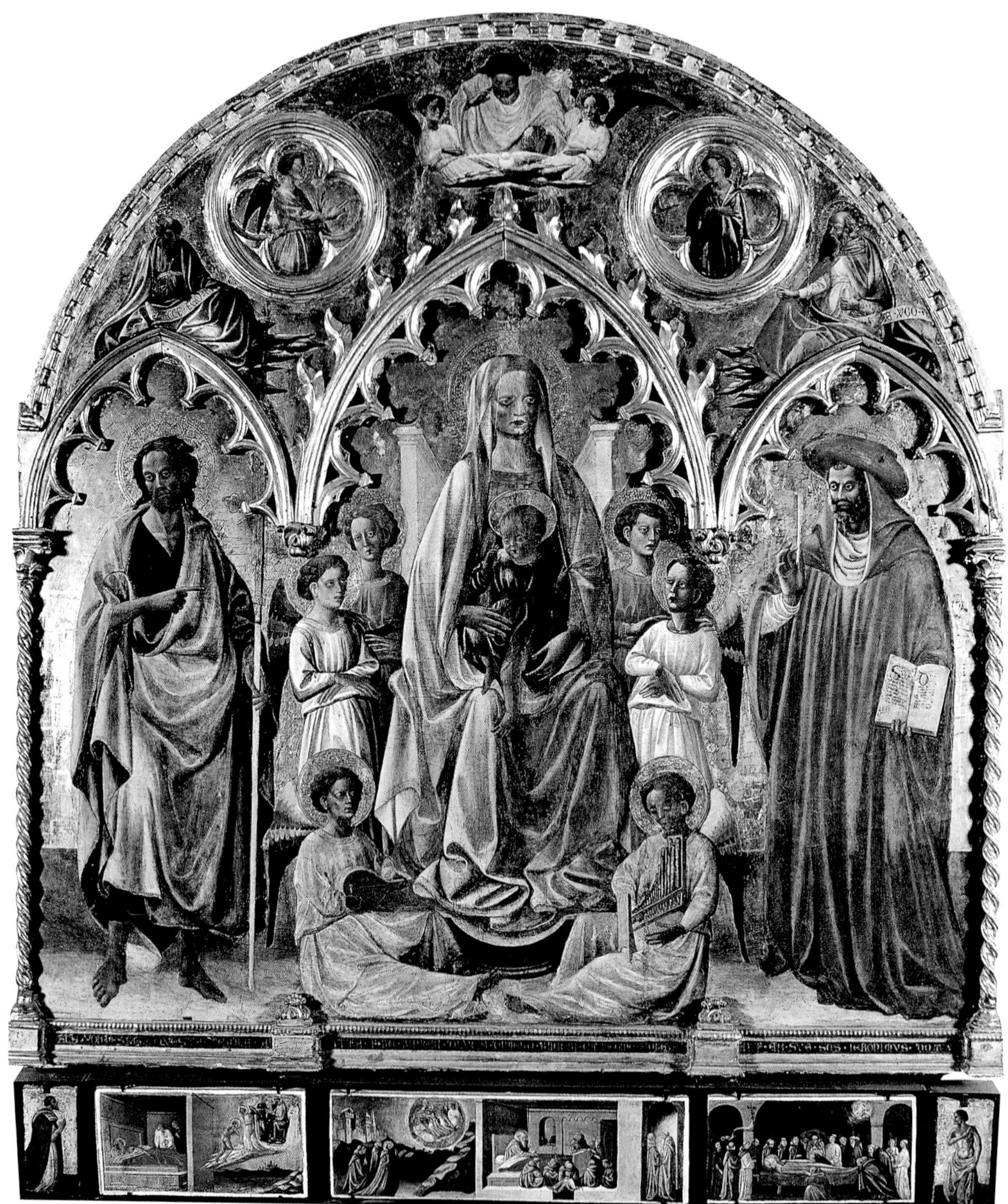

Figure 35. Francesco d'Antonio. *Virgin and Child Enthroned, with Angels and Saints John the Baptist and Jerome* (Rinieri Altarpiece). About 1430. Musée du Petit-Palais, Avignon

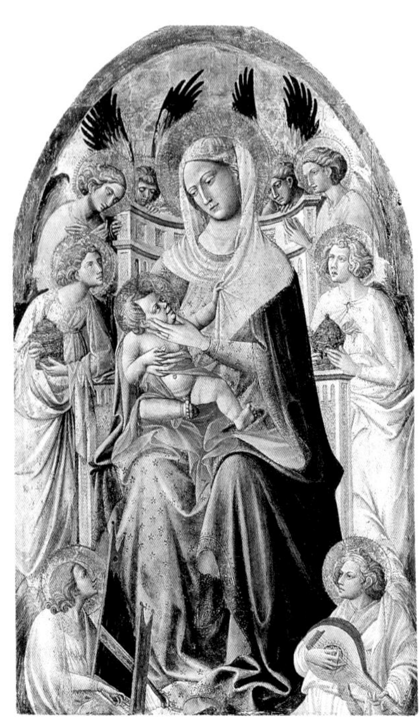

Figure 34. Giovanni dal Ponte. *Virgin and Child Enthroned, with Angels.* About 1427–30. Fitzwilliam Museum, Cambridge

Stephen—documented in 1412–15—the designs for which are attributed to Lorenzo Ghiberti.[12] More significantly, however, the niche and its canopy may be compared with the niches on the façades of Or San Michele, which, like the back of the throne, are not curved in a fluid semi-circular shape, but in segments. The similarity between the tabernacle-like throne of Fra Angelico's early painting of the Madonna (fig. 55) in the Städelsches Kunstinstitut, Frankfurt am Main, and the tabernacle of the Arte dei Medici e Speziali at Or San Michele was first remarked upon by Mario Salmi.[13] Apparently, in the San Domenico high altarpiece Fra Angelico sought to achieve a similar three-dimensional architectural effect with a satisfactorily monumental crowning element. A comparison with the niches at Or San Michele makes clear why Fra Angelico struggled with exactly this aspect of the composition, and probably also why other painters did not even bother to try, preferring to omit this element altogether. Customarily, a gable is set over the arch, but if this were employed in the case of the San Domenico high altarpiece, the crowning structure would have become quite tall, and as a consequence the Virgin would have had to be reduced in size in order to fit into the limited space of the polyptych's central compartment. This solution,

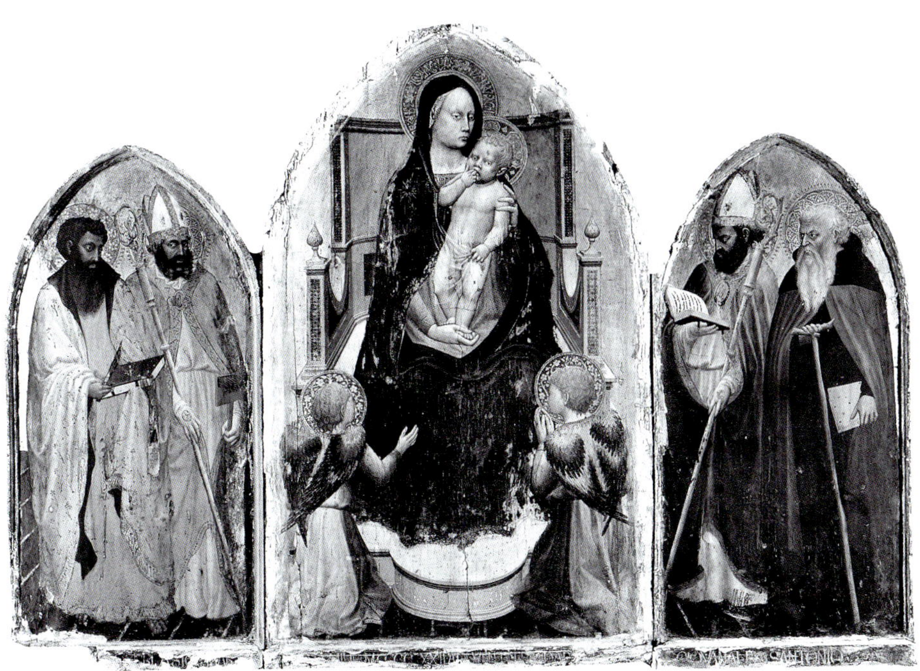

Figure 36. Masaccio. *Virgin and Child Enthroned, with Two Angels and Saints Bartholomew, Blaise, Giovenale, and Anthony Abbot* (San Giovenale Altarpiece). 1422. San Giovenale, Cascia di Reggello

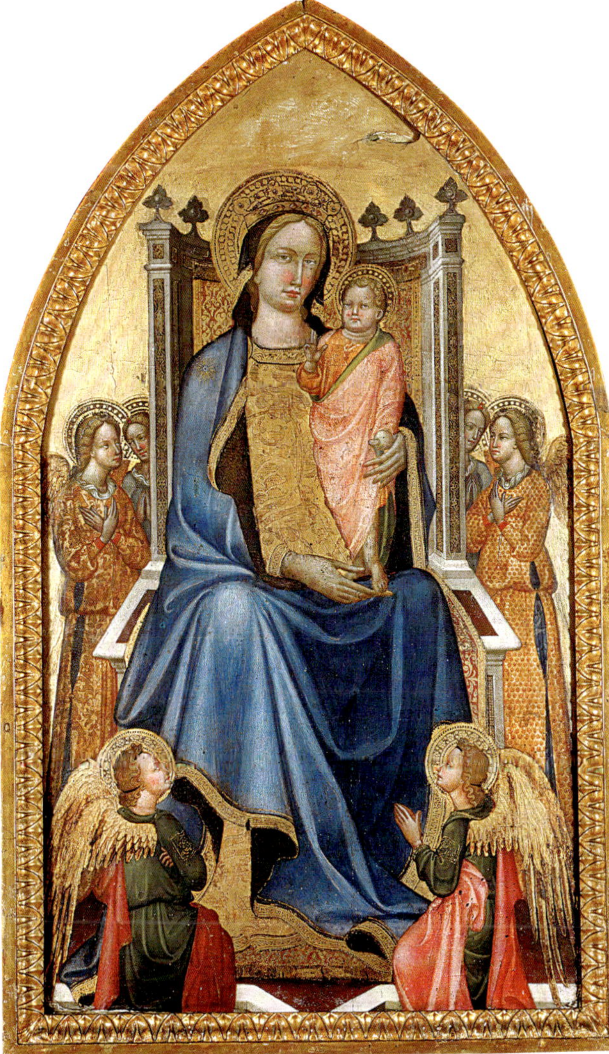

Figure 37. Master of Borgo alla Collina. *Virgin and Child Enthroned, with Angels.* About 1425–30. Ateneum, Helsinki

however, would have been a breach of the conventions of the polyptych, whereby the size of a figure is determined by the height of the compartment it occupies, each figure filling up its allotted space to the fullest, with the central figure often slightly larger than those on the lateral panels, thus emphasizing the importance of the former. In order to solve this problem, Fra Angelico not only made the gable as flat as possible, but it is very likely that he chose a round rather than a pointed arch for this reason as well, as the polyptych's frame clearly had pointed arches. Similar arches were also used on the niches of Ghiberti's *Saint Matthew* (1419–21) and of Donatello's slightly earlier *Saint George* (about 1415–17). Yet, it may well be that Fra Angelico was not satisfied with the squat, unimposing result. Moreover, a painted canopy was really an unnecessary device, for the frame of a polyptych served the purpose of sheltering the enthroned figure.

It, therefore, may come as no surprise that Fra Angelico did not repeat his experimental inclusion of a canopied throne in his subsequent polyptychs of the 1420s. However, such a throne does occur in his polyptych for San Domenico in Perugia (cat. 30), which is probably datable to the late 1430s—if, indeed, it was commissioned in 1437, as recorded in a sixteenth-century document[14]—and represents an alternative to the crowning solution arrived at for the San Domenico high altarpiece. In the latter, a throne with a classicizing entablature is extended to comply with the proportions of the figures, and, consequently, is rather brutally cut off by the ogival arch of the polyptych's frame.[15] The first successful instance of a monumental, unreservedly classicizing architectural canopy is found in the high altarpiece for San Marco (cat. 34) of about 1440–42. It is the earliest example in Fra Angelico's oeuvre of an altarpiece with a rectangular, undivided picture plane, where the elaborate canopy takes on the function of the frame of the polyptych: it helps to articulate the composition and emphasizes the importance of the central figure, who is no longer larger than the lateral saints; in fact, reducing all the figures to the same scale is a logical consequence of the *sacra conversazione* type of composition and the natural result of a unified picture field.

A significant aspect of the San Domenico high altarpiece, then, is that its now-hidden parts reveal attempts to achieve a degree of monumentality to which the polyptych, with its narrow compartments and heavy framework, was ill suited. Fra Angelico's experiments with this form could be interpreted as marking the imminent demise of the polyptych. It is not surprising that his inclination in this direction displays a sensitivity toward contemporary developments in sculpture. The group of similar compositions created in the wake of the San Domenico high altarpiece is interesting for a number of reasons: they suggest that Fra Angelico's contemporaries were following his earliest achievements, but they also indicate that their adoption of Renaissance elements was limited to those that did not violate the format of the polyptych. The experimental nature of the center panel of Fra Angelico's San Domenico high altarpiece, as discussed here, shows him to be a different kind of painter and the altarpiece itself a first step in an artistic development that would soon become a "velvet" revolution.

1. See note 1 in the entry for catalogue 10 by Laurence Kanter in this volume.
2. Baldini and Dal Poggetto 1972, p. 25.
3. Baldini 1977, pp. 236–46; see, most recently, Gordon 2003, pp. 2–31.
4. Frosinini 1986, pp. 5–15, and p. 13 doc. 16.
5. Stubblebine et al. 1980, pp. 217–25.
6. The same is true for some other compositions not mentioned by Stubblebine. Several works by Paolo Schiavo, all datable to the 1430s, include a heavy marble throne: a fresco formerly in San Piero a Sieve; the tabernacle in the Lindenau-Museum, Altenburg; and the fresco, signed and dated 1436, in San Miniato al Monte, Florence. The same characteristics may be found in a painting of the Madonna attributed to Giovanni dal Ponte in the Städelsches Kunstinstitut, Frankfurt; this work which was recently dated to about 1410–20 by R. Hiller von Gaertringen (2004, p. 213), but I see no reason to place it earlier than about 1425.
7. Dunkerton and Gordon 2002, pp. 89–109, esp. p. 97.
8. Becattini 1990, pp. 17–26, reprinted in Caneva 2001, pp. 267–77; L. Berti, in Berti and Paolucci 1990, p. 118; Padoa Rizzo 2001, pp. 155–59. Becattini noted that the triptych is not mentioned in the records of the 1436 pastoral visit to San Giovenale; the suggestion that it was on view in San Lorenzo and that it was not sent to Cascia straightaway because of its innovative character is Berti's.
9. Bernacchioni 2003, pp. 233–44, esp. pp. 234–35; see also Marchi 2002, pp. 160–69.
10. Shell 1972, pp. 41–46.
11. Laclotte and Mognetti 1987, pp. 89–91.
12. Poggi 1988 ed., vol. 1, pp. 98–100, docs. 522–531.
13. Salmi 1958, p. 12. For the panel, see Hiller von Gaertringen 2004, pp. 220–22.
14. See Laurence Kanter's catalogue entry 30 in this volume for stylistic considerations favoring this date. A canopied throne also appears in the polyptych in Cortona (fig. 143), which is problematic in terms of its date and authorship as well as its condition. See Kanter's remarks in note 11 of the same entry; see also Israëls 2003, pp. 760–76.
15. For a photograph of the center panel without the modern frame, showing the ogival shape of the picture field, see Garibaldi 1998, p. 31.

FRA ANGELICO

The High Altarpiece from San Domenico, Fiesole

10.

A.
Saint Alexander

Tempera on panel, 15.9 x 15.6 cm (6¼ x 6⅛ in.)
The Metropolitan Museum of Art, New York. Bequest of Lucy G. Moses, 1990 (1991.27.2)

B.
Eighteen Blessed of the Dominican Order

Tempera on panel: overall, 32.2 x 22.8 cm (12⅝ x 9 in.); picture surface, 31.8 x 21.9 cm (12½ x 8⅝ in.)
National Gallery, London (NG663.4)

C.
Seventeen Blessed of the Dominican Order and Two Dominican Tertiaries

Tempera on panel: overall, 32.6 x 22.8 cm (12⅞ x 9 in.); picture surface, 31.6 x 21.9 cm (12⁷⁄₁₆ x 8⅝ in.)
National Gallery, London (NG663.5)

These three panels, together with one other in the National Gallery, London (*Saint Romulus* [NG 2908], fig. 38), two in the Musée Condé, Chantilly (*Saint Mark* [inv. 4], fig. 39, and *Saint Matthew* [inv. 5], fig. 40), and two in the Rau Collection (*Saint Nicholas of Bari* [inv. GR 1.696], fig. 41, and *Saint Michael* [inv. GR 1.697], fig. 42), are fragments of the original framing structure of the high altarpiece from San Domenico in Fiesole, Fra Angelico's first major commission from his own Dominican Observant order. The altarpiece itself, the principal panels of which are still in situ in San Domenico—although now installed in the first chapel on the left upon entering the church—underwent at least two major reconfigurations before the early nineteenth century. In 1501, Lorenzo di Credi was commissioned to convert the Early Quattrocento triptych form of the altarpiece into an updated, Renaissance *pala quadrata* by providing it with a unified pictorial field framed beneath a classical entablature and overpainting its gold ground with a continuous landscape view and naturalistic blue sky (see fig. 28). Alterations to the original carpentry of the panel support (which was reconstructed with considerable accuracy, but with some questionable additions, by Umberto Baldini following the cleaning of the altarpiece in the 1970s)[1] entailed adjustments to the frame as well—specifically, the elimination of the shaped pinnacles and the rebuilding of the molding surrounds of the predella (described by Baldini as a *gradino* rather than a true predella) and of the lateral, buttressing pilasters.

In the course of these alterations it appears that Lorenzo di Credi retained as many of the original framing elements painted by Fra Angelico as possible but the painted pinnacles could not be preserved, as their primary panel support is still incorporated into the structure of the altarpiece, covered with Lorenzo di Credi's later gesso and repainting.[2] Angelico's predella and painted pilasters were reused and were only removed sometime after 1792, when copies of the predella and various unrelated pilaster panels from the workshop of Lorenzo Monaco[3] were substituted for them. The three original predella panels (fig. 43, 44, 45) and two panels reasonably supposed to be pilaster bases (B and C) were sold shortly before 1827, entering the collection of the Prussian consul in Rome, from whose heirs they were acquired by the National Gallery in 1860. The four full-length pilaster figures in painted niches (now in Chantilly and in the Rau Collection) bear inscriptions on the reverse identifying them as part of a series of ten such panels from San Domenico, Fiesole. That they did, indeed, once decorate the pilasters of the San Domenico high

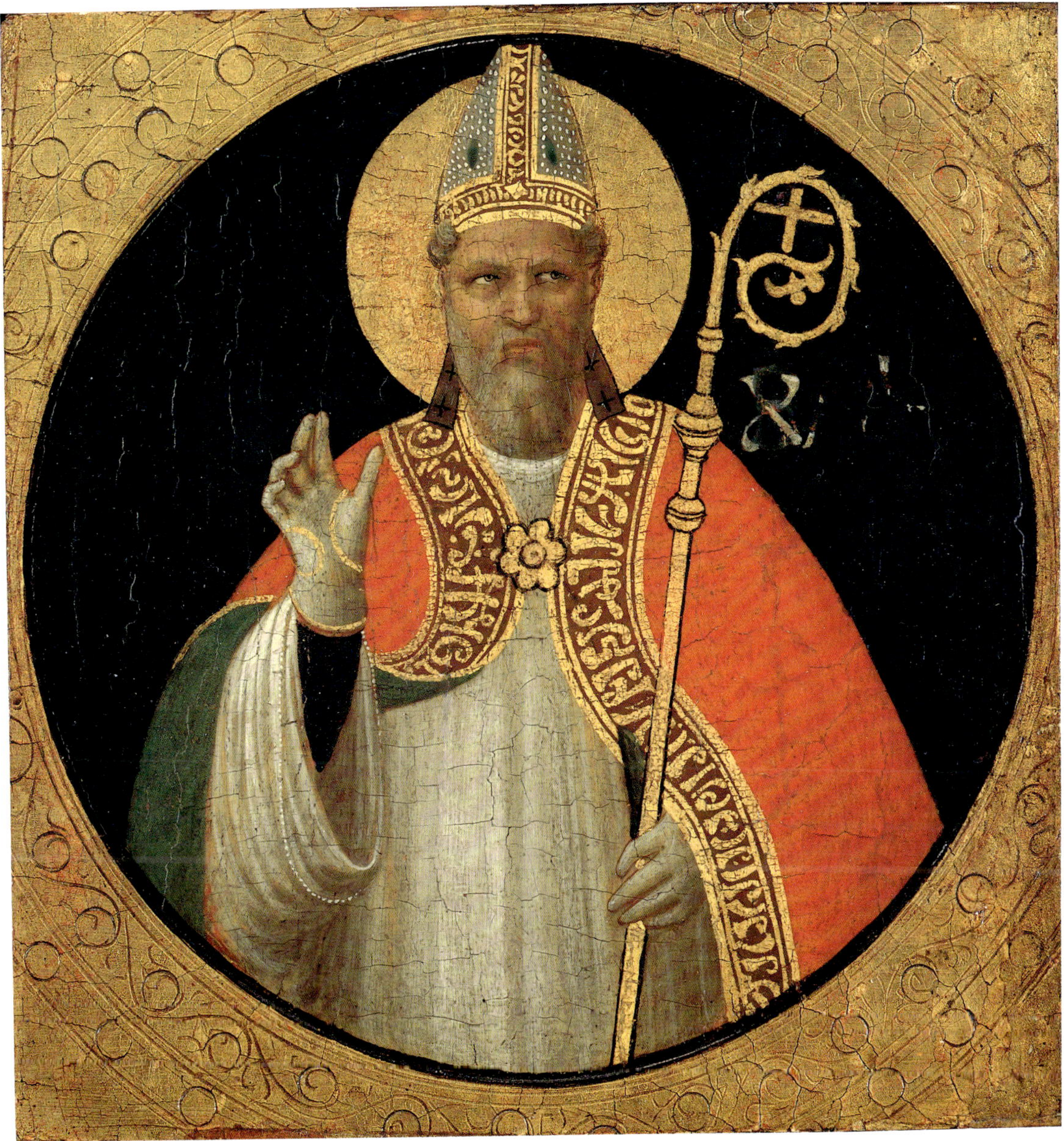

10: A

altarpiece was demonstrated by the discovery of a fragment of Lorenzo di Credi's painted decoration still surviving in situ at the top of the right pilaster, which, in form, corresponds to the painted decoration that surrounded these figures prior to their recent cleaning. Angelico must have painted eight such figures: two on the front of each pilaster (as reconstructed by Baldini) and two on the outer, lateral surfaces, given that the pairs of panels in the Rau Collection and in Chantilly significantly differ in width (14 and 11 centimeters, respectively). With the substantial increase in the height of the pilasters necessitated by the new format of the altarpiece, Lorenzo di Credi would have added a third pair of saints at the top of each pilaster. It should be noted that none of the Chantilly or Rau panels is cropped at the top in a manner consistent with the fragmentary painted surround still visible on the right pilaster in San Domenico, so it must be assumed that additional figures by Lorenzo di Credi, either not surviving or as yet unidentified, occupied these positions.

The association of the Metropolitan Museum's *Saint Alexander* and the National Gallery's *Saint Romulus* with the San Domenico high altarpiece has been more controversial. Variously accepted, on the basis of Langton Douglas's assertion that the Metropolitan Museum's panel came from San Domenico, or rejected in the early literature on the subject, and doubted more authoritatively on the grounds of style and format by Carl Strehlke,[4] their inclusion in the reconstructed

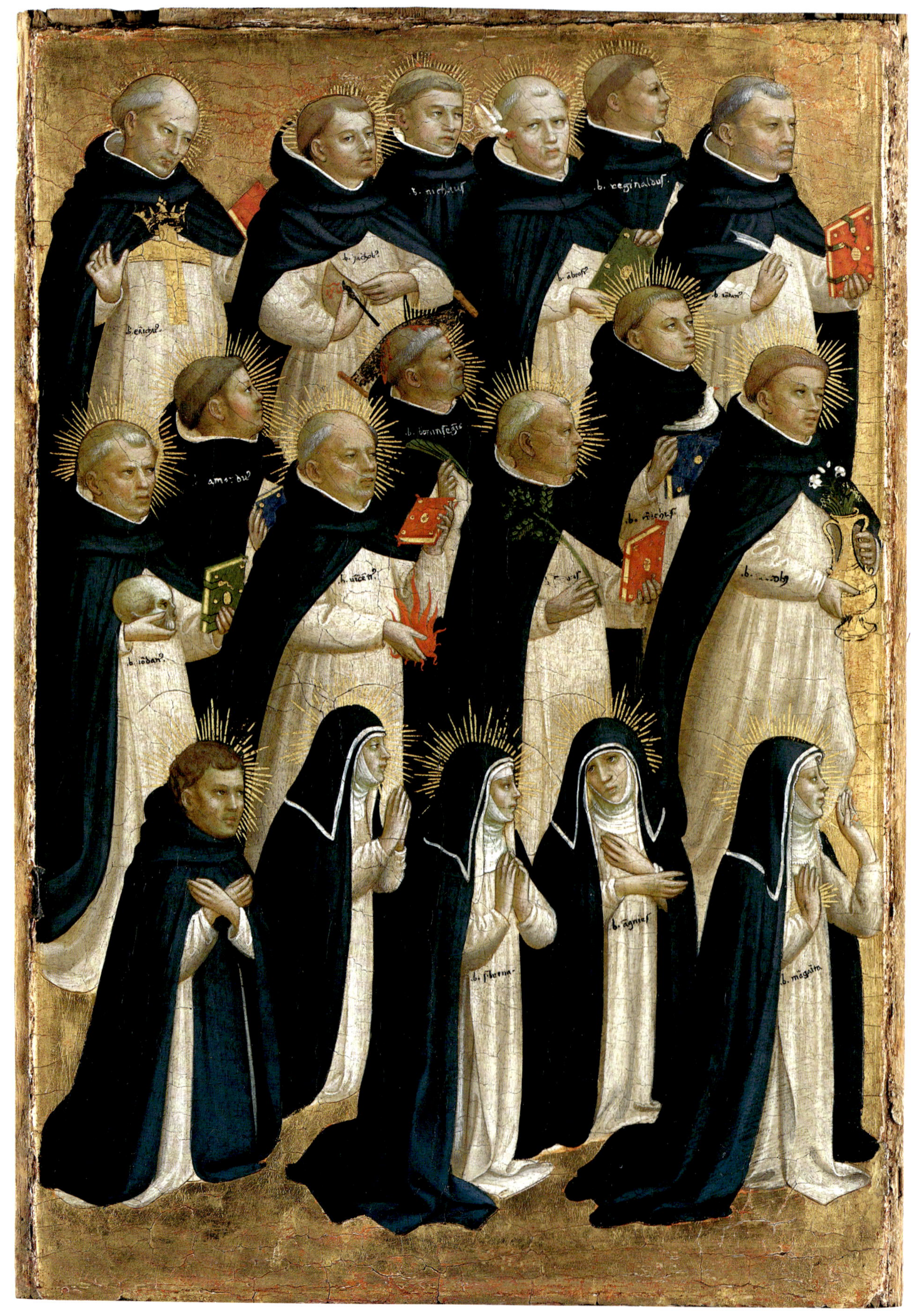

10: B

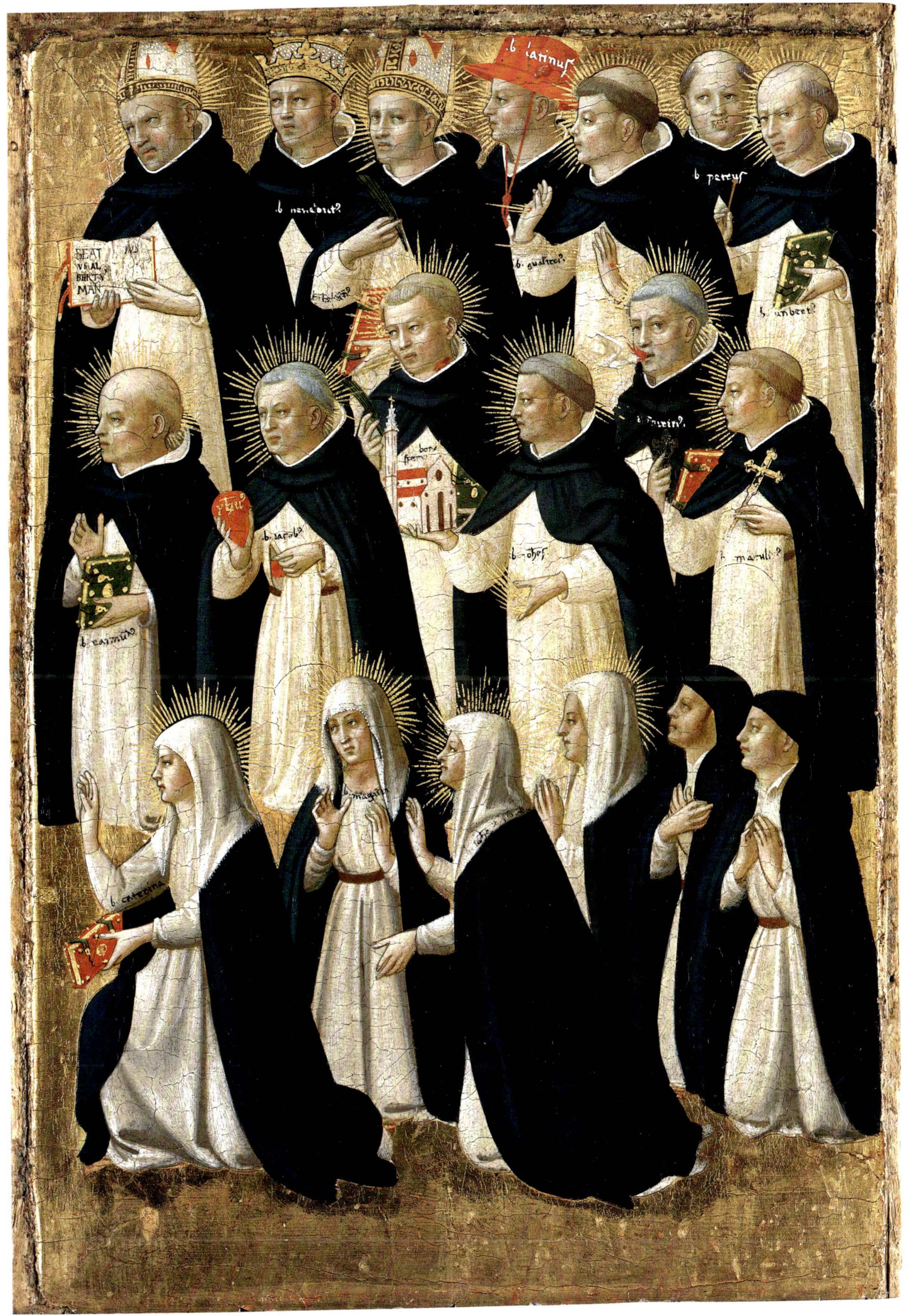

10: C

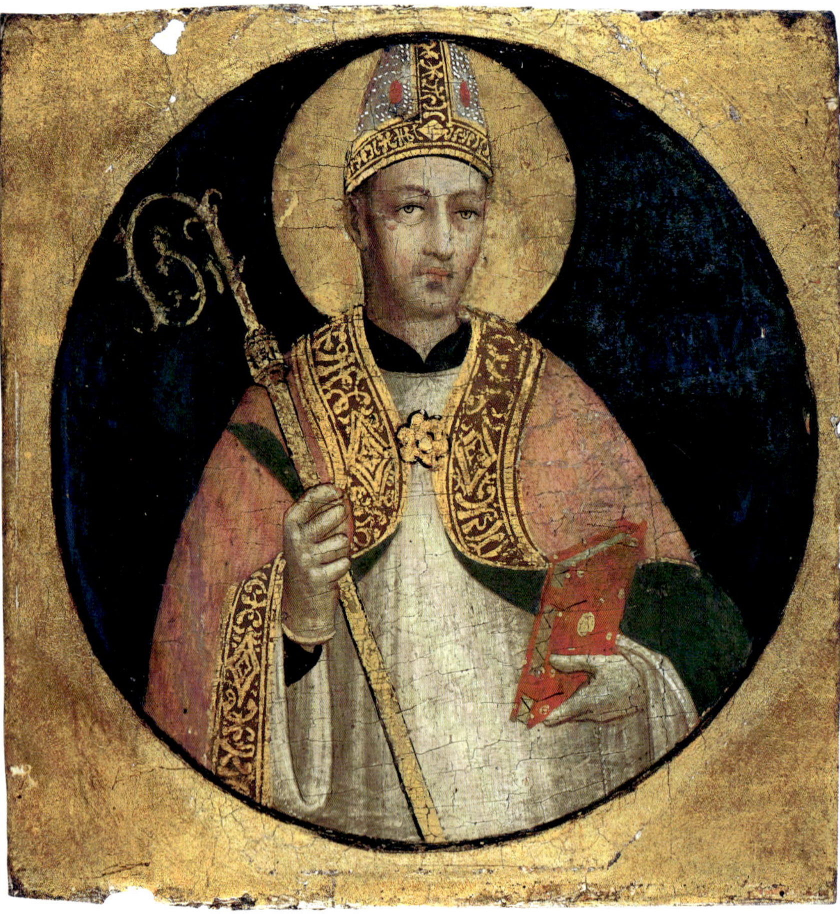

Figure 38. Fra Angelico. *Saint Romulus.* About 1419–21. National Gallery, London

altarpiece seemed to have been demonstrated conclusively with the recent identification of their subjects by Christa Gardner von Teuffel.[5] Identifying Saints Alexander and Romulus as patrons of Fiesole and its cathedral, however, only establishes the origin of these panels in that town, not necessarily in this specific complex. Strehlke cites a notice of 1769, before the dismemberment of the altarpiece frame, of two small panels by Angelico in the sacristy of San Domenico, "*con due Santi in campo d'oro assai diligentemente lavorati*," which may well have been the present pair. It should be noted, however, that the inscriptions identifying the Rau and Chantilly saints as part of a set of ten imply that two pilaster figures already were missing before the altarpiece was definitively dismantled, as they must logically have numbered either eight or twelve originally. The 1769 notice could, therefore, have referred to two panels that were initially painted for the high altarpiece but were removed at an early date, and are lost or unidentified today.

Based on the example of Angelico's later altarpiece of the *Deposition* from Santa Trinita in Florence (about 1430–32), Baldini's reconstruction of the San Domenico high altarpiece showed the Metropolitan's and the National Gallery's roundels occupying the tops of the lateral framing piers, which appears to be substantially correct. Following more closely the structure of the Santa Trinita altarpiece or of the slightly later Guidalotti altarpiece in Perugia (about 1437; see cat. 30), it is necessary to amend Baldini's reconstruction to allow for four roundels originally, one on the front of each pilaster and one on each outer, lateral face. The present pair is unlikely to have occupied the two fronts of the pilasters, as the light depicted in them is cast from opposite directions. Furthermore, the London panel is composed of two vertical members, the narrower of which, at the left, is four centimeters wide. This slender piece of wood probably was the edge of the adjoining face of the pilaster, abutting the front at right angles, with the seam between them covered in linen and gessoed over to provide a continuous paint surface. A vertical strip of exactly the same width at the right of the New York panel is a modern fill, supporting the original canvas, gesso, and paint layers where the wood was completely removed. It is probable then that these two panels were originally contiguous, occupying the front and side of one of the two pilasters: the conformity in the direction of the cast light depicted in each panel suggests that they may have been on the front (London) and outside (New York) of the left pilaster.[6]

The association of the two panels of Dominican Blessed in London with the San Domenico high altarpiece is less problematic in that they have always been together with the three predella panels that demonstrably stood below that structure. Whereas the latter were painted on a single plank of wood with a continuous, horizontal grain, the panels of the Blessed have a vertical grain, the original thickness of which seems to have been less than one centimeter. As their light source is consistent with that of the rest of the predella panels, it is reasonable to assume that their reconstruction as pilaster bases is correct, but the possibility must be left open that they could have been added to the surface of the already constructed frame, when the altarpiece was installed in the church. That they might not have been an integral part of the original pictorial program is suggested by the radical differences in scale of the figures and by the evident maturity of their style, compared with that of the rest of the predella, as well as by the measurably greater solidity of their painting technique,[7] all of which more closely resemble such slightly later works by Fra Angelico as the Santa Maria degli Angeli *Last Judgment* (about 1424) or the predella of the Prado *Annunciation* altarpiece (about 1425). It is, however, equally possible that these discrepancies simply reflect a protracted period of execution for the altarpiece as a whole. Strehlke regarded the pilaster panels in New York, London, Chantilly, and in the Rau Collection as also more stylistically mature than the rest of the altarpiece, although, in fact, there exist close parallels for them among the figures in the right-hand panel of the predella, which, in turn, seems to be more carefully organized and the figures more sensitively modeled than in the other two predella panels. At

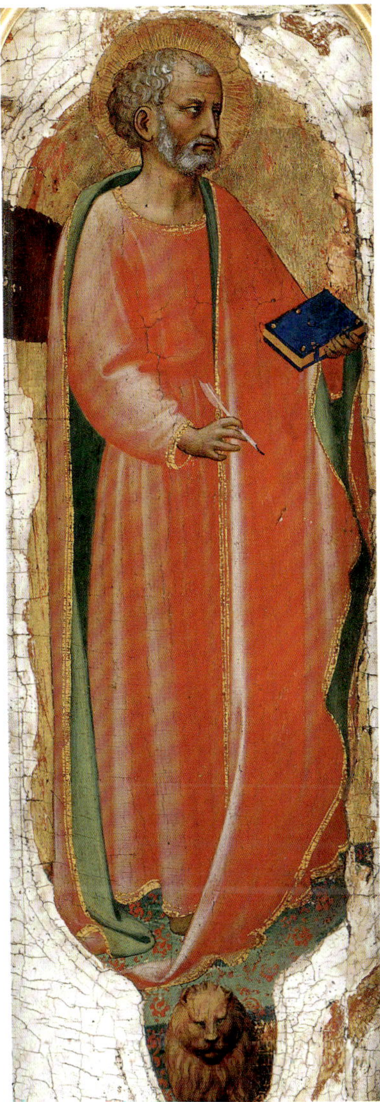

Figure 39. Fra Angelico. *Saint Mark*. About 1419–21. Musée Condé, Chantilly

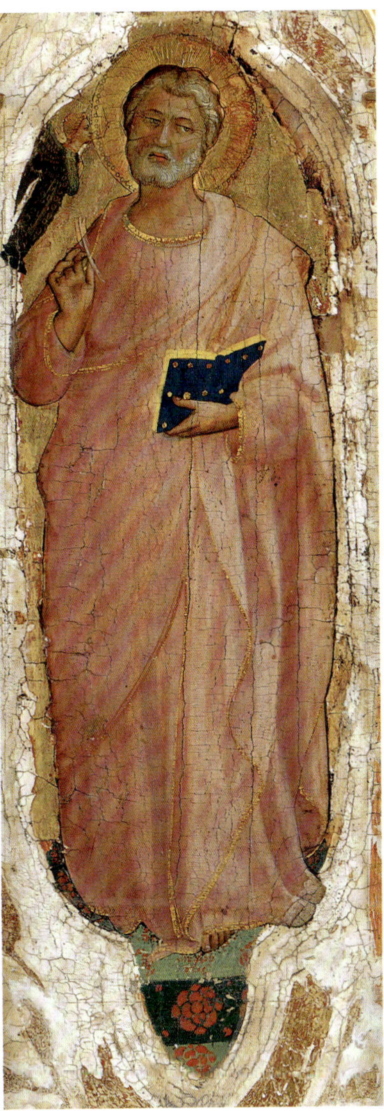

Figure 40. Fra Angelico. *Saint Matthew*. About 1419–21. Musée Condé, Chantilly

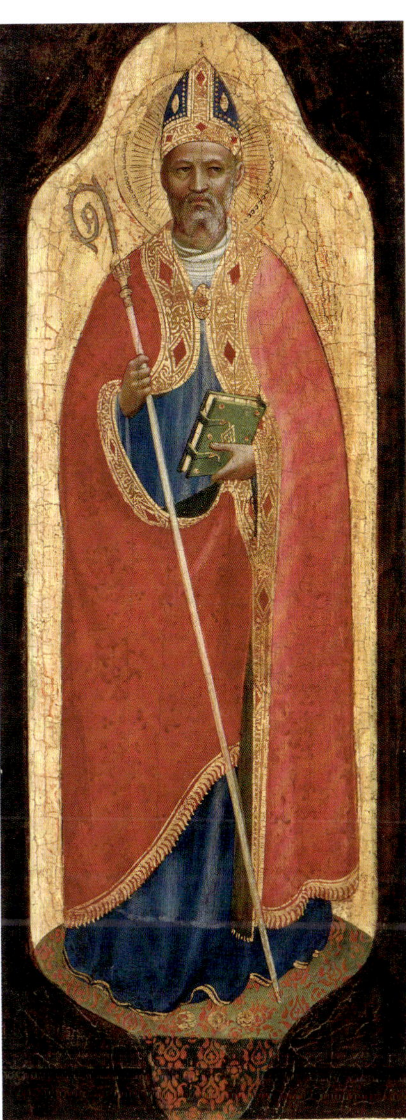

Figure 41. Fra Angelico. *Saint Nicholas of Bari*. About 1419–21. Fondation Rau, Rielasingen-Worblingen, Germany

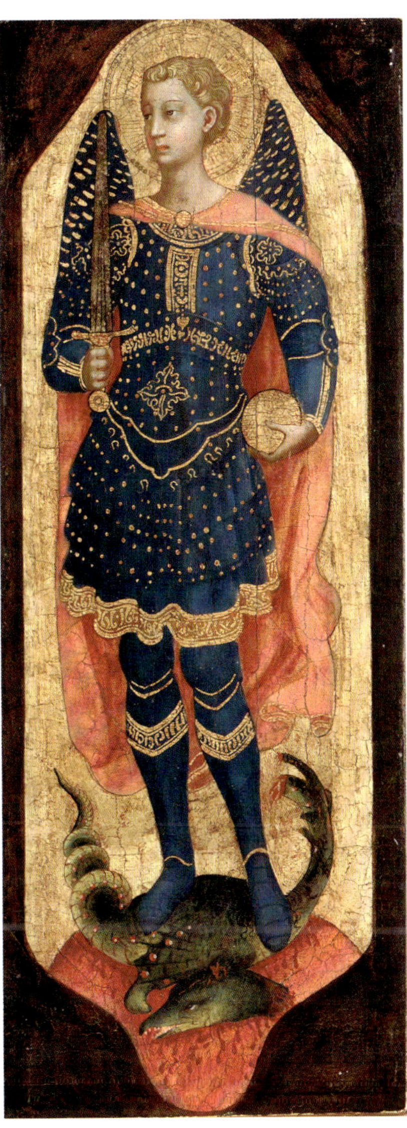

Figure 42. Fra Angelico. *Saint Michael*. About 1419–21. Fondation Rau, Rielasingen-Worblingen, Germany

this date in Angelico's career, none of these differences is attributable to workshop intervention: they reflect his evolving experience as a designer and technician and the rapidity with which he mastered the complexities of his craft.

Circumstantial considerations establish a range of possibility for dating the San Domenico high altarpiece between 1418, the date of Barnaba degli Agli's will providing for the financing of the construction of the church and convent of San Domenico, and 1435, when the church and its three altars were formally consecrated by Bishop Tommaso Parati of Venice. The terminus ante quem could be advanced a decade if a notice of 1424/25 concerning the completion of an altar cloth (pallium) for the high altar is interpreted to mark the date of the installation of the altarpiece or of the first celebration of the Mass before it.[8] Such a date is consonant with the style of the Dominican Blessed portrayed on the pilaster bases, although most of the work on the altarpiece is significantly earlier in style. While Miklós Boskovits has suggested a plausible date of 1422–23, there is no *a priori* circumstantial or stylistic reason to suppose that the design of the major components of the altarpiece could not date to the immediate vicinity of its probable commission in 1419. Indeed, the progression of Angelico's artistic development in this period implies that much of the labor of its execution may have been completed as early as 1420 or 1421.

The iconography of this altarpiece, especially of its predella, has been discussed in detail in an exemplary study by Dillian

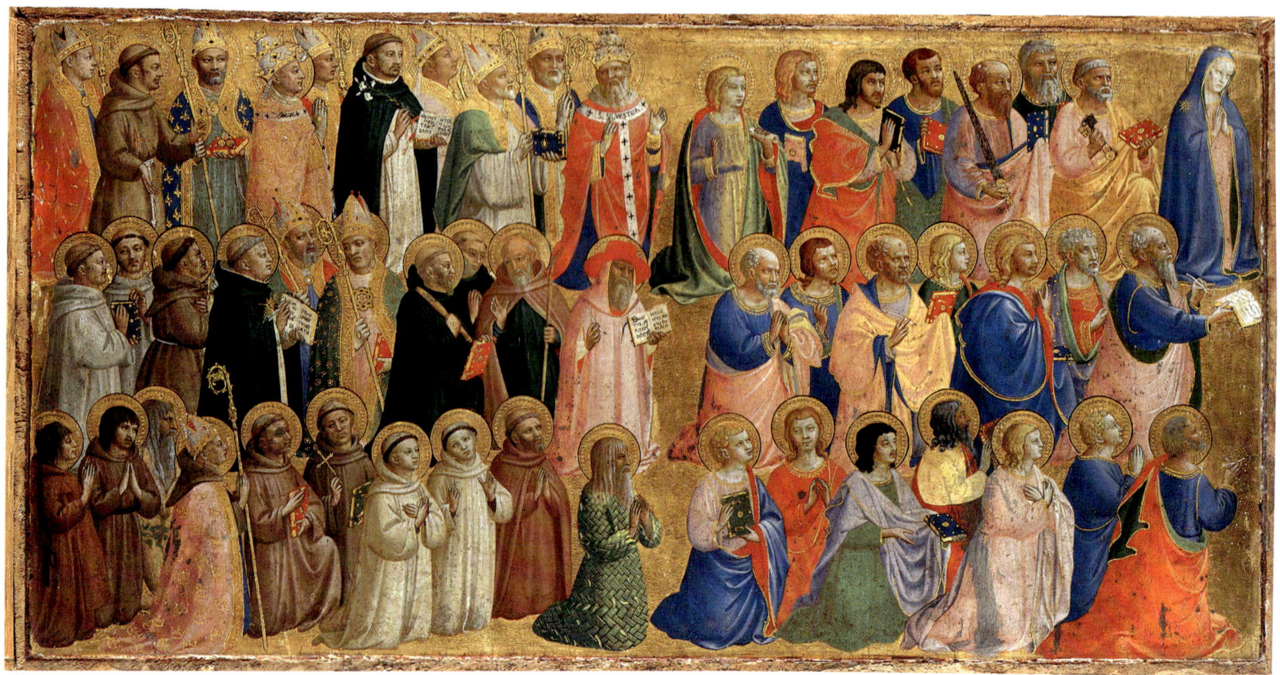

Figure 43. Fra Angelico. *The Virgin Mary, with the Apostles and the Doctors of the Church.* About 1419–21. National Gallery, London

Gordon.[9] To her observations it is useful to add only that the crowds of saints in the three main panels of the predella are organized according to the same principles that determined the design of Angelico's ceiling frescoes in the Chapel of San Brizio in Orvieto Cathedral (1447), completed by Luca Signorelli following a plan devised by Dominican theological advisers. To the left of the Glorified Christ and angels is the Virgin with the Apostles and the Doctors of the Church. To the right are the Patriarchs, Prophets, Martyrs, and Virgins, completing the chorus of All Saints. The great majority of figures in this multitude represent specific individuals rather than merely being emblematic of a particular category or type. In the case of the pilaster bases with the Dominican Blessed, each figure is meant to be individually identifiable, although they are clearly not portraits in the modern sense. Primarily from the evidence of original inscriptions, Gordon has proposed the following identifications:

Left panel, from right to left, beginning in the top row: Jordan of Saxony, second Master General of the Dominican order (d. 1237); Reginald of Orléans (d. 1220); Ambrogio Sansedoni of Siena (d. 1286/87); Nicholas of Palea or Nicholas of Giovanazzo (?) (d. 1255); unknown (inscribed, "*b. jachob*"); Henry Teutonicus (?) (d. 1217); James of Salamonio (d. 1314) or James of Bevagna; Henry of Cologne (?) (d. 1225); unknown (inscribed, "*B. sinuus*"); Buoninsegna (martyred about 1268); Saint Vincent Ferrer (d. 1419); Henry Suso (?); Jordan of Pisa or Jordan of Rivalto (d. 1311); Margaret of Hungary (d. 1271); Saint Agnes of Montepulciano (d. 1317); Sibyllina de Biscossis (d. 1367); unknown; unknown.

Right panel, from left to right, beginning in the top row: Saint Albert the Great (d. 1280); Pope Benedict XI (d. 1304); Bertrand (?); Cardinal Latino Malabranca (d. 1294); Walter of Strasbourg (d. before 1260); Peter Gonzalez (?) (d. 1246); Humbert of Romans, fifth Master General of the Dominican order (d. 1277/78); Saint Raymond of Penafort, third Master General of the Dominican order (d. 1275) or Raymond of Capua; unknown (inscribed, "*b. iacob*"); unknown (inscribed, "*b. bona/speme*"); John of Salerno (d. 1242); Venturino of Bergamo (d. 1346); Marcolino of Forlì (d. 1397); Saint Catherine of Siena (d. 1380); Margaret of Città di Castello (d. 1320); Joanna of Florence (fl. 1333); unknown; perhaps Jacopo and Domenico di Barnaba degli Agli. LK

1. Baldini 1977, pp. 236–46. The *Blessing Redeemer* in the English Royal Collection and the two *Adoring Angels* in the Galleria Sabauda, Turin, cannot have been parts of this altarpiece, as proposed by Baldini (see note 2, below, and cat. 25), and the Hermitage tabernacle and two angels, now in the Louvre, also formed an independent complex. The latter may or may not have been installed on the high altar of San Domenico, but it was completed later than—and did not form part of—the high altarpiece itself. It may also be observed that in addition to the obvious alterations made by Lorenzo di Credi and accurately described by Baldini, the receding pavement in the right-hand panel, the feet and the robes of Saints Dominic and Peter Martyr in the same panel, and the blue of Saint Barnabus's robe in the left panel and of the Virgin's robe in the center panel were repainted by Lorenzo di Credi in oil over Angelico's original tempera surface.
2. It is reasonable, therefore, to doubt the frequently proposed association with this reconstruction of a pair of roundels by Fra Angelico portraying the Annunciation (fig. 16), last recorded in the collection of Baron von Tucher (sometimes cited as Tucker) in Vienna (Salmi 1958, pp. 11, 98;

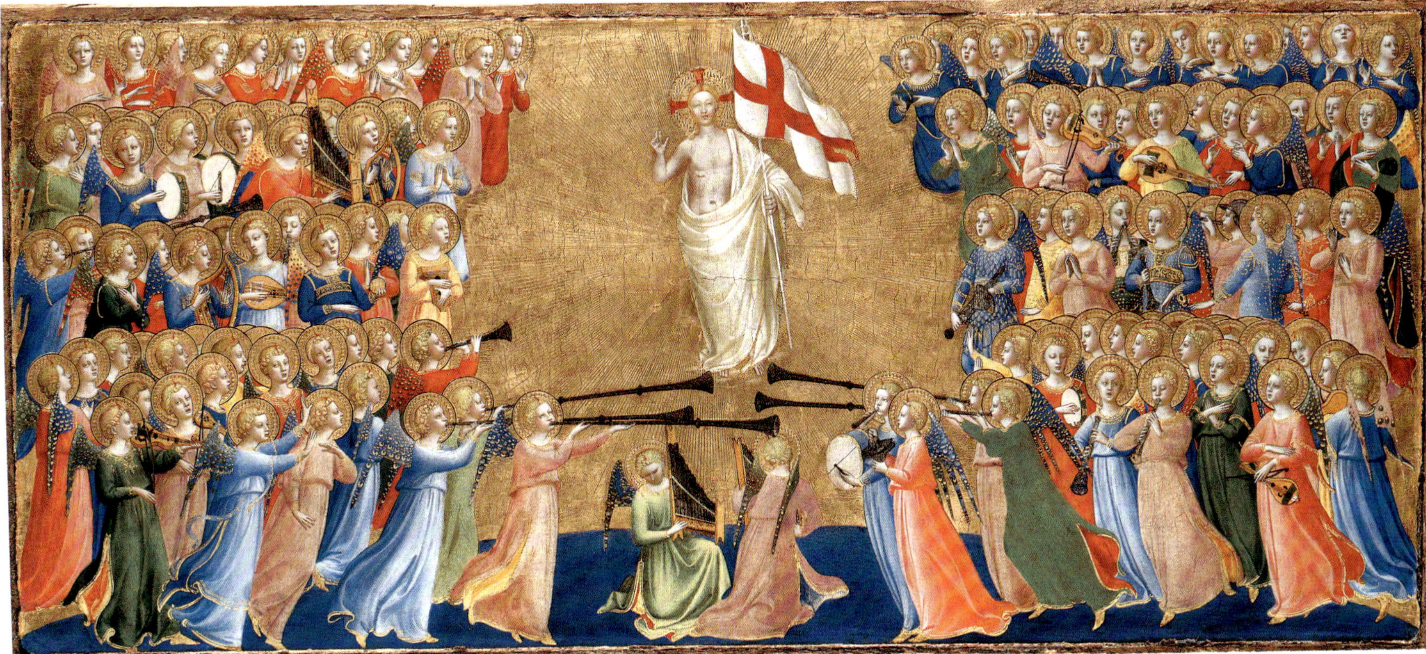

Figure 44. Fra Angelico. *Christ Glorified in the Court of Heaven*. About 1419–21. National Gallery, London

Baldini 1970, pp. 88–89). C. B. Strehlke (in Kanter et al. 1994, p. 341) is the only modern author to doubt that the Tucher panels originally were parts of the frame of the San Domenico high altarpiece. It is possible that these roundels could have been painted on separate framing members applied to the pinnacles, in which case they would have been removed by Lorenzo di Credi and kept separately, elsewhere in the convent, although similar cases of historic preservation in Late Renaissance Florence are rare: the pinnacle of Giotto's Baroncelli altarpiece (now in San Diego) is an exceptional example. If these two panels were removed from the frame of the high altarpiece in 1501, they would be likely candidates for the pair of paintings given by the friars of San Domenico to Cardinal Scaglia in 1621 (Orlandi 1964, p. 196). There is no reason to maintain the association, sometimes proposed, of the *Annunciatory Angel* and the *Virgin Annunciate* in Detroit (cat. 25, F, G) with the panels formerly in San Domenico.

3. Eisenberg 1989, p. 97. The altarpiece to which these six pilaster figures originally belonged has not been identified, although it is likely to have been painted for a female monastic house, probably in the immediate environs of Fiesole.

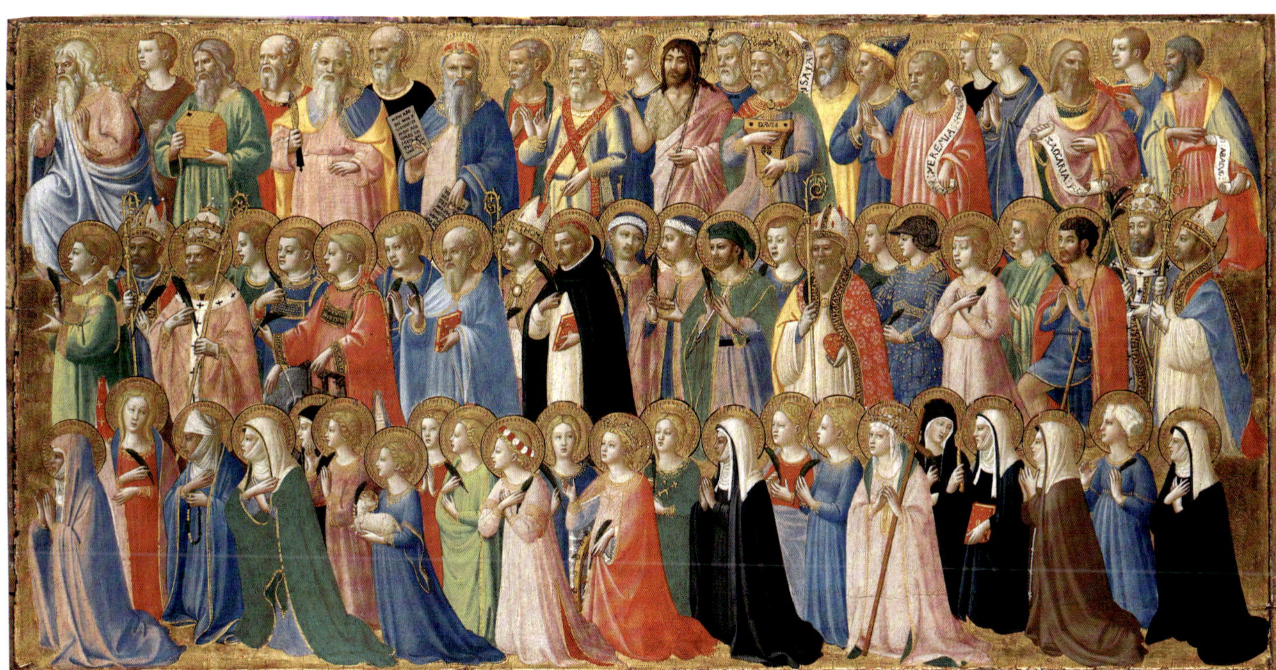

Figure 45. Fra Angelico. *The Forerunners of Christ (Patriarchs and Prophets) with the Martyrs and the Virgins*. About 1419–21. National Gallery, London

4. C. B. Strehlke, in Kanter et al. 1994, p.341 (with earlier bibliography).
5. Gardner von Teuffel 1997, pp. 463–65.
6. This proposal assumes that the front of each pilaster was lit from the same direction as the main panels of the altarpiece, which may or may not have been the case. As the light in the Rau panels also enters from the right, they, too, may have adorned the front of one or both pilasters, but the narrower Chantilly panels are not consistent with each other: Saint Matthew is lit from the right and Saint Mark from the left, suggesting that they were painted for the outer, lateral edges of the pilasters. It should be noted, however, that the predella of the altarpiece is lit from the center: the source of illumination is not external but radiates outward from the figure of the risen Christ in the middle of the central panel. The pilasters flanking the altarpiece today measure 15.4 centimeters in width within their framing moldings on both the front and lateral faces. The structure of the London panel of *Saint Romulus* includes, in addition to the two wood members discussed in the text above, a modern mahogany (?) insert along the left edge, trapezoidal in section, that undoubtedly is a replacement for the wood lost as a result of the angled saw cut that was necessary to separate the London from the New York panels.
7. D. Gordon (2003, p. 18) also records the opinions of other scholars reinforcing the visual differences between the images of the Blessed and the other predella panels.
8. Ibid., pp. 12, 23 n. 67.
9. Ibid.

FRA ANGELICO

11.

Virgin and Child Enthroned

Tempera on panel: overall, 101.6 x 58.6 cm (40 x 23⅛ in.); picture surface, 100.5 x 57.9 cm (39⅝ x 22¾ in.)
The Barbara Piasecka Johnson Collection Foundation

This majestic image of the Virgin seated on a low faldstool was first made known to scholars in 1963, when it was published as the work of Fra Angelico assisted by Zanobi Strozzi.[1] Only John Pope-Hennessy and Richard Fremantle entirely rejected this proposal, the latter suggesting, in recognition of its exceptionally high quality, that the painting should be reattributed to Masaccio.[2] Richard Offner classified the painting as "San Domenico Angelican," while P. J. Cardile referred to it as an early work by Zanobi Strozzi alone.[3] All other scholars who knew the picture have considered it a fully autograph work by Angelico, of the highest quality; for Miklós Boskovits, "all that needs to be determined is its chronological position in Fra Angelico's oeuvre."[4]

Most arguments for dating the Johnson *Virgin and Child* have focused on the motif of the Child reaching for the bunch of grapes in his mother's right hand and its presumed derivation from the similar iconography of the center panel of Masaccio's Pisa polyptych of 1426. To suppose, however, that in the Johnson panel the gentle motion of the Child acknowledging the symbolism of his sacrifice represents Angelico's timid response to the aggressive earthiness of Masaccio's image, which shows the Christ Child hungrily devouring the Eucharistic fruit, is to underestimate the power, vitality, and originality of Angelico's narrative imagination. Nor is it necessary to understand the imposing three-dimensionality of the Virgin in this painting as a paean to Masaccio's prior accomplishments. As Boskovits and, implicitly, Offner pointed out, the composition and style of the Johnson *Virgin and Child* are related not to works by Angelico from the second half of the 1420s but rather to the San Domenico high altarpiece: the only variation is in the object of the Christ Child's gesture and the fact that he is shown seated rather than standing in his mother's lap in order to rationalize the raised position of the Virgin's knee. Boskovits correctly observed that this motif creates an ambiguity in the Johnson painting, bridging the formulas of the Madonna enthroned and the Madonna of Humility. It is not to the example of Masaccio that this painting should be linked—as a respectful but watered-down adaptation—but to that of Lorenzo Monaco, which it seems to critique and to improve upon at the same time. Even the motif of the faldstool in the form in which it appears here seems to derive from earlier paintings by Lorenzo Monaco, such as panels now in the Museo della Collegiata, Empoli, and in the National Gallery of Scotland, Edinburgh.[5]

The Johnson *Virgin and Child* is more, however, than merely a domesticated reprise of the composition of the San Domenico high altarpiece; it also shares with that painting nearly all of the details of its execution, including such supposedly mechanical elements as the manner of rendering eyelids with a single, pronounced, horizontal stroke of the brush; the elongated, oval proportions of the heads; and the engraved patterns of the Virgin's halo, which also resemble those in the Rotterdam (cat. 6), Pisa, and Saint Petersburg images of the Madonna. Indeed, in all these respects the present panel more closely resembles paintings reasonably supposed to precede the San Domenico high altarpiece than it does Angelico's immediately successive works: only the powerful tactility of the image is suggestive of the artist's later achievements. Consequently, it is necessary to date the painting closer to 1420 or 1422 than to 1426, and, as such, its relationship to Masaccio becomes moot. Perhaps more appropriate would be to speculate on whether Masaccio (or his friends and mentors,

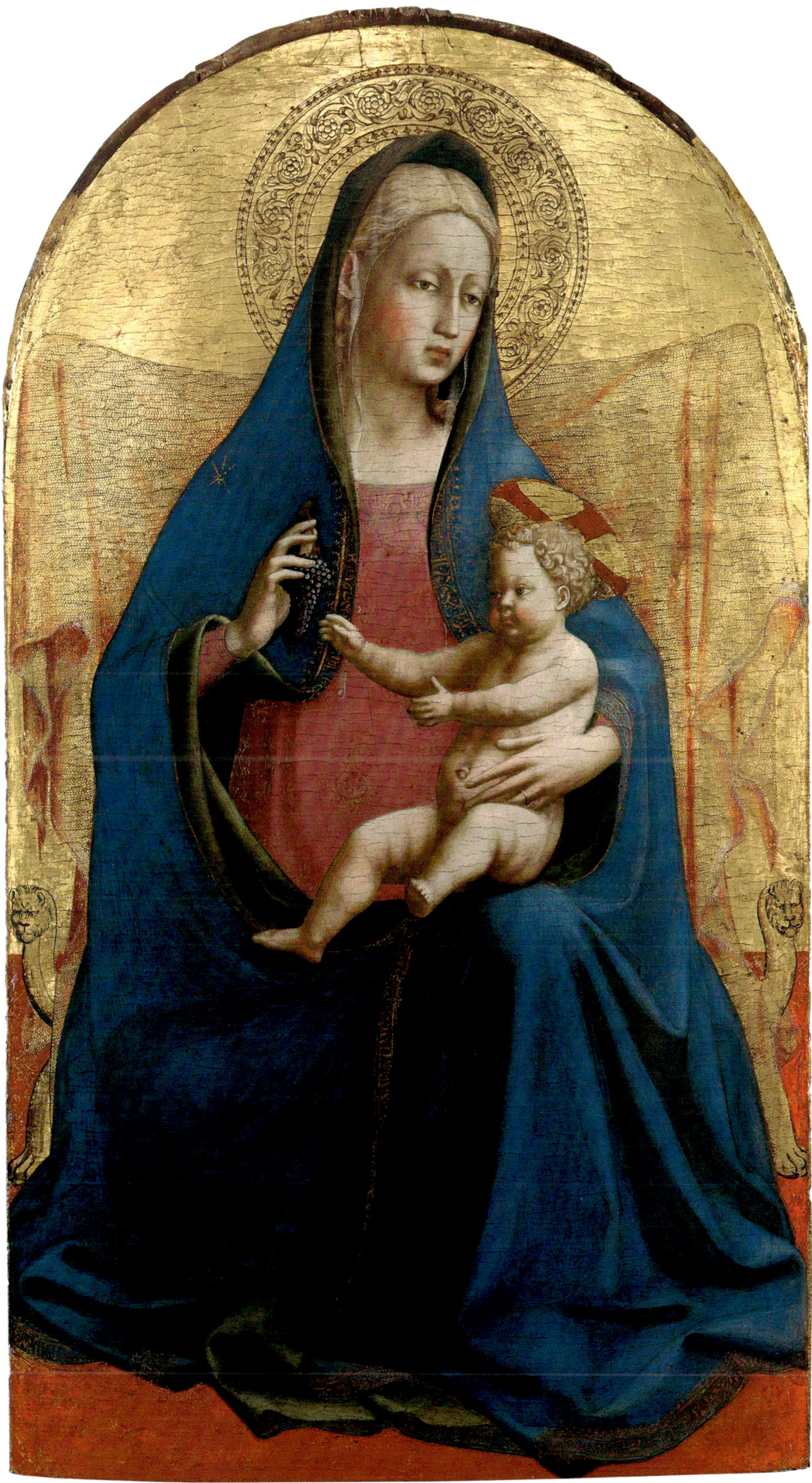

Donatello or Brunelleschi) knew of the present *Virgin and Child* and may have consciously had it in mind as a point of departure when designing the Pisa polyptych.

The current shape of the Johnson panel is an alteration of its original profile, the upper part of which may have terminated in an ogival arch. The panel has been cut across the top at a level tangent to the upper arc of the Virgin's halo, and it has been trimmed along both lateral edges and at the bottom, although a raised gesso barb at the left and right indicates that the picture field has not been reduced at either side. The reverse of the panel, which has been thinned only along its outer edges to accommodate its warp to a later frame, bears no traces of the attachment of horizontal battens. It is therefore likely that the picture was originally an independent painted tabernacle like Angelico's Pisa *Madonna,* rather than the center panel of a polyptych.[6]

LK

1. Berti 1963, p. 22, fig. 12.
2. Fremantle 1970, pp. 39–40; Pope-Hennessy 1974, p. 226 (as possibly by Andrea di Giusto). Pope-Hennessy later (in a verbal communication) retracted this opinion and was persuaded that the painting was an autograph work by Angelico.
3. Cardile 1976, p. 307, fig. 115. Offner's opinion is recorded in an autograph notation on the back of a photograph in his archives at the Institute of Fine Arts, New York University.
4. M. Boskovits, in Grabski 1990, pp. 56–61 (with earlier bibliography).
5. Eisenberg 1989, pp. 93, 95–96, fig. 156, 158.
6. The suggestion of Baldini (1977, pp. 240–41, 245 n. 23) to identify the images of Saints Catherine and John the Baptist and Saints Zenobius (?) and Agnes, in a private collection (cat. 12), as the lateral panels of an altarpiece that included the Johnson *Virgin and Child* cannot be defended on the basis of style, size, or format.

11

12.

A.
Saint Catherine and Saint John the Baptist

Tempera on panel, transferred to plywood,
50.3 x 30.5 cm (19¾ x 12 in.)
Private collection

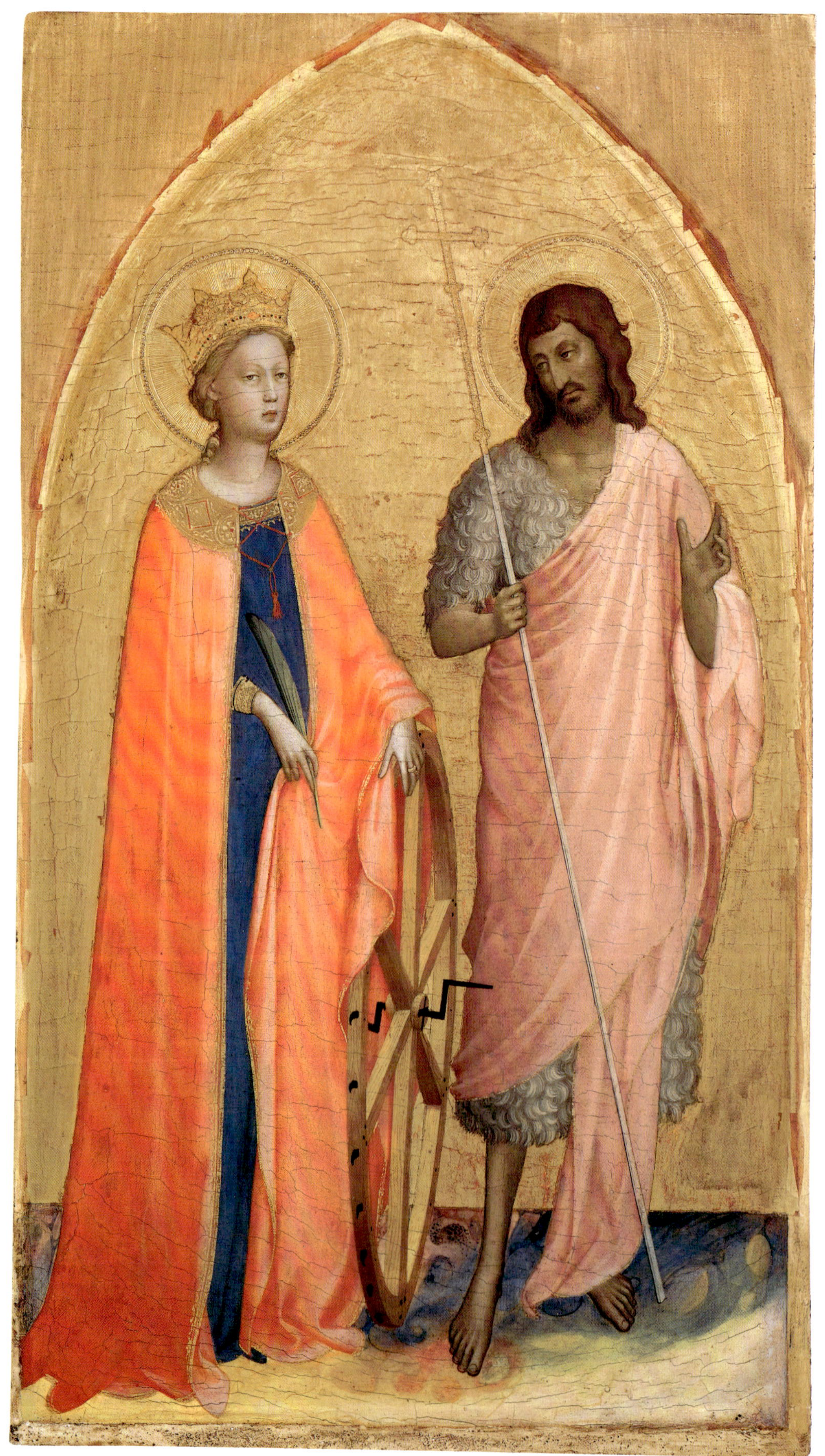

12: A

B.
Saint Zenobius (?) and Saint Agnes

Tempera on panel, transferred to plywood,
50.6 x 30.2 cm (19⅞ x 11⅞ in.)[1]
Private collection

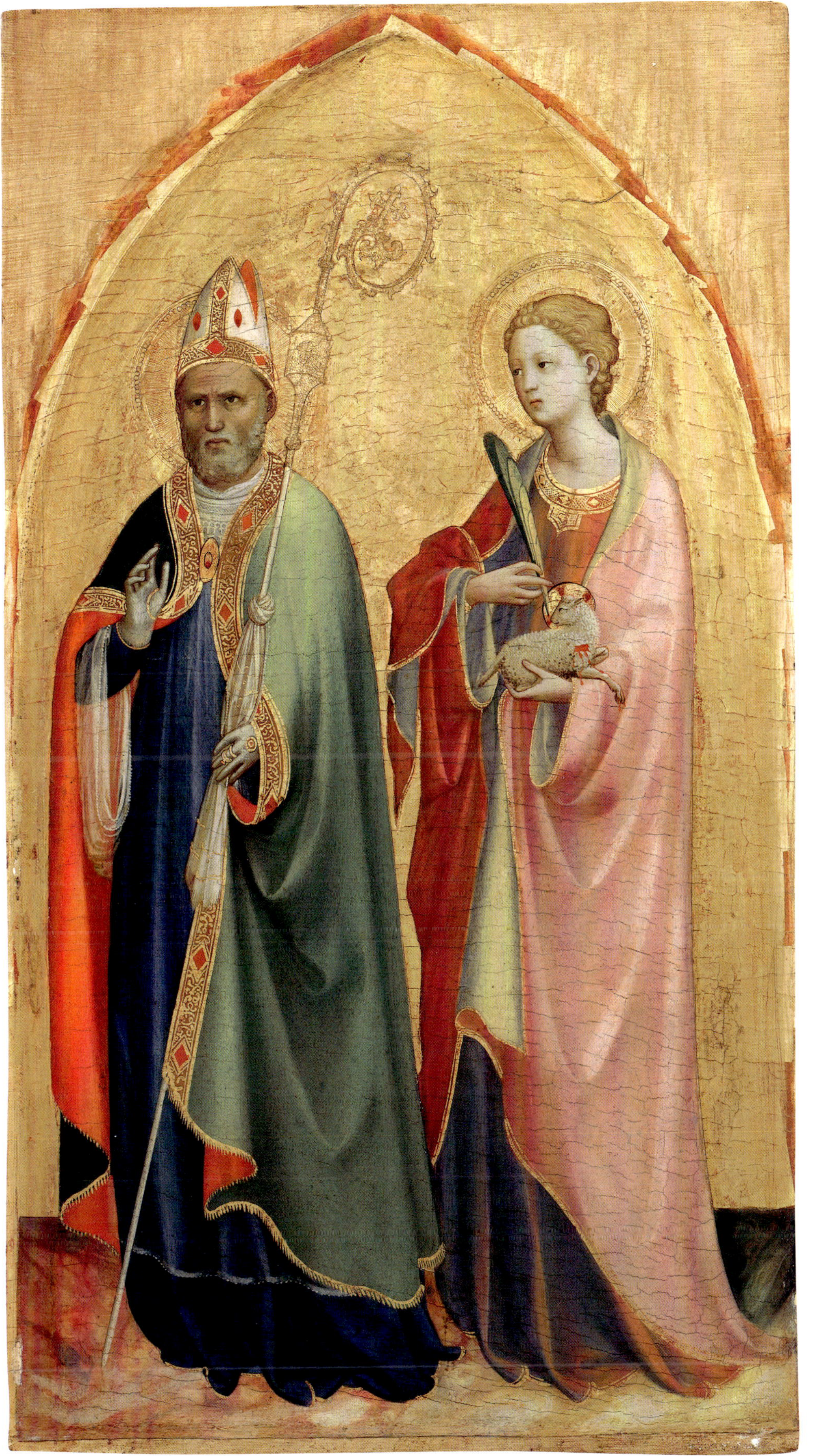

12: B

These two beautifully preserved panels representing Saint Catherine of Alexandria with Saint John the Baptist and Saint Agnes with a bishop saint are reputed to have once formed part of the Esterhazy collection in Hungary, passing from there, through the Liechtenstein collection in Vaduz, to their present owner. They were first published by John Pope-Hennessy,[2] who described them as "cut horizontally at the top" but also as bearing "traces of an earlier enframing arch beside the figures." This arch, visible as a shadow probably formed by the removal of an engaged molding, in photographs of the panels before their transfer, is lined along its inner edge by a diagonal craquelure pattern that implies that it bordered the original extension of the paint surface on each panel. Further traces of craquelure outside this arch may indicate the continuation of the original gesso beneath decorated spandrels, but all traces of craquelure disappear at the corners of each panel, which originally may have been cropped, either diagonally or along the curve of an ogival or mixtilinear arch, and would have been made up to complete the present rectangular format in a later restoration. Evidence of such alteration, however, was lost in the process of transferring the panels to their present supports, during which both were also enlarged by some six centimeters in height and from one to two centimeters in width. Notwithstanding their transfer, the restorations to each panel are largely confined to releafing the gold ground. The figures are remarkably free of abrasion or repaints, and may be considered among the finest preserved examples of Angelico's early work.

The original function of these panels is not absolutely certain. They are painted with a monumentality of form and an evocation of depth appropriate to the side panels of an altarpiece, but their small size is more suggestive of the folding wings of a tabernacle (see cat. 16). While the latter possibility cannot be ruled out entirely, their exceptional width relative to their height implies that they probably served as the lateral panels of a small, fixed altarpiece—an impression underscored by the fact that they appear once to have borne engaged-frame moldings along their entire perimeter (uncommon on the wings of a folding triptych in this period). A proposal to identify the center panel from such a complex was first advanced by Miklós Boskovits,[3] who associated them with a large *Madonna of Humility* (fig. 12) in the Museo Nazionale di San Matteo in Pisa. Aside from being grander in scale and earlier in style than the present panels, however, the Pisa *Madonna* is preserved with its original frame moldings intact, and these indicate that it was originally an independent tabernacle with no lateral attachments. A subsequent proposal by Umberto Baldini, associating the panels with a *Virgin and Child Enthroned* in the collection of Barbara Piasecka Johnson (cat. 11), must similarly be rejected.[4] Although these paintings are more closely related in style and thus, probably, in date, they are utterly incompatible in size, and it is impossible to visualize their reconstruction in any conventional form of triptych or other multi-panel complex.

Among the known works by Fra Angelico, only one panel is of approximately the right date and size to be considered a plausible candidate for completing a reconstruction of this triptych. Representing Christ on the cross with the Virgin, Saint Mary Magdalene, and Saint John the Evangelist (fig. 46), this recently rediscovered painting,[5] formerly in the Ashburton collection, documents a moment in the career of Fra Angelico nearly contemporary with his work on the high altarpiece for San Domenico in Fiesole, in the early 1420s. Like the lateral panels, it is anomalous in size: measuring 25 x 15 inches (63.5 x 38.1 centimeters), it is somewhat small for an independent tabernacle yet too wide for a wing and too narrow for the center of a conventional folding triptych. It is, however, appropriate in format for the center of a small altarpiece, and the difference in size between this painting and the present lateral panels is well within the range of standard practice for the period. The projection of its ground plane, the viewing angle of the figures, and the tooling of the gold ground, which is unusual among Angelico's early works in its simplicity, all correspond almost exactly to the lateral panels with standing saints. Perhaps equally significant is the comparable condition of the *Crucifixion,* whose paint surface is beautifully preserved, with restorations largely confined to the gold ground; pre-transfer photographs of the standing saints reveal that they were restored in much the same manner.

All three of these panels are, like the predella to the San Domenico high altarpiece, remarkable examples of Angelico's interest in naturalism and his precocious mastery of its rendering in paint. Infrared reflectography discloses very simple, schematic underdrawing in the figures of the four standing saints, but the fall of their robes where the pleats meet the marble pavement is studied in complex yet confident and carefully hatched detail. The engraved lines of Saint Catherine's crown as it curves around her head, the meticulously depicted nails that fix the spokes of the wheel of her martyrdom to its rim, and the beaten ironwork handle that is slotted into its hub are sufficiently persuasive in their immediacy to distract the viewer's attention from such pictorial conventions as the projection of the Baptist's feet parallel to the picture plane or the stridently opulent coloration of the marble pavement. These panels are also ambitious in their spatial illusionism, although not as aggressively so as Masaccio's first mature works will be just a few years later. The projection of Saint Catherine's wheel dramatically backward in space, or—in the center panel (fig. 46)—the angle of vision upward to the knees, chest, and face of the crucified Christ, and the view of Saint John the

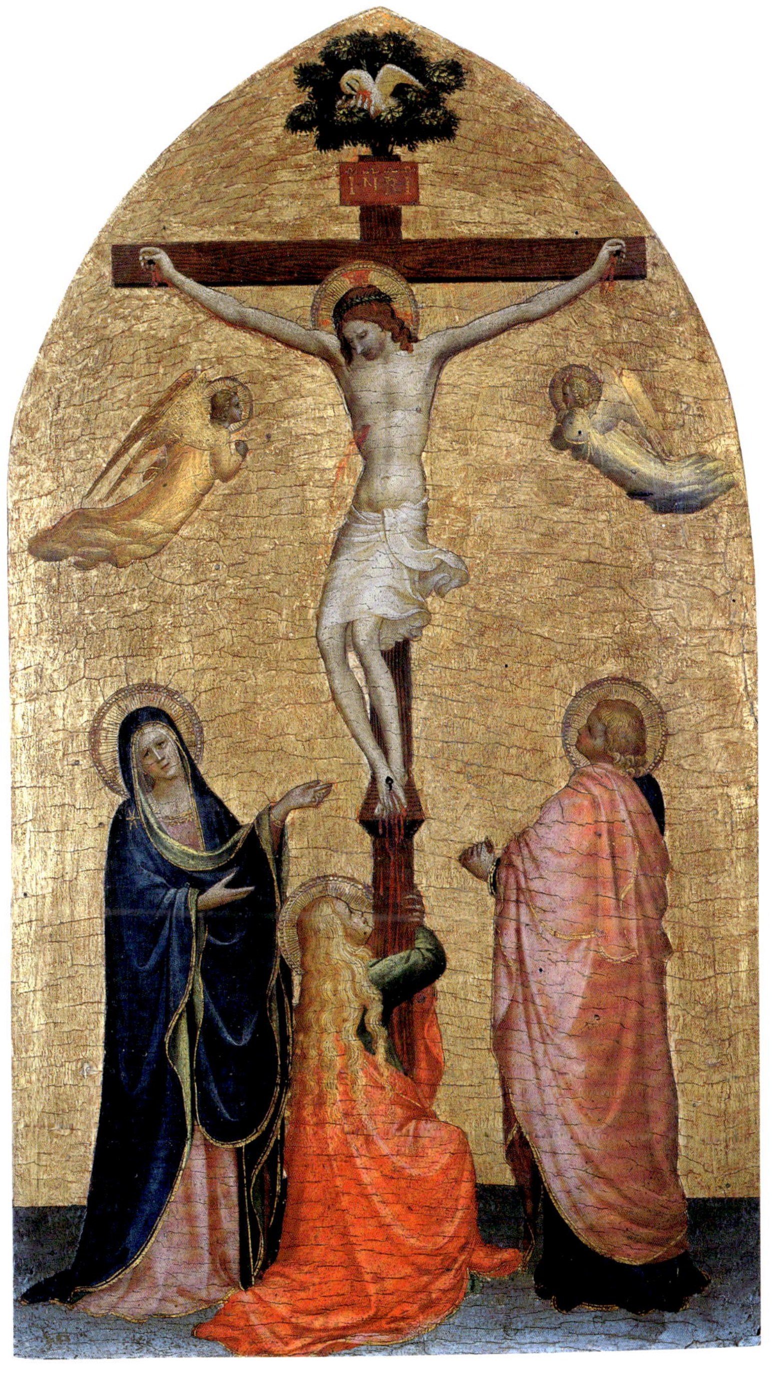

Figure 46. Fra Angelico. *The Crucifixion*. About 1421–22. Private collection

Evangelist from behind, his head turned sharply back over his left shoulder, are novelties in Florentine painting at this date, and a subtle advance over slightly earlier works such as the Griggs *Crucifixion* (cat. 8). Most of the limited discussion of these panels has focused on whether they immediately precede or follow work on the San Domenico high altarpiece, and, indeed, it is the figures, both large and small scale, in that painting that provide the closest frame of reference for those in the present triptych. The balance of probability suggests that this triptych would almost immediately postdate the San Domenico high altarpiece and precede the design of the San Pier Martire triptych, therefore placing its execution possibly about 1421 or 1422.[6]

In discussing the four standing saints as the lateral panels to the *Madonna of Humility* in Pisa, Boskovits hypothesized a provenance for the resulting altarpiece from the Giugni family of Florence, whose coat of arms appears on the distaff side of the frame of the Pisa panel. He tentatively suggested that the commission for the paintings could have been related to the entry of Giovanna di Filippo Giugni into the Dominican convent of San Pier Martire in 1423. Redating the panels slightly earlier and disassociating them from the Pisa *Madonna* leaves open the question of their possible original destination. The bishop saint in the right-hand panel is usually identified as Nicholas of Bari, but the absence of any attributes specific to that saint makes this identification doubtful. It is at least as likely that he is meant to portray Saint Zenobius, who, with John the Baptist, was one of the protector saints of Florence but who lacks a fixed iconography in painting beyond his episcopal vestments. The presence of Saints Catherine of Alexandria and Agnes alongside John the Baptist and Zenobius (?) could suggest the patronage of a female institution, but with no monastic saints in the central or lateral panels it is difficult to specify to which order such a house might have belonged. Catherine and Agnes are paired in the right-hand section of the predella to the San Pier Martire triptych (cat. 13), and appear together again on the predella to the reliquary of the *Annunciation and the Adoration of the Magi* from Santa Maria Novella (see cat. 28). The latter was commissioned from Angelico by the prominent Dominican Fra Giovanni di Zanobi Masi (for whom, see p. 97), whose name saints might be identified with the two male saints in these panels. Although Fra Giovanni Masi came from a wealthy Florentine family, the possible extent of his patronage beyond the four painted reliquaries mentioned by Vasari is unknown.

LK

1. The dimensions are approximate and reflect the maximum apparent extension of the original paint surface and gold ground in each direction. Regilding after the panels were transferred enlarged their picture fields to 56 x 31.5 centimeters (A) and 55.5 x 32 centimeters (B), respectively; these are the dimensions recorded in published sources.
2. Pope-Hennessy 1974, pp. 12, 190.
3. Boskovits 1976a, pp. 23–25; Boskovits 1976b, pp. 33–34.
4. Baldini 1977, pp. 240–41, 245 n. 23.
5. Russell 1996, pp. 315–17.
6. Although this author finds a date of about 1423, as suggested by Pope-Hennessy, Boskovits, and Baldini, too late, he agrees with most of their arguments for relative dating within Fra Angelico's oeuvre. D. Cole Ahl (1980, pp. 374–76) opts for a date after 1425, citing the influence of Gentile da Fabriano's Quaratesi altarpiece. Presumably, this observation was meant to contrast the four standing saints with more Masaccesque works by Angelico, but no direct influence from the panels of the Quaratesi altarpiece is evident in these paintings.

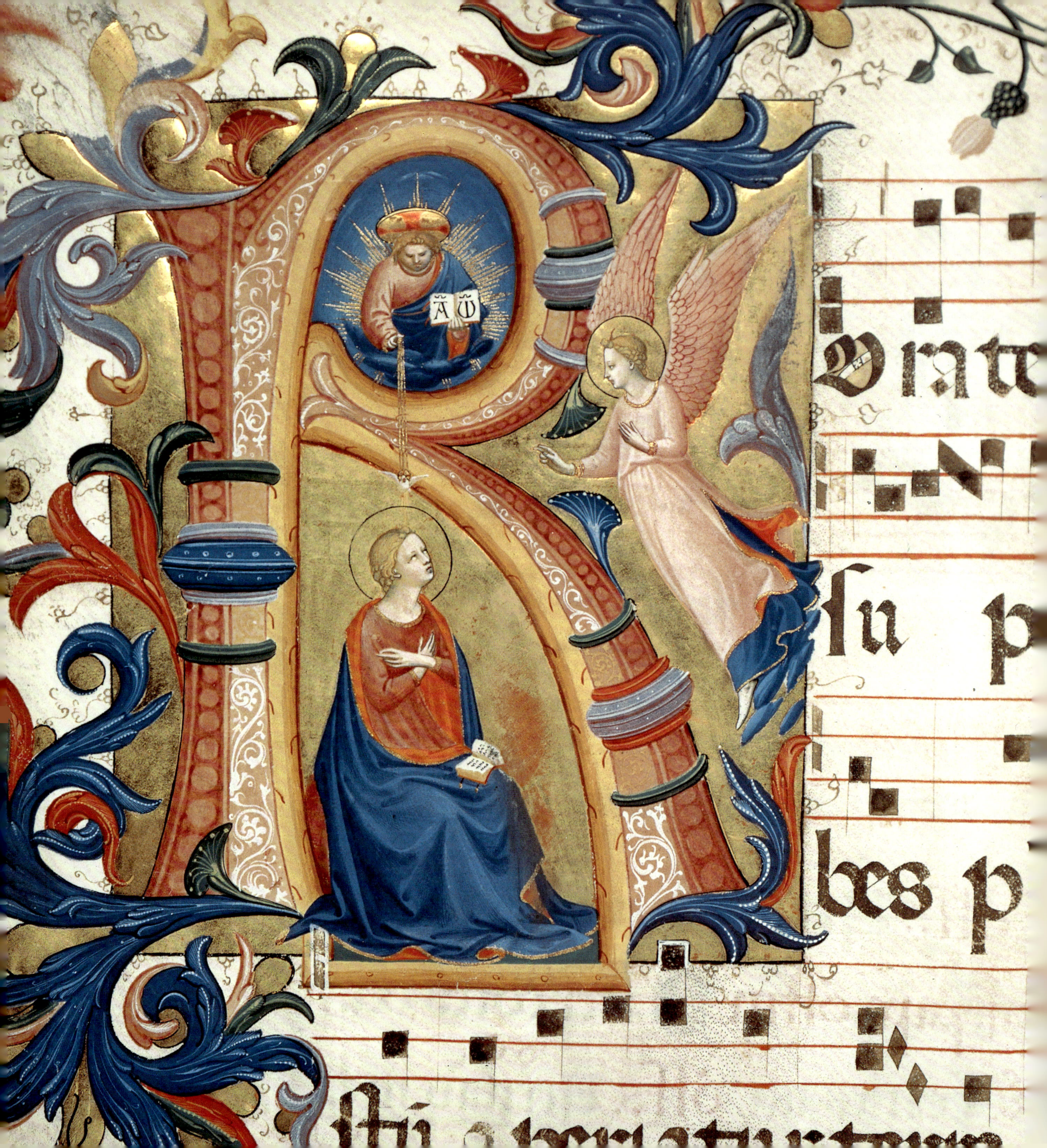

Chapter IV
Fra Angelico: A Decade of Transition (1422–32)

LAURENCE KANTER

Opposite:
Figure 47. Fra Angelico. *The Annunciation* (detail). About 1423. Biblioteca del Convento di San Marco, Florence (Cod. 558, fol. 33*v*.)

It is frequently repeated, as part of the legend of the painter's sanctity, that Angelico's decision to join a mendicant order, and specifically an Observant community of that order, was motivated purely by spiritual concerns. This may well be true, at least in large measure, but it can surely be no coincidence that at the moment that he took vows, the Dominicans represented one of the two leading communities of intellectual activity in Florence, along with the Camaldolese at Santa Maria degli Angeli. Furthermore, with the election of Martin V Colonna as pope, the Dominicans were poised on the threshold of a period of great influence and expansion. The decision in 1418 to build a convent in Fiesole to house the Observant community founded more than a decade earlier by Giovanni Dominici but until then resident in exile in Foligno, and the flurry of commissions to redecorate and embellish Santa Maria Novella in advance of the arrival there of the newly elected pope in 1419, translated, in an immediate and practical sense, into a steady stream of patronage and opportunity for a young artist. Angelico's former master, Lorenzo Monaco, already enjoyed a monopoly on commissions funneled through the Camaldolese community and its brilliant and charismatic leader, Ambrogio Traversari, at Santa Maria degli Angeli. Guido di Pietro, or Fra Giovanni as he was called in religious orders, soon achieved the same success with the even more industrious Dominicans.

As far as can be ascertained with any confidence, the first fruit of Angelico's labors for the Dominicans was the commission to paint the high altarpiece for the new convent at San Domenico in Fiesole (see cat. 10). It is reasonable to assume, however, that this was not the artist's first contact with the order. As has been argued (see pp. 27–39, and cat. 5), the *rotulus* of Petrus de Cruce's pilgrimage guidebook to the Holy Land, to which the young Angelico contributed at least two illustrations, was undoubtedly intended for a Dominican patron, and it is possible that the Uffizi *Thebaid* (fig. 19) was produced in a Dominican context as well—or, at the very least, commissioned as a copy of an earlier painting that was, itself, from a Dominican context. Also, as Carl Strehlke recently has suggested, Angelico's youthful *Adoration of the Magi* now in Riggisberg (fig. 27) may have been painted for Santa Maria Novella, and the young artist may have been involved, possibly before he began his Dominican novitiate, in the campaign to fresco the Chiostro Verde in preparation for the arrival of Martin V in February 1419.[1] Before 1419, Angelico, then known as Guido di Pietro, was merely one of a number of local painters available to be called upon by Dominican patrons; after 1420 he was their artist of choice.

Directly following the San Domenico high altarpiece, and possibly even before the completion and installation of that ambitious work, Angelico was engaged on a series of major and minor commissions from Dominican institutions for paintings intended both for public and private display. His situation as a friar seems not to have constrained him to work exclusively for his own order, and, indeed, he may well have been encouraged to accept commissions from other orders, as well as from secular patrons, as a source of income for the fledgling community at Fiesole. It was the Dominicans, however, who proved to be his most dependable, continuous, and demanding supporters, beginning with the commission of a painting for the high altar of another recently established convent, the female house of San Pier Martire in Florence. A much more modest undertaking than the San Domenico high altarpiece, the "*tabula*" for San Pier Martire (cat. 13) is recorded in a receipt of residual payment to the prior of San Domenico in March 1429, and has frequently been accepted as a work of approximately that date. In fact, it must have been painted considerably earlier, probably not long after 1421, when the first nuns took up residence in the new convent. Immediately following or perhaps even concurrently with this commission, the artist was asked to provide thirty-three historiated initials for a gradual (Bibl. San Marco, cod. 558; fig. 47, 48, 49) for San Domenico in Fiesole that may have been executed over time but whose outside date is surely no later than 1423 or perhaps 1424.[2] Slightly later still is the first of four painted reliquaries (fig. 80), popularly known as the *Madonna della Stella,* commissioned, on the testimony of Giuseppe Richa more than three centuries later, by Fra Giovanni di Zanobi Masi, sacristan of Santa Maria Novella (see cat. 28), as well as a handful of

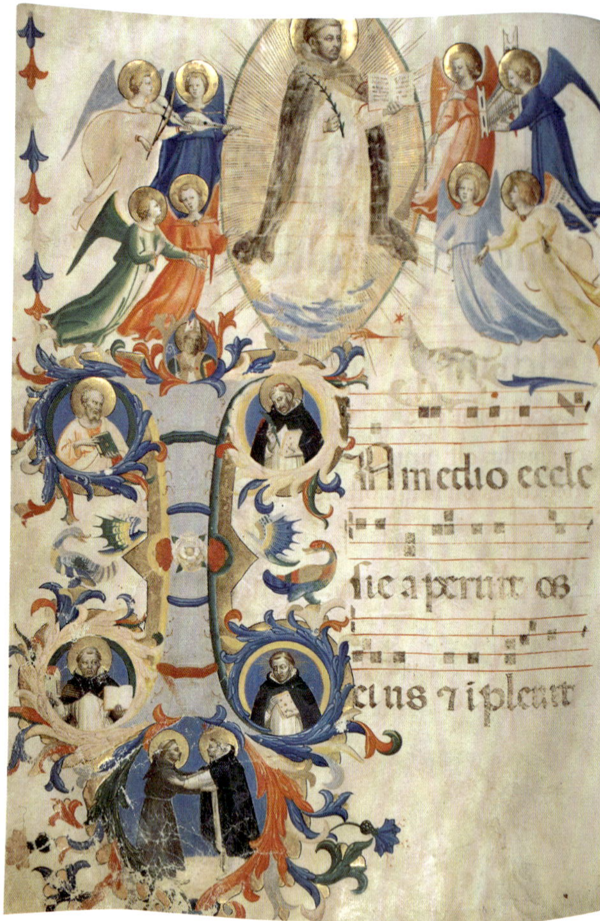

Figure 48. Fra Angelico. *The Glory of Saint Dominic.* About 1423. Biblioteca del Convento di San Marco, Florence (Cod. 558, fol. 67*v.*)

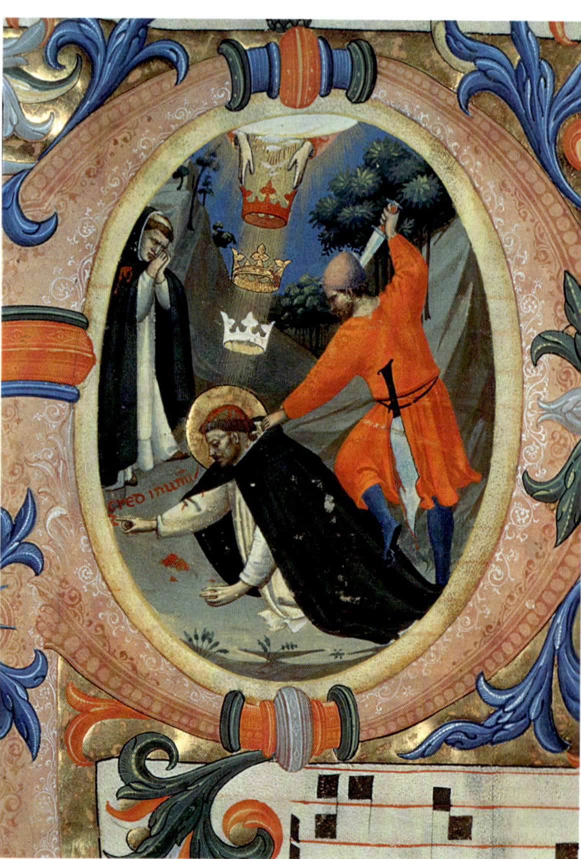

Figure 49. Fra Angelico. *The Assassination of Saint Peter Martyr* (detail). About 1423. Biblioteca del Convento di San Marco, Florence (Cod. 558, fol. 41*v.*)

paintings for private devotion that may also have been made for Fra Giovanni Masi or for other Dominican patrons (see cat. 16).

Frequently associated with a document of 1431 but surely completed well before that date is one of Angelico's best-known images, the *Last Judgment* (fig. 50), now in the Museo di San Marco, Florence. The relatively archaic compositional structure of this image was in part determined by the demands of its unusual lobed shape—it was said to have functioned as the back of a presbyter's chair at Santa Maria degli Angeli[3]—but it is equally a conscious reflection of the artist's interest in Lorenzo Ghiberti's experiments with organizing space in his narrative reliefs. Angelico's familiarity with Ghiberti and his artistic principles was a longstanding and continuous one. Undoubtedly, their "association" may be traced back to the time of Angelico's apprenticeship in Lorenzo Monaco's studio, but its impact on his own painting style was highly selective after about 1425. The *Last Judgment* clearly dates before this—the last moment in which the artist was interested in such devices as the strictly centralized, tilted perspective of the open tombs in the middle foreground of the scene. The *Last Judgment,* furthermore, may not have been designed by Angelico with an entirely free hand. The raised *pastiglia* halo of Christ in Judgment at the top center of the composition is an unusually archaic feature that is not repeated in any other work by the artist, and the punishments of the damned at the right are adopted fairly literally from the *Last Judgment* fresco in the Camposanto at Pisa. Other than the Uffizi *Thebaid,* which was made specifically as a replica, Angelico is not known ever to have copied another work of art in generating his own compositions, and there is reason to believe that this *Last Judgment* may have been planned and left incomplete by another artist. If so, considering its provenance from Santa Maria degli Angeli, it is reasonable to suppose that the commission may originally have been awarded to Lorenzo Monaco, whose death in 1423 or 1424 might have occasioned its transfer to Fra Angelico. A similar situation a few years later would lead to the creation of one of Angelico's greatest masterpieces, the Strozzi *Deposition* for Santa Trinita (fig. 53).

The culmination of this phase of rapid development in Fra Angelico's visual imagination and painting style is represented by the second, and smallest, of his three great altarpieces for San Domenico, Fiesole: the *Annunciation* altarpiece (fig. 51), now in the Museo del Prado, Madrid. In this painting, for the first time, Angelico seems to betray an awareness of the pictorial innovations evident in Masaccio's early works, but not in a closely imitative manner. It is essentially his own intrinsic predilection for the description of visual phenomena that informs the structure and the details of this composition, and the language with which he expresses this interest is at this date based more on the example of Gentile da Fabriano than

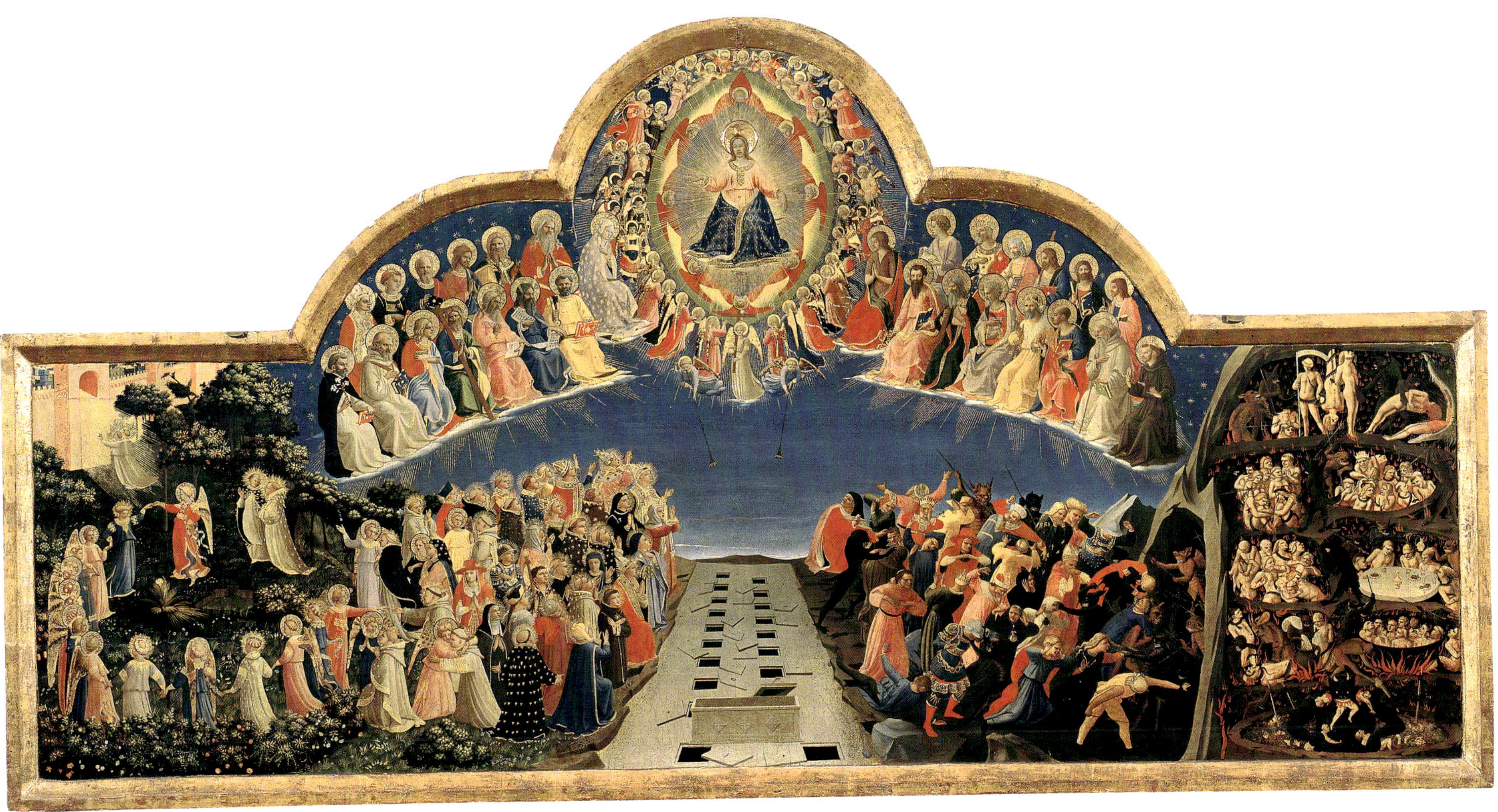

Figure 50. Fra Angelico. *The Last Judgment.* About 1424. Museo di San Marco, Florence

of Masaccio. The simple, single-point perspective of the predella narratives and the teeming abundance of almost microscopic detail compressed into the landscape of the main panel of the *Annunciation* altarpiece have sometimes been interpreted as evidence of an imitator borrowing Angelico's formal vocabulary without fully comprehending its meaning.[4] It is, in fact, an indicator of the precedence in date of this composition over the other monumental versions of the theme painted or designed by the artist, and specifically of its execution in about 1425 or 1426. The intricacy of the delicate glazes of color defining the feathers of the archangel's wings or highlighting the gilt embroidery on his robe, gently distorted along the crease of each pleat to indicate the motion of genuflection; the mathematical precision of the receding gold dots on the carefully shaded blue sail-vaults of the loggia; or the reflected highlights cast upon the floor and back wall in the small chamber behind the Virgin are a sure indication not only of the presence here of the mind and hand of Angelico but also of the subtlety and technical sophistication of that mind and hand.

A coincidence of dating and of iconography suggests the possibility that the Prado *Annunciation* from San Domenico in Fiesole may be identifiable with a painting mentioned in a document of December 15, 1425. On that date, Alessandro di Simone di Filippo Rondinelli specified in his last will and testament his intention to supply an altarpiece for the Chapel of Saint Lawrence in the church of San Lorenzo in Florence, "*in qua tabula pingi debeat Beata Virgho Maria cum Angelo Anuntiante eidem conceptionem domini nostri Jesu Christi et sanctus Alessander*."[5] A marginal note in Italian further specifies that "*per rimedia dell'anima sua si debi fare una tavola con la Nu[n]ziata e con santo Alesandro . . . di spesa di fiorini venti, ne' cholonegli da llato, santo Giovanni batista, san lorenzo, santo antonio, san nicholò e san Giuliano . . . vuole la facci frate* [?] *de' frati di san domenicho di Chamerata*." The moderate cost of this altarpiece may be an indication of its relatively modest size, but also that it was probably not intended to be an elaborate polyptych with a gold ground but rather a single painted panel with six pilaster figures, including the donor's namesake, Alexander, and the dedicatee of the church and chapel, Lawrence, as well as John the Baptist, Anthony Abbot, Nicholas, and Julian.

In the event, the painting described in this document was either not executed or not delivered, and Alessandro Rondinelli's successive will, dated October 9, 1429, voided all the bequests and obligations of his first will without any further discussion of an altarpiece for this or any other chapel. It is possible, however, that the painting he wished to have made

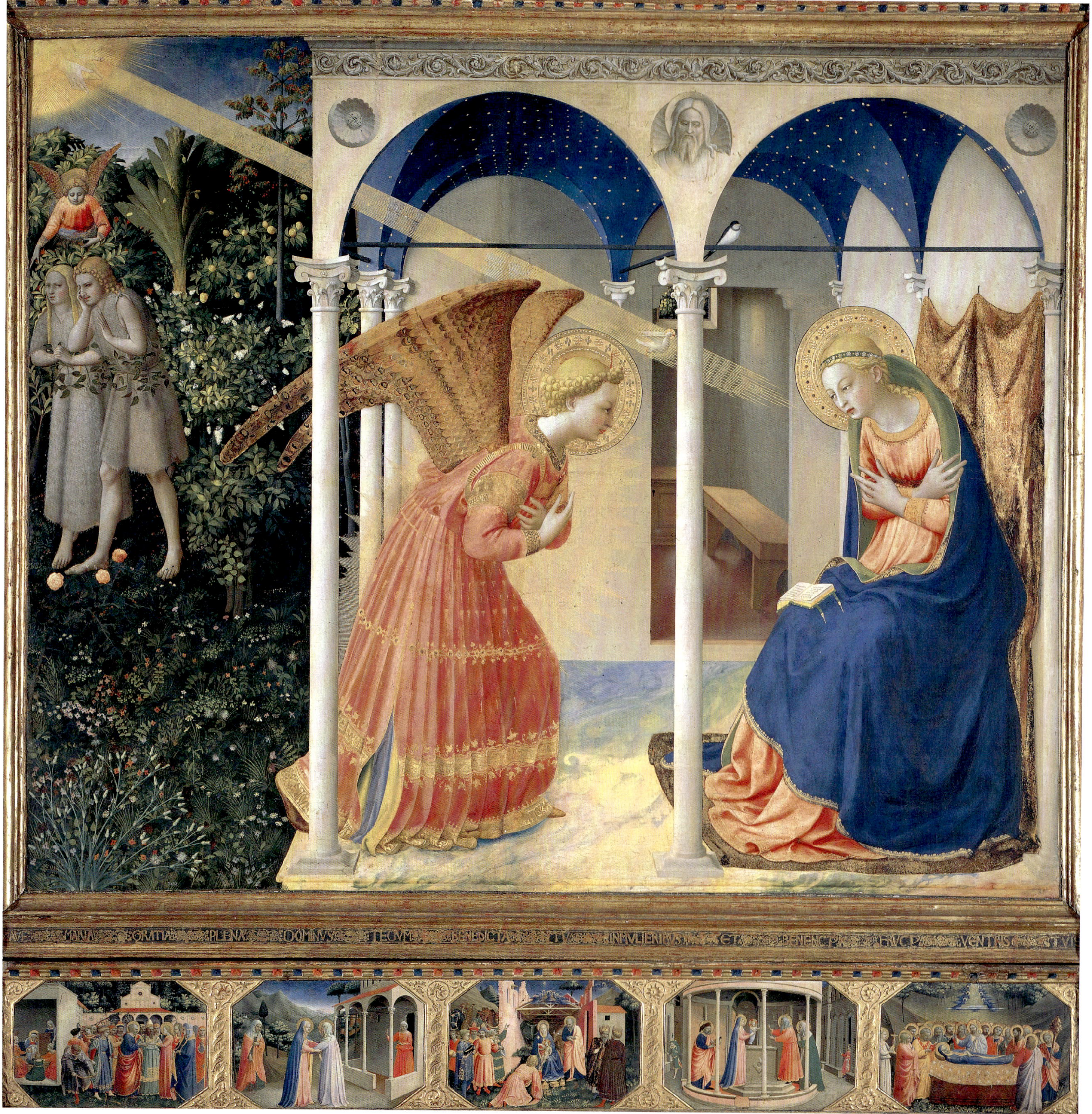

Figure 51. Fra Angelico. *The Annunciation*. About 1425–26. Museo Nacional del Prado, Madrid

by the "*frate* [?] *de' frati di san domenicho di Chamerata*" (that is, Fra Angelico) was, in fact, completed but for some reason was not paid for by Alessandro Rondinelli, and perhaps subsequently was installed elsewhere—specifically at San Domenico in Fiesole. Perched on an iron tie rod spanning the front arch of the loggia above and to the left of the Virgin's head in the Prado altarpiece is a swallow (*rondine* in Italian). This detail may not be entirely irrelevant to Annunciation iconography,[6] but it does not appear in any other version of the *Annunciation* by Fra Angelico. It is tempting in this case to construe the "*rondine*" as a punning reference to the name of the original patron of the altarpiece, Alessandro Rondinelli.

Angelico's response to the new style of painting introduced by his younger contemporary Masaccio was, as Roberto Longhi argued so eloquently, both more intelligent and more profound than that of any other master of his generation; yet it was also more selective. Those of Masaccio's innovations that paralleled his own prior interests, such as the construction of credible pictorial space and the rationalization of the effects of light on modeling, he understood intuitively, and he adopted them as refinements of his own experiments. Other aspects of Masaccio's art, such as the massive, sculptural monumentality of his figures (derived perhaps from his association with Donatello), or the reductive simplicity of his palette, Angelico approached with greater skepticism, toying briefly with some of their implications without entirely abandoning his own predilection for descriptive surfaces and textural verisimilitude, more in keeping with his earlier training in the orbit of Lorenzo Ghiberti and his admiration for Gentile da Fabriano. Above all others, the painting that most perfectly synthesizes these two competing interests is the *Virgin and Child, with Two Angels,* of about 1426 in the Alba collection. Loosely reflecting in its composition the sobriety and solemnity of Masaccio's Sant'Anna Meterza altarpiece from Sant'Ambrogio, it retains the decorative virtuosity of Angelico's immediately preceding works, such as the Prado *Annunciation* altarpiece, but here it is softened, almost chastened, by his exposure to the spare aesthetic of the young Masaccio.

Even more overtly dependent on Masaccio's example are two large paintings of the Madonna of Humility—in the Thyssen Collection at the Museu Nacional d'Art de Catalunya (cat. 18), and in a Swiss private collection (fig. 61). Painted between 1426 and 1428, the years of Masaccio's undisputed ascendancy in the Florentine artistic community, these two works are unabashed paeans to the younger artist's stylistic and compositional innovations: the first of them a sincere effort of emulation, the second an accomplished critique. The period bracketed by their execution also saw the production of more intimate compositions, such as the almost miniaturist *Virgin and Child, with Four Angels,* in Detroit (cat. 20), or the second of four reliquaries painted for Santa Maria Novella at the behest of Fra Giovanni Masi: the *Coronation of the Virgin* in the Museo di San Marco (fig. 81). In paintings such as these, the innate delicacy of Angelico's vision combines with the monumental aspirations of his "temporary" mentor to produce images of a classicizing serenity and a direct, human appeal. Perhaps the most complete statement of this tendency in Angelico's art is the imposing tabernacle of which the *Virgin and Child, with Four Saints,* in Parma, formed the center (cat. 21). The loss of as many as five narrative scenes from the fragmented and dispersed wings of this triptych obviates any meaningful comparison to Masaccio that might lie behind its ideation, but it is not difficult to imagine that when it was intact and in situ it must have been instantly recognized as one of the monuments of the new style of painting in Florence.

Following Masaccio's death in 1428 in Rome, no Florentine painter could seriously contest Angelico's dominance of the field until Filippo Lippi's maturation as an independent master near the end of the following decade. This period of ten or so years saw the production by Fra Angelico of a major altarpiece almost every year, alongside a scarcely diminished output of smaller devotional works, as well as several fresco commissions for which he was either wholly or in part responsible. Inevitably, it was also at this time that the first intimations of the collaboration of assistants became apparent in his works, although it was only toward the middle of the 1430s that he came to rely on them for substantial contributions to his paintings, in some cases delegating the execution of entire projects to his studio. The viability of this method of production depends in no small measure on the clarity of the master's example and the patience with which he can codify his ideas for interpretation by less talented hands. Angelico never descended to the level of formulaic invention in the interests of greater productivity, but the restless experimentation underlying his paintings from the mid-1420s gradually gave way to an assured continuity of expression that sometimes makes it difficult to specify a date for his mature works with unwavering confidence or precision. Fortunately, a not insignificant number of both firmly and circumstantially documented works survives from the period of the artist's maturity, and while some controversies over the dating or attribution of key paintings persist, it is possible to construct a fairly reliable chronology of his development after 1428.

Angelico's immediate response to the departure—and, ultimately, to the death—of Masaccio does not, ironically, seem to have been a renunciation of competition. In many respects those of his works that can with the greatest plausibility be dated to 1428, 1429, and 1430 represent his most maturely cogitated reflections on the principles of Masaccio's art. In his entire oeuvre, few paintings make so direct and overt a reference to

Masaccio's example as the Madonna of Humility in a Swiss private collection (fig. 61) discussed above, which was probably painted in 1428. From the same year or perhaps 1429, and presumably identifiable with part of a "*tabula*" mentioned in a document of that date, are the severe, uncharacteristically restrained narratives of a Franciscan predella (cat. 24) and the moody, almost ungainly, full-length saints on the lateral panels of an altarpiece triptych generally associated with them. The precarious state of preservation of these saints and the possibility that Fra Angelico may have relied on some degree of assistance in their execution (the angel and the Virgin Annunciate painted in the pinnacles above them are certainly by an assistant, possibly Battista di Biagio Sanguigni) compromise close analysis of their style. Yet, the enthroned Virgin and Child that occupied the center of the altarpiece (fig. 68) is easily the most self-consciously monumental image Angelico had painted up to that point in his career. It is possible to claim, as has been done,[7] that the lack of decorative ornament and reduction to visual essentials apparent in these panels, and even more so in the five predella panels with scenes from the legend of Saint Francis, is a response to the spiritual sobriety of Franciscan culture, but the claim rings hollow when applied to an artist who was also an Observant Dominican and who, furthermore, only one year later may have painted another Franciscan altarpiece that moves decidedly away from this extremist position. It is at least equally likely that the minimalist detail in the staging of the narratives in the panels of the Franciscan predella, with their simplified, blocky figures and clearly organized spatial volumes, came about as the result of a stylistic rather than an iconographic experiment, and is a measure of the restless, probing intelligence of their creator.

More than sixty years ago, Roberto Longhi pointed out the striking Masaccesque references in two panels (cat. 25 A, B) from the predella to an unknown altarpiece[8] that subsequent research has revealed may have been intended for another chapel in the Franciscan church of Santa Croce. The limpid atmospheric effects, structural solidity, and rationally constructed spaces in Masaccio's paintings are deployed in these two panels, and in three others that have since been recognized as parts of the same complex, beneath a veneer of descriptive naturalism that strikes an unmistakable note of continuity with Angelico's earlier style. However, the decorative exuberance of those earlier works is tightly controlled in these five predella panels to produce an air of austerity that contributes to a noticeable heightening of the emotive pathos of the scenes. Rather than predating the Franciscan predella, as was once thought, this hybrid of two opposing tendencies represents a maturation—a step forward toward the anecdotal sophistication of Angelico's works from the 1430s. For this and for other reasons, including the development of his figure style beyond the softly rounded or blocky but always squarely proportioned forms characteristic of his paintings in the 1420s, it is likely that these five predella panels mark what might be termed a point of transition in Angelico's work that probably took place in 1429 or 1430. From that point on, Angelico's intrinsic interest in the descriptive and his preference for a proliferation of detail reasserted itself, although tempered always by the compositional lessons he had learned from Masaccio.

The first, and perhaps greatest, instance of this blend of experiences is the famous *Annunciation* altarpiece (fig. 52), painted for the church of San Domenico in Cortona, a work that is undocumented but likely on stylistic grounds to have been executed about 1430 or 1431. There, all the subtlety and pictorial sophistication of Angelico's Prado *Annunciation* of five years earlier is heightened and made more urgent and dramatically expressive as a result of Masaccio's influence. The Virgin and the archangel Gabriel do not merely assume poses appropriate to the narrative they are enacting but strain toward each other, fully aware of their roles within the evolving history of salvation as symbolized by the vignette of the expulsion from Eden in the upper-left corner of the composition. Concentrating on the spiritual intensity of his protagonists, Angelico reduced the distraction of surface detail in the rendering of the landscape and architectural setting, which figured so prominently in the Prado altarpiece; at the same time, the Cortona *Annunciation* also incorporates the greatest elaboration of decorative detail in engraved and mordant gilding—particularly apparent in the angel's wings and robe—that Angelico had yet attempted. Notwithstanding the technical virtuosity of its execution, however, this painting reveals the first certain traces of Angelico's reliance on assistants' work, which increasingly would become a feature of his production in the 1430s. The uncertain resolution of the ellipses that define the bases of the columns of the portico in which the Annunciation is set is clearly not due to Angelico himself, and the seven scenes on the predella and pilaster bases of the altarpiece are largely the efforts of an assistant, who may possibly be identifiable with the young Zanobi Strozzi. It is likely that Angelico was willing to concede so important a role in this painting's execution to his studio because the work was not destined for a Florentine patron.

The Cortona *Annunciation* must have been painted all but concurrently with the last great altarpiece of this middle period of Angelico's career: the *Deposition* (fig. 53), formerly in the sacristy of Santa Trinita in Florence and now in the Museo di San Marco. Intended as a pendant to Gentile da Fabriano's *Adoration of the Magi* altarpiece, which had been unveiled in 1423, the *Deposition* was initially commissioned from Lorenzo Monaco, who, in the event, is thought to have completed only the predella and the pinnacles of the altarpiece frame before

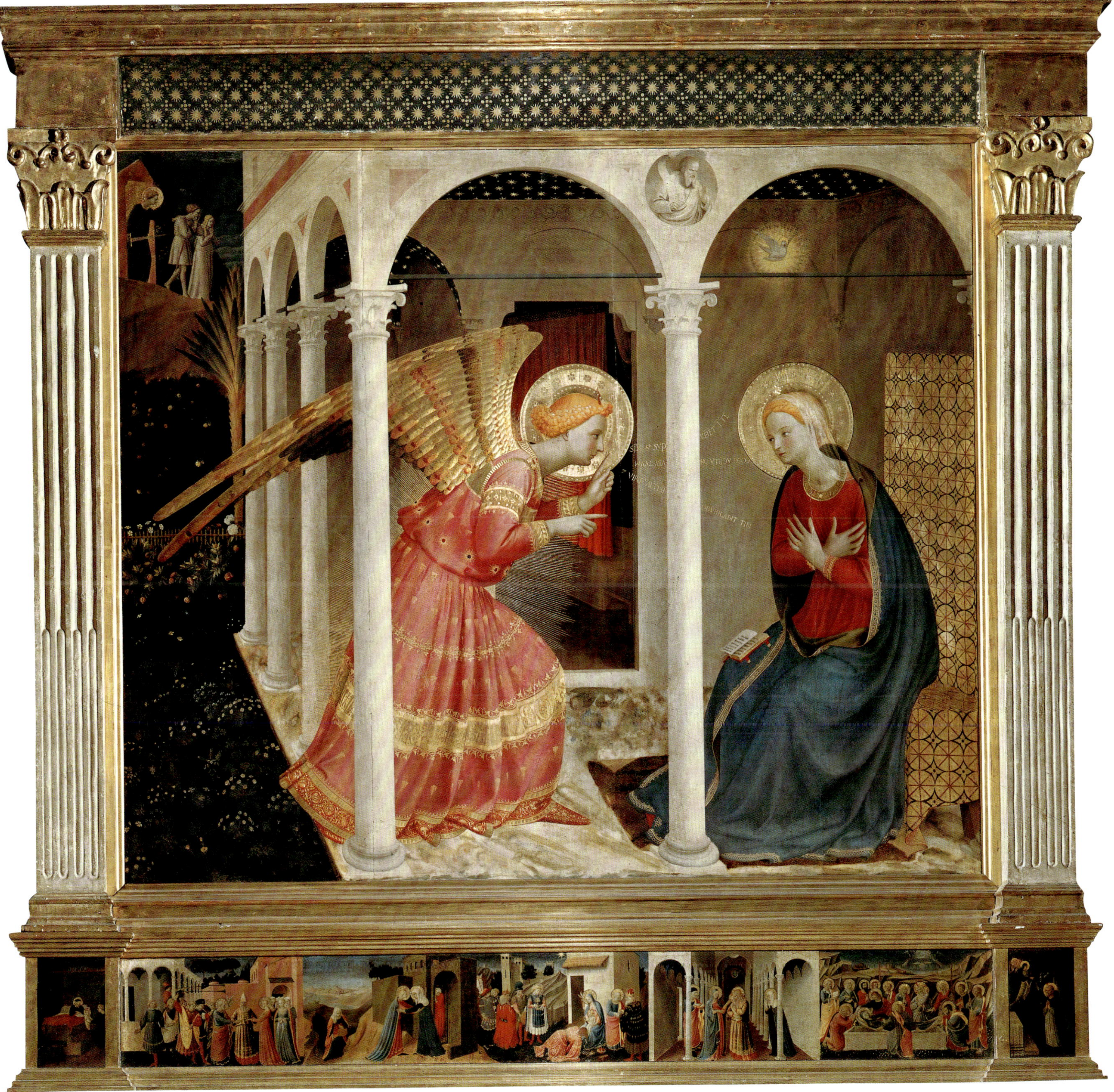

Figure 52. Fra Angelico. *The Annunciation*. About 1430–31. Museo Diocesano, Cortona

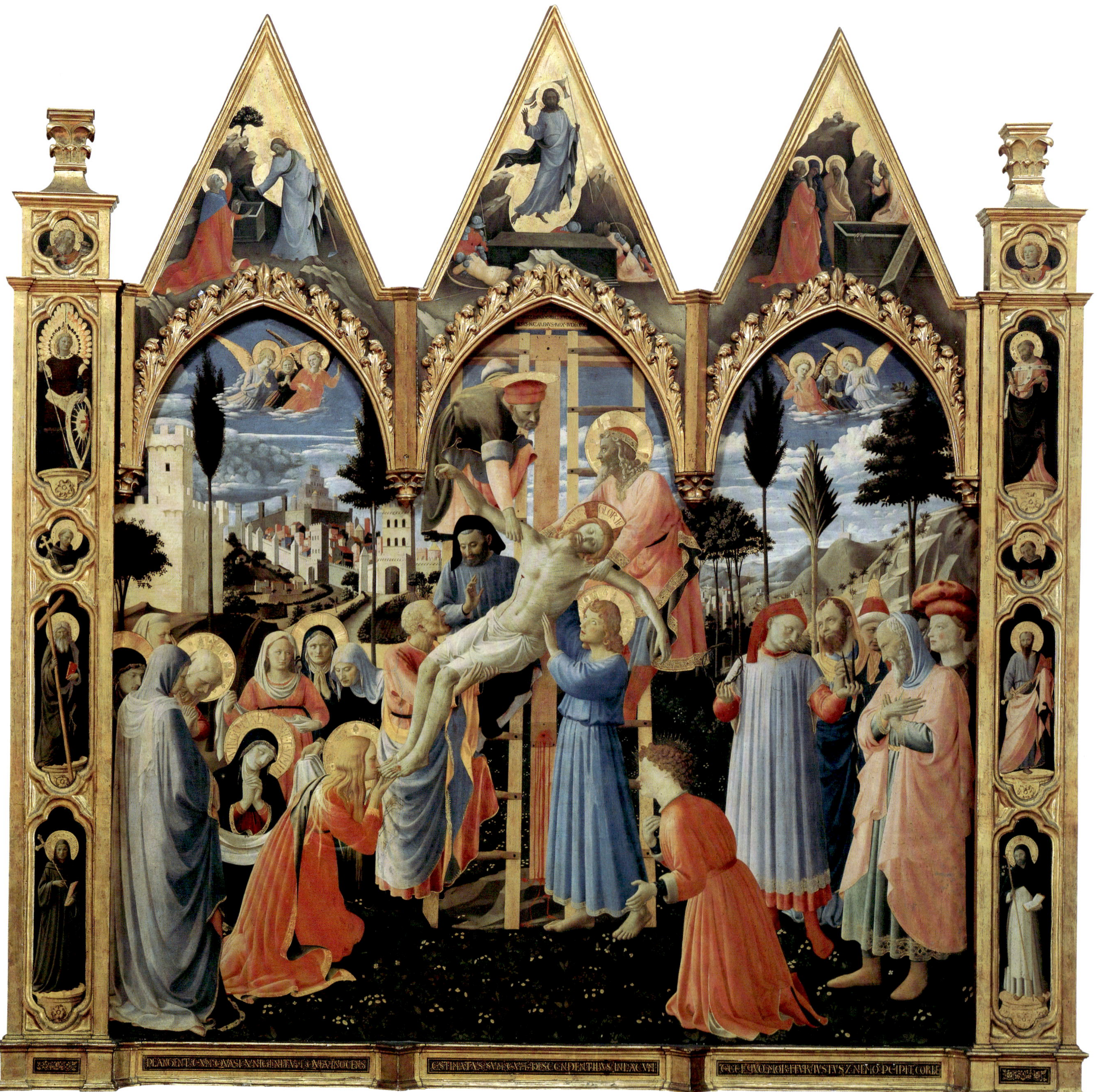

Figure 53. Fra Angelico. *The Deposition*. About 1430–32. Museo di San Marco, Florence

his death in 1423 or 1424. The three predella panels—representing the Nativity and scenes from the legends of Saint Onophrius and Saint Nicholas—conform in iconography to the dedication of the altar that this painting once adorned, and have led to speculation that Lorenzo Monaco's original design for the main panel of the structure may have comprised a traditional Virgin and Child enthroned with saints. It should be noted, however, that conventional altarpieces with this subject are composed of a central picture field that is substantially taller and, generally, wider than are the fields of the lateral panels, whereas in this case the three arches of the main panel are essentially equal in height and width. Furthermore, Lorenzo Monaco's pinnacle paintings of the *Resurrection,* the *Three Maries at the Tomb,* and the *Noli me Tangere* presuppose a Passion scene as the altarpiece's principal subject.

That these pinnacles and the predella—although peripheral parts of the altarpiece—were completely finished by Lorenzo Monaco may also imply that, whatever its subject, the main panel could have been finished by the artist as well, and not, as is generally supposed, left incomplete at his death. Such a contention would explain why Angelico, or any other artist, was not called upon to rework the painting immediately, as may have been the case with the Santa Maria degli Angeli *Last Judgment*. In style the *Deposition* altarpiece conforms exactly to the Cortona *Annunciation* of about 1430–31, and it has recently been shown that expenditures recorded in Lorenzo di Palla Strozzi's account books indicate that the *Deposition* was installed above its altar in 1432.[9] The implication, not susceptible to proof, is that Angelico was asked to revise the subject of the painting in some fashion rather than to bring it to completion. Carl Strehlke has persuasively argued that the decision to rework the painting may have been occasioned by a desire to incorporate within it portraits of Palla and of his son Lorenzo, as well as to shift the focus of the narrative toward the relic of the crown of thorns—prominently displayed in the foreground of the panel—with which the Strozzi had come to associate themselves after 1425.[10]

Whatever the reasons for Angelico's intervention, the result is a narrative masterpiece of greater complexity than any attempted previously by the artist, conceived with a grandeur and panoramic sweep normally encountered only in monumental frescoes yet enlivened with a range of naturalistic detail nearly impossible to achieve in that medium. The lash wounds on Christ's body, the wood grain of the cross and of the ladders and the tapered ends of the ladders' rungs, the nails that hold them in place, and the carefully described foliage of the trees in the middle distance all bring the viewer into immediate contact with the scene, which is set before an evocation of the historical city of Jerusalem but is attended by at least four Florentines in contemporary dress. The seemingly casual overlap of figures among the onlookers at either side—the Virgin is nearly lost among the Holy Women who surround her—coupled with the deeply receding line of hills at the right, the cityscape at the left, and the blue, cloud-filled sky above also add to the illusion of immediacy, and serve to heighten rather than distract from the emotional pathos and drama of the scene.

The contrasting effect of Angelico's *Deposition* and Gentile's elegant but raucous *Adoration of the Magi* set opposite it in the sacristy of Santa Trinita must have been fully intentional and could hardly be more extreme. Both a paean to and a critique of the master who had been such an inspiration in his early career, Angelico's painting amplifies the radical, descriptive naturalism of Gentile's picture through the lessons he had gleaned from Masaccio's dramatic and heroic images. Created within ten years of each other, the two altarpieces are supreme examples of diametrically opposed trends in Italian Renaissance painting and remained highly influential on subsequent generations of artists in Florence, although few imitators or admirers of either work successfully rose to a comparable level of quality before the advent of Leonardo and Raphael at the end of the fifteenth century.

1. Strehlke 2003b, pp. 19–22.
2. C. B. Strehlke, in Kanter et al. 1994, pp. 332–39; M. Scudieri, in Scudieri and Rasario 2003, pp. 86–88.
3. Described as in Santa Maria degli Angeli in 1568 by Vasari (Milanesi ed.) 1878–85, vol. II, pp. 514–15, this painting was identified by V. Marchese (1845–46, vol. I, p. 279) as the back or *spalliera* of the priest's throne near the high altar, and this article of furniture was, in turn, associated by S. Orlandi, O.P. (1964, pp. 27–30, 184), with a documented commission of August 1431. A. Santagostino Barbone (1989, pp. 255–78) convincingly refutes this identification.
4. Muratoff 1930, p. 35; Bazin 1949, p. 185; Collobi-Ragghianti 1950b, p. 458; Pope-Hennessy 1974, p. 194; Kanter 2001a, pp. 28–30.
5. Ladis 1981, pp. 378–79. I am indebted to Dillian Gordon for suggesting the association of this document with the Prado altarpiece.
6. A swallow is included in two *Annunciation* altarpieces by Giovanni del Biondo: in the Museo dell'Ospedale degli Innocenti, Florence, no. 122 (formerly in Santissima Annunziata d'Orbatello, Florence), and in the Cappella dell'Annunziata, Poggio di Croce di Preci, Perugia.
7. Henderson and Joannides 1991, pp. 3–6.
8. Longhi 1940, p. 175 (reprinted in Longhi 1975).
9. Jones 1984, pp. 9–106.
10. Carl Strehlke, in a paper delivered at a conference on May 21, 2005, suggested that Lorenzo Monaco's original altarpiece might have been commissioned in 1418—when funds were first committed for the decoration of the chapel—and finished by 1421, when the chapel was formally consecrated. Such a range of dates accords well with the style of the predella panels and pinnacles by Lorenzo Monaco.

13.

A.

The Blessed Catherine of Siena and Saint Cecilia

Tempera on panel, 20.2 x 49.3 cm (8 x 19⅜ in.)
Courtauld Institute of Art Gallery, London
(Inv. no. P.1966.GP.10)

B.

Christ as the Man of Sorrows, with Saint Mary Magdalene and Saint John the Evangelist

Tempera on panel, 20.3 x 54.8 cm (8 x 21⅝ in.)
Courtauld Institute of Art Gallery, London
(Inv. no. P.1966.GP.10)

C.

Saint Catherine of Alexandria and Saint Agnes

Tempera on panel, 20.5 x 50.9 cm (8⅛ x 20 in.)
Courtauld Institute of Art Gallery, London
(Inv. no. P.1966.GP.10)

Sold in 1860 with an attribution to Starnina and a putative provenance from the church of the Carmine in Florence, these three panels were recognized by Roberto Longhi in 1940 as works from Fra Angelico's early career.[1] Their supposed Carmelite provenance must have been deduced from the traditional attribution to Starnina, who is known to have frescoed the Chapel of Saint Jerome in Santa Maria del Carmine. However, the inclusion of four female saints on the lateral panels and the substitution in the center panel of Saint Mary Magdalene for the Virgin, who normally occupies the space to the left of the Dead Christ in images of the Pietà or the Man of Sorrows, implies that this predella was painted for a female monastic community; that this community must have been Dominican is indicated by the prominence afforded Catherine of Siena, who was not canonized until 1461. As the style, aggregate width, and *pastiglia* decoration of the predella all conform to those of the San Pier Martire triptych (fig. 54), their common origin—first proposed by Umberto Baldini— seems certain. These panels, then, are the "*figure piccole assai*" Vasari described, when he saw the San Pier Martire

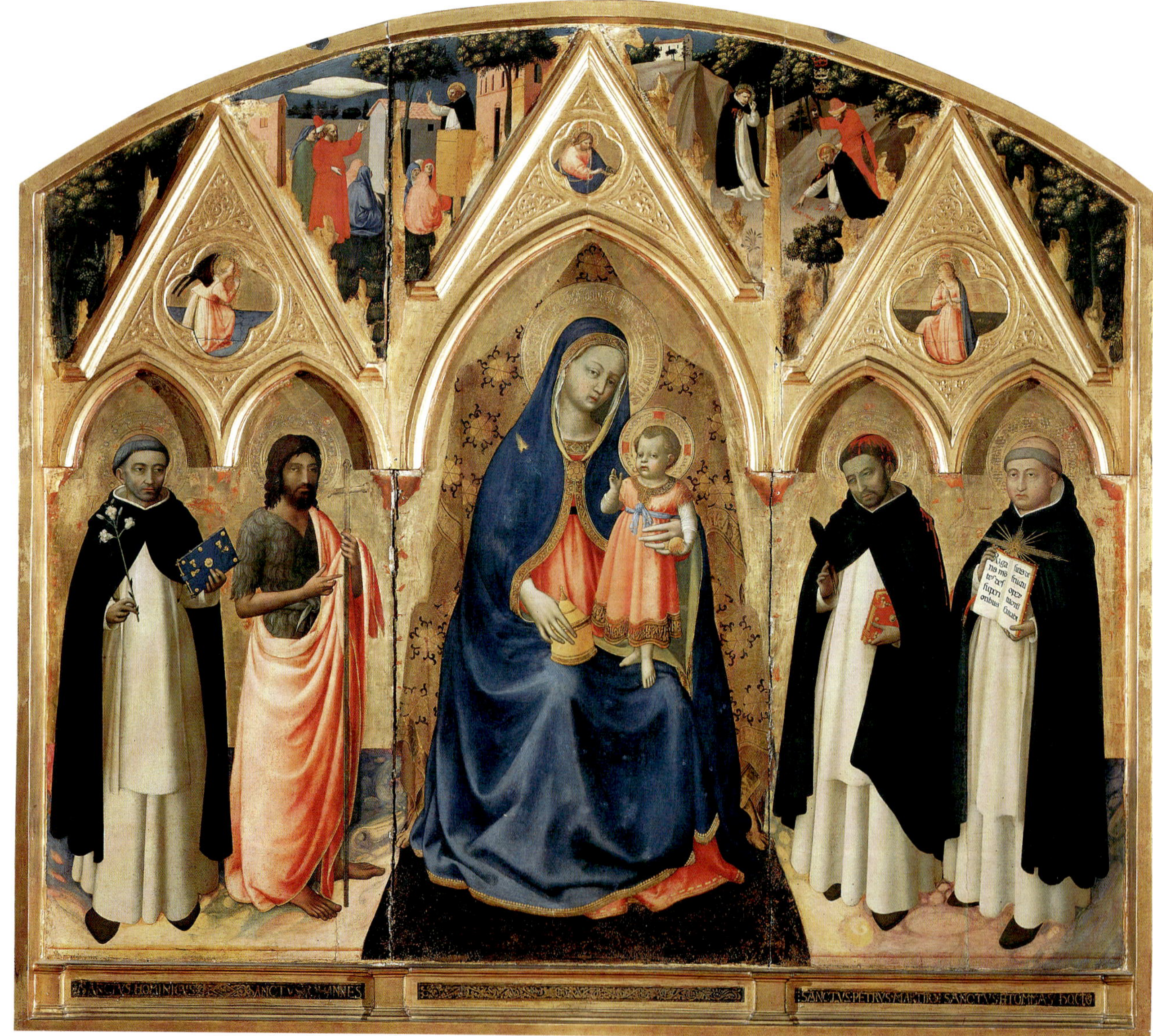

Figure 54. Fra Angelico. *Virgin and Child, with Saints Dominic, John the Baptist, Peter Martyr, and Thomas Aquinas* (San Pier Martire Triptych). About 1422–23. Museo di San Marco, Florence

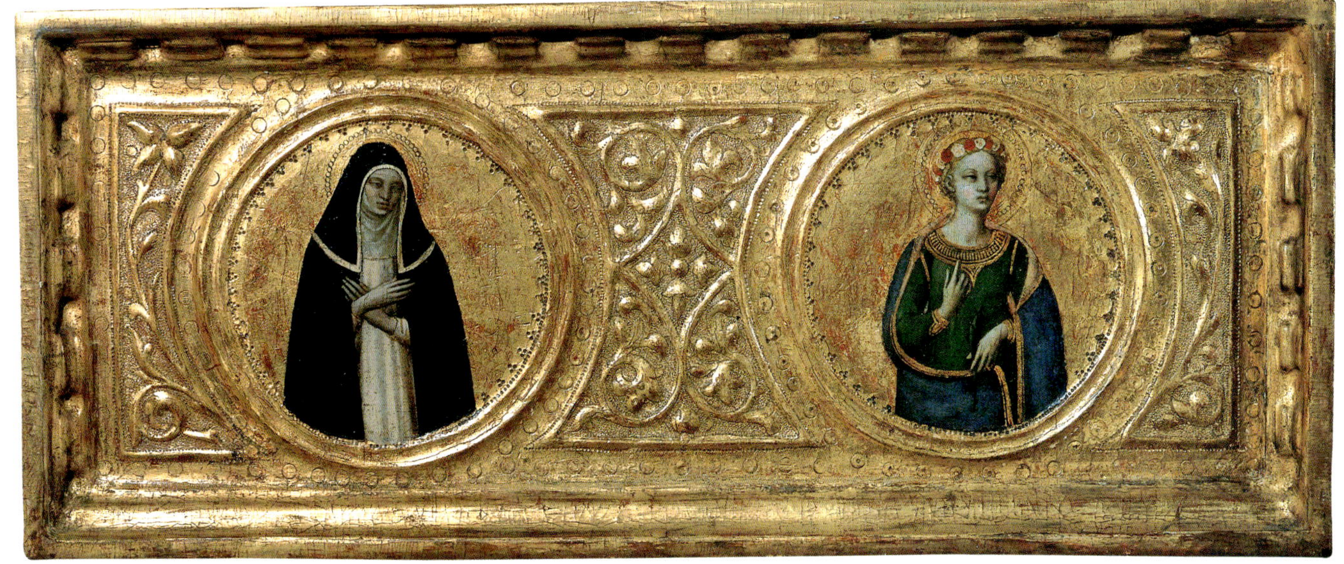

13: A

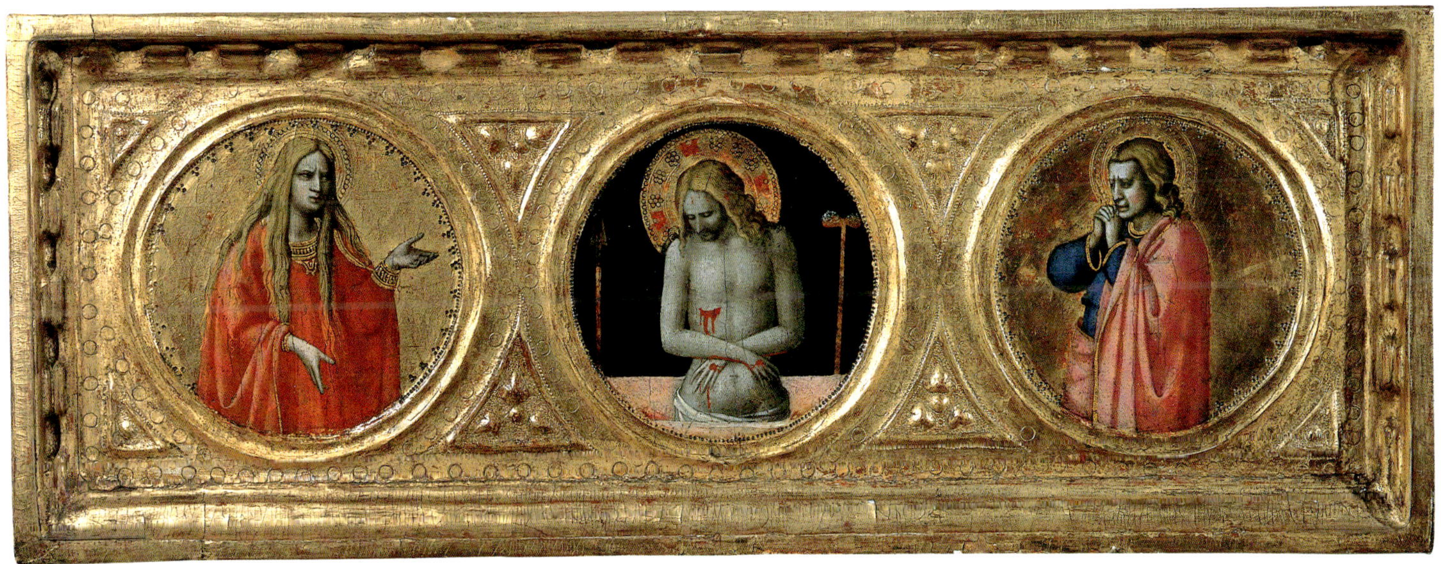

13: B

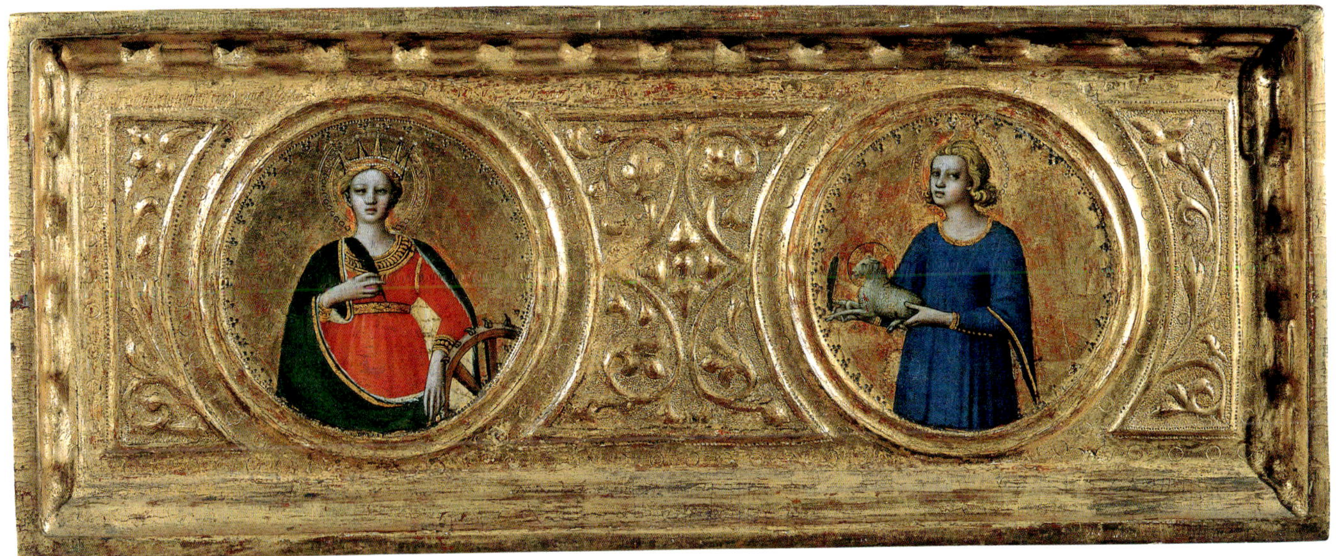

13: C

triptych reinstalled in the church of San Felice in Piazza after 1557.[2]

While a reconstruction of the original situation of these panels is relatively unproblematic, their dating remains a subject of little agreement. A consensus of opinion in accepting the altarpiece itself as an autograph work by Fra Angelico was reached only after its cleaning in preparation for the centenary exhibition of 1955 in Florence. While Angelico's authorship has not been doubted since then, the range of dates proposed for this work encompasses much of the decade of the 1420s and includes the suggestion that the small painted scenes of the Preaching and Martyrdom of Saint Peter Martyr in the spandrels of the frame might have been added later, perhaps in the 1440s, by Benozzo Gozzoli.[3] On documentary grounds, the execution of the altarpiece must be confined to the period between March 1417, when land was purchased from the nuns of San Gaggio to found a convent for Dominican sisters dedicated to Saint Peter Martyr,[4] and March 1429, when Fra Pietro di Antonio, Prior of San Domenico in Fiesole, recorded a residual payment of ten florins from "*Monasterium Sancti Petri Martiris adhuc tenetur dare de pictura tabule sue*."[5] For Pope-Hennessy this notice implied that the altarpiece was completed only shortly before, and he accepted 1428 as its relatively firm date.[6] In actuality, however, it is more likely that the painting, which stood on the high altar of the small church, was commissioned close to the period of the convent's founding, and that it was finished and installed not too long after 1421, when three sisters from the Pisan convent of San Domenico, Suor Margherita degli Spini, Suor Piera (widow of Niccola dell'Ossa), and Suor Maddalena di Bartolommeo di Scolaio Usimbardi, were transferred to Florence and became the first residents at San Pier Martire.[7]

The chief obstacle in recognizing 1421 or 1422 as a terminus a quo for the execution of the San Pier Martire altarpiece has been the persistent belief that the solid modeling of the figures and the unified spatial plan of the main panels reflect the young artist's response to the example of Masaccio, and therefore could not predate 1424 at the earliest. Yet, the sequence of Angelico's earlier works, as presented in this exhibition, demonstrates the artist's interest in spatial and tactile illusion well before the advent of Masaccio. Angelico's first overt response to Masaccio's pictorial innovations appears only after the San Domenico *Annunciation* altarpiece (now in the Prado), of about 1425. The San Pier Martire triptych is a significantly less mature work than the latter, as is evident in the exaggerated tilt of its painted marble pavement, the disproportionately large and imperfectly foreshortened feet of the standing saints, and the slight inconsistencies in the positioning of these figures in depth relative to each other. In all these respects it resembles the larger and more complex composition of the San Domenico high altarpiece, to which it is closely related in details of the figure types as well. Probably, Angelico was called upon to execute the San Pier Martire triptych immediately following the commission for the high altarpiece for his own convent church, and it is likely that he began work on it shortly after 1421.

The choice of saints to fill the predella of the San Pier Martire triptych may have been dictated by the presence of relics donated to the church perhaps from Santa Maria Novella. All the figures portrayed here also occur on the predella to the reliquary of the *Annunciation and the Adoration of the Magi* now in the Museo di San Marco—one of four reliquary panels commissioned for Santa Maria Novella by Fra Giovanni Masi before 1434 (see cat. 28). Painted labels below the half-length figures on that predella confirm the identities of the two saints in the left-hand panel from San Pier Martire as Catherine of Siena, shown with a halo notwithstanding the fact that she would not be canonized until forty years later, and Cecilia, although she is constantly referred to as Dorothy in published references to the Courtauld panels.[8] LK

1. Sold at Christie's, London, June 9–11, 1860, lots 32–34, from the collection of Samuel Woodburn; Christie's, London, June 12, 1863, lot 134, from the collection of the Reverend Walter Davenport-Bromley. See Longhi 1940 (1975 ed.), p. 38.
2. Baldini 1970, p. 86; Vasari (Milanesi ed.) 1878–85, vol. II, pp. 515–16.
3. M. Salmi (1950, pp. 146, 154) identifies them as by Gozzoli in the 1440s; L. Collobi-Ragghianti (1955 b, pp. 38, 46 n. 5) dates them about 1420–22; Longhi (1940) dated them about 1424–25, and Longhi later noted (1960 b, p. 60) that they were earlier than the San Domenico high altarpiece; M. Boskovits (1976 a, p. 30) dated them to the first half of the 1420s; and G. Bonsanti (1998, p. 124) dated them to 1429.
4. Richa 1762, vol. X, p. 202.
5. Orlandi 1954 a, p. 180.
6. Pope-Hennessy 1974, pp. 190–91.
7. Richa 1762, vol. X, p. 204.
8. The fact that all the saints represented on the predella to the Santa Maria Novella reliquary are female has not previously elicited comment. While there is no evidence that it might have been painted for San Pier Martire, and only later was transferred to Santa Maria Novella where it was seen by Vasari, the possibility cannot be dismissed. The first governor of San Pier Martire was Fra Andrea di Giovanni da Palaia from Santa Maria Novella, who may have brought some relics to the new church to enable the consecration of its main altar. See Richa 1762, vol. X, p. 203. Fra Andrea was succeeded by Fra Benedetto Domenichi and Fra Maestro Giovanni da Mantova, both residents of San Marco.

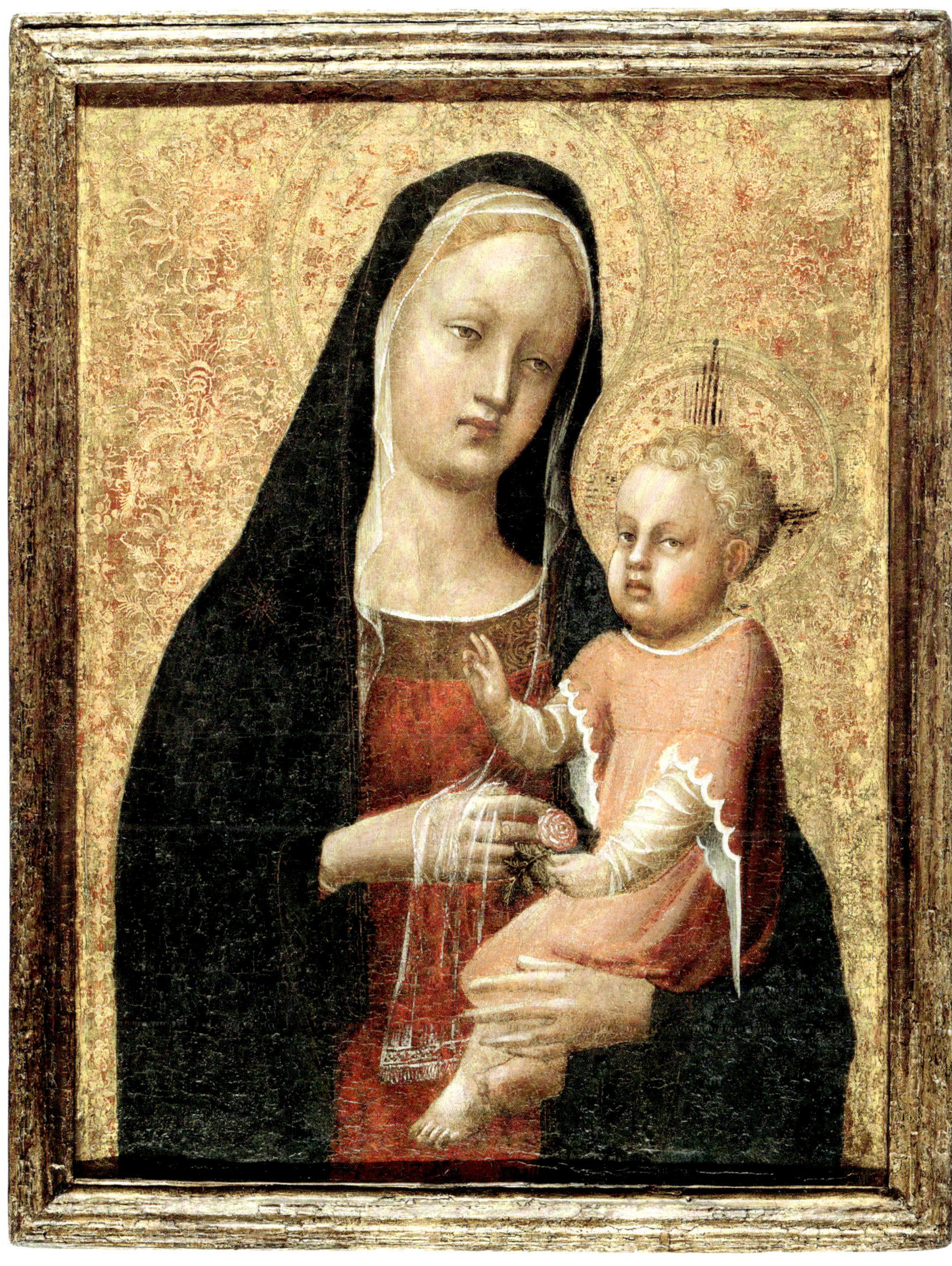

14

FRA ANGELICO

14.
Virgin and Child

Tempera on panel, transferred to Masonite, 40.4 x 30.8 cm (15⅞ x 12⅛ in.)
Fogg Art Museum, Harvard University Art Museums, Cambridge, Massachusetts. Bequest of Lucy Wallace Porter (1962.277)

This beautiful but rarely discussed panel, which was first recorded in the collection of Elia Volpi with an attribution to Masolino, was listed by Berenson as by an unidentified Florentine artist close to that master.[1] Everett Fahy initially recognized it as an early work by Fra Angelico, but later withdrew this suggestion in favor of the attribution to Zanobi Strozzi that had been proposed by Licia Collobi-Ragghianti.[2] Close examination of the panel, whose condition has been compromised by the transfer from its original support, reveals that its identification as an autograph work by Fra Angelico is, indeed, correct. The surface of the painting was flattened in the process of its transfer; the draperies of both figures are damaged, and a certain coarseness of their facial features is largely the result of restoration. Nevertheless, the impressive spatial effect of the Virgin's extended arms encircling the Child is still fully legible, while the refined modeling of the figures' faces and hands and the glancing highlights on the transparent veil lining the Virgin's cowl and trailing over her left hand (still

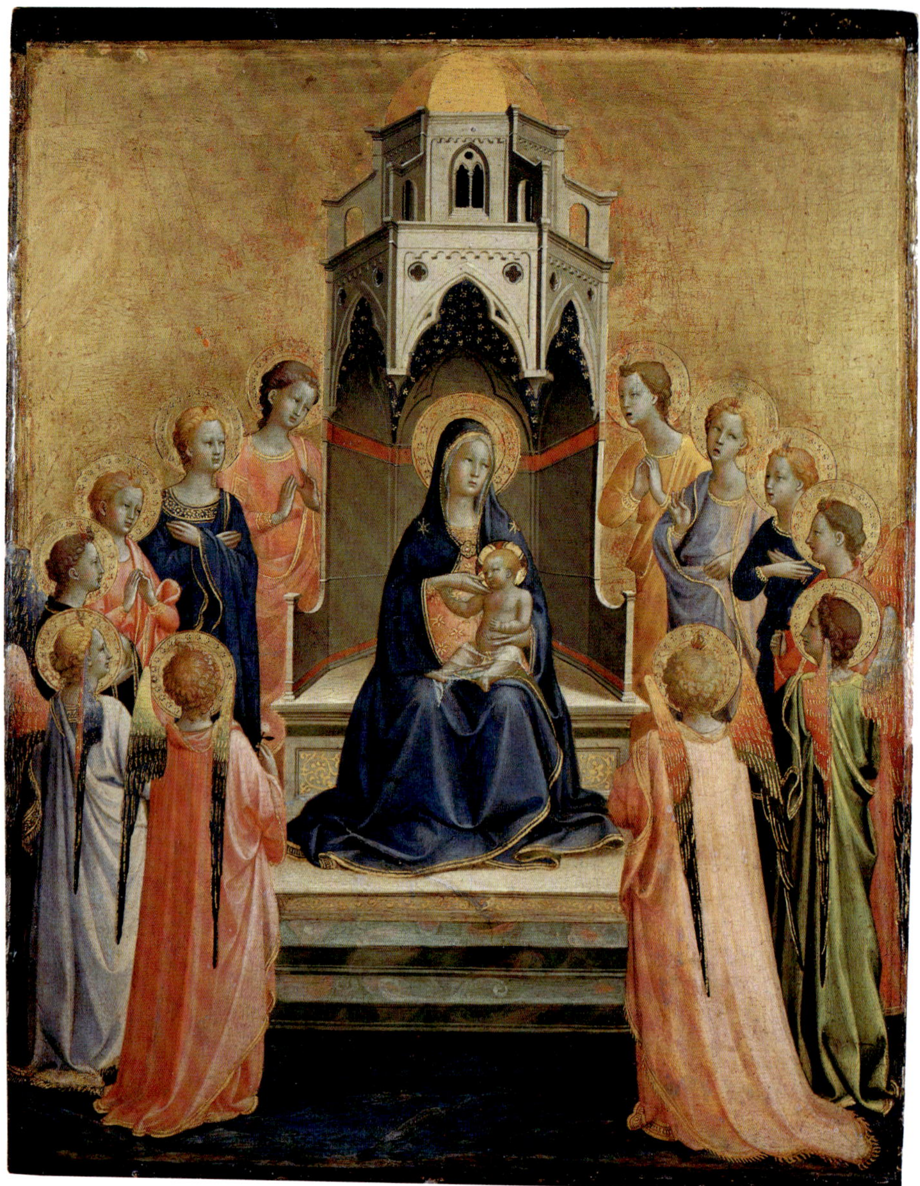

Figure 55. Fra Angelico. *Virgin and Child Enthroned, with Twelve Angels.* About 1421. Städelsches Kunstinstitut, Frankfurt

visible despite abrasion) indicate the original subtlety of the picture's design. Furthermore, the elaborate floral pattern tooled into the gold ground of the panel is reminiscent of—although more complex than—those employed in the brocade draperies of both the Pisa *Madonna* and the Rotterdam *Virgin and Child* (cat. 6), and is closely comparable in the sophisticated naturalism of its motifs to the pen-and-ink borders of the initials added, probably by the young Angelico, to an incomplete choir book on which he worked while in the studio of Lorenzo Monaco (cat. 1).

In his biography of Fra Angelico, Giorgio Vasari confessed his amazement that one man could have painted the many remarkable pictures that were to be seen in the houses of Angelico's Florentine compatriots, even taking into account that the artist's work spanned many years: "*Lavorò tante cose questo Padre che sono per le case de'cittadini di Firenze, che io resto qualche volta maravigliato, come tanto e tanto bene potesse, eziandio in molti anni, condurre perfettamente un uomo solo.*"[3] By way of example only he singled out three paintings in the collection of Bartolommeo Gondi: "*un quadro grande, un piccolo, ed una croce,*" and one in the collection of "*il molto reverendo Don Vincenzo Borghini, spedalingo degl'Innocenti, . . . una Nostra Donna piccola, bellissima.*"[4] The majority of images of the Virgin and Child painted by Angelico as objects of private devotion are relatively large tabernacles (see cat. 6, 11, 18, 31), but he did produce a limited number of more intimate pictures of this subject, one of which could well have been the painting owned by Vincenzo Borghini. The smallest of these represent the Virgin and Child enthroned with angels: three such pictures survive, all of them painted before 1440 (see cat. 20). Somewhat larger than these three but closely related in size among themselves are three other paintings that show the Virgin and Child alone, in half-length, the execution of which seems to have been spread over nearly the entire length of the artist's career. In shape, size, and composition, these panels suggest a type commonly encountered, from the thirteenth century on, as the left—or, less often, the right—valve of a diptych, but none of the examples by Fra Angelico can be paired with a companion scene and none shows certain evidence of the removal of hinges that would indicate such a function.

The earliest of Fra Angelico's experiments in this genre is certainly the *Virgin and Child Enthroned, with Twelve Angels,* now in Frankfurt (fig. 55)—a panel that seems to have been painted while the artist was at work on the high altarpiece for San Domenico in Fiesole (cat. 10). This must have been followed, at no great distance of time, by the Fogg *Virgin and Child,* a painting that shares its figure style and manner of rendering with the San Pier Martire triptych (cat. 13), but that seems to betray a first, tentative interest in the contemporary efforts of Masolino and the young Masaccio. In the immediately successive *Last Judgment* from Santa Maria degli Angeli (about 1424) and in the predella to the Prado *Annunciation* altarpiece (about 1425), the artist adopts a much more compact and classicizing figure canon. Along with the San Pier Martire triptych, the Fogg *Virgin and Child* probably can be dated about 1422 or 1423.

LK

1. Sold, American Art Association Galleries, New York, November 27, 1916, lot 991; Berenson 1963, vol. I, p. 217.
2. Collobi-Ragghianti 1955 b, p. 43. Fahy's original attribution is recorded in Pope-Hennessy 1974, p. 222, and his subsequent opinion, in Bowron 1990, p. 130.
3. Vasari (Milanesi ed.) 1878–85, vol. II, p. 512.
4. Ibid.

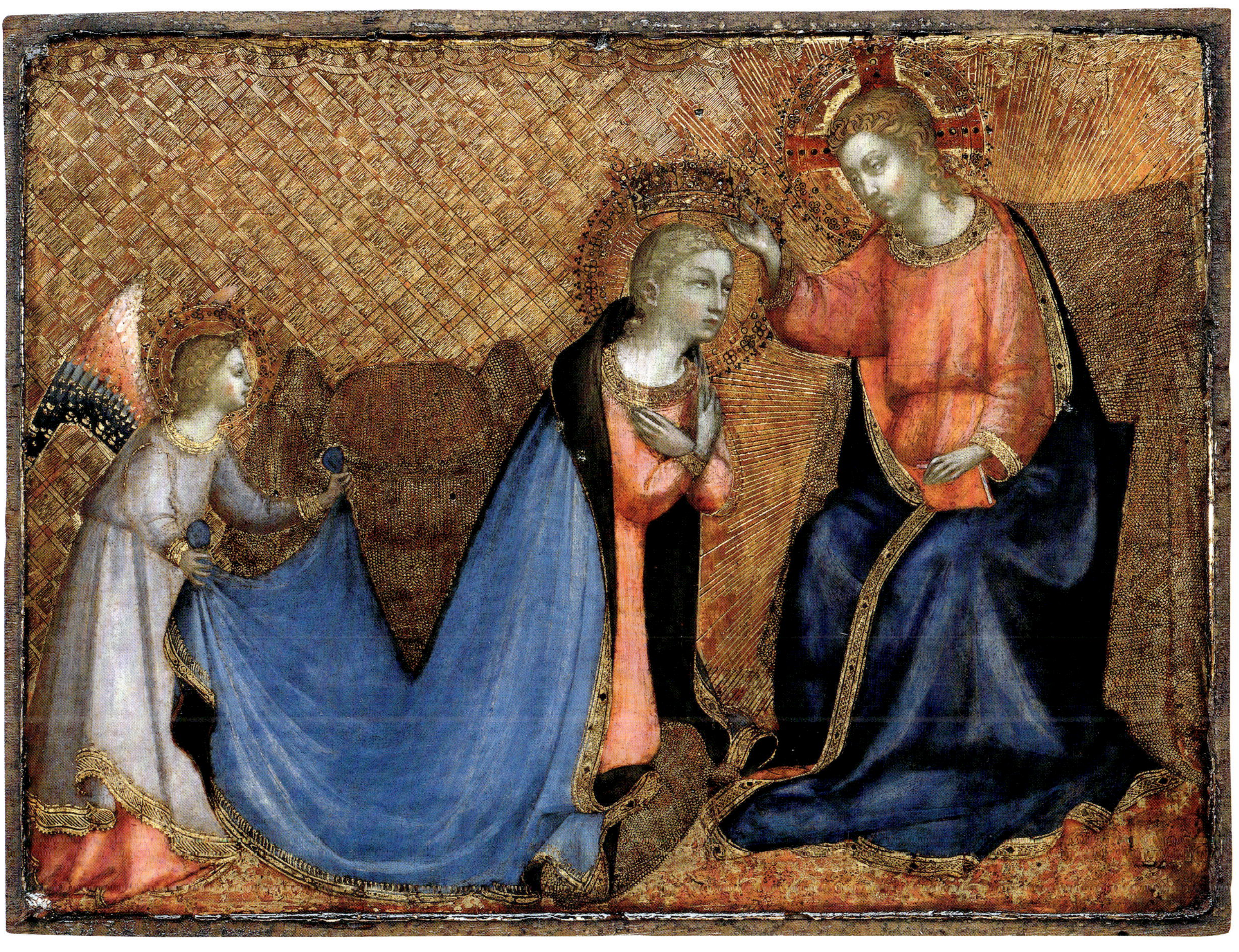

15

FRA ANGELICO

15.
The Coronation of the Virgin

Tempera on panel: overall, 28.3 x 38.4 cm (11⅛ x 15⅛ in.); picture surface, 27 x 37.2 cm (10⅝ x 14⅝ in.)
The Cleveland Museum of Art. Elisabeth Severance Prentiss Collection, 1944 (1944.79)

Although accepted as an early work of Fra Angelico by a number of authors,[1] this surprisingly complex panel is overlooked in much of the literature concerning the artist[2] in part because of its uneven state of preservation. It has been severely abraded across most of its surface, resulting in the loss of modeling glazes that originally softened the contrast between highlights and areas of shadow, while the faces of both principal figures are worn down to the level of the green underpaint and have lost nearly all their individual character. The blues of the mantles of Christ and the Virgin, furthermore, are thin and exaggeratedly intense in tone, and the draperies have thus lost most of the sense of volume once conveyed by the patterning of their folds. Unimpaired is the technical mastery apparent in the engraving of the gold ground to simulate a cloth hanging stretching across the full width of the scene in the back; the cloth-of-gold draped thrones of Christ and the Virgin—the latter seen frontally and the former in three-quarter profile; and the gilt cushion on which the Virgin kneels to receive the crown from her son. These details alone would be adequate to demonstrate Angelico's authorship of

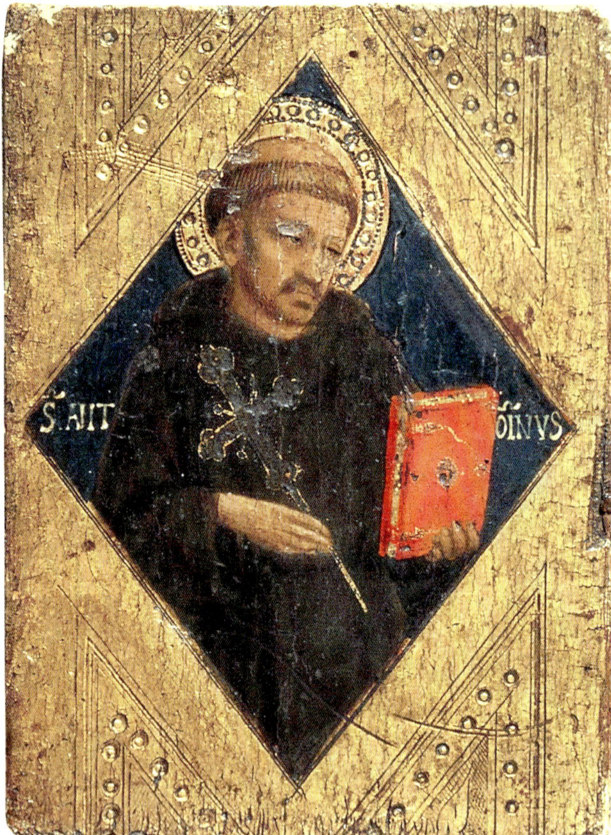

Figure 56. Fra Angelico. *Saint Francis*. About 1422–25. Collection F. M. Perkins, Assisi

the panel, but coupled with the delicacy with which the draperies of all three figures are painted and the ambitious spatial conceits of the composition, the attribution becomes all but self-evident. Dating the painting is a less easy task, given its present condition. However, the unmistakable relationship of the single well-preserved figure—the angel at the left—to counterparts in the Santa Maria degli Angeli *Last Judgment* or the Dominican missal (Ms. 558) in the Museo di San Marco suggests a likely date for this panel before 1424.

No less difficult to determine with certainty is the original function of the panel or the nature of the larger complex from which it might derive. The survival of a barb along all four edges of the paint surface indicates that the composition has not been altered in size or format, and the horizontal wood grain of the support suggests the probability that this panel was once part of a predella. The Coronation of the Virgin, however, is an unusual subject for a predella, and no other panels by Fra Angelico are known that might have accompanied this one in a narrative sequence. If this panel did come from a predella, it is not clear whether it might have been the only scene in an unusually tall one, below a tabernacle with the *Virgin and Child*, or whether it was flanked by other, now-lost scenes from the life of the Virgin or the legends of one or more saints and belonged to an as-yet-unidentified altarpiece. Supporting the former hypothesis is the existence of a small panel by Fra Angelico representing Saint Francis (Perkins Collection, Assisi; fig. 56)[3] that is not very different in style from the Cleveland *Coronation of the Virgin* and may well have been painted on the pilaster base of a devotional tabernacle, alongside a single-panel predella. It is difficult to reconstruct the original height of this panel, however, for although it is unaltered in width, it has been severely reduced at both top and bottom, and, furthermore, it is hard to imagine the saint, who is depicted looking slightly downward, flanking the present scene.

The thinning paint layers of the Cleveland *Coronation of the Virgin* have made visible to the naked eye some of Fra Angelico's very loose and confident underdrawing, especially in the robes of Christ at the right. These reveal a number of changes to the design of this figure, which at first was intended to be shown in left profile, closing off the composition as a symmetrical accent to the ministering angel on the opposite side. As finally painted, Angelico rotated Christ in space to form a right angle (as viewed from above) with the figure of the Virgin kneeling before him, creating a pronounced movement backward and forward in depth more in keeping with the processional nature of this composition, which departs from traditional, static images of the Coronation that show the Virgin seated alongside her son. Angelico reverted to this more iconic formula in three later versions of the subject: a reliquary panel (fig. 81), painted sometime about 1427 or 1428, from Santa Maria Novella (now in the Museo di San Marco, Florence); an altarpiece (fig. 74), painted between 1432 and 1434, from San Domenico, Fiesole (now in the Musée du Louvre, Paris); and another, smaller altarpiece (fig. 75), painted after 1434, from Santa Maria Nuova (now in the Galleria degli Uffizi, Florence).

LK

1. Longhi, in a written opinion, 1924; Boskovits 1976a, p. 38; Bonsanti 1998, p. 115; Spike 1996, p. 259 ("but the question remains open").
2. Pope-Hennessy (1952, p. 197) assigns the painting to an artist close to Arcangelo di Cola da Camerino, and it is catalogued by E. de Fernandez-Gimenez, in Cleveland Museum of Art 1974, pp. 39–40, as "Workshop of Fra Angelico." It is ignored in most biographies of the artist published since the panel's discovery in 1924.
3. L. Kanter and P. Palladino, in Morello and Kanter 1999, pp. 108–9.

16.

A.
Saint Francis and a Bishop Saint [Zenobius ?]

Tempera and gold on panel, 52.7 x 23.2 cm (20¾ x 9⅛ in.)
J. Paul Getty Museum, Los Angeles (Acc. no. 92.PB.111.1)

B.
Saint John the Baptist and Saint Dominic

Tempera and gold on panel, 52.7 x 21 cm (20¾ x 8¼ in.)
J. Paul Getty Museum, Los Angeles (Acc. no. 92.PB.111.2)

C.
The Annunciatory Angel

Tempera and gold on panel, 18.1 x 13.5 cm (7⅛ x 5⁵⁄₁₆ in.)
Yale University Art Gallery, New Haven (1959.15.6a)

D.
The Virgin Annunciate

Tempera and gold on panel, 18.4 x 17.8 cm (7¼ x 7 in.)
Yale University Art Gallery, New Haven (1959.15.6c)

The attribution of each of these pairs of panels to the young Fra Angelico was first proposed by Miklós Boskovits,[1] although their reconstruction as the wings of a single triptych (fig. 57) was only recognized later.[2] In addition to an affinity of style that links the Getty and Yale fragments, the four panels are the same thickness, their reverse sides are identically painted, and X-radiographs reveal a continuity of wood grain between the top and bottom elements of each pair. While it has not yet been possible to identify a plausible candidate for the missing central panel of the Getty/Yale triptych among the surviving works from this period by Fra Angelico—or even to specify its subject—physical evidence suggests that it was probably between eighty and ninety centimeters in height and approximately forty-five centimeters in width. It may also be presumed to have included an image of the Blessing Redeemer on its pinnacle, completing the scene of the Annunciation in the pinnacles of the wings.

A case has been made to date the Getty/Yale triptych to about 1424, based on the presumption that the San Domenico high altarpiece was painted only shortly before that. If, however, the execution of at least a large part of the San Domenico altarpiece were moved back to the beginning of the decade, as argued above (see cat. 10), the date of the Getty/Yale triptych would be slightly earlier as well. The principal stylistic references in these panels are largely to the predella of the San Domenico altarpiece, where the closest parallels for both the figure types and the manner of their realization in space are to be found, and to the illuminations in the Dominican missal (Ms. 558) in the Museo di San Marco. The highly sophisticated and naturalistically observed details in both the Getty and the Yale fragments, such as the suggestion of a step before the Virgin's throne barely visible through the folds of her robe or the textures of the fabrics worn by the standing saints, juxtaposed with conceptual lapses such as the inaccurate foreshortening of the feet of Saints Francis, John the Baptist, and Dominic, argue that this triptych must anticipate Angelico's more consistently successful efforts in such paintings as the Santa Maria degli Angeli *Last Judgment* and the Prado *Annunciation*, which may be dated about 1424 and 1425, respectively.

As the Getty/Yale triptych was painted soon after Angelico entered the convent of San Domenico in Fiesole, the question of the identity of its patron naturally arises. The identity of the bishop saint on the left wing—who may be presumed to indicate the name or patronymic of the triptych's original owner—is unclear. While this figure bears no attributes that might specifically identify him, in practice very few holy bishops were frequently invoked as name saints in Early Renaissance Florence. The two such figures most commonly represented are Nicholas and Zenobius (see cat. 12). Saint Nicholas has a well-established iconography that seldom varies in Italian painting, regardless of region or period, and which is conspicuously absent here. Zenobius often has an embroidered fleur-de-lis on his robes or liturgical apparel (a reference to his role as a protector saint of Florence), but it cannot be said that he ever acquired a fixed iconography in Italian painting, and thus he could easily be the figure depicted here.

If the bishop saint can be identified as Zenobius, there is the possibility that this triptych was commissioned from Angelico by Fra Giovanni di Zanobi Masi, one of the artist's few early

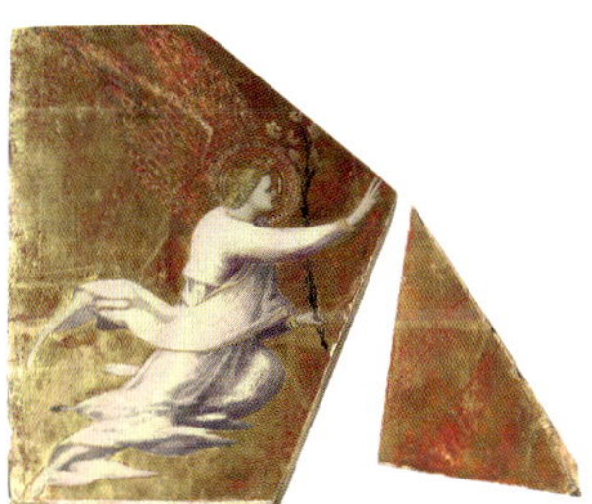

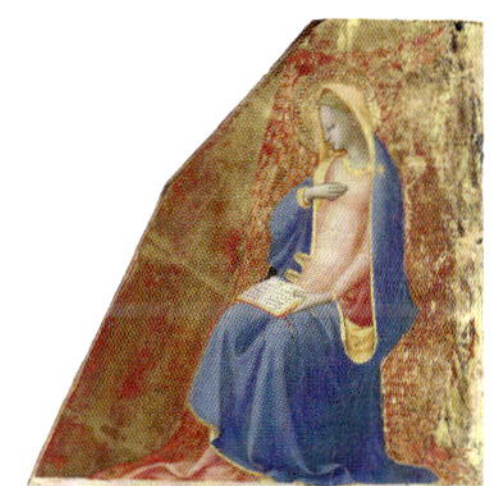

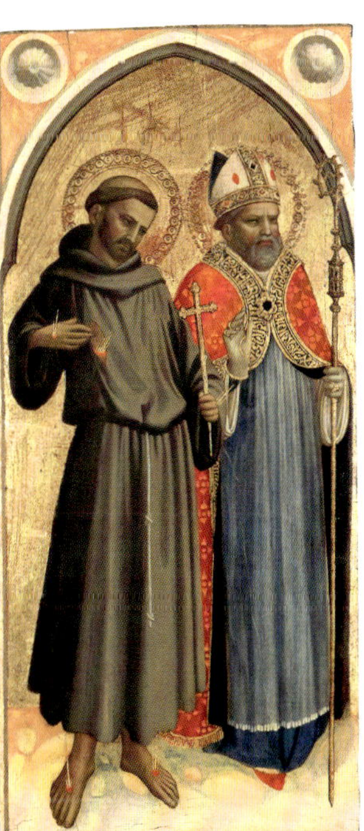

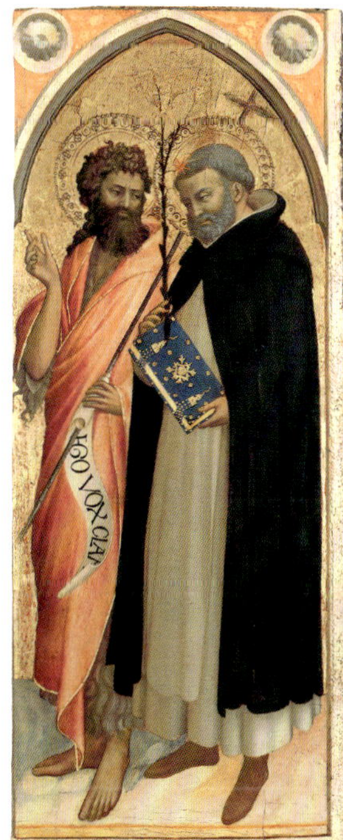

Figure 57. The Getty and Yale panels reconstructed as the wings of a triptych

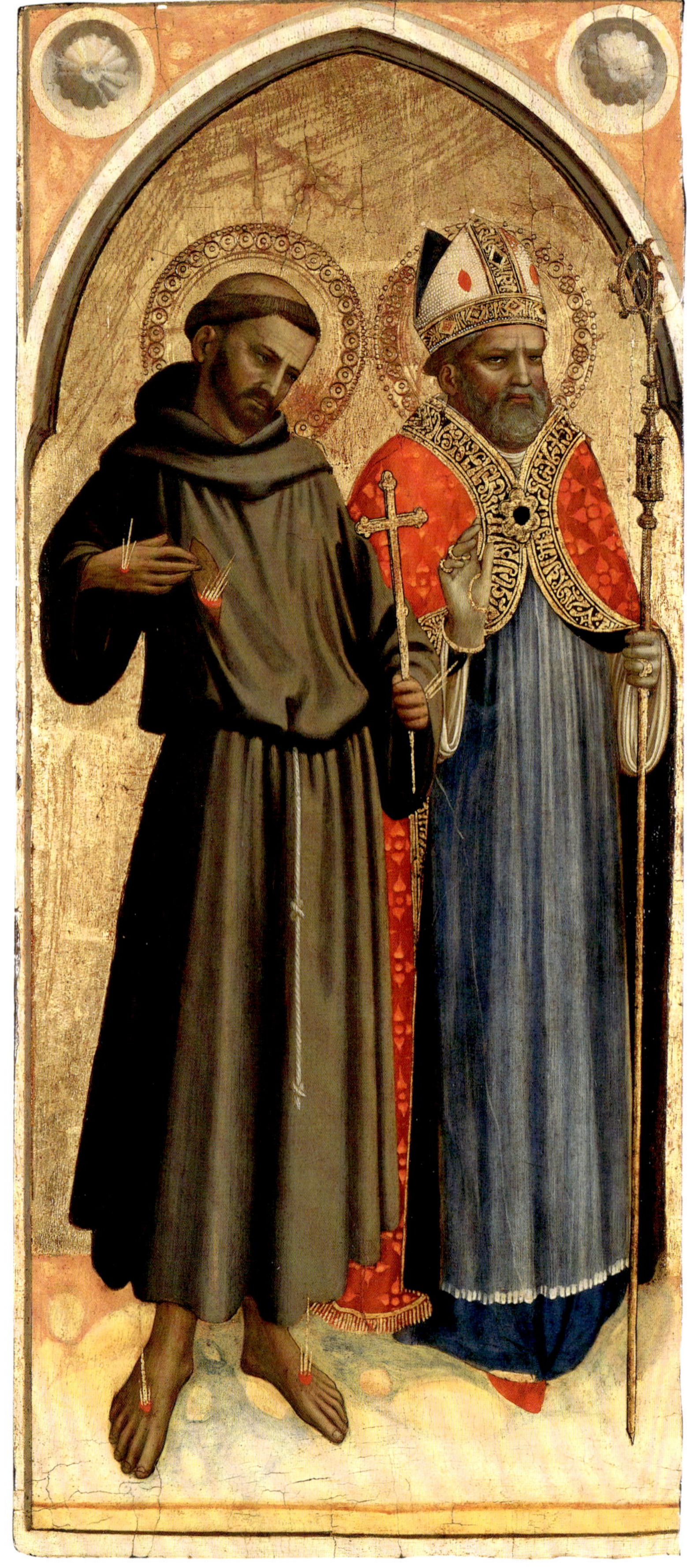

16: A

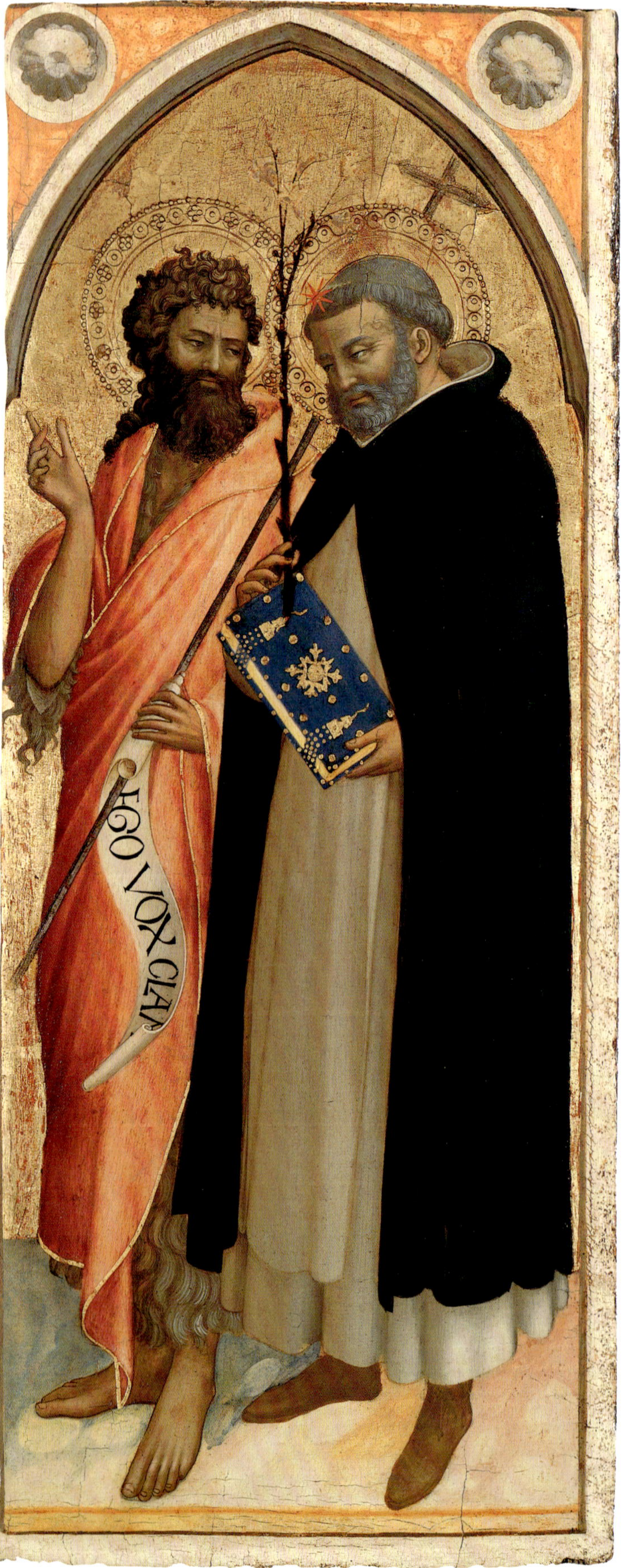

16: B

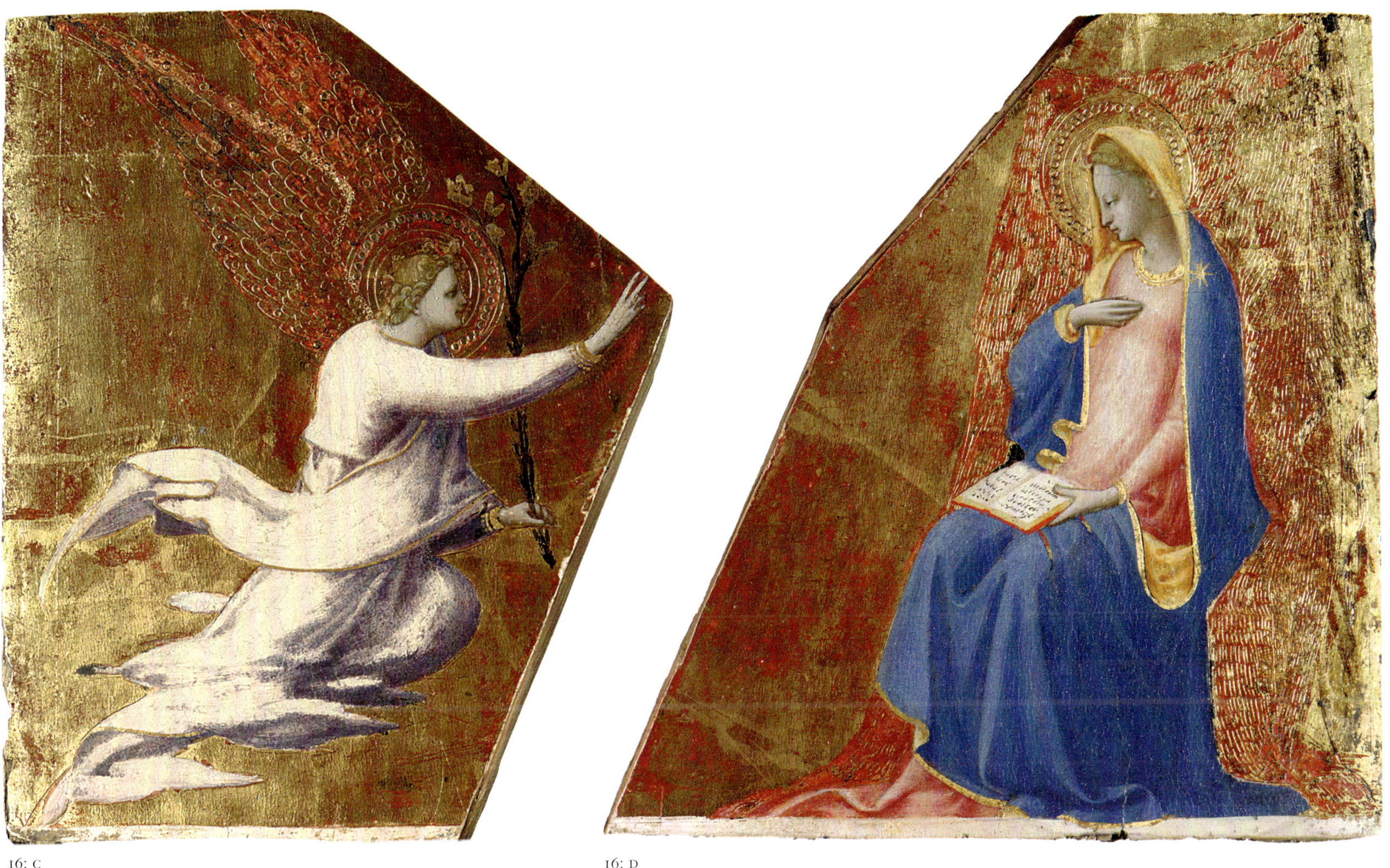

16: C

16: D

patrons known to us by name. The Masi were conspicuously wealthy members of Florence's commercial bourgeoisie, their fortune derived from the ships that they owned and leased to Florentine merchants.[3] Fra Giovanni di Zanobi, who chose to pursue a religious life rather than business, passed his novitiate in the company of Antonino Pierozzi (later, Bishop of Florence and canonized as Saint Antoninus). He was a founding member of the Dominican Observant community at San Domenico in Fiesole in 1419, after which he returned to the Conventual community at Santa Maria Novella and became a prominent spiritual leader there, serving in 1424 as sacristan.[4] It was Fra Giovanni di Zanobi Masi who, on the testimony of Richa, commissioned the four reliquaries for the sacristy of Santa Maria Novella (see cat. 28), but it is possible—given his family's great private wealth, to which he had access—that these reliquaries represented neither the exclusive focus nor the full extent of his patronage of the young Dominican painter.

LK

1. Boskovits 1983, pp. 11–23; Boskovits 1976 a, p. 38.
2. Kanter 2001 a, pp. 13–39.
3. Ciabani 1992, p. 78.
4. Orlandi 1955 b, pp. 167–71.

17.
The Nativity

Tempera on panel, 28.3 x 16.5 cm (11⅛ x 6½ in.)
The Minneapolis Institute of Arts. Bequest of Miss Tessie Jones in memory of Herschel V. Jones (68.41.8)

This little-known panel was first published as the work of Fra Angelico in 1924, when it was in the collection of Marczell von Nemes in Munich.[1] Acquired shortly afterward by the Minneapolis collector Herschel V. Jones—and, thereafter, virtually inaccessible to European scholars—it quickly passed out of the canon of Angelico's widely accepted autograph works. Licia Collobi-Ragghianti included it in her study of the panel paintings of Zanobi Strozzi,[2] and John Pope-Hennessy dismissed it as the work of an imitator of Fra Angelico, a derivation from the same scene on the Annunziata Silver Chest (fig. 58).[3] An attribution to Fra Angelico himself was revived in 1976 by Miklós Boskovits, who regarded the Minneapolis *Nativity* as a typical example of Angelico's style in the decade of the 1420s. This opinion has been confirmed more recently by Giorgio Bonsanti, Everett Fahy, and Carl Strehlke.[4]

Based on its size, shape, and subject, Boskovits suggested that the Minneapolis *Nativity* probably was painted as the wing of a portable triptych—possibly the same one from which the *Annunciation* pinnacles (cat. 16 C, D) in the Yale University Art Gallery were excised. Although it can now be shown that the Yale pinnacles came from a different complex, the assumption that the Minneapolis *Nativity* probably was once the wing of a small triptych seems likely to be correct. The panel retains its original thickness and bears no traces of hinges at either side, but the partial remains of a barb along the left and right edges of the paint surface coupled with visible evidence of trimming along the lateral edges indicate that an engaged frame has been cut away, and any hinges that might have secured the panel to another one would have been affixed to this frame molding. The bottom edge of the paint surface, while damaged, seems also to retain partial remnants of a barb, implying that the composition is largely complete in this direction as well. There is extensive damage and repair in the gilding across the top of the picture surface, however, eliminating any evidence of the possible vertical extension of the picture field.

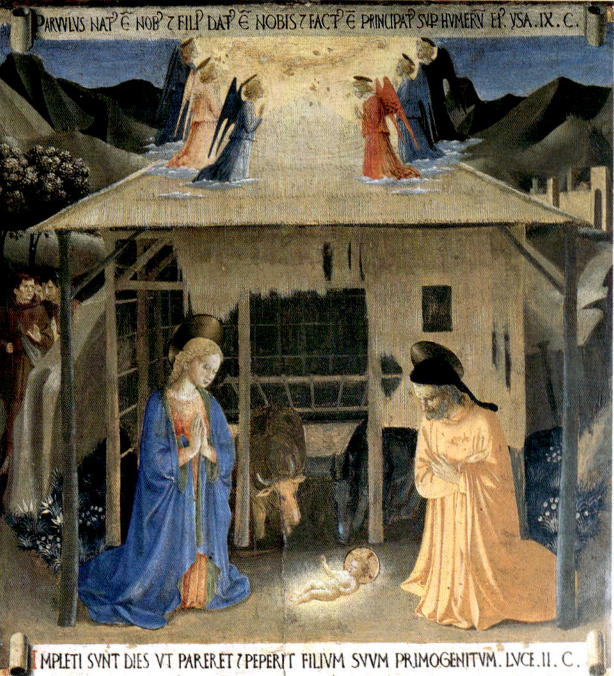

Figure 58. Fra Angelico. *The Nativity* (from the Santissima Annunziata Silver Chest). About 1448–50. Museo di San Marco, Florence

The logical point of comparison for evaluating the composition of the Minneapolis *Nativity,* as John Pope-Hennessy contended, is the *Nativity* scene on the Annunziata Silver Chest (fig. 58). Both compositions are centralized around the recumbent form of the Christ Child on the ground beneath the projecting straw roof of a rustic shed, with the Virgin and Saint Joseph symmetrically disposed on either side of him. In both scenes, a glory of angels hovers at the top, over the roof of the shed and directly above the Christ Child, and a hilly landscape completes the visible portion of the scene in the middle ground and the far distance, at the upper left and right. As the Silver Chest *Nativity* is more nearly square in format than the pronouncedly vertical composition in Minneapolis, it includes the figures of the shepherds appearing from around the shoulder of an outcropping of rock behind the Virgin at the left, whereas the Minneapolis scene alludes to their presence only through a miniaturist vignette in the distant background, in the upper-left corner. The spatial structure of the scene on the Silver Chest, based on a semi-circular arrangement of the figures within a centrally foreshortened cube, is much more sophisticated than that of the Minneapolis *Nativity,* where the figures are disposed along a diagonal vaguely situated in front of a similar cube. This difference, however, does not imply that the latter is a weak derivation of the former; it is typical of the development of Angelico's interest in illusionistic pictorial space, before and after his initial exposure to the experiments of Masaccio and Brunelleschi on the walls of the Brancacci Chapel. Such naturalistic details in the Minneapolis *Nativity* as the rope ties securing the ends of the projecting canes that define the sides of the shed, as well as the studied irregularity of those canes and of the rough-cut supporting poles to which they are attached, can only be ascribed to Angelico himself—and, specifically, to a moment close in time to the date of the predella of the San Domenico *Annunciation* altarpiece (now in the Museo del Prado).

A comparison of the Minneapolis *Nativity* with the scene of *The Adoration of the Magi* on the predella of the San Domenico

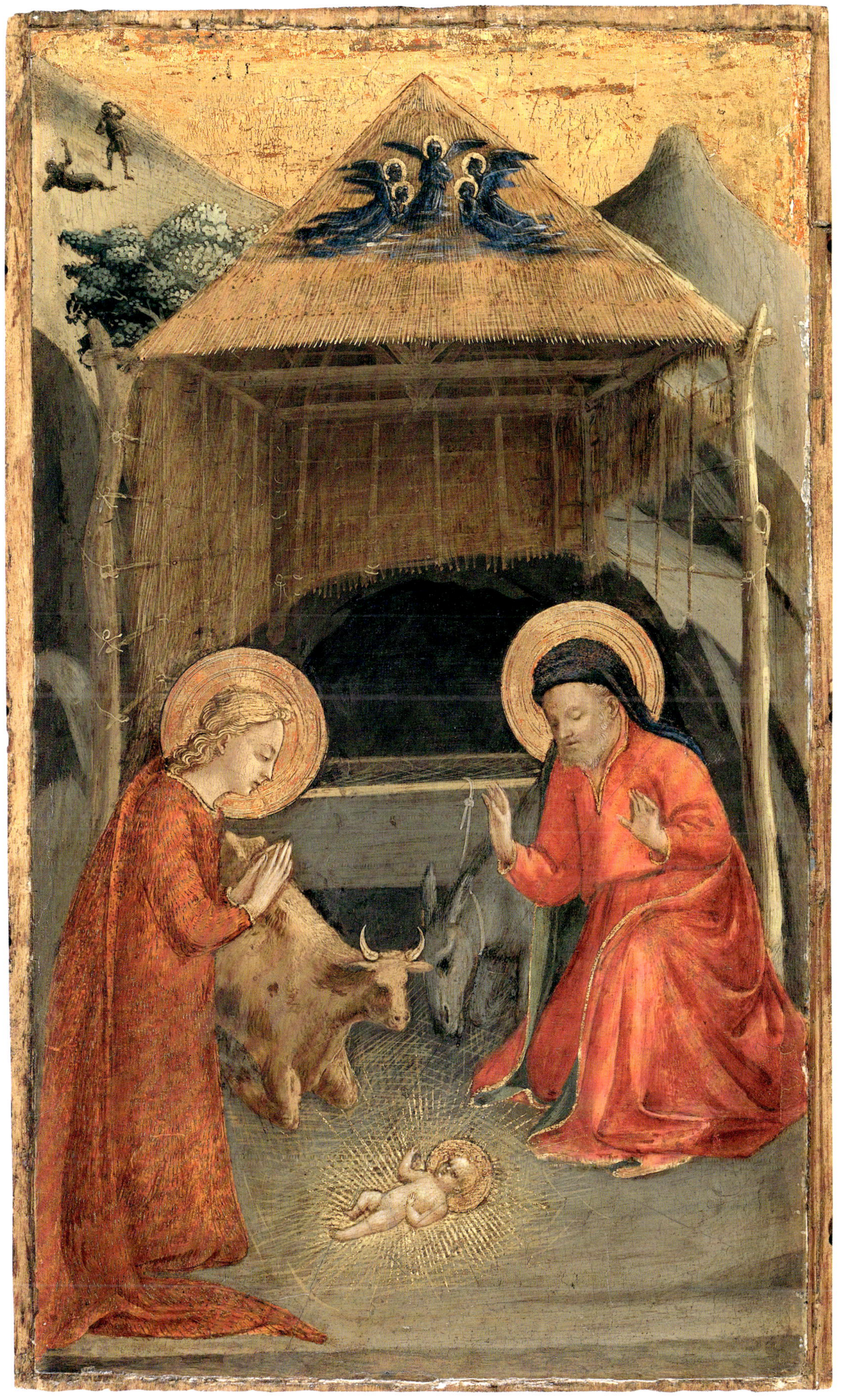

17

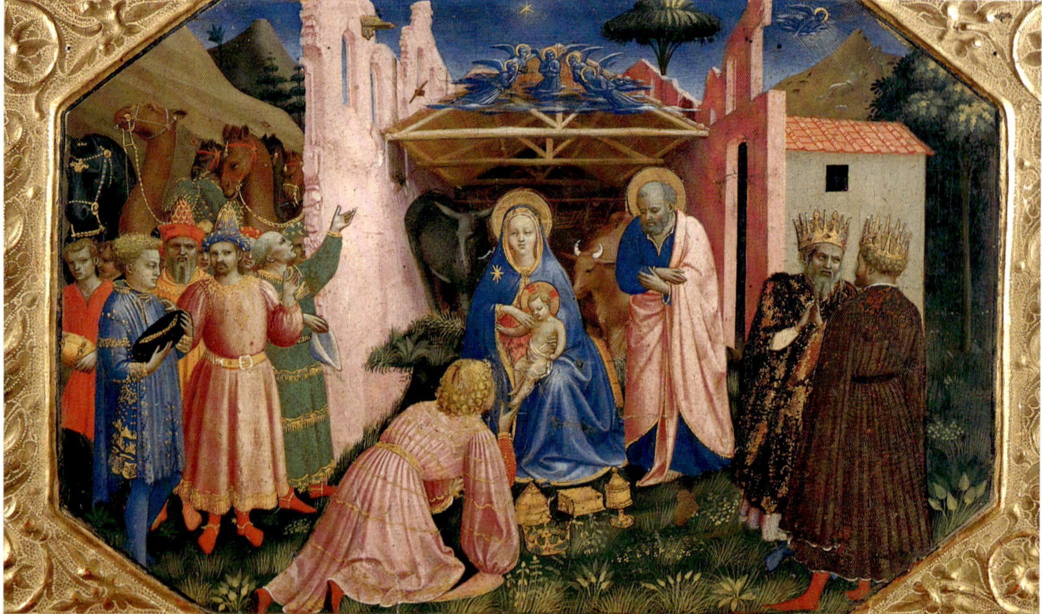

Figure 59. Fra Angelico. *The Adoration of the Magi*. About 1425–26. Museo Nacional del Prado, Madrid

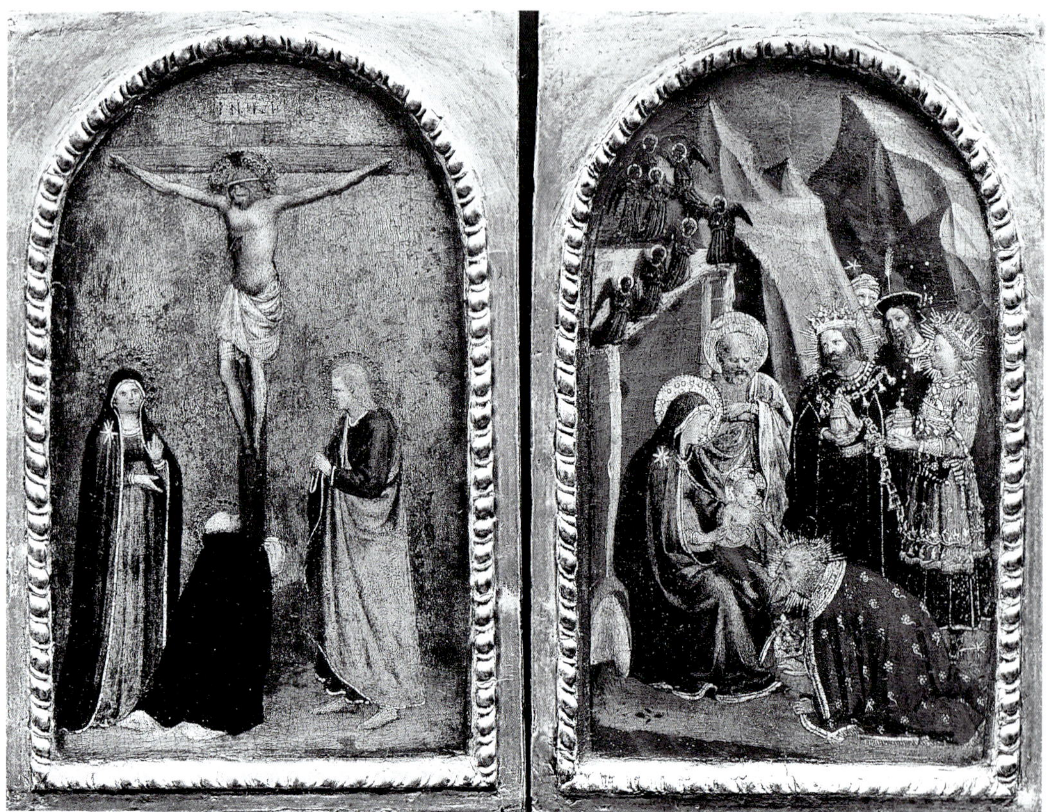

Figure 60. Fra Angelico. *The Crucifixion* and *The Adoration of the Magi*. About 1425. Formerly, Collection Marczell von Nemes, Munich (1927)

Annunciation (fig. 59) reveals a nearly identical compositional plan in both, although elaborated in a horizontal format in the case of the *Adoration*. The figure types in the two paintings are closely related, as is the spatial structure and the microscopic attention to detail in depicting the setting. An argument has been made for dating the *Annunciation* altarpiece to 1425—a date that seems accurate for the Minneapolis *Nativity* as well. Shortly afterward, undoubtedly in response to Masaccio's accomplishments in the Carmine, Fra Angelico's staging of narrative becomes more simplified: still unremittingly naturalistic, but purged of the dense patterning and detail that may well have been inspired by the unveiling at Santa Trinita in 1423 of Gentile da Fabriano's *Adoration of the Magi* altarpiece for Palla Strozzi. In paintings postdating 1426, such as the five scenes from the legend of Saint Francis from the Franciscan altarpiece of 1429 (cat. 24) or the five panels of the *Saint Lucy* predella (cat. 25), the artist employs some of the same perspectival devices he experimented with here but they are realized with greater subtlety. His figures are grander, more statuesque, and more successfully integrated into the architectural spaces they occupy rather than disposed before them. All this must be seen as a direct response to Masaccio's influence—a response that would be tempered in the following decade by a gradual but increasinlgy mature resumption of his own intuitive sense of descriptive naturalism.

Another, unpublished painting by Fra Angelico of the *Adoration of the Magi* (fig. 60) was also in the Marczell von Nemes collection, but at a later date (1927) than the panel now in Minneapolis.[5] This *Adoration*—which was part of a diptych that included a much-damaged *Crucifixion*—must date from only a year or two earlier than the Prado altarpiece and the Minneapolis *Nativity*. It is possible that the Minneapolis painting similarly was intended to be part of a diptych, rather than the wing of a folding triptych, but until other panels are identified that might have been associated with it in a single structure, the question must remain unresolved.

LK

1. Schottmüller 1924, p. 242.
2. Collobi-Ragghianti 1950b, p. 463.
3. Pope-Hennessy 1974, p. 229: "the panel, though influenced by Angelico . . . originates outside his shop." The painting is illustrated as figure 92, alongside the *Nativity* by Zanobi Strozzi in The Metropolitan Museum of Art (cat. 51), but the captions for the two paintings are reversed.
4. Boskovits 1976a, pp. 41, 43, 53 n. 45; Bonsanti 1998, p. 117; Everett Fahy (1980; 1996) and Carl Strehlke (1992), in notes in the archives of The Minneapolis Institute of Arts.
5. Annotation on photographs in the Richard Offner Photo Archive at the Institute of Fine Arts, New York University.

18.
Virgin and Child, with Five Angels

Tempera on panel: overall, 98.6 x 49.2 cm (38⅞ x 19⅜ in.); picture surface, 95 x 46.5 cm (37⅜ x 18¼ in.)
Museu Nacional d'Art de Catalunya, Barcelona. Thyssen-Bornemisza Collection

The iconography of the Madonna of Humility, in which the Virgin is shown seated on a cushion placed directly on the ground, was first taken up by Fra Angelico in one of his earliest surviving paintings, the *Virgin and Child, with Four Angels,* in the State Hermitage Museum, Saint Petersburg (fig. 11). In that painting, which probably can be dated shortly before 1417, the cushion rests on an elaborately brocaded carpet that extends continuously from the "horizon" to the foreground, following a model employed on several occasions by Angelico's master, Lorenzo Monaco. Two small angels kneel in lost profile in front of the Virgin, and two more hover in adoration at either side and, notionally, behind her, simultaneously complementing the line of her silhouette, which is traced against the gold ground of the panel, and establishing the corners of the box-like space in which she is contained. For the Thyssen panel, painted perhaps ten years later, Angelico's model shifted decisively from the Late Gothic masterpieces of Lorenzo Monaco to the revolutionary new style of Masaccio. Here, the Virgin's cushion is situated on a raised marble step or dais, and its gilt and glazed pattern is expertly foreshortened and seen from a lower viewing point than that adopted in the Hermitage panel (in which pictorial space is constructed empirically, not perspectivally). Three angels hold up an embroidered cloth of honor behind the Virgin—a device not unknown in fourteenth-century Florentine painting but in this specific configuration obviously a direct reference to Masaccio's *Virgin and Child with Saint Anne* in the Uffizi. Two music-making angels are seated in the foreground: the one on the left, in three-quarter profile, is playing a portative organ, and the angel on the right, shown frontally, is strumming a lute.[1] Their heads are tilted upward and their eyes are rolled back as they glance toward the Virgin and her son. The Christ Child stands on his mother's raised left knee, leaning on her shoulder and pressing his forehead against her cheek as he proffers her a lily, symbolic of her purity. The Virgin holds a vase of red and white roses in her right hand.

The Thyssen *Madonna* was among the first of Fra Angelico's paintings to enter an English collection, having belonged to Princess Charlotte of Wales not later than 1816, when it possibly was presented to her as a wedding gift by her father, King George IV.[2] Upon the death of Princess Charlotte in 1817, the painting remained in the possession of her husband, Leopold of Saxe-Coburg—from 1831, King of Belgium—and was sold by his son, Leopold II, in 1909, at which time it entered the collection of J. Pierpont Morgan in New York.[3] It was acquired by Baron Thyssen in 1935 from The Pierpont Morgan Library, and only recently has been on public display: first at the Museu Thyssen at Pedralbes, and now in the Museu Nacional d'Art de Catalunya. While scholars have always been aware of its existence, opinions regarding its authenticity and date have vacillated widely due in large measure to the painting's relative inaccessibility. A thorough summary of these opinions was included by Miklós Boskovits in his exemplary catalogue of Italian paintings in the Thyssen Collection;[4] the author offered a vigorous and fully justified defense of the painting's autograph status and proposed a date for it between about 1433 and 1435, contemporary with the Linaiuoli tabernacle (see cat. 29).

Although accepted in the latest literature on the artist, a date in the mid-1430s for the Thyssen *Madonna* is problematic. The evidence adduced by Boskovits in support of this contention is on the one hand subject to alternative interpretations and on the other based on an unconvincing late dating of such paintings by Angelico as the Santa Maria degli Angeli *Last Judgment,* once thought to be a documented work of 1431 but now recognized as a considerably earlier effort, possibly from about 1424 (see p. 80). The figure types employed in the Thyssen *Madonna,* with their short, rounded proportions, do not occur in any paintings securely datable in the fourth decade of the fifteenth century. They are, instead, encountered regularly, and exclusively, in paintings reasonably situated between about 1425 and 1428/29—a dating that also conforms better to the type of Gothicizing capital letters used by the artist to embellish the Virgin's halo (inscribed, AVE MARIA GRATIA PLENA), the border of her mantle, or the Child's halo (inscribed, ALFA/OM[EGA]).[5] Only the round-arched, "Renaissance" format of the Thyssen *Madonna* and its sophisticated depiction of space might be said to justify a later date, but assuming that Angelico's model for this painting was, indeed, Masaccio's Sant'Anna Meterza altarpiece of 1424, it becomes difficult to explain why a full decade might have passed before Angelico formulated a response to this example when he otherwise appears to have reacted almost immediately to the younger painter's innovations.

A more compelling argument can be advanced for accepting the Thyssen picture among Angelico's earliest experiments with this compositional model, immediately following the Prado *Annunciation* altarpiece and the Alba *Madonna* of about 1426—the artist's first clearly articulated responses to Masaccio's radical approach to the construction of pictorial space and

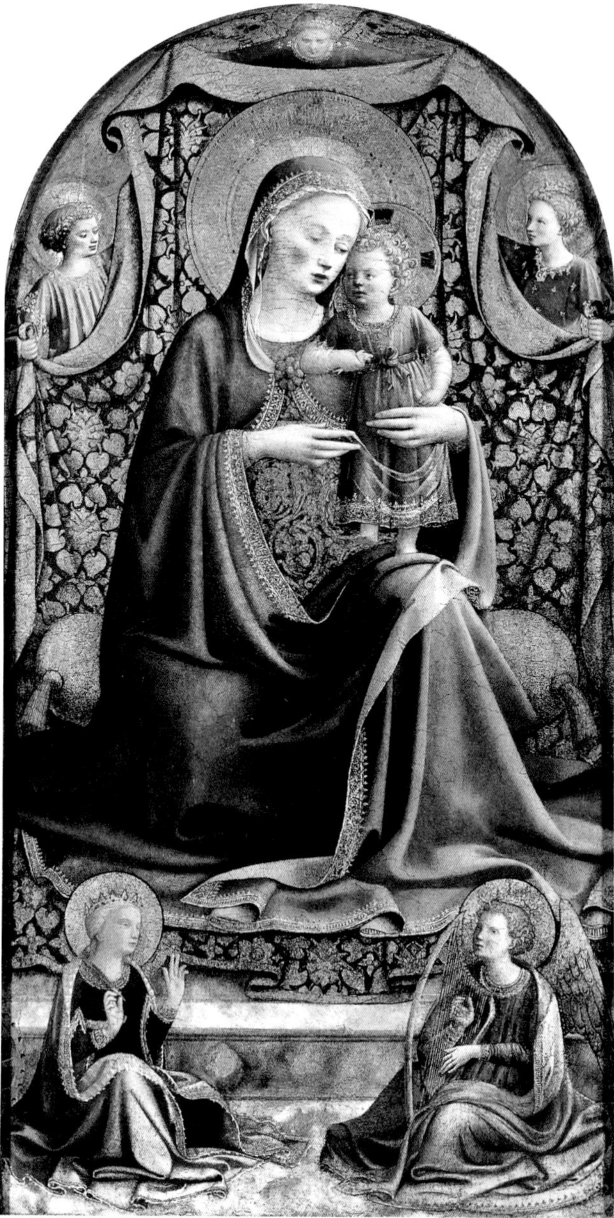

Figure 61. Fra Angelico. *Madonna of Humility*. About 1427–28. Private collection, Switzerland

tactile form (see pp. 81–83). The virtual identity of figure types in the Alba and Thyssen panels tends to confirm this hypothesis, as do the uncompromising frontality of the Thyssen *Madonna,* which has been described as "archaizing,"[6] and the relatively tentative solution adopted to justify the poses of the two foreground angels, whose heads are tipped up and slightly backward to glance at the objects of their devotion. Angelico painted a second, more successfully thought out version of this composition; now in a private collection in Switzerland (fig. 61), it is, however, less well preserved. In this work, all of the experimental uncertainties of the Thyssen panel have been resolved. The Virgin is turned noticeably to her left, engaging her son in a more active embrace, in a pose that breaks with the rigid frontality of the Virgin in the Thyssen painting. The two figures seated in the foreground, Saint Catherine of Alexandria and a harp-playing angel, no longer make a pretense of looking back at the Virgin, and the three angels holding up the cloth of honor are more aggressively foreshortened as they strain forward in a touchingly realistic effort to see around the loops of cloth that separate them from the Virgin and the Child. The figure types in this painting associate it unmistakably with the Franciscan altarpiece of about 1428/29 (cat. 24), which thus becomes a terminus ante quem for the Thyssen *Madonna*. Given the latter's striking resemblance to the Alba *Madonna,* a date of about 1426/27 seems reasonable for it.

Based on its scale and exceptionally elongated proportions—its painted surface is almost exactly twice as tall as it is wide—Collobi-Ragghianti as well as Boskovits proposed that the Thyssen *Madonna* probably originally was the center panel of an altarpiece.[7] This contention is not borne out by comparison with Angelico's other paintings from the 1420s that demonstrably served this purpose, such as the center panel of the San Pier Martire triptych, which is proportionately wider (107 x 57 centimeters), or the *Pontassieve Madonna* in the Uffizi, which is proportionately much taller (132 x 57 centimeters). Additionally, no surviving polyptych by Angelico is composed of round-arched panels. It is more likely that the Thyssen *Virgin* and its "replica" in Switzerland were conceived as independent devotional panels framed by an aedicular tabernacle of the type then being popularized by Brunelleschi and his followers. Sometime between the execution of these two paintings, probably in 1427, Angelico was called upon to paint a more traditionally Gothic, ogival-arched tabernacle with movable shutters (cat. 21); he reverted to a round-arched format in his later, Linaiuoli tabernacle (see cat. 29), designed in 1433 to fit a frame carved in Lorenzo Ghiberti's workshop that employs an ornamental vocabulary of decidedly Gothic proportions. Whether the frames of the Thyssen and Swiss panels similarly were designed by Ghiberti or in his style, or whether, instead, they more closely followed Brunelleschi's classicizing models cannot now be determined. A third possibility is that both panels were framed by simple casetta-type moldings and were designed to be hung on piers in a church, on the model of two paintings presumed to be copies of a lost *Virgin of Humility, with Angels,* by Orcagna—one by Jacopo di Cione in the National Gallery of Art, Washington, and one by Don Silvestro dei Gherarducci in the Galleria dell'Accademia, Florence.

LK

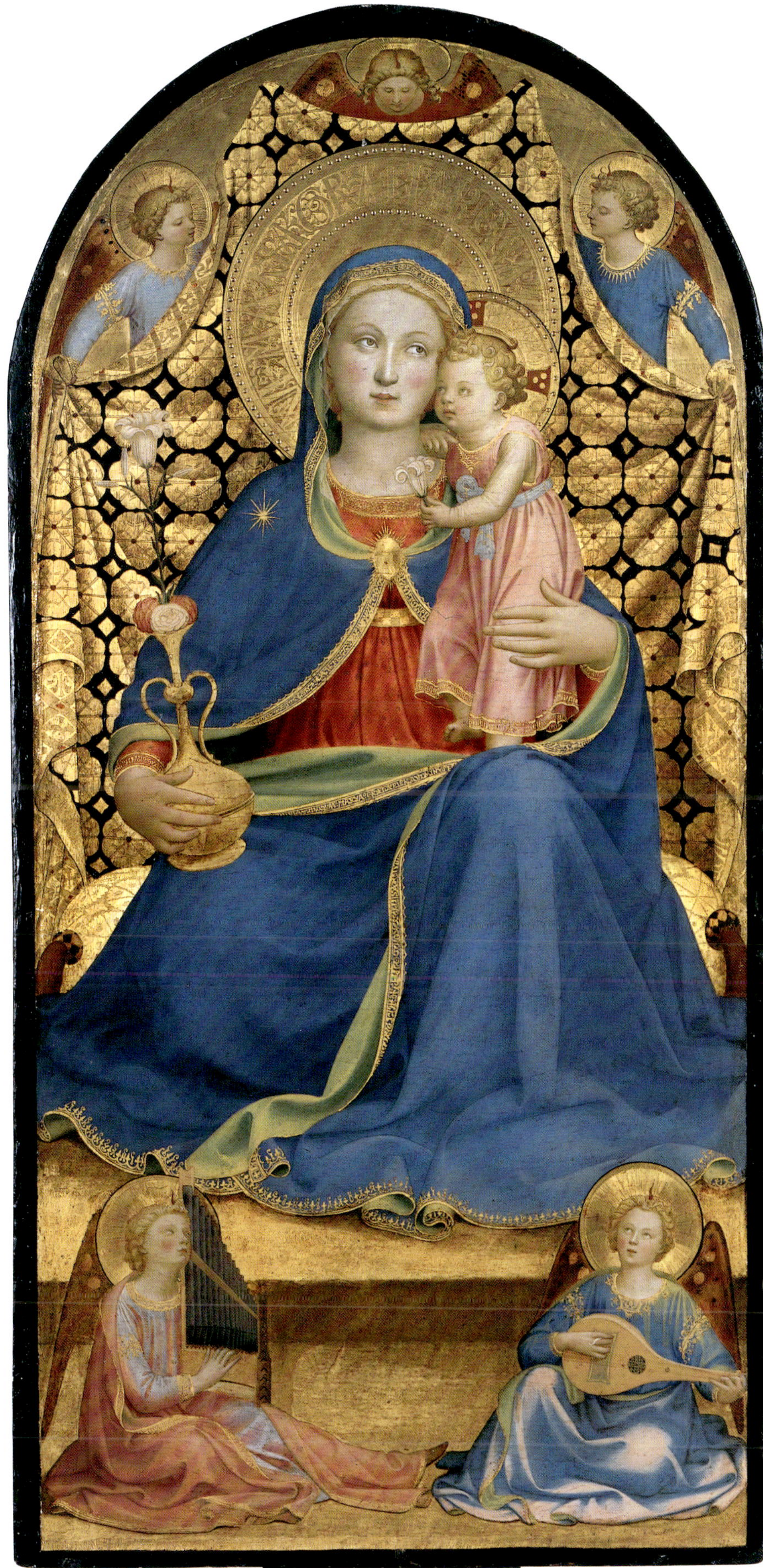

18

1. The angels may have been adapted from the composition of a relief by Donatello known in three surviving examples: a stucco squeeze and a later marble replica in the Victoria and Albert Museum, London (Pope-Hennessy 1964, nos. 74, 73), and a stucco squeeze in a New York private collection (Butterfield 2000, no. 1; Giurescu Heller 2002, no. 2). The lost prototype for this relief, possibly a bronze meant to decorate the door of a sacrament tabernacle, seems to have provided the model for the center panel of Masaccio's Pisa altarpiece of 1426, and either that prototype or a replica almost certainly was known to Angelico by this date as well. The three reliefs in London and in New York differ from one another in minor details, suggesting that they are the surviving members of a once more numerous class of object rather than direct copies either of the lost original or of each other. The stucco version in New York, the earliest of the three, retains its original frame and some of its original pigmentation.
2. Boskovits 1990, p. 26. Among the known paintings by Angelico, only the Gardner *Dormition and Assumption of the Virgin* (cat. 28) can be shown to have been in an English collection so early in the nineteenth century. In 1857 (Cartier 1857, p. 444), it was claimed that the Thyssen painting came from the Palazzo Gondi in Florence, but it cannot be ascertained whether this provenance was based on documentable information or was simply a fanciful reference to Vasari's statement that three paintings by Angelico, "*un quadro grande, un piccolo, ed una croce,*" were the property of Bartolomeo Gondi, "*amatore di queste arti al pari di qualsivoglia altro gentiluomo,*" in 1568 (Vasari [Milanesi ed.] 1878–85, vol. II, p. 512).
3. Boskovits 1990. The purchase of the painting for his own collection by Morgan, then Chairman of the Board of Trustees of The Metropolitan Museum of Art, was the cause of a rift between him and the Museum's curator of paintings, Roger Fry, who had been trying to procure the painting for the Museum. See Pope-Hennessy 1984, p. 238.
4. Boskovits 1990, pp. 22–29.
5. Boskovits (1990, p. 27 n. 21) observed that this type of lettering forming the words of prayers first appears in paintings by Angelico beginning with the Alba *Madonna,* which is here dated about 1426 (see p. 83). C. Gómez-Moreno (1957, pp. 188–89) argued that this lettering does not recur in Angelico's oeuvre after the early 1430s, a contention accepted by Boskovits with some reservations. It should be noted that the system employed in the Thyssen *Madonna* of modeling the folds of the cloth of honor with translucent glazes superimposed on a continuous, uninflected fabric pattern is also more typical of Angelico's early works than of his paintings of the mid-1430s, as was specifically observed by Boskovits although not pursued by him to its logical conclusion.
6. Boskovits 1990, p. 29.
7. Ibid., p. 24; Collobi-Ragghianti 1950 b, p. 25.

19.
Saint Anthony Abbot

Tempera on panel, 89 x 33 cm (35 x 13 in.)
Collection T. Robert and Katherine States Burke

This moving image of Saint Anthony Abbot, shown holding a book and a staff and standing in a barren, rocky landscape enlivened by a single branch of foliage at the right, and powerfully lit by a strong raking light from the left, was first made known to scholars in 1976 by Miklós Boskovits,[1] who identified it as a lateral panel from an unknown altarpiece and associated it with a predella panel of the *Temptation of Saint Anthony* (fig. 62) in the Museum of Fine Arts, Houston, widely attributed to Fra Angelico. Reaffirming the connection between these two panels, Carolyn Wilson published an engraving, preserved in the Musei Civici, Pavia, which reproduces a figure virtually identical to the Burke *Saint Anthony Abbot,* surrounded by eleven episodes from his life; among the scenes is one of Saint Anthony tempted by a heap of gold portrayed just as it is in the Houston panel.[2] Wilson acknowledged that these two panels might have belonged to a conventional altarpiece of the type envisioned by Boskovits, but left open an alternative possibility that they formed members of a *vita retable* of which the engraving might have been a direct record. Close consideration of the engraving, however, suggests that the images depicted in it were probably derived from a variety of sources rather than copied from a single model. Furthermore, at least four scenes the size of the Houston *Temptation* would be required to match the height of the Burke *Saint Anthony,* whereas only three are shown alongside it in the engraving. Damages to the panel support and to the gold ground at the upper right of the Burke *Saint Anthony* are more consistent with its hypothetical reconstruction as half of the lateral panel of an altarpiece, where it would have been paired with another full-length standing saint, on the model of the San Pier Martire triptych (cat. 13), the Franciscan altarpiece of about 1428–29 (see cat. 24), or the later Cortona triptych (fig. 143), painted about 1440 by an assistant over a design by Fra Angelico. A third possibility is that the panel might have been the folding wing of a large tabernacle triptych, similar to Nardo di Cione's *Saint Peter* in the Yale University Art Gallery—a painting of the same size and format as the Burke *Saint Anthony*—or to Angelico's own, more monumental Linaiuoli tabernacle (see cat. 29); this appears to be discounted, however, by X-radiographs of the panel (kindly provided by Jeanne and Andrea Rothe), which show what seems to be a nail hole near its bottom edge that perhaps secured a batten across the reverse, but that reveal no traces of the attachment of iron strap hinges large enough to support a panel of this weight.

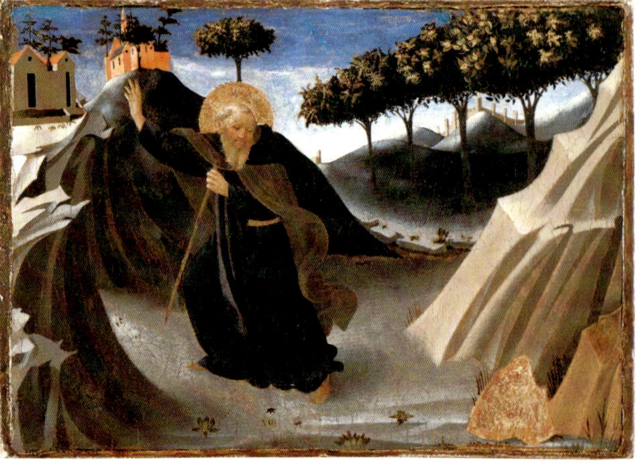

Figure 62. Zanobi Strozzi. *The Temptation of Saint Anthony.* About 1445. Museum of Fine Arts, Houston

A consideration of the authorship and date of the Burke *Saint Anthony* must first of all recognize that it bears no stylistic relationship to the Houston *Temptation of Saint Anthony,* and that even iconographic connections between the two works are tenuous: the depiction of the saint differs in figure type and in habit in the two panels, and it is highly unlikely, therefore, that they came from a single complex. Reconstruction of the predella to which the Houston panel might have belonged has been the subject of wide-ranging but largely fruitless discussion, which, most recently, has been dismissed by Wilson and by Strehlke.[3] The Houston *Temptation of Saint Anthony* is a typical work by Zanobi Strozzi of about 1445. It almost certainly formed part of the same predella as a panel of similar size in the Musée du Louvre, Paris, representing the Dance of Salome, which is also by Zanobi Strozzi and of the same date, although, like the Houston panel, sometimes incorrectly discussed as an autograph work by Fra Angelico. No other panels by Zanobi Strozzi are known that are of an appropriate size or format to have completed this predella, nor is an altarpiece by him depicting Saints Anthony Abbot and John the Baptist.

There can be no doubt, by contrast, that the Burke *Saint Anthony,* although damaged, is an autograph work by Fra Angelico and of a considerably earlier date than the Houston *Temptation of Saint Anthony.* The strong modeling of the saint's head and, especially, of his beard; the subtle play of raking light across the folds of his cloak and habit; and the fall of those folds in a carefully described ellipse around his feet, or curling back from the fingers of his left hand, are typical of Angelico's early interest in emulating Masaccio's techniques for simulating plasticity and volume. The isolation of the saint within a highly abstracted landscape setting recalls similar effects on the lateral panels of the Franciscan altarpiece of about 1428–29 (cat. 24), but the softer, more rounded and compact figure type

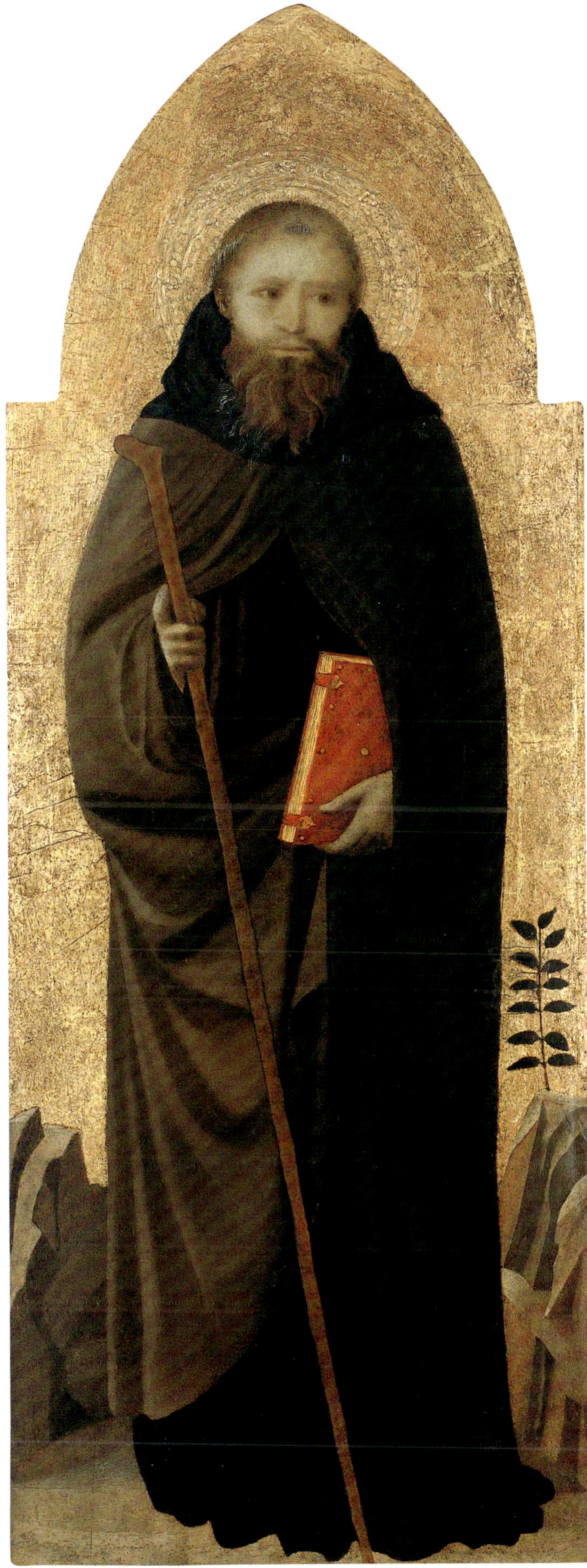

19

employed here implies that the painting was executed slightly earlier, closer to the Parma tabernacle of about 1427 (cat. 21) or even to the Thyssen Virgin of Humility of perhaps the year before (cat. 18). No other works by Fra Angelico of this date are known that might have joined the Burke *Saint Anthony Abbot* in a single altarpiece. A tentative suggestion to consider a full-length image of Saint James, formerly in The Minneapolis Institute of Arts, as a possible companion panel may be dismissed;[4] although it is close in size and format to the *Saint Anthony Abbot,* it is lit from the opposite direction and, in addition, the paint surface has been extensively repaired, compromising any definitive judgment of its date.

LK

1. Boskovits 1976b, pp. 43, 52 n. 27.
2. See Hind 1938, vol. I, no. 68, pl. 64. Wilson 1995, pp. 737–40; Wilson 1996, pp. 130–45. Wilson illustrates the Burke *Saint Anthony Abbot*, then in an English private collection, in its heavily overpainted state, before its recent cleaning in 2003 by Andrea Rothe, who more accurately reconstructed the folds of the saint's robes utilizing surviving traces of the original paint that had been covered over.
3. Wilson 1996, pp. 130–45; Strehlke 2004, pp. 59–60. The Houston panel was associated by L. Berti (1963, p. 38 n. 108) with a *Penitent Saint Julian* (identified as Saint Augustine) in the Musée des Beaux-Arts, Cherbourg. Pope-Hennessy (1974, p. 227) added two other works to the Cherbourg panel: a *Saint Benedict in Ecstasy* in the Musée Condé, Chantilly, and a *Saint Romuald Appearing to the Emperor Otto III* in the Koninklijk Museum voor Schone Kunsten, Antwerp. That these four panels formed part of a single predella was accepted by Boskovits (1976b, p. 52 n. 27), and that they are by a single painter was supported by D. Cole (1977, vol. II, pp. 475–77, 499–500, 503–4, 530–32, 567, no. 96). K. Christiansen (1984, pp. 61–62) proposed that an *Adoration of the Christ Child* in The Metropolitan Museum of Art, New York (cat. 44 C), formed the center of this predella. Ann Leader (oral communication, July 1999) first recognized that the Cherbourg, Chantilly, and Antwerp panels were fragments of a *Thebaid* rather than a predella. Michel Laclotte associated a fourth, larger fragment in a private collection (now on loan to the Musée Condé, Chantilly) with them, and Carl Strehlke (2004, pp. 59–60) added yet another panel, in the Philadelphia Museum of Art, to the group, depicting an episode from the life of Saint Celestine V or Saint Gregory the Great.
4. Kanter 2000, p. 8.

20.
Virgin and Child, with Four Angels

Tempera on panel, 16.2 x 9.7 cm (6⅜ x 3⅞ in.)
The Detroit Institute of Arts. Founders Society Purchase, Ralph Harman Booth Bequest Fund (56.32)

Few paintings by Angelico are as jewel-like in scale or in delicacy of execution as this miniaturist treatment of a common devotional theme. The artist has portrayed the Virgin not as the enthroned Queen of Heaven or the Madonna of Humility but with a greater naturalistic immediacy, seated on an unadorned stone bench. She holds a beautifully painted rose and spray of leaves in her right hand, and with her left hand supports the Christ Child, who stands on her lap. Her head inclines very slightly toward her son, although her eyes

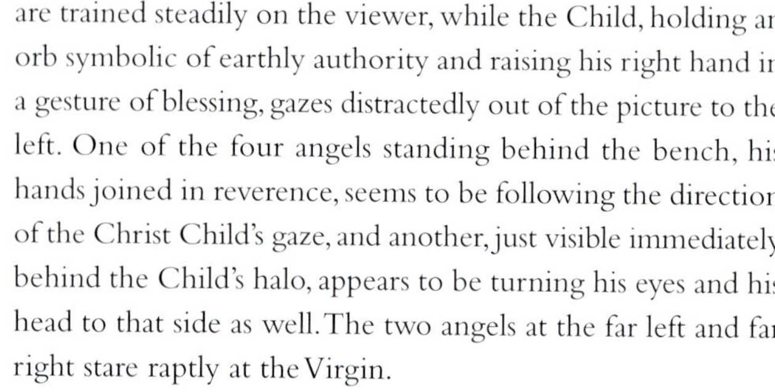

are trained steadily on the viewer, while the Child, holding an orb symbolic of earthly authority and raising his right hand in a gesture of blessing, gazes distractedly out of the picture to the left. One of the four angels standing behind the bench, his hands joined in reverence, seems to be following the direction of the Christ Child's gaze, and another, just visible immediately behind the Child's halo, appears to be turning his eyes and his head to that side as well. The two angels at the far left and far right stare raptly at the Virgin.

The original function of the Detroit *Virgin and Child* is not known, although it may be half of a diptych or part of the wing of a small portable triptych; more likely, however, is that it is complete in its present form, except for the loss of its engaged frame. Three other panels by Fra Angelico portraying the Virgin and Child with angels, all intimate in scale yet not as small as this one, also appear to have been conceived as independent works rather than as parts of a larger complex. The earliest of these (fig. 55), showing the Virgin enthroned beneath an elaborate marble canopy and adored by a ring of twelve angels (Städelsches Kunstinstitut, Frankfurt), dates from approximately the time of the San Domenico high altarpiece: probably about 1420 or 1421. Like that altarpiece, it is still essentially Late Gothic in tenor, but a number of progressive spatial devices prefigure the development of Angelico's style through that decade. In a somewhat later version in the Pinacoteca Vaticana (fig. 91), dating to the mid- or late 1430s, the carved baldachin of the Frankfurt painting is replaced with a gilt cloth of honor, which stretches across the back of the entire composition. The Virgin is more monumental in scale in relation to the tightly compressed crowd of angels at either side, and two kneeling figures of Saints Dominic and Catherine of Alexandria are introduced in the foreground. In the artist's final version of the theme, probably painted in 1447 (Museum of Fine Arts, Boston; cat. 36), the format of a major *sacra conversazione* altarpiece has been adapted to the reduced scale of a domestic furnishing. While these three paintings might be viewed as maturing solutions to a single artistic problem, none of them pretends to the emotional intimacy of the Detroit panel, and it is difficult to consider that work as part of a series with them.

The few scholars to have written about the Detroit *Virgin and Child* since it first came to public attention in 1956 have been unanimous in considering it among Angelico's early works and proposing a date ranging from the 1420s to as late as 1432.[1] Umberto Baldini associated it stylistically with the San Pier Martire triptych (see cat. 13), which he regarded as one of the artist's earliest paintings.[2] The structural solidity of

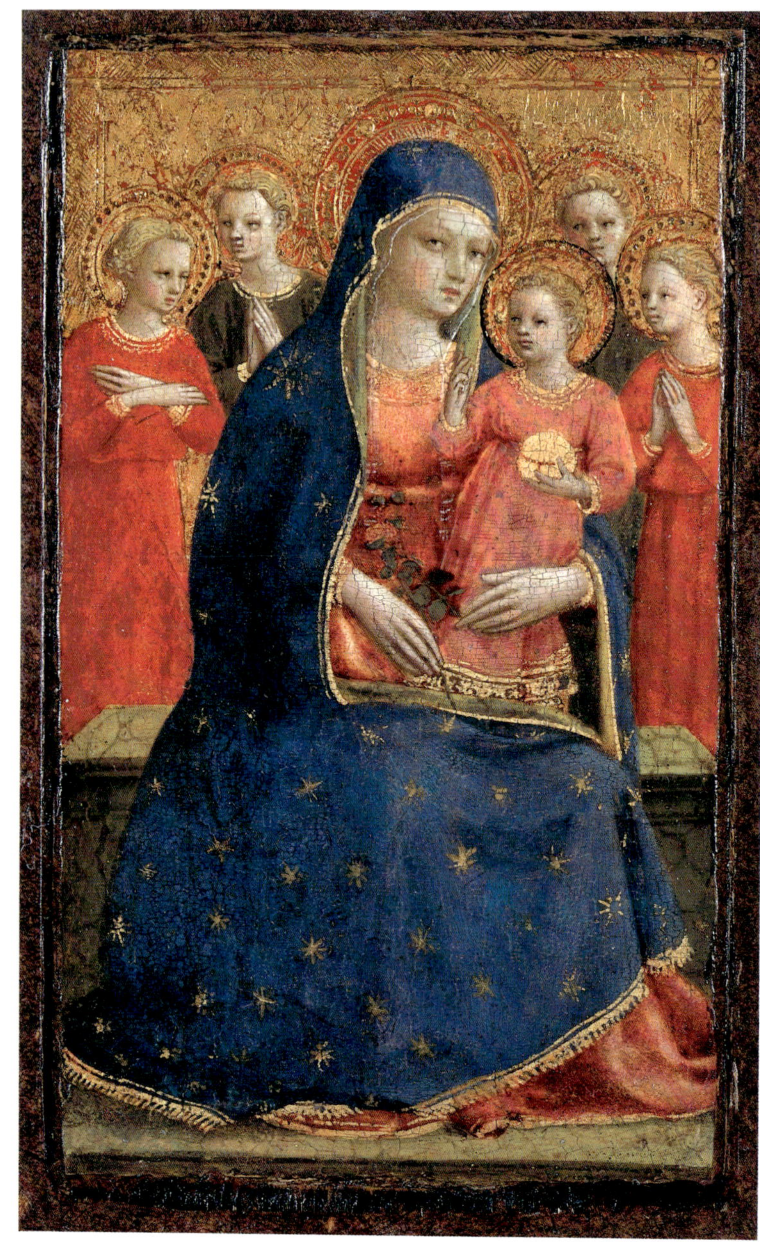

20

the figures in the Detroit panel and their sophisticated psychological interaction argue for an even later date, however—closer to the execution of the *Saint Lucy* predella (cat. 25), dated here about 1429 or 1430, or the *Saint Francis* predella (cat. 24) of perhaps a year earlier. Exact parallels for the style, for the poses of the figures, and (although on a more elaborate scale) for the spatial structure of the Detroit *Virgin* are to be found in the *Coronation of the Virgin* reliquary from Santa Maria Novella—the second of four reliquaries that, according to Richa, were painted by Angelico for Fra Giovanni Masi (see cat. 28). This painting, too, can be dated by inference only, but like the Detroit panel it must immediately precede the *Saint Francis* predella, and probably was executed about 1427 or 1428. A date of about 1427 for the present painting seems the most plausible. LK

1. Richardson 1955–56, pp. 86–88; Berti 1963, p. 38 n. 102; Orlandi 1964, pp. 14–15; Pope-Hennessy 1974, p. 223; Boskovits 1976a, p. 31; Boskovits 1976b, p. 35; Bonsanti 1998, p. 121.
2. Baldini 1970, p. 86.

FRA ANGELICO

21.

A.

The Virgin of Humility, with Saint John the Baptist and Saint Paul, and the Meeting of Saint Francis and Saint Dominic

Tempera on panel: overall, 128.8 x 68.2 cm (50 ¾ x 26⅞ in.); picture surface, 101 x 56 cm (39¾ x 22 in.)
Galleria Nazionale, Parma (Inv. no. 429)

B.

The Vision of the Dominican Habit

Tempera on panel, 24.4 x 32.3 cm (9⅝ x 12¾ in.)
National Gallery, London (NG3417)

C.

The Annunciatory Angel

Tempera on panel, 32.1 x 18.8 cm (12⅝ x 7⅜ in.)
Alte Pinakothek, Bayerische Staatsgemäldesammlungen, Munich (no. 1019)

D.

The Virgin Annunciate

Tempera on panel, 32.2 x 19 cm (12⅝ x 7½ in.)
Alte Pinakothek, Bayerische Staatsgemäldesammlungen, Munich (no. 637)

The subject of the London *Vision of the Dominican Habit* was elegantly summarized by Dillian Gordon in her recent catalogue of fifteenth-century Italian paintings in the National Gallery: "Reginald, Dean to the Bishop of Orléans, came to Rome in 1218, learned of the new religious Order and sent for Saint Dominic. Hearing that Reginald had fallen ill, Dominic prayed to the Virgin on his behalf. She appeared to Reginald with two beautiful damsels and offered him anything he wanted. One of the damsels suggested he should not ask for anything but should commit himself to the will of the Virgin. She anointed him with healing balm and showed him the habit of the Order, saying it was for him."[1] This vision is described in numerous thirteenth-century chronicles of the life of Saint Dominic, but apparently the representation of the vision appearing to both Saint Dominic and the Blessed Reginald, as here, derives specifically from the account of Roderigo of Cerrato, written after 1280.[2] In the London panel, again according to Gordon, "The Virgin in both episodes is ostentatiously holding out the scapular, signifying that this is her particular gift to the Order."[3]

The *Vision of the Dominican Habit* has received only summary attention from students of Fra Angelico's work: most of them assign it to the master's workshop and one author attributes it to Battista di Biagio Sanguigni.[4] Most negative opinions of the painting, however, are based on its abraded condition. There can be little doubt either from the complex organization of the composition, which unfolds in a continuous interior space viewed obliquely from the left, or from the sophistication of the representational details, such as the folds of the scapular as it falls from the Virgin's hand, the pull of the bed curtains on their rings, the somewhat casual disarray of Reginald's bed linens, or the shadows cast by the bed itself, that this is a fully autograph painting by Angelico. It remains only to determine the panel's function and approximate date. Although most scholars assume the work to be from the mid- to late 1430s,[5] the reductive simplicity of its setting is typical of only a brief moment in Angelico's career: close to the time that he executed the Franciscan altarpiece (about 1428–29) and certainly before he painted the predella to the Louvre *Coronation of the Virgin* altarpiece in the early 1430s.

The format of the London panel has led to the general assumption that it was once part of the predella of an altarpiece.[6] The vertical wood grain of its support, the original painted geometric pattern on the reverse, and the remains of a wire hinge on its left edge, however, indicate that it did not belong to a predella but, rather, to a cupboard door or the wing of a folding triptych. In the latter case, given the placement of the hinge and the discontinuity of the geometric pattern at the top of the panel, the London scene would have been positioned at the bottom of the right wing of the triptych, with at least one, but—in view of its proportions—probably two other scenes above it. There is no certainty, of course, that an additional episode from the legend of Saint Dominic was situated above the London panel rather than a *Crucifixion* or another Christological subject, but since the Vision of the Dominican Habit is among the earliest events in the saint's biography, and one infrequently represented except in the context of an extended hagiographical cycle, the strongest probability is that the structure of which it formed part was dedicated entirely to the life and miracles of Saint Dominic or to the early history of the Dominican order.

As was common practice on Florentine tabernacles, the triptych's wings are likely to have terminated in pinnacles containing figures of the Annunciatory Angel and the Virgin Annunciate: specifically, the two panels—C and D—now in the Alte Pinakothek, Munich. The exceptional width of the London panel relative to other works that served the same function (see, for example, cat. 16) implies that the complex to which

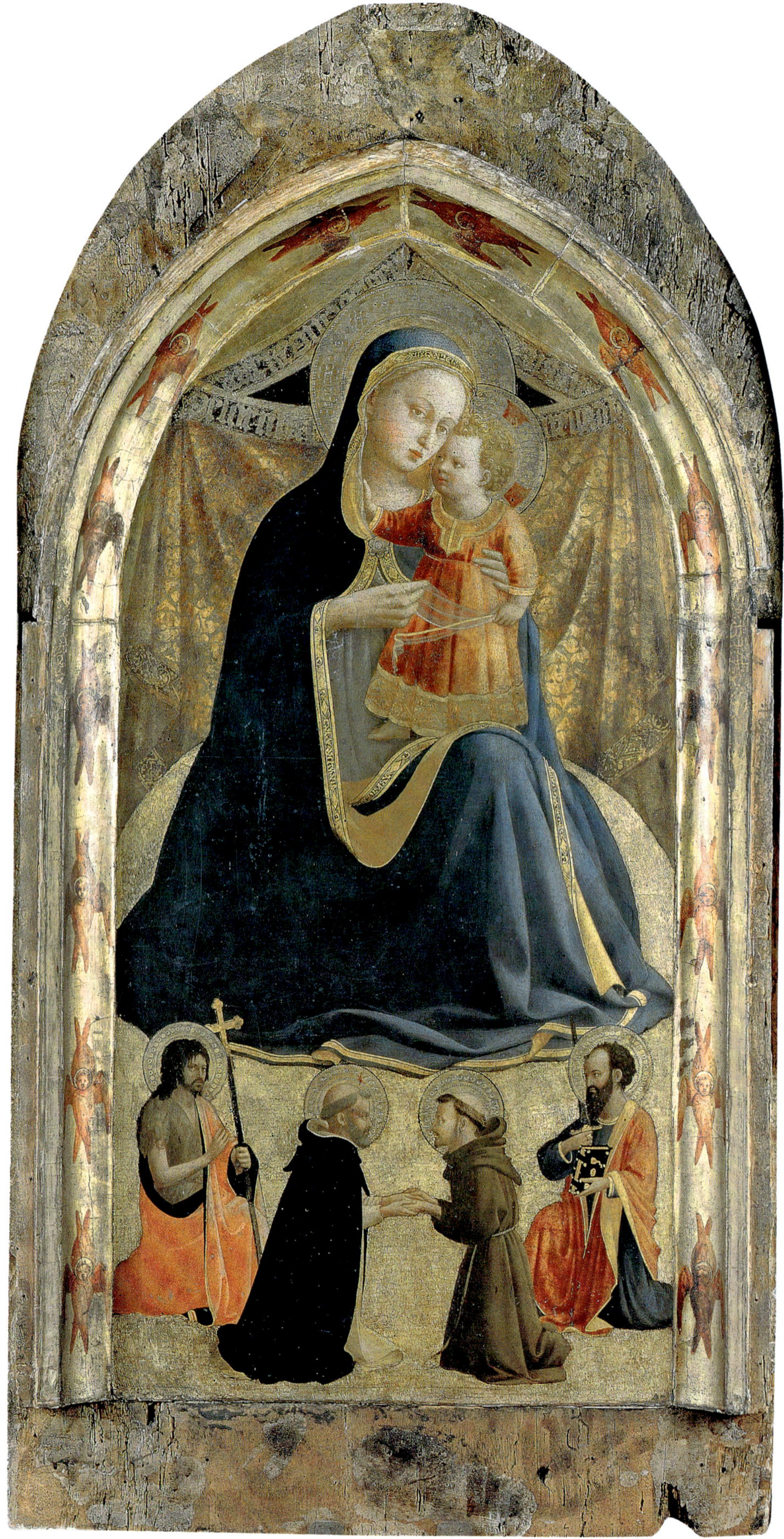

21: A

it belonged was unusually large. This is true of the Munich pinnacles as well, which even in their present fragmentary state are wider and significantly taller than other, similar panels by Angelico. Reconstructing their probable original size by completing the truncated arc at their top and inner edges, and allowing for the cropping of the figures along their straight, outer edges as well, results in panels approximately 37 to 38 centimeters tall and approximately 30 to 32 centimeters wide. These dimensions correspond neatly with the width of the London *Vision of the Dominican Habit,* which has white framing bands painted along its left and right margins precisely like that along the bottom of each panel in Munich. Unfortunately, the Munich panels have been thinned to a depth of one centimeter, and thus have lost the painted decoration on their reverse sides that could have demonstrated their association with the London panel (which measures 2.4 centimeters in depth). As they exactly match the style of the London *Vision of the Dominican Habit,* however, the conclusion that all three are fragments of the wings of a single folding triptych is inescapable.

Two wings of approximately the width of the London *Vision of the Dominican Habit* (the wings of triptychs were often of slightly unequal widths, and a two-centimeter or more discrepancy is not uncommon) would have a combined width of approximately 60 to 64 centimeters. Only four surviving paintings by Fra Angelico that may have served as the center panel of a tabernacle with folding wings are this large. All four represent the Virgin and Child, and are today divided among the collections of the Duchess of Alba in Madrid, the Galleria Nazionale in Parma, the Rijksmuseum in Amsterdam, and the Galleria Sabauda in Turin. Of these four paintings, only one is of exactly the same date as the London and Munich panels: the *Virgin of Humility* in Parma.[7] The small scene of the meeting of Saints Dominic and Francis painted in the "foreground" beneath the seated Virgin in the Parma picture establishes an iconographic link with the London panel. Finally, only the Parma panel is of an appropriate height to have accommodated the likeliest reconstruction of the London and Munich wings. Two scenes the size of the London *Vision of the Dominican Habit* and an *Annunciation* pinnacle atop each wing would have resulted in an unusually squat format: approximately 87 to 90 by 60 centimeters for the central panel, while three scenes and a pinnacle on either side would have extended the overall height to approximately 110 to 115 centimeters. The area of the Parma *Virgin of Humility* including the flat, top edge of its projecting surround painted with cherubim and the (missing) sloped ledge that must have completed the bottom of the tabernacle (fig. 63), and over which the wings would have folded,[8] measures 111 to 112 by 59.5 centimeters.

Although it has come down to us diminished by the fragmentation of its wings and by the loss of its frame and of some

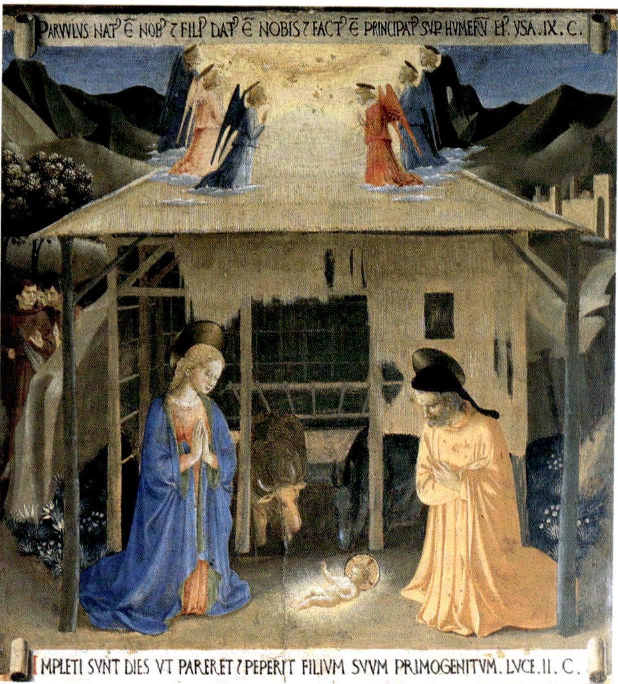

Figure 58. Fra Angelico. *The Nativity* (from the Santissima Annunziata Silver Chest). About 1448–50. Museo di San Marco, Florence

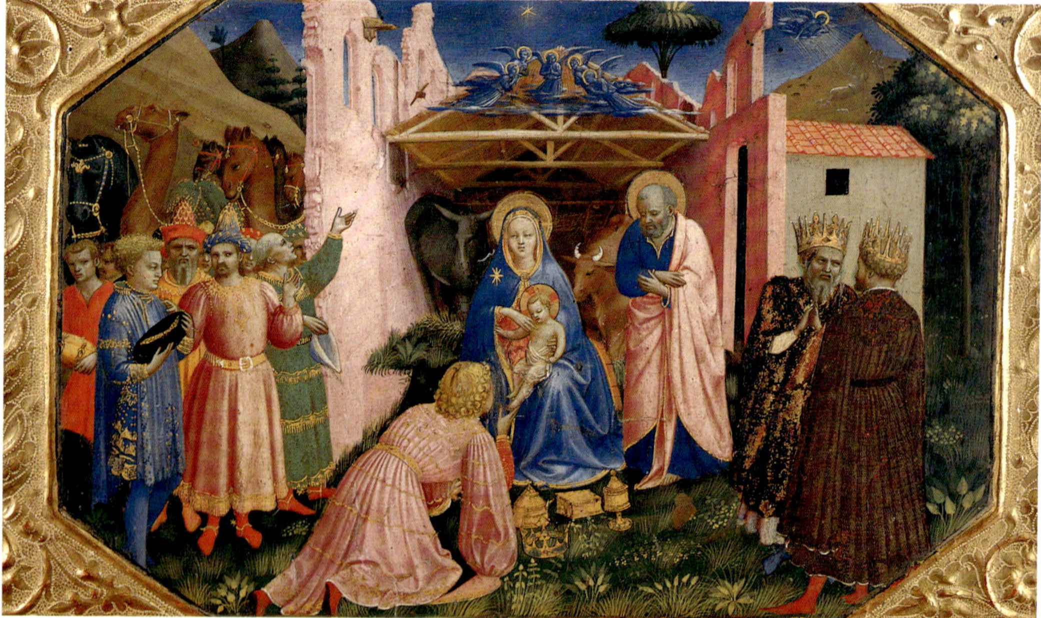

25.

A.

The Apostle Saint James the Greater Freeing the Magician Hermogenes

Tempera and gold on panel: overall, 25.4 x 22.5 cm (10 x 8⅞ in.); picture surface, 25.4 x 21.9 cm (10 x 8⅝ in.)
Kimbell Art Museum, Fort Worth (AP 1986.03)

The magician Hermogenes summoned devils to ensnare Saint James, but the apostle turned them on Hermogenes instead. The devils bound Hermogenes, but James ordered him freed as an act of Christian charity, and offered him his own staff as an amulet against the demons.

B.

The Naming of Saint John the Baptist

Tempera and gold on panel, 27.3 x 24.9 cm (10¾ x 9¾ in.)
Museo di San Marco, Florence (Uffizi Inv. no. 1499)

Struck dumb for doubting the angelic message of his son's birth, Zacharias wrote on a tablet, "John is his name," and he was immediately cured.

C.

The Burial of the Virgin and the Reception of Her Soul in Heaven

Tempera, gold, and silver on panel: overall, 26.2 x 52.5 cm (10⁵⁄₁₆ x 20⅝ in.); picture surface, 24.5 x 48.2 cm (9⅝ x 19 in.)
Philadelphia Museum of Art. The John G. Johnson Collection (no. 15)

D.

The Appearance of Saint Agatha to Saint Lucy

Tempera and gold on panel: overall, 25.7 x 21.5 cm (10⅛ x 8 ½ in.); picture surface, 25.1 x 21.5 cm (9⅞ x 8½ in.)
Collection Richard L. Feigen, New York

According to *The Golden Legend,* Saint Lucy, a princess of Siracusa, brought her mother, Eustochia, to the shrine of Saint Agatha to be healed from an unstoppable flow of blood. Falling asleep before the tomb, Lucy beheld Saint Agatha in a vision, and was told that she herself had the power to cure her mother if she would dedicate her life to the poor.

E.

The Meeting of Saint Dominic and Saint Francis of Assisi

Tempera and gold on panel: overall, 26.7 x 25.7 cm (10½ x 10⅛ in.); picture surface, 25.5 x 23.5 cm (10 x 9¼ in.)
The Fine Arts Museums of San Francisco. Gift of the Samuel H. Kress Foundation (61-44-7 [K289])

The episode of Saint Dominic recognizing and embracing Saint Francis, who had been commended to him by the Virgin in a dream, was popularized by Jacopo da Varagine's account in *The Golden Legend,* although it was rarely portrayed in art before Angelico's many paintings of the subject.

F.

The Annunciatory Angel

Tempera and gold on panel, 31.4 x 25.5 cm (12⅜ x 10 in.)
The Detroit Institute of Arts. Bequest of Eleanor Clay Ford, 1977 (77.1.1)

G.

The Virgin Annunciate

Tempera and gold on panel, 31.4 x 25.5 cm (12⅜ x 10 in.)
The Detroit Institute of Arts. Bequest of Eleanor Clay Ford, 1977 (77.1.2)

H.

The Blessing Redeemer

Tempera on panel, 28 x 22 cm (11 x 8⅝ in.)
H. M. Queen Elizabeth II

I.

Two Adoring Angels

Tempera on panel: each, 25.2 x 13.2 cm (9⅞ x 5³⁄₁₆ in.)
Galleria Sabauda, Turin

The reconstruction of the altarpiece to which these ten panels belonged has evolved gradually over the past several decades. Roberto Longhi first intuited a connection between the *Naming of the Baptist* and *Saint James the Greater Freeing the Magician Hermogenes,*[1] and a connection between these two panels and the *Meeting of Saint Dominic and Saint Francis* and the *Burial of the Virgin* was established by Keith Christiansen and Everett Fahy.[2] The present writer added the fifth panel of the predella, *The Appearance of Saint Agatha to Saint Lucy,*[3] and also suggested that *The Blessing Redeemer* from the English Royal Collection (H), together with the *Two Adoring Angels,* now in the Galleria Sabauda, Turin (I), may have formed the central pinnacle of the altarpiece.[4] The Turin and Hampton Court panels had previously been associated with the cropped central pinnacle of the San Domenico high altarpiece (see cat. 10), but they are somewhat later in style than that work, and are closer in this respect to the predella panels reunited here; furthermore, their combined width corresponds approximately to that of the Philadelphia panel.

X-radiographs of the Hampton Court *Redeemer* show the structure of the panels of which it is composed as well as evidence of the removal of engaged moldings along its top edges, clearly indicating that it originally formed the central pinnacle of an altarpiece rather than of a smaller triptych or tabernacle,[5] and that the frame of this altarpiece conformed in type to that of the polyptych (fig. 143) attributed to Fra Angelico in the Museo Diocesano, Cortona, or to the *Trinity* altarpiece of 1429 now in the Museo di San Marco, Florence (see cat. 24). As in these altarpieces, it is likely that the lateral panels—combining two standing saints beneath ogival arches on each panel: Saints James and John the Baptist on the left and Saints Lucy and Dominic or Francis on the right—also contained images of the *Annunciatory Angel* and the *Virgin Annunciate* on their pinnacles. It now seems that this was the original disposition of the two fragmentary panels in Detroit,[6] which, additionally, are stylistically related to the Hampton Court *Redeemer* and to the five predella panels reunited here, and are of an appropriate size to have joined them in a single complex.

Dates proposed for all these panels have generally hovered in the vicinity of the later 1420s, on account of their similarities to Masaccio's spatial experiments in the Brancacci Chapel first pointed out by Roberto Longhi. The five predella panels were specifically discussed by the present writer as midpoints in the development of Angelico's style between the Prado *Annunciation* altarpiece and the Louvre *Coronation of the Virgin* altarpiece,[7] but assigning them to 1426–27, based on an overly

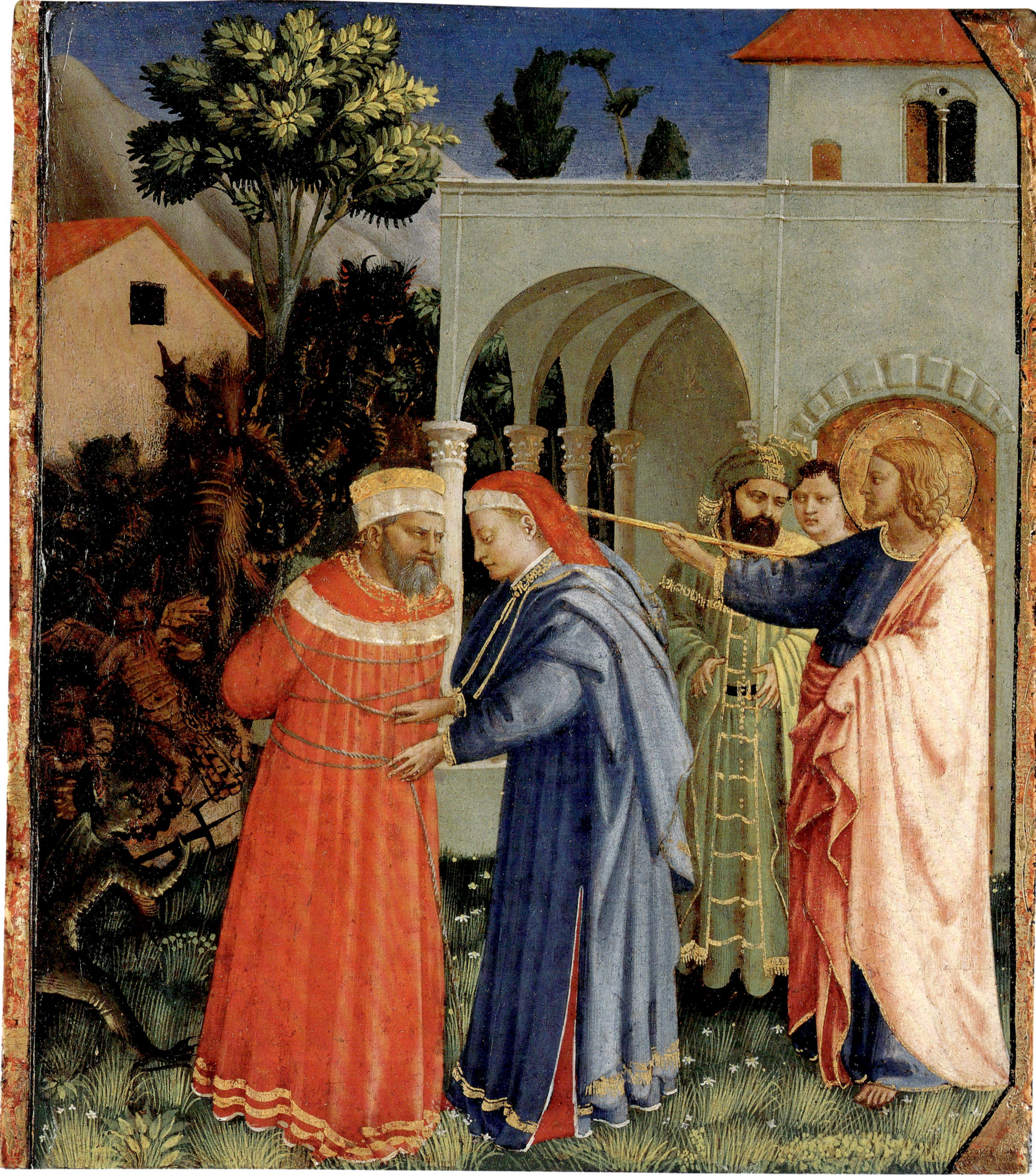

25: A

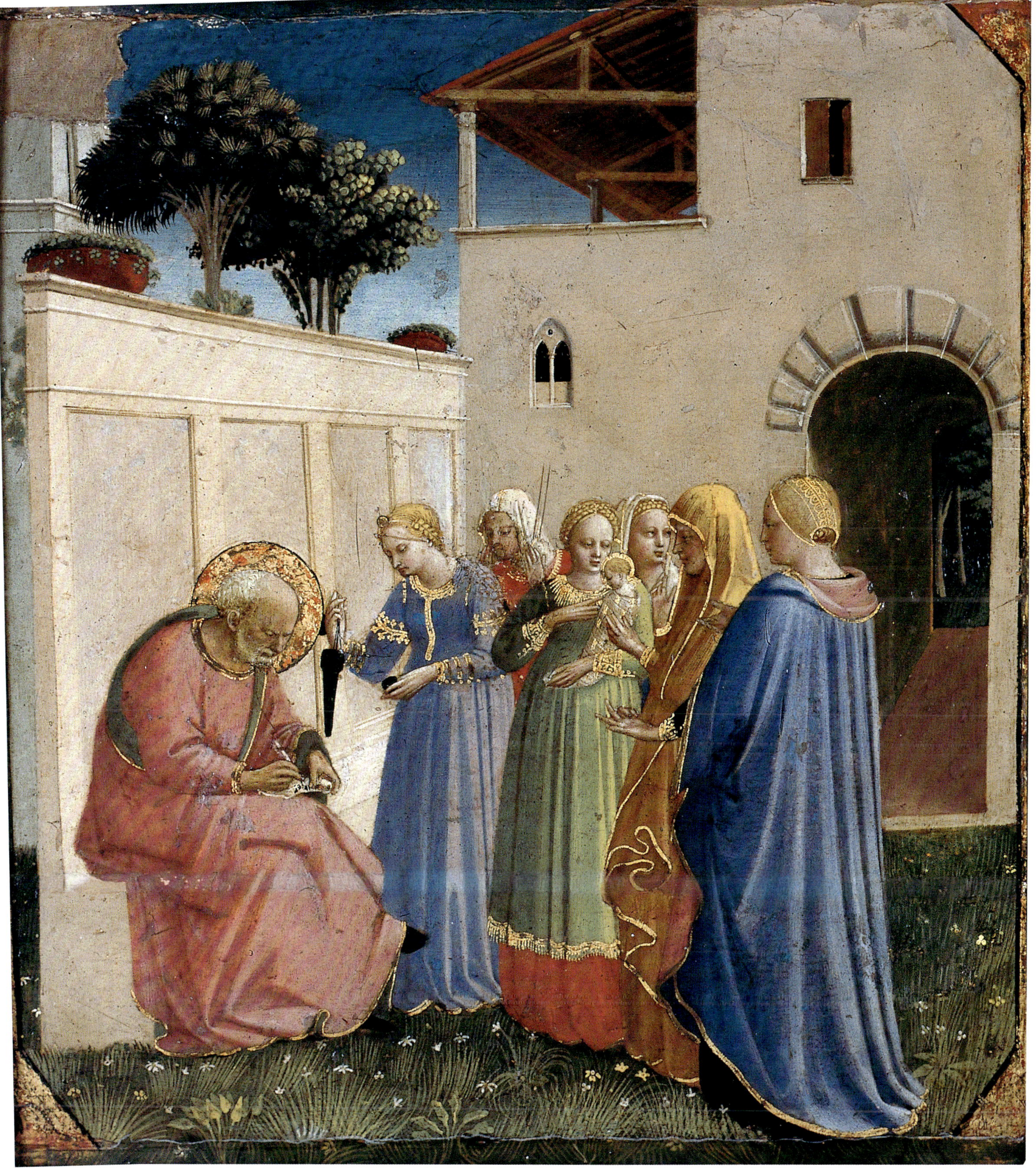

25: B

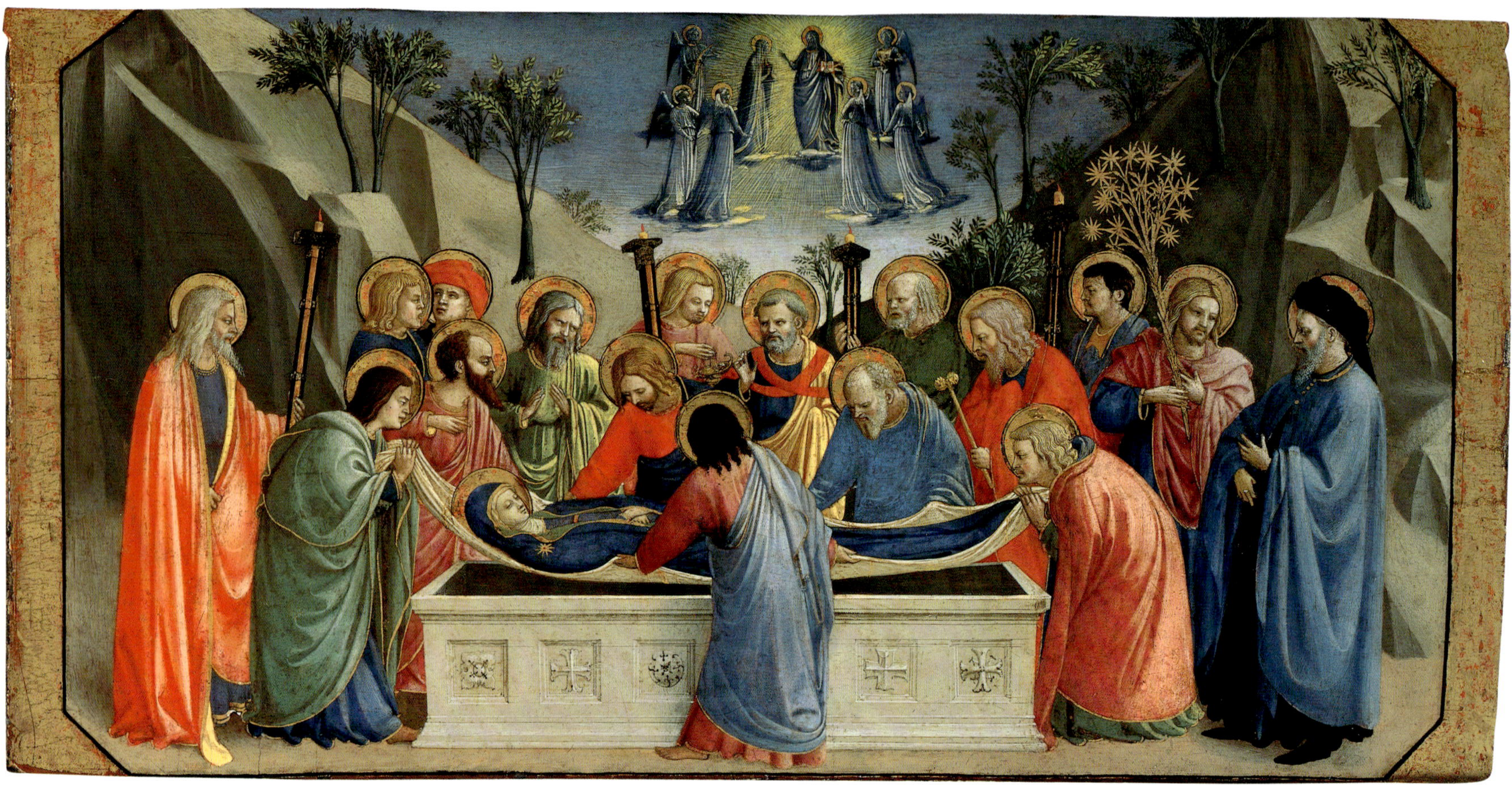

25: C

precocious dating of the Louvre *Coronation*, now seems to be too early. Considering the more sophisticated treatment of ambient detail and the more solid modeling of the figures in these panels, it would seem that they followed rather than preceded the otherwise closely related panels from the Franciscan predella of about 1428–29 (cat. 24). At the same time their figure canon does not reveal the greater attenuation evident in such slightly later paintings as the reliquary of the *Annunciation and the Adoration of the Magi* (see cat. 28) of about 1431–32, or the predella of the Louvre *Coronation of the Virgin* of about 1432–34. A date of about 1429–30 for this partially reconstructed altarpiece seems most likely.

The identification of the panels from the main tier of this altarpiece remains elusive. While it is now possible to specify the subjects of the lateral panels, it is doubtful that the full-length *Saint James* formerly in The Minneapolis Institute of Arts and sometimes associated with the Kimbell predella panel could have been among them. Its relation to the other panels is exclusively iconographic: it is divergent in size and format, while its style is impossible to judge from its apparently damaged and liberally retouched state. The central panel of this complex probably represented the Virgin and Child and certainly terminated in an ogival arch. The only surviving panel by Fra Angelico of this subject and of a suitable size and format is the so-called *Pontassieve Madonna* in the Uffizi, Florence (fig. 70). Although this painting is traditionally dated to a more mature period in the artist's career,[8] its gold ground and ogival-arched shape, coupled with the flat projection of the Virgin's throne, make it unlikely to have been painted later than the second half of the 1420s. More specifically, the incipient attenuation of the figures and the modeling of their heads and facial features situate this panel midway between the Madonna from the Franciscan altarpiece (1428–29), now in the Museo di San Marco, and the Cortona *Annunciation* (about 1430), making it a highly plausible candidate for the missing central panel of this complex (fig. 71).

The presence within the predella of this altarpiece of two relatively uncommonly portrayed saints—James, and, in a position of honor, Lucy—led this writer to speculate that its original location might have been the Florentine church of San Jacopo (James) in Campo Corbolini. This church was the seat both of the Knights of Malta, dedicated to Saint John the Baptist, and of the Compagnia di Santa Maria del Giglio (or dei Ciechi), dedicated to Saint Lucy.[9] While the suggestion

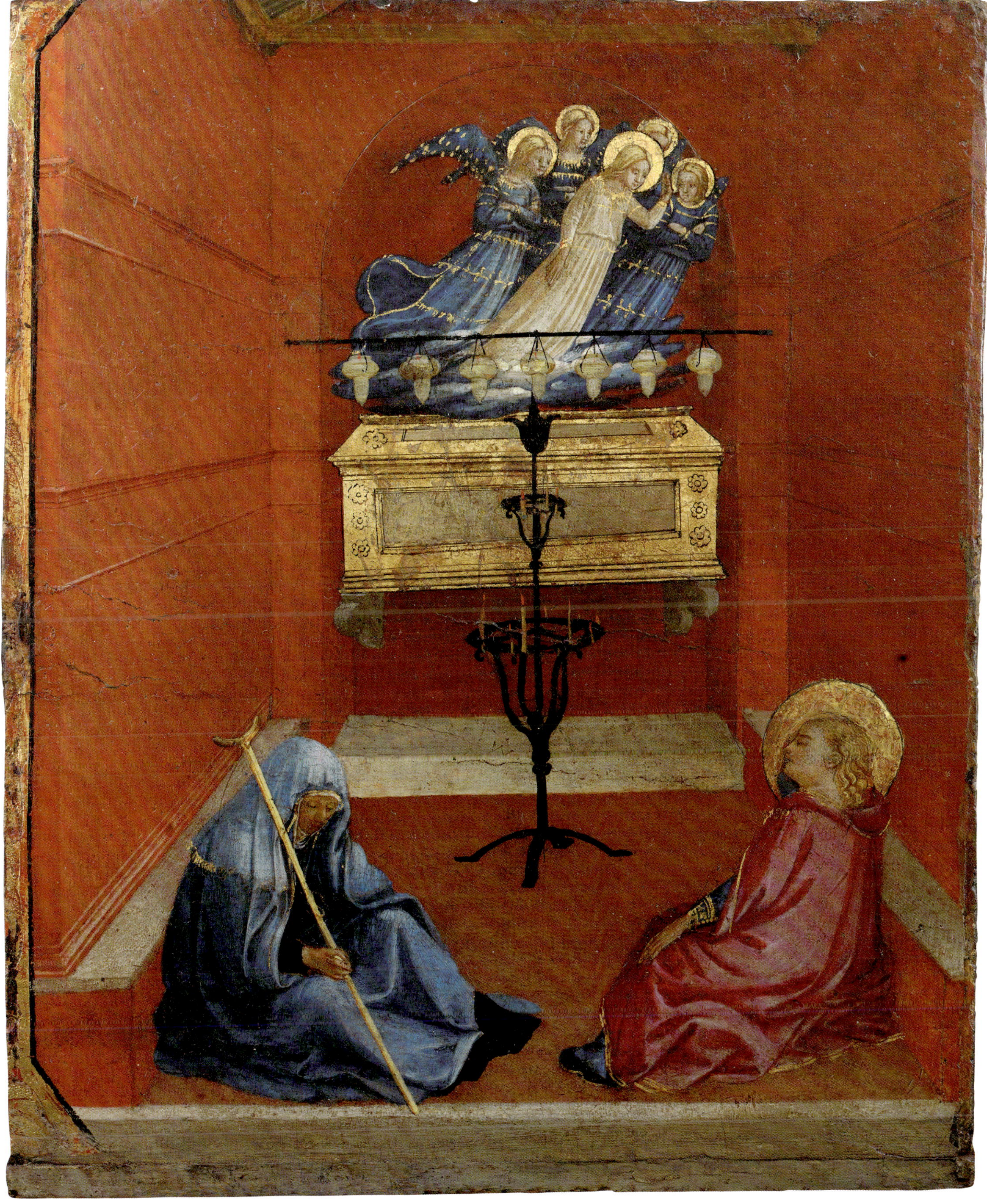

25: D

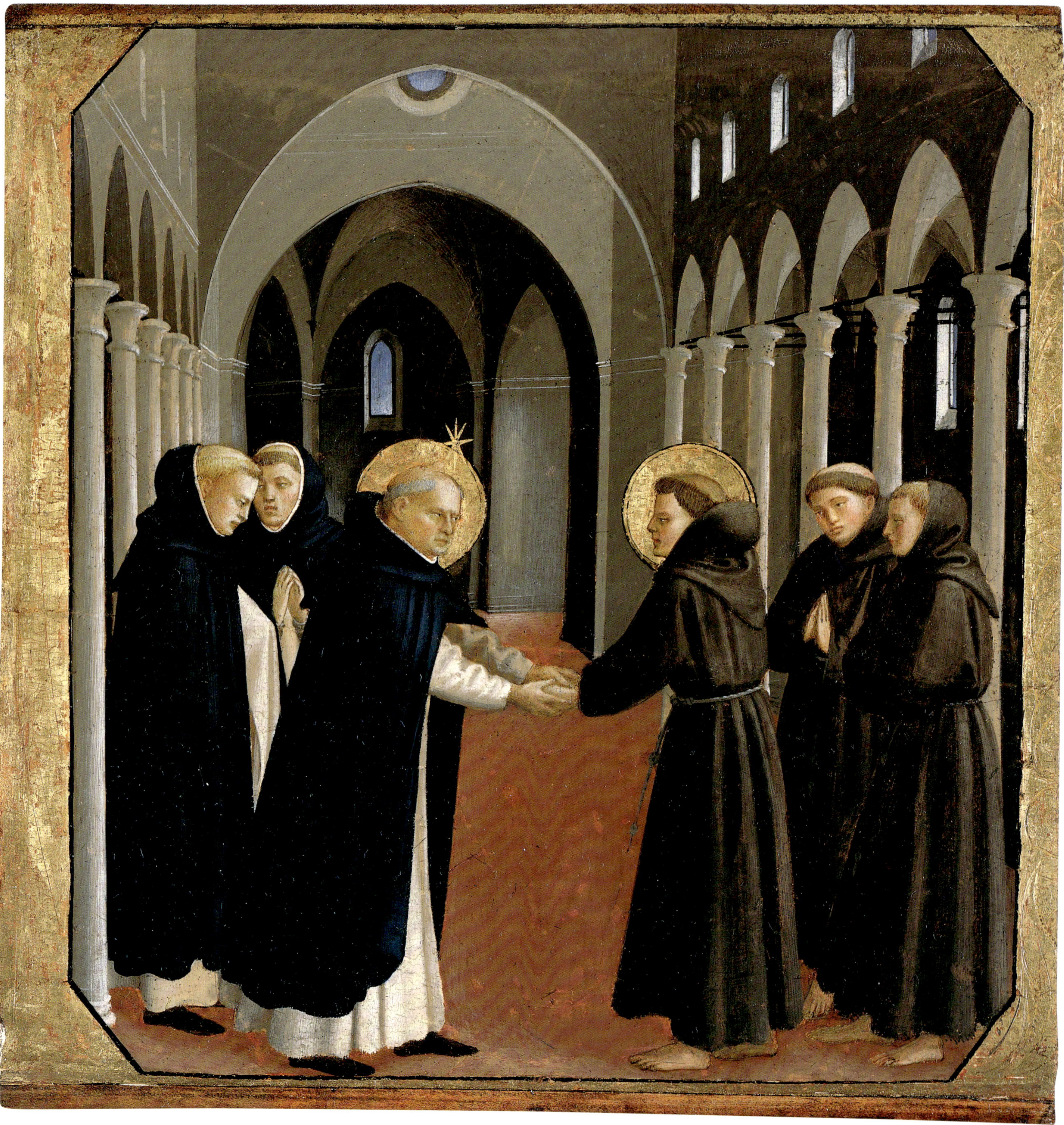

25: E

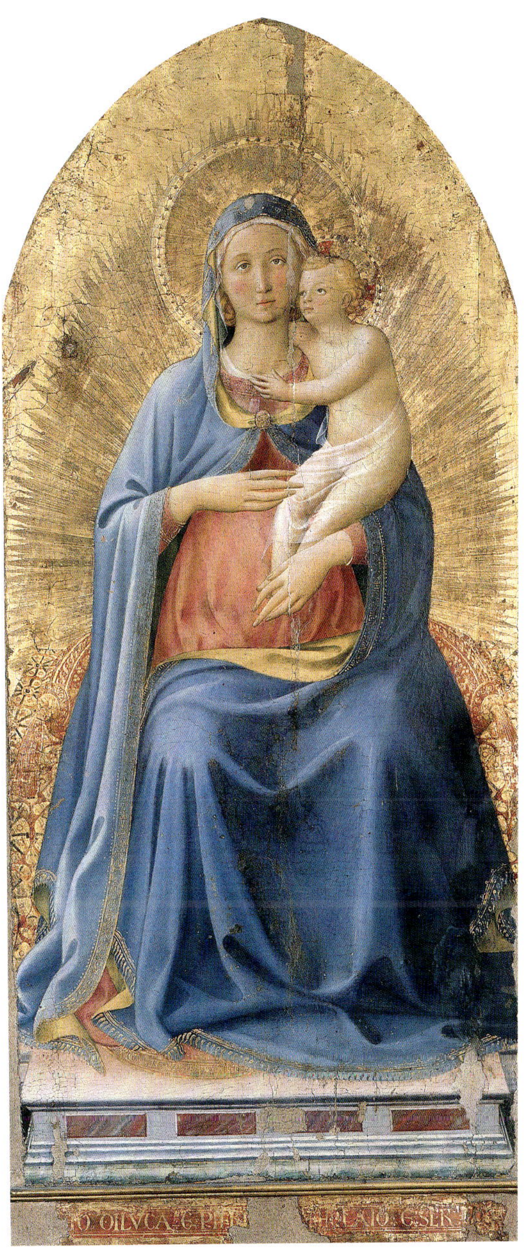

Figure 70. Fra Angelico. *Virgin and Child (Pontassieve Madonna)*. About 1429–30. Galleria degli Uffizi, Florence

remains plausible, no documentary confirming evidence has emerged, and therefore other circumstantial possibilities for the provenance must remain open. Among these is the church of San Domenico in San Miniato al Tedesco, which originally was dedicated to Saints James and Lucy. Like many Dominican establishments in outlying areas of Tuscany, this church underwent a program of renovation in the early years of the fifteenth century.[10] However, the fact that the *Naming of Saint John the Baptist* was copied by Andrea di Giusto in 1435 for the predella of an Olivetan altarpiece (now in the Museo Comunale, Prato) that otherwise borrows heavily from Lorenzo Monaco's altarpiece from San Benedetto fuori della Porta a Pinta in Florence[11] might argue that Angelico's altarpiece was publicly accessible in Florence rather than in San Miniato al Tedesco, which was more frequented by painters from the provinces of Pisa.

If it is possible to accept the *Pontassieve Madonna* as the central panel of this altarpiece, yet another solution may be considered. This panel was discovered in the Prepositura di San Michele Arcangelo at Pontassieve in the suburbs of Florence, and while it is conceivable that it was originally intended for that site, more likely, given its fragmentary state, is that it was transferred there from a Florentine church following the Napoleonic suppressions (or some other calamity) of the late eighteenth century, probably as the property of the largest landowners at Pontassieve, the Da Filicaia family. Along the base of the *Pontassieve Madonna* is a partial inscription recording the names of three men who may be presumed to have been the donors of the altarpiece: "... TONIO DI LVCA E PIERO DI NICHOLAIO E SER PIERO ..."; almost certainly, the references are to Antonio di Luca di Manetto da Filicaia (b. 1389–d. before 1449), Piero di Niccolò di Manetto da Filicaia (b. 1399–d. before 1438), and Ser Piero di Betto di Marco da Filicaia (1384–1443).[12] These men, the heads of three branches of the Da Filicaia family, were all residents of the Gonfalone della Chiavi in the *quartiere* di San Giovanni, in the parish of San Pier Maggiore, and traced their lineage to a common great-great grandfather. The circumstances under which they might have come together to sponsor the commission for an altarpiece about 1429 or 1430 are mysterious, but it may be assumed that they were in some way related to an ancestral chapel.

Three churches in Florence are known to have housed Da Filicaia chapels in the fifteenth century: Santa Maria degli Angeli, San Pier Maggiore, and Santa Croce. The Da Filicaia chapel in Santa Maria degli Angeli, dedicated to Saint Nicholas, was established in 1388 by the endowment of Monna Gemma, widow of Manetto da Filicaia, mother of Luca and Niccolò di Manetto, and therefore the paternal grandmother of two of the signatories of Angelico's painting. Completed in 1390 at a cost of 416 florins, the chapel was provided with an altarpiece by Mariotto di Nardo representing the *Virgin and Child Enthroned, with Saints Anthony Abbot, Nicholas, Lawrence, and Francis,* which is recorded as in situ until shortly before 1657.[13] Monna Gemma and her descendants were not buried in the chapel she established at Santa Maria degli Angeli, however, but rather in the family vault at Santa Croce, from which some of them were later translated to San Pier Maggiore. Little is known of the Da Filicaia chapel in San Pier Maggiore other than that it was located in the north aisle between two Albizzi family chapels, that it was dedicated to Saint Julian, that the family was obligated to pay for annual Masses there on the feasts of Saint John the Evangelist and Saint Mary Magdalene, and that it often is mistakenly supposed to have contained the

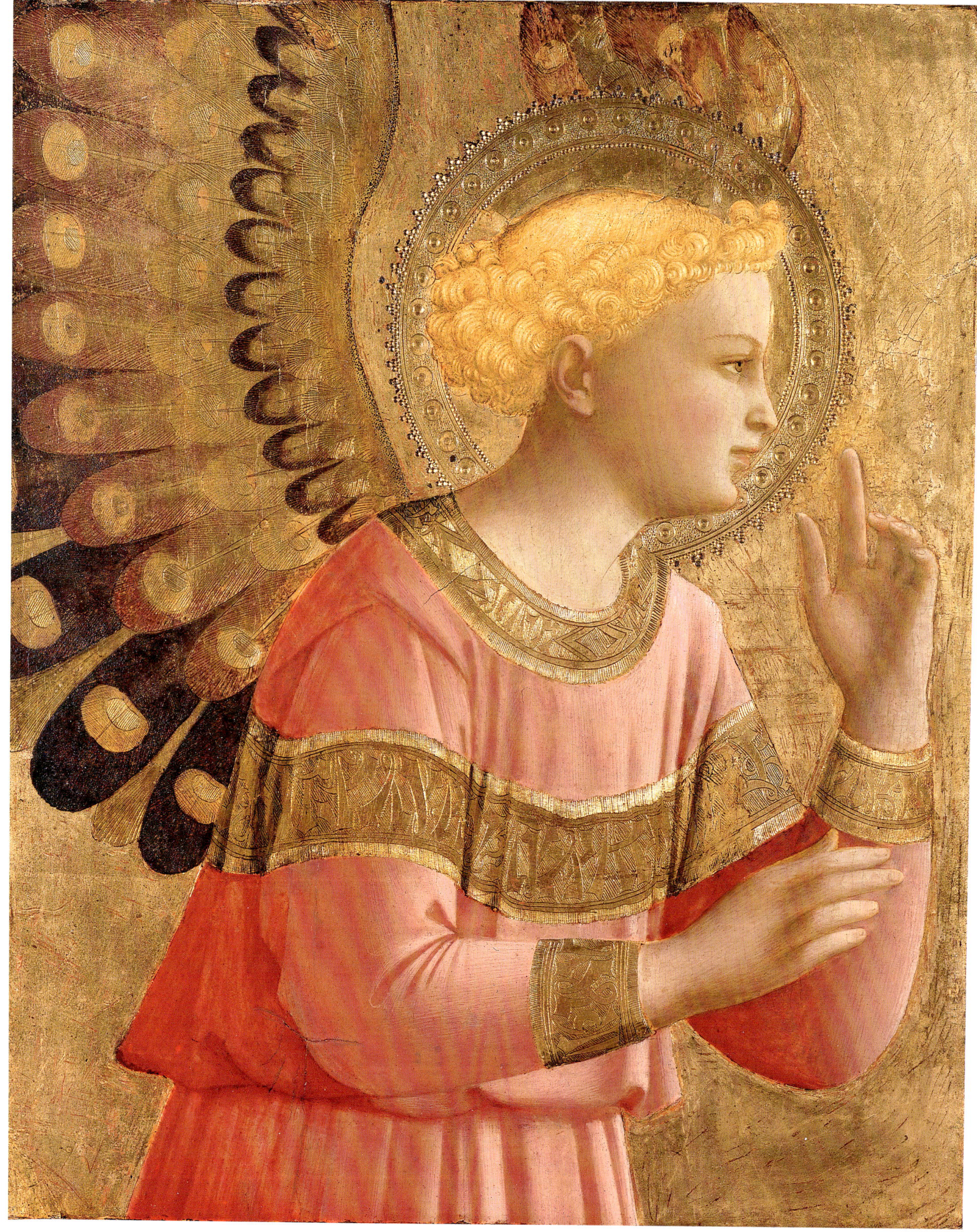

25: F

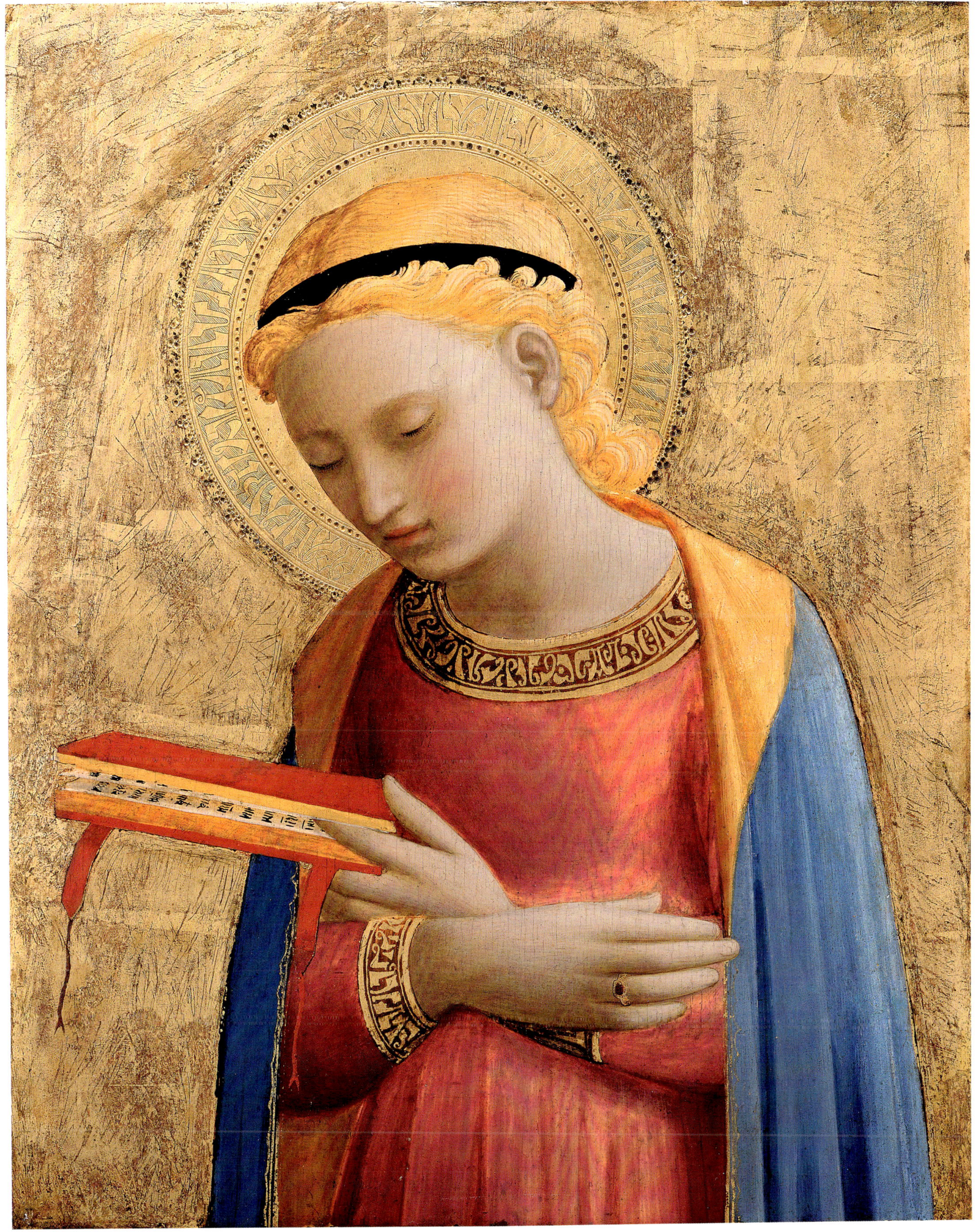

25: G

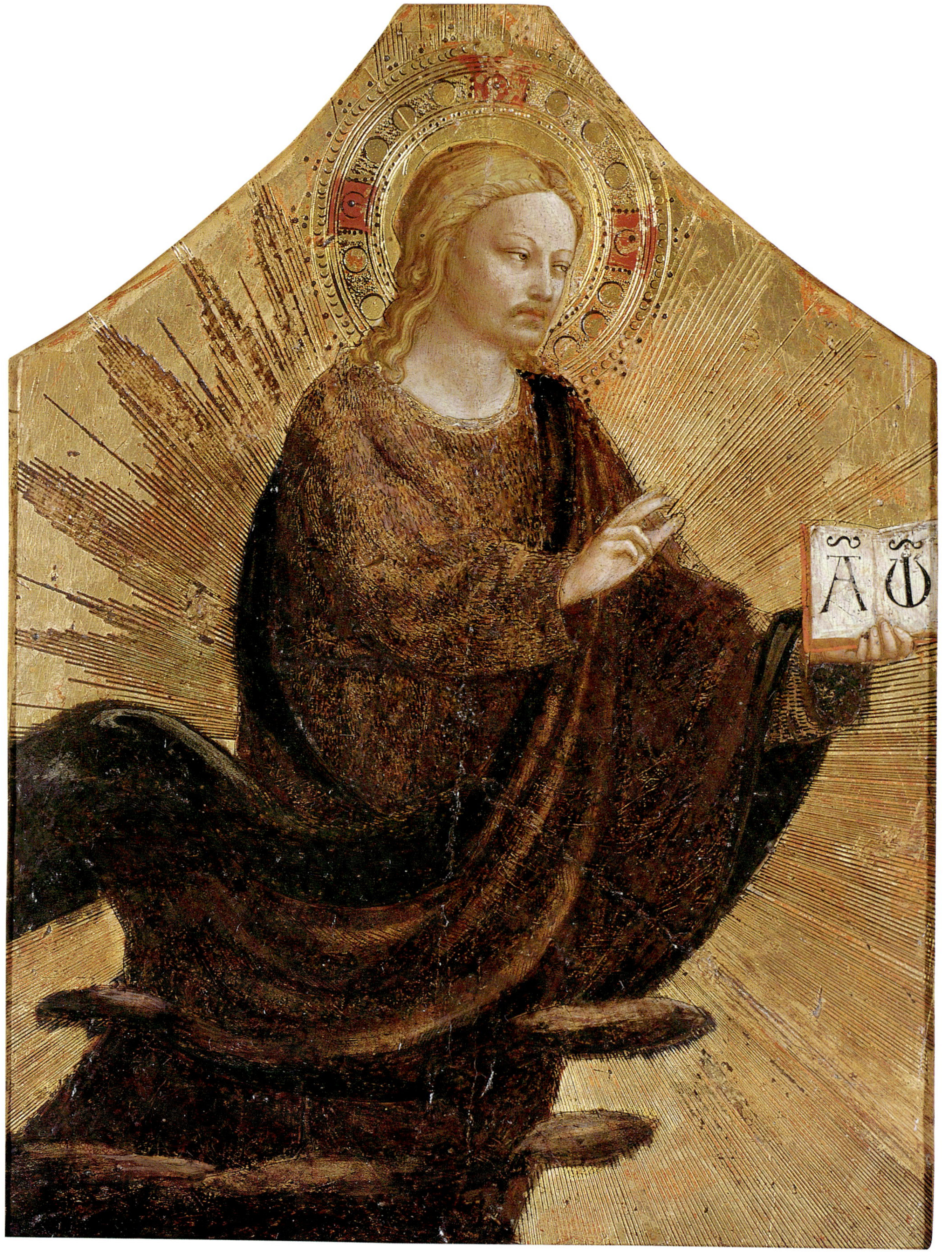

25: H

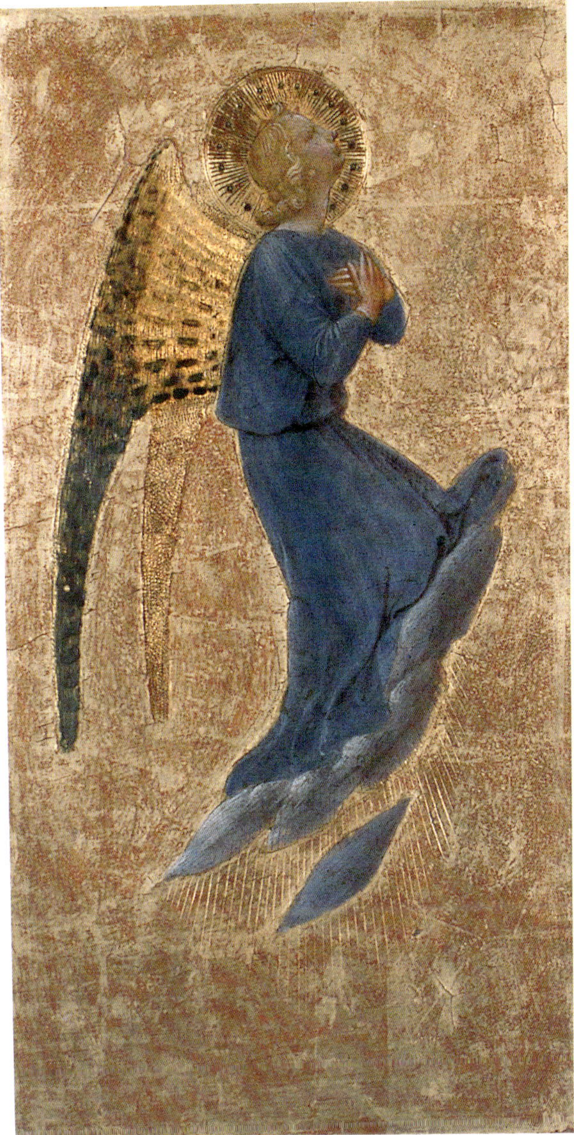

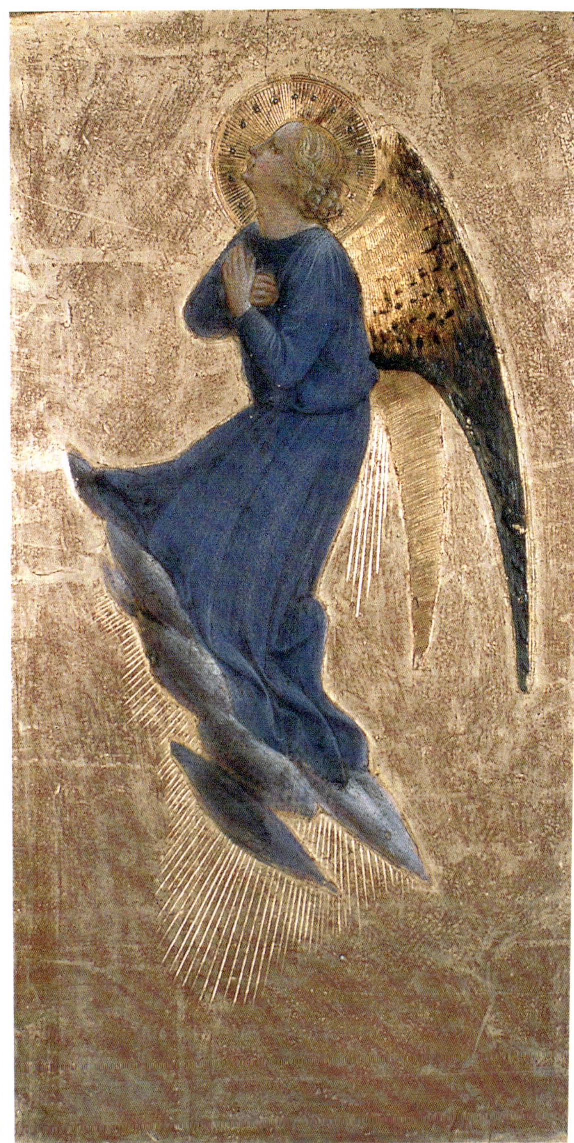

25: 1

late-thirteenth-century altarpiece of *Saint Peter Enthroned* by the Master of Saint Cecilia that was subsequently moved to the nearby church of San Simone.[14] It is unlikely that this chapel was ever dedicated to Saint Lucy, the principal saint in Angelico's altarpiece, since another chapel at San Pier Maggiore, the rights to which were owned by the Albizzi, bore that dedication. Even less is known of the chapel in Santa Croce, except that it was located "*sotto le volte*," presumably in the crypt. At least one early document records the presence there of a tomb marker engraved with the coat of arms of Antonio di Luca di Manetto da Filicaia, the principal signatory of Angelico's altarpiece, and identifies the locale as "Santa Lucia da Filicaia."[15] If the fourth saint portrayed in Angelico's altarpiece, above the San Francisco *Meeting of Saint Dominic and Saint Francis,* was Francis rather than Dominic, it is not unrealistic to suppose that Santa Croce may have been the painting's original location.

LK

1. Longhi 1940, p. 175.
2. Fahy 1987, pp. 178–83.
3. Kanter 2000, pp. 3–13.
4. Cited in Kanter et al. 1994, p. 327 n. 2.
5. The proposal by Kanter (2001a, pp. 34–37) that the Hampton Court *Redeemer* might have formed the central pinnacle of the triptych to which the Getty *Saints* and the Yale *Annunciation* belonged (see cat. 16) is mistaken.
6. See C. B. Strehlke, in Kanter et al. 1994, pp. 345–48, for a summary of earlier proposals.
7. Kanter 2001a, p. 30.
8. U. Baldini (1970, p. 96) dates it about 1435; J. Pope-Hennessy (1974, p. 226) dates it after 1450; and G. Bonsanti (1998, pp. 107, 154) dates it about 1450.
9. Kanter 2000, pp. 10–11.

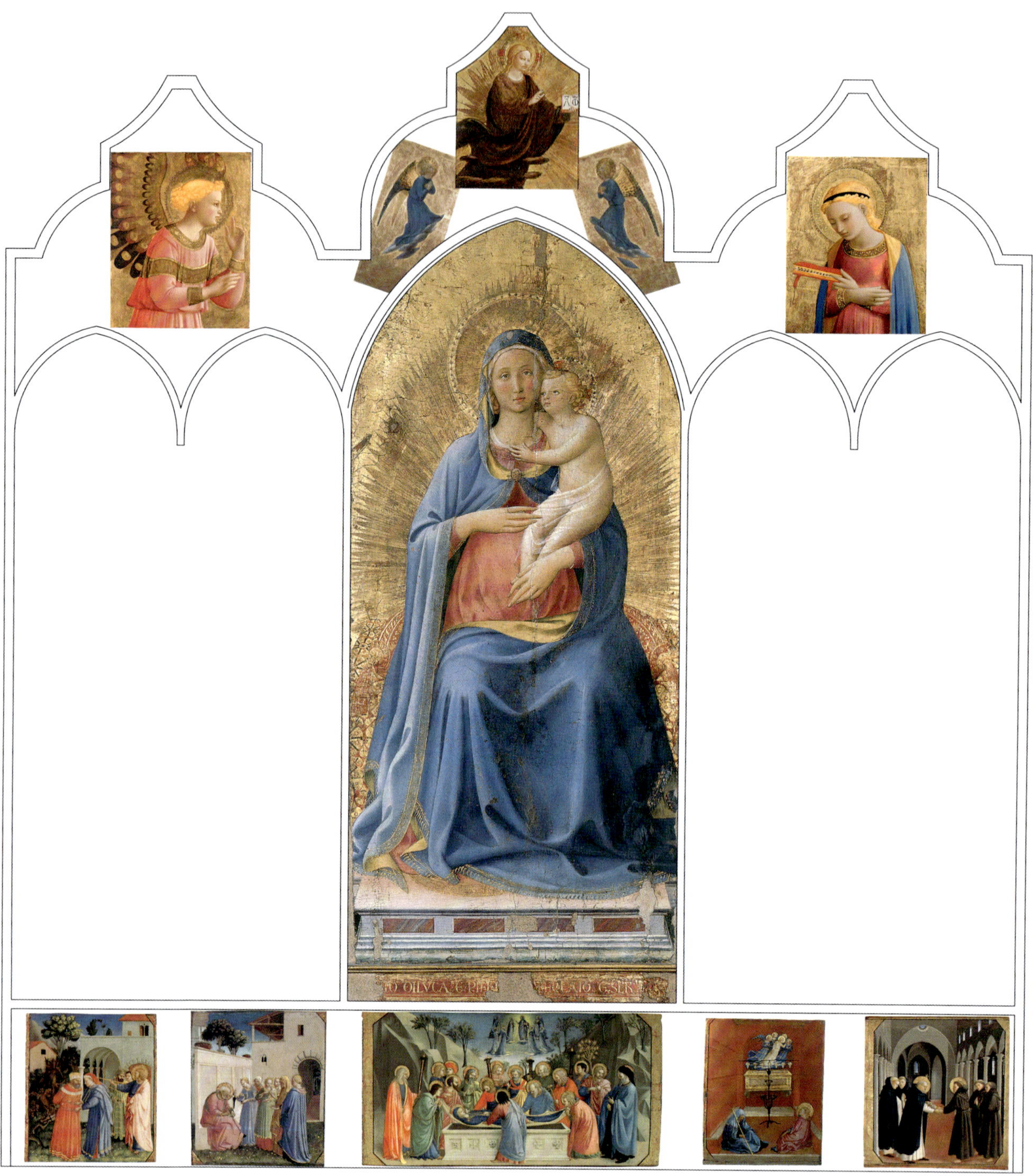

Figure 71. Fra Angelico. Santa Lucia (Da Filicaia) Altarpiece (reconstruction)

10. Pasquinucci 1998, pp. 112–19.
11. Datini 1972, p. 17; Eisenberg 1989, pp. 100–101.
12. The correct identification of the third signatory was kindly provided by Alessandro Cecchi, who is preparing an in-depth archival study of the Da Filicaia family.
13. Spinelli 1988, pp. 44–51.
14. W. Paatz and E. Paatz (1952, pp. 640–41) note also that the *Saint Peter* altarpiece may have been in the sacristy of San Pier Maggiore, whose patrons were the Benvenuti family; M. Bietti Favi (1990, p. 243) identifies the *Saint Peter Enthroned* as the original high altarpiece of that church. The Da Filicaia apparently owned rights to a second chapel in San Pier Maggiore, in the *tramezzo*.
15. ASF ms. 624, Sepoltuario Rosselli, I, p. 424 n. 268; also ASF, Carte Ceramelli Papiani, 2017, and ASF, Raccolta Sebregondi, 2209, which includes a complete genealogy of the family.

26.
King David Playing a Psaltery
(cutting from a psalter)

Pen and brown ink, with purple wash, on parchment, 19.7 x 17.9 cm (7¾ x 7 in.)
British Museum, London (1895-9-15-437)

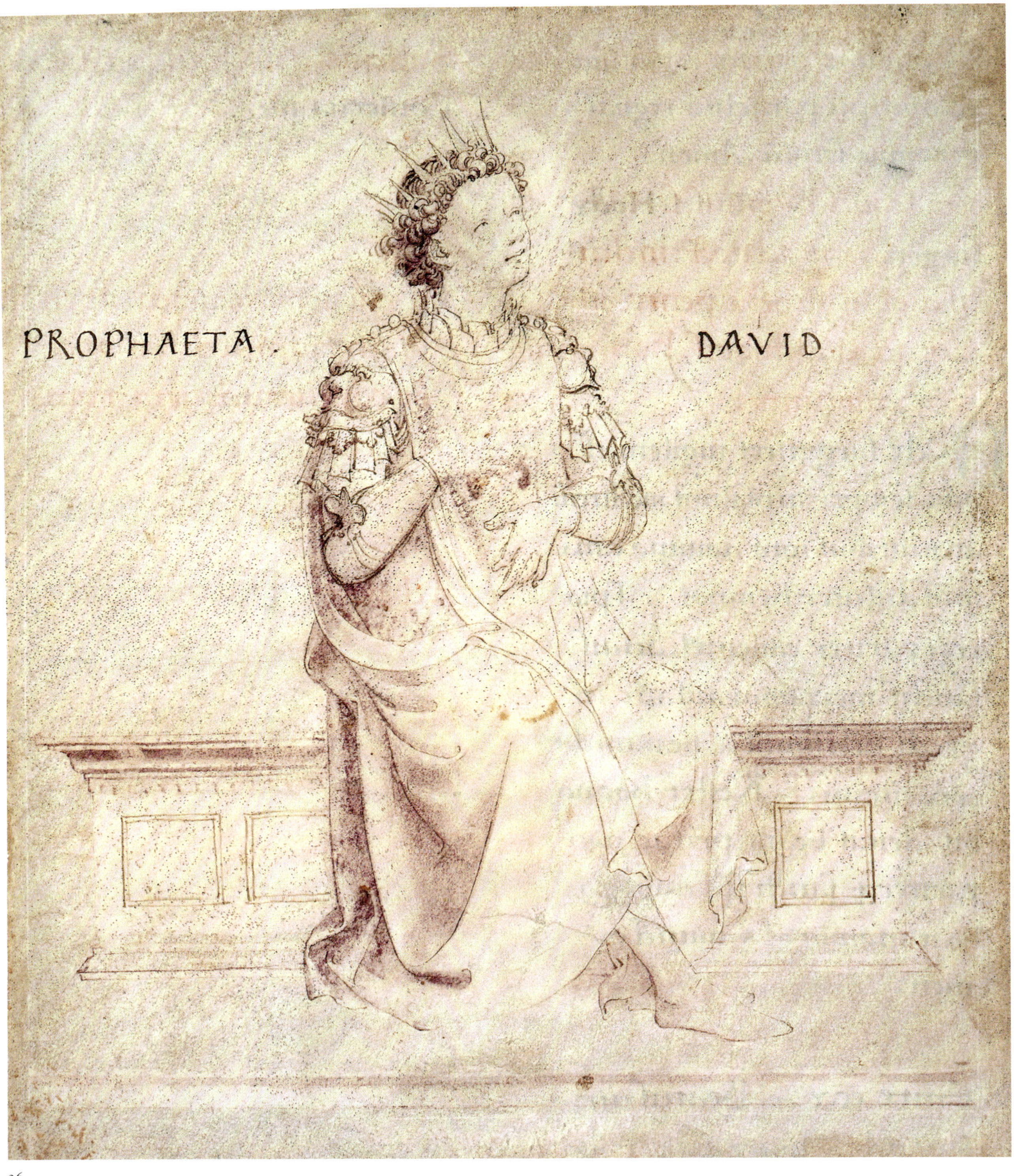

26

First described by Berenson as "the only drawing by Fra Angelico which leaves no ground for doubt,"[1] the British Museum *David* is unanimously recognized by scholars as one of the artist's small-scale masterpieces. Against the creamy white parchment preparation is the exquisitely elegant figure of the prophet King David dressed in royal armor, his face turned upward to God as his fingers move nimbly along the strings of a psaltery. He is seated on an impressively carved stone seat raised on a platform. The figure is identified by a Latin inscription, possibly added at a later date: PROPHAETA. DAVID. A delicately applied purple wash, now partially faded, highlights the prophet's hair and the deep folds

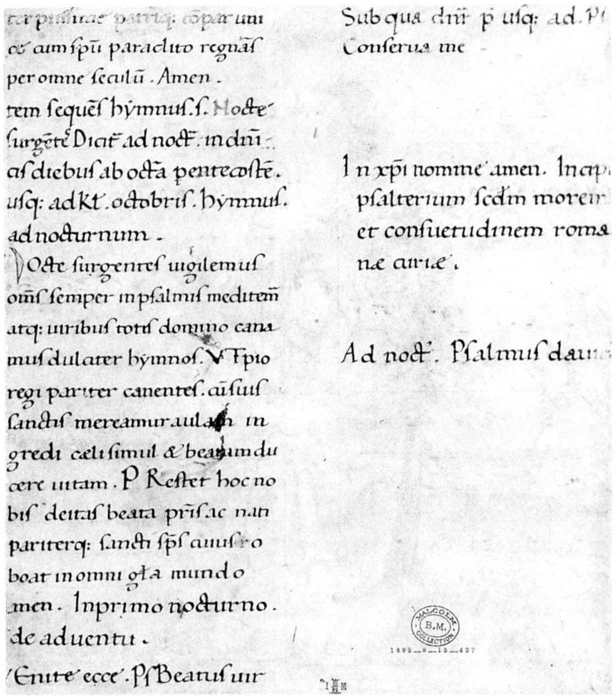

Figure 72. Verso of catalogue 26

of his mantle, and articulates the architectural details of the stone seat.

Although sometimes placed in the category of model-book drawings, and believed by Popham and Pouncey to have been executed on "a piece of waste parchment,"[2] the British Museum's *David* was correctly identified by Berenson as a cutting from a psalter, or Book of Psalms. On the reverse of the image, the original recto of the folio (fig. 72), is the continuation of the missing volume's index,[3] containing the list of hymns and Psalms to be recited at the appropriate times of day, followed by the incipit: "*In Christi nomine amen. Incipit psalterium secundum morem et consuetudimen romane curiae*" ("In the name of Christ. Amen. Here begins the psalter according to the customs and usage of the Roman curia"). Below this text is the rubric: "*Ad nocturnum. Psalmus David*" ("At nocturns. The Psalm of David"). Fra Angelico's illustration, which takes up virtually the entire space on the verso, presumably faced the text of Psalm 1, located on the following leaf of the same volume. In most medieval and Early Renaissance illuminated manuscripts, Psalm 1, "*Beatus vir*" ("Blessed is the man"), opens with a historiated initial *B* containing an image of King David, traditionally believed to have been the author of the Psalms. One such example also excised from a psalter is the initial *B* with David looking up to God, by Zanobi Strozzi (cat. 46), included in the present exhibition. Fra Angelico's illustration, on the other hand, is more typical of the so-called prefatory full-page miniatures, showing the seated prophet as a musician, which appear in the introductory pages of early medieval psalters.[4]

Most authors have concurred in dating the British Museum *David* to about 1430 or only slightly later.[5] In fact, the lucidly articulated structure of the prophet's seat finds a close precedent in other works produced by the artist during this period, such as the remarkable series of predella panels centered around the Philadelphia *Burial of the Virgin,* which are here dated around 1429 (cat. 25 C). Like the drawing, these works are distinguished above all by the artist's confident display of his absolute mastery of one-point perpective and of the classically inspired, Early Renaissance architectural idiom developed by Brunelleschi and Masaccio. In terms of its figural style, however, the drawing reflects a slightly more mature phase in the artist's career than this predella, anticipating the formal vocabulary of such images as the Louvre *Coronation of the Virgin,* from about 1432–34. This would confirm a date for Angelico's intervention in the decoration of the psalter between 1430 and 1432.

If the British Museum *David* is to be viewed within the context of Fra Angelico's activity as an illuminator rather than as an independent drawing, it may be worth speculating on the possible circumstance of its commission. While it is tempting to associate the original psalter with the same Florentine Dominican establishments that sponsored the production of other liturgical books decorated by the artist, the fact that it was written according to the Use of Rome, as stated in the incipit, would seem to preclude a monastic provenance. Like privately owned Books of Hours, whose function the psalter sometimes replaced, the volume may have been commissioned by a powerful cleric or Florentine aristocrat, perhaps with ties to the Dominican order.[6]

PP

1. Berenson 1903, p. 4.
2. Popham and Pouncey 1950, no. 2, p. 2.
3. From the top of the leaf, the full text on the verso (the original recto) reads as follows: "[*pa*]*ter piissime patrique co*[*m*]*par uni / ce cum sp*[*irit*] *uparaclito regna*[*n*]*s/per omne seculu*[*m*]. *Amen.* / [*rub.*] [. . .]*tem seque*[n]s *hymnus.s.* Nocte surge[n]tes [rub.] *Dicit*[*ur*] *ad noct*[*urnum*] *in d*[*omi*]*ni/cis diebus ab octa*[*va*] *pentecoste*[*m*] / *usq*[*ue*] *ad Kl. octobris. hymnus./ ad nocturnum.* / Nocte sugentes vigilemus/ om[ne]s semper in psalmis meditem[ur] / atque viribus totis domino cana/mus dulciter hymnos. Ut pio / regi pariter canantes cu[m] suis/sanctis meramur aulam in/gredi caeli simul et beatam du/cere vitam. Prestet hoc no / bis deitas beata p[at]ris ac nati/pariterque sancti sp[iritu]s cuius ro/boat in omni gl[ori]a mundo/amen. [rub.] *In primo nocturno./ de adventu.*/Venite ecce. [rub.] *Ps.* Beatus vir / [. . .] / [rub.] *Sub qua dominicis per usque. ad. Ps.*/Conserva me. / In christi nomine amen. Incipit / psalterium s[e]c[un]d[u]m morem / et consuetudinem roma/nae curiae. / [rub.] *Ad noct*[*urnum*]. *Psalmus david.*"
4. Corrigan 1996, pp. 87–95.
5. Degenhart and Schmitt (1968, pp. 446–48), followed by Bonsanti (1998), suggest a date of about 1430. For Pope-Hennessy (1974, p. 235), "the architecture of the seat is consistent with a dating ca. 1433."
6. Rosemary Muir Wright (2000, p. 6) aptly notes that "some of the most famous illuminated psalters were made for lay people of high status."

27.

A.
The Nativity

Tempera and gold on panel, 29 x 18.9 cm
(11⅜ x 7 7/16 in.)
Pinacoteca Civica, Forlì

B.
The Agony in the Garden

Tempera and gold on panel, 29 x 18.9 cm
(11⅜ x 7 7/16 in.)
Pinacoteca Civica, Forlì

These two small panels, identical both in size and support—and now missing their original engaged frames—are presumed to have once formed part of a portable altarpiece for private devotion. Still visible on the reverse of each painting is the *faux-marbre* pattern that often decorated such objects and that would have been evident when the panels were folded or closed. First identified as autograph works by Fra Angelico when they entered the Pinacoteca in Forlì as part of the Missirini Bequest, in the late nineteenth century, this attribution has been accepted by most subsequent scholars. There have been divergent opinions, however, regarding their placement in the earlier or later part of the artist's career, with varied proposals for dating them ranging from between as early as 1422 and as late as 1446–48.[1]

The most cogent and penetrating discussion of the Forlì panels to date was published by Roberto Longhi in 1940.[2] While acknowledging Angelico's debt to Gentile da Fabriano in the evocative nocturnal setting of the *Nativity,* Longhi identified Masaccio's powerful monumental vocabulary as the immediate source for the advanced spatial and formal solutions that distinguish both of the present compositions, and, accordingly, ascribed them to the period of the artist's greatest receptivity to Masaccio's models, between 1425 and 1430. Describing the massive, solidly articulated bodies in the *Agony in the Garden* as the "most Masaccesque persons that one may be given to find outside of Masaccio," Longhi drew a pointed comparison between the figure of the pensively absorbed Saint Peter, in particular, and the detail of the same apostle kneeling before the water in Masaccio's fresco of *The Tribute Money.*

No less impressive than the statuesque figure types that inhabit these scenes, as Longhi observed, is the ambitious, monumental spatial structure of the compositions, despite their reduced scale. In a brilliant display of technical virtuosity, the steeply foreshortened hut that occupied center stage in the earlier, Minneapolis *Nativity* (cat. 17), as well as in Angelico's later versions of the subject, is here rotated, so that it is viewed at a sharp angle from the right, with the same rigorously observed recession in depth characterizing all of its architectural components. Possibly executed in conscious consideration of the panel's position on the left in the original structure, this solution reflects the artist's keen exploration of the laws of one-point perspective and the principles of realistic representation. Similarly, in the *Agony in the Garden,* Angelico's intelligent adaptation of the scene to the vertical format of the panel results in a more psychologically charged and complex version of the traditional subject. Rather than following the typical iconography for the sleeping apostles, who are usually presented as an isolated group in the foreground, the composition is unified by the carefully orchestrated placement of the figures in different, superimposed zones, articulated in depth by the orchard fences and by the receding roof of the garden hut. From the beautifully depicted, recumbent Saint John in the foreground, enveloped in ample blue robes and leaning on his arm like a fallen soldier of antiquity; to Saint Andrew and Saint Peter in the middle distance above him; to the praying figures of Christ and the angel at the upper left, the eye is made to linger over each and every detail of the narrative.

Of the other works by Angelico from the same "Masaccesque" period identified by Longhi, the closest to the Forlì panels is the series of predella scenes centered around the Philadelphia *Burial of the Virgin* (cat. 25 C), here dated to about 1429. The stringent correspondences, both in figure types and spatial conceits, among the Forlì paintings and the two other panels from that predella now in San Marco and in the Kimbell Art Museum, Fort Worth, in particular, prompted Longhi to suggest that they were part of the same complex. While recognizing that all these works must, indeed, be contemporary in date, Pope-Hennessy[3] rightly noted that they could not, in fact, have belonged to one altarpiece, simply based on technical considerations, and proposed that the Forlì panels might, instead, have comprised the wings of a small triptych.

Physical evidence indicates that whether included in a dip tych, triptych, or larger narrative structure, the present panels, which preserve their original edges, were never hinged together. The existence of portable altarpieces made up of independent elements that were intended to be installed side by side, with no permanent connecting device, recently has been highlighted by Victor Schmidt,[4] who cites surviving fourteenth-century Sienese examples with two or more scenes. Among existing diptychs composed of narrative scenes, both with and without hinges, there seems to be none, however, which combines the subject of the Nativity with that of the Agony in the Garden—an espisode depicted with less frequency than others, and normally included only in complete cycles of the Passion. While this would appear to confirm that the Forlì panels were once part of a more extensive complex, it is worth citing a famous Florentine exception, in which the Agony in the Garden was made the focus of a major altarpiece: the panel by Lorenzo Monaco in the Galleria dell'Accademia. Although presumably made for Santa Maria degli Angeli, the

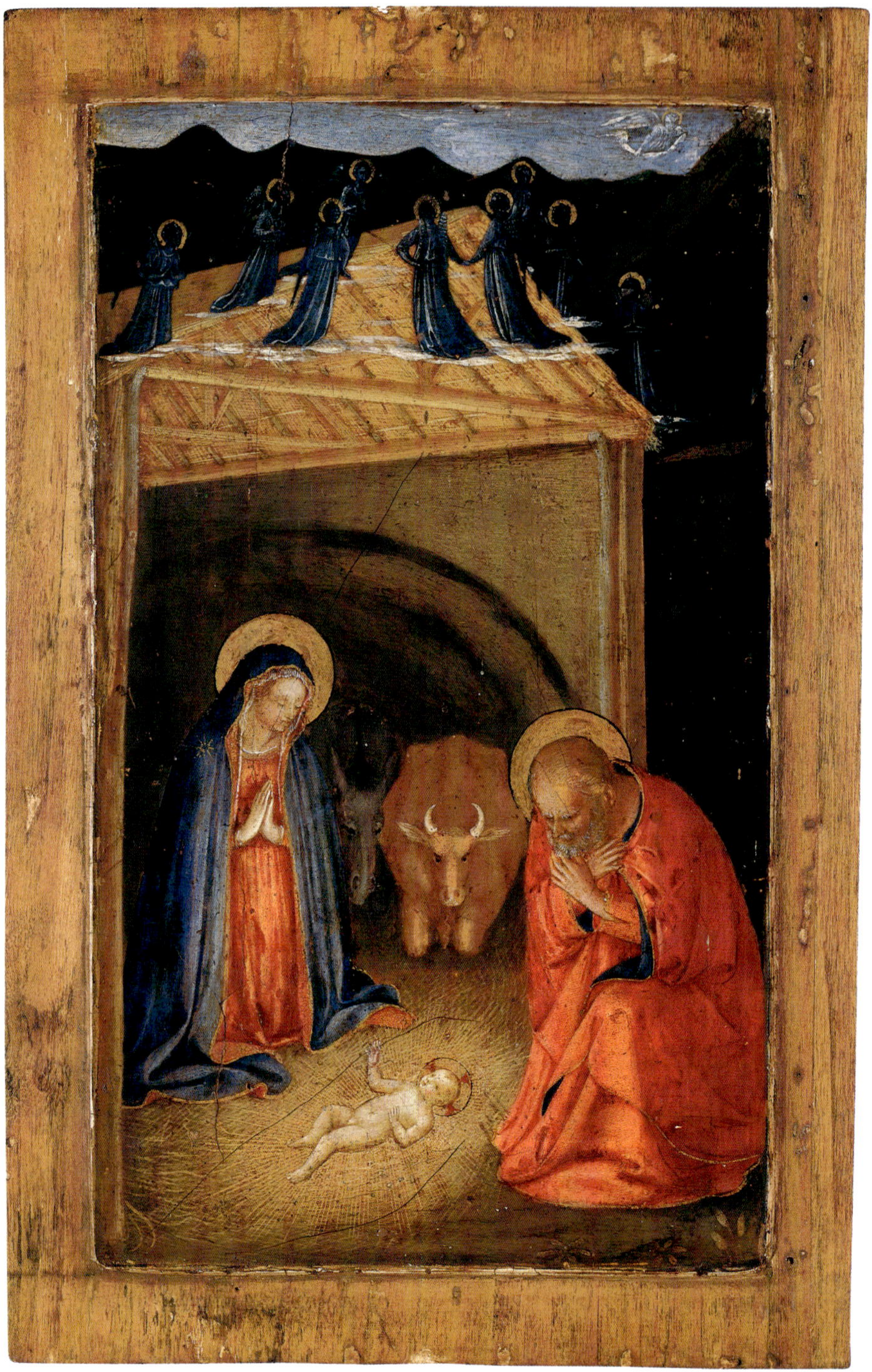

27: A

precise function and exact original location of this impressive seven-foot-high icon is not known, nor is the identity of its secular donor, shown in prayer next to the sleeping apostles. Marvin Eisenberg and George Bent have related the image to the devotions of Holy Week—specifically, to the liturgical passages recited during services on Maundy Thursday.[5] In Pseudo-Bonaventure's text of the *Meditations on the Life of Christ*, in fact, it is the account of Christ's spiritual struggles in the Garden of Gethsemane that marks the beginning of the meditations on the Passion, "before the morning"—the first of the numerous agonies, both mental and physical, that are endured by Christ as a "real man."[6] Viewed within such a context, rather than as one of the many episodes in painted cycles of the Passion, the Forlì *Agony in the Garden* takes on an added relevance as a vehicle for prayer and meditation on Christ's humanity, complementing the accompanying *Nativity* scene.[7]

PP

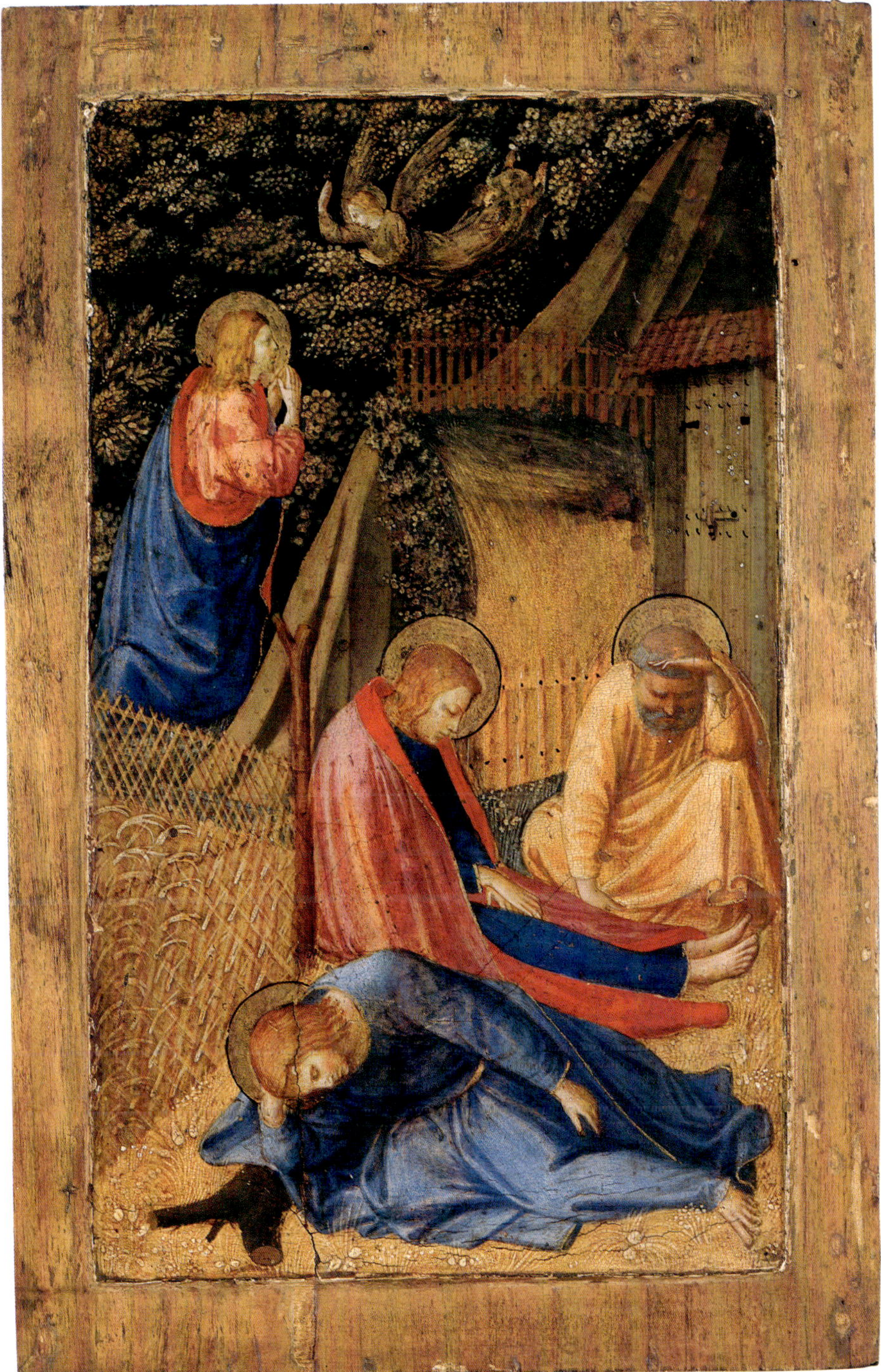

27: B

1. See Viroli 1980, pp. 32–34 (with earlier bibliography); Spike 1996, pp. 236–37; Bonsanti 1998, pp. 114–15.
2. Longhi 1940 (1975 ed.), pp. 40–41.
3. Pope-Hennessy 1974, p. 226.
4. Schmidt 2002, pp. 395–419, esp. pp. 403–6.
5. Eisenberg 1984, pp. 271–89; Bent 1984, vol. I, pp. 388–91.
6. "Therefore, since he was a real man and placed in great anguish as a man, pity Him as intimately as possible. Consider and see with perseverance all the actions and afflictions of your Lord" ("Meditation on the Passion of Christ Before the Morning," in Bonaventure 1977 ed., p. 324).
7. Another scene that may perhaps be of some relevance for this interpretation of the Agony in the Garden is a panel attributed to Masaccio in Altenburg, Germany (Penndorf 1998, p. 46), in which the *Agony in the Garden* is paired with the *Communion of Saint Jerome,* highlighting the Eucharistic significance of the theme. Equally of some interest is the mention of a small tablet with "Christ on the Mount of Olives" ("*una tavoletta dipintovi storia di Cristo di Monte Uliveto*") in the 1492 inventory of the Medici palace (Spallanzani and Gaeta Bertelà 1992, p. 80); the painting, then located in Piero's bedroom, is listed together with a small panel of the *Annunciation,* described as "*opera grecha.*"

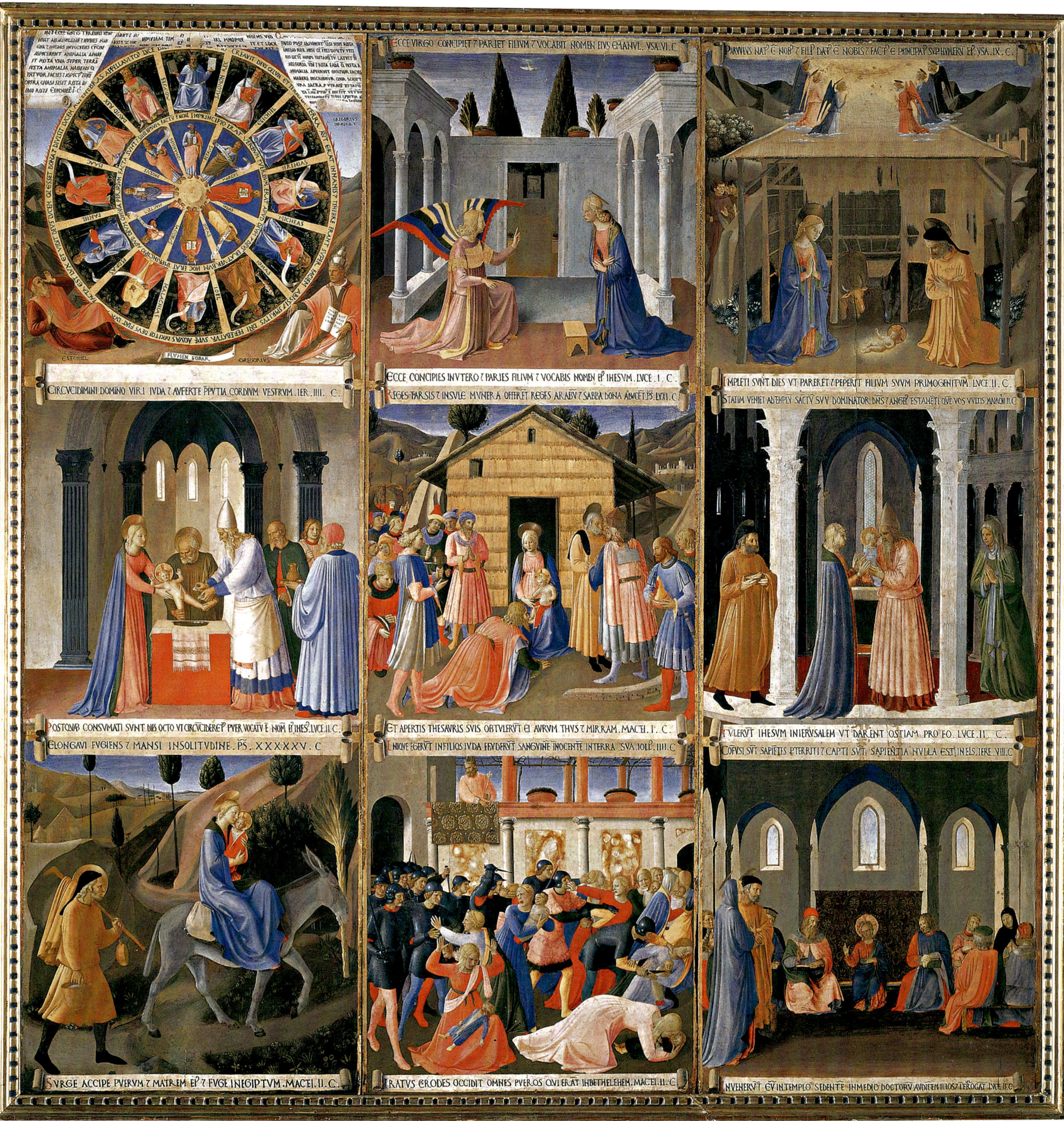
ECCE VIRGO CONCIPIET 7 PARIET FILIVM 7 VOCABIT NOMEN EIVS EMANVEL. YSA. VII. C.
FLVMEN COBAR
CIRCVCIDIMINI DOMINO VIRI IVDA 7 AVFERTE PPVTIA CORDIVM VESTRVM. IER. IIII. C.
ECCE CONCIPIES INVTERO 7 PARIES FILIVM 7 VOCABIS NOMEN EP IHESVM. LVCE. I. C.
REGES TARSIS 7 INSVLE MVNERA OFFERET REGES ARABV 7 SABBA DONA ADVCET. PS. LXXI. C.
IMPLETI SVNT DIES VT PARERET 7 PEPERIT FILIVM SVVM PRIMOGENITVM. LVCE. II. C.
STATIM VENIET AD TEMPLV SACTV SVV DOMINATOR DNS 7 ANGEL TESTAMETI QVE VOS VVLTIS. MALACHI. II. C.
POSTQVAM CONSVMATI SVNT DIES OCTO VT CIRCVCIDERET PVER VOCATV E NOM EI IHES. LVCE. II. C.
ELONGAVI FVGIENS 7 MANSI INSOLITVDINE. PS. XXXXXV. C
ET APERTIS THESAVRIS SVIS OBTVLERVT EI AVRVM THVS 7 MIRRAM. MACTEI. I. C.
INIQVE EGERVT INFILIOS IVDA EFVDERVT SANGVINE INOCENTE INTERRA SVA. IOEL. IIII. C.
TVLERVT IHESVM INIERVSALEM VT DARENT OSTIAM PRO EO. LVCE. II. C.
COFVSI SVT SAPIETES PTERRITI 7 CAPTI SVT. SAPIENTIA NVLLA EST IN EIS. IERE. VIII. C.
SVRGE ACCIPE PVERVM 7 MATREM EI 7 FVGE INEGIPTVM. MACTEI. II. C.
IRATVS ERODES OCCIDIT OMNES PVEROS QVI ERAT INBETHELEHEM. MACTEI. II. C.
INVENERVT EV INTEMPLO SEDENTE INMEDIO DOCTORV AVDIEEM ILLOS 7 IEROGAT. LVCE. II. C.

Chapter V
Fra Angelico: Artistic Maturity and Late Career (1433–55)

LAURENCE KANTER

The third and final chapter of Fra Angelico's career opens with a painting regarded by some as the artist's greatest masterpiece, the *Coronation of the Virgin* altarpiece (fig. 74) from San Domenico, Fiesole, now in the Musée du Louvre, Paris. The Louvre *Coronation* is so sophisticated in its spatial structure that John Pope-Hennessy was led to conclude that it must be dependent upon the example of Domenico Veneziano's paintings of the 1440s, and, therefore, that the complexity of its figural arrangement and decorative details must be typical of Angelico's latest works.[1] Other scholars, however, have recognized that it was probably completed before the formal consecration of the church of San Domenico in 1435; on the basis of its figure style alone it is most likely datable to the years between 1432 and 1434. Thus, the nature of its relationship to such paintings as Domenico Veneziano's *Saint Lucy* altarpiece, or Filippo Lippi's Barbadori or Sant'Ambrogio altarpieces, needs to be reformulated, acknowledging that the compositional novelties of this painting—its exceptionally low viewpoint; its faultless, sweeping perspective; the foreground occupied by saints seen almost completely from behind—are all inventions of Fra Angelico, designed by the artist to situate the worshiper within the fictive space of the mystical event he has portrayed. The intellectual component of the illusion is reinforced by the breathtaking precision and abundance of veristic detail throughout the painting: the pleats, ripples, textures, and gilt ornament of the saints' robes; the patterns of the steeply foreshortened floor tiles and the brightly colored marble steps of the dais; and the strings, bridges, sound-hole carvings, and belled tubes of the angels' instruments are perhaps matched in their accomplishment—taking into account all of European painting in the first half of the fifteenth century—only by the altarpieces of Jan van Eyck in Bruges and Ghent.

The predella to the Louvre *Coronation of the Virgin* recounts six episodes from the life of Saint Dominic with, at the center, an image of Christ as the Man of Sorrows: it is the first complete series by Angelico, so far as is known,[2] of scenes from the legend of the founder of his order. Following the example of the main panel of the Cortona *Annunciation* altarpiece, each scene is oriented parallel to the picture surface, opening out at one side with a steep diagonal recession into depth. The third scene, *Saint Dominic Raising Napoleone Orsini,* is set in what is essentially a replica of the painted architecture of the Cortona *Annunciation*. The last three scenes—the *Miracle of the Book, Saint Dominic and His Companions Fed by Angels,* and the *Death of Saint Dominic*—are in part derived from earlier experiments on the *Saint Francis* (cat. 24) and *Saint Lucy* (cat. 25) predellas but also anticipate the designs of the Linaiuoli (cat. 29) and Guidalotti (cat. 30) predellas later in the 1430s, as well as of the Orange Cloister frescoes painted at about the same time by Angelico's studio (see pp. 291–94). The initial predella scene, the pope's vision of Dominic supporting the crumbling walls of the Lateran Basilica, continues a tradition descended from Giotto's frescoes of the legend of Saint Francis, at Assisi, where a similar episode in the life of that saint is portrayed; it established an iconographic prototype from which even Angelico himself hardly strayed in two later versions of the subject (see cat. 37). In many ways the most remarkable of the predella scenes—Dominic's vision of Saints Peter and Paul inside the Vatican basilica—is unprecedented in its aggressive spatial effects and sophisticated interior lighting. In this episode, and again in the fourth one, depicting the *Miracle of the Book,* it is not only the mathematical precision with which the architectural perspective is realized but the palpable density and temperature of the atmosphere and the tireless attention to minute, realistic details that set Angelico apart from (and ahead of) any painter among his contemporaries in Italy.

Although radically different in scale, only one other work by Fra Angelico incorporates a spatial structure similar to that of the Louvre *Coronation of the Virgin* altarpiece and approaches the same obsessive level of naturalistic detail: the small *Dormition and Assumption of the Virgin* in the Isabella Stewart Gardner Museum, Boston (cat. 28), the last of four reliquaries painted by the Dominican master for Santa Maria Novella, reputedly commissioned by Fra Giovanni di Zanobi Masi (d. 1434). Following shortly after these two works, Angelico produced a painting that is perhaps a compromise between them, both in size and in the blending of compositional ideas:

Opposite:
Figure 73. Fra Angelico. Annunziata Silver Chest (detail). About 1448–50. Museo di San Marco, Florence

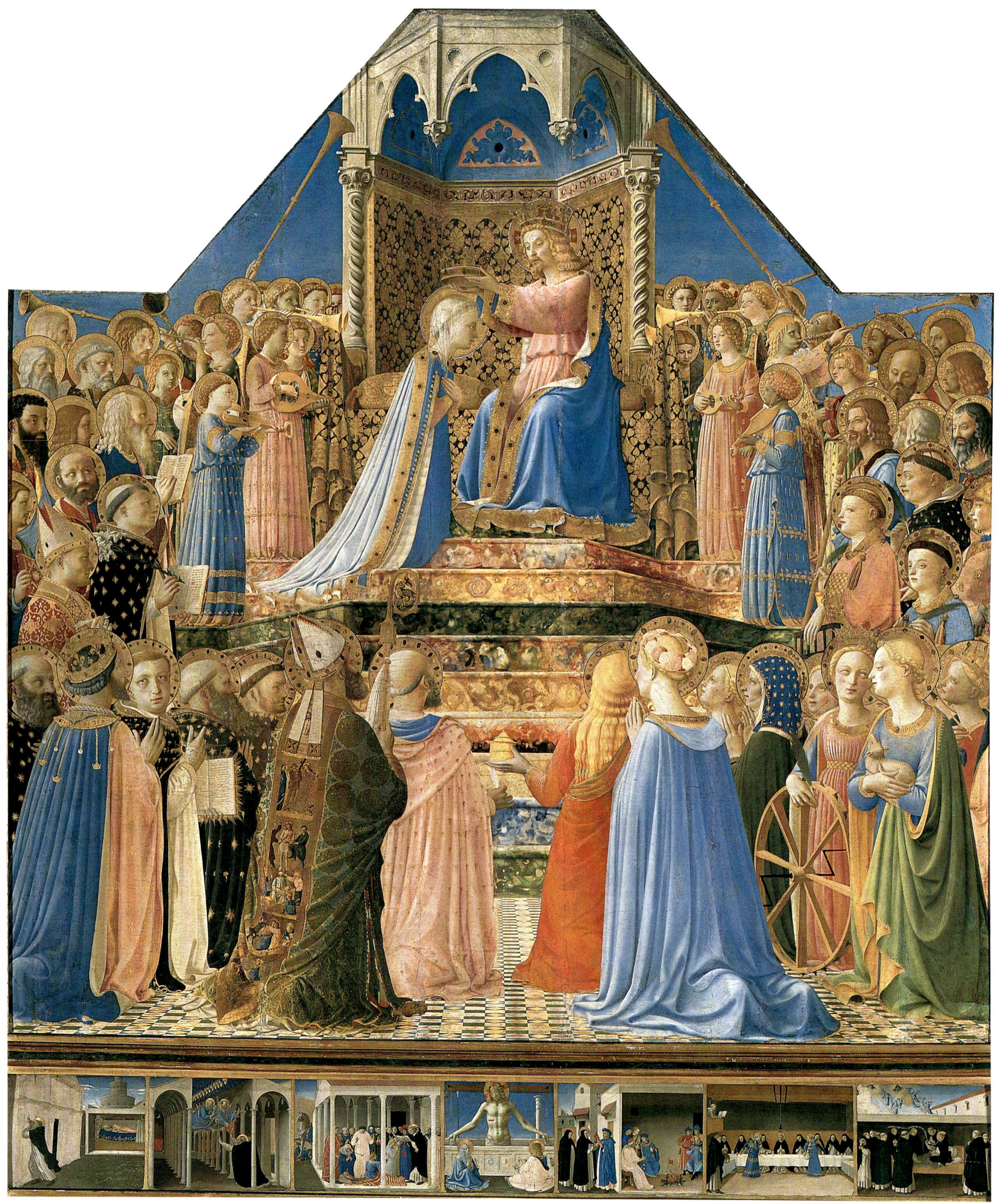

Figure 74. Fra Angelico. *The Coronation of the Virgin*. About 1432–34. Musée du Louvre, Paris

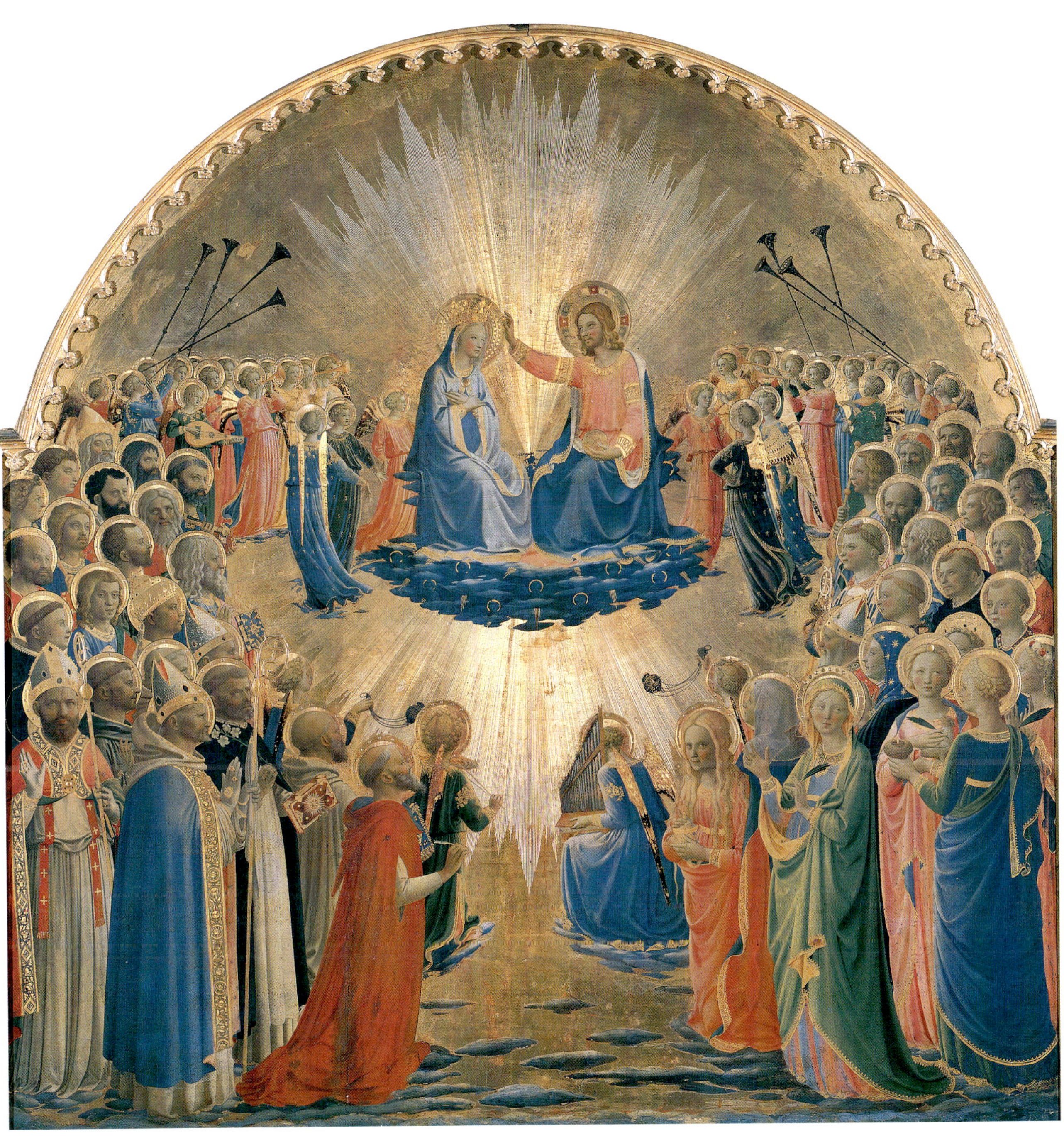

Figure 75. Fra Angelico. *The Coronation of the Virgin.* About 1434–35. Galleria degli Uffizi, Florence

a small altarpiece of the *Coronation of the Virgin* formerly installed on the rood screen in the hospital church of Santa Maria Nuova in Florence, and now in the Galleria degli Uffizi (fig. 75). The elaborate throne and stone canopy of the Louvre altarpiece are eliminated, as are the flight of colored marble steps, the intricately patterned floor tiles, and any other indication of physically measurable space. Instead, the artist evokes the celestial realm encountered in the upper half of the Gardner panel, densely populated here not only by a ring of dancing and music-making angels but also by ranks of saints—none of them seen entirely (and indecorously) from behind—deployed along radiating orthogonals with Christ and his mother at their focal center.

The elevation of the Virgin in the Uffizi *Coronation* to a position of honor in which she is level with Christ rather than kneeling before him as in the Louvre altarpiece, and the heightened abstraction of the elaborately engraved gold ground behind them may have been concessions on the artist's part to the demands of his patrons—a community of female oblates—or may indicate a trend in his pictorial thinking that

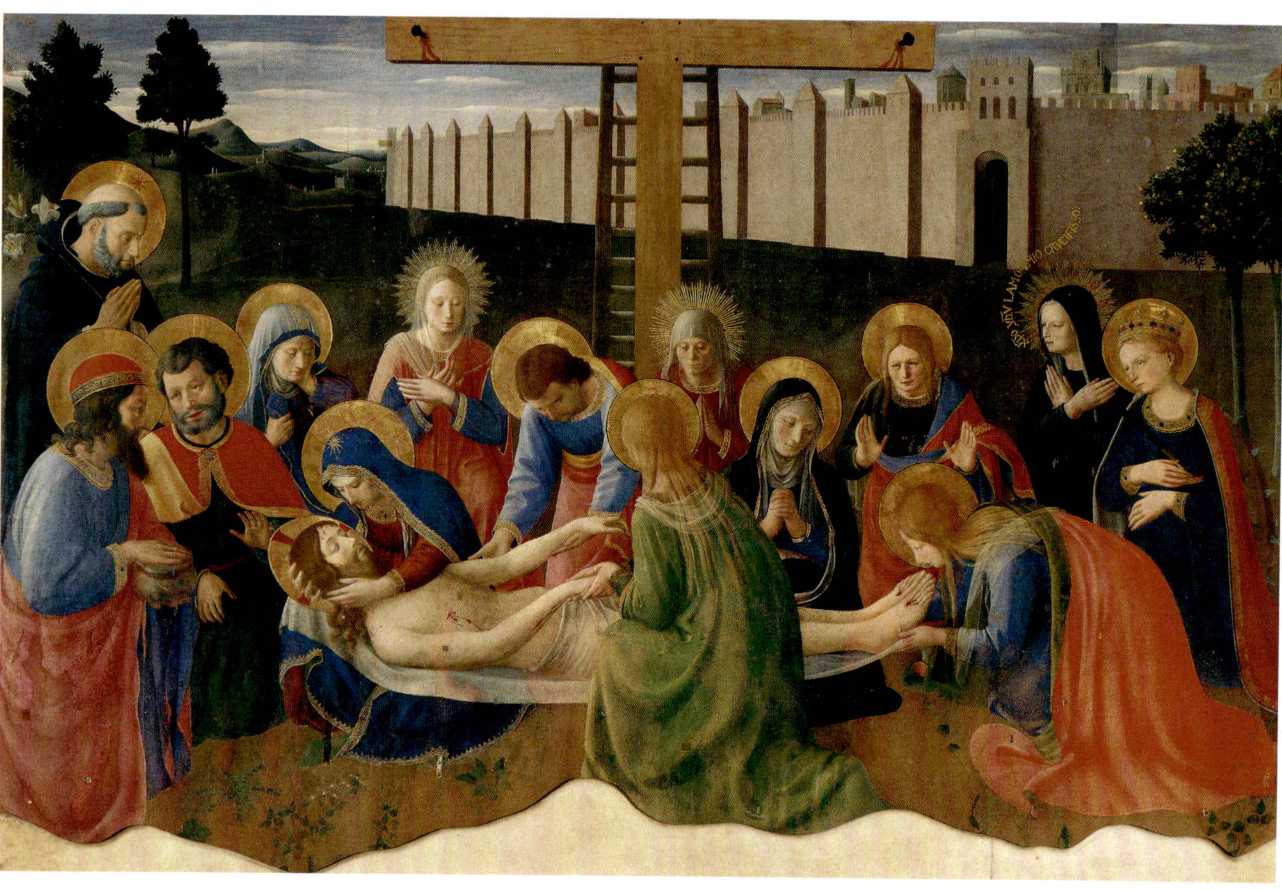

Figure 76. Fra Angelico. *The Lamentation over the Dead Christ*. 1436–41. Museo di San Marco, Florence

evolved over the last half of the 1430s. The debate could be framed in this particular case to support either argument, but that Angelico's style did develop in the direction of a preference for reduced visual detail in his settings, more rigorous and classicizing symmetry in his compositions, and greater concentration of dramatic focus in his narratives is undeniable. The progress of this development can be charted in a comparison of the predella scenes from the monumental Linaiuoli tabernacle (cat. 29), its commission documented in 1433; the Guidalotti altarpiece in Perugia (cat. 30), only indirectly documented by secondary sources but datable on stylistic grounds to about 1437; and the San Marco high altarpiece (cat. 34), which appears to have been begun about 1439 or 1440 and was complete by the end of 1442. The same trend is evident on a more monumental scale in the contrast between the *Deposition* altarpiece from Santa Trinita (about 1431–32) and the damaged but moving altarpiece of the *Lamentation* from the church of Santa Maria della Croce al Tempio (fig. 76), commissioned in 1436 but completed only in 1441.[3] Where the former is panoramic in vision, brightly lit, teeming with veristic detail, and almost exuberant in the activity of its cast of numerous characters, the latter is somber and severe in mood; its landscape setting is spare, distilled only to descriptive essentials; and the emotional pathos of its subject is emphasized by positioning the saints and beati, who enact the scene, in the foreground, close to the picture plane, and minimizing the importance of their placement in rational, measurable space. Again, differences such as these might be attributable to variables in context or patronage, but it is difficult to escape the impression that they are also intrinsic to Angelico's maturation as an artist.

While perhaps the result of a natural trend in his thought processes, it is altogether possible that this development in Angelico's style was precipitated—or at least facilitated—by the experience of creating the remarkable series of frescoes in the cloister, chapter house, and dormitory corridors and cells at the newly restored convent of San Marco, the works for which he is undoubtedly best known today. Angelico was no stranger to the peculiar technical demands of fresco painting when, about 1438, he began this massive project—analyzed in detail by Magnolia Scudieri elsewhere in this catalogue. In addition to a standard training in the medium that he undoubtedly received as a young man,[4] he could boast of previous experience in the fresco decoration of San Domenico in Fiesole and San Domenico in Cortona, as well as of a role in the design and perhaps overseeing the frescoes in the Orange Cloister at the Badia Fiorentina (see pp. 291–94). None of these projects, however, entailed the need, which Angelico

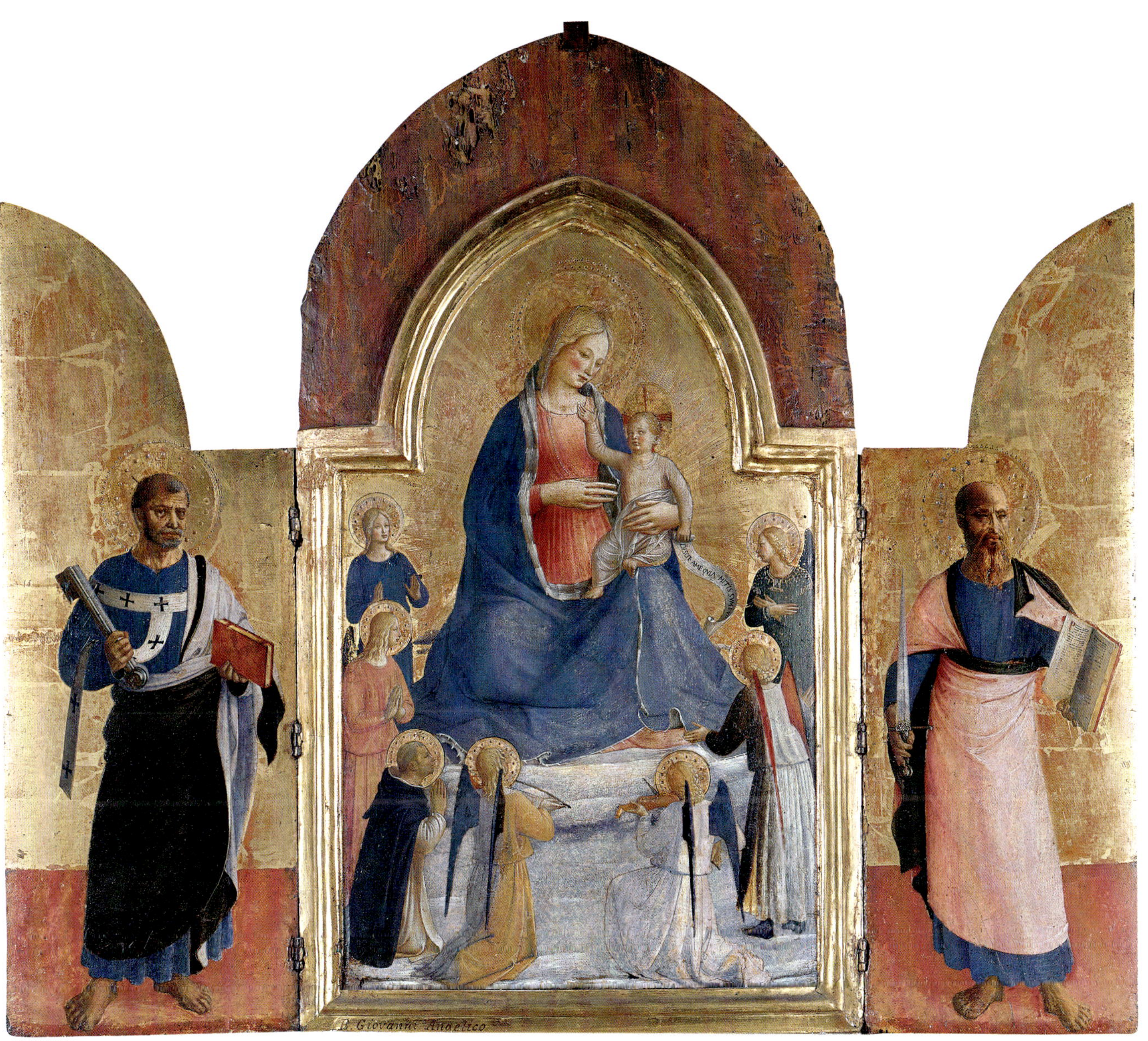

Figure 77. Fra Angelico. *Virgin and Child Enthroned, with Angels and Saint Dominic, between Saints Peter and Paul.* About 1446–48. Ashmolean Museum, Oxford

encountered at San Marco, to invent a new, reductive vocabulary of symbolic and meditative imagery, nor did they present the restrictions of format and picture-field size imposed by the dormitory cells there. The contrast between the spare aesthetic of the San Marco frescoes and the almost irreverent decorative excesses of Angelico's later frescoes in the Cappella Niccolina at the Vatican (1447–48) could hardly be more exaggerated, yet the compositional principles that underlie these two disparate series—as well as most of Angelico's late panel paintings—are fundamentally the same.

The campaign to embellish San Marco with frescoes and a new high altarpiece was so consuming a task and represents so complete a caesura within Angelico's career that it is not inaccurate to mark the date of the formal dedication of the church and convent—January 6, 1443—as the beginning of the artist's late period. The last twelve years of his life also constitute the only truly peripatetic period of Angelico's career: although he is documented in Cortona in 1438, he can otherwise scarcely be shown to have journeyed far from his home convent in Fiesole until he moved to Rome in 1445, back to Fiesole in 1449 (having also traveled for work to Orvieto in 1447 and Florence in 1448), and in 1453 to Rome once again, where he died on February 18, 1455. It is also a period in which he devoted more time to the responsibilities of conventual administration than had previously been required of him, having been elected prior of San Domenico in Fiesole for two years, beginning in the summer of 1450. Most of the major projects that occupied him in Rome at this time, many of which do not survive, are described by Carl Strehlke in his essay in this catalogue, and others that he undertook in

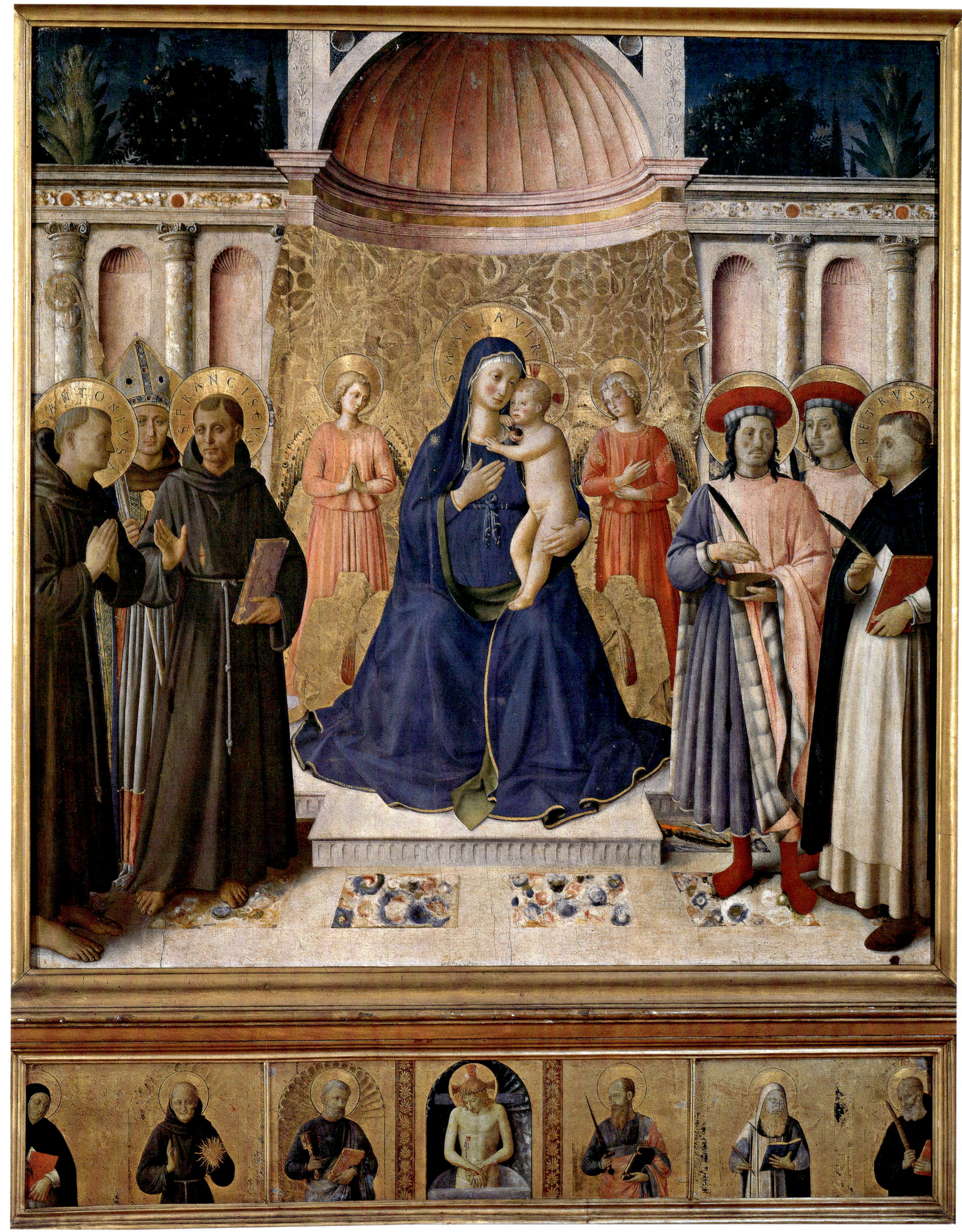

Figure 78. Fra Angelico. *Virgin and Child Enthroned, with Angels and Saints Anthony of Padua, Louis of Toulouse, Francis, Cosmas, Damian, and Peter Martyr* (Bosco ai Frati Altarpiece). About 1449–51. Museo di San Marco, Florence

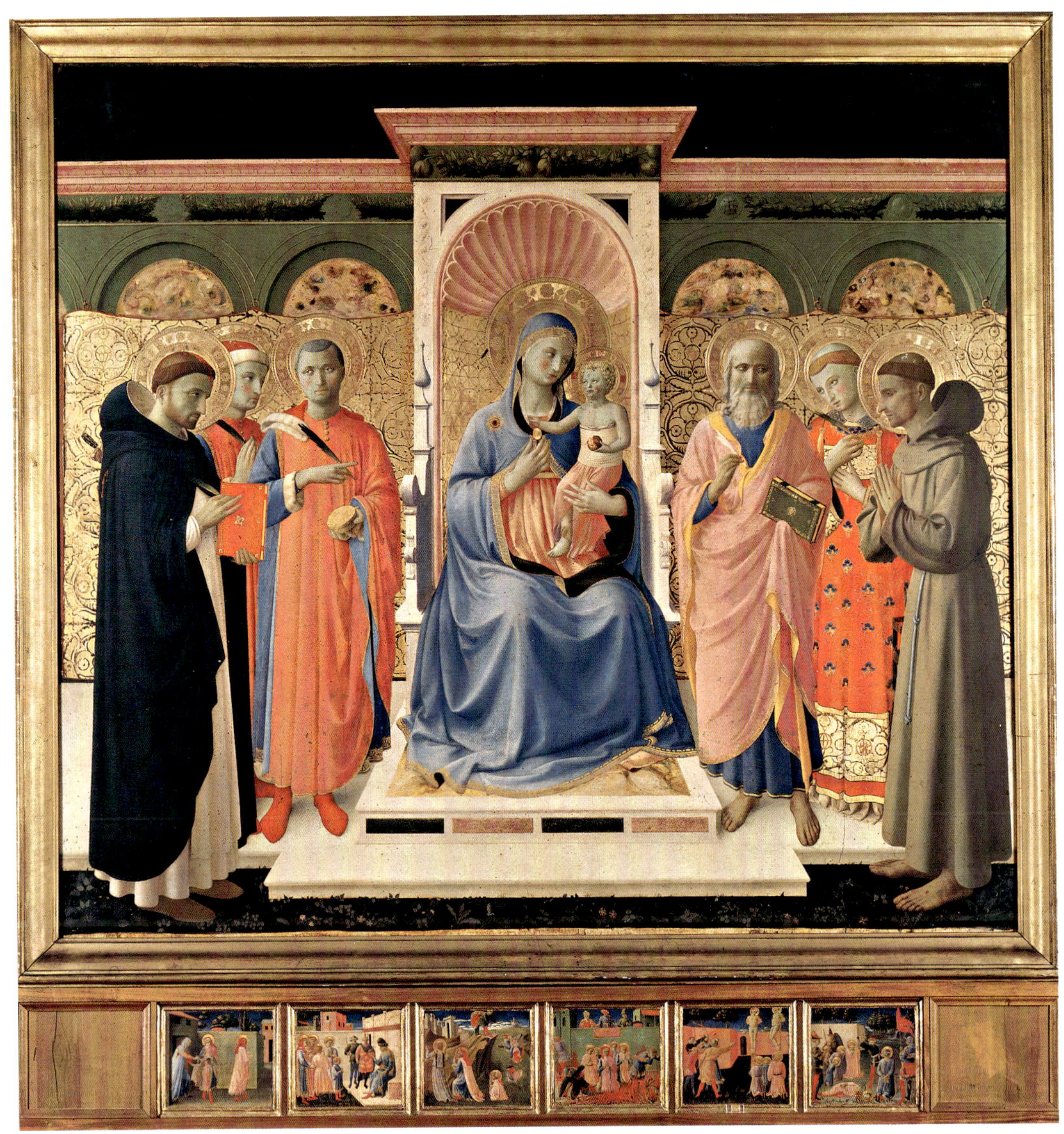

Figure 79. Fra Angelico and Zanobi Strozzi. *Virgin and Child Enthroned, with Saints Peter Martyr, Cosmas, Damian, John the Evangelist, Lawrence, and Francis* (Annalena Altarpiece). About 1453. Museo di San Marco, Florence

Florence can be briefly touched upon here. It is interesting to note what might be deemed a change in Angelico's working habits in this period: he can be credited with having painted only two altarpieces in this entire twelve-year span, a fraction of his output in any earlier period in his career. At the same time, the complex nature of the fresco commissions he accepted constrained Angelico to employ a large number of assistants—notwithstanding his frequent travels and relocations—and, perhaps inevitably, much of the work of these assistants became increasingly autonomous over the years.

Alongside the San Marco and Vatican frescoes, the *locus classicus* for discussions of Angelico's dependence on assistants in his late works has become the three large panels with scenes from the life of Christ that were painted to decorate a reliquary cupboard—known as the Armadio degli Argenti—for the church of Santissima Annunziata in Florence, now in the Museo di San Marco (fig. 73). According to contemporary tradition, the commission for these panels, received from Piero di Cosimo de' Medici, has been assigned to the year 1448,[5] although this date has frequently been disputed since Angelico was presumed not to have returned to Florence from Rome until the following year, and work on the ceiling of the chapel that housed the reliquary was not completed until 1451. The uneven state of preservation of the panels, furthermore, has led to almost as wide a variety of opinion regarding the authorship of individual scenes, and of the extent of Angelico's contribution to their design or execution, as have the frescoes at San Marco. That more than one artist contributed to this series is clear simply from a comparison of figure types between scenes—as, for example, those in the *Presentation in the Temple* and the *Circumcision*. Which scenes were painted by Angelico himself, whether they were all designed by the master, who his assistants might have been, and whether the work was protracted over an extended period of time all remain open questions. It does seem possible to suggest, however, that the first panel (fig. 73)—comprising scenes from the Infancy of Christ, from the *Vision of Ezekiel* through the *Dispute in the Temple*—might have been painted somewhat earlier than the other two, possibly during Angelico's brief return to Florence from Rome in 1448, when he may have been accompanied by Benozzo Gozzoli (see p. 306), and, in turn, that it may have been Gozzoli who was at least in part responsible for several of its images. This hand does not reappear in the other two panels, which, additionally, are far more uniform in conception and quality of execution.

Whatever had been the previous relationship of Gozzoli and Angelico, documents inform us that they worked together in Rome with the legal status of partners rather than as master and assistant. It is not surprising, therefore, to find Angelico scholarship preoccupied with attempts to isolate Gozzoli's work among the Cappella Niccolina or Orvieto frescoes, following the assumption that he participated in both contexts more as an equal and independent contributor than as an amanuensis. Fewer attempts have been made to recognize panel paintings produced at this time that might further reveal the nature of the collaboration between the two artists, but two such works must be the double-sided *desco* of the *Virgin and Child Enthroned* and the *Volto Santo* (cat. 36), now divided between the Museum of Fine Arts in Boston and a private collection, and a little-studied triptych in the Ashmolean Museum, Oxford (fig. 77), representing on its center panel the *Virgin and Child Enthroned, with Angels and Saint Dominic,* and on its wings *Saint Peter* and *Saint Paul.* This object has in the past been considered a pastiche, but physical evidence reveals that the three panels do belong together, having been only cosmetically altered with the reattachment of frame moldings to the center panel. The style, iconography, and unusual shape of this triptych all point to its having been painted in Rome, and the differences in quality of execution and compositional sophistication between the center panel on the one hand and the two wings on the other are the result of the latter being autograph works by Fra Angelico, while the former is very likely an all but independent effort of Benozzo Gozzoli.

Vasari claimed that Fra Angelico painted an altarpiece of the *Deposition* for the Cappella Niccolina at the Vatican,[6] as well as the high altarpiece and another altarpiece of the *Annunciation* for the Dominican convent church of Santa Maria sopra Minerva in Rome (see cat. 37). None of these can be certainly identified with a known work of art, however; the only late altarpiece by Angelico that survives nearly intact[7] was painted for the Franciscan Observant convent of San Bonaventura at Bosco ai Frati in the Mugello (fig. 78), a Medici dependency close to Cosimo's villa at Cafaggiolo. Probably commissioned by Piero rather than Cosimo de' Medici—judging from the inclusion of Saint Peter Martyr alongside Saints Cosmas and Damian on the main panel—possibly on the occasion of the convocation of the General Chapter of the Franciscan Observants at Bosco ai Frati in 1449, the predella of this altarpiece includes an image of Saint Bernardino, who was canonized in 1450. Loosely following the format of the high altarpiece from San Marco (see cat. 34), or even more closely the fresco popularly known as the *Madonna of the Shadows* (fig. 127) in the upper corridor of the dormitory at San Marco, the most unusual feature of this painting is the exaggerated proportions and unexpected colors of the aedicula in which the Virgin's throne is set and of the architectural screen behind the standing saints. The warm pinks, bright reds, and soft blues of the marble structures and many of the complicated decorative motifs that enliven their surfaces derive from the fantastic architectural forms inserted in the background of the Cappella Niccolina frescoes, and reappear elsewhere in Angelico's oeuvre only in the so-called Annalena altarpiece also now in the Museo di San Marco (fig. 79). Although this last painting is frequently thought to have been commissioned by Cosimo de' Medici from Fra Angelico in the mid-1430s,[8] there can be no doubt that it is, instead, contemporary with the Bosco ai Frati altarpiece, and, like that work, was probably also commissioned by Piero di Cosimo de' Medici. In the event, only the design of this painting may be attributed directly to Fra Angelico. Whether he never intended to execute it entirely by himself, or left it incomplete in 1453 when he abandoned Florence for his final trip to Rome, cannot be determined. It is clear, however, that the paint surface of this altarpiece, as well as the design and execution of all of its predella panels, are the work of Zanobi Strozzi: his last collaboration with the master for whom he had begun working over twenty years before.

1. Pope-Hennessy 1974, pp. 34–35, 215–16.
2. Two events from the life of Saint Dominic, his investiture and his birth, were depicted on the pilaster bases of the Cortona *Annunciation* altarpiece, probably painted about 1430–31. A scene of the investiture of Saint Dominic also appeared on the wing of a tabernacle triptych possibly painted for the Spedale di San Paolo in Florence, about 1427–28 (cat. 21), where it was undoubtedly accompanied by other episodes from the founder's life: as none of these survives, however, their subjects cannot be ascertained, although there may have been as many as five such scenes.
3. See Bonsanti 1998, pp. 141–42. The altarpiece was commissioned on April 13, 1436, by Fra Sebastiano Benintendi, a descendant of the Beata Villana, who is portrayed in the painting, the second figure from the right. A payment registered on December 2, 1436, was once thought to indicate the painting's completion, but the date 1441, inscribed in mordant gilding on the hem of the Virgin's robe, is now recognized as the terminal date of the work.
4. See Strehlke 2003b, pp. 21–22.
5. *Cronaca di Firenze di Benedetto Dei,* Biblioteca Nazionale, Florence, Cod. Magl. xxi, f. 96).
6. This painting was hesitantly identified by M. Salmi (1958, p. 88) with a panel now in the National Gallery of Art, Washington, D.C. (1939.1.260), sometimes attributed to Jacopo del Sellaio. M. Boskovits (in Boskovits and Brown 2003, pp. 31–35), reaffirming an attribution to Angelico for the Washington *Deposition* or *Entombment,* acknowledged Salmi's suggestion that a Florentine provenance seems more likely than a Roman one for this work, but added that he "would not exclude the possibility that the panel was painted for the chapel in the Vatican." It is conceivable that the fragmentary triptych wings by Angelico with the *Pentecost* and the *Ascension,* presently mounted alongside the *Last Judgment* in the Galleria Nazionale d'Arte Antica di Palazzo Corsini in Rome (see cat. 32), could have been painted as part of an altarpiece for the Cappella Niccolina, if Vasari's description of the subject of the latter is correct. They are complementary in iconography and congruent in date with the fresco decoration of the chapel.
7. According to U. Baldini (in Florence 1955, pp. 88–90), the main panel of the Bosco ai Frati altarpiece was reduced by approximately twelve centimeters at either side—a loss that is sufficient to accommodate the missing half-length figures of Saints Dominic and Benedict cropped from either end of the predella.
8. See Hood 1993, pp. 102–7, for arguments dating the Annalena altarpiece to 1434–35 and suggesting its original provenance from a Medici chapel in the church of San Lorenzo. Annalena Malatesta, a ward of Cosimo de' Medici, was widowed at the age of fifteen in 1441, and in 1450 she lost her only son to the plague. With Cosimo's support she obtained from Pope Nicholas V, on December 12, 1450, license to receive a cloistered community of Dominican pentitential tertiaries in her home. On August 4, 1452, she and twelve companions received the habit of tertiaries from Saint Antoninus, in a formal ceremony at Santa Maria Novella, and in June 1453 they moved into the premises that would later, in 1455, be consecrated as the Oratory of San Vincenzo. Angelico's altarpiece must have been commissioned in 1452 or 1453; the absence within it of any reference to Saint Vincent Ferrer, canonized in 1455, suggests that it must predate the reconsecration of the oratory to him, by Pope Calixtus III, in that year. See Richa 1762, vol. X, pp. 128–40.

28.
The Dormition and Assumption of the Virgin

Tempera on panel: overall, 61.8 x 38.3 cm
(24⅜ x 15⅛ in.); picture surface, 55.9 x 35.2 cm
(22 x 13⅞ in.)
Isabella Stewart Gardner Museum, Boston

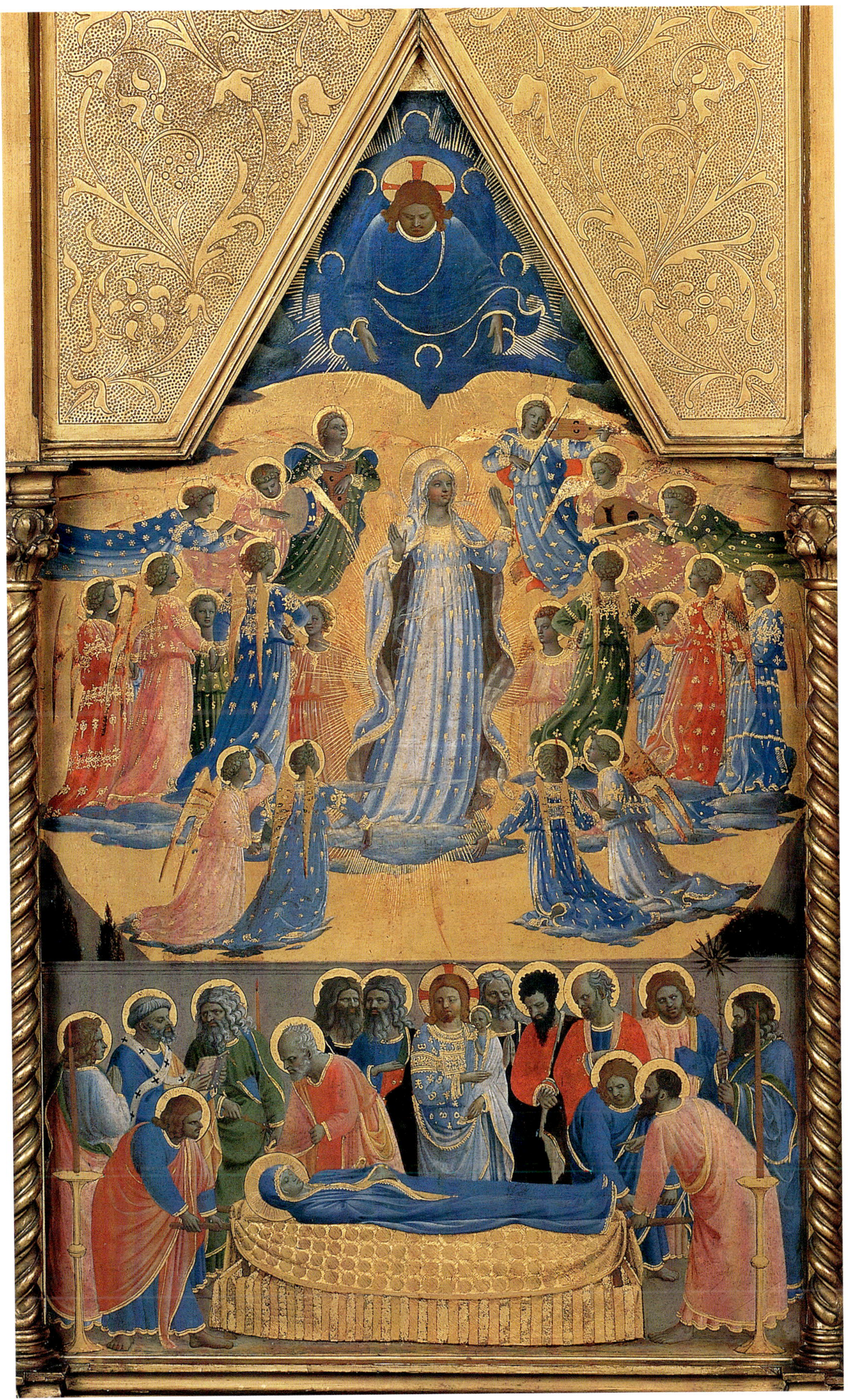

28

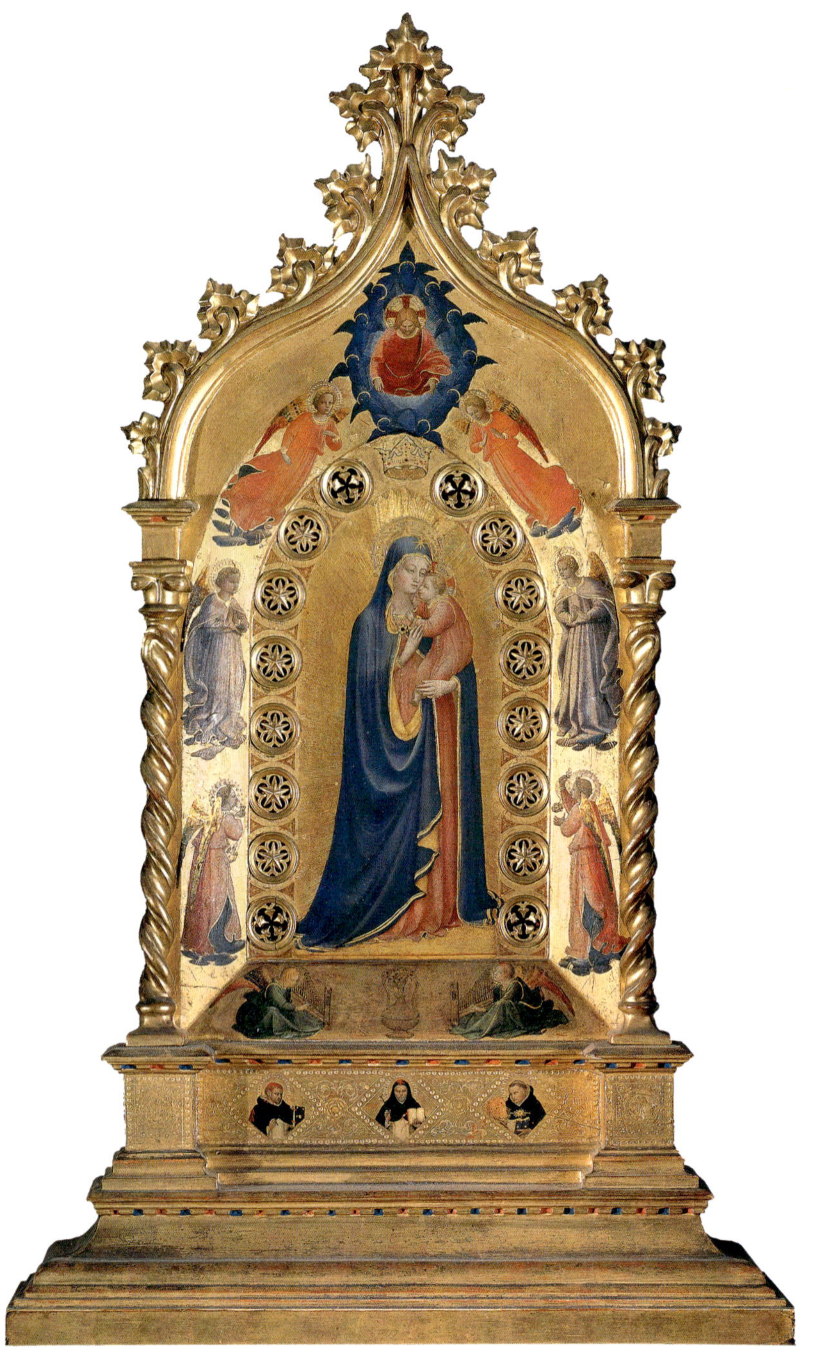

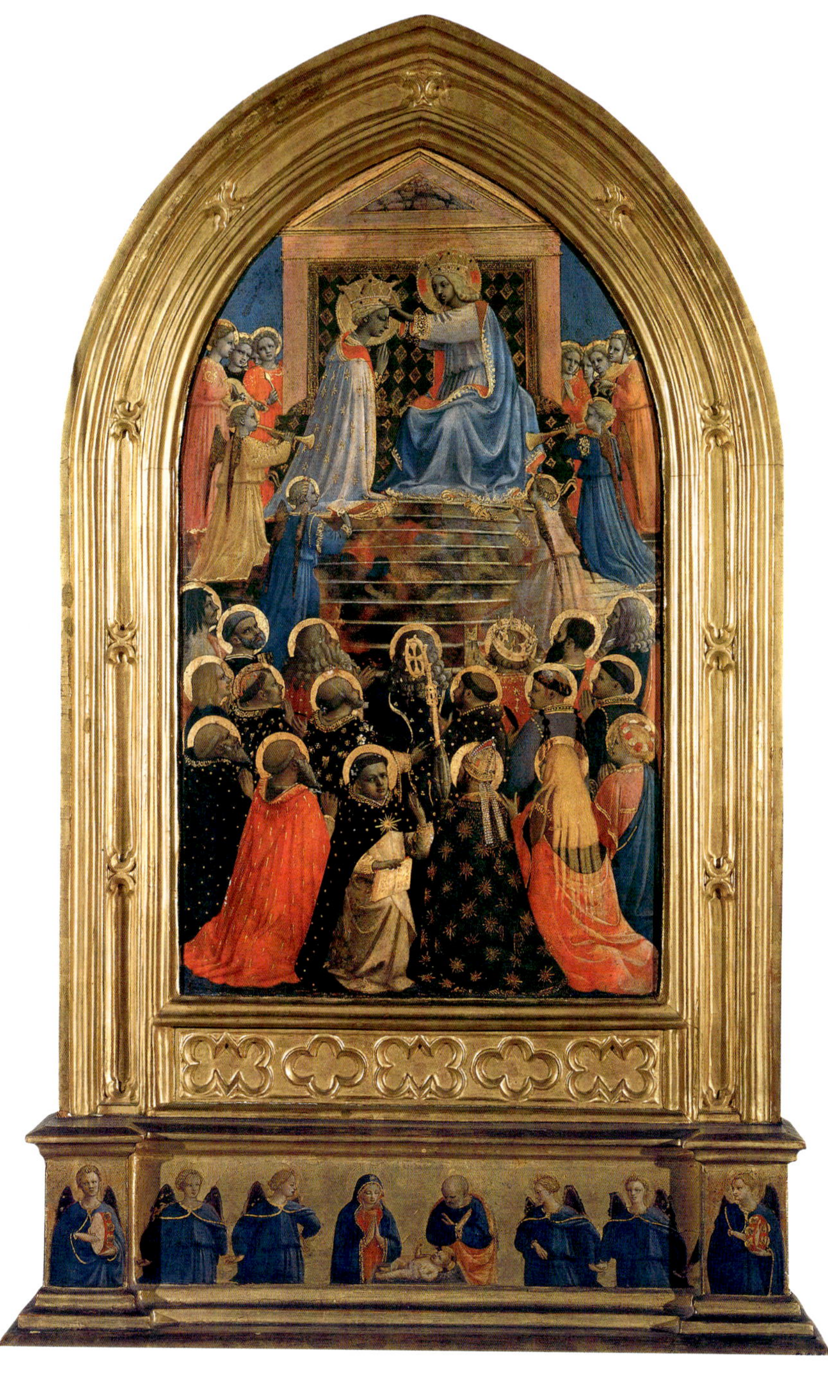

Figure 80 (above left). Fra Angelico. *Virgin and Child, with Saints Dominic, Thomas Aquinas, and Peter Martyr (Madonna della Stella)*. About 1425. Museo di San Marco, Florence

Figure 81 (above right). Fra Angelico. *The Coronation of the Virgin*. About 1428. Museo di San Marco, Florence

Across the bottom of the panel, before a high stone wall, fourteen holy figures, including all the apostles except Saint Thomas, stand in a circle around the Virgin's bier, which is draped in a cloth of gold, as is the catafalque on which it rests. Saint Peter, at the left, dressed in the robes of a priest and with a pallium crossed over his chest, reads the Office of the Dead, while Saint John the Evangelist, at the far right, holds the palm presented to him by the Virgin, which, in turn, had been brought to her by the Annunciatory Angel as a sign of her impending death. Four apostles in the foreground bend forward to lift the poles of the bier, one pulling back his sleeve for the task, another pointing toward the unmanned pole opposite him. Behind the bier, Christ cradles the soul of the Virgin, represented as a small, child-like figure, in the crook of his arm. Above the wall, set against a symbolic gold ground and portrayed on a larger scale than the scene below, the Virgin ascends bodily to Heaven, encircled by twenty-one singing, dancing, and music-making angels. The triangular pinnacle at

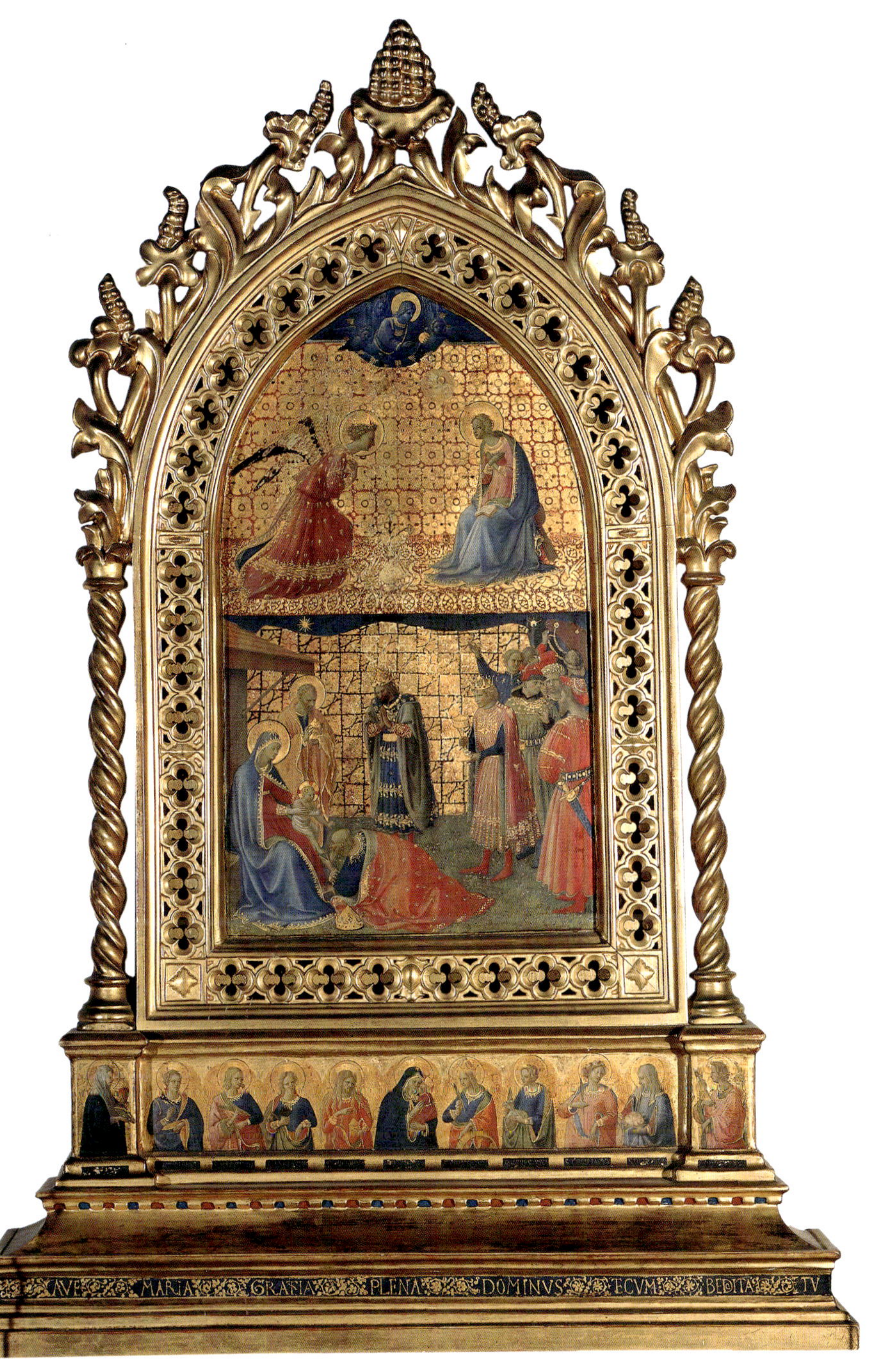

Figure 82. Fra Angelico. *The Annunciation* and *The Adoration of the Magi*. About 1431–32. Museo di San Marco, Florence

the top of the panel is filled with a dramatically foreshortened figure of Christ in a mandorla of blue cherubim waiting to receive his mother in Paradise.

The Gardner *Dormition and Assumption of the Virgin* is commonly believed to belong to a series of four reliquaries painted by Fra Angelico for Santa Maria Novella, which were described by Vasari in both editions of his *Vite* (1550 and 1568) and were said by Richa to have been commissioned by the sacristan of the church, Fra Giovanni di Zanobi Masi: "... *quattro tavole, o sieno tabernacoli di legno pieni nelle cornici di Sante Reliquie, e dipinti dal B. Fra Giovanni Angelico, fatti fare da Fra Giovanni Masi; e veggonsi effigiati in minute figure, che sembrano miniature, i Misterj della vita di Maria Vergine.*"[1] The date of Fra Giovanni Masi's death, reasonably considered a terminus ante quem for the commission of the reliquaries, was reported as 1430 in Father M. Billiotti's sixteenth-century chronicle of Santa Maria Novella,[2] and corrected to 1434, following a notice in the *Necrologia di Santa Maria Novella*, by Stefano Orlandi in 1955. Consequently, references to the four panels prior to 1955 consider them among Angelico's earliest known paintings, whereas later authors treat them as works from the artist's maturity.

Three of the four reliquaries from Santa Maria Novella were described in 1847 when they were still housed in the sacristy of the church.[3] Now in the Museo di San Marco, these represent: 1) the Virgin and Child with angels and, in the predella, Saints Dominic, Thomas Aquinas, and Peter Martyr, popularly known as the *Madonna della Stella* (fig. 80); 2) *The Coronation of the Virgin* with, in the predella, an unusual representation in half-length of the Nativity with six angels (fig. 81); and 3) *The Annunciation* and *The Adoration of the Magi* with, in the predella, the Virgin and Child and ten half-length female saints (fig. 82). There is no documentary or incontrovertible physical evidence that the Boston panel, which was in the collection of the Reverend John Sanford at Nynehead, Somerset, by 1816,[4] is the missing fourth reliquary except that it corresponds to the others in size, and its subjects complement those of the other paintings, supplying important episodes from the life of the Virgin otherwise conspicuously absent from the series (the church of Santa Maria Novella is dedicated to the Assumption of the Virgin). None of the three reliquaries now in San Marco preserves its original frame wholly intact, although neither do they seem to have been significantly altered in format. Triangular inserts were added at the upper corners of the Gardner Museum panel to complete a rectangular shape; these inserts, and a four-centimeter-wide border of the triangular gable, now covered by the frame, have been overpainted with a blue sky and clouds, and a two-centimeter-wide border along the sides and bottom of the panel has been regilt. Otherwise, this panel differs from the others chiefly in its lack of a predella and of any remnants of compartments for relics, which, however, would have been lost with the destruction of its original frame.

Diane Cole Ahl adduced the evidence of a later niello pax by Donato di Leonardo and Antonio di Salvi in the Walters Art Museum, Baltimore, to contend that the Gardner *Dormition and Assumption of the Virgin* had undergone more extensive changes than in shape alone.[5] The pax copies both the overall composition of the Gardner panel and many of its details, omitting others in order to compress the spatial content of the scene into the more limited pictorial surface available to the engraver. Cole Ahl's assertion that the landscape elements visible above the wall in the Gardner panel are modern additions because they do not appear on the pax is untenable. Equally, the round-arched top of the Baltimore pax is not a reliable guide to the probable original shape of the Gardner panel since it is typical of late-fifteenth-century paxes but not of early-fifteenth-century painted or carved reliquaries. It is likely that the Gardner panel was not significantly different in shape from the *Madonna della Stella* in the Museo di San Marco, which, of all Fra Angelico's paintings, is also the one it most closely corresponds to in size and proportions.

Discussions of the authorship and dating of the *Dormition and Assumption of the Virgin* reveal a contentious divergence of opinion in part reflecting the biases of successive generations of students of Fra Angelico's work and in part the Gardner panel's relative inaccessibility to European scholars, other than in photographs. Among early writers, few besides Berenson and Langton Douglas, both of whom knew the picture well and at firsthand, considered it substantially autograph.[6] A majority of scholars attributed its design to Angelico but its execution, particularly in the lower scene of the *Dormition,* to assistants in his studio, while several[7] ascribed it to Zanobi Strozzi or to another illuminator active in Angelico's immediate circle. Based only on considerations of quality and technique, it cannot be doubted that the Gardner *Dormition and Assumption of the Virgin* is wholly autograph—one of Fra Angelico's most ambitiously conceived and meticulously rendered works. The sophisticated organization of space in the lower scene and the carefully calibrated ring of angels seen *di sotto in su* in the upper register parallel the accomplishment of Angelico's majestic *Coronation of the Virgin* altarpiece in the Louvre (fig. 74), while such details of naturalistic observation as the modeled shadows in the cloth-of-gold drapery where it is pulled over the poles of the Virgin's bier (realized in translucent glazes over engraved gold leaf), the subtle narrative psychology of the four apostles bending to lift the bier, or the individualized features and expressions of all nineteen figures in the lower scene are only encountered in Florentine painting in the mature works of Fra Angelico.

Ironically, it was precisely these characteristics of insistent naturalism that led numerous early scholars to assign the execution of the lower half of the Boston panel to an assistant of Fra Angelico, its accurate and detailed physicality at odds with the then prevailing notions of Angelico as a master of abstraction and ideal form. Confusing the choice and treatment of a subject with the quality and manner of its execution, this traditional view of Angelico—which had its roots in the artist's nineteenth-century rediscovery by such spiritualist critics as A. F. Rio, but which persists even in some recent monographs—accepts only the scene of the *Assumption of the Virgin* at the top of the panel, with its balletically posed angels, gracefully swirling draperies, and pastel palette, as betraying Fra Angelico's direct intervention. Modern reaction to this traditional view, beginning with Roberto Longhi and John Pope-Hennessy, has tended to emphasize the rational, intellectual basis of Angelico's work. For many of these scholars, the abundant decorative gilding and the highly refined figure types throughout the four reliquary panels from Santa Maria Novella contradict a perceived trend within Angelico's paintings toward the spare and monumental, arguing instead for the intervention of a miniaturist painter operating within the Dominican master's circle, such as Zanobi Strozzi. Recent scholarship has recognized the fundamental role of naturalism in the development of Angelico's early style and his reconciliation of the conflicting demands of decoration, symbolism, and illusionism—a development within which the Gardner *Dormition and Assumption of the Virgin* may be inserted as a key work.[8]

In considering both the attribution and the dating of the four Santa Maria Novella reliquaries, scholars have tended to treat them as a unified group. It was pointed out by Strehlke,[9] however, that, while they were apparently conceived as parts of a single decorative program, their manufacture may have been protracted over a period of time. Liana Castelfranchi Vegas,[10] following a suggestion by Roberto Longhi, observed that the patron of the panels, Fra Giovanni Masi, was provost of the sacristy of Santa Maria Novella in 1424 for one year only, and she proposed that year as the likeliest date for the commissioning of all four. One of them, the *Madonna della Stella,* does conform somewhat, in figure style, to other paintings of this period, although its closest analogies are to the Prado *Annunciation* altarpiece of about 1425–26. The remaining three reliquaries are significantly more mature efforts. The *Coronation of the Virgin,* for example, displays more sophisticated handling of space and chromatic range than does the *Madonna della Stella* and its figure style relates closely to that employed in the Parma tabernacle (cat. 21) or, more approximately, in the Franciscan predella of about 1428–29 (cat. 24); it probably was painted about 1427 or 1428—the second in the series to be finished. The *Annunciation and Adoration* reliquary, on the other hand, is clearly an even later work, dating from the period after 1430 when the influence of Masaccio on Fra Angelico was visibly waning. Its figure types, spatial structure, and modeling technique correspond to those in the pilaster panels from the Santa Trinita *Deposition* altarpiece, known to have been completed by 1432, and even more so to the predella scenes below the *Coronation of the Virgin* altarpiece in the Louvre, very likely painted in 1432 or 1433 (see p. 139). A date of about 1432, immediately preceding work on the Louvre altarpiece, seems most plausible for this reliquary.

The Gardner *Dormition and Assumption of the Virgin* is in many respects the most original and complex of the four reliquaries from Santa Maria Novella. It was probably the last of them to be painted and may have been commissioned only shortly before Giovanni Masi's death in 1434. The lucidity of its spatial structure and the precision and density of its textural and decorative detail obviously call to mind the Louvre *Coronation of the Virgin* altarpiece and its remarkable predella. The Gardner panel advances even beyond these, however, toward a full and seemingly effortless assimilation of naturalism that characterizes the predella to the Linaiuoli tabernacle (cat. 29), commissioned in 1433 and presumably completed by 1436. Assuming the Gardner reliquary was not—as contended by Pope-Hennessy and Berti[11]—commissioned after Giovanni Masi's death, and was simply grouped together with the other reliquaries for lack of reliable information to the contrary, a date for it of about 1433–34 seems convincing. LK

1. Vasari (Milanesi ed.) 1878–85, vol. II, p. 513; Richa 1755, p. 49.
2. Archivio di Santa Maria Novella, *Chronica pulcherrimae Aedis Sanctae Mariae Novellae,* fol. 24; first published in Marchese 1845–46, vol. I, p. 270.
3. Kugler 1847, vol. I, p. 358.
4. Sanford collection, 1847, no. 29. The panel was lent by Sanford to the British Institution in London in 1816, the first Italian Quattrocento painting known to have been publicly exhibited in the British Isles.
5. Cole 1977, pp. 306–12.
6. Douglas 1900, pp. 34–38, 196–97; Berenson 1904 p. 99; Berenson 1909, p. 104; Schottmüller 1911, pp. xviii, 23, 228, 239, 241, 247.
7. Van Marle 1928, pp. 46, 50; Collobi-Ragghianti 1950b, part 2, p. 25 n. 20; Collobi-Ragghianti 1955b , p. 43; Pope-Hennessy 1952, pp. 199–200; Pope-Hennessy 1974, pp. 222, 224–25; Berti 1963, p. 38 n. 101.
8. Boskovits 1976a, p. 47 n. 11; C. B. Strehlke, in Kanter et al. 1994, pp. 342–45.
9. C. B. Strehlke, in Kanter et al. 1994, pp. 342–45.
10. Castelfranchi Vegas 1989, p. 43 n. 27.
11. L. Berti, in Florence 1955, pp. 7–8. In the first edition (1952) of his monograph on Fra Angelico, Pope-Hennessy dated the reliquaries between 1435 and 1440; he revised this dating to "about 1430–34" in the second edition (1974).

FRA ANGELICO

29. *Saint Peter Preaching*

Tempera on panel: overall, 35.8 x 53 cm (14⅛ x 20⅞ in.); painted surface, 33 x 51.5 cm (13 x 20¼ in.)
Museo di San Marco, Florence

On July 11, 1433, Fra Angelico received the only monumental public commission of his career for an entity other than a church, monastery, or chapel. He was engaged to paint "inside and out, with the finest colors, gold, blue, and silver that can be found,"[1] a tabernacle triptych for the guild hall of the Arte dei Linaiuoli. Apparently, the tabernacle was to replace an earlier image of the Virgin, of the colossal type known from surviving examples dating from the end of the thirteenth or the beginning of the fourteenth century by artists such as Cimabue, Duccio, Lippo di Benivieni, and Bernardo Daddi. Planning began at least as early as the middle of the preceding year: on October 29, 1432, the massive panel supports that comprise the tabernacle, based on a construction design of surprising complexity provided by Lorenzo Ghiberti, were commissioned from the woodworker Jacopo di Piero, called il Papero.[2] Once these were delivered to Angelico for painting, work commenced on the carving of the marble frame to house the painting, again according to a design by Ghiberti, which, in turn, was commissioned on August 11, 1433.[3] No unequivocal documentation survives of the project's completion, although a notice of August 6, 1436, recording payment for painting, brickwork, and glazing "*allato al tabernacolo*" ("alongside the tabernacle") is generally assumed to imply that the work was finished and installed.[4] It may be safe to claim that these costs were part of, or occasioned by, the installation of the marble tabernacle frame, since, among other items, the document specifies payment for bricks, mortar, stone, and ironwork "*per murare in decto tabernacolo*" ("for walling in the said tabernacle"), but it reads as a summary of various accounts already disbursed, which had begun at least as early as November 23, 1435, with the reimbursement to a certain Piero di Lorenzo for painting "around the tabernacle."[5] Furthermore, Angelico's work was entirely independent of the carving or installation of the marble frame, and could have been completed at any time either before or after 1435/36.

The main panel of the Linaiuoli tabernacle contains an image of the Virgin and Child Enthroned (fig. 83), conceived on a scale that dwarfs all but the largest of Angelico's monumental fresco commissions. Above the Virgin's halo hovers the dove of the Holy Spirit against a painted blue vaulting with gold stars, and at either side of her are heavy gold draperies depicted as though pulled open and pinned to the painting's frame—a projecting molding similar to the one that surrounds the Parma *Virgin of Humility* (cat. 21 A). The twelve music-making angels painted on the frame have become icons in the popular imagination: a seemingly inexhaustible supply of

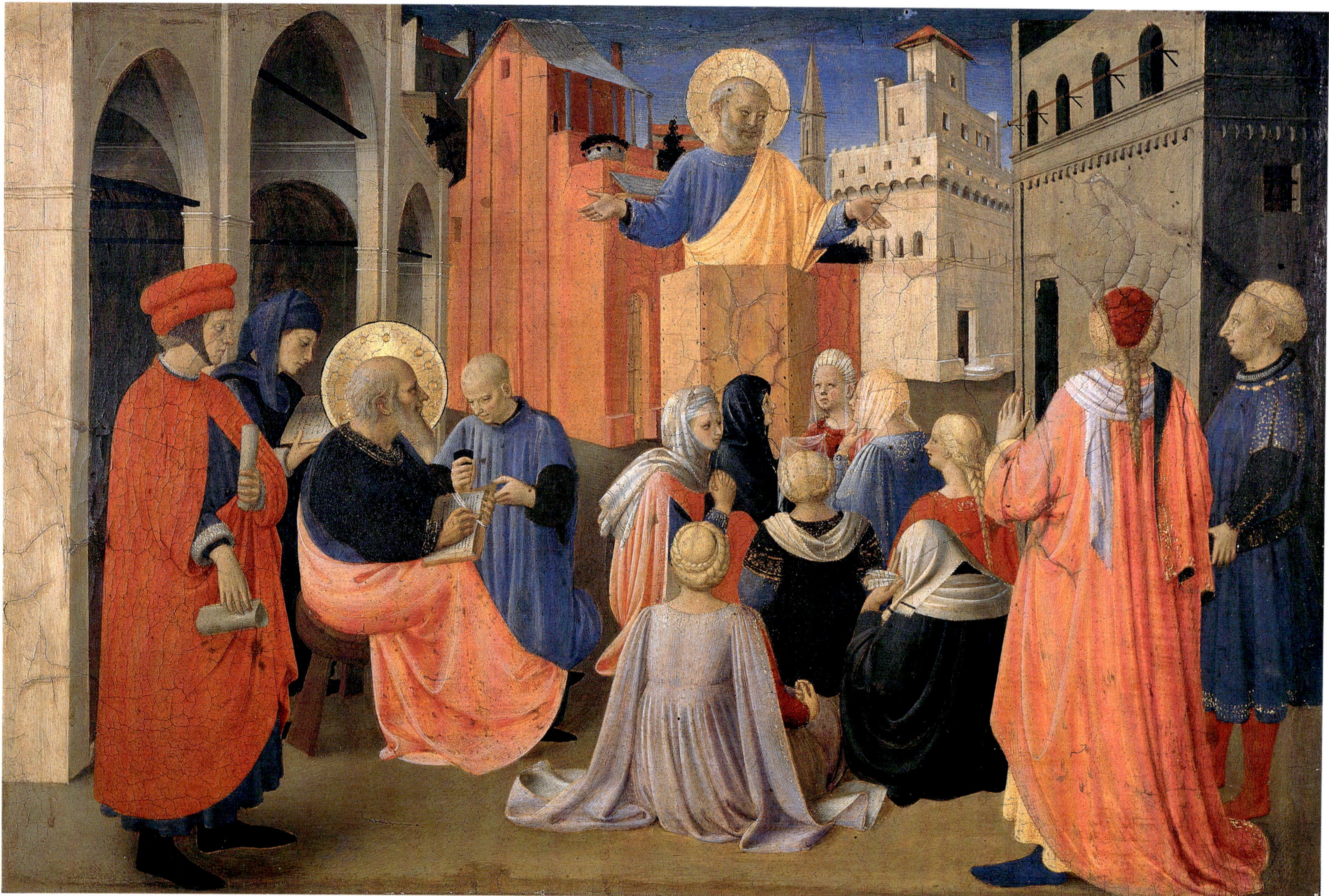

29

painted or photomechanical reproductions of them have been sold as souvenirs in Florence from the nineteenth century on. Affixed to the outer edge of this frame are large (290 x 88.5 centimeters) folding wings that close over the center panel; on their inner surfaces are over-life-size painted figures of Saints John the Baptist (left) and John the Evangelist (right) and on the outer surfaces, visible when the wings are closed (fig. 84), are images of Saints Mark (left) and Peter (right). Below the tabernacle, but still set within Ghiberti's marble frame, are three predella panels, which represent the Adoration of the Magi (fig. 85) in the center; on the right the martyrdom of Saint Mark (patron saint of the Arte dei Linaiuoli), whose body is being dragged through the streets of Alexandria in a hailstorm (fig. 86); and on the left Saint Peter dictating the Gospel of Saint Mark—the present work.

A passage in Ghiberti's *Commentari,* in which he boasts of having assisted painters in depicting figures enlarged "*fuori de la naturale forma*" ("beyond their natural size"),[6] coupled with our knowledge of his involvement in designing the frame and support structure for the Linaiuoli tabernacle have led to widespread speculation on the likelihood of his direct intervention in the ideation of Angelico's paintings for the tabernacle as well. Certainly, the monumental painting of Saint Mark on the exterior wing of the tabernacle bears no relationship to Donatello's marble standing figure of the saint (1411–13) in the niche of the Linaiuoli on the façade of Or San Michele, but there is no reason to assume that it therefore is a reflection of a model by Ghiberti rather than an invention by Angelico himself. To be sure, Angelico's early figure style and compositional methods owe a substantial debt

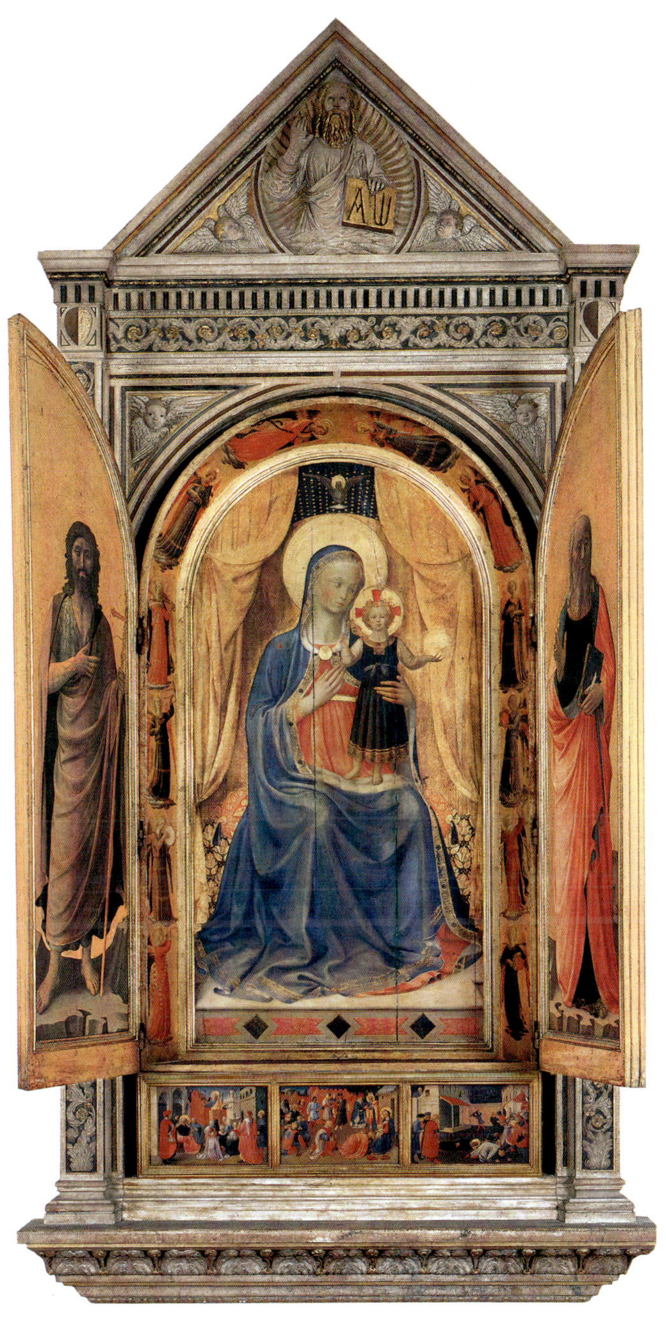

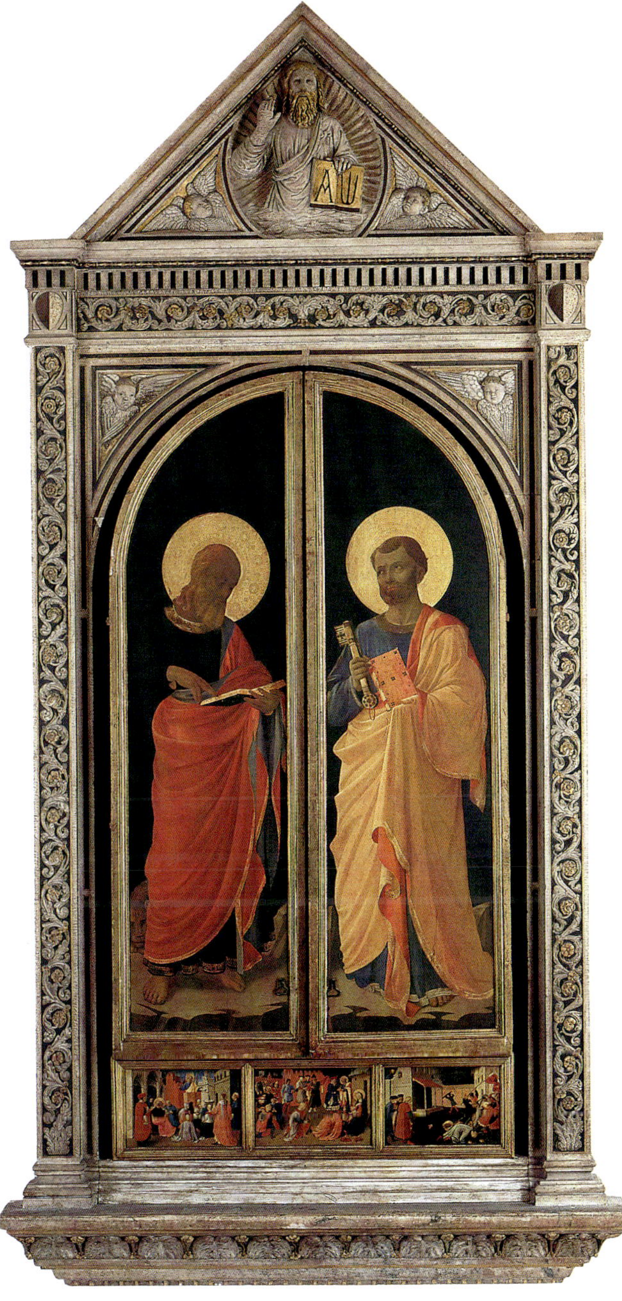

Figure 83 (above left). Fra Angelico. *Virgin and Child Enthroned, with Saint John the Evangelist and Saint John the Baptist* (Linaiuoli Tabernacle: open). 1433–35. Museo di San Marco, Florence

Figure 84 (above right). Fra Angelico. *Saint Mark and Saint Peter* (Linaiuoli Tabernacle: closed). 1433–35. Museo di San Marco, Florence

to Ghiberti's example, but by 1433 the Dominican master was firmly established—and, indeed, unchallenged—as the most accomplished painter in Florence, and there is nothing about the large figures in the Linaiuoli tabernacle, either in their overall conception or in specific details, that is incompatible with the course of his artistic development at this date. The same is true of the three predella scenes, although they—and the central *Adoration of the Magi* especially—do reveal in their execution the hand of an assistant first discernible in the predella to the Cortona *Annunciation* altarpiece of about 1430–31. This assistant's intervention in paintings by Angelico appears to have been sporadic rather than continuous, and with varying degrees of responsibility, ranging from the insertion of minor details into larger compositions to the virtually complete execution of the master's designs, functioning as Angelico's amanuensis. Given the chronology of his work for Angelico (from about 1430 to perhaps the mid-1440s) and its irregularity, it would seem that he was not a traditional apprentice or journeyman assistant as much as an occasional collaborator. There is also reason to believe, on the basis of style and of the incidentals of his biography, that this assistant can be identified as Zanobi Strozzi (see pp. 228–30).

If Zanobi Strozzi's intervention can be detected in the panel of the *Saint Peter Preaching,* it would be limited to some

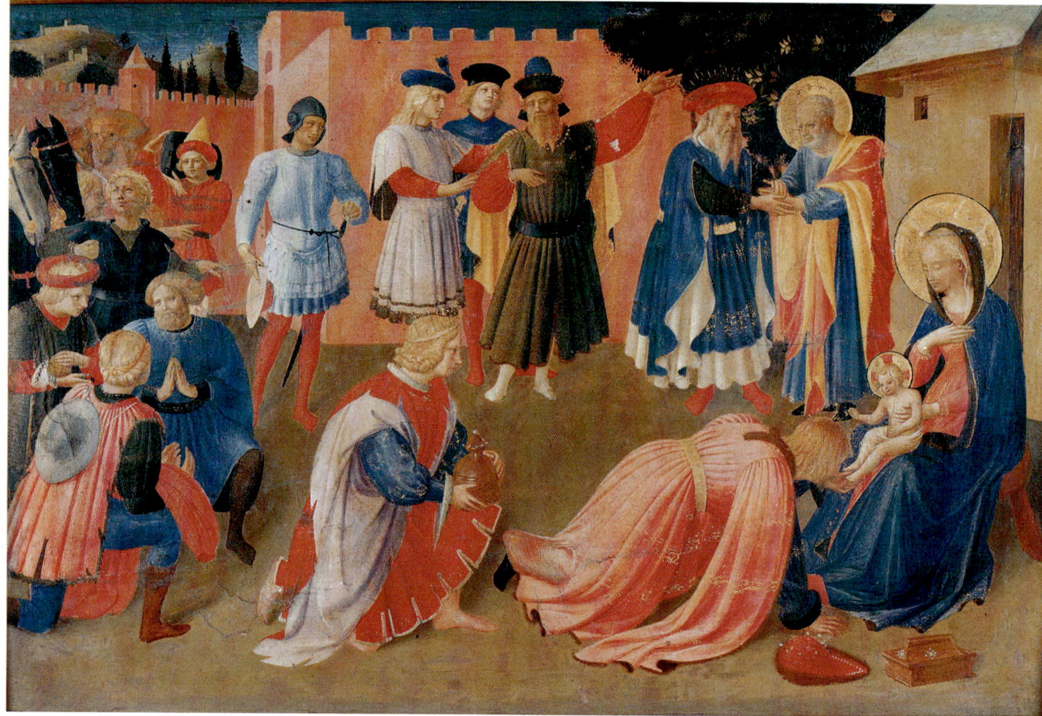

Figure 85. Fra Angelico. *The Adoration of the Magi*. 1433–35. Museo di San Marco, Florence

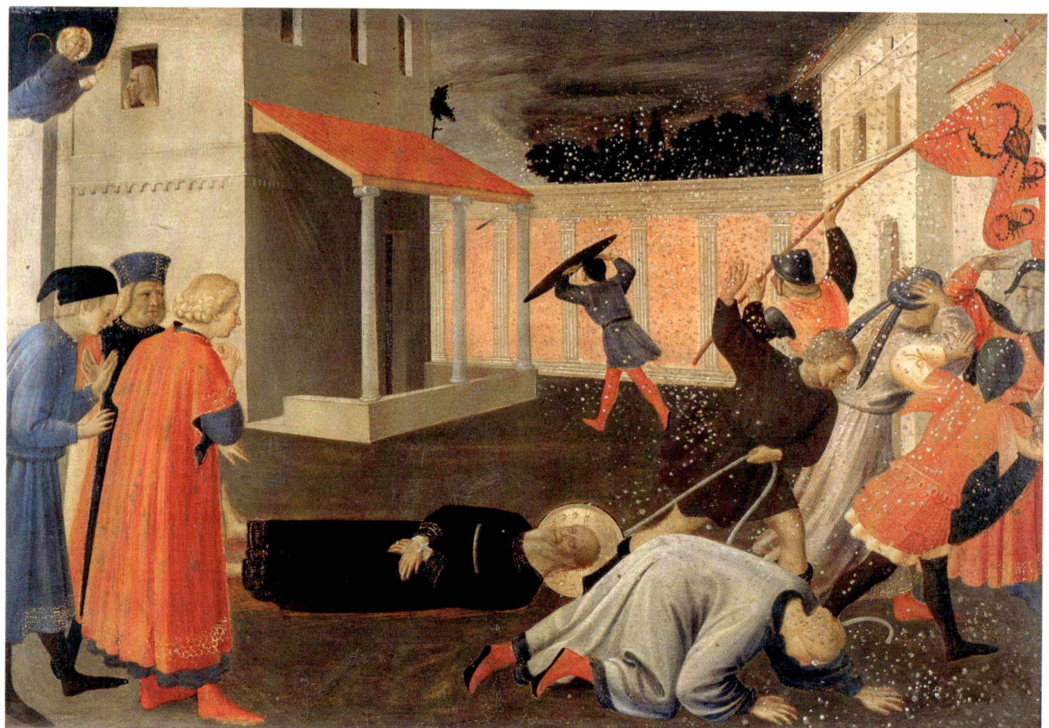

Figure 86. Fra Angelico. *The Martyrdom of Saint Mark*. 1433–35. Museo di San Marco, Florence

mechanical details of the background. Yet, even in these passages—if they are, indeed, by him—he must have been scrupulously following a detailed drawing by Fra Angelico, for the organization of space and the staging of the narrative is masterful.[7] The naturalism of the figure of Saint Mark, seated on a three-legged stool with his legs crossed, taking dictation, and of the page kneeling behind him holding an inkwell, is entirely in keeping with that of the predella to the *Saint Lucy* altarpiece (cat. 25) or the Louvre *Coronation of the Virgin* altarpiece. Yet, such details as the braid wrapped carefully around the head of the seated woman seen from behind, in the foreground of the composition; the gauzy headdress of the seated woman in front of her and slightly to the right; and the painstakingly rendered nailheads in Saint Peter's pulpit or in the heavy wooden door behind him to the left betray an intimate awareness of the minutiae of everyday existence that informs all of Angelico's work but not that of any other Florentine artist prior to the emergence of Francesco Pesellino in the middle years of the century (see pp. 269–89).

LK

1. Archivio di Stato, Florence, Arte dei Rigattieri, Linaiuoli, e Sarti, N. 20, *Campione dei debitori e creditori,* 1418–1511, fol. 98*v*. (July 11, 1433). First published in Baldinucci 1768, pp. 91–92.
2. Ibid., *sub datum*. First published in Gualandi 1843, p. 109. This entry in the account books of the Arte records the commission to Jacopo di Piero "*a fare el legname del tabernacolo grande di detta arte, dove oggi è dipinta la figura di Nostra Donna, avendo fattone fare de tutto uno modello per mano di Lorenzo di bartoluccio*." This work is sometimes said to have involved executing a wooden model of the tabernacle frame, but it is clear that Ghiberti had already made and been paid for such a model. The reference to "*la figura di Nostra Donna*" suggests that this tabernacle was designed to replace an existing image, undoubtedly explaining its unusual and archaic type and scale.
3. Ibid., *sub datum*.
4. Ibid., fol. 99*r*., *sub datum*; Cole 1977, vol. II, p. 596.
5. Baldinucci 1768, *sub datum*; Cole 1977, vol. II, p. 595.
6. *Commentari* II, vi, 1: "*Etiandio chi avesse avute a ffare figure grandi, fuori de la naturale forma, dato le regole a condurle con perfetta misura*"; published in Ghiberti 1998 ed., p. 97.
7. A replica of this scene that appeared consecutively in the sales of the Bournenville (Hôtel Drouot, Paris, May 21–22, 1883, lot 127), Aynard (Galerie Georges Petit, Paris, December 1–4, 1913, lot 36), and Spiridon (Muller, Amsterdam, June 19, 1928, lot 15) collections seems to be modern.

30.

A.

Saint Nicholas Calms a Tempest at Sea and The Miracle of the Ration of Grain

Tempera on panel, 35 x 61.5 cm (13¾ x 24¼ in.)
Vatican Museums, Vatican City (Inv. 40252)

B.

Saint Nicholas Saves Three Innocent Men Condemned to Death and The Death of Saint Nicholas

Tempera on panel: overall, 34 x 60.1 cm (13⅜ x 24⅝ in.); picture surface, 32.8 x 59.3 cm (12⅞ x 23⅜ in.)
Galleria Nazionale dell'Umbria, Perugia (Inv. no. 96)

C.

The Blessing Redeemer

Tempera on panel: diameter, 12 cm (4¾ in.)
Musée du Louvre, Paris (D.L. 1973-22)

One of the most beautiful and well-preserved[1] paintings by Fra Angelico, from any period in his career, is the altarpiece that he painted for the Guidalotti chapel in the church of San Domenico, Perugia. The main panels of this majestic work (fig. 87), now in the Galleria Nazionale dell'Umbria, Perugia, represent the Virgin and Child enthroned with four angels and Saints Dominic, Nicholas, John the Baptist, and Catherine of Alexandria. The chapel in which this altarpiece originally was located[2] was dedicated to Saint Nicholas of Bari—hence the prominence of that saint, who stands immediately to the Virgin's right in the main register, and whose legend is recounted in seven scenes on the three panels that comprised the predella below it. Shown at left in the first panel (fig. 88) is the miraculous birth of Saint Nicholas in the town of Patera in Greece: according to his legend, on the first day Nicholas was bathed he was able to stand by himself in the washbasin. In the scene in the center of the panel the youthful saint ignores the games and vanities of his friends and, instead, listens intently to a bishop preaching in front of a church. At the right is the well-known episode of the charity of Saint Nicholas: hearing of the plight of a poor man who could not arrange for the marriage of his three daughters, as they lacked suitable dowries, Nicholas resolved to save the girls from prostitution by secretly throwing sacks of gold, one for each girl, through the bars of their window at night. From this story, a sack or ball of gold came to be a standard attribute of Saint Nicholas, and Angelico painted three wrapped-and-tied bags of gold at the feet of the saint in the main panel of this altarpiece.

Two further scenes from the legend of Saint Nicholas occur in the second panel of the predella (A), now also separated from the altarpiece and exhibited alongside the first panel in the Pinacoteca Vaticana. Elected Bishop of Myra, Nicholas had quickly become known for his sanctity and charity. At the right of the panel, a boat full of sailors prays for salvation from a fierce tempest at sea; Nicholas appears to them in a vision, calming the winds and leading their boat to safety. At the left, Nicholas approaches another group of sailors bringing grain for the emperor from Alexandria to Rome. Nicholas pleaded for a ration of one hundred measures of grain to relieve the starvation of his town, which was suffering through a drought, but was told that the grain had been carefully measured and that a full tally had to arrive at the imperial granaries. After Nicholas assured the sailors that sharing their grain would not diminish the emperor's portion, they measured out one hundred sacks to be carried into Myra (on the left). When the ships subsequently reached their destination in Rome, the full tally of grain aboard miraculously was found to be intact. In

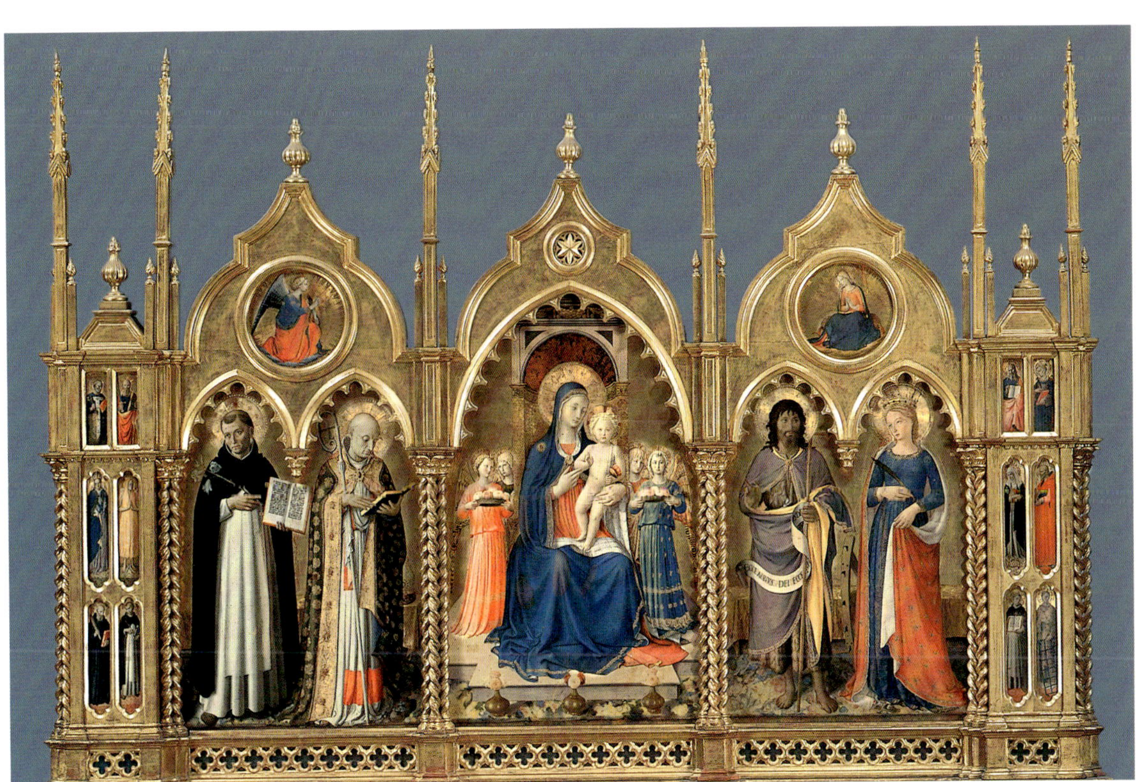

Figure 87. Fra Angelico. *Virgin and Child Enthroned, with Four Angels and Saints Dominic, Nicholas, John the Baptist, and Catherine of Alexandria* (Guidalotti Altarpiece). About 1437. Galleria Nazionale dell'Umbria, Perugia

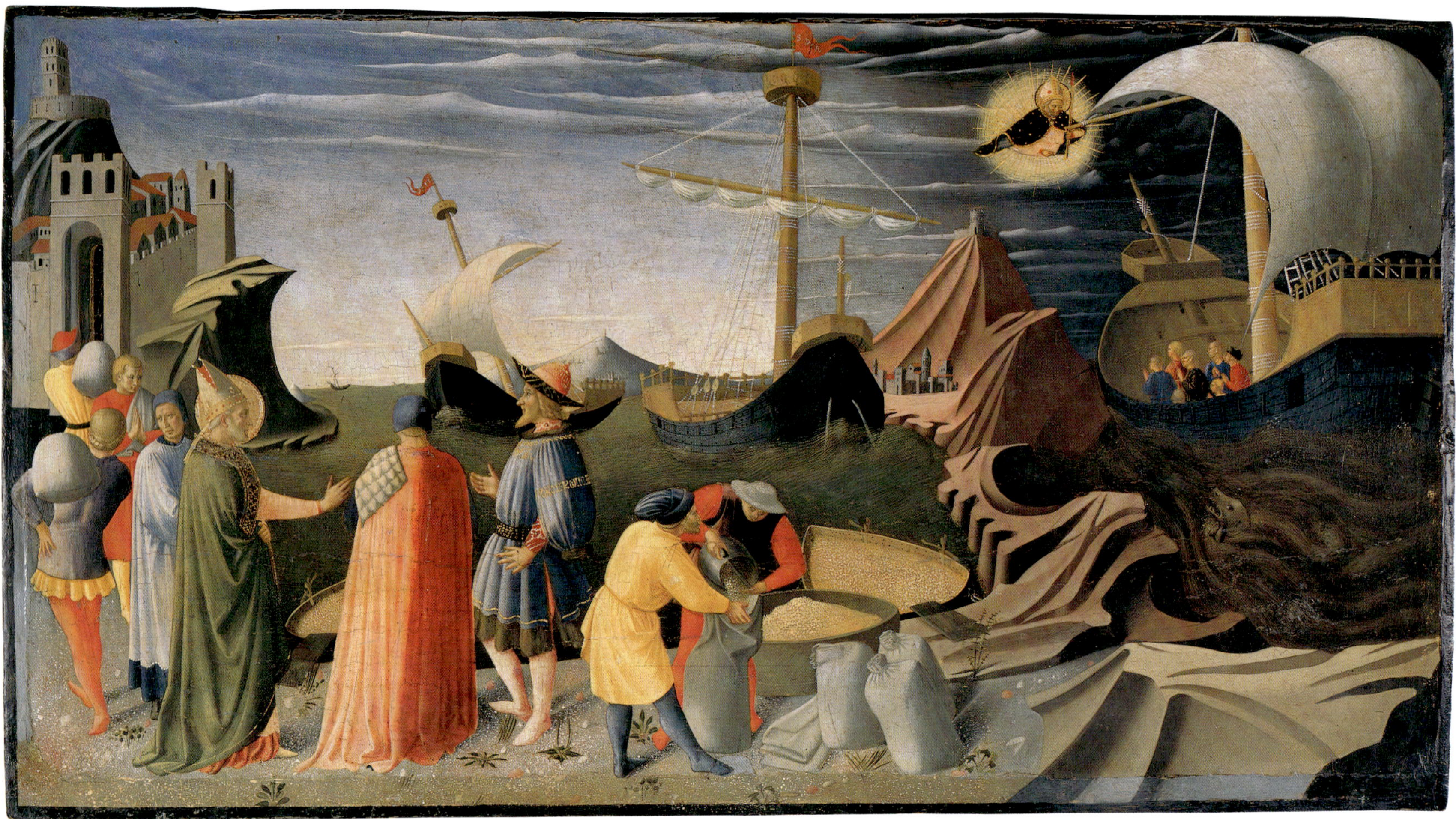

30: A

the final panel of the predella (B)—the only one to remain with its original structure—Saint Nicholas, in the presence of three princes of the Roman Empire, halts the execution of three innocent men condemned to death by a corrupt prefect. At the right in the panel, the death of the saint is portrayed: Nicholas's body is arrayed on a bier covered with a red-and-gold cloth of honor and surrounded by mourning acolytes and pilgrims; above, his soul is borne heavenward by four angels.

Arranged in a traditional polyptych format with each full-length saint standing before a burnished gold background and beneath an ogival arch—two on either side of the Virgin and angels in the center panel—the overall design of this altarpiece is not significantly different from the high altarpiece from San Domenico in Fiesole (cat. 10), the San Pier Martire triptych (cat. 13), or the Franciscan altarpiece of 1428–29 (cat. 24). In the Guidalotti altarpiece, however, the artist made a significantly more sophisticated effort to create a sense of unified pictorial space than he had in any of those earlier works. In addition to employing the conventional device of a brightly colored marble pavement extending across the foreground, he continued the projecting corners of the dais on which the Virgin's throne rests, from the center panel into the lateral panels, and introduced a low bench draped with a cloth of gold spanning the full width of each lateral panel, behind the saints. The bench serves as a spatial anchor for the entire composition by delimiting the depth of the pavement on either side and placing it in an exactly measurable relationship with the recession of the dais in the center panel. Angelico also exploited the bench as an opportunity to heighten the richness of his painted light effects—specifically, the luminescence of the reflected highlights and shadows delicately stamped and glazed along the pleats of its covering fabric—and to increase the sense of anecdotal veracity otherwise created by the tactile illusionism of the painted draperies, providing a perch for Saint Nicholas's miter, casually propped on top of it rather than at the saint's feet. As a final contravention of the restrictions of the Gothic picture field in which he had (or chose) to work, Angelico painted a shadow cast by the frame of the altarpiece that stretches along the pavement behind the figure of Saint Dominic in the left-hand panel.

Completing the painted portion of the altarpiece was the decoration of its original frame. The present frame is a neo-Gothic structure designed and carved for the altarpiece

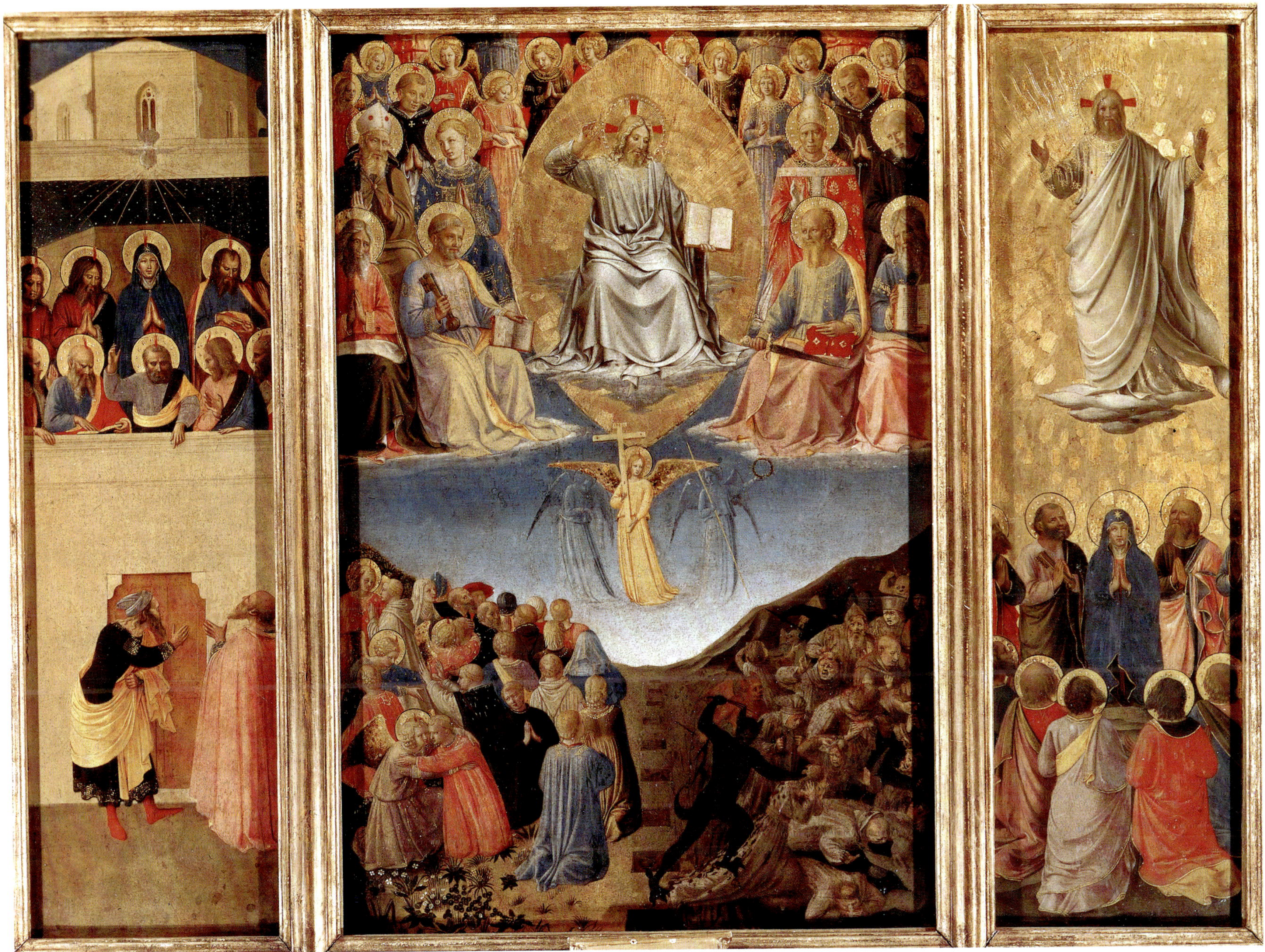

Figure 94. Fra Angelico. *Pentecost, The Last Judgment, and The Ascension.* About 1447–50. Galleria Nazionale d'Arte Antica di Palazzo Corsini, Rome

picture, and their reintroduction here, as pointed out by Jérôme Baschet, is indicative of the decidedly more didactic character of this version.[18]

Stylistically, the Berlin *Last Judgment* may be compared with works produced by Angelico in the mid to late 1430s, in which one finds the same rounded figures, in contrast to the more attenuated forms that distinguish the paintings from the next decade, as well as the brilliant palette and precious decorative effects. The intensely emotive quality of the gestures and facial expressions that distinguishes the tumultuous crowd of fleeing and persecuted souls brings to mind, in particular, the narrative vivacity of the predella to the Linaiuoli tabernacle (cat. 29), as well as the dramatically charged scenes—most notably, *The Attempted Martyrdom of Saints Cosmas and Damian*—of the later San Marco altarpiece (fig. 118). The most stringent comparisons, however, may perhaps be found in the small *Virgin and Child* in the Pinacoteca Vaticana (fig. 91), dated by Kanter (p. 106) to the second half of the 1430s, which is characterized by nearly identical figure types and by a similar loose handling of forms and sketchier definition of facial features.

Dating the Berlin *Last Judgment* between 1435 and 1440 raises several possibilities with regard to its patron, who, as suggested by the overriding presence of Dominicans among the blessed, was most probably a member of that order. Bode's

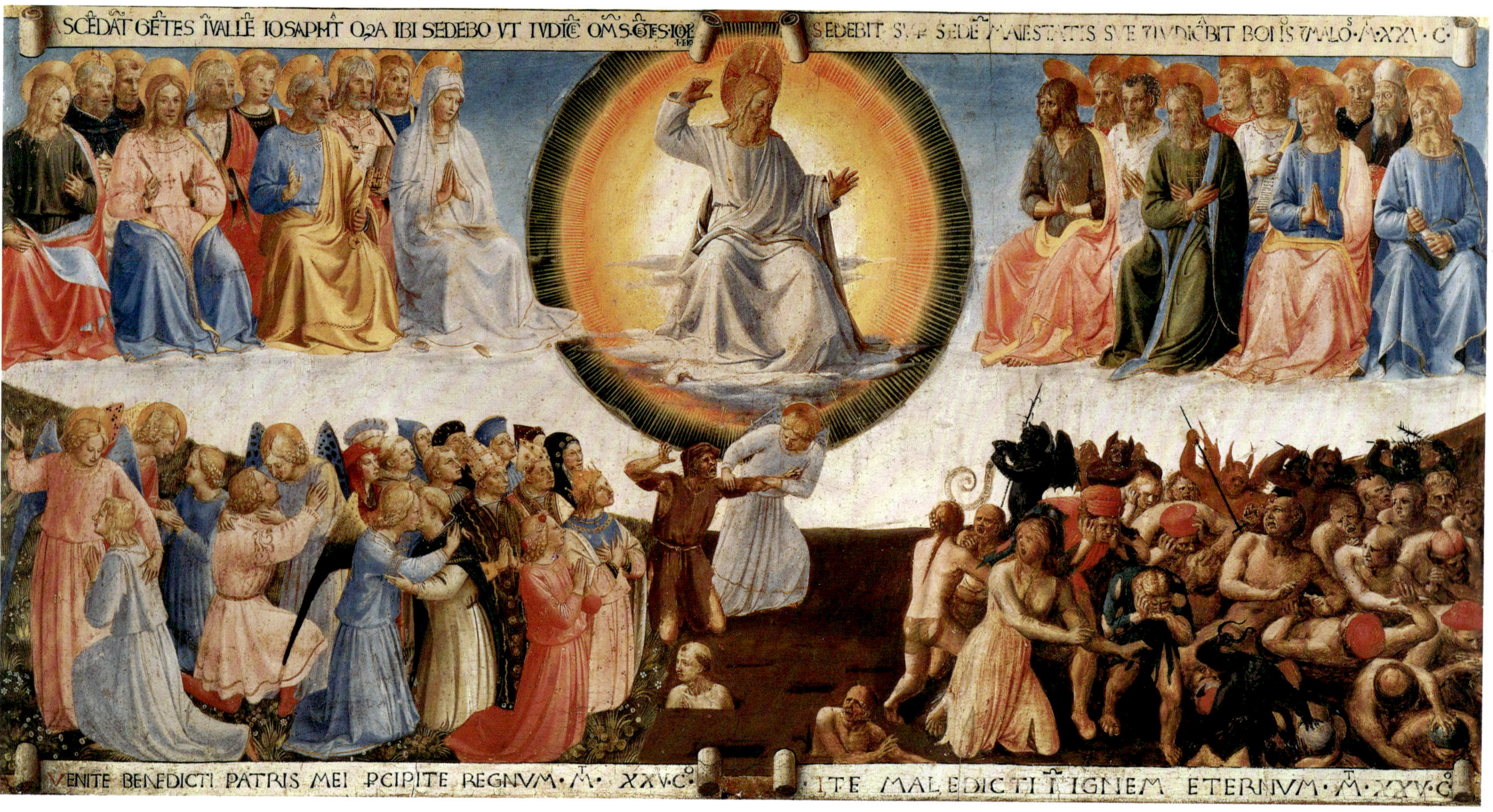

Figure 95. Fra Angelico. *The Last Judgment* (from the Annunziata Silver Chest). About 1450–52. Museo di San Marco, Florence

identification of him as the Dominican cardinal prominently situated next to a pope in the upper left of the garden leading up to Paradise[19] deserves proper consideration, especially in light of the pointing gesture of Saint Augustine, clearly directed at them. Given the painting's execution during the pontificate of Eugenius IV (r. 1431–47), it may be safe to presume that he is the pope shown with his back to the viewer (and thus probably not the picture's patron). The role accorded Saint Augustine might be explained in terms of Eugenius's first affiliation with the Augustinian order, as a former canon of San Giorgio in Alga in Venice. It is tempting to speculate, in this context, that the cardinal depicted here might be the famous Juan de Torquemada, who received the title in Florence in 1439, and who would later commission the *Christ on the Cross* now in the Fogg Art Museum (cat. 39). Barring such a late date for the painting's execution, the remaining possibility is to identify the patron with the only other known Dominican cardinal during the reign of Eugenius IV, the Spaniard Juan de Casanova of Aragon, who, like Torquemada after him, held the title of *Magister Sacri Palatii* (master theologian of the Vatican palace), received the cardinal's hat in 1431, and died in Florence in 1436.[20] Regardless of the cardinal's identity, most likely the painting was commissioned in Florence, during the pope's prolonged residence in the Dominican convent of Santa Maria Novella, between 1434 and 1436, and again between 1439 and 1443.[21] The fact that Spranger's copy of the Berlin *Last Judgment* was executed in Rome for a Dominican pope, Pius V, suggests, however, that the painting may have been intended to decorate a cardinal's private chapel or residence in the same city, perhaps located in one of the two major Dominican convents, that of Santa Maria sopra Minerva or of San Sisto.

PP

1. As reported in Staatliche Museen Preussischer Kulturbesitz 1978, p. 27.
2. Fesch collection, 1841, no. 565, p. 27; Königliche Museen zu Berlin 1898, pp. 8–9.
3. It is worth noting that the earliest descriptions of the Berlin *Last Judgment,* in the 1841 Fesch catalogue and in the 1864 edition of Crowe and Cavalcaselle (vol. I, p. 587 n. 3) appear to refer to a continuous, uninterrupted composition, albeit "altered in form and impaired by some retouching" (Crowe and Cavalcaselle). The hypothesis recently proposed by M. G. Ciardi Dupré Dal Poggetto (1996, pp. 140–41) that the Berlin picture may be identified with a tondo, presumably of the *Last Judgment,* which is listed without attribution in the 1492 inventory of the Medici palace, fails to convince on both technical and circumstantial grounds.
4. Bona 1909, p. 74.
5. Van Mander 1603–4 (1994 ed.), pp. 341–42 (cited in Bona 1909): "When

he got to Rome the Cardinal [Farnese] brought him to Pope Pius the Fifth. Arriving there the Cardinal and Don Giulio [Clovio] went together before His Holiness and shortly afterwards Sprangher was also called in and after he had kissed the Pope's feet and received the benediction, Sprangher was—after some talk and discussion about a piece that His Holiness wished him to paint—appointed there as painter to the Pope; he was allocated a grand place to live in the Belvedere, directly above the *Laocoon* sculpture, and there he made a piece with the *Last Judgement*, six feet tall, on a sheet of copper, so full of detail that five hundred faces appeared in it, which can still be seen in the monastery at Il Bosco, between Pavia and Alessandria, on the Sepulchre of Pius V, and this was painted within fourteen months."

6. To Spranger's copy perhaps may be added a mysterious panel of the *Last Judgment* (to my knowledge never published) in a private collection in Sicily, which was first cited by Crowe and Cavalcaselle (1864, p. 588 n. 1) as a much repainted, contemporary replica of the Berlin painting. According to these sources the painting, then in the Capuchin church at Leonforte, near Catania, was the gift of the Branciforti Trabbia family. The 1931 Staatliche Museen zu Berlin catalogue notes that the same panel, then owned by Baron Lidestri of Artesinella, appeared for sale in Rome in 1914. (See also Pope-Hennessy 1974, p. 221; Staatliche Museen Preussischer Kulturbesitz 1978, where it is stated that the painting, in a private collection, was on loan to the Museo Civico di "Castello Ursino," Catania, in 1970.) I have not been able to see or obtain a photograph of this work. The present curator of the Museo Civico, Anna Quartarone, kindly informs me (written communication) that the painting was on loan from the Li Destri di Rainò family between 1956 and 1972. It was then sent by the owners to the Istituto Centrale per il Restauro in Rome for technical examination. Nothing is known of the panel's subsequent history or location.
7. Spike 1996, p. 193 (with earlier bibliography).
8. M. Minardi, in Toscano and Capitelli 2002, pp. 176–79.
9. Crowe and Cavalcaselle 1864, pp. 587–88; Schottmüller 1911, p. 234.
10. Magnanimi 1980, p. 118.
11. Ibid., p. 77.
12. The *Pentecost* and the *Ascension* also appear to be fragmentary and may be assumed to have been reduced substantially in width. Each scene includes only a fraction of the number of figures normally required to appropriately illustrate the textual sources, and several figures in each are cropped inexplicably at the lateral edges of the composition.
13. The entire estate of Sommaia, located about fourteen kilometers northwest of Florence, was bequeathed to the Dominicans at San Marco by del Pugliese, who specified in his will that he was leaving to the chapel and church of Sant'Andrea at Sommaia, "five pictures painted on panel . . . that is: a picture on which is painted a head of Christ made in Flanders, with two wings at either side, painted by the hand of Filippo di fra Filippo; and a picture on which is painted a Judgement painted by the hand of Fra Giovanni, with two wings at the side, painted by the hand of Sandro di Botticello; and another picture on which is painted the Transition of Saint Jerome, by the hand of the aforementioned Sandro; and another small painting, by the hand of Pesellino; and another large painting, by the hand of the aforementioned Filippo, where is painted the Nativity with Magi" (as cited in Burke 2004, p. 159 [with earlier bibliography]). The hypothesis that the Corsini *Last Judgment* is the painting owned by del Pugliese was first advanced by C. Gamba (1936, p. 165), who identified as its lateral panels two paintings by Botticelli now in the State Pushkin Museum, Moscow, of the *Angel of the Annunciation* and the *Virgin Annunciate,* and two other works by the same artist in the State Hermitage Museum, Saint Petersburg, of *Saint Jerome in Penitence* and *Saint Dominic Preaching.* Gamba's suggestion was considered plausible by R. Lightbown (1978, pp. 94–96), who, however, accepted only the Pushkin paintings, the dimensions of which closely correspond to those of the Corsini picture, as the lateral panels in the proposed reconstruction. The del Pugliese document has been ignored, to my knowledge, by Angelico scholars.
14. Referring to del Pugliese's apparent predilection for surrounding small works by renowned older masters with lateral panels by younger contemporaries, J. Burke (2004, pp. 175–76) has suggested that by this date a painting like Angelico's *Last Judgment* may have attained the status of an icon, to be protected as something sacred and precious.
15. Gilbert 2003, pp. 46–47.
16. Traversari's possible role in determining the iconography of the painting was also highlighted by A. Santagostino Barbone (1989, pp. 272–73).
17. The principles underlying Thomist thought about the Last Judgment, and their influence on the Orvieto frescoes, in particular, are eloquently discussed by E. Paoli (1996, pp. 65–77, esp. pp. 66–67).
18. Baschet 1993, p. 366.
19. Bode 1888, p. 473.
20. Eubel 1960, vol. 1, p. 34 n. 8, vol. II, p. 7 notes 1–2.
21. For the various relocations of the papal court during this period, see ibid., vol. II, p. 7 n. 4.

33.
Christ Crowned with Thorns

Tempera and gold on panel, 55 x 39 cm (21⅝ x 15⅜ in.)
Parrocchia di Santa Maria del Soccorso, Livorno (on deposit in the Museo Civico Giovanni Fattori, Livorno)

This exceptionally powerful devotional image of Christ crowned with thorns and bleeding from his wounds was first attributed to Fra Angelico by Roberto Longhi, who saw it in the eighteenth-century church of Santa Maria del Soccorso in Livorno, where it was attributed to the "School of Giotto."[1] Nothing is known of the painting's earlier provenance prior to entering the Livornese church in 1837 as a gift of Silvestro Silvestri.[2]

Although Longhi's attribution has been unanimously accepted by scholars, both the dating and the unusual iconography of this work—considered one of Angelico's most intensely devout creations—have been the source of debate. Longhi, who dated it between 1430 and 1435, in close proximity to the Linaiuoli tabernacle, viewed it as Angelico's entirely original invention of a new prototype, in which the image of the suffering Christ crowned with thorns, derived from larger compositions, was adapted to the rectangular, portrait-like format of paintings of the Holy Face (*Sancta Facies*), which had been widely circulated in Europe, especially in the Northern countries, since the early fourteenth century.[3] The unique character of the Livorno *Christ* was also emphasized by Liana Castelfranchi Vegas,[4] who dated the panel to about 1438, and considered it the model for other nearly contemporary Netherlandish versions of the subject, such as the image on the reverse of Rogier van der Weyden's *Portrait of a Woman* in the National Gallery, London, and Petrus Christus's *Head of Christ* of about 1445, in The Metropolitan Museum of Art.

While Baldini and Pope-Hennessy also proposed a date for the Livorno *Christ* in the mid- to late 1430s, Boskovits individuated its closest points of reference in the so-called *Madonna delle Ombre* fresco in San Marco, and in the Perugia polyptych, a work that he dated to about 1447–48.[5] Based on the existence of an exact replica of the present picture, probably painted by Benozzo Gozzoli, in Assisi (Museo-Tesoro della Basilica di San Francesco), and of a second copy by a follower of Bonfigli, in Perugia (Pinacoteca Nazionale), Boskovits suggested that Angelico may have taken the painting with him during his Umbrian sojourn, or that he may actually have executed it in Perugia. An even later date for the Livorno *Christ* was proposed by De Marchi, who situated its execution in close proximity to that of the Bosco ai Frati altarpiece—about 1450—and cited Netherlandish examples such as the portrait by van der Weyden in the National Gallery, London, as its possible source of inspiration rather than as an image derived from it.[6] De Marchi's dating was accepted by Spike and Bonsanti, and it remains unquestioned in the most recent considerations of the painting.[7]

As suggested by the above arguments, a point of departure for any discussion of the Livorno *Christ* is provided by its unusual iconography and its presumed relationship to Netherlandish models, beginning with the vividly realistic image of Christ as *Rex Regum* (King of Kings) formulated by Jan van Eyck. In this work, now known only through copies, the earliest of which, in Berlin (fig. 96), is dated 1438, van Eyck transformed the iconic, two-dimensional type of Holy Face paintings into a life-like portrait of Christ "as a living being," situated behind a trompe-l'oeil frame that further heightens the illusionistic quality of the image.[8] Wearing a regal red robe inscribed with the words "REX REGVM," his face uniformly bathed in light, van Eyck's Christ became the most immediate, "true likeness" of the Redeemer in all his triumphant glory.

Pointing to the intense naturalism of the Livorno *Christ* and to such iconographic similarities as the inscribed red robe, Paula Nuttall has postulated that Angelico must have known a version of the Eyckian painting, "which was perhaps conflated with a more emotive type," integrating the details of blood and thorns. Among the possible sources, according to Nuttall, may have been one of the paintings by van Eyck reputedly owned by Eugenius IV or, more specifically, the Netherlandish *Head of Christ* listed in the Medici inventory of 1492.[9] Since none of these works survives or has been identified, Nuttall's suggestion must remain speculative. Moreover, the idea of a lost Netherlandish prototype fails to take into consideration the possibility that Angelico himself—as Longhi noted—may have been responsible for this new conception of the suffering Christ as *Rex Regum,* which represents, in effect, the earliest known example of a specific fusion between the Eyckian model and Veronica type of images, showing the head of Christ bleeding and crowned with thorns against the white sudarium.[10]

That Angelico probably did have access to a version of the Eyckian *Head of Christ* is suggested both by the portrait-like quality of the image—emphasized by the intentional cutting off of the halo along the top edge—and by the elaborately decorated collar of Christ's red robe, which integrates the inscription found in the Berlin painting with the gemstone decoration seen in other examples. At the same time Angelico further developed the message of the Eyckian model, as Beate Fricke points out, by completing the inscription "REX REGVM" with the words "DOMINVS DOMINANTIVM" (Lord of Lords), in accordance with the text of the Apocalypse (19: 16).[11]

The exceptional character of the Livorno painting is defined, however, by the way in which Angelico intensified

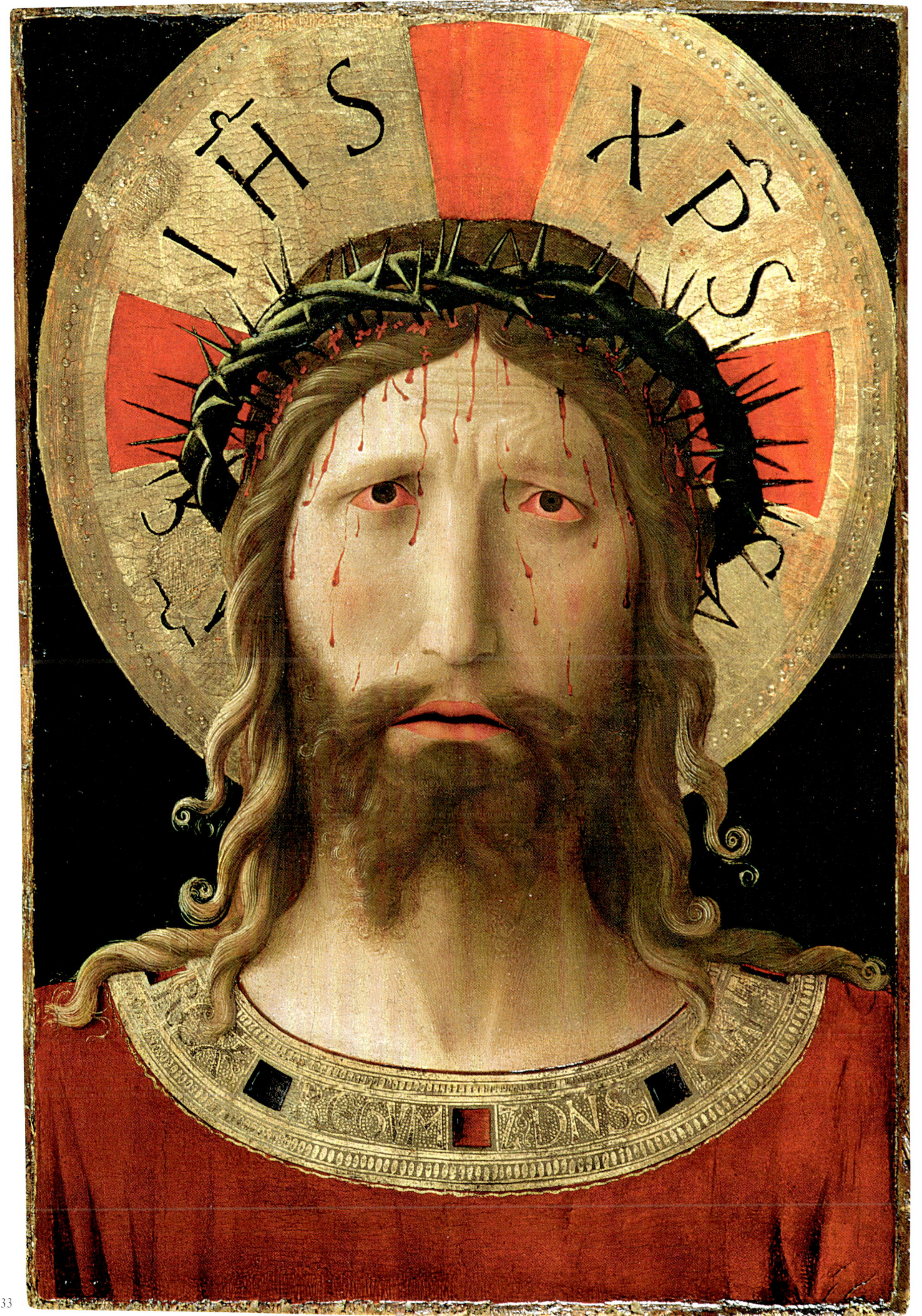

33

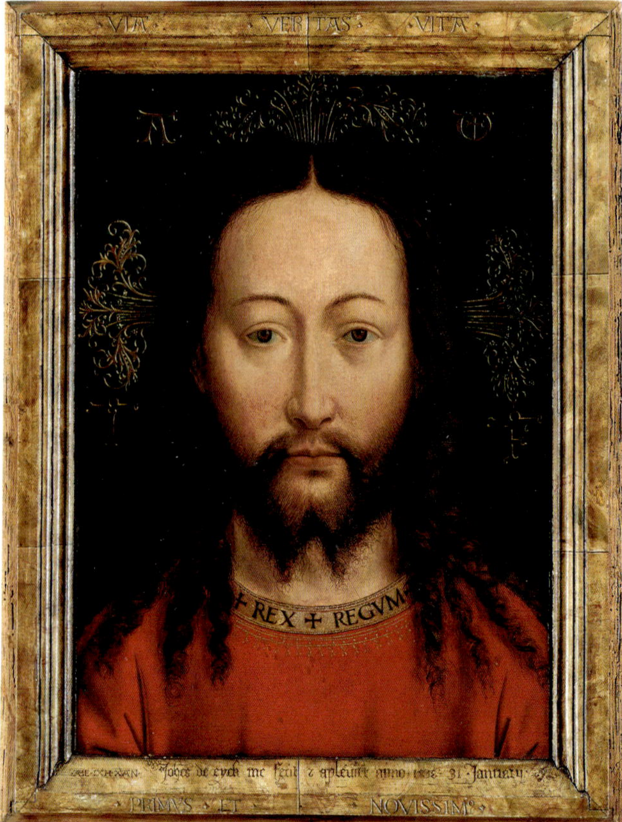

Figure 96. Copy after Jan van Eyck. *Head of Christ* (Rex Regum). 1438. Gemäldegalerie, Staatliche Museen Preussischer Kulturbesitz, Berlin

the emotive content of Veronica images of the suffering Holy Face by depicting the redness of Christ's blood-filled eyes and mouth. The source for this detail, absent from any of the various Netherlandish versions of the subject, was traced by Scarpellini[12] to the *Revelations* of Saint Bridget of Sweden (about 1304–1373), who recounted how the Virgin had vividly described her son's torments on the cross and said of the crown of thorns that, "It pricked so hard that both my son's eyes were filled with the blood that flowed down, and the ears were stopped up and His beard was thick with blood."[13] One of the most popular texts of the Middle Ages, the *Revelations* may, in turn, have inspired the writings of the Dominican archbishop of Florence and friend of Angelico, Saint Antoninus (1389–1459), whose *Opera a ben vivere* was cited by Boskovits in relationship to the Livorno *Christ*.[14] In this guide on how to lead a Christian life, written for a devout lady, Antoninus advises that "you should meditate a little every day on the passion of our Lord Jesus Christ . . . kneel down before a Crucifix and with the eyes of the mind, more than with those of the body, consider his face. Beginning first with the crown of thorns, pressed into his head, down to his skull; next the eyes, full of tears and of blood; the mouth, frothing and full of bile and of blood; the beard, similarly full of spit and of blood and of bile . . . . And in reverence of all these things, you should recite the Lord's prayer with a Hail Mary."[15]

Although the gruesome, graphic details of such descriptions are included in Angelico's depiction, they do not distort the idealized beauty of Christ's face and perfectly chiseled features, highlighted by the brilliant light illuminating the composition from the left. Lending the image a preciousness that overrides the distressing subject matter is the luminous quality of the painted surface and the meticulous handling of such details as the golden highlights enlivening the curly locks of Christ's hair and beard or the translucent glow of the gems set in the elaborate gilt border of his dress. These elements were placed by Nuttall in direct relationship to the Eyckian model and viewed in terms of Angelico's conscious decision to create a "Netherlandish" image. They are, however, consistent with other paintings produced by the artist in the late 1430s and early 1440s, such as the Perugia altarpiece, for which Kanter accepts the traditional dating of 1437 (see cat. 30), and the San Marco high altarpiece, generally situated between about 1438 and 1442. Both these works, executed at the same moment as Filippo Lippi's Netherlandish-inspired *Tarquinia Madonna* of 1437, were recently singled out by Keith Christiansen as reflecting, in their luminous intensity, Angelico's own, broader response to Netherlandish painting at this date.[16] In fact, the same "reflective brilliance and luster" that are cited by Christiansen as marking the rendering of individual details in the Perugia and San Marco altarpieces may be considered the hallmarks of the Livorno *Christ*, which should be viewed as from the same period in Angelico's career. Beyond the analogies with these works, final confirmation for a dating of the Livorno *Christ* in the late 1430s or early 1440s may be found in the stringent, formal correspondences between it and the type of Christ depicted by Angelico on the walls of San Marco, as was first observed by Boskovits,[17] or in the *Lamentation* from Santa Maria della Croce al Tempio (now in the Museo di San Marco), executed between 1436 and 1441.[18]

The original destination of the Livorno *Christ*, as well as its specific function, are unknown. Saint Antoninus's text, cited above, might suggest that the image was intended to fulfill the same function as a Crucifix, as an object for private meditation on the Passion of Christ. Placed on an altar, it could have served a purpose similar to that of more traditional Veronica paintings, whose role in the daily devotions of cloistered women, in particular, recently has been discussed by scholars.[19] On the other hand, the confirmation of an early date for the painting's execution leads to a reconsideration of the compelling hypothesis, put forward nearly thirty years ago by

Giulia Brunetti (but ignored in the subsequent literature), that this might be the "*volto sancto*" listed in an old inventory of the furnishings of the Altar of the Annunziata in the Servite church of Santissima Annunziata in Florence.[20] Compiled between 1439 and 1441—that is, before the altar underwent the radical transformations carried out by Michelozzo on behalf of Piero de' Medici—the inventory refers to "*uno volto sancto dipinto sta in su il dicto altare bello e divoto*" ("a holy face which is on the said altar, beautiful and pious"). According to Brunetti, despite the apparent discrepancy in subject matter, this reference could apply to the Livorno painting, which is identified in an inscription on the reverse as a "Holy Face of Jesus Christ."

Significantly, in the sixteenth century, the Altar of the Annunziata contained another painting of the Holy Face, by Andrea del Sarto, which was described by Vasari in the following terms: "Shortly after . . . Andrea del Sarto painted a Head of Christ, which is now preserved by the Servite monks on the altar of the Annunciation; and this is so beautiful, that for my part I do not know whether the human imagination could possibly conceive any more admirable representation of the head of the Redeemer."[21] In the seventeeth century this image was inserted into an elaborate tabernacle commissioned by the Medici.[22] According to nineteenth-century sources the new tabernacle had been built so that Andrea's painting would be movable, and could serve as a temporary replacement for the silver door with the monogram of Christ that was removed when the Host was not inside. On this basis, it has been suggested that Andrea's painting may, in fact, have been designed originally as a tabernacle door rather than as an independent devotional object;[23] whether or not Fra Angelico's *Christ Crowned with Thorns* is, indeed, the painting mentioned in the 1439–41 inventory of the same altar, it is worth speculating whether it might have served a similar function.

That the Livorno *Christ* was produced for a patron of some note, or that it was on public display on the altar of as important a Florentine church as that of Santissima Annunziata, is perhaps confirmed by the existence of the copy in Assisi attributed to Benozzo Gozzoli. Somewhat smaller in size and executed in ink and tempera on parchment, this work was probably commissioned as a less-expensive replica of the Livorno *Christ,* possibly the gift of a pilgrim specifically intended for the basilica of San Francesco. It may have been this image, in turn—rather than Angelico's—that served as a model for the two other Umbrian versions of the same subject painted by a follower of Bonfigli.[24] PP

1. Longhi 1928a, pp. 153–59 (ill. in Longhi 1928a [1968 ed.], pp. 37–45).
2. L. Berti, in Florence 1955, p. 34, no. 19.
3. For a discussion of the evolution of this image, see G. Wolf, in Kessler and Wolf 1998, pp. 153–79.
4. Castelfranchi Vegas 1983, p. 70.
5. Baldini 1970, p. 96, no. 45 (dated 1435); Pope-Hennessy 1974, p. 227 (about 1436); Boskovits 1994, pp. 386–87 n. 25.
6. A. De Marchi, in Bellosi 1990a, pp. 104–5.
7. Spike 1996, p. 238, no. 83; Bonsanti 1998, pp. 154–55, no. 82; B. Fricke, in Morello and Wolf 2000, pp. 188–89; Nuttall 2004, p. 235.
8. See Ainsworth 1994, p. 86; and, most recently, Wolf 2000, pp. 111–12; K. Gludovatz, in Morello and Wolf 2000, pp. 187–88.
9. Nuttall 2004, p. 235. In support of Eugenius IV's taste for Netherlandish painting, Nuttall (ibid., p. 32) mentions a letter written from Rome by Cardinal Jean Jouffroy, Bishop of Arras, in 1468, in which the prelate refers to the genius of "John of Bruges, whose paintings you have seen in Pope Eugenius' palace." As noted by Nuttall, the Medici inventory (Spallanzani and Gaeta Bertelà 1992, p. 72) refers to a painting in Giuliano's room: "*uno colmetto picholo, cornicie messe d'oro, dipintovi una testa d'uno Cristo, opera fiandrescha*" ("a small panel with a gilt frame in which is painted the head of Christ, Netherlandish work").
10. This version of the Veronica type, with the suffering Christ, appears to have made its first appearance about 1400 in the work of the Netherlandish painter known as the Master of the Veronica; see Wolf 2000, pp. 111–12. Citing the portrait in the National Gallery, London, Panofsky (1956, p. 112) credited the invention of this particular conflation of images to the workshop of Rogier van der Weyden. The National Gallery panel, however, like the Petrus Christus painting in the Metropolitan Museum, shows Christ dressed in a gown, rather than the regal red robe. Angelico's image (not cited by Panofsky) appears to be the one most closely indebted to the *Rex Regum* portraits.
11. "And he hath on his garment, and on his thigh written: King of Kings, and Lord of Lords"; B. Fricke, in Morello and Wolf, 2000, p. 189.
12. P. Scarpellini, in Ciardi Dupré Dal Poggetto 1980, p. 56.
13. *Revelations,* Book VII, as cited in Butkovich 1969, p. 62.
14. Boskovits 1994, p. 386; see also L. Kanter and P. Palladino, in Morello and Kanter 1999, p. 110 (reprinted in Morello and Wolf 2000, pp. 189–90).
15. "*Conforto anco la carità vostra che ogni dì pigliate una poca di meditazione della passione del nostro Signore Gesù Cristo* [. . .] *inginocchiatevi dinanzi ad uno Crocifisso e cogli occhi della mente, più che con quelli del corpo, considerate la facia sua. Prima, alla corona delle spine, fitteglele in testa, insino al célabro, poi gli occhi pieni di lacrime e di sangue; la bocca, piena di fiele e di bava e di sangue; la barba, similmente piena di bava e di sangue e di fiele* [. . .] *E a reverenzia di tutte queste cose direte un paternostro con avemaria*" (Sant'Antonino, *Opera a ben vivere* . . . , part III, chap. XI, p. 149 [as cited in Boskovits 1994, p. 138]).
16. K. Christiansen, in Ainsworth and Christiansen 1998, p. 49.
17. Boskovits 1994, p. 386.
18. For the correct interpretation of the date of this work, see Bonsanti 1998, pp. 141–42.
19. Hamburger 1998, pp. 229–46.
20. Brunetti 1977, pp. 228–35.
21. Vasari 1911 ed., vol. III, p. 261.
22. For this painting and the tabernacle, still in Santissima Annunziata, see C. Caneva, in Florence 1986, pp. 103–4, no. IX; D. Liscia Bemporad and E. Nardinocchi, in Casalini et al. 1987, pp. 302, 331–34.
23. C. Caneva, in Florence 1986, pp. 103–4, no. IX.
24. For these images, attributed to a so-called Master of the Pietà di San Costanzo, see Todini 1989, vol. I, p. 165.

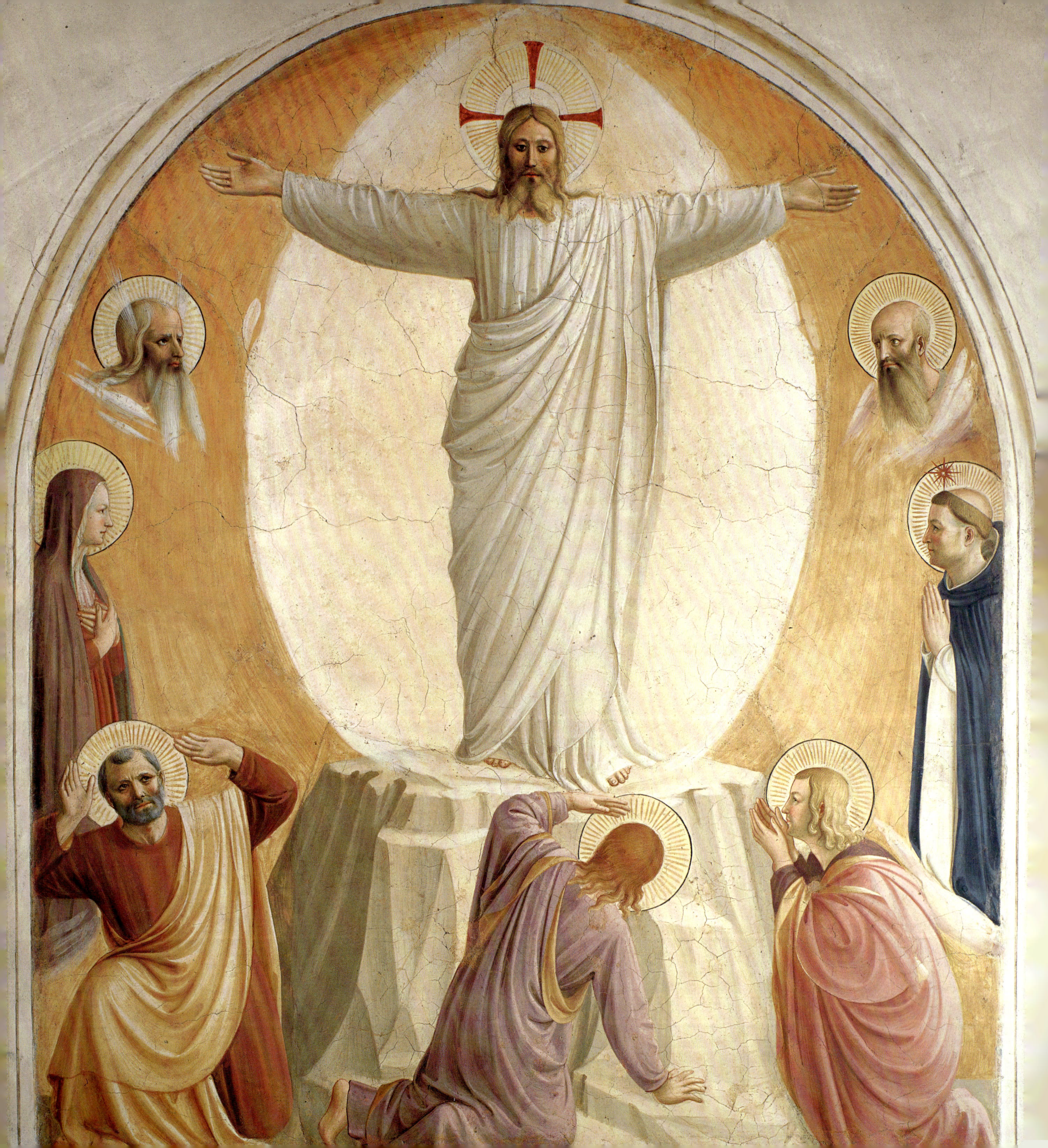

Chapter VI
The Frescoes by Fra Angelico at San Marco

MAGNOLIA SCUDIERI

Opposite:
Figure 97. Fra Angelico. *The Transfiguration* (cell 6). Convento di San Marco, Florence

Throughout its critical history the fresco cycle at the convent of San Marco has provoked endless questions regarding the participation of assistants or collaborators in its execution, their identity, and the extent of their responsibilities, even though the series has the rare distinction of being recorded in an authoritative contemporary source, the *Cronaca*—the fifteenth-century chronicle of the convent—which attributes it unequivocally entirely to Fra Giovanni da Fiesole.[1] To anyone studying the frescoes attentively, these questions, as well as the sometimes contradictory answers that have been proposed for them, must appear to be completely justified.

Since the nineteenth century, along with scholars like Berenson,[2] who assigned all or almost all the frescoes to the hand of the master, there have been others who discerned differences in style or quality—even though frequently not in the same passages—which might be imputed to the intervention of collaborators;[3] the latter were referred to either generically or as anonymous personalities, and only occasionally were identified hypothetically with artists known to have worked with Angelico, such as Zanobi Strozzi and Benozzo Gozzoli.[4] In the mid-1950s, the perception of inconsistencies throughout the cycle led to some highly restrictive positions, such as that of John Pope-Hennessy, for whom Angelico's contribution was relatively limited compared to that of several anonymous artists active at his side.[5] Others, like Mario Salmi,[6] reaffirmed Angelico's overall responsibility, even while recognizing notable variations in quality—especially in the frescoes on the upper floor—which they felt could be explained not only by the presence of assistants but by developments in Angelico's own style over time, presupposing a broad range in dates among the various parts of the cycle. This more inclusive avenue of interpretation, which credited the master with the conception and layout of the frescoes even in those parts executed by others—by virtue of the designs (*sinopie* or cartoons) he provided for them—was also accepted by Francini Ciaranfi,[7] Collobi-Ragghianti,[8] and by Umberto Baldini in the catalogue of the Angelico exhibition of 1955.[9] While acknowledging the discrepancies in execution, Baldini sought to emphasize, on the occasion of that exhibition, that "the collaboration—which undoubtedly took place—was never a substitution [for the master]." This reassertion of the uniformity of vision that informs the cycle, determined by Angelico's role in the conception and supervision of work on every fresco, has been accepted by virtually all subsequent scholars, and remains to this day a basic assumption, even in the search to identify different hands involved in the execution of the series.

The notion that all of the frescoes reveal the constant and continuous presence of Angelico as the one responsible for the invention, composition, and design of the *sinopie*—no less than as the supervisor of the work of his collaborators—was reaffirmed by Giorgio Bonsanti in 1983, following the restoration of the frescoes undertaken by Dino Dini in that year.[10] Among the cells in the upper dormitory, Bonsanti restricted Angelico's intervention in the execution of the frescoes to those situated on the left side of the eastern corridor alone (up to cell 10 but to varying degrees in each) and to the figure of Saint Dominic in the *Crucifixion* in cell 25; he also postulated a larger role to Benozzo Gozzoli in the decorative program than that normally accorded this artist, acknowledging the presence of his hand in the *Adoration of the Magi* in Cosimo's cell.[11] By 1983, in effect, scholars had already advanced numerous suggestions regarding Benozzo's possible intervention in the frescoes. The most recent proposal had been that of Anna Padoa Rizzo, who identified Benozzo's hand in the *Crucifixion* in cell 29 and in cell 22,[12] adding these works to others already accepted as by the artist: the *Crucifixion* in cell 38, the *Adoration of the Magi* in cell 39, and the figure of the saint in the *Saint Dominic before the Crucifix* along the corridor.[13]

The increased interest in Benozzo Gozzoli during the last several years resulting in several monographic studies and in the recent exhibitions in Perugia and in Montefalco[14]—and the efforts to reconstruct the less certain, early phase of his career, have led scholars to acknowledge the circumstantial likelihood of the artist's presence at San Marco, and to extend the limits of his participation in the execution of the frescoes. Thus, Bonsanti[15] has identified Benozzo as the number one assistant, who supposedly collaborated with Angelico in some sections of the frescoes in the cells on the outer wall of the east corridor (he is presumed to be the author of the *Virgin* in cell 7, of the *Three Maries* and the *Christ* in cell 8, and of the *Two Saints* in cell 11) and on the decorative band framing the *Crucifixion* in the Chapter House. Over the master's design, he would also have executed all of the frescoes on the opposite side of the east corridor (in cells 22 to 30), and, probably, with some assistance, all of the frescoes in the north corridor and in the south corridor as well. In substance, this hypothesis has gained the support of Padoa Rizzo,[16] who, like Bellosi,[17] is more prudent, however, in her assessment of the cells on the inner wall of the east corridor and of part of those along the north corridor. The recognition of Gozzoli's intervention in the cycle—albeit not so extensive—is implicit in the opinions of Paolo Morachiello, Diane Cole Ahl, and Cristina Acidini Luchinat,[18] all of whom also favor the notion of the artist's increased independence, in the design as much as in the execution of the frescoes, following his activity in the Chapter House: first in the cells of the east corridor, then in the south corridor, and finally in the north corridor.

An isolated voice in this debate is that of Miklós Boskovits,[19] who appears never to have been in doubt about Angelico's substantial authorship of the frescoes, and, in the most recent consideration of the argument, has strongly disputed the role attributed to Benozzo at San Marco,[20] reasserting Angelico's responsibility for the entire cycle—excepting the decorative band surrounding the Chapter House *Crucifixion*—and regarding those differences that others have imputed to the intervention of assistants as, instead, the result of distinctions in date and the evolution of the master's style.

The existence of such a range of scholarly opinion is unquestionably an indicator of the complexities inherent in the interpretation of the San Marco frescoes, suggesting the need for a general reconsideration of this work, in light of the various arguments fueling the debate. Above all, I am convinced that the discussion would profit from a more in-depth analytical study of the frescoes that took the technical data into proper account alongside the stylistic evidence and situated the arguments within a chronological framework that, itself, perhaps deserves to be reconsidered. In this regard, I believe it might be useful to begin by reexamining the historical circumstances under which the frescoes originated, through a critical reading of the documentary sources, in order to circumscribe better the possible chronogical parameters of the project.

In 1436, with the bull of Pope Eugenius IV and the support of Cosimo and Lorenzo de' Medici, the Dominican Observants of Fiesole finally obtained their sought-after home in Florence: the convent of San Marco, formerly inhabited by the Silvestrine monks. While still retaining their ties to San Domenico, the small community of brothers—which, a few months before, had settled in San Giorgio sulla Costa, on the opposite side of the city—immediately took possession of their new headquarters with an official ceremony on February 4, 1436.[21] As related in minute detail in the *Cronaca,*[22] the convent was in a ruinous state, and the monks had to wait almost two years (until the end of 1437) before any part of the building was repaired or reconstructed, living, in the meantime, in partially destroyed, simple wooden cells. It is the *Cronaca*, again, which relates that in 1437 the first dormitory, with twenty cells, was built above the refectory, preserving the ancient lateral walls of the convent.[23] This must have been at the end of the year, if, as the *Cronaca* states, the Medici—who had promised their financial support for the entire reconstruction project, entrusting its execution to their favorite architect, Michelozzo—decided to postpone the start of work until hearing the outcome of the petition brought by the Silvestrines before the Council of Basel; the council's decision, in favor of the Dominicans, came only at the end of 1437.[24] It, therefore, seems probable that the first twenty cells and the refectory—where Angelico painted a *Crucifixion* (destroyed in the sixteenth century)—were ready to be frescoed in the first months of 1438, and that given the small number of *giornate* (from three to six) required to paint every fresco in that dormitory, it is possible that the entire job, including the technical preparations, was carried out by the end of 1438. This is, it must be understood, a purely theoretical conclusion, which should be borne in mind within the larger context of the general reconsideration of the project; we do not know, for example, how long Fra Giovanni remained in Cortona, where he is recorded in the same year,[25] at work on the frescoes above the portal of the church of San Domenico, which are very close stylistically to those in the first dormitory at San Marco.[26]

The *Cronaca* is silent with regard to the period and the circumstances surrounding construction of the other dormitories and remaining parts of the convent. Following its narrative thread, which appears to be chronological (although one cannot exclude the possibility of some omissions), we learn that in 1438, the Medici turned their attention to the church, which resulted in the commissioning of a new altarpiece from Angelico. Having obtained the patronage of the main altar of the church, Cosimo and Lorenzo had proceeded to promote the construction of the new tribune with an altar ornamented with marble intarsia decoration, "*totum de lapidibus sectis ac politis,*" which unfortunately has been lost.[27] The same year also witnessed the Medici's decision to award to the convent of San Domenico in Cortona the polyptych by Lorenzo di Niccolò that had decorated the old altar, substituting a new altarpiece by Angelico for it, which would adequately celebrate their new patronage.[28] An inscription added at the base of Lorenzo di Niccolò's painting, alongside the Medici arms, records that the transfer took place in 1440, even though Angelico's new altarpiece, as the *Cronaca* states, was not yet completed.[29] One of the predella panels now in the Museo di San Marco in Florence, portraying *The Burial of Saints Cosmas and Damian and Their Brothers* (fig. 119), is set before the church in the Piazza San Marco and provides a useful chronological point of reference for the altarpiece. There, the convent is depicted in a specific phase of the reconstruction: on the right is a building block with the first dormitory; the dormitory in the south building block, facing the piazza, still remains to be erected. Construction on the north wing and on the church does not appear to have been completed. Visible, projecting from the right side of the nave, is an extension to the building with an elegant Gothic window (similar to those extant today on the exterior of the right façade of the church), which can be clearly identified as the preexisting right arm of the transept, subsequently demolished by Michelozzo in order to complete the north wing of the convent and allow space for the second dormitory. We may deduce from this that Angelico's panel was painted between 1438 and 1439, when, according to the *Cronaca*, the church underwent many major transformations, especially in the tribune; these renovations perhaps were already in progress by the end of 1440, when Lorenzo di Niccolò's old altarpiece certainly had been removed, and were terminated in 1441, when the new sacristy, located next to the tribune, appears to have been finished. While documenting the completion of the first dormitory, Angelico's predella panel also confirms the hypothesis, suggested by the account in the *Cronaca,* that work on the convent was suspended following the construction of that dormitory, only to be resumed after the alterations to the church—that is, surely from 1440 on.[30] This is indirectly implied in the *Cronaca,* which, although not specific about the dates of the work on the other dormitories, notes that after the death of Lorenzo in 1440 Cosimo took it upon himself to oversee the completion of all parts of the convent. Construction of the dormitory in the north wing probably had already been terminated by 1441, given that the new sacristy, situated in an area below the far side of that wing, was finished by then; work on the dormitory preceded the completion in August 1442 of the Chapter House (including the fresco), located a short distance from the sacristy within the same building block.[31] Once again, the *Cronaca* reports that the program had proceeded with such speed that by 1443 the convent—albeit not entirely completed—essentially was ready to be occupied (specifically, the three-part dormitory with forty-four cells, the workshops, and the garden),[32] and that Pope Eugenius IV—who had arrived for the consecration of the new church on the feast of Epiphany (January 6), 1443—was housed in the cell destined for Cosimo, at the end of the north corridor.[33] The *Cronaca* does not designate which parts of the convent remained unfinished; the library undoubtedly was one such place, as we know that its furnishings (benches, cupboards, and books) were not installed until 1444.[34] Were there others? A margin of doubt surrounds the frescoes; although it seems logical to presume that they were substantially finished by the time of the consecration of the church in 1443, it is possible that the execution of minor areas continued until 1445, when Angelico is still documented in Florence. In that year, his signature appears among those of the monks who voted in favor of separating the convent of San Marco from that of San Domenico.[35]

In theory, this period would have been sufficiently long for Angelico to have carried out the project even single-handedly, given the limited number of *giornate* required for each fresco; that the execution took place in successive phases would also account for certain stylistic variations among the frescoes that are considered autograph. On the other hand, it should be noted that the actual time available to the artist to execute the frescoes is significantly reduced if one considers the intervals between the various stages of construction and the artist's concurrent activity at the churches of San Marco, San Domenico in Cortona (where he is documented in 1438), and San Domenico in Perugia (albeit over a protracted period)[36]—all of which perhaps made the collaboration with other painters indispensable in order for the work to have been completed by 1443. Visual evidence, indeed, suggests that this collaborative enterprise cannot be reduced to the intervention of a single assistant (identified as Benozzo Gozzoli), since it entailed the creation of a stylistic idiom generically indebted to Angelico and, despite its various manifestations, sufficiently uniform in vision as to make the distinction of individual hands difficult. A fresco cycle such as this one surely demonstrates how the notion of individual authorship by necessity should be extended to include those parts of the series not executed directly by the master, but—as was the case with Angelico—invented, drawn, and overseen by him.

An examination of the frescoes, and of their division into working *giornate,* allows one to discern with a greater assurance the intervention of different painters, even within a single scene, and provides a sufficiently informative picture of a fully developed workshop—one that included perhaps four or five collaborators working alongside Angelico, who was active sometimes as author, sometimes as coordinator, and sometimes as supervisor of the project. However, before proceeding with the identification of these collaborators, it is necessary to isolate their respective contributions, and, as yet, these have not been clearly determined.[37] Even the attributions to Gozzoli, unanimously regarded as having been the main assistant, seem less obvious to me than others have proposed—especially in light of the stylistic heterogeneity of those passages that have been assigned to him over the years, and of the difficulty in

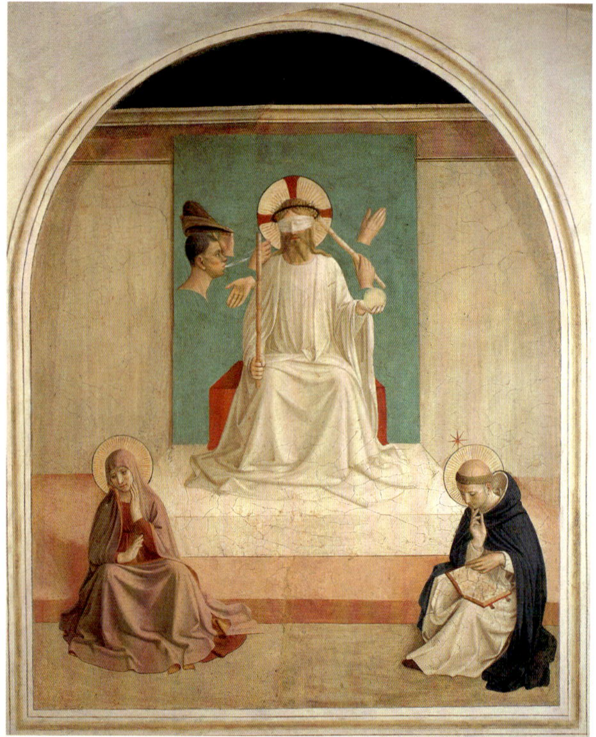

Figure 98 (near right). Fra Angelico and Assistants. *The Mocking of Christ* (cell 7). Convento di San Marco, Florence

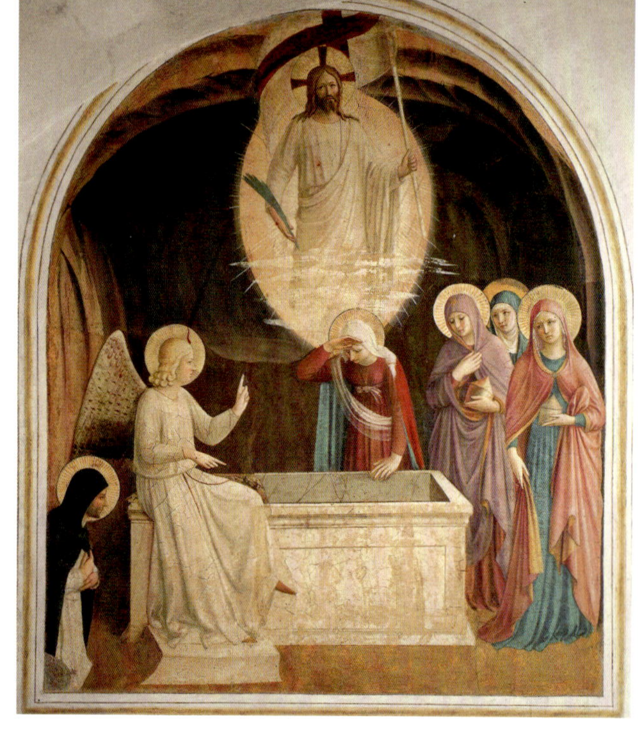

Figure 99 (far right). Fra Angelico and Assistants. *The Holy Women at the Sepulcher* (cell 8). Convento di San Marco, Florence

comparing them to works that are securely autograph—although perhaps distant in date. The latter—such as the frescoes in Montefalco, of 1450–52, and those in the Medici Chapel, of 1459—are themselves the product of collaborations with other artists.

The intervention of assistants is discernible, albeit to varying degrees, throughout the San Marco cycle, even in the frescoes in cells along the outer wall of the east corridor, where, by common admission, the hand of Angelico predominates. The *Mocking of Christ* in cell 7 (fig. 98) offers a pertinent example of the decisive impact that examination of the *giornate* can have on our understanding of the creative process. In the seated figure of Saint Dominic one observes a noticeable variation in style, quality, and technique between the right hand—clear, translucent, and modeled like the head—and the left hand, which is differently proportioned and made ponderous by its dense coloring and heavily drawn outlines. These distinctions were difficult to explain until more careful scrutiny of the wall surface revealed that the upper portion of the figure, including the right hand, was included in one *giornata* (painted section) of intonaco, and the rest of the figure in another. It becomes possible, therefore, to attribute the stylistic discrepancies between the two parts to the intervention of an assistant—obviously gifted in the painting of draperies—to whom Fra Giovanni would have entrusted the completion of the figure. The same opaque palette and unmodulated contrasts of light and shadow also characterize the figure of the Virgin—painted on another *giornata*—which has generally been regarded as the work of a collaborator identified by most scholars as Gozzoli.[38] The attribution appears confirmed in the present case by a comparison with Benozzo's frescoes in the church of San Francesco in Montefalco—especially with a figure such as that of Saint John the Evangelist in the vault, whose robe echoes the dense chiaroscuro and the voluminous folds of the Virgin's mantle, and is spread out around him in the same way.

Gozzoli's hand has also been identified in the execution of the Three Maries in the fresco of the *Holy Women at the Sepulcher* (fig. 99) in cell 8. However, while there is no doubt that the author of the *Virgin* in cell 7 was responsible for the two figures in the background of this scene, it is questionable whether he also painted the third figure in the foreground, distinguished by a less opaque palette and by a crisp drawing technique that may be ascribed directly to Angelico—the author, in my opinion, of the rest of the fresco. In support of such a hypothesis is the discovery that this figure occupies its own *giornata,* separate from the one on which the other two are painted.

Yet another significant example of the subdivision of labor within a single fresco, and its significance for our interpretation of the resulting image, is offered by the *Crucifixion* in cell 4 (fig. 100); only an accurate mapping of the six working *giornate* that constitute this fresco would allow us to speculate on the intervention of assistants, thus justifying certain lapses in quality that sometimes are evident within the same figure. This would seem to be the case with the figures of Saint Dominic

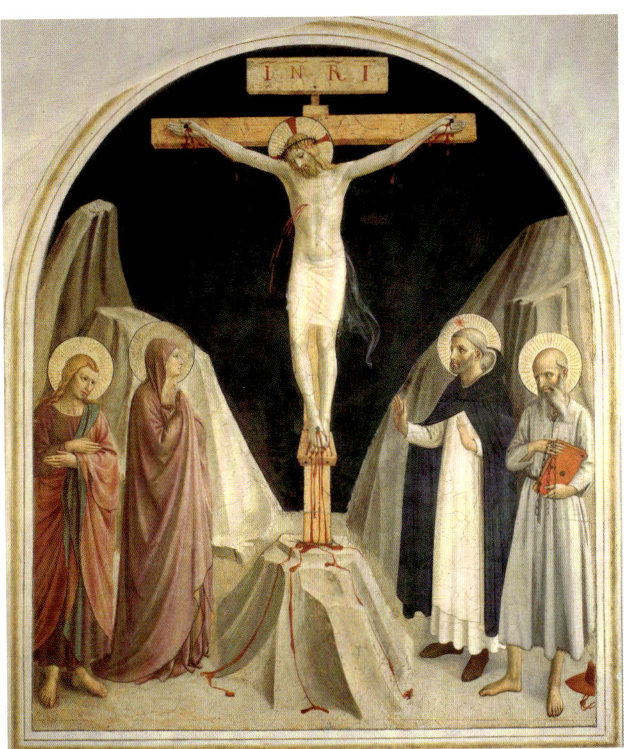

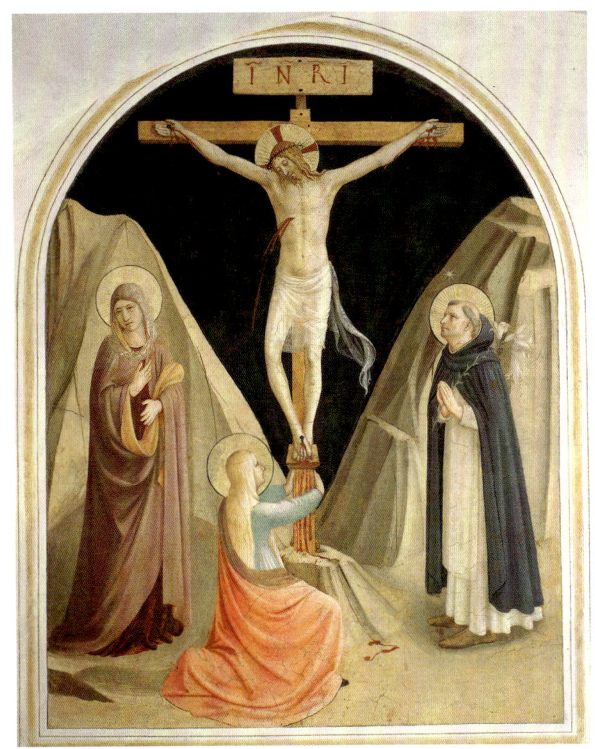

Figure 100 (near right). Fra Angelico and Assistants. *The Crucifixion, with the Virgin, Saint John the Evangelist, Saint Dominic, and Saint Jerome* (cell 4). Convento di San Marco, Florence

Figure 101 (far right). Fra Angelico and Assistants. *The Crucifixion, with the Virgin, Saint Mary Magdalene, and Saint Dominic* (cell 25). Convento di San Marco, Florence

and Saint Jerome, in which the high level of execution of the heads, painted at the same time in a single *giornata,* unquestionably by Angelico, does not appear to relate to the slightly rigid, schematic treatment of the rest of the bodies; this is especially apparent in the poorly attempted foreshortening of the hands of Saint Dominic. Doubts about authorship are also raised by the rendering of the head of Saint John the Evangelist, which is painted on a different *giornata* than the body; while reflecting Angelico's manner in its general outlines, the proportions appear somewhat too reduced and the expression too exaggerated for the hand of the master, suggesting the intervention of another artist, even though a plausible candidate remains to be named.

In other instances, such as the *Madonna and Child Enthroned between Saint Augustine and Saint Thomas* in cell 11, the subdivision of the *giornate* corresponds to whole figures or groups, making it easier to distinguish the hand of the master—recognizable in the figure of Saint Augustine—from that of a mediocre assistant, whose intervention may be detected here for the first time; that same artist may be identified again in the decorative surround of the Chapter House *Crucifixion,* where he was responsible at least for the depiction of the blessed in the first medallion on the right. In any case, this is not the same assistant who executed the slackly painted figure of Saint Dominic in the *Lamentation* in cell 2 (fig. 149), and perhaps also that of Saint Peter Martyr in the *Annunciation* in cell 3.

The frescoes on the other side of the corridor are quite different. Their more simplified and repetitive compositions are marked by a generally more archaizing tendency characteristic of Angelico's vocabulary of a decade earlier, which still reflected the influence of Lorenzo Monaco.[39] Late Gothic prototypes underlie most of the depictions of the Crucifixion, defined by a slender, ethereal Christ far removed from the solid, all-too-human type painted by Angelico in the Cloister (fig. 108). At the same time, the images of the Virgin echo examples by Angelico from the early 1430s. The intensely dramatic features of the *Virgin* in cell 30 recall those of her counterpart in the *Deposition* from Santa Trinita (fig. 53), while the simplified forms of the *Virgin* in cells 23 and 25 (fig. 101) are still in the Trecento tradition, and are reminiscent of the figures of Adam and Eve in Angelico's even earlier *Annunciation* for San Domenico (fig. 51). Objectively, it seems unlikely that toward the end of the 1430s Angelico would have employed such a *retardataire* style, which is more plausibly understood as the effort of a follower who was not quite as accomplished as his master. Angelico's direct participation in the execution of these frescoes should, nonetheless, not be excluded, and, moreover, it is confirmed in many instances by one or more insertions, each corresponding to a *giornata,* and often, but not exclusively, devoted to the representation of Saint Dominic. Certainly to be counted among these is the beautiful image of the saint in cell 25—cited by Bonsanti[40]—the rendering of whose face, sculpted by light, anticipates the intensely observed naturalism of the Chapter House *Crucifixion*; to this may be added the figures of the same saint in the *Crucifixion* in cell 23 and in *The Way to Calvary* in cell 28, which, in their typology

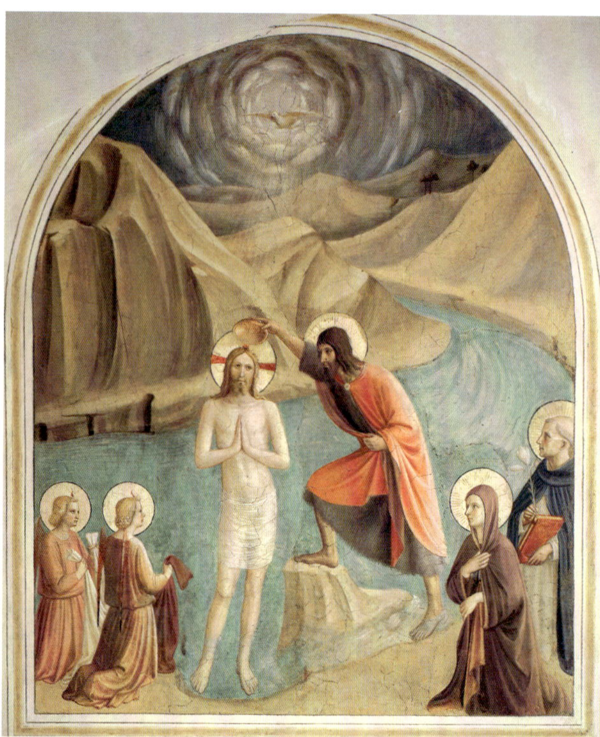

Figure 102 (near right). Fra Angelico and Assistants. *The Baptism of Christ* (cell 24). Convento di San Marco, Florence

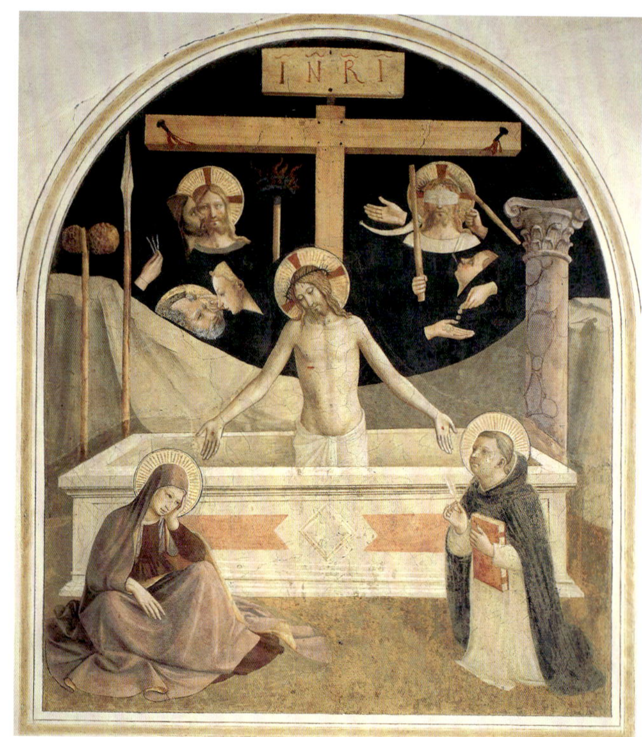

Figure 103 (far right). Fra Angelico and Assistants. *The Man of Sorrows* (cell 26). Convento di San Marco, Florence

and modeling with light, recall the Magdalene in the *Noli me tangere* in cell 1. Angelico's hand may again be recognized in the portrayal of the grieving Virgin Mary in the *Man of Sorrows* (fig. 103) in cell 26, which is distinguished from other images of the Virgin painted on this side of the dormitory by its elegant outlines and compact modeling, and perhaps also in the figure of Christ in the *Crucifixion* in cell 23 and in 25, in which the delicacy of execution is combined with a softness of form that is absent from the depictions of the Crucifixion in the nearby cells.

The apparent unity of conception nevertheless fails to obscure noticeable variations in style that cannot be attributed to the intervention of Gozzoli alone, suggesting a more extensive participation of collaborators—some of them new—than in the frescoes on the other side of the corridor. The identification of Gozzoli's hand in the frescoes on this side is, moreover, especially problematic for several reasons. The only fresco that unmistakably reflects the artist's style—the *Crucifixion with the Sorrowing Virgin* in cell 22—bears no evident relationship to his intervention in the paintings on the other side but appears, instead, to reveal a more advanced phase in his development: one that is marked by a decidedly more graphic and expressive idiom, characterized by strong contrasts of light and color, such as we find in the Medici Chapel frescoes. This would suggest a more advanced date, toward the end of the cycle or even after its completion,[41] both for this fresco and for those stylistically related to it, in the Dormitory of the Novices (cells 15 to 21). In the frescoes in the other cells on this side of the corridor, those passages that display a stylistic continuity with the sections ascribed to Gozzoli on the opposite side are few in number, and the identification of the artist's hand in specific areas remotely evocative of his manner, such as the figures of the Virgin in cells 23 and 25, is questionable due to the more archaic quality of these details.

Among the new collaborators, whose artistic vocabulary is very different with respect to the other frescoes, is the painter whose hand may be identified in most of the *Baptism of Christ* in cell 24 (fig. 102). The composition, in which the sweeping landscape becomes the dominant element, is more descriptive in tone. The slender inconsistency of the figures, painted with calligraphic precision and a linear emphasis that reduces their expressivity but heightens their decorative effect, is an element that distances this work from Angelico and brings to mind the style of another follower of Fra Giovanni, known until now only from panel paintings and miniatures—Zanobi Strozzi—whose intervention in the frescoes in this dormitory has already been identified in the execution of the angels in the *Nativity* in cell 5. It is in Strozzi's work that we find not only the same interest in minutely described landscapes but also the same graphic approach, schematic highlighting, and fixed facial expressions, as in the depiction of Christ. Among the most pertinent comparisons are the panel with *God the Father Enthroned, with Two Angels,* in the Musée Jacquemart-André, Paris, datable to 1440–45, and certain miniatures in Gradual A of the San Marco choir books (Museo di San Marco, ms. 515), such as *The Calling of Peter and Andrew* (folio 1r.), *Christ and the*

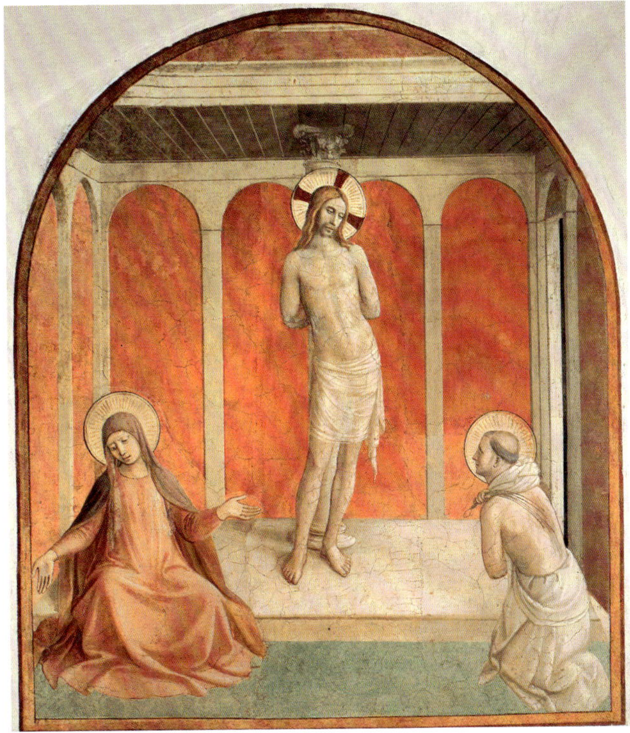

Figure 104. Fra Angelico and Assistants. *Christ at the Column, with the Virgin and Saint Dominic* (cell 27). Convento di San Marco, Florence

Apostles (folio 58*r.*; fig. 138), and *Saint Agnes* (folio 19*v.*), or the *Saint John the Baptist* on folio 1*r.* of antiphonary F (Museo di San Marco, ms. 520), datable, respectively, to 1448/49 and 1447.[42] It is worth recalling that these choir books were illuminated by Strozzi (together with Filippo di Matteo Torelli) at Cosimo de' Medici's expense, between 1446 and 1453–54, with Angelico providing an estimate of the cost of the miniatures[43]—which would appear to confirm that the two artists enjoyed a working relationship of mutual respect. The only two figures in the *Baptism* fresco that may be ascribed to Angelico by virtue of their more incisive rendering are those of the Virgin and Saint Dominic,[44] whereas the thickly painted, kneeling angels at the left, which display an affinity with the figure of the Virgin in cell 7, reveal the hand of Gozzoli.

It is Gozzoli, again, who appears to have intervened in the execution of the *Man of Sorrows* in cell 26 (fig. 103), in the *giornata* that includes Christ rising from the tomb and the figure of Saint Dominic, both of which are characterized by full, rounded forms. To Angelico's hand, in addition to the figure of the Virgin, perhaps may be attributed the upper section of the fresco with the symbols of the Passion.

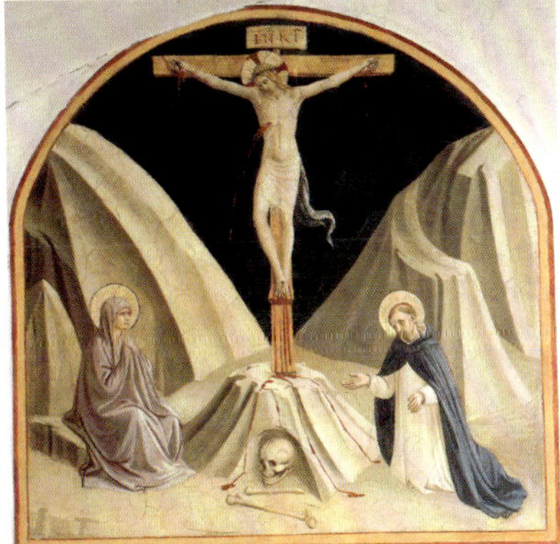

Figure 105. Fra Angelico and Assistants. *The Crucifixion, with the Virgin and Saint Peter Martyr* (cell 29). Convento di San Marco, Florence

More difficult to accept is the attribution to Gozzoli of a fresco that departs from all the others not only by virtue of its considerably smaller dimensions but also in its style and technique: the *Crucifixion, with the Virgin and Saint Peter Martyr,* in cell 29 (fig. 105).[45] This image seems to betray, instead, the salient characteristics of a different personality at work. The figures lack the volume and plasticity that distinguish Gozzoli's manner: their bodies disappear under ample capes and mantles, the illusion of solidity below which is conveyed by summarily outlined folds executed with broad striations of pale color, following a technique employed in manuscript painting. The debt to Angelico's illuminations in missal 558 (Museo di San Marco) is especially pronounced, even in terms of the expressivity and typology of the figures—as evidenced from a comparison of the Saint Peter Martyr and Christ on the Cross with miniatures from that codex, such as the *Glory of Saint Dominic* on folio 67*v.* (fig. 48), the *Saint Dominic in Prayer* on folio 68*v.*, or the *Crucifixion* on folio 45*v.* One immediately calls to mind a miniaturist who was both a friend of Angelico and strongly influenced by him (yet from whom, it cannot be excluded, Angelico, himself, may have learned the art of illumination): Battista di Biagio Sanguigni. It seems to me that an interesting comparison may be made between the fresco and the miniature of *Saint Augustine Presenting His Rule to the Nuns* (fig. 137) on folio 19*v.* of the San Gaggio antiphonary (Museo di San Marco, ms. 10073), in which we observe the same treatment of light and the same sorrowful expressions on the faces of the saints, while the severe facial type of the nuns resembles that of the Virgin in the fresco.[46]

A pronounced archaism, along with other elements derived from manuscript illumination, is discernible in the *Christ at the Column, with the Virgin and Saint Dominic* (fig. 104) in cell 27. This is especially evident in the slender fragility of the figure of Christ, who leans against the column in an unnatural pose that is reminiscent of Gothic models; in the inconsistency of the architecture, which still possesses an unreal quality despite the attempts at perspectival foreshortening; and, finally, in the schematic rendering of the facial features, defined with dark outlines and heavy white highlights. Even the figure of the Virgin—which, like that of Saint Dominic, is distinguished by a greater physical presence perhaps because it might have been executed by another painter—betrays echoes of the late manner of Lorenzo Monaco and of artists in his circle. A comparison of this fresco with the miniature in the San Gaggio antiphonary of the *Beheading of Saint Catherine* (folio 32*v.*) sheds further light on the issue.

Also the result of a collaboration, it would appear, is the fresco of *The Way to Calvary* in cell 28, in which the luminous solidity of the figure of Saint Dominic, executed by the master, is juxtaposed with the delicately conceived Christ, of uncertain attribution; clearly distinguished from them both is the figure of the Virgin, which, in its excessive proportions, reads as a flat and rigid reinterpretation on the part of a collaborator of a prototype by Angelico.

The archaic style encountered in the frescoes on this side of the east corridor is widespread, suggesting that a rethinking of the chronology of the decoration of this dormitory is in

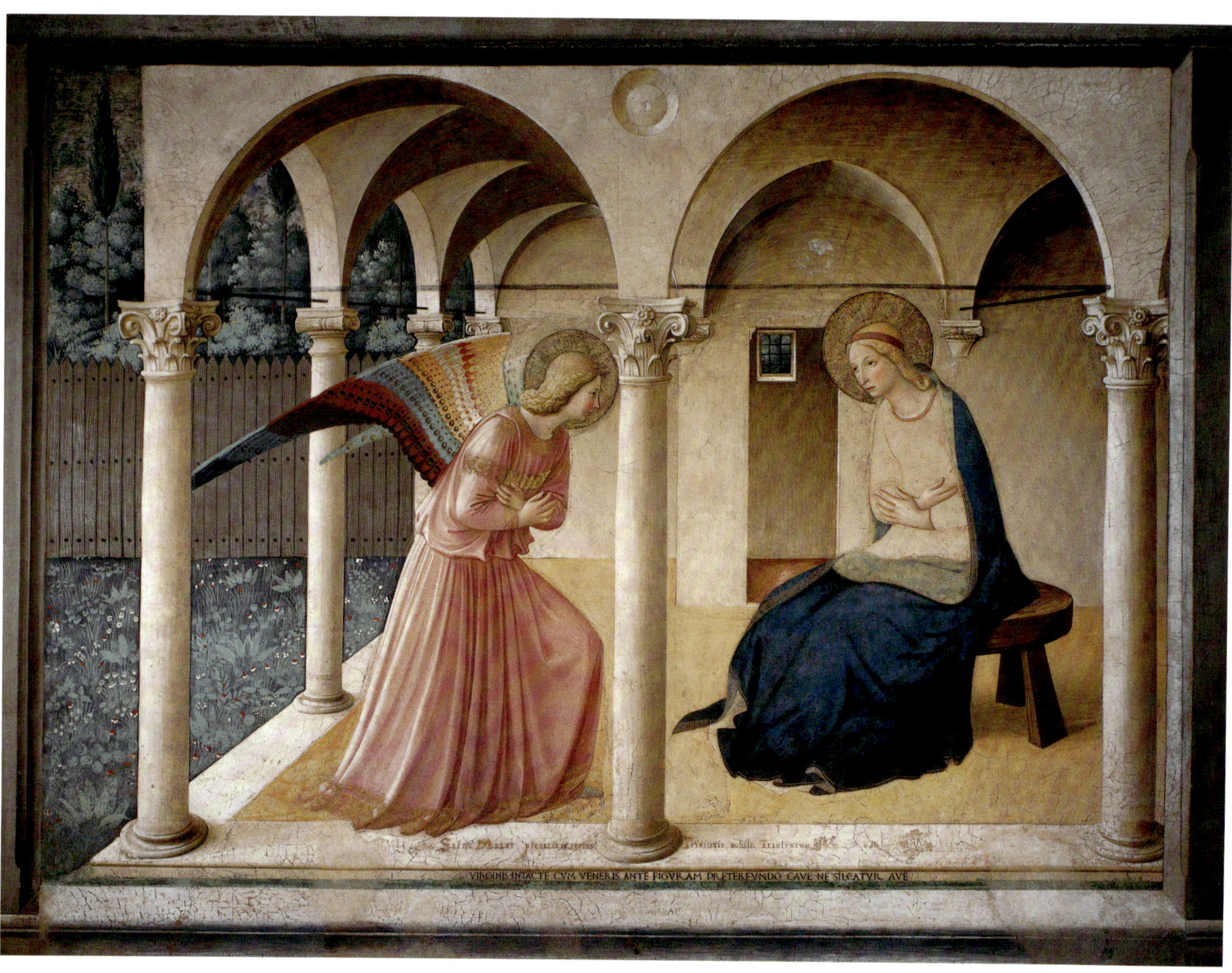

Figure 106. Fra Angelico. *The Annunciation* (north corridor). Convento di San Marco, Florence

order. It is not a given, in fact, that the frescoes along the outer wall were executed before the ones on the inner wall,[47] if only because the dating of the former, as a whole or in part, may be advanced after considering the unquestionable stylistic relationship between the *Lamentation* in cell 2 (fig. 149) and the *Lamentation* panel for Santa Maria della Croce al Tempio (fig. 76), completed in 1441, as well as the stylistic continuity that links such frescoes as *The Transfiguration* in cell 6 (fig. 97) with the *Madonna of the Shadows* (fig. 127) on the opposite side of the same corridor—a work unanimously regarded as late in date and executed, in any event, after 1440.

To a new phase of work, which includes the *Annunciation* (fig. 106) on the wall of the north corridor, belongs the *Noli me tangere* in cell 1, located in a space that is part of the same building block. These paintings are enriched by the treatment of light, which bathes the colors in a luminous glow—especially the finely modeled flesh tones—and lends brilliance and luster to the halos, while the landscape and the architectural setting take on added significance along with the figures. The dating of these two frescoes should be contiguous to that of the *Crucifixion* in the Chapter House (fig. 107) and of the frescoes on the ground floor.

Angelico's direct involvement in the execution of the *Crucifixion* extends to most, if not all, of the fresco. The painted figures are characterized by the slow, rhythmic movements and gestures that we have come to recognize as a constant quality of the master's style, and their draperies fall in soft folds, defined by highlights that further accentuate the already pale, translucent palette. The finely sculpted faces—in which every single feature and plane is defined by subtle hatchings and by effects of light created by revealing the base tone, rather than by the addition of white—are animated by a new expressive intensity and by a piercing naturalism that has recently led to the hypothesis, as fascinating as it is bold, of the collaboration of Jean Fouquet (who passed through Florence in the entourage of René d'Anjou) in their execution.[48] Despite this intriguing notion, I think it is more probable that the importance assumed by light in the work of Angelico at this date, culminating in the fresco of *Saint Dominic in Adoration before the Crucifix* (fig. 108) in the cloister, is the result of the further evo-

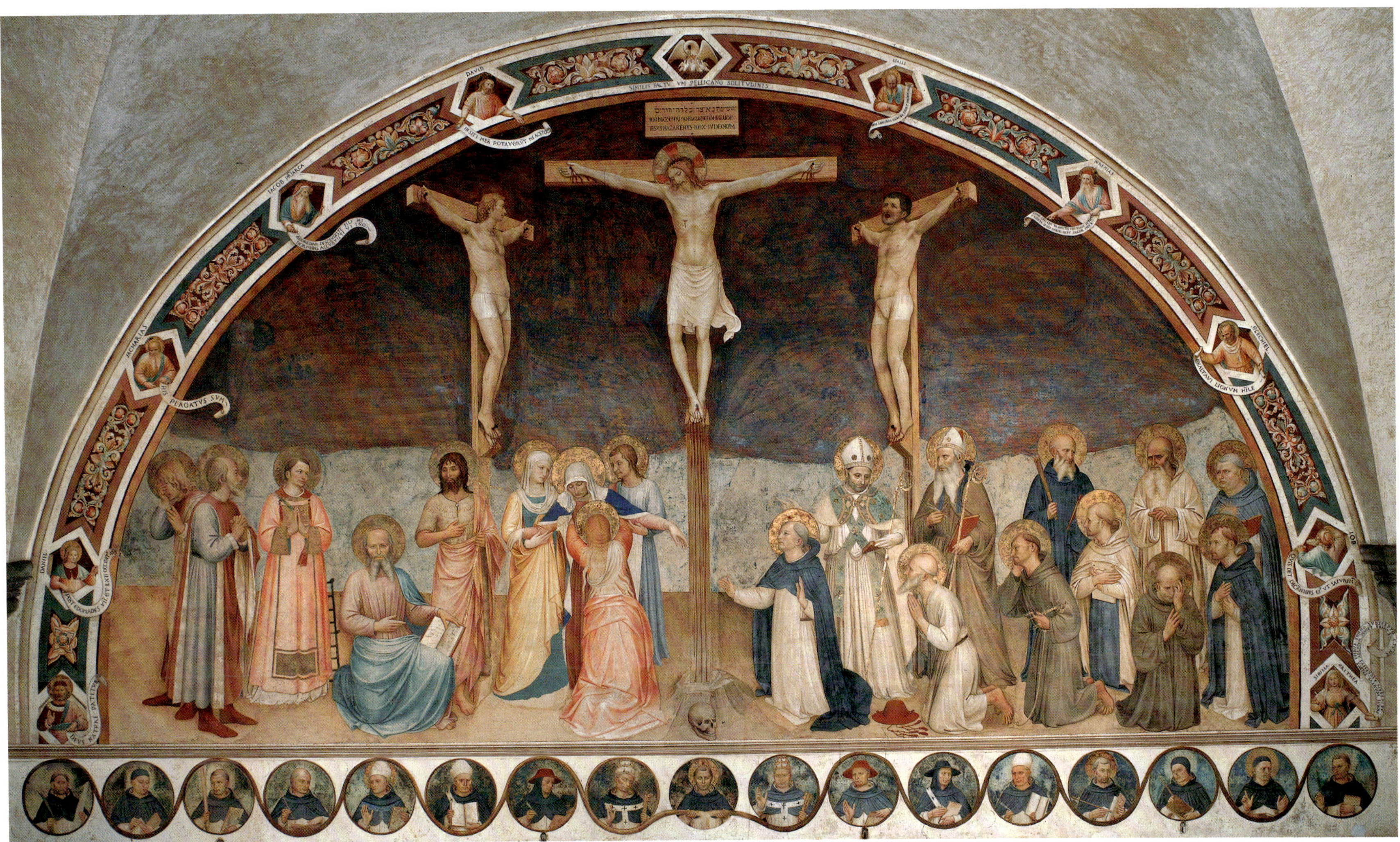

Figure 107. Fra Angelico. *The Crucifixion* (Chapter House). Convento di San Marco, Florence

lution of his art, in which the circulation of Netherlandish paintings, surely increased by the foreign presence at the Council of Florence of 1439, certainly played a role; to this may perhaps be added a specific awareness of works by Fouquet, who, for his part, must also have been receptive to Angelico's innovations.

It is my view, although contrary to widespread opinion, that Angelico's refined approach may also be discerned in the execution of many of the figures painted, in separate *giornate*, in the hexagons of the decorative band around the *Crucifixion*: specifically, Zacharias, Isaiah,[49] Jacob, Jeremiah, Pseudo-Dionysius the Areopagite, and, perhaps also Job and Ezekiel (fig. 111), whose linear but intense features recall those of some of the figures in the frescoes in the upper cells. The images of David and Daniel (fig. 112) may be ascribed to an anonymous collaborator with a cursory style, whereas the hand of Gozzoli—possibly the author only of the Erythraean Sibyl—may be identified in many of the realistic physiognomies of illustrious personalities of the Dominican order, painted in the medallions below the *Crucifixion*.

The decoration of the cells in the north corridor, intended for lay brothers and non-religious guests, must have taken place contemporary with—or shortly after—the frescoes on the ground floor. In these works we sense a noticeable change in style: the overall tone is more descriptive; the landscape acquires greater importance; the palette becomes clearer and more varied, enriched by new color harmonies; and the technique is more rapid, concerned with the overall effect rather than with the particulars. Angelico, still in charge of the compositions, seems, on the one hand, to have adjusted his pictorial vocabulary to fit the changed audience for these images, and, on the other hand, to have been hard pressed by time constraints, thus assigning increasingly greater parts to his collaborators and limiting himself to only a few autograph passages.

The presence of the hands of assistants in the frescoes in these cells is so evident as to leave no doubt as to their intervention. Closer scrutiny of the frescoes and identification of the different *giornate* would be warranted here as well, in order to better assign specific sections to the various assistants—a task too lengthy to be carried out in the present context.

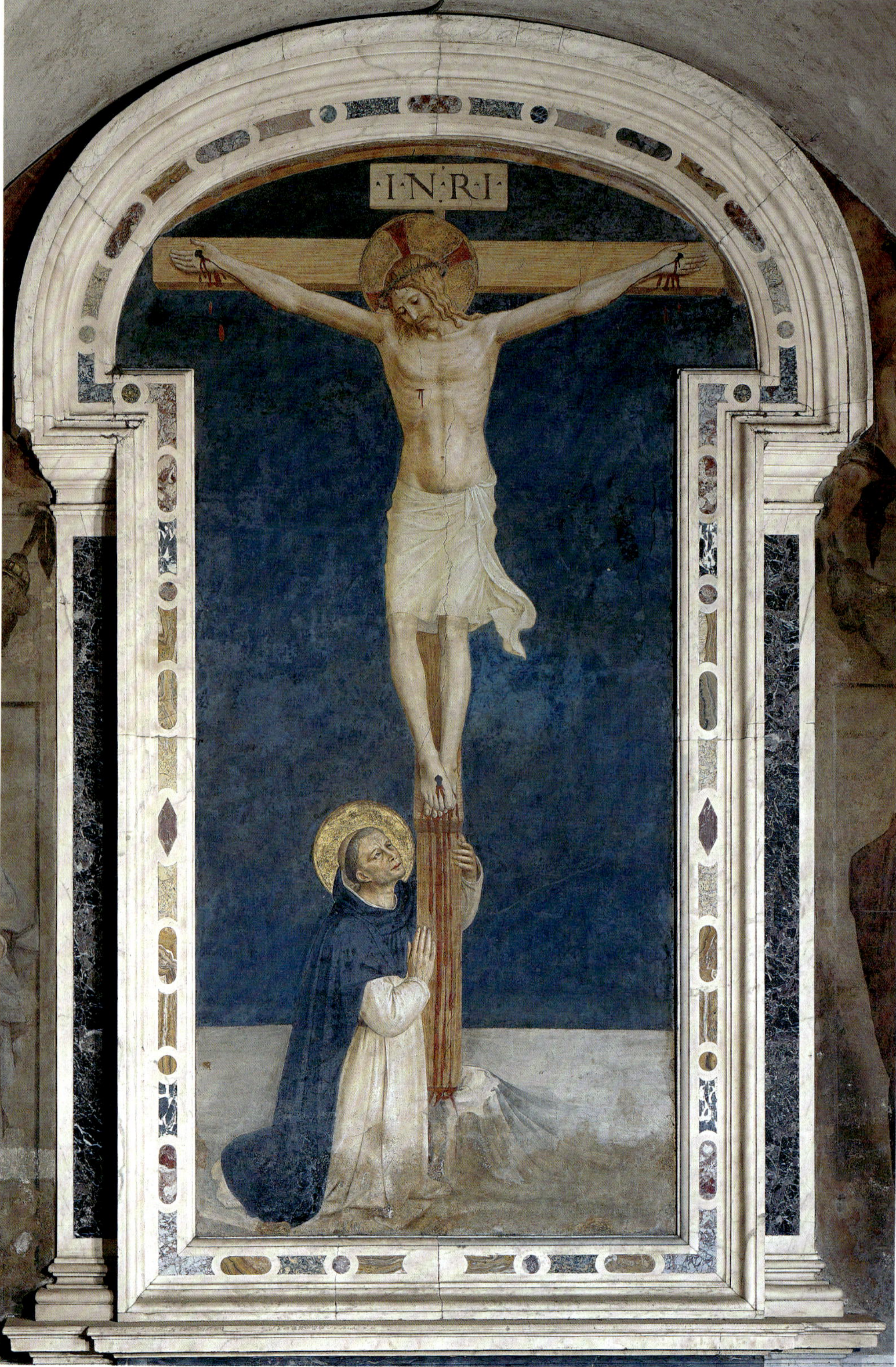

Figure 108. Fra Angelico. *Saint Dominic in Adoration before the Crucifix* (Cloister). Convento di San Marco, Florence

Starting with the premise that, in this wing, the possibility of Zanobi Strozzi's participation may be proposed only for the fragment with the *Entry into Jerusalem* in cell 33—in which may be recognized the same calligraphic approach already encountered in the *Baptism*—and disregarding, for the moment, those passages in which the intervention of less-talented assistants is beyond question, what remains essential is to identify the sections executed by Angelico alone and those by Gozzoli. Only through such a process will it be possible to interpret the remaining frescoes, and to address some of the questions they still pose.

It should be noted that three of the frescoes—the *Agony in the Garden* (fig. 110) in cell 34, the *Adoration of the Magi* (fig. 109) in cell 39, and the *Crucifixion, with the Virgin and Saints Cosmas, John the Evangelist, and Peter Martyr* in cell 38—in which scholars have repeatedly claimed to recognize Gozzoli's whole or partial intervention, are not, in fact, stylistically homogeneous. In the first fresco, the attribution to Gozzoli of the figures of Mary and Martha may be justified by a comparison with the frescoes in Montefalco; at the same time, the luminous clarity and spatial depth of the fragment of interior in which they are shown praying, and the close analogy, even in technical terms, between the face of Mary and that of the Virgin in the Chapter House *Crucifixion* also speak in favor of Angelico's authorship. It could be reasoned, therefore, that at the time of the north corridor frescoes, Gozzoli was a faithful imitator of Angelico—however, not in the same way as in the frescoes in cells 38 and 39. In the *Crucifixion* in cell 38, only the face of the Virgin is comparable in style and technique to the faces of the two figures in cell 34, while the rest of the scene is painted in a much more cursory manner and with a calligraphic style that is found only rarely in the work of Gozzoli: for example, as in some of the background figures in the Medici palace fresco of the procession of the Magi.

In the *Adoration of the Magi* in cell 39, only the figures in the procession, to the right, painted in the space of two working *giornate* (out of a total of fifteen), are characterized by this abbreviated, calligraphic style. These figures are highly expressive, nevertheless, even if partially incomplete, corroborating the hypothesis of a hurried, unfinished execution. The treatment of the four adjacent figures appears similar, with the exception of the heads, which are distinguished by carefully lit and precisely modeled features, indicated with finely hatched lines, in much the same way as the head of the young king (fig. 113), whose profile recalls that of the angel Gabriel in the *Annunciation*. The mapping of the *giornate* aids in the process of interpretation, clarifying that the heads of the four individuals engaged in discussion were painted on a single *giornata,* distinct from those on which the rest of the figures were painted, exactly as was done for the head of the young king, thus providing a

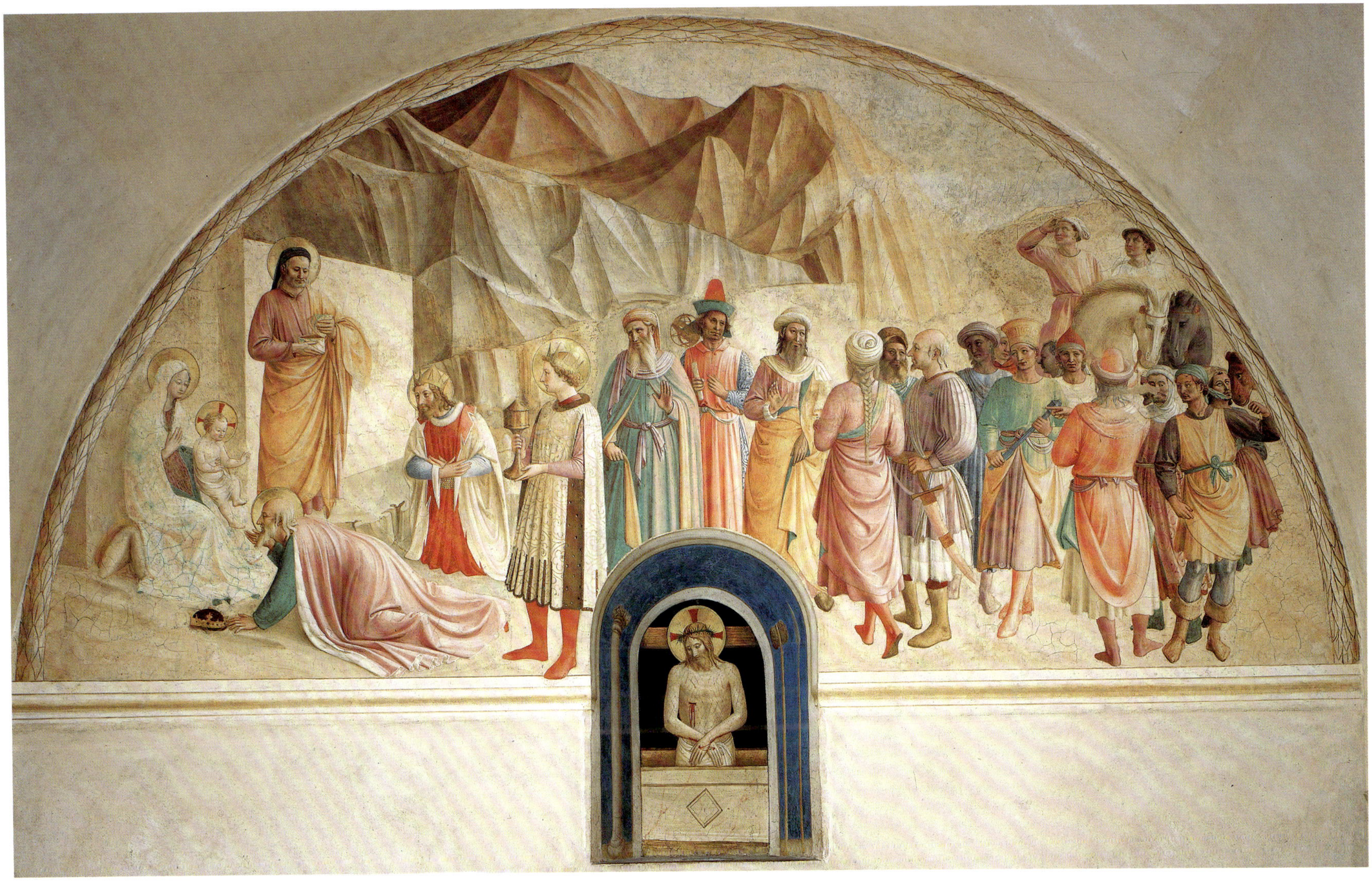

Figure 109 (above). Fra Angelico and Assistants. *The Adoration of the Magi* (cell 39). Convento di San Marco, Florence

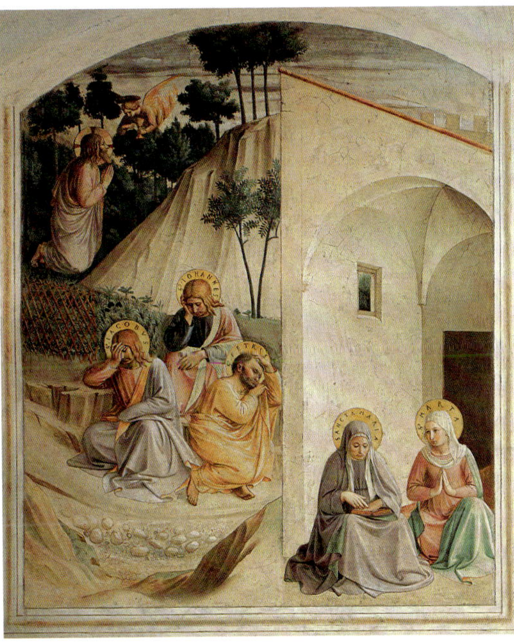

Figure 110 (right). Fra Angelico and Assistants. *The Agony in the Garden* (cell 34). Convento di San Marco, Florence

solid foundation on which to base the hypothesis of another artist's intervention.

A different idiom informs the execution of the nearby figures in the center, which were painted on one *giornata* (with the exception of the head with the turban, on the right, and that of the aforementioned young king), as well as the execution of the other two kings, one kneeling and one prostrate before the Virgin, which were painted on two separate *giornate*. The figures, here, have lost all plastic credibility; the modeling is flattened by the unmodulated juxtapositions of brilliant color; and the quick touches of highlights on the faces fail to achieve the same level of expressivity observed in the previously cited heads. There is sufficient evidence to assign these parts to another, unidentified collaborator, who may also have been responsible for the figures of the Virgin and Child and of Saint Joseph; perhaps the same artist who intervened in the execution of the Patriarchs, in the *Descent into Limbo*, as well as in other frescoes on the inner wall of this corridor.

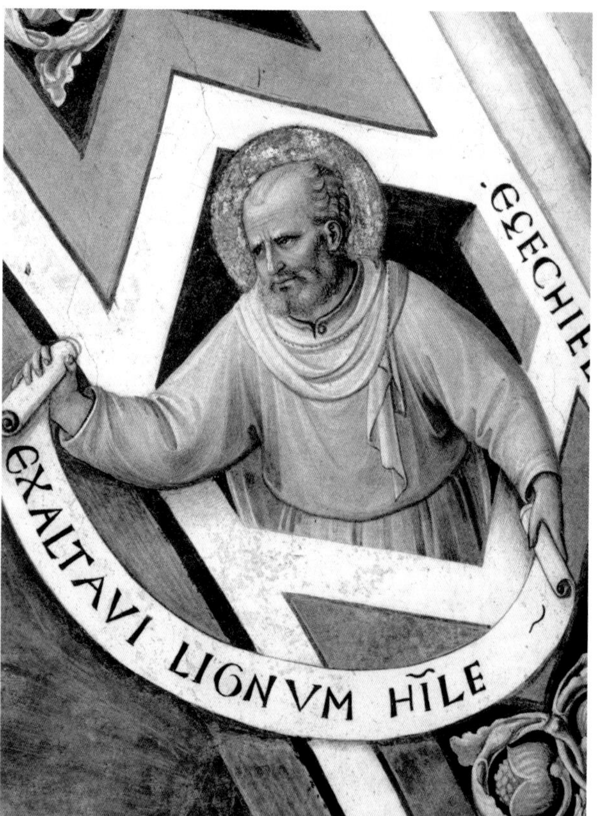

Figure 111. Fra Angelico. *Ezekiel* (detail of fig. 107)

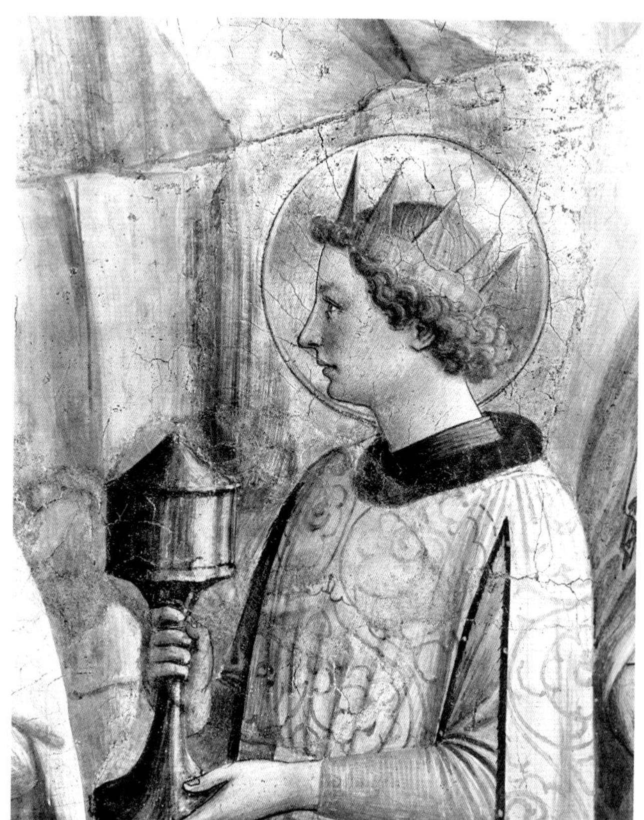

Figure 113. Fra Angelico. *The Magus Jasper* (detail of fig. 109)

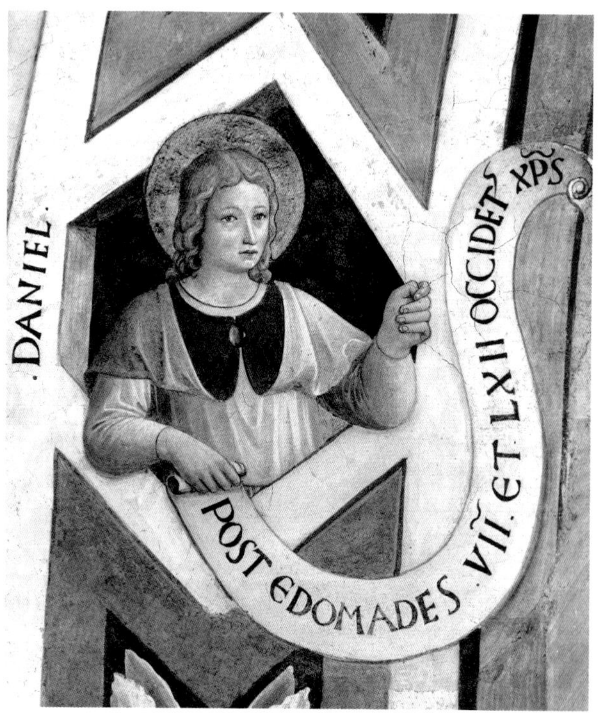

Figure 112. Assistant of Fra Angelico. *Daniel* (detail of fig. 107)

One of the possibilities to emerge from these observations is that Gozzoli was the author of the individuals on the right, and that, with the exception of the heads, he also painted the two figures in the center, shown from behind and in profile, whose draperies are similarly constructed and colored. Another, unknown assistant may have painted the remainder of the scene, while it would appear that Angelico left his imprint on a few splendid details: the head of the young king, and probably those of the four bystanders in conversation. This is not, nor has it previously been the only hypothesis that may be advanced to explain the structure of Angelico's workshop—an issue that is hardly resolved—but it is merely intended to serve as a starting point for further inquiry and investigation.

1. The fifteenth-century *Cronaca* of Fra Giuliano Lapaccini, a resident in San Marco until his death in 1458, is inserted in the *Cronaca* written by Fra Roberto degli Ubaldini da Gagliano, which he began in 1509 (San Marco n.370, Biblioteca Medicea Laurenziana, Florence); Lapaccini's text is published in Morçay 1913, pp. 3–31. In reference to the San Marco frescoes, Lapaccini writes: "*Nam tabula altaris maioris et figurae capituli et ipsius primi claustri et omnium cellarum superiorum et Crucifixi refectorii omnes pictae sunt per quendam fratrem ordinis praedicatorum et conventus Fesulani qui habebatur pro summo magistro in arte pictoria in Italia, qui frater Iohannes Petri de Mugello dicebatur, homo totius modestiae et vitae religiosae*"

(p. 16). Other sources, discussing the paintings by Angelico in San Marco, explicitly name only those in the Chapter House as well as the high altarpiece, and refer to the rest in general terms (see A. Manetti 1490 [?] [1887 ed.], p. 166; Albertini 1510 [1863 ed.], p. 12; *Il libro di Antonio Billi* 1516– [1991 ed.], pp. 77, 128; *Il codice magliabechiano* 1536–46 [1892 ed.], pp. 94–95).

2. Berenson 1896, pp. 23–26, 99–100; Berenson 1932a, pp. 20–22.
3. Among the first to notice the presence of collaborators were J. A. Crowe and G. B. Cavalcaselle (1883, pp. 383–84), followed by Wurm (1907), Venturi (1911), Van Marle (1928), Muratoff (1930), Schottmüller (1911; 1924), and Bazin (1949). For an extensive bibliography related to each fresco, see the recent monograph by Spike (1996, pp. 203–16).
4. The possibility of Strozzi's participation in the frescoes in the cells of the north corridor (numbers 31–35) was advanced by P. D'Ancona (1908, p. 12), followed by F. Schottmüller (1924, p. XXIX). A. Francini Ciaranfi (n.d., p. 12) subsequently discerned Strozzi's involvement in the execution of the angels in the fresco in cell 5, although she rejected the parts identified by P. D'Ancona (1908). M. Salmi (1958, pp. 44, 46) reiterated P. D'Ancona's proposals, adding the suggestion that Strozzi might also have been responsible for parts of the frescoes in cells 8, 36, and, alongside Benozzo Gozzoli, in other cells in the north corridor. To Gozzoli were attributed, initially, the *Crucifixion with Saints* in cell 38 (Venturi 1911, part 1, pp. 58, 70–72), the *Adoration of the Magi* in cell 39, and some of the figures in the Chapter House *Crucifixion* (Gengaro 1944). A. Francini Ciaranfi (n.d., p. 9) associated Gozzoli with the series of frescoes of *Saint Dominic at the Foot of the Cross* in the cells of the south corridor, and M. Salmi (1950, p. 154) attributed to him the female figures in the painting in cell 34 and in parts of the one in cell 36.
5. According to Pope-Hennessy (1952, pp. 17–23, 179–87; 1974, pp. 19–29, 202–10), a total of three assistants were involved in the cycle: the Master of Cell 2 and the Master of Cell 36, who closely followed Angelico, in addition to the more independent Master of Cell 31.
6. Salmi 1958, pp. 40–50, 113–14.
7. Francini Ciaranfi n.d.
8. Collobi-Ragghianti 1955b, pp. 40–41.
9. U. Baldini, in Florence 1955, pp. 120–32, and reiterated in Baldini 1970, pp. 104–7.
10. Bonsanti 1983, pp. 25–34.
11. G. Bonsanti essentially accepts the view previously expressed by L. Berti (in Berti, Bellardoni, and Battisti 1966), while at the same time limiting the extent of Angelico's direct participation.
12. Padoa Rizzo 1969a, pp. 52, 62; A. Padoa Rizzo (1969b, pp. 9–13) cites cell 23, but from the illustration it seems that she intended to refer to cell 22; Padoa Rizzo 1972, pp. 17–19.
13. See Padoa Rizzo 1972, pp. 17–19.
14. Padoa Rizzo 1992; Cole Ahl 1996; Garibaldi 1998; Toscano and Capitelli 2002.
15. Bonsanti 1990, pp. 165–72; Bonsanti 1998, pp. 144–46; Bonsanti 2003, pp. 47–62.
16. Padoa Rizzo 1992, pp. 6–7, 27–29; Padoa Rizzo 2002b, p. 20; Padoa Rizzo 2003, pp. 23–29.
17. Bellosi 1996, pp. 26–28. W. Hood (1993, p. 211) also remains cautious about the various attributions to Gozzoli, with the exception of the fresco of the *Noli me tangere* in cell 1.
18. Morachiello 1995, pp. 294–98; Cole Ahl 1996, pp. 8–18, 285–86; Acidini Luchinat 1994, pp. 4–6.
19. Boskovits 1983, pp. 11–23; Boskovits 1994, pp. 369–96.
20. Boskovits 2002b, pp. 41–56.
21. See Centi 1989, pp. 13–14. For a summary of the early history of the Dominicans at San Marco, see Scudieri 2000, pp. 9–43.
22. Morçay 1913, p. 13.
23. The account is confirmed by the discovery of some fragments of fourteenth-century decoration on the wall facing the cloister. See M. Scudieri, in Damiani, Marchetti, and Scudieri 1995, pp. 13–22.
24. Centi 1989, p. 15.
25. Cole 1977, pp. 95–100.
26. Illustrated in Spike 1996, p. 197.
27. Morçay 1913, p. 14.
28. Ibid. The notice of the gift of Lorenzo di Niccolò's altarpiece to the convent in Cortona is confirmed by the letter of thanks addressed by the priors of Cortona to Cosimo de' Medici in 1438; Vasari (Milanesi ed.) 1878–85, vol. II, p. 533.
29. For the inscription, see Vasari (Milanesi ed.) 1878–85, vol. II, p. 533.
30. The question has been addressed by the present author on several occasions (M. Scudieri, in Rykwert and Engel 1994, pp. 523–25; Scudieri 1998, pp. 107–13), also taking into consideration the studies of the building complex by F. Carbonai and M. Salmi (in *La Chiesa e il Convento di San Marco* 1989–90, vol. I, pp. 266, 290–93), who already had speculated about the original existence of an east arm of the transept, after noticing a reduction in the thickness of the wall in that area, which could be explained by a later repair.
31. See U. Baldini, in Florence 1955, p. 132.
32. Morçay 1913, pp. 14–16.
33. Ibid., p. 18.
34. Ibid., p. 21. On the library of San Marco, see Scudieri and Rasario 2000.
35. Orlandi 1955a, pp. 3–37.
36. De Marchi 1985, pp. 53–57.
37. The existence of fully developed workshops employing a significant number of assistants, whose presence may be detected not just in minor passages in the cycle—and whose names are sometimes recorded in documents—was recently reconfirmed by the results of the latest restorations, in the case of fresco projects directed by Angelico as well as by Benozzo Gozzoli (see Giantomassi and Zari 2001, pp. 99–109; Testa 1996, pp. 26–31; Toscano 2002, pp. 57–77).
38. See Bonsanti 1990, p. 165; Padoa Rizzo 1992, p. 27; Cole Ahl 1996, p. 14; Acidini Luchinat 1994, p. 4.
39. The presence of elements distantly derived from Lorenzo Monaco was noted by L. Bellosi (1996, p. 23).
40. Bonsanti 1983, p. 31.
41. The possibility of a later dating was also advanced by L. Bellosi (1996, p. 27).
42. The illuminations are reproduced in Scudieri and Rasario 2003, pp. 174, 179, 176, 171, respectively.
43. See A. Di Lorenzo, in Di Lorenzo 2001, pp. 16, 20–21.
44. The same opinion is shared by L. Bellosi (1996, p. 22).
45. The fresco was first attributed to Gozzoli by A. Padoa Rizzo (1969a, p. 52), who dated it 1442–44.
46. On the relationship between Sanguigni and Angelico, see Scudieri 2003, pp. 33–43.
47. Bellosi 1996, p. 25.
48. Sricchia Santoro 2003, pp. 55–56.
49. They reflect a strong affinity with the figures of Saint John the Evangelist and Saint Paul painted on the pilasters of the Perugia polyptych.

34.

The High Altarpiece from San Marco

A.

Saint Romuald

Tempera on panel, 40.5 x 13.3 cm (16 x 5¼ in.)
The Minneapolis Institute of Arts. The Putnam Dana McMillan Fund (62.9)

B.

Saint Thomas Aquinas

Tempera on panel, 39 x 14 cm (15⅜ x 5½ in.)
Fondazione Giorgio Cini, Venice

C.

Saint Anthony Abbot

Tempera on panel, 39.3 x 13.8 cm (15½ x 5⅜ in.)
The Art Institute of Chicago (2001.329)

D.

Saint Roch

Tempera on panel, 39 x 14 cm (15⅜ x 5½ in.)
Lindenau-Museum, Altenburg, Germany (Inv. no. 92b)

E.

Saint Benedict

Tempera on panel, 39 x 14 cm (15⅜ x 5½ in.)
Lindenau-Museum, Altenburg, Germany (Inv. no. 92c)

F.

Saint Jerome

Tempera on panel, 39 x 14 cm (15⅜ x 5½ in.)
Lindenau-Museum, Altenburg, Germany (Inv. no. 92a)

G.

The Healing of Palladia by Saints Cosmas and Damian

Tempera on panel, 38.1 x 47.5 cm (15 x 18¾ in.)
National Gallery of Art, Washington D.C. Samuel H. Kress Collection (1952.5.3)

H.

The Attempted Martyrdom of Saints Cosmas and Damian

Tempera on panel, 37 x 46 cm (14⅝ x 18⅛ in.)
National Gallery of Ireland, Dublin (NGI 242)

I.

The Decapitation of Saints Cosmas and Damian

Tempera on panel, 37.3 x 46.1 cm (14 11/16 x 18⅛ in.)
Musée du Louvre, Paris (R.F. 340)

Having completed the high altarpiece and two lateral altarpieces for the church of San Domenico in Fiesole, as well as altarpieces for the sister houses of San Domenico in Cortona and San Domenico in Perugia, Angelico's next major commission from his own order in Florence was to provide a new high altarpiece for the restored convent church of San Marco. In 1435 the local parish priests, together with the Dominican Observant community in Fiesole, petitioned Pope Eugenius IV for an investigation of the Silvestrine monks who had long occupied the convent annexed to San Marco. The Silvestrines—a reformed branch of the Benedictine order—were determined to be living "with neither poverty nor chastity," and were ordered to leave the premises of the convent, which, reportedly, were in ruinous condition; afterwards, the property was transferred to the Dominicans. The Silvestrines appealed the judgment, and while litigation continued (the Dominican cause was argued before the Council of Basel by Fra Juan de Torquemada, the official theologian of Eugenius IV; see cat. 39), the Dominicans were awarded the parish church of San Giorgio sulla Costa in the Oltrarno, in July 1435, as their temporary quarters in Florence. Although the dispute was not finally settled for a number of years, in January 1436 Pope Eugenius IV ordered the Silvestrines and Dominicans to exchange premises immediately—an order supported by Cosimo de' Medici and the Florentine civic councils. The Silvestrines then moved into San Giorgio sulla Costa and the Dominican Observants of Fiesole took possession of San Marco.[1]

The refurbishment of the church and convent of San Marco was largely financed by Cosimo de' Medici and his brother Lorenzo, and began in 1436 with the restructuring of the dormitory and cloisters. Only two years later did the Medici finally succeed in purchasing from the Caponsacchi family patronage rights to the high altar in the church and in negotiating the relocation of several lay confraternities that owned the land north of the apse.[2] Rebuilding efforts were transferred to the apse and choir of the church at that point, the expansion of which was finished in 1439. Construction at San Marco continued well into the following decade. Although the library was completed only in 1444, the church and convent were solemnly consecrated by Eugenius, accompanied by the principal members of the Roman Curia and the Florentine government, on the feast of Epiphany, January 6, 1443.

The painting installed above the high altar of San Marco when the Dominicans took possession of the church, Lorenzo di Niccolò's monumental *Coronation of the Virgin*, was removed in 1438 to facilitate construction in the apse and the choir chapel. The painting had become the property of Cosimo and Lorenzo de' Medici, with the purchase of patronage rights that year, and they promised it as a gift to the Dominicans of Cortona, where they delivered it in 1440.[3] It is reasonable to assume that the contemplation of bestowing such a gift implies that plans to replace it with a new painting were already formulated. It is even likely that a new high altarpiece had been projected from as early as 1436, although serious work on its design cannot have begun much, if at all, before 1438. Independent of its design, the precise period in which the new high altarpiece was executed remains a much-debated topic, with most scholars assuming the consecration of the church in January 1443 to be a terminus ante quem, and a majority argu-

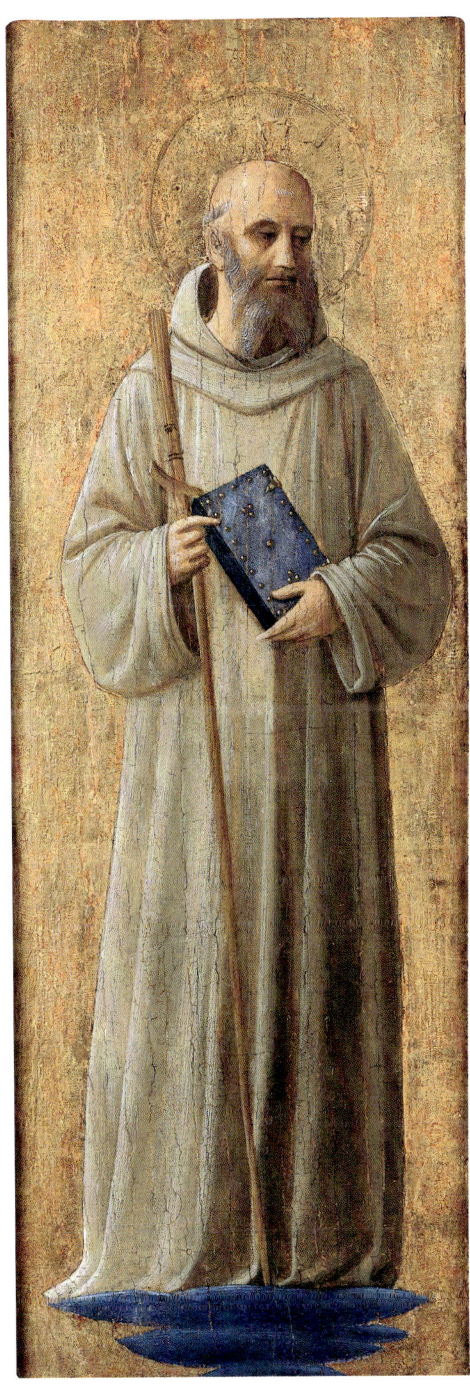

34: A

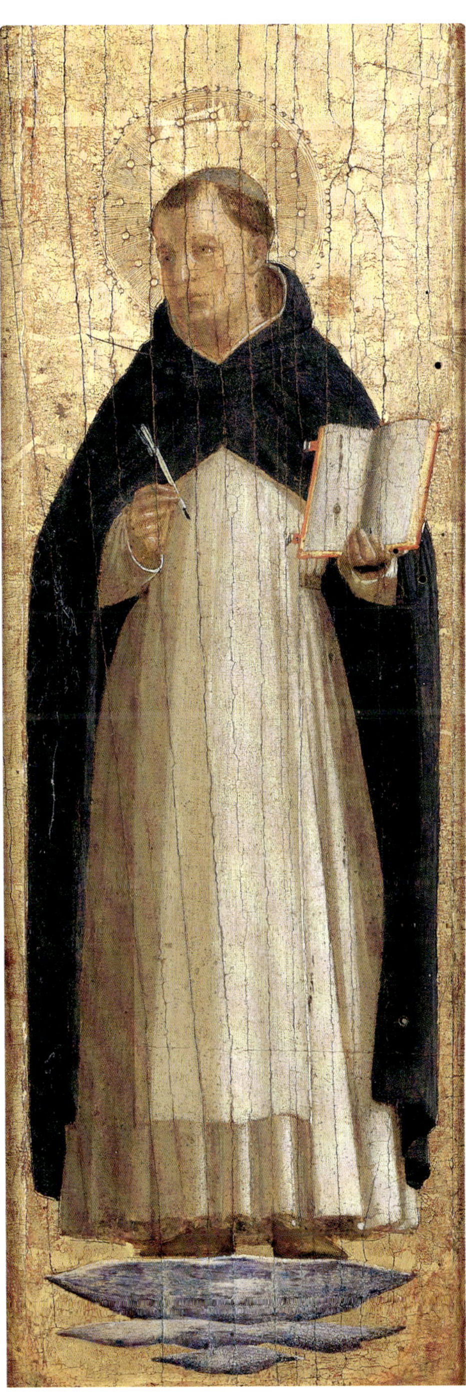

34: B

ing for the likelihood of its completion within the years 1438 to 1440. The entire chronology of Angelico's work on the decorative complex at San Marco, including the painting for the high altar and the frescoes in the chapter house, cloister, dormitory corridors, and in the cells of the forty-three friars, lay brothers, and novices, remains unresolved. There is no *a priori* reason to assume that an altarpiece was the most urgently required liturgical furnishing for a new church or chapel, as Mass could be celebrated at any altar with or without a painting installed above it. Furthermore, the spatial innovations introduced by Angelico in the composition of the main panel of the high altarpiece and in most of its predella panels represent a decided break from his work in the 1430s but form the basis of all his subsequent production. Consequently, while it is perhaps most prudent to opt for a date for the altarpiece between 1438 and 1442, in all likelihood the period of its execution comprised only the later part of that time span.

The subject assigned to Angelico for the San Marco high altarpiece was conventional: the Virgin and Child enthroned, with angels and saints in attendance around them. His solution to the assignment, however, was a radical departure from convention that was to become the prototype for nearly all Florentine altarpieces of this subject through the end of the fifteenth, and into the sixteenth, century. Instead of adopting the traditional Gothic polyptych format of, for example, the Guidalotti altarpiece in Perugia (cat. 30), Angelico composed, or was instructed to compose, his image within the large square picture field of the *pala quadrata* form favored by Brunelleschi for the altars in Santo Spirito and San Lorenzo. The open field of the painting (fig. 114) is organized architectonically around the central vertical of the Virgin's aedicular throne and the horizontal band of a patterned curtain extending over the full width of the panel, behind the standing saints and angels, and reminiscent of the cloth of gold drawn across the benches behind the figures in the Guidalotti altarpiece. Instead of the symbolic gold ground of that painting, however, the curtain in the San Marco high altarpiece is surmounted by a painted landscape of poplar and fir trees and a naturalistic blue sky, the whole closed off at the top by swagged garlands of roses and, at the upper corners, gold curtains painted as if they were suspended from the altarpiece's frame and had been pulled open to reveal the scene behind. The angels stand on the steps of the Virgin's throne as they do in the Perugia altarpiece, although in this case there are four on either side. An equal number of saints in the foreground,

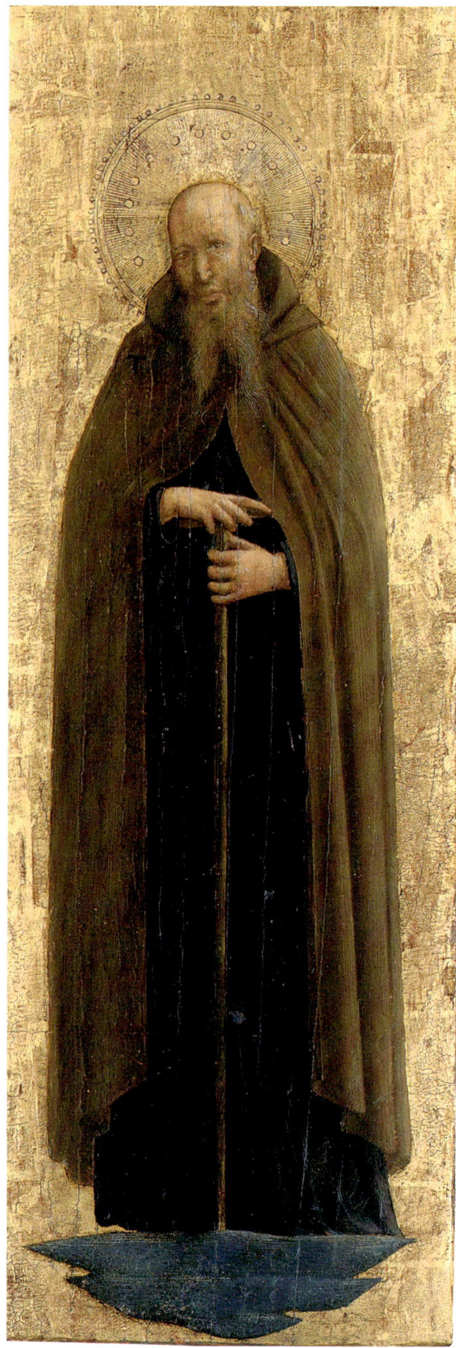

34: C

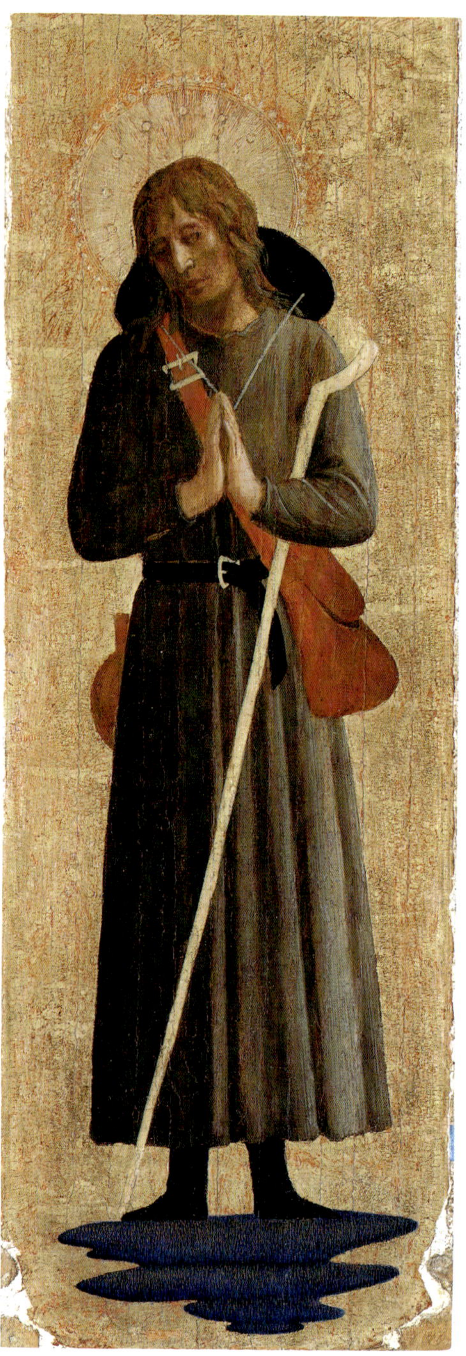

34: D

standing or kneeling on an elaborately patterned Anatolian carpet that covers the lower third of the composition, are ranked in converging diagonals leading back toward the throne and the objects of their veneration.

The spatial ambitions of this monumental painting, still clear despite its severely damaged condition, are more far-reaching than anything Angelico, or any other artist, had attempted before this, and the geometry he employed to achieve his goals is more rigorous and tightly controlled. This disciplined geometric order pervades the nine panels of the predella of the altarpiece as well. Now dispersed among collections in Florence, Munich, Dublin, Paris, and Washington, these panels illustrate eight scenes from the legend of Saints Cosmas and Damian—who, as patron saints of the Medici family, are shown kneeling prominently in the foreground of the altarpiece—surrounding an image of the Entombment of Christ. The latter scene (Alte Pinakothek, Munich, Inv. no. WAF 38a; fig. 115), one of Angelico's most poetic creations, is uncompromising in the severity of its formal abstraction, casting an image that is both narrative and devotional into the same bilaterally symmetrical format as the composition of the main panel of the altarpiece once directly above it. The result is a triumph of design in which nothing of the emotional pathos inherent in this dramatic subject is sacrificed to artifice.

The eight episodes from the legend of the third-century saints Cosmas and Damian, brothers and physicians, commenced on the outer face of the left framing pilaster with a scene of the miraculous healing of a woman named Palladia and with Palladia insisting that Damian accept the gift refused by Cosmas (G). The latter renounced his brother when he learned that Damian had taken Palladia's offering, and he swore that when they died they should not be buried together. The following night, in a divine vision, Cosmas was urged to reconcile with Damian. In the next scene (now in the Alte Pinakothek, Munich, Inv. no. WAF 36; fig. 116), originally situated perpendicular to the first one, at the left end on the front of the predella, Saints Cosmas and Damian, with their brothers, Antimus, Leontius, and Euprepius, stand before the proconsul Lycias. For having refused to sacrifice to idols, Lycias orders them to be bound and thrown into the sea: this is shown in the background of the third scene (also now in Alte Pinakothek, Munich, Inv. no. WAF 37; fig. 117). Their rescue by an angel made Lycias resolve to convert to Christianity, but the pagan gods sent devils to slap him in the face, among other torments, for his infidelity; the saints prayed for his release and the devils flew off. In the fourth scene (H), Lycias repented and renounced his decision to convert, condemning Cosmas, Damian, and their brothers to be burned at the stake. The saints, however, were spared the flames, and were left unharmed, and the executioners were burned instead.

The legend of the saints continued to the right of the central *Lamentation* scene with another episode of attempted martyrdom (Alte Pinakothek, Munich, Inv. no. WAF 38; fig. 118) in which Lycias ordered Cosmas and Damian to be tied to crosses and their brothers thrown into prison. When the people stoned the saints, however, the stones were turned back on their tormentors. In a rage, Lycias commanded that the three brothers be taken from prison and made to stand at the foot of the two crosses, whereupon his soldiers were to shoot arrows at all five of them, but, again, the arrows were turned

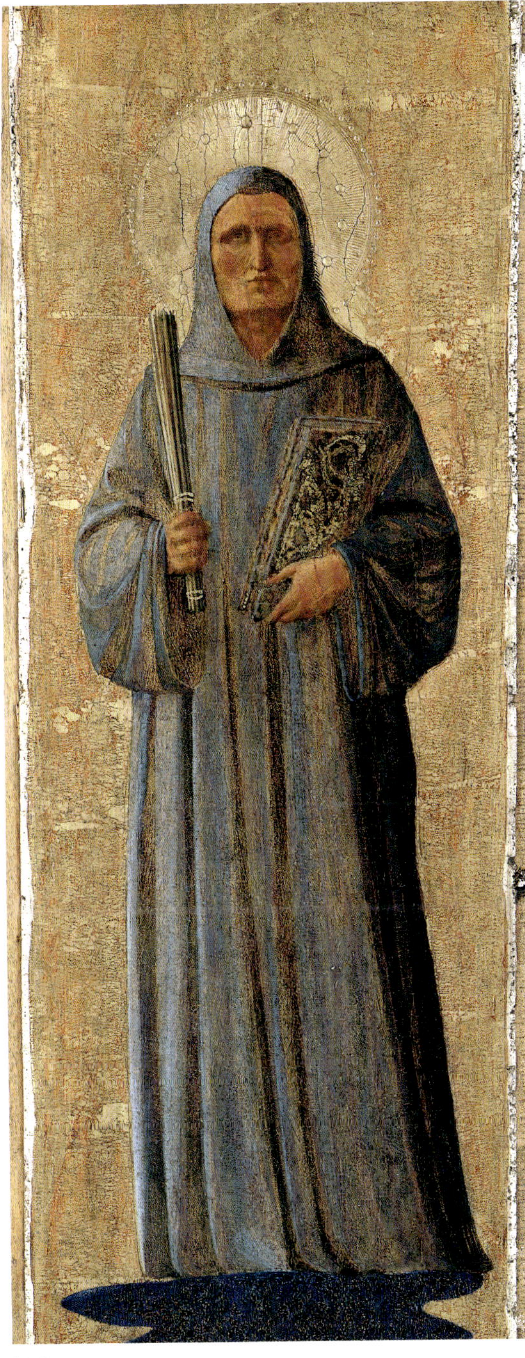
34: E

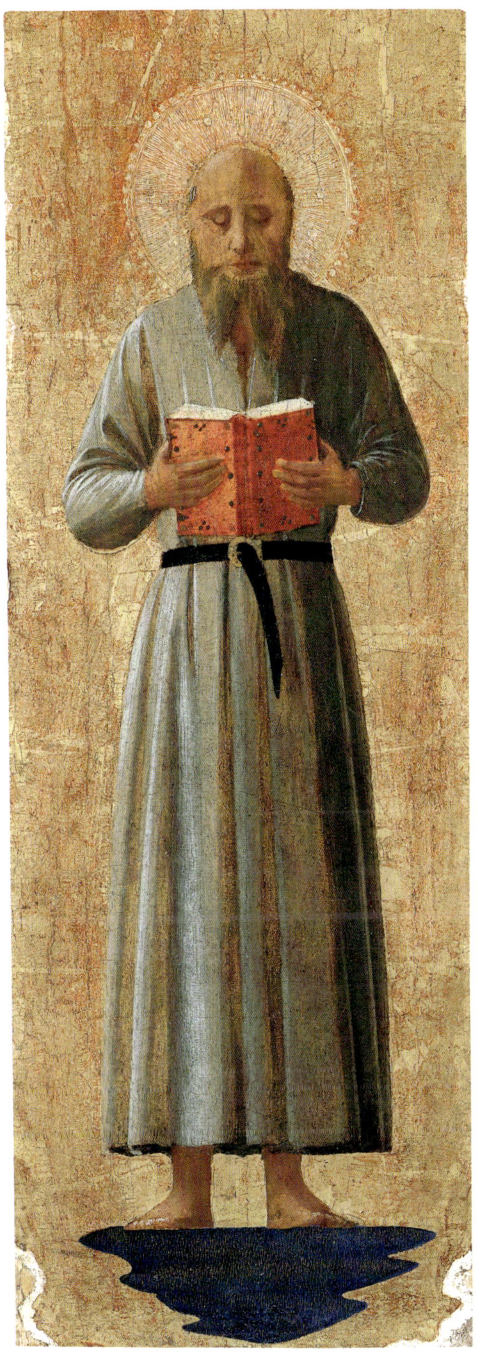
34: F

back on the archers, and the saints remained unhurt. Lycias then ordered the beheading of all five brothers—the episode portrayed in the next scene of the predella (I). After the saints' martyrdom, their followers set out to bury them in accord with Cosmas's expressed wishes, resolving to ensure that his grave be separate from Damian's. In the next panel (Museo di San Marco, Florence, Inv. 1890, no. 8494; fig. 119), they are shown being stopped in their efforts by a camel, who, miraculously, speaks to them and reports that the brothers had reconciled and desired to be buried together. One of the saints' posthumous miracles was portrayed in the final scene of the predella, installed originally on the outside edge of the right framing pilaster and now in the Museo di San Marco, Florence (Inv. 1890, no. 8495; fig. 120): Justinian, a deacon of the church of Santi Cosma e Damiano in Rome, dreamt one night that the two saints appeared to him, applying ointments to his cancerous leg and then replacing it with the leg of an Ethiopian from the cemetery of San Pietro in Vincoli; the following morning the vision was found to have been real.

In a marked departure from his earlier practice, as revealed by the Perugia (cat. 30) and Linaiuoli (cat. 29) predellas or the predella to the Louvre *Coronation of the Virgin* altarpiece, all of the compositions of the San Marco predella save one are oriented parallel to the picture planes and are either centralized (scenes 2, 4, 5, 6, 8, and 9) or carefully balanced from left to right (scenes 1 and 3). Only the *Decapitation of Saints Cosmas and Damian* (I), the seventh panel, reverts to a formula more familiar in Fra Angelico's earlier works: the narrative action is developed more dynamically along pronounced diagonals receding in depth, as though witnessed by a viewer entering the scene casually from one side. In all of the other panels, including the centrally placed *Entombment,* the setting is closed off by a carefully articulated architectural form (those in the first and last scenes are less detailed than the others) in front of which the figures are disposed along the orthogonals of a centrally foreshortened cube of space. Some of the compositions introduce diagonally positioned architectural forms intruding at the margins, but these do not materially alter the essentially planar organization of each scene except in the case of the third panel, where the demands of a continuous narrative required the artist to open out the landscape at the left to allow two further moments in the story to be incorporated into the middle distance and background. The novelty and sophistication of this approach may best be underscored by comparing the compositions of these predella scenes to their inept transcriptions, painted, apparently, by Zanobi Strozzi, on the predella to the slightly later Annalena altarpiece (now in the Museo di San Marco),[4] where none of the subtleties of Angelico's geometric abstractions have been either understood or retained. Only in Angelico's own later compositions for the Annunziata Silver Chest and for the San Marco and Cappella Niccolina frescoes were these principles of spatial and compositional organization realized with an even more rigorous degree of consistency.

Completing the San Marco altarpiece at either side of the main panel were massive buttressing pilasters decorated with standing figures of saints, similar to those included in Angelico's earlier altarpieces in the Guidalotti chapel in Perugia (cat. 30) and in the sacristy of Santa Trinita in Florence (fig. 53). Six of these figures—Saints Romuald,[5] Thomas

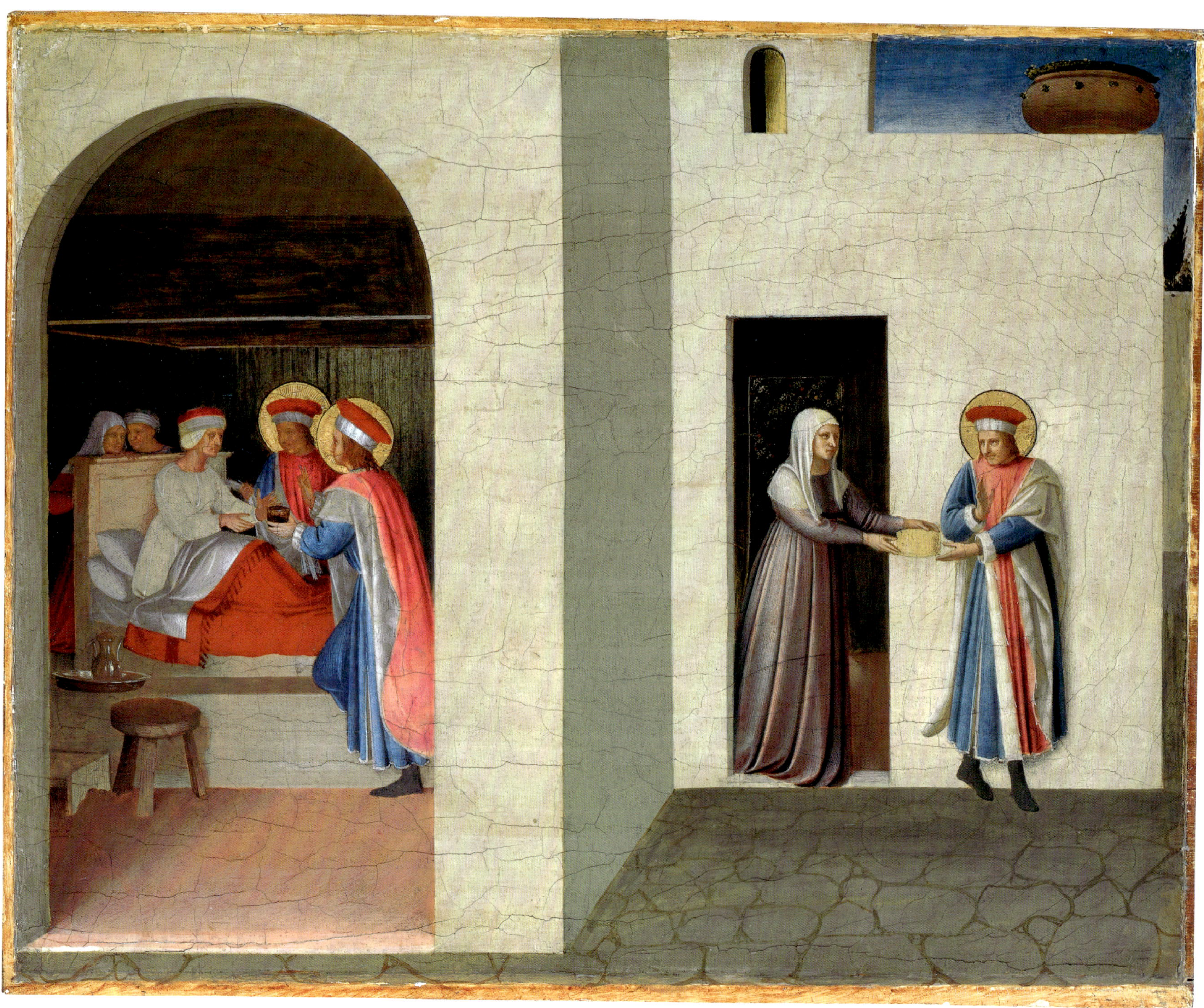

34: G

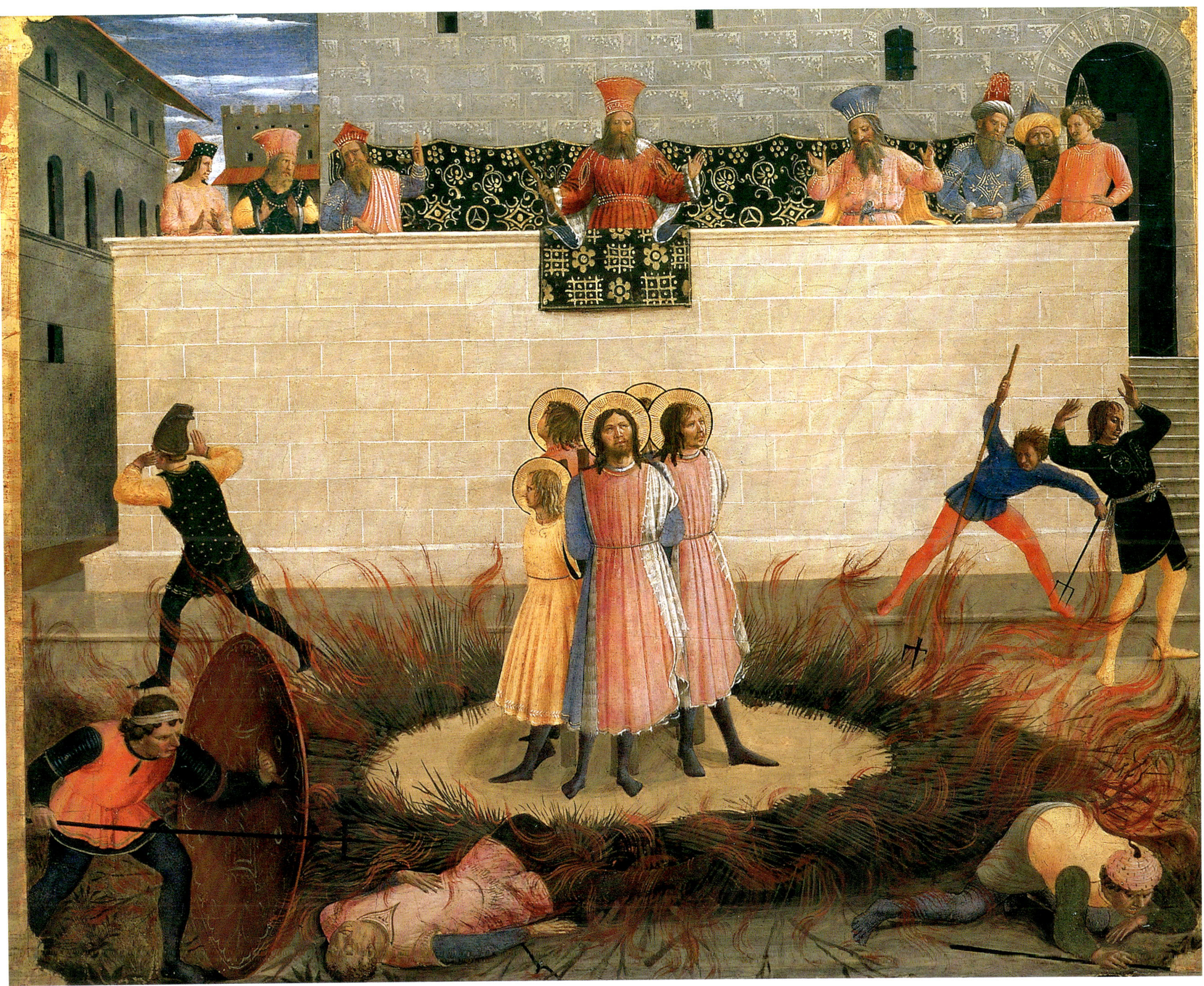

34: H

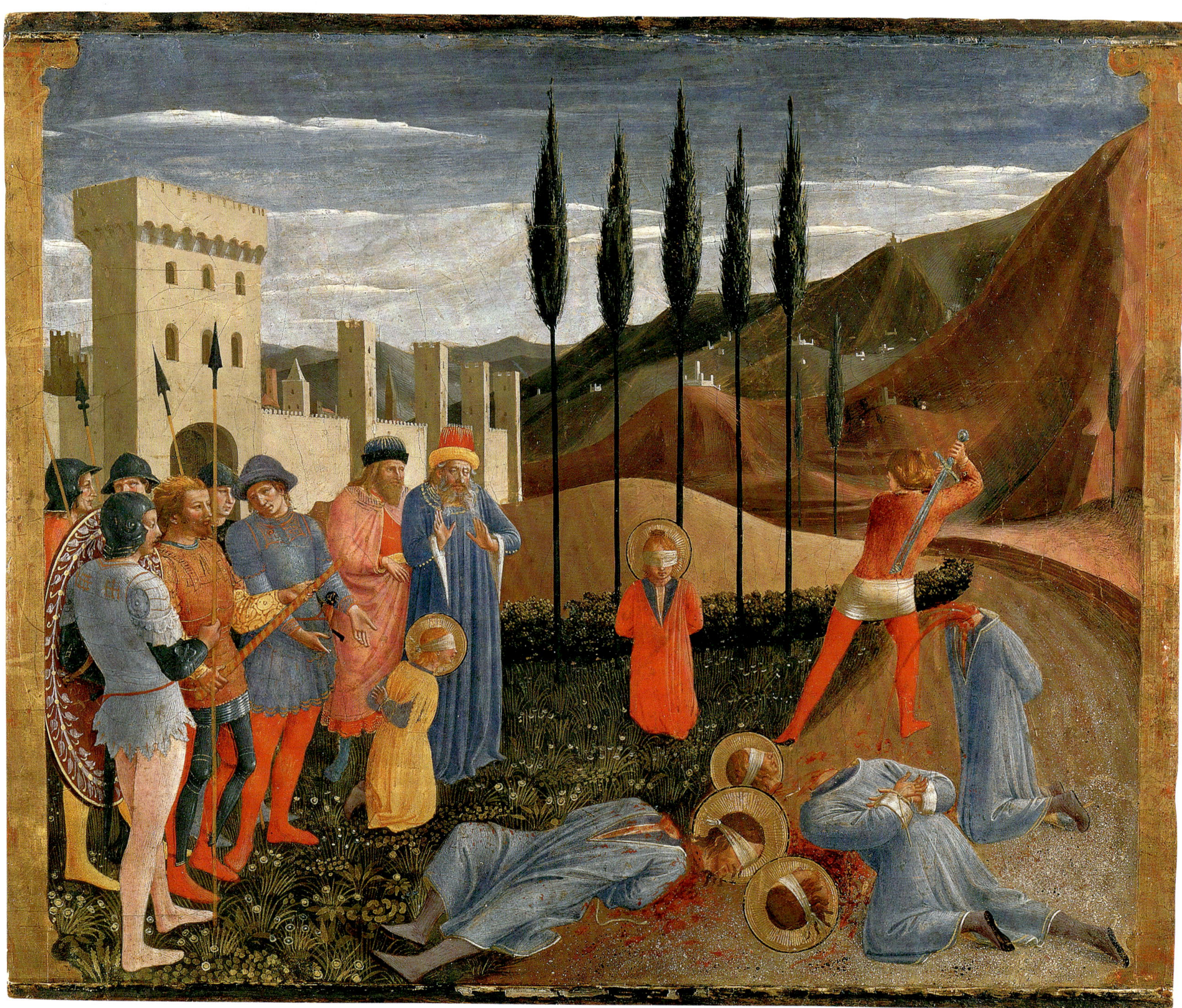

34: 1

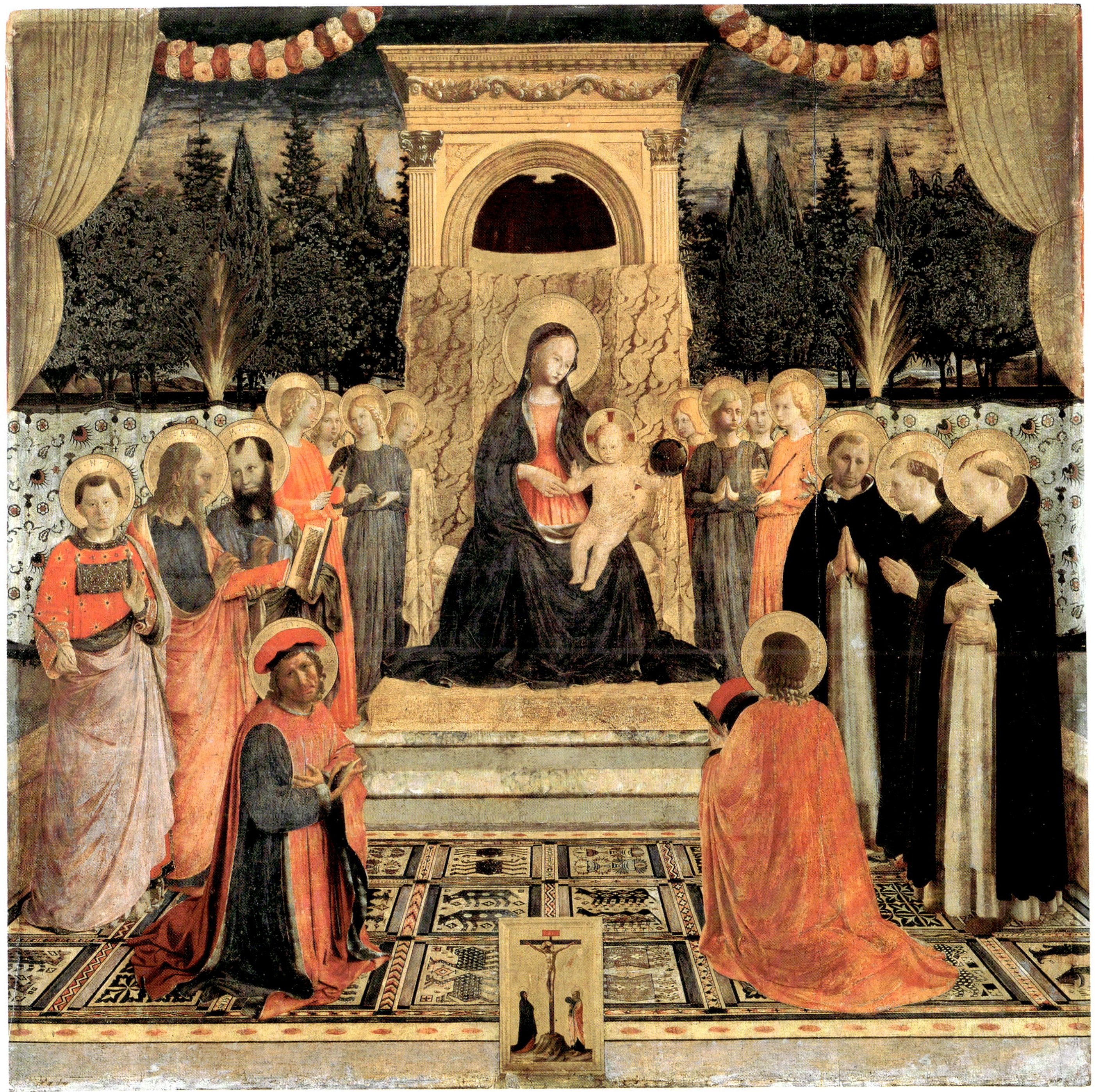

Figure 114. Fra Angelico. *Virgin and Child Enthroned, with Eight Angels and Saints Lawrence, John the Evangelist, Mark, Dominic, Francis, Peter Martyr, Cosmas, and Damian* (San Marco High Altarpiece). About 1440–42. Museo di San Marco, Florence

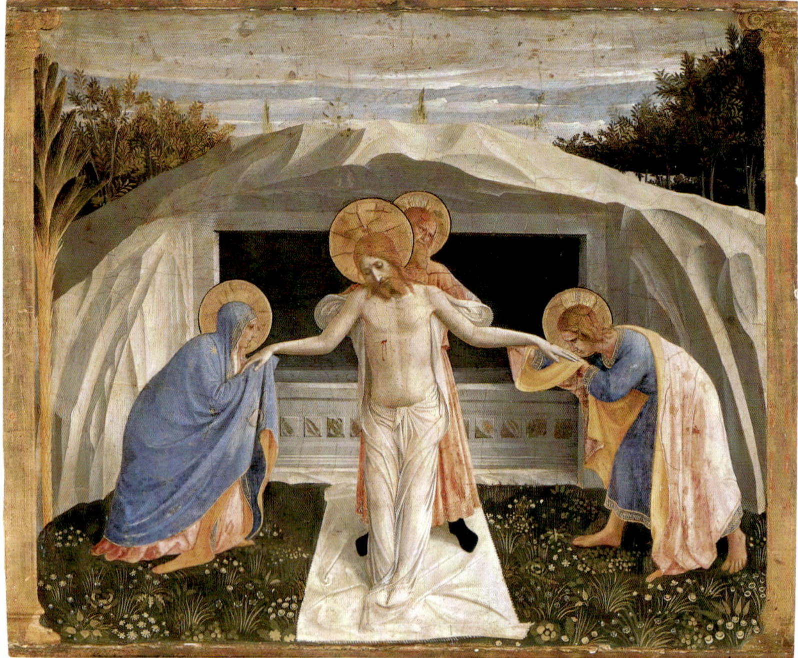

Figure 115. Fra Angelico. *The Entombment*. About 1440–42. Alte Pinakothek, Munich

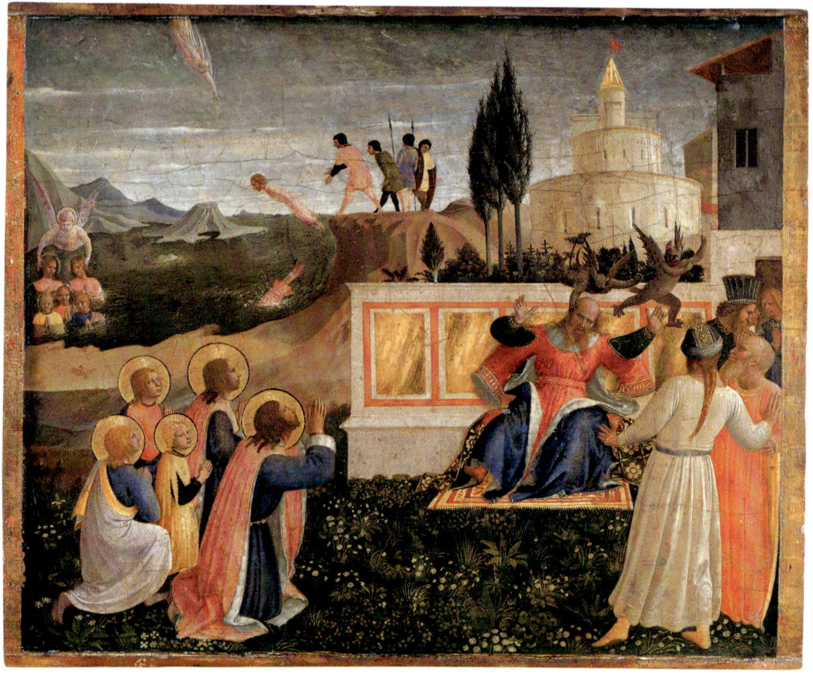

Figure 117. Fra Angelico. *Saints Cosmas and Damian Thrown into the Sea*. About 1440–42. Alte Pinakothek, Munich

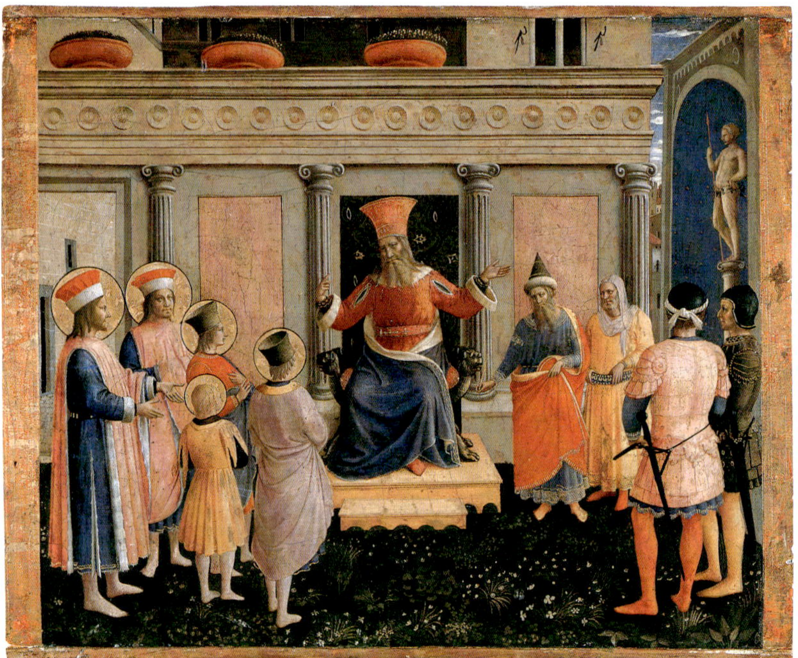

Figure 116. Fra Angelico. *Saints Cosmas and Damian before the Proconsul Lycias.* About 1440–42. Alte Pinakothek, Munich

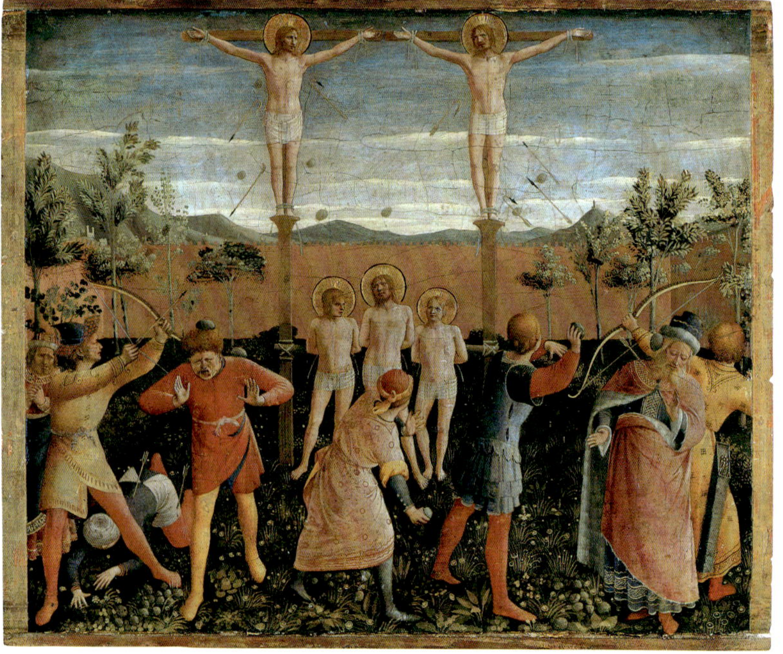

Figure 118. Fra Angelico. *Saints Cosmas and Damian Tied to Crosses.* About 1440–42. Alte Pinakothek, Munich

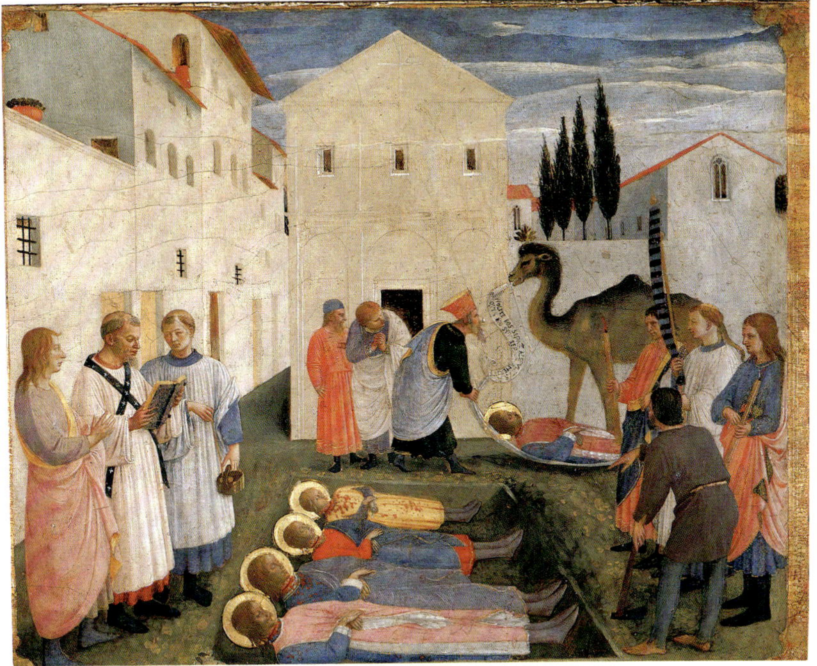

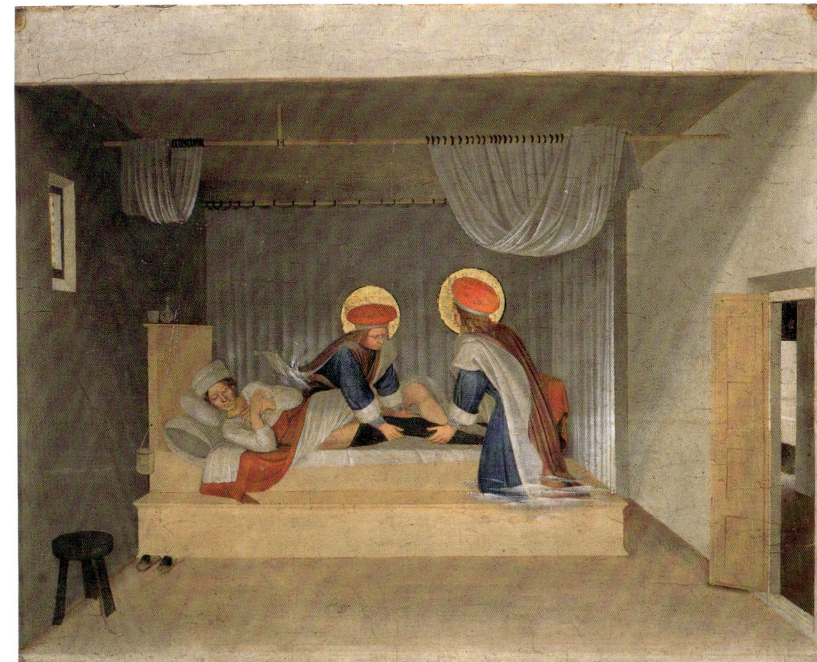

Figure 119 (above left). Fra Angelico. *The Burial of Saints Cosmas and Damian and Their Brothers.* About 1440–42. Museo di San Marco, Florence

Figure 120 (above right). Fra Angelico. *Saints Cosmas and Damian Healing the Deacon Justinian.* About 1440–42. Museo di San Marco, Florence

Aquinas,[6] Anthony Abbot, Roch, Benedict, and Jerome (A–F)—are known to survive, although there once may have been as many as twelve. In a recent reconstruction by Miklós Boskovits,[7] these six figures were arranged in two columns, with Saints Benedict, Jerome, and Romuald on the left of the main panel and Saints Roch, Thomas Aquinas, and Anthony Abbot on the right. Such an arrangement is perhaps suggested by the poses of the figures but not by their lighting. In the main panel of the altarpiece and in all seven predella scenes that originally occupied its front face, the light consistently enters from the right, while in the first and last predella scenes those that have been plausibly situated on the outer faces of the framing pilasters—the light source is at the left. Three of the figures of saints—Benedict, Jerome, and Romuald—are also lit from the left, and it would follow that they must have occupied the outer face of a pilaster. Romuald, who faces right, was probably painted on the left pilaster, while Benedict and Jerome, who are both portrayed frontally, could have appeared on either side of the altarpiece. The other three saints—Roch, Thomas Aquinas, and Anthony Abbot—are all lit from the right and turn slightly to their left; it therefore is possible that they were situated on the front of the right pilaster.

LK

1. Morçay 1913, p. 7; Hood 1993, p. 30.
2. Hood 1993, p. 33.
3. Libreria del Seminario, Cortona, Libro di Ricordanze di Frate Giovanni Tommaso Minerbetti, San Domenico di Cortona, 1703: "*Cosimo e Lorenzo Medici ad insistanza di S. Antonino, donano a questo convento un quadro in Tavole, che e quello che sta nella facciata al Coro ebbe levato di San Marco, come si vede nelle ricordanze di questo Convento in Firenze*"; reprinted in Cole 1977, vol. II, p. 612.
4. Although this altarpiece is frequently dated to the early 1430s, especially in the more recent literature on Fra Angelico, Pope-Hennessy (1974, p. 211) was correct to observe that its predella scenes cannot precede those of the San Marco high altarpiece. Difficulties in dating this work have arisen in large measure because it is not generally recognized to have been painted entirely by an assistant, probably Zanobi Strozzi, over a design by Fra Angelico. The relationship of its architectural backdrop to details incorporated in the Cappella Niccolina frescoes and in the Bosco ai Frati altarpiece suggests the likelihood that it dates after 1448–49, the year of Angelico's return to Florence from Rome. During this period, the services of Benozzo Gozzoli, who is documented at Orvieto and Montefalco, were unavailable to Angelico.
5. This panel, first published by R. Oertel (1961), usually is referred to as an image of Saint Benedict, whose attributes are also a book and a birch rod; however, the saint in Altenburg (E), who bears these attributes and wears a gray habit, is clearly a representation of Benedict. Romuald, the founder of the Camaldolese order, is identified by his white habit.
6. This panel was incorrectly noted by J. Spike (1996) and by all subsequent scholars as formerly in a private collection in Italy and later (having been confused with C) in a private collection in Lake Bluff, Illinois; the present painting had already entered the Cini collection by the 1950s.
7. M. Boskovits (in Boskovits and Brown 2003, p. 17) argues that the pilasters must have contained four figures each rather than three, and four more on their outer, lateral faces, for a total of sixteen. Boskovits appears to have reconsidered his first proposal for recontructing the pilasters and to have arrived at a result largely in conformity with that suggested here (cited by A. Labriola, in Boskovits 2005, p. 50). Part of this reconstruction was recently confirmed by Holger Manzke, in a paper delivered on May 21, 2005, in which he demonstrated that the wood grain of the panels of *Saint Benedict* (E) and *Saint Jerome* (F) is continuous and that the *Saint Benedict* was situated at the bottom of its pilaster, while the Saint Roch (D) was painted on a different plank of wood.

35.
Virgin and Child

Tempera on panel, 46.6 x 35.1 cm
(18⅜ x 13⅞ in.)
Kunstmuseum, Bern. Bequest of Adolf von Sturler, 1881

Although little discussed in the literature on Fra Angelico, the Bern *Virgin and Child* is one of the artist's most beautiful and moving late creations. The intimacy of the image is accentuated by the absence of any hieratic gestures of blessing or suggestions of benedictional function: the Child is shown lifting his head and left hand to disengage himself from his mother's embrace. He turns slowly toward the spectator, of whose presence he seems to have just been made aware, while his mother's attention is still entirely focused on her son. The viewer's sense of privileged access to this very private scene is further emphasized by the painting's format and scale: the Virgin's torso fills the full width of the picture field, the arc of her halo tangent to the top molding of the (now missing) engaged frame, while the Child's left foot stretches down to the bottom molding. The restricted, strongly contrasting palette of blue and red, the warm raking light falling across the image from the left, and the highly plastic modeling of the forms complete the impact of this deceptively simple composition.

Among the few modern scholars to have discussed the Bern *Virgin and Child,* most have described it as a product of Fra Angelico's workshop or of a follower.[1] For Diane Cole Ahl, none of the three surviving half-length images of the Virgin and Child by Fra Angelico—the Bern picture, a heavily repainted example in the Norton Simon Collection in Pasadena, and a damaged and restored painting of the Madonna in the Fogg Art Museum at Harvard University (cat. 14)—is autograph, although each may possibly represent a workshop replica of a lost image by the master.[2] John Spike, on the other hand, conceded the possibility of an attribution to Angelico of the Bern *Virgin and Child,* which he knew from a photograph only, and proposed a date for the painting close to 1432, roughly contemporary with the *Deposition* altarpiece from Santa Trinita, now in the Museo di San Marco.[3] Gaudenz Freuler correctly noted that the sophistication of the painting's composition alone would justify its direct ascription to Fra Angelico as an autograph work, and further observed that the color and the quality of its light effects indicate that it dates from late in the artist's career. For Freuler this date was likely to be about 1450, based on the assumption that the Guidalotti altarpiece in Perugia (cat. 30) was completed only a few years earlier and that the Bern *Virgin and Child* represented an advancement beyond the accomplishments of that majestic work.[4] The Guidalotti altarpiece, however, probably dates to 1437, rather than to the last half of the 1440s; therefore, the date of the Bern panel remains a matter of discussion.

The closest point of reference for the figure types in the Bern picture and for their emotional presence is to be found in the main panel of the San Marco high altarpiece (cat. 34), probably executed between 1440 and 1442, but the formality and reserve of the Virgin's posture and the Child's gesture in that altarpiece are completely at odds with the intimacy and spontaneity of the Bern painting. This difference is probably less a matter of chronology than of function, and may be explained by the liturgical demands required of an altarpiece in contrast to the private, devotional purpose served by the smaller panel. The central group of the Virgin and Child in the Bosco ai Frati altarpiece at San Marco (fig. 78), generally (and reasonably) dated between 1449 and 1452, follows the composition of the Bern painting more closely, but it, too, displays concessions to its liturgical context: the Virgin's gaze directly engages the spectator and the Christ Child holds a pomegranate, a symbol of the Resurrection, in his right hand. Although the compositions of the Bern and Bosco ai Frati paintings may seem, at first glance, similar enough to suggest their contemporaneity, the altarpiece reflects, in its measured disengagement and brooding, monumental calm, the final development of Angelico's figure style as first expressed on the walls of the Cappella Niccolina at the Vatican, and refined in the best of the scenes painted on the Annunziata Silver Chest. The Bern panel, by contrast, is still redolent of the emotional urgency that climaxed in Angelico's work on the predella of the San Marco high altarpiece. On balance, it seems preferable to date the Bern *Virgin and Child* just prior to Angelico's departure from Florence for Rome in 1445, rather than shortly following his return in 1448, although works from this period are so scarce that precise judgments in this regard must remain tentative.

LK

1. Berenson 1963, vol. I, p. 11; Pope-Hennessy 1974, p. 221; Baldini 1970, p. 116, no. 119.
2. Cole 1977, vol. II, pp. 487–88.
3. Spike 1996, p. 258.
4. G. Freuler, in Fehlmann and Freuler 2001, pp. 124–29. G. Bonsanti (1998, pp. 138–39) also accepts the autograph status of the painting and its relation to the Guidalotti altarpiece, but dates it on that basis to about 1437.

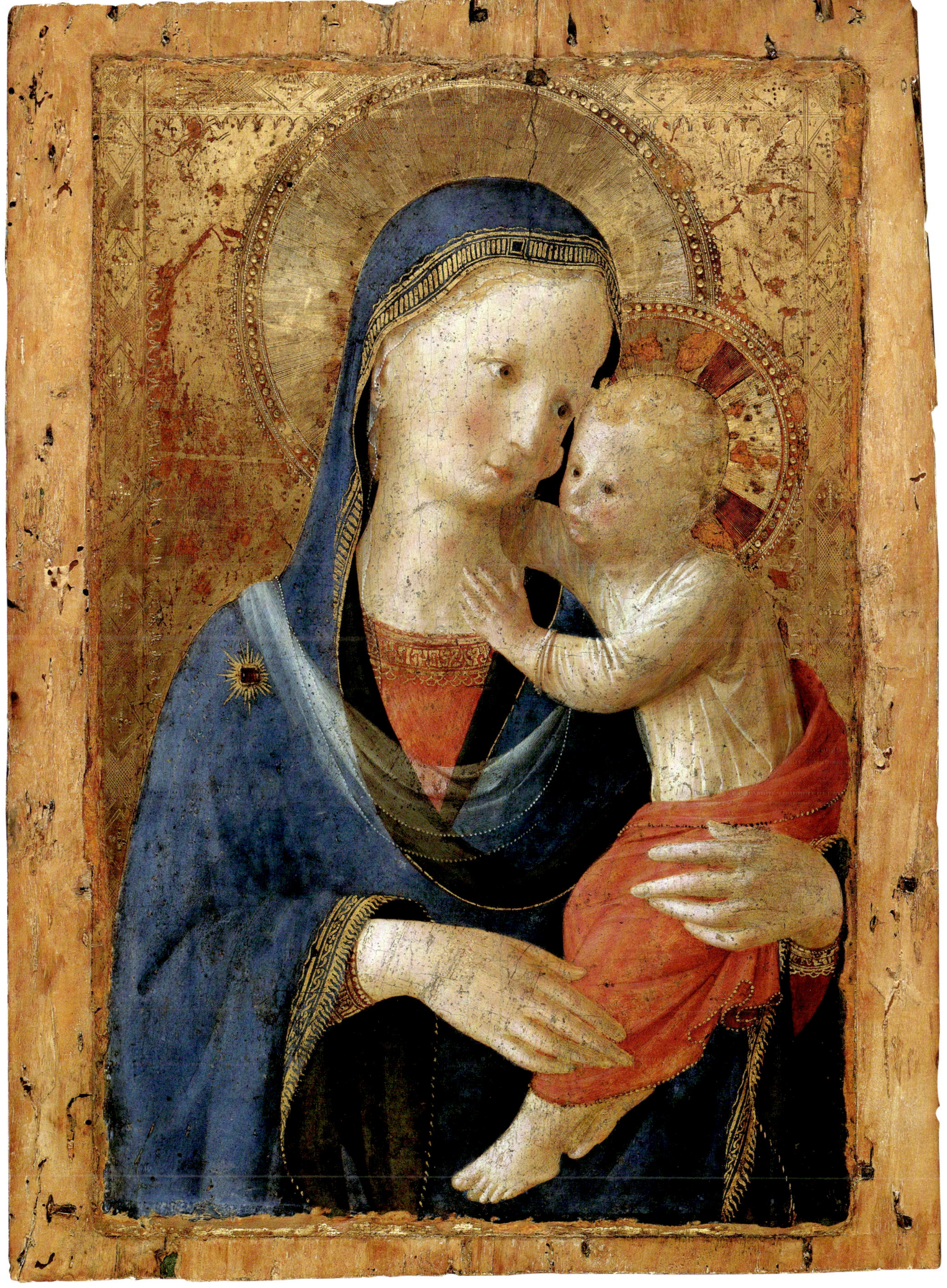

35

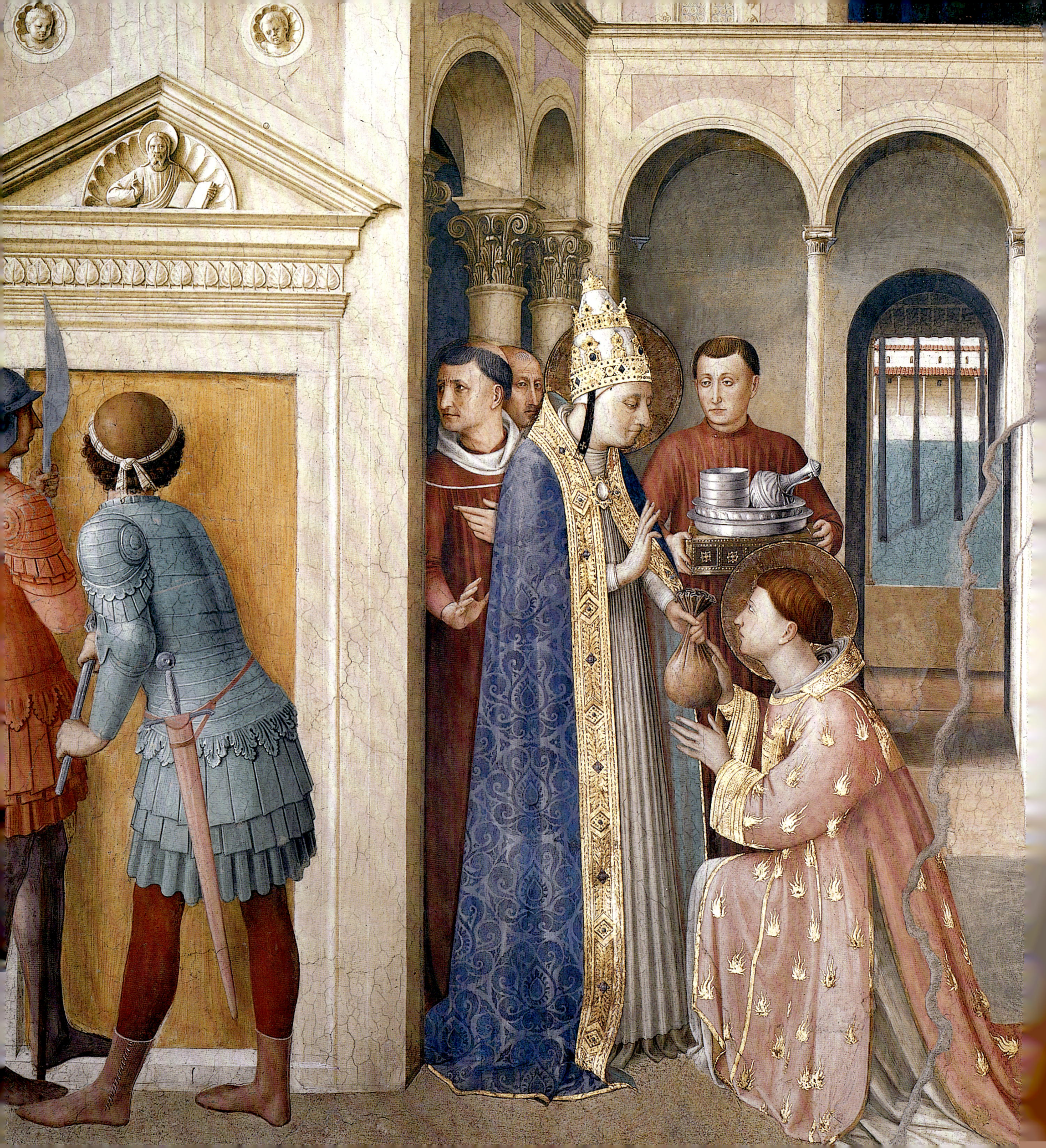

Chapter VII
Fra Angelico: A Florentine Painter in "Roma Felix"

CARL BRANDON STREHLKE

In his biography of Pope Nicholas V, written shortly after the pontiff's death on March 24, 1455, the humanist Giannozzo Manetti related the pope's deathbed defense of his ambitious building projects.[1] His aspirations for Rome had been great—a commemorative medal of the Jubilee of 1450[2] bore the inscription *Roma felix* ("the happy city, Rome")[3] in honor of the city's renewal under his guidance. According to Manetti, Nicholas assailed the critics of his schemes as insignificant men unable to appreciate their greatness, and expressed regret at not finishing the Vatican palace, which he had intended to transform into a magnificent residence. The pope visibly shocked the cardinals gathered at his bedside, yet, unrepentant, enjoined them to continue his building campaign. In the final review of his accomplishments, Nicholas recorded donations of precious objects to churches, codices that he had translated, and the learned men in his employ, but he was silent on the subject of painting, despite his commissions to the Tuscan artist Fra Giovanni da Fiesole (Fra Angelico) for a chapel and a studio in the Vatican palace. In fact, the chapel and studio were located just a few yards from where the pope lay dying. Neither did Manetti mention Angelico, who had died a month before the pope. Manetti spoke only of the pope's close personal relationship with Bernardo Rossellino, the Florentine architect who oversaw the building projects and renovations. Except for Angelico's frescoes in the chapel, little of Nicholas's *Roma felix* survives today.

Nicholas had inherited Fra Angelico from his predecessor, Eugenius IV, for whom the artist had begun the frescoes in the Chapel of the Sacrament, also in the Vatican palace. The date of this chapel, which no longer exists, can be ascertained from two documented events: in May 1446 officials of Orvieto Cathedral, then seeking a painter to fresco the Chapel of San Brizio, were informed that Angelico might soon be available. Secondly, a diarist, recounting that Eugenius's body was laid out in the Vatican chapel after his death on February 23, 1447, made mention of the fact that the chapel was newly painted.[4] Work may have continued into the next papacy as Angelico's sixteenth-century biographer Giorgio Vasari noted that the frescoes contained portraits of contemporary individuals, and that the collector Paolo Giovio (1483–1552) had copies made of the likenesses of Nicholas V; the German Frederick III, crowned Holy Roman Emperor in 1452; and even Ferrante of Naples, who would succeed his father, Alfonso V of Aragon, in 1458 (Ferrante's rights to the Neapolitan throne had been recognized by Eugenius IV in July 1444 and had also been confirmed by Nicholas V). Copies of some of these portraits still exist, indicating that Vasari's information is correct.[5] The main work would thus have been completed before 1447, and some portraits updated or added later.[6] When the chapel was destroyed during the reign of Pope Paul III (1534–49) to make a proper antechamber for the Sistine Chapel, collectors were able to obtain fragments of the frescoes. Michelangelo, an admirer of Angelico, treasured one of a Madonna (now lost),[7] and a detached fresco of a head of the young Christ, in the Museo Nazionale di Palazzo Venezia in Rome, may be such a

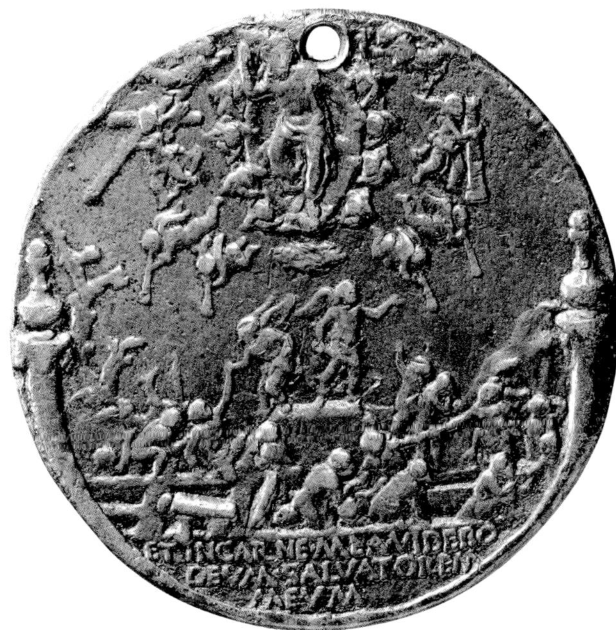

Figure 122. Bertoldo di Giovanni (?). *The Last Judgment*. About 1468–69. The Metropolitan Museum of Art, New York. Rogers Fund, 1974 (1974.166)

Opposite:
Figure 121. Fra Angelico. *Saint Sixtus Consigning the Goods of the Church to Saint Lawrence*. 1447–48. Cappella Niccolina, Vatican Palace, Vatican City

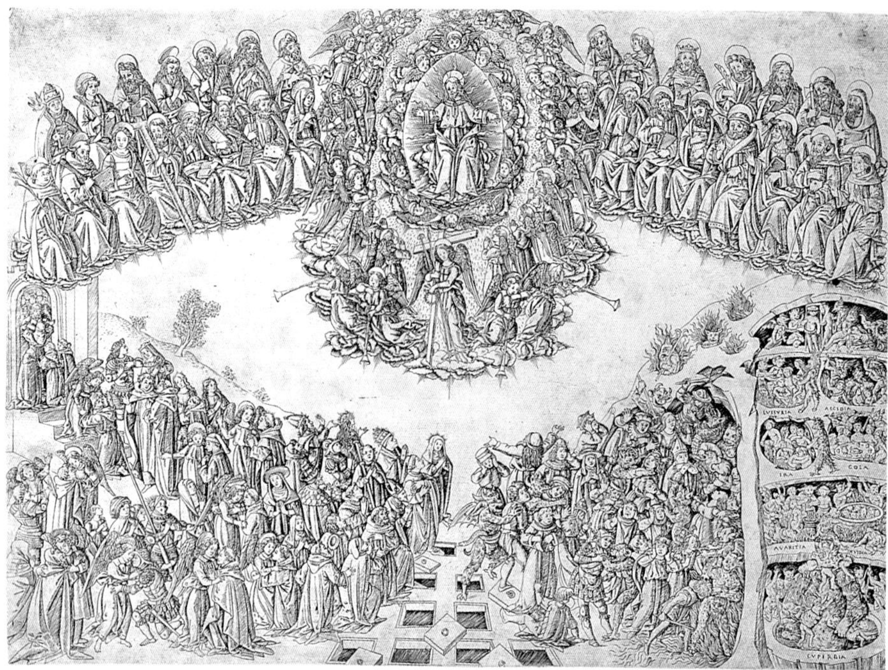

Figure 123. Francesco Rosselli. Engraving after Fra Angelico's *Last Judgment* from Santa Maria degli Angeli. About 1475–80. National Gallery of Art, Washington, D.C.

souvenir.[8] The *Christ* appears to have been executed by Angelico's assistant Benozzo Gozzoli, who is not documented in Rome until May 1447—yet another indication that work on the chapel continued after Eugenius's death.

The subject of the chapel's frescoes was the life of Christ. An early Florentine source (the *Anonimo magliabechiano*) described the chapel as truly a "paradise"[9]—a reference to its beauty but perhaps also to the principal scene: the Last Judgment with a vision of Christ the Judge surrounded by the heavenly host. As is known from various derivations, the most distinct feature of Angelico's lost *Last Judgment* in the Chapel of the Sacrament at the Vatican was the depiction of Christ with his left arm raised in condemnation of the damned. Michelangelo famously adopted the gesture in the Sistine Chapel *Last Judgment*. Angelico repeated this same depiction of Christ in Orvieto Cathedral, probably because the patrons there desired something similar to the new Vatican frescoes. In the 1460s, Filippo de' Medici, Archbishop of Pisa, had a portrait medal made by Bertoldo on the reverse of which is an image of Christ gesturing as in Angelico's paintings (fig. 122). While one of the few precedents for this pose is the fresco of the *Last Judgment* in the Camposanto in Pisa,[10] the medal dates to about the time of the archbishop's trip to Rome in 1468–69 as Florentine ambassador to Pope Paul II.[11] The archbishop hoped to be named a cardinal, and perhaps this is why a Vatican source was used for the medal rather than Angelico's early Florentine *Last Judgment* in Santa Maria degli Angeli (now in the Museo di San Marco), which showed Christ with one arm extended to the blessed and the other turned down in condemnation of the damned. In the 1470s Francesco Rosselli would adapt the Florentine version of the image of Christ for the composition of a large print (fig. 123).[12] It is one of the first examples of a reproductive engraving of a work of art, but it was to Angelico's Vatican fresco that the Florentines Bertoldo and Michelangelo looked as a model.

Angelico's lost cycle of frescoes in the cloister of the Roman church of Santa Maria sopra Minerva included a version of the subject of Christ in Glory, but, as a drawing recording the composition shows, with Christ blessing and holding an orb in his other hand—suggesting that the compositions of the Last Judgment with Christ's more active pose were specifically associated with the Vatican and the papacy, and were infrequently utilized in other contexts.[13] This raises the questions of the owners and dates of the two triptychs of the *Last Judgment* by Angelico now in Rome and in Berlin (cat. 32) in which Christ is depicted in the distinctly active "Vatican" pose.[14] The Berlin painting, which was originally a single panel, merits particular attention. John Pope-Hennessy attributed it to Angelico's collaborator Zanobi Strozzi,[15] whereas, as Laurence Kanter has pointed out to me, it is, indeed, an autograph work by Angelico from the 1430s. The adaptation of its iconography for the papal project in Rome would indicate that the original owner was a member of the Curia, if not Pope Eugenius IV himself, who—after he had been forced out of Rome in May 1434—settled in the Dominican convent of Santa Maria Novella in Florence, where he lived until September 1443, when he returned to the Vatican. The Berlin painting has a Roman provenance, but it can be traced only to 1811.[16] However, Bartholomaeus Spranger copied the panel (Galleria Sabauda, Turin) for Pope Pius V (r. 1566–72), suggesting that the original might, in fact, have once been in the Vatican collections. Angelico would have painted the picture for Eugenius or a member of his Curia during the pope's Florentine sojourn. It would have been taken back to Rome by the pope, serving as a model for the principal scene in the Chapel of the Sacrament.

In the other triptych (fig. 94),[17] now in the Palazzo Corsini in Rome, Miklós Boskovits identified one of the saints surrounding Christ as a portrait of Eugenius IV,[18] making a connection with Eugenius's chapel even more compelling. It is also possible that the *Pentecost* and the *Ascension* depicted on the wings of that triptych are reductions of the frescoes as well. The only other record is a drawing in the Louvre of *Christ Calling the Apostles*.[19] However, it is also probable that some of the scenes are reflected in a group of small drawings (cat. 47), now divided between the Museum Boijmans Van Beuningen, Rotterdam, and the Fogg Art Museum, Cambridge, Massachusetts, of scenes from the life of Christ. Their compositions are usually related to the silver chest commissioned by Piero de' Medici for Santissima Annunziata in Florence and executed in 1451–53. Yet, while there are many similarities, the compositions are not the same, indicating that they were based on another model.

The drawings are on vellum tinted purple. Colored backgrounds are not unusual for drawings from this period,[20] but the purple used in these studies specifically recalls certain precious manuscripts on *porpora*-stained vellum, largely from the Carolingian and Ottonian periods, which were being rediscovered in the mid-fifteenth century and became objects of fascination. These manuscripts were usually thought to be antique.[21] The Renaissance practice of tinting manuscripts purple in direct imitation of the early examples began in Padua in the early 1460s,[22] but, in a public sermon, Saint Bernardino of Siena already had commented on the beauty of a famous *porpora* Gospel, which he had seen in the sacristy of Verona Cathedral. He provided a Christological interpretation of the color of the vellum by calling it the "*vestimento di Jhesù*" (the vestment of Jesus).[23] A similar manuscript was owned by the monastery of Santa Giulia in Brescia.[24]

If the drawings do record Angelico's frescoes in the Chapel of the Sacrament, they might have been prepared for an important object, such as a reliquary, as Pia Palladino suggests in the present catalogue (see cat. 47). Alternatively, they could have been excised from a volume perhaps made for a distinguished personage as a papal gift; the German emperor Frederick III, who was crowned by Nicholas V in Saint Peter's on March 19, 1452, is one possibility.[25] A miniature portrait of him against a deep blue background was made about this time,[26] and there is evidence of his curiosity about Italian art.[27] The interest of Northern European patrons in the art of papal Rome is borne out by the copies of Masolino's frescoes of *uomini famosi* (famous men) in the Palazzo Orsini at Montegiordano prepared by Barthélemy d'Eick for King René d'Anjou and by Leonardo da Besozzo for an unidentified Lombard or Neapolitan patron.[28] The Rotterdam and Cambridge drawings may have served a similar purpose.

Tinted backgrounds distinguish several drawings by Angelico's collaborator Benozzo Gozzoli. His drawing in the British Museum of one of the statues of the Dioscuri[29] located on Rome's Quirinal hill has a deep blue ground, indicating that Gozzoli was experimenting with colored grounds during his sojourn in Rome with Angelico. The similarly intensely colored drawings with violet backgrounds by Angelico's workshop must date to the master's Roman period. A hallmark of those drawings and Gozzoli's is the white gouache used to delineate outlines. Leon Battista Alberti's *De pictura,* written in the early 1430s in Florence, contains a long discussion on the use (and abuse) of white as a color.[30] Alberti is critical of excessive use of white in painting, but notes that it should be employed to outline the illuminated side of a surface, with black applied opposite it, in the shaded areas: "With such balancing, as one might say, of black and white a surface rising in relief becomes still more evident."[31] Although speaking of painting, Alberti's ideas seem to find particular resonance in Gozzoli's remarkable drawings, in which the surfaces of objects, highlighted with white and a minimum of black, appear to "rise up in relief" against the colored background.

In the present catalogue, Palladino ascribes the Christological drawings to Zanobi Strozzi, Angelico's closest Florentine collaborator. This does not exclude *a priori* a Roman origin for the compositions, because the relationship between the artists continued beyond Angelico's first Roman period; as late as May 1449, by which time Angelico had returned to Florence, he was supervising Strozzi's work on the choir books for San Marco in Florence. In addition, members of Angelico's out-of-town workshop made trips to Florence for supplies, proving that contacts were ongoing. In 1447, for example, Angelico sent an assistant named Giovanni (possibly his nephew Giovanni d'Antonio) from Orvieto to Florence to buy ultramarine and other colors.[32]

Eugenius IV, Angelico's first papal patron, would have met the artist in Florence, where the pope lived intermittently from 1434 to 1443. At the beginning of his last year there, Eugenius spent the night of Epiphany (January 6) in a cell (one actually frescoed by Gozzoli) in the Dominican Observant convent of San Marco, which Angelico and his *équipe* had just finished decorating. The experience would have made the pope appreciate not only Angelico's talents as a painter but also his skill as a manager. In a short number of years, a highly disciplined team painted the frescoes in the convent, comprising forty-five cells, the chapter house, and the cloister, as well as the altarpiece in the church. Eugenius would have realized that only an organization like that one could handle the projects on the scale of what he was planning for Rome. However, Angelico did not move his whole Florentine team to Rome and Orvieto. He brought his nephew Giovanni d'Antonio, and after January 1447, if not before, Benozzo Gozzoli, whom Angelico had come to rely on in San Marco, joined them.[33] His other collaborators Zanobi Strozzi and Domenico di Michelino, who were mainly engaged in illumination and panel painting, seem to have remained at home.[34] The three additional assistants named in Roman and Orvietan documents were not Florentine, indicating that Angelico set up a new operation when he relocated.[35]

The interregnum after Eugenius's death in early 1447 may have resulted in a suspension of work at the Vatican. That summer, Angelico's workshop moved to Orvieto, where the artist signed a three-year contract, perhaps not envisioning that the new pope would be employing him. At this time he may have also begun the altarpiece for San Domenico in Perugia. The date of this painting, executed for the sepulcher chapel of Bishop Benedetto Guidalotti (d. 1429), is much debated.[36] A Perugian chronicle places it in 1437, but Andrea De Marchi (with whom I agree) has argued for a later date, noting that the style recalls Angelico's surviving Vatican frescoes and that the figure of Saint Nicholas bears the features of Nicholas V, elected pope on March 6, 1447.[37] The Perugian chapel was commissioned by the bishop's sister Elisabetta whose husband was buried there in 1441, the most probable terminus ante quem for the commission. The deceased's family name was Bartolini, but it is not known if he was related to the same Bartolini of Florence that had two members as friars at Angelico's convent in Fiesole.[38] The Perugian Bartolini did own property at Santa Maria a Soffiano, near Florence, on which, in 1442, Florentine relations collected rent.[39]

Exactly where the Perugia altarpiece was executed is unknown. The form is that of a Gothic polyptych, a type that Angelico had not employed for commissions in Florence, preferring the *tavola quadrata,* or rectangular format. An examination of the edges of the panels shows that they were painted without any attached moldings, and, therefore, that the parts were easily portable and could be sent from afar, assembled, and framed on location. These pictures could also be worked on piecemeal. Laurence Kanter has perceptively observed (see p. 159) that Angelico's Florentine associate Zanobi Strozzi painted (on the master's design) the central scene of the predella.[40] This would indicate that Angelico was willing to delegate important parts of the commission to his assistants, and suggests, but does not prove, that the altarpiece was produced in Florence. While such a collaboration could argue for a date in the late 1430s, when Strozzi assisted Angelico on a number of paintings, their working relationship lasted through the late 1440s, if not longer. Strozzi, for instance, executed the predella with stories from the lives of Saints Cosmas and Damian for Angelico's Annalena altarpiece.[41] In fact, Strozzi's contribution to the Perugian predella resembles most his *Journey of the Magi: Jasper Riding from the Kingdom of Tharsis* (cat. 54 B) in Strasbourg, part of a group of pictures painted in the late 1440s, possibly, in my opinion, for Alfonso of Aragon, King of Naples.[42]

The conclaves that elected Eugenius IV and Nicholas V pope took place in the Dominican convent of Santa Maria sopra Minerva, where Angelico lived when in Rome. The most prominent member of that convent was the Spanish cardinal Juan de Torquemada, whom Angelico depicted kneeling at the foot of the cross in the Fogg Art Museum *Christ on the Cross, between the Virgin and Saint John the Evangelist* (cat. 39). This was part of a triptych (now disassembled) on one wing of which was an image of Saint Sixtus (Private collection; fig. 131),[43] indicating that the altarpiece must have been executed after Pope Eugenius nominated Torquemada as cardinal of the basilica of San Sisto in 1439 and possibly before the change in his title to that of cardinal of the basilica of Santa Maria in Trastevere sometime before October 7, 1446—a period of time in which Angelico was still largely in Florence.[44] Torquemada had been with the papal entourage in Florence, but after he became a cardinal he moved to Rome; there, in the 1450s, he commissioned from Angelico the cloister frescoes for which the cardinal composed a book of meditations, published in 1467, a year before his death.[45] Torquemada remained devoted to his original *titulus,* and was shown kneeling before Saint Sixtus in one of the cloister frescoes, signifying that Angelico's painting in the Fogg could date even after Torquemada's title had changed in 1446 (see p. 224).[46] Torquemada's nephew Fray Tomás de Torquemada, the Spanish Inquisitor and confessor to Queen Isabella, must have inherited Angelico's painting, as the large *Crucifixion* he commissioned from Pedro Berruguete between 1495 and 1498 for the Dominican convent of Segovia is obviously inspired by it.[47]

The elevation of Cardinal Tommaso Parentucelli to the papacy in 1447 as Nicholas V brought Angelico a new patron, but one whom he would have known already from Parentucelli's stays in Florence in the entourage of Cardinal Niccolò Albergati. Angelico could certainly have met Parentucelli in 1441 at San Marco, where the great bibliophile had been given the task of organizing the library. Their first contacts might even date to their youth, when in the mid-1410s Parentucelli was a tutor in the houses of the powerful Florentines Rinaldo degli Albizzi and Palla Strozzi.[48] It is likely that a relative of Rinaldo degli Albizzi, Jacopo di Alessio, who was governor of Angelico's native Vicchio in 1401–2, provided the artist with an introduction to Florence.[49] For Palla Strozzi, Angelico later painted the Santa Trinita *Deposition* (fig. 53). Pope Nicholas would have seen this picture, which was installed in the church in 1431, when he was in Florence in the 1430s and 1440s even though by then Strozzi—as well as many members of the Albizzi family—had been exiled for their anti-Medicean activities. The lost Angelico altarpiece for Nicholas's chapel in the Vatican palace depicted the same subject, and, as derivations of it suggest, the composition was close to that earlier work.[50]

Nicholas had depended heavily on Medici patronage. Always impecunious as a young prelate, even before becoming a cardinal, he borrowed money from the Medici bank, and, after becoming pope, he reestablished the Medici, temporarily out-of-favor in the last years of Eugenius's papacy, as the papal bankers,[51] with Roberto Martelli, his former personal banker, heading the Roman branch. (Martelli controlled the accounts out of which Angelico was paid.)[52] However, Nicholas remained loyal to the exiled Strozzi and to others in the same position. The pope was particularly solicitous of Felice Brancacci, Strozzi's son-in-law and Masolino's and

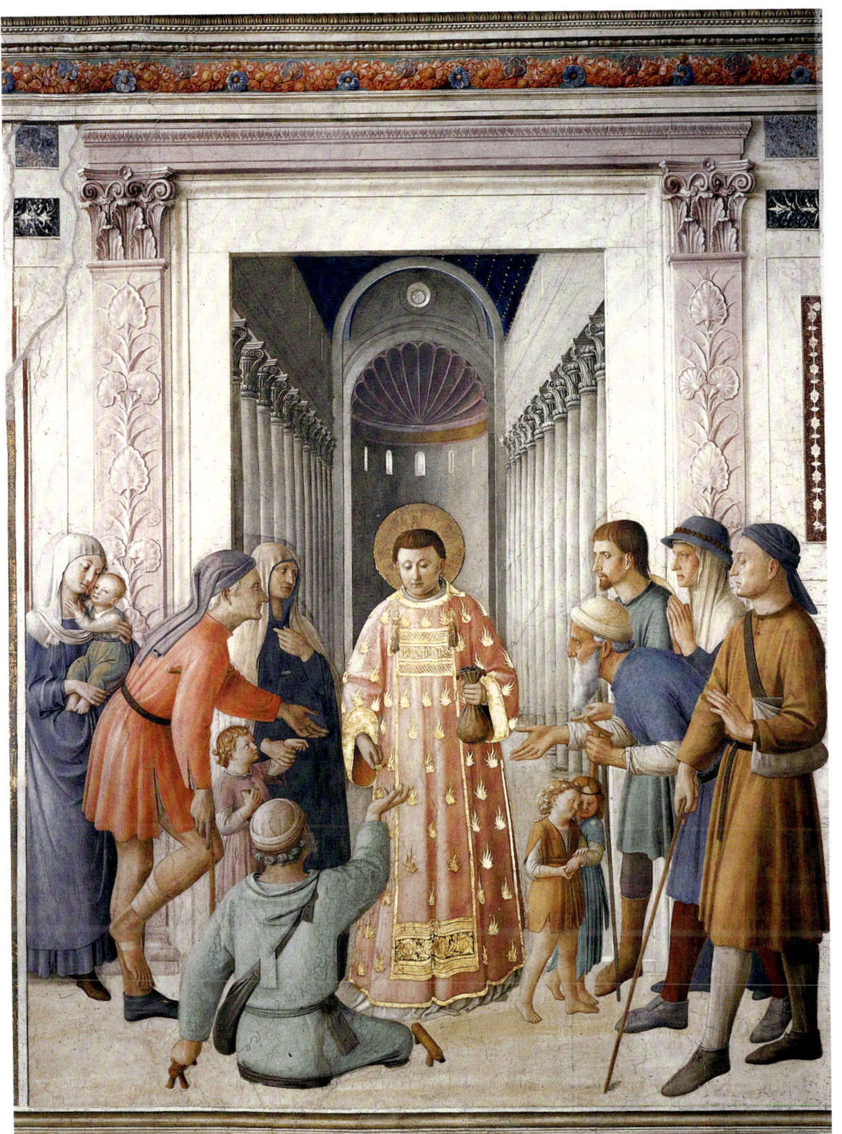

Figure 124. Fra Angelico. *Saint Lawrence Distributing the Goods of the Church.* 1447–48. Cappella Niccolina, Vatican Palace, Vatican City

Masaccio's former patron,[53] and Strozzi's son Carlo became the pope's private chamberlain.

For Nicholas V, Angelico frescoed the Chapel of Saints Stephen and Lawrence and a study in the Vatican palace;[54] only the chapel, painted about 1448–49[55] in close collaboration with Benozzo Gozzoli, survives.[56] Their subject was particularly dear to Nicholas, who, in August 1447, had initiated an official inquest into the legitimacy of the relics in the Roman basilica of San Lorenzo fuori le Mura, where the two saints, each deacons of the Church, were said to repose in a common tomb.[57] The relics of Stephen, whose life and martyrdom are recounted in the Acts of Apostles, had been transferred to Rome in the fifth century; Lawrence, a Roman deacon, was martyred during the anti-Christian persecutions of the third century.

Nicholas's interest in the legends of Early Christian martyrs led him to commission the Florentine cleric Antonio Agli to write a new martyrology (*De viris et gestis sanctorum*) based on contemporary humanist scholarly grounds. Agli was highly critical of medieval hagiographers, who embellished tales to such an extent that "less pious men, puffed up by secular letters and learning . . . ridicule not only the writings, but also the naïveté of all Christians who could believe and accept such artless and childish stories."[58] Agli considerably edited the legends of Saints Stephen and Lawrence, which the thirteenth-century hagiographer Jacopo da Varagine had popularized in *The Golden Legend* (his text was the source for the medieval fresco cycle in the portico of San Lorenzo fuori le Mura).[59] Yet, Agli's text, which was never finished, was not the basis for the Vatican cycle, for Agli had eliminated a central character in the legend of Saint Lawrence: Pope Sixtus II.[60] Sixtus lived during the reign of Valerian (253–60), whereas Lawrence was reputedly martyred under that of Decius (249–51). This had already caused a problem for Jacopo da Varagine, who acknowledged the disparity in dates. However, the Vatican cycle required the inclusion of a pope, and Sixtus was depicted with the features of Nicholas V.

Sixtus appears in two scenes: the *Ordination of Lawrence as a Deacon* (a counterpart to *Saint Peter's Ordination of Stephen*) and in the *Consigning of the Goods of the Church to Saint Lawrence* (fig. 121). In the second scene, Sixtus just manages to consign the treasures to Lawrence before soldiers break down the door and arrest the pope. The subsequent incident, the pope's martyrdom by beheading, is conspicuously absent, and, in fact, there was no tradition for its representation. Sixtus was a martyr, but his administration and care of the Church is the central feature of his legend. Humanists close to Nicholas V also praised him as a martyr, but as a martyr to his position. In a life of the pontiff written four years before his death, the *De laudibus et divina electione,* Michele Canensi,[61] a scholar and Church canon, stated that Nicholas was a martyr not because of the blood that he shed but because of the cares and anxieties that he suffered tending to his flock; the French prelate Jean Jouffroy, who delivered an oration at Nicholas's funeral, called him a "living martyr."[62] Angelico's frescoes underscore this. The scene of Sixtus giving Lawrence the Church treasure, depicted in the lower tier of the entrance wall, is paired with Lawrence distributing the riches to the poor (fig. 124). Of the many paired narratives in the chapel, it is the only one in which the scenes are separated by a painted border; all the others have a continuous background. The border suggests a break between the two scenes and, specifically, the absent episode of the papal martyrdom.

Nicholas's martyr-like care for the Church was embodied in his many reconstruction projects for Rome. The cycle's architectural settings beautifully express his vision for the Vatican and for Rome, then in intense preparation for the

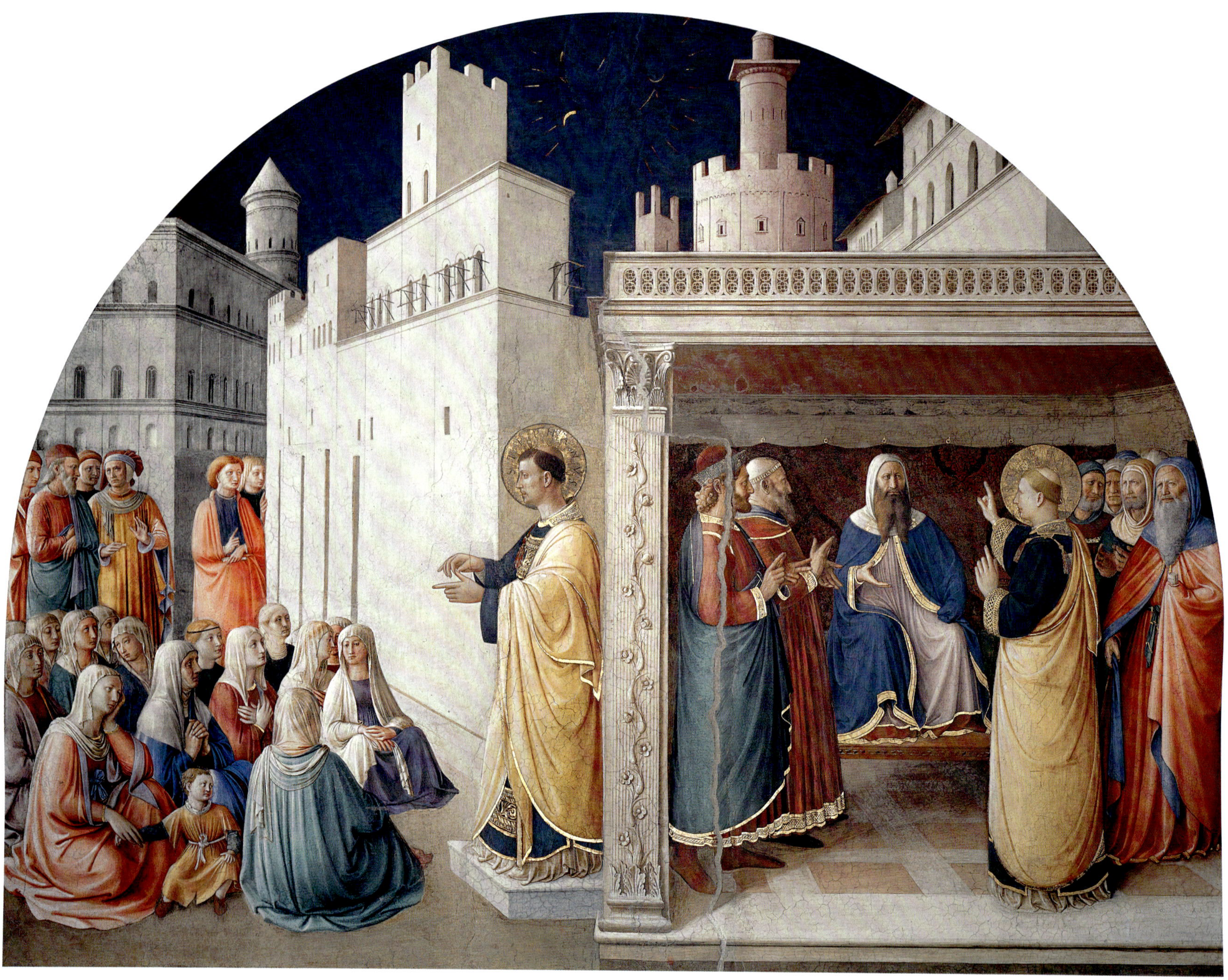

Figure 125. Fra Angelico. *Saint Stephen Preaching and Saint Stephen Addressing the Sanhedrin.* 1447–48. Cappella Niccolina, Vatican Palace, Vatican City

upcoming Jubilee of 1450. The pope would have known that in the biblical account of Saint Stephen defending himself before the Sanhedrin (Acts 7: 44–50), depicted in the upper tier on the chapel's entrance wall (fig. 125), the saint admonished the Jewish elders that by rebuilding the Temple the primitive, more spiritual Judaism embodied in Moses' Ark of the Covenant was being destroyed.[63] However, the inclusion of the scene is certainly not a veiled criticism of Nicholas. As evidenced by Manetti's account of Nicholas's deathbed defense of his papacy, the pope believed that building strengthened and glorified the Church and that the restoration of Rome's Early Christian monuments rekindled a return to the origins of Christianity. Indeed, orators at the pope's funeral celebrated his restoration of Rome. Jouffroy called him an "amazing builder of temples," listing them and declaring that "all the temples of this city, earlier squalid and in ruins, under Nicholas's guidance now delight to be shining, happy, gleaming."[64]

In the frescoes it is impossible to work out an exact topography of the *urbs* (the legend of Saint Stephen is set in Jerusalem), but modern Rome is present throughout. Angelico's buildings

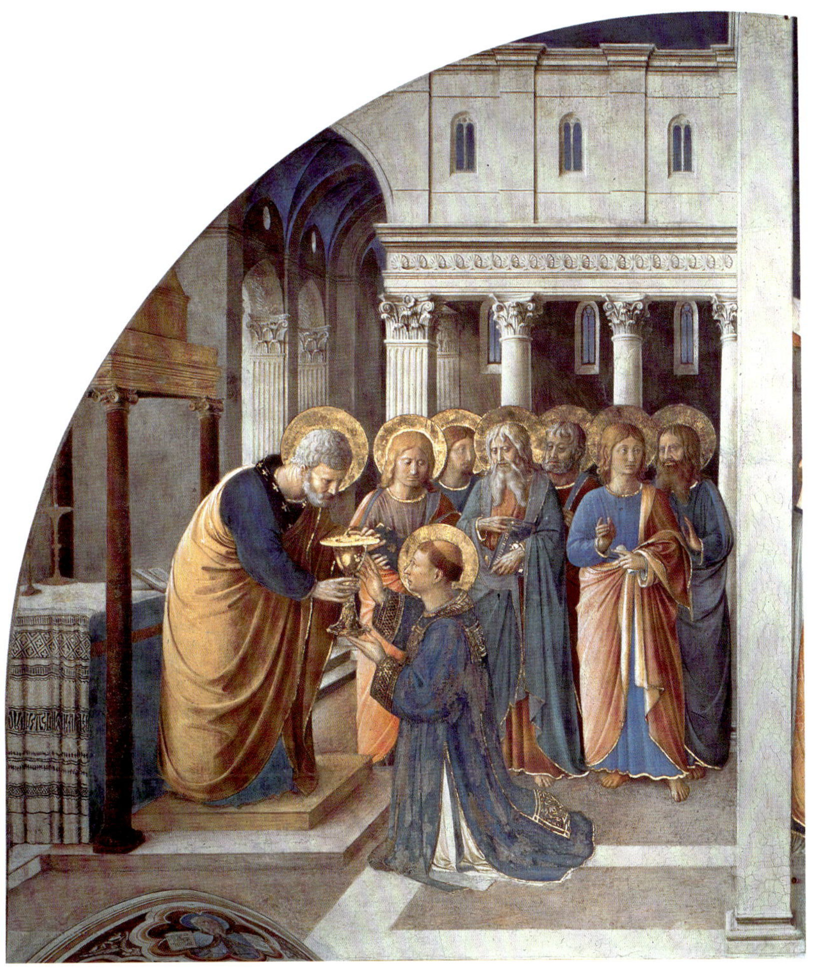

Figure 126. Fra Angelico. *Saint Peter Ordaining Saint Stephen*. 1447–48. Cappella Niccolina, Vatican Palace, Vatican City

would not stand up to the inspection of a structural engineer: the architecture is imaginary and the styles are mixed, but to the privileged viewer of the chapel, Pope Nicholas—a practicing architect himself, who had rebuilt the bishop's palace in Bologna—the panoply of constructions and urban spaces would have had great resonance. The epitaph on the pope's tomb noted that he had restored morals, walls, churches, and buildings ("*mores, moenia, templa, domos*").[65] There are numerous references to his renovation of such well-known landmarks of Rome as its ancient walls, prominently depicted in the *Expulsion and Stoning of Saint Stephen,* and the Castel Sant'Angelo, whose exterior walls—Manetti writes—the pope had plastered and painted. The round-towered building in the background of *Saint Stephen Addressing the Sanhedrin* may refer to the latter project. Nicholas also transformed the Vatican palace, adding a tower to the Vatican's walls, and enclosing a garden, which Manetti called a "paradise." Structures like this one appear in *Saint Stephen Distributing Alms.*[66]

Nicholas's most ambitious project was for the basilica of Saint Peter. Angelico set three scenes (*Saint Peter Ordaining Saint Stephen* [fig. 126]; *The Ordination of Saint Lawrence*; and *Saint Lawrence Distributing Alms*) in Early Christian basilicas, which are obvious references to Saint Peter's and to Nicholas's plans for allowing more light into the dark church. Manetti describes the basilica as if the transepts and tribune had been opened up with oculi, or round windows, noting that they illuminated not only the cupola but showed all the faithful a visible example of the glory of God.[67] Work on the church did not take place until 1450–51, after Angelico's frescoes were executed, but the system of oculi described by Manetti was never actually realized (only Gothic-style mullioned windows were constructed).[68] However, the windows and, especially, the modern oculi depicted in the basilicas in Angelico's frescoes reflect the most current thinking about how the illumination of Saint Peter's might be improved.

Oculi were an architectural element that interested builders and architectural theorists in this period, and in 1453 Bernardo Rossellino installed oculi in the Early Christian Roman basilica of Santo Stefano Rotondo (another reconstruction paid for by Nicholas V in 1453).[69] In Leon Battista Alberti's treatise on the art of building, the *De re aedificatoria,* presented to the pope about 1450–52, he noted that the ancients only used the quadrangular shape—perhaps a criticism of the round windows that were being proposed for Saint Peter's and were appearing elsewhere.[70] They were a prominent feature of the dome of Florence Cathedral, and in 1443 Rossellino had served on a committee, also including Brunelleschi, Ghiberti, and Paolo dal Pozzo Toscanelli, which debated whether the glass of these windows should be clear or colored and with or without figural representations.[71] All but one member of the committee (a Franciscan friar, who later changed his mind) opted for colored glass with figures. Toscanelli argued that the oculi were more for ornament than for light ("*più tosto ad adorneza che per lume*"), and even Brunelleschi clearly stated that they would appear richer with images.[72] However, they were discussing a well-worn topic, for, from the start, Brunelleschi's project for the cupola had been criticized for not allowing enough light into the church.[73] In 1426, its principal opponent, Giovanni di Gherardo da Prato, citing medieval optical treatises, had argued that natural light not broken by the refraction of a window would fall flat and not illuminate the cupola.[74] The play of light across space and over surfaces was an important concern of architects, but one that they shared with painters, who had to calculate the source of light carefully in order to give form and dimensionality to the figures.

Alberti asserted that windows in sacred buildings should be placed in the upper part of the wall so that only the sky was visible: "The awe that is naturally generated by darkness encourages a sense of veneration in the mind; and there is always some austerity about majesty. What is more, the flame,

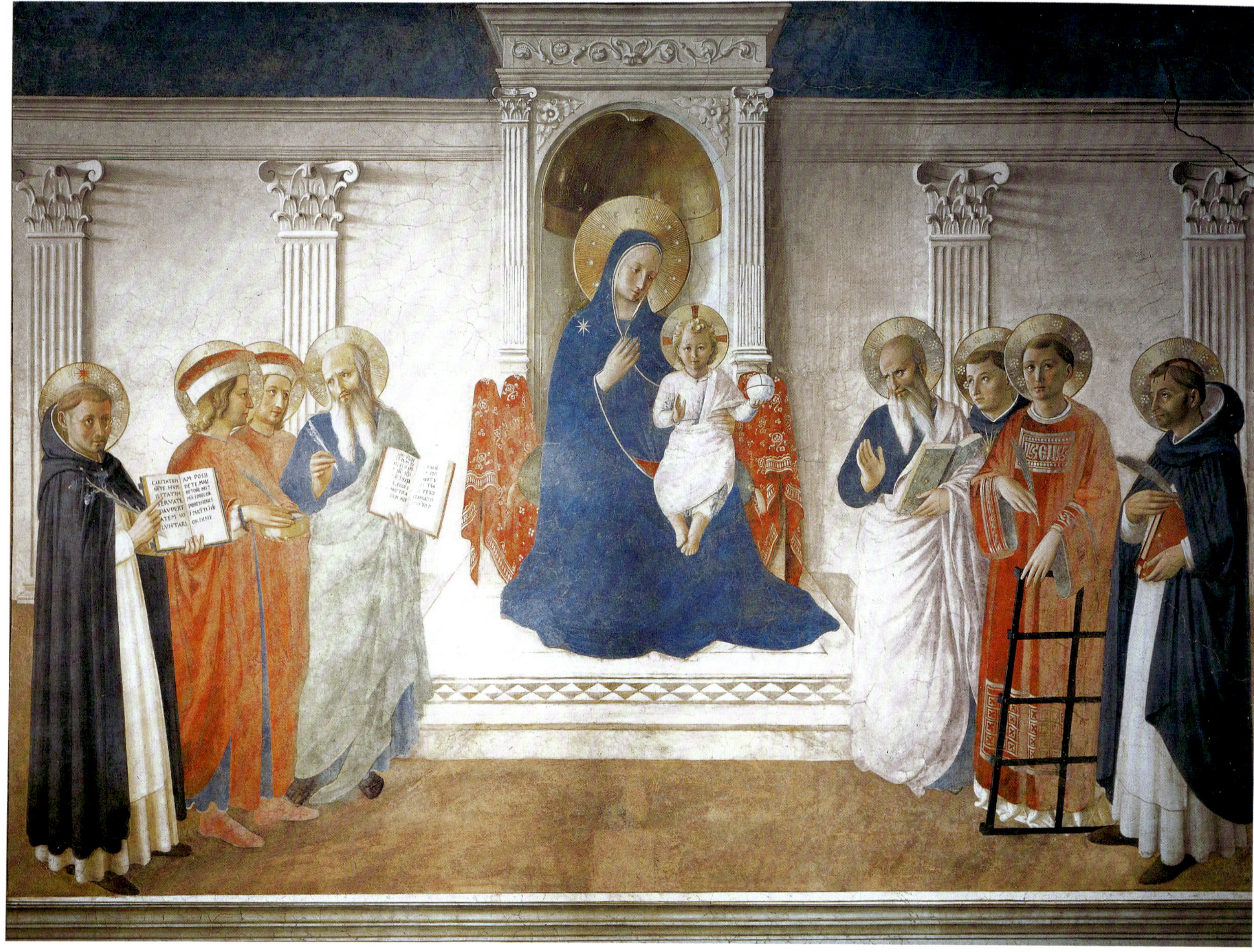

Figure 127. Fra Angelico. *Virgin and Child Enthroned, with Saints Dominic, Cosmas, Damian, Mark, John the Evangelist, Thomas Aquinas, Lawrence, and Peter Martyr (Madonna of the Shadows)*. Museo di San Marco, Florence

which should burn in a temple, and which is the most divine ornament of religious worship, looks faint in too much light."[75] Although there are no candles depicted in Angelico's Vatican frescoes, the contrast between the darkness of the interior and the light in the distant reaches of a sacred building is particularly well expressed in *Saint Peter Ordaining Saint Stephen* (fig. 126).

Of course, light was not only a concern of architects, but an essential quality in painting, and of Angelico's work in particular. In *De pictura* Alberti wrote at length about how to depict the fall of light across an object as well as in a *historia*, or a painted scene. He defined the problem as the "reception of light" (*luminum receptione*), which he described as one of the three principal elements of the art of painting (circumscription and composition being the others).[76] Angelico had been particularly attentive to the painting of light in the frescoes in San Marco. The fresco known as the *Madonna of the Shadows* (fig. 127) in the long corridor of the dormitory, as its title implies, shows the shadows cast by a raking light from the window at the end of the hall. A specific light source and a fleeting moment in the time of day is rendered in a way that Alberti might have found too literal and that Angelico avoids in the Vatican frescoes, but that seems to echo earlier artistic concerns; Cennino Cennini in his *Craftsman's Handbook,* written about 1400, had instructed artists to be aware of the source of light (particularly in the windows of chapels) and to apply relief and shadow accordingly.[77] Rarely, however, was light depicted as so fugitive as in Angelico's San Marco frescoes. In those on the cell walls, each painted near or next to a window, Angelico played on the temporal quality of natural light—often contrasting it with light from a divine source (as in the *Annunciation* in cell 3)—by making it appear to shimmer across surfaces. He might have been taking up the idea, here, also elucidated by Alberti, that when an artist wishes to study the play of light on a three-dimensional object, it helps if he dims his vision by half closing his eyes to make the light appear less strong.[78] In general, the effects of light depicted in the Vatican frescoes are much less temporal than at San Marco. Light has a unifying effect, but only, as Alberti recommended, in the way in which it picks out surface details and sets them in relief. Such is the case in the Vatican frescoes, giving the figures a statuesque appearance and the scenes an intentionally timeless quality.

The Vatican chapel bears Angelico's name, and, through the ages, its decoration has been his most famous work,[79] but the frescoes nevertheless are a product of his workshop. The settings, the distribution of the figures, and the unified lighting bespeak Angelico, but much of the execution appears to have been entrusted to Benozzo Gozzoli. There exist three Gozzoli drawings related to the chapel, one for figures in the scene of *Saint Lawrence Distributing the Goods of the Church* and *Saint Lawrence before Decius* (Windsor Castle, Royal Library), and studies for the *Saint Matthew* (Fitzwilliam Museum, Cambridge) and the *Saint Mark* (Musée Condé, Chantilly) on the vault of the ceiling. While the drawings may have been made as records of the frescoes, they are copies of the parts of the frescoes by Gozzoli himself—proof, in my mind, of Gozzoli's participation in the design stage of the cycle. The Windsor drawing includes figures that were used in two different scenes, indicating that he was involved in the overall planning from the beginning and was not just assigned individual areas to paint; indeed, the frescoing would have begun with the vaulting, for which Gozzoli designed the two saints.[80]

The attitudes of the Dominican order toward work and the regulation of its convents and its activities might have influenced how Angelico organized his workshop. The Dominicans are the Order of Preachers. Although the artist was not trained to be a professional preacher, which required a three-year study of theology, he did attain the position of prior vicar and then served as a prior of his convent in Fiesole.[81] This meant that he reached a level of responsibility that was on par with that of a qualified preacher, because priors controlled who could preach.[82] In fact, his activity as an artist should be viewed in the context of the preaching profession. The Dominican *Constitutions,* or Rules, required that each preacher be given a socius when he was sent out in the world: "The socius given to a preacher was to obey him like his own prior."[83] Gozzoli was documented in the payments for the Orvieto frescoes as Angelico's "*consotio,*" and he clearly acted as such in the execution of the Vatican frescoes.[84] In the 1442 tax declaration of Gozzoli's grandfather, when the painter was already a mature twenty-four, it is stated that Benozzo "was learning to paint." The Florentine tax authorities did not accept this explanation, but given Gozzoli's role within the Angelico workshop, it was a truthful statement.[85] Gozzoli's subordinate yet easily recognizable full participation in Angelico's major projects at San Marco, the Vatican, and Orvieto suggest a new interpretation of workshop organization, and one that might well be informed by the close preacher/socius relationships that the Dominican order encouraged. Certainly, Angelico's reliance on Gozzoli or on such other collaborators as Zanobi Strozzi would have been in no way frowned upon in the order.

The relationship between Angelico and Gozzoli appears to have been different from the usual early-fifteenth-century Florentine artistic partnerships, which for the most part were business oriented and lasted for circumscribed periods of generally three years.[86] A stylistic unity even on a common project was not necessarily required, the most famous example being Masolino's and Masaccio's widely different frescoes in the Brancacci Chapel. The pattern established in Trecento Florence of large family workshops like those of the Cioni (Orcagna) and Gaddi, which engaged many assistants and outside partners for important undertakings, had died out by the mid-fifteenth century. Unable to assemble a workshop along those lines, Angelico created a new type of organization following a model adapted from his religious order.

From the time of the San Marco project in Florence, Angelico had become a superb administrator and manager of artistic enterprises. Cosimo de' Medici, Saint Antoninus, Eugenius IV, and Nicholas V all recognized these abilities. No other workshop in Florence, or elsewhere in Italy, could have handled such complex projects. Angelico's membership in the Dominican order made his workshop thrive and endowed it with special resources. While his collaborators, such as Gozzoli, were not members of the order, the organization to which Angelico belonged provided him with a built-in administrative structure and stellar political and ecclesiastical contacts, allowing him to expand his activities throughout Central Italy. He also operated outside the restrictions imposed by guild rules, so that he could take on major assistants like Strozzi or Gozzoli without them being accountable to the guild.[87]

With the able Gozzoli working as his *consotio,* Angelico could concentrate on his roles as overseer, theoretician, and theologian, functioning essentially as a preacher and employing not words but pictures. After his death, the artist was revered as a theologian, and was given the name Angelico in direct homage to the greatest theologian of his order, Saint Thomas Aquinas, who was known as the Angelic, or Seraphic, Doctor.[88] During the last decade of his activity Angelico created three cycles of paintings of episodes in the life of Christ (the frescoes in the now destroyed Chapel of the Sacrament for Eugenius IV; the doors of the silver chest at Santissima Annunziata for Piero de' Medici; and the now destroyed frescoes in the cloister at Santa Maria sopra Minerva, Rome, for Cardinal Juan de Torquemada) and one cycle devoted to Early Christian history (the legends of Saints Stephen and Lawrence in the Vatican). In each, Angelico's exploration of new ways of depicting sacred events was equivalent to the sermons of a Dominican preacher. In 1452, Aeneas Sylvius Piccolomini (later Pope Pius II) wrote a letter to the Swiss humanist scholar and amateur painter Niklas von Wyle in which he associated painting with oratory, noting that the aims of the two disciplines in effect mirrored each other. Piccolomini also recounted the history of pagan and Christian oratory up to the time of Petrarch, and examined the revival of painting under Giotto, comparing the similar trajectories of the two arts.[89] This would not have been lost on Angelico, who was intimately familiar with the practice of preaching and its humanist conterpart, oratory, as well as with the by-then commonly held theories about the revival of painting by the Florentine master Giotto. Working for a pope intent on the *renovatio* of Rome, Angelico found an outlet for his voice as a modern painter on the walls of the Vatican, and participated fully in the humanist project to further the art of painting.

1. G. Manetti 1999 ed., pp. 178–91.
2. The medal is recorded in Buonanni 1699, pp. 51–53, ill. on pl. after p. 48. N. T. Whitman (1991, p. 820) claims that only Andrea Guazzalotti's 1455 medal of Nicholas V was made during the pope's lifetime or shortly after his death; the subject has not otherwise been very well investigated. See B. Paolozzi Strozzi, in Paolozzi Strozzi 2000, pp. 81–82. Some of the medals were made about 1664 by Girolamo Paladino. See Modesti 1988, pp. 7–57, esp. pp. 29–32; Attwood 1989, pp. 24–27.
3. The inscription is found on ancient Roman coins (*Urbs Roma Felix*), but the term has long had Christian associations. Paulinus of Aquileia's eighth-century hymn to the apostle Peter contains the much-repeated verse: "*O Roma felix, quae tantorum principum / Es purpurata pretioso sanguine*" ("O Happy Rome, which is made purple by the prized blood of so many princes").
4. Gilbert 1975, p. 260.
5. Strehlke 1998, p. 54.
6. This was common practice. For an example in Monza, see C. B. Strehlke, in B. Agosti et al. 1998, pp. 24–27.
7. G. Agosti and Hirst 1996, p. 683 n. 7.
8. M. Boskovits, in Toscano and Capitelli 2002, pp. 174–75.
9. Ficarra 1968, p. 130.
10. Meiss 1951, pp. 76–77.
11. Draper 1992, pp. 82–86.
12. Many details differ from the original. Some, such as the presence of several Franciscan friars being received by angels at the gates of Paradise, might be an indication of the patronage or original purpose of the print. Rosselli also made engravings after works by Uccello and by Botticelli. The plate of the *Last Judgment* is listed in the inventory of the workshop of Rosselli's son Alessandro (d. 1525). J. A. Levenson, in Levenson, Oberhuber, and Sheehan 1973, pp. 60–62.
13. De Simone 2002, p. 55, fig. 46.
14. Galleria Nazionale di Palazzo Venezia, and Gemäldegalerie, Staatliche Museen Preussicher Kulturbesitz.
15. Pope-Hennessy 1974, p. 221.
16. The painting was bought from a Roman baker in 1811 and then owned by Cardinal Fesch. It was sold at the auction of the Fesch collection in 1845 to Prince Musignano (probably Charles-Lucien Bonaparte, Prince of Canino and Musignanon [1803–1857]). It then is recorded in England and later in Berlin in 1884. A copy of it, in the Museo Civico, Catania, most likely dates to the nineteenth century and has not been properly studied or published. It shows slight changes in the composition, which might indicate the copyist knew the Berlin painting before it was cut down (see the Alinari photograph, neg. no. 55340; *edizione* 1952). Pope-Hennessy (1974) records another variant of the composition attributed to the Master of Marradi. This is actually the *Last Judgment* by Zanobi Strozzi (cat. 45), which is derived from the Berlin and Florence paintings of the same subject and was partially repainted in the fifteenth century with figures added.
17. The painting was inventoried in 1750 in the Roman collection of Cardinal Neri Maria Corsini (1685–1770), nephew of Pope Clement XII (r. 1730–40), as having been presented to the cardinal by Baron Mantica, a Roman nobleman. See Magnanimi 1980, p. 118, inv. nos. 220–222, p. 124. A note added by Corsini's curator, Gaetano Bottari, contains the information "*e dal Cardl Bardi*" ("and by Cardinal Bardi")—a reference to Cardinal Girolamo Bardi, a Florentine, whose career had been linked to that of the Corsini pope; he was nominated a cardinal in 1743. See Moroni 1840–61, vol. III (1840), pp. 123–24. The original owner and place of production are not known.
18. Boskovits 1976b, pp. 43, 45.
19. Pope-Hennessy 1974, pp. 235–36, fig. 115.
20. Pia Palladino (see p. 251) quotes Cennino Cennini about drawing on tinted paper: he specifically mentions the colors pink and violet.
21. Several passages from the writings of Saint Jerome, which Renaissance ecclesiastics and humanists would have known, describe purple codices as great vanities. In the preface to the Book of Job in the Vulgate, he wrote: "Let those who will keep the old books with their gold and silver letters on purple skins, or, to follow the ordinary phrase, in 'uncial characters,' loads of writing rather than manuscripts, if only they will leave for me and mine, our poor pages and copies which are less remarkable for beauty than for accuracy." Jerome 1893 ed., p. 492. Saint Jerome also mentions such luxurious codices in epistles XXII (32) and CVII (12).
22. G. Mariani Canova, in Alexander 1994, pp. 23–25. See the manuscript of Petrarch's *Canzoniere* and *I Trionfi* (Victoria and Albert Museum, London, L. 101-1947), illuminated in Padua about 1463–64: J. J. G. Alexander, in Alexander 1994, pp. 152–54, no. 71; Alexander 1970, pp. 27–40. See, recently, on the revival of Renaissance purple manuscripts, Mariani Canova 1998, pp. 339–71.
23. "*A Verona vidi in Libro antico nella sacristia, el Vangelistario in carte del vestimento di Jhesù, tutte le lettere d'ariento e ove si nominava Jhesù erano lettere d'oro*"; quoted in Lowe 1934–66, vol. IV (1947), no. 481, p. 22; cited in Alexander 1970, pp. 27–40.
24. Lowe 1934–66, vol. III (1938), no. 281, p. 3.
25. There is little information on the provenance of the drawings. When they were sold at auction in Amsterdam in 1927 they were in an eighteenth-century volume bearing "the royal arms"—presumably those of the Dutch royal house of Nassau-Orange.
26. The miniature is in the Galleria degli Uffizi. Recently, Andrea De Marchi attributed it, with some question, to the Perugian Benedetto Bonfigli. Seemingly dating before Frederick's coronation as emperor, the portrait, De Marchi suggests, might have been a present for Frederick's betrothed, Eleanor of Portugal, whom he married by proxy in 1451 and whom he finally met in Siena in February 1452. See A. De Marchi, in Christiansen 2005, pp. 210–12.
27. It is said that in Padua, which Frederick III visited in January 1452, he invited the painter and antiquarian Francesco Squarcione to call on him:

see Scardeone 1560, p. 370. M. Meiss (1961, p. 61) is dismissive of this notice.

28. C. B. Strehlke, in B. Agosti et al. 1998, pp. 29–30.
29. Cole Ahl 1996, colorpl. 1.
30. Alberti 1972 ed., pp. 89, 91.
31. Ibid., p. 89.
32. Pope-Hennessy 1974, p. 214. In my 1998 monograph on Fra Angelico (p. 51), I mistakenly confused this nephew with the worker Antonio di Giovanello, who fell from the scaffolding in Orvieto Cathedral and died; see Orlandi 1964, p. 111.
33. Gozzoli had a contract with Ghiberti, which lasted until January 1447. He is first documented in Rome in May of that year, but could have arrived earlier.
34. Actually, Strozzi's whereabouts in 1446–47, when he rented his house in Fiesole to a group of widows, is unknown. Lillie 1986, pp. 142–43, 150 n. 62.
35. They were Pietro Giacomo from Forlì in Romagna, Carlo di ser Lazzaro from Narni in Umbria, and Jacopo d'Antonio from Poli, a town just outside Rome.
36. Garibaldi 1998; reviewed by the present author (1999, pp. 477–79). See also catalogue number 30.
37. De Marchi 1985, pp. 53–57.
38. The brothers Bernardo and Marco di Bartolomeo Bartolini. See Orlandi 1964, pp. 20 n. 2, 47.
39. T. Biganti, in Garibaldi 1998, p. 111 n. 56.
40. An X-radiographic analysis of the three existing sections of the predella has not been undertaken to determine if they were originally painted on a single plank, as would likely have been the case. The predella would also have had elements at the ends, probably with coats of arms, as well as between the scenes (possibly with representations of angels, as on the predella with scenes from the life of Saint Dominic, in Cortona); these are now missing.
41. The date and original location of this work has been much discussed: see Pope-Hennessy 1974, pp. 211–12; Hood 1993, pp. 102–7; Strehlke 1998, pp. 44–45. See also pages 146, 229–30.
42. The other surviving panel from this complex is Pesellino's *The Journey of the Magi: Melchior Crossing the Red Sea* in Williamstown, Massachusetts. Alfonso's heraldic colors are displayed on several boats, indicating the possible destination of the paintings—or, at the very least, referring to the king and to the conquest of Naples. For a discussion of the attributions, see E. Fahy, in Di Lorenzo 2001, pp. 71–75; and catalogue number 54 A.
43. Boskovits 1976 b, pp. 43–45, fig. 16.
44. Eubel 1901, p. 74. San Sisto remained without a titular cardinal until 1471 (ibid., p. 65).
45. Barstow 1990; Hood 1993, pp. 227–28; De Simone 2002, pp. 41–87.
46. De Simone 2002, p. 46, fig. 2.
47. Strehlke 2003a, p. 541, fig. 62.
48. G. Manetti's biography of the pope (1999 ed., pp. 88–89) mentions the period he spent as a tutor without identifying the patrons because of their subsequent disgrace. The later biographer Vespasiano da Bisticci (1963 ed., p. 32) is less circumspect and identifies the men.
49. Strehlke 2003 b, p. 16. Angelico's and Albizzi's families remained in contact until at least 1441, when Angelico's sister received an inheritance from Jacopo's widow.
50. Padoa Rizzo 1981, pp. 15–17; Strehlke 1998, p. 53.
51. In his later years, angry with the Medici, Eugenius had engaged another Florentine banker, Tommaso Spinelli; De Roover 1963, p. 198.
52. Orlandi 1964, p. 189.
53. Pandimiglio 1987, pp. 100–101.
54. He also did some unspecified work on the tribune at Saint Peter's, which seems to have been located under the apse where there was an Early Christian mosaic that had been restored in Late Medieval times.
55. The chapel may have been finished earlier as Angelico seems to have been in Florence in October 1448 (see cat. 60). However, trips to and from Rome and Florence may have been more frequent than we have documents for, and, as discussed below, Gozzoli actually executed most of the frescoes. It is interesting that, in 1450, when he commissioned an altarpiece for the Certosa in Bologna, Nicholas did not turn to the Angelico team but rather to the Venetian Vivarini. This may well be because the Florentines were not available. On Nicholas's commissioning of that altarpiece, see Aurigema 2000, pp. 415–24.
56. For an analysis of Gozzoli's role in the cycle, see Cole Ahl 1996, pp. 24–33. Two books on the chapel were published after its restoration and illustrate it fully: see Venchi et al. 1999; Buranelli 2001. A. Nesselrath's essay, in Venchi et al. 1999 (esp. pp. 80–92), places great importance on Gozzoli's participation.
57. Borsook 1980, pp. 81, 103.
58. Salatino 1992, p. 197. This unpublished dissertation is a superb study of the humanist world of Nicholas V and its importance for the Vatican frescoes. On Agli, see D'Addario 1960, pp. 400–401.
59. S. Romano 1992, pp. 25–26.
60. Salatino 1992, p. 202.
61. Miglio 1975, pp. 10–12.
62. Salatino 1992, p. 115. See also Stinger 1985, pp. 170–74.
63. Burroughs 1990, pp. 58–59.
64. Salatino 1992, pp. 219–20.
65. Pastor 1938–61, vol. II (1949), p. 314.
66. Cantatore 2000, pp. 399–410; Frommel 2004, pp. 144–68.
67. G. Manetti 1999 ed., pp. 147–48.
68. Mack 1982, p. 63; Frommel 1997, p. 107.
69. Mack 1987, pp. 35–36, 50–51.
70. Alberti 1988 ed., p. 223 (7:12).
71. The document is published in Guasti 1857, pp. 76–77, document 201. See also Haines 1983, pp. 126–27.
72. Guasti 1857, p. 77.
73. Saalman 1959, pp. 11–20.
74. Giovanni di Gherardo wrote: "If the sun should enter the window without being interrupted by glass and was broken on the opposite pier, it would light [the octagon] by reflection. Now, does anyone think that this reflection is of such force that it would reflect upwards a distance of more than seventy *braccia*. I am certain that it would not. All reasoning makes clear to me and you could find it [written] in the treatises *De speculis* and *Prospettivis*. Now imagine how much light the windows will give when the light is interrupted by glass. You have an example of that in Santa Liperata [Florence Cathedral] in the front windows over the doors" (Saalman 1959, p. 13).
75. Alberti 1988 ed., p. 223 (7:12). For an analysis of Alberti's ideas on sacred architecture, see Lawson 2001, pp. 45–68.
76. Alberti 1972 ed., pp. 66–67, 86–93.
77. Cennini 1960 ed., p. 6 (chap. 9).
78. Alberti 1972 ed., pp. 100–101.
79. Strehlke 1998, pp. 91–93.
80. Cole Ahl 1996, pp. 32–33.
81. Angelico was prior vicar in 1432, 1433, and 1436, and prior from April 1450 to June 1452; see Orlandi 1964, pp. 40–41, 114–15.
82. Hood 1993, p. 299.
83. Ibid.
84. Cole Ahl 1996, p. 38.
85. D. Cole Ahl (ibid., p. 283 n. 16) interprets the statement as a tax dodge, but it seems, in fact, to reflect Gozzoli's actual situation in Angelico's shop.
86. On partnerships in Florence, see Procacci 1960 a, pp. 3–70. For the partnership of Masolino and Masaccio, see R. Bellucci and C. Frosinini, in Strehlke and Frosinini 2002, p. 86.
87. Strozzi was never a guild member and Gozzoli was enrolled only in the Florentine Compagnia dei Pittori, not the painters' guild.
88. Strehlke 1998, p. 8.

89. "*Gaudeo igitur, quod te pictorem et oratorem simul video.*" Piccolomini 1918 ed., pp. 100–101; Spencer 1957, p. 27; Salatino 1992, p. 207. Piero della Francesca gives a similar account of the art of literature during the reign of Emperor Augustus and of the pictorial arts—in particular, his own painting—under the patronage of Federigo da Montefeltro, in the preface to the *Libellus de quinque corporibus regularibus* (Piero della Francesca 1995 ed., vol. I, fol. 1r.). Comparisons with ancient glories were equally valid for Angelico. In the epitaph on the tomb of Fra Angelico in Santa Maria sopra Minerva, Rome, the name of Apelles is evoked. See Strehlke 1998, pp. 8, 67 n. 1.

FRA ANGELICO AND BENOZZO GOZZOLI

36.

A.

Virgin and Child Enthroned, with Saints Peter, Paul, and George (?), Four Angels, and a Donor

Tempera on panel: overall, 29.7 x 29.1 cm (11 ¾ x 11 ½ in.); picture suface, 25.8 x 24.8 cm (10 ⅛ x 9 ¾ in.)
Museum of Fine Arts, Boston. Gift of Mrs. W. Scott Fitz (14.416)

B.

The Holy Face (Volto Santo)

Tempera on panel, 29.5 x 29 cm (11 ⅝ x 11 ⅜ in.)
Private collection

Originally the front and reverse sides of a single painted panel, these two images remained together until the middle of the nineteenth century. When they were seen by J. A. Crowe and G. B. Cavalcaselle in 1869 in the collection of Baron Triqueti of Paris, the two sides had already been separated; they are illustrated side by side in the sale catalogue of the collection of Mme Lee-Childe in 1886.[1] From that point on their histories diverged: the *Virgin and Child* remained largely accessible to scholars and the public, first in the collection of Édouard Aynard in Lyon,[2] and then, from 1914, in the Museum of Fine Arts, Boston, while the *Holy Face* "disappeared," until its rediscovery only twenty years ago;[3] the two paintings are reunited here for the first time, as far as is known, since 1886.

In explaining some of the peculiarities of the composition of the Boston *Virgin and Child*—specifically, the prominent isolation of the figure of a warrior saint, presumed to be Saint George, on the right side of the painting—Stefano Orlandi advanced a hypothesis associating this panel with the cession of the church of San Giorgio sulla Costa in Florence to the Observant Dominicans of Fiesole in January 1435 (see cat. 34). According to this theory, the kneeling donor at the left would be the parish priest, Tonnero de' Castellani, whose renunciation of his benefice allowed the Dominicans to take possession of San Giorgio pending resolution of their dispute with the Silvestrines at San Marco.[4] Although accepted by a number of scholars,[5] this proposal is unlikely for a number of reasons. First, the kneeling donor is shown wearing an ermine almuce, indicative of his rank as a canon—a dignity to which Tonnero de'Castellani is not known to have been elevated—and he is presented by Saints Peter and Paul, who are neither his name saints nor patrons of his other benefice, Sant'Andrea a Mosciano.[6] Furthermore, the date of 1435 is entirely inappropriate for the style of the painting, which should, instead, be situated among the late works of Angelico's Roman period. The octagonal form of the panel, its scale, and the fact that it was painted on both sides also argue for its manufacture somewhere other than in Florence, where this category of object had no precedent and generated no following.

A Roman provenance for the Boston panel, appropriate to the presence of Saints Peter and Paul on the left, also is suggested by the subject of the reverse side. The *Volto Christi,* or face of Christ, was an image much venerated in Rome, especially in the form seen here, which follows the Greek type of the Mandylion. Supposed to be the "*vera icon,*" or true image, of the face of Christ, it is distinguished from other representations of the Holy Face—such as a painting by Angelico now in Livorno and also included in this exhibition (cat. 33)—by the expression of passive, non-suffering dignity. The image of the *Volto Christi* as painted on the reverse of the Boston panel, framed by an octagonal surround, appears as a prominent feature of the silver cover of the principal icon in the Lateran basilica in Rome, the Acheropita—an image of Christ enthroned that is installed on the altar in the pope's private oratory, known as the Sancta Sanctorum. Throughout the Late Middle Ages, the pope celebrated Easter Mass at this altar, and it was here that a newly elected pope was vested and the keys to the Lateran and Vatican basilicas were delivered to him.[7] Although he remains unidentified, it is not difficult to imagine that the donor portrayed in the Boston panel was a canon either of the Lateran basilica or of Saint Peter's, and that the commission of this painting may have been roughly coincidental with the election of Nicholas V as pope on March 6, 1447.

In 1447 Fra Angelico was documented at work on the frescoes in the vault of the Cappella di San Brizio in Orvieto Cathedral and on the (now lost) frescoes in the Chapel of the Sacrament in the Vatican palace with Benozzo Gozzoli as his independently paid partner, or "*consotio.*" Benozzo may

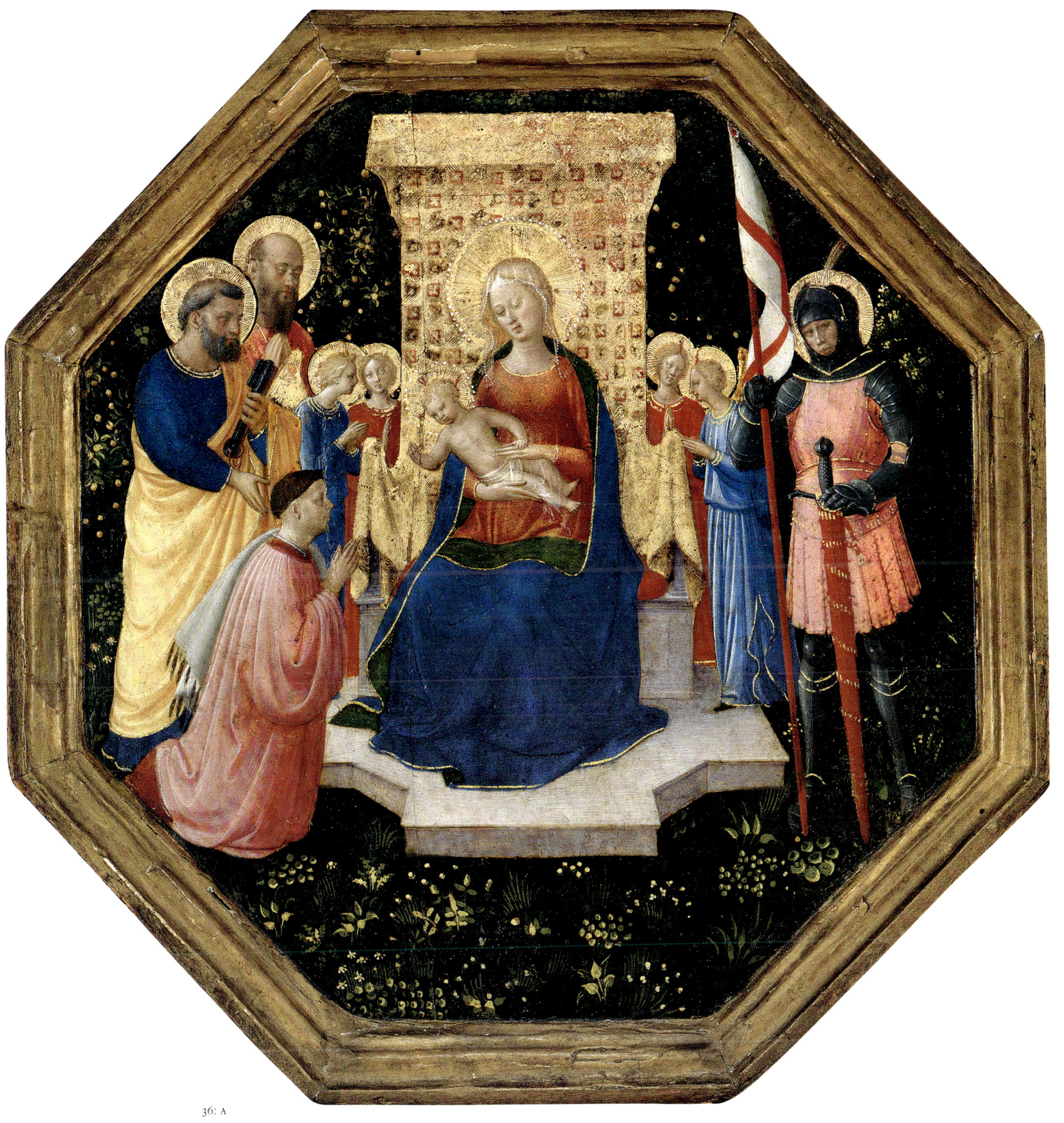

36: A

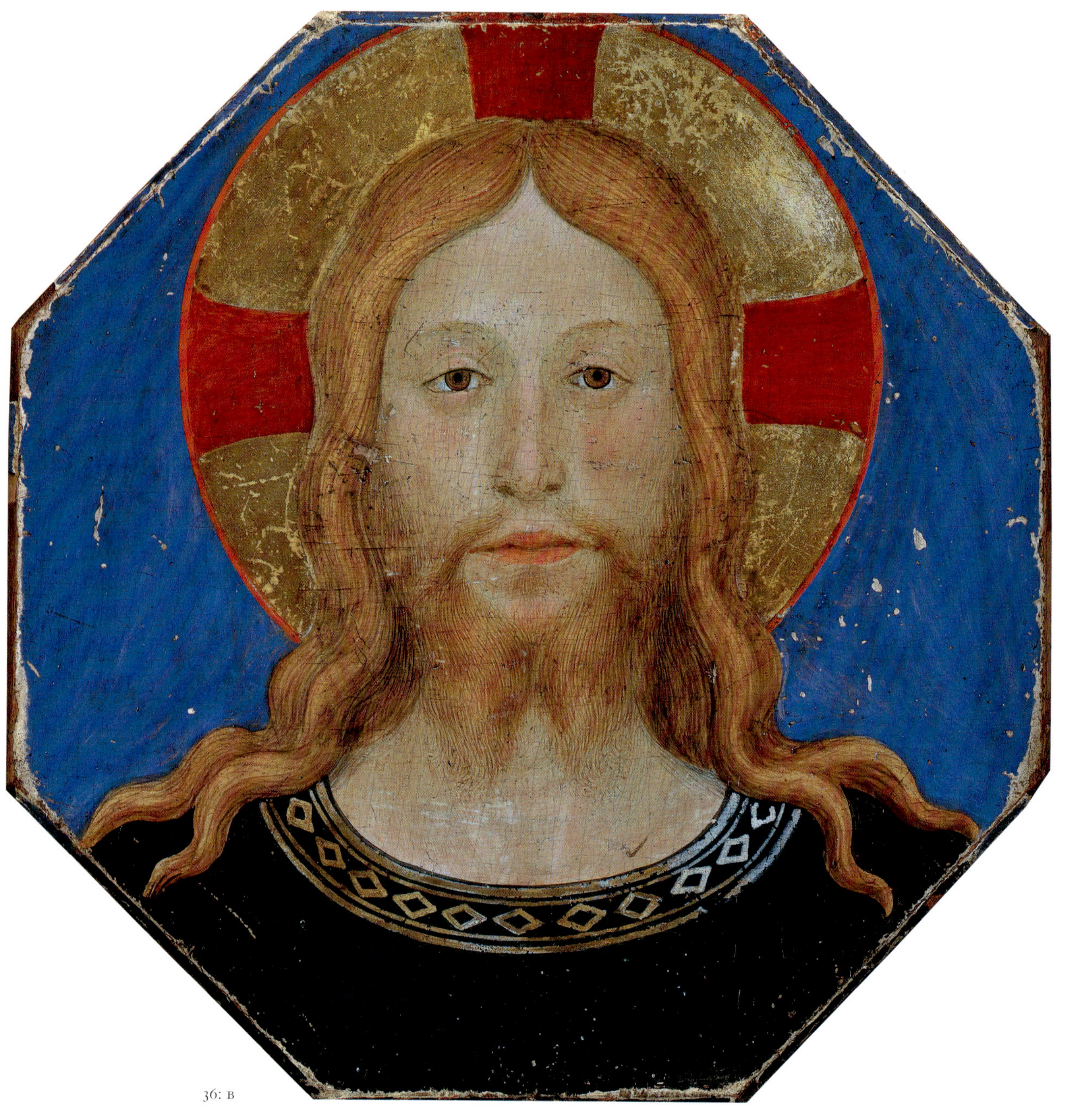

36: B

also have actively participated in the execution of the frescoes in the Cappella Niccolina at the Vatican, which, although not documented, must date to 1447 or the following year; it is these works that provide a context for the figure style and spatial structure of the Boston panel. Furthermore, while only three scholars have doubted the attribution to Fra Angelico of this painting,[8] it should be acknowledged that its attenuated, weightless figures and the comparative uncertainty of their spatial relationships, as well as the decorative use of highlighting, especially in the background foliage, more closely relate to Benozzo Gozzoli's earliest identified efforts as a painter than to Angelico's mature production. The same affectations, although more pronounced, are found in a small and exceptionally delicate *Madonna of Humility* in the Accademia Carrara in Bergamo (fig. 186) and in an even more intimate *Virgin and Child Enthroned, with Saints Dominic and Sixtus (?)* in the Courtauld Institute of Art Gallery in London (fig. 187), astutely recognized by Miklós Boskovits as early works by Gozzoli.[9] These paintings and the Boston panel are certainly by the same hand, but it is reasonable to assume that whereas the Bergamo and Courtauld pictures are conceived as imitations of works by Angelico, in the case of the Boston panel the young painter may have been working directly over a detailed drawing provided by Fra Angelico, given that the perspective of the

Virgin's throne is more ambitious and more accurately resolved than in any independent painting by Gozzoli.

The image of the head of Christ, from the reverse of the Boston panel, also seems to reflect the participation of two artists—presumably, Angelico and Gozzoli, or possibly another of Angelico's assistants named in documents of 1447[10]—one serving as designer and one as executant. Such details as the flatly embroidered collar of Christ's tunic or the symmetrical waves of hair falling on his shoulders lack the sophistication to be expected from an autograph work by Angelico at this date. However, close scrutiny of Christ's eyes reveals that the left one is expertly rendered as a carefully inflected orb while the right eye is an uninspired copy of the first. Again, it is not unreasonable to assume that Angelico provided a drawing for this figure and may have contributed some details of its final form, but it is otherwise correct to classify the painting as a workshop product. LK

1. Crowe and Cavalcaselle 1869–76, vol. II, p. 164 n. 78; sold, Hôtel Drouot, Paris, May 4, 1886, lot 1.
2. Sold, Galerie Georges Petit, Paris, December 4, 1913, lot 35.
3. Boskovits 1983, pp. 12–13; Corsini 1984, pp. 16–19.
4. Orlandi 1964, pp. 63–64.
5. Baldini 1970, p. 95; Pope-Hennessy 1974, p. 222; Boskovits 1983.
6. Kanter 1994, pp. 144–47.
7. S. Romano 2000, pp. 39–41.
8. Van Marle 1928, pp. 156, 164; Muratoff 1930, p. 59; Pope-Hennessy 1952, p. 197; Pope-Hennessy 1974, p. 222.
9. Boskovits 2002b, pp. 48–50.
10. The documents cite Pietro Jachomo da Furli [Forlì], Giovanni d'Antonio de la Checa, Carlo di ser Lazzaro da Narni, Jachomo d'Antonio da Poli (see Orlandi 1964, pp. 188–89).

FRA ANGELICO

37.

A.

The Dream of Pope Innocent III and Saints Peter and Paul Appearing to Saint Dominic

Tempera on panel, 33.2 x 41.9 cm (13 1/16 x 16 1/2 in.)
Yale University Art Gallery, New Haven. Edwin Austin Abbey Memorial Collection (1937.343)

B.

Christ on the Cross, with the Virgin and Saints Mary Magdalene, John the Evangelist, Monica (?), Augustine (?), Peter Martyr, Thomas Aquinas, Francis, and Elizabeth of Hungary (?)

Tempera on panel, 33.9 x 50.1 cm (13 3/8 x 19 3/4 in.)
The Metropolitan Museum of Art, New York. Bequest of Benjamin Altman, 1913 (14.40.628)

C.

Saint Dominic and His Companions Fed by Angels

Tempera on panel, 35 x 47.7 cm (13 3/4 x 18 3/4 in.)
Staatsgalerie, Stuttgart (Inv. no. 3118)

These three panels, previously not associated with each other, may be supposed to have formed part of a single predella dedicated to episodes from the life of Saint Dominic. All three are approximately the same height; they are closely related to each other stylistically; and all are preserved in a comparably damaged state. Primarily on account of their compromised condition, each of them has been relegated at one time or another to the status of an imitative or studio work, but each is demonstrably an autograph painting of exceptional quality and invention from the period of Fra Angelico's full maturity, following the completion of the San Marco high altarpiece.

The Yale panel (A), the first in narrative sequence, compresses two episodes from the early ministry of Saint Dominic into a relatively constricted pictorial space. Pope Innocent III was initially reluctant to grant Dominic's petition for approval of a rule for a new order of Preachers. One night, dreaming of the ruin of the Lateran basilica, the pope had a vision of Dominic supporting the crumbling church on his shoulder and was immediately persuaded to embrace the new movement. In the event, Dominic and his followers chose to adopt the rule of Saint Augustine, but Innocent III died before their petition could be granted and his successor, Pope Honorius III, eventually approved the rule. Praying afterward in Saint Peter's basilica in Rome, Dominic had a vision of Saints Peter and Paul presenting him with a staff and a book, and instructing him to go forth and preach—a symbolic commission to his order to teach and perform missionary work. In the center of the Yale panel, in the middle distance, Pope Innocent III is visible through a doorway, asleep and dreaming, his vision of Saint Dominic unfolding before him at the left. Dominic, whose black cloak is thrown back over his shoulders to free his arms for his work, braces the crumbling walls of a church, which is rendered in steep foreshortening. The incisive shadow cast by Saint Dominic, the crisp highlights on the moldings and doorframes, and the realistic fissures in the masonry are all affectations characteristic of Fra Angelico's style in this period. The same precise rendering is carried over to the architectural details on the classicizing façade of the building at the right, through the doorway of which Saint Dominic can be seen receiving his vision of Saints Peter and Paul. Although their legibility has been blunted by abrasion, the inventive sophistication of these details, including the elegantly undercut cornice of the doorframe, the exuberant acanthus decoration of the pilaster capitals, and the (now) barely visible niche-like chapel where the vision is enacted are paralleled elsewhere in Fra Angelico's oeuvre only on a monumental scale, in the fresco of the enthroned Madonna (fig. 127) on the east wall of the upper corridor at San Marco or in those in the Cappella Niccolina at the Vatican.

The two episodes portrayed in the Yale panel recur in the first two scenes at the left on the predella to the San Domenico *Coronation of the Virgin*, now in the Louvre, probably painted between 1432 and 1434. The scene of *Saints Peter and Paul Appearing to Saint Dominic* in the Yale panel omits the elaborate colonnaded architecture of the nave of Old Saint Peter's, so beautifully evoked in the Louvre predella (fig. 129),

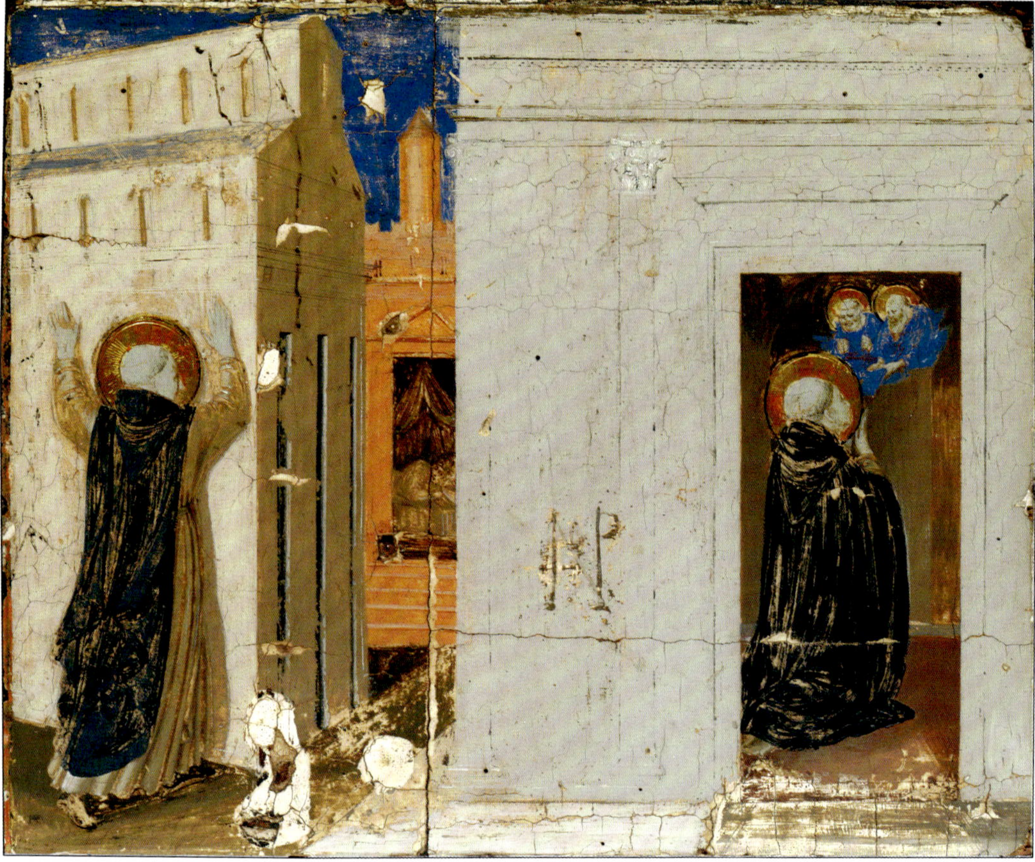

37: A

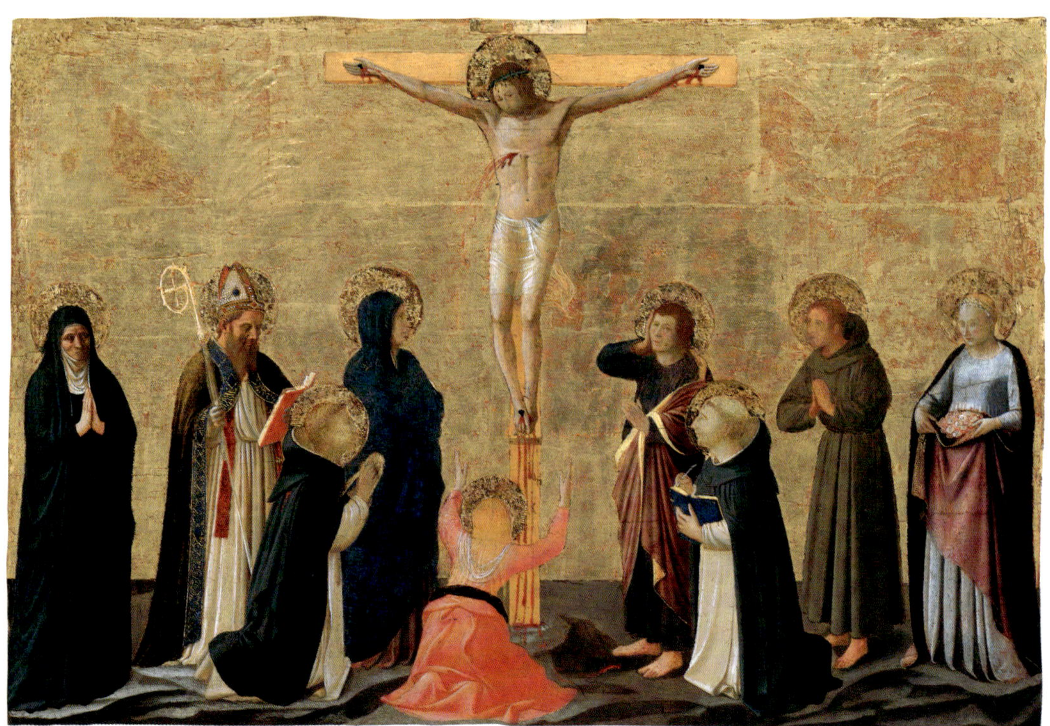

37: B

substituting for it a view through a doorway that is more difficult to render, with its elaborate coordination of shifting scales and light values, but that, at the same time, is better suited to the more restricted horizontal format of the panel. In this form the scene more closely resembles the same episode in the predella to the Tommasi altarpiece, painted for San Domenico in Cortona.[1] The narrative sequence of the Cortona predella also begins at the left with *The Dream of Pope Innocent III,* but that scene and *The Vision of Saints Peter and Paul* are separated there by a vignette of Saint Dominic meeting Saint Francis, which is omitted from the Yale panel.

In both the Louvre and Cortona predellas, the *Vision of Saints Peter and Paul* is followed by a scene of *Saint Dominic Raising Napoleone Orsini,* and then by the *Disputation of Saint Dominic* and the *Miracle of the Book.* A version of the last subject (fig. 128), which certainly formed part of the same predella as the Yale panel, was formerly in the collection of Sir Thomas Barlow; this panel, measuring 34.3 x 46.4 centimeters (13½ x 18¼ inches), was—to judge from photographs of it published early in the last century—also much damaged from abrasion, and was extensively repainted.[2] Its soberly organized scene was centered about a fireplace in the house of the heretics of Montpellier, six of whom recoil in astonishment as a book of Saint Dominic's sermons miraculously floats above a fire and is not burned. Once again, the image is conceived as a simplification and clarification of the much busier, more crowded episode portrayed in the Louvre predella, with a deeper and more measured sense of pictorial space and with less agitated but more dramatic gesturing figures.

Following the *Miracle of the Book* in both the Louvre and Cortona predellas is a scene of Saint Dominic and his companions being fed by angels, the subject of the Stuttgart panel exhibited here (C). This scene, the most extensively damaged of the present series insofar as the losses encompass the complete lower quarter of the composition, is in many ways the most sophisticated in its narrative details. It transpired one day, in the convent church of San Sisto Vecchio in Rome, that not enough bread was available to feed the forty friars of the community. Dominic enjoined the brothers to divide equally what little bread there was among themselves, but as they prepared to dine on these tiny morsels, two angels miraculously appeared with aprons full of bread, which they spread before Dominic. In the Stuttgart panel, a refectory table is set against the back wall of a simple box-like room with two doors and six carefully rendered windows high up in the lateral walls. Along the rear wall and turning the corners onto the lateral walls is a plain wooden *spalliera* with a remarkably delicate cornice molding, and above this, suspended from three nails near the ceiling, is a black cloth standard with an image of the *Crucifixion.* A lay brother entering through the doorway at the

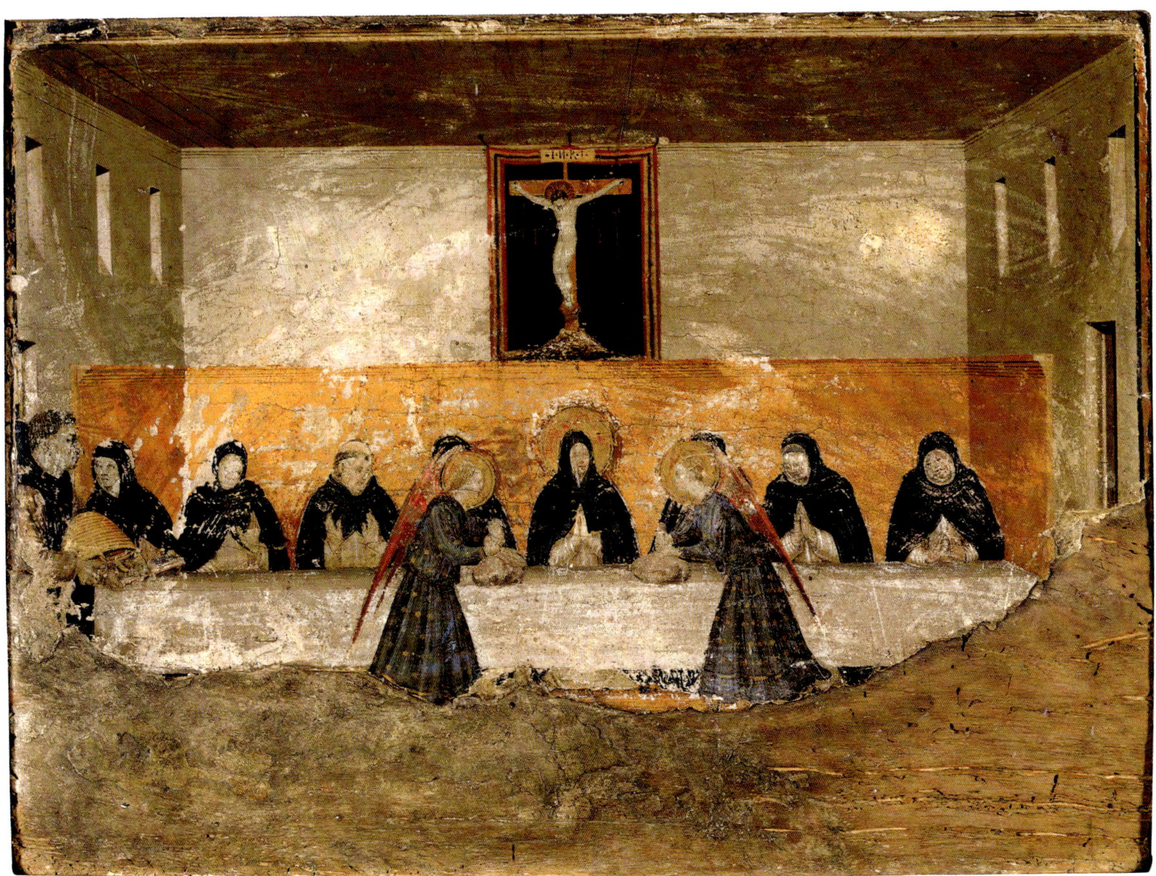

37: C

left turns an empty basket upside down to show how little bread there was in the convent's pantry, while two angels place bulging cloth sacks on the table at either side of Saint Dominic, who is seated at its center. The spare setting of the miracle contrasts dramatically with that of the same scene in the Louvre predella (fig. 130), where the recession of the realistic wood rafters of the ceiling, the texture and folds of the embroidered linen tablecloths, and a pulpit and lectern (with a novice reading from the Scriptures) are painstakingly represented. The architectural backdrop of the Stuttgart panel is made more subtle by simplification, and the human drama of the event portrayed is greatly heightened—an indication of the painting's significantly later date. In both these respects the composition of the Stuttgart panel is far more satisfactory than that of the Cortona predella, where the scene is implausibly set out of doors and the figures resemble inexpressive mannequins.

Echoing the example of the Paris and Cortona predellas, the narrative of Saint Dominic's life could have been completed either with a scene of the Raising of Napoleone Orsini (situated to the right of the Yale panel), or with a scene of the Death of Saint Dominic (following the Stuttgart panel), although no other versions of these subjects by Fra Angelico are known.[3] It is also likely that, just as the Louvre predella contains an image of the *Pietà* at the center, the present predella might also have included a Passion scene at its center—specifically, the panel (B) depicting the Crucifixion and various saints, in The Metropolitan Museum of Art, New York. This painting, which was transferred to canvas and then back again to a panel support, is undoubtedly the best known and most controversial of the series. The original, although now-much-repaired gold background was overpainted at an early date with a naturalistic sky and two large palm trees, "shadows" of which are still visible impressed in the gesso and bole of the ground. It is possible that they were added to cover voids created by the removal of two angels that once hovered alongside the cross, as well as to repair or modernize the gold ground. The removal of the overpainted landscape elements by conservators at The Metropolitan Museum of Art in 1951 significantly altered the appearance of the panel, and while this perhaps eliminated a degree of uncertainty in previous discussions of its attribution, it also revealed the extremely abraded state of all but the two figures at the left of the scene, presumed to be Saints Augustine and Monica, representing the adoption of the Augustinian rule by the Dominican order. The two Dominican saints kneeling at the foot of the cross are universally identified as Dominic and Thomas Aquinas, whereas

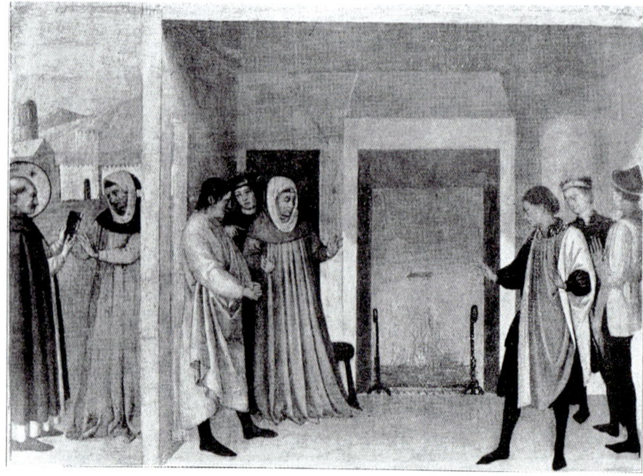

Figure 128. Fra Angelico. *The Miracle of the Book*. About 1446–55. Formerly, Collection Thomas Barlow, London

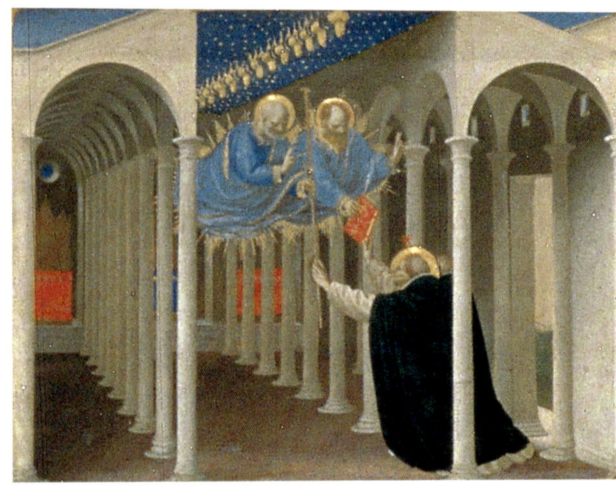

Figure 129. Fra Angelico. *Saints Peter and Paul Appearing to Saint Dominic*. About 1432–34. Musée du Louvre, Paris

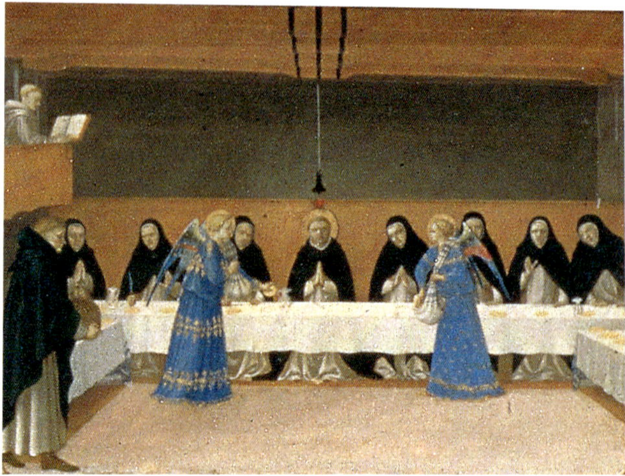

Figure 130. Fra Angelico. *Saint Dominic and His Companions Fed by Angels*. About 1432–34. Musée du Louvre, Paris

the figure on the left is unequivocally Saint Peter Martyr, the wound in his skull clearly visible on close inspection. Although the figure at the far right is usually described as Saint Elizabeth of Hungary, patroness of the third order of Saint Francis, she does not wear a Clarissan habit, and she could equally be meant to portray Saint Dorothy or Saint Cecilia.

The precise identification of the figures in the Metropolitan Museum *Christ on the Cross* is of some importance in that they may ultimately establish the probable origin of this predella. The combined width of the five known or presumed panels—approximately 240 centimeters[4]—is equaled only by the predella to the San Marco high altarpiece (cat. 34), among all of Fra Angelico's production. Its iconography, coupled with its size, implies that the structure to which it belonged was likely to have been the principal altarpiece of a major Dominican church, and that Saint Dominic, who is conspicuously absent from the New York Crucifixion scene, was included in the main panel or elsewhere in the complex. No altarpiece by Fra Angelico of this date, size, or description is known, however, which can be linked to this predella, and documents make no concrete allusions to any likely candidates that might now be lost.[5] Vasari does claim that the high altarpiece in the Dominican church of Santa Maria sopra Minerva in Rome was painted by Angelico, and, if this were true (no independent confirmation of this claim in documents or in other early sources has been found), it would not be unreasonable to suggest that the present predella could be a surviving element of this undoubtedly major work. On the other hand, the inclusion of Saints Monica (?)—neither this figure nor the bishop alongside her wears a leather belt, which would establish their identity as Augustine and his mother—and Cecilia (or Dorothy) in the New York *Christ on the Cross* might suggest that the altarpiece was intended for a female house of the Dominican order, but no further deductions based on the evidence of the panels themselves seem possible at present.

It has been proposed that the Metropolitan Museum *Crucifixion* might have been an independent devotional work rather than the center panel of a predella,[6] and that it might be identical with a painting by Fra Angelico in the *anticamera* of Piero di Lorenzo de' Medici recorded in a 1492 inventory of the Palazzo Medici: "*una tavoletta quadra dipintovi . . . uno Christo in croce con 9 figure d'attorno*."[7] Despite the interesting coincidence of its subject, the high value placed on this painting—twelve florins—suggests that it describes a larger panel; Angelico's *Thebaid* (now in the Uffizi), which measures over two meters in length, appears in the same inventory with a valuation of fifteen florins.

LK

1. See Israëls 2003, pp. 760–76. For further discussion of the dating and authorship of this altarpiece, see p. 160 n. 11.
2. This panel was published by Berenson (1932b, p. 524) as by Fra Angelico, about 1440. The dimensions of the panel are generally—and incorrectly—recorded as 24 x 33.5 centimeters; the correct dimensions are given by M. Davies (1961, p. 36). Further confusion was introduced by Pope-Hennessy, who catalogued the painting as having been exhibited by Lord Rothermere at the Burlington Fine Arts Club in 1919, as a work by Masolino; Lord Rothermere did own this painting, but he acquired it sometime after 1923 and sold it in 1941 (Christie's, London,

December 19, 1941, lot 92, as a *Miracle of Saint Mark* by Masolino; 13¼ x 18½ in.). The painting was purchased at the Rothermere sale by Agnew's, London, who, presumably, sold it to Sir Thomas Barlow. Previously—but not known on what authority—it is said to have belonged to John Bowyer Nichols (1779–1863), to R. C. Witt, and to the Honorable Robert Bruce. It was purchased by Colnaghi, London, on March 31, 1922, from Tancred Borenius (again as a *Miracle of Saint Mark* by Masolino, measuring 13½ x 18¾ in.), and sold by them to C. F. U. Meeks on October 1, 1923. The panel was last exhibited in Birmingham from August to October 1955, in "Exhibition of Italian Art from the 13th Century to the 17th Century," no. 4; its present whereabouts are unknown.

3. A fragmentary replica of the right third of the scene of the *Raising of Napoleone Orsini* as portrayed in the Cortona predella was exhibited in Stuttgart in 1950 ("Frühe italienische Tafelmalerei," no. 80, as by the Master of the Griggs Crucifixion; 23.3 x 18.1 cm). It is impossible to judge from the illustration in the Stuttgart catalogue whether this panel might have been a fake or a heavily overpainted original fragment by Fra Angelico missing from the predella reconstructed here.
4. The Yale panel preserves a narrow strip of black paint and gilding along its left margin but has been cropped within the picture field at the right. It is likely that approximately five centimeters are missing from this side, which would have centered the portico of Old Saint Peter's within its façade and brought the panel into greater conformity with the width of the Stuttgart and ex-Barlow panels. A similar border of black paint and gilding is visible at the right of the Stuttgart panel, which might imply that this was the final scene of the predella. Photographs of the ex-Barlow panel mask its edges.
5. W. Bombe (1912, p. 77) quotes a statement in the *Annali* of Padre Bottonio (Ms., Bibl. Com., Perugia, ii, c. 72), ascribing "*l'altra tavola posta in chiesa Vecchia* [*San Domenico, Perugia*] *sopra l'altar maggiore*" to "*F. Gio. da Fiesole padre nostro et famosissimo pittore de l'ordine nostro*." S. Orlandi (1954b, pp. 199–201) identifies this altarpiece, instead, with a lost painting commissioned from Fra Filippo Lippi in 1451.
6. Zeri and Gardner 1971, pp. 78–79.
7. Salmi 1958, p. 89; Muntz 1888, p. 86. It is tempting to identify this painting with the "*Crocifisso con altre figurine, di fra Giovanni da Fiesole domenicano*," listed in a seventeenth-century inventory (undated, but after 1658) of the Guicciardini collection in Florence (Fallani 1992, p. 188), which includes several other paintings formerly in the Palazzo Medici (see p. 283 n. 8). What appears to be the same painting is described in an earlier (1643) Guicciardini inventory as "*un quadretto entrovi un Crocifisso con più figure, alto br. 1⅓ et largho br. 1.1.8, tutto col fondo d'oro*" (ibid., p. 182).

FRA ANGELICO

38.
Saint Peter Martyr and Saint Thomas Aquinas before the Crucifix

Tempera on panel, 19.9 x 12.1 cm
(7⅞ x 4¾ in.)
Private collection

Among the most interesting recent additions to Fra Angelico scholarship was the publication in 1998 of this previously unknown work.[1] Its subject may best be described as a mystical vision embodying the two poles of Dominican spirituality: the passionate and the cerebral, or, in a more secular and metaphoric vein, the Dionysian and the Apollonian. The two principal saints of the Dominican order—after the founder himself—Peter Martyr and Thomas Aquinas, kneel in a carefully articulated church interior: specifically, in the crossing of a Brunelleschian or Michelozzan basilica. Rising in front of the apsidal chapel, above the table of the high altar—which is covered in a blue cloth with red fringe—is a life-size crucifix with blood spilling from the wounds in the hands, feet, and side of the crucified Christ. Behind the cross is a black drapery that sets it off dramatically from the gold back wall of the chapel. At the right, Saint Thomas Aquinas kneels in lost profile, presenting a volume of his theological writings to Christ, who replies (in words inscribed in white on the panel): "*Bene scripsisti de me Thomma* [sic]" ("You have written well of me Thomas").[2] At the left, Saint Peter Martyr, holding a martyr's palm, kneels in profile, as blood drips from the wounds in his head and shoulder; the message to him from Christ reads, "*Petre, et ego quis*" ("Peter, I too [suffered] thus").[3]

In first calling scholarly attention to this panel—intimate in scale and so loose and impressionistic in handling as to blur the distinction between a brush drawing and a finished painting—Luciano Bellosi speculated that it might originally have decorated a painted reliquary or the base of a paschal candlestick such as those described by Vasari as having been executed by Angelico for Santa Maria Novella.[4] The vertical wood grain and relative thinness (1.2 centimeters) of its panel support suggest, instead, that it is likely to be a fragment of the wing of a triptych. That it has been trimmed in width may be deduced from the glimpses of arches springing to either side of the crossing piers and, at the left, the oblique view of an altar table in the lateral chapel, gratuitously cropped at the edges of the panel. The angle at which the lateral altar table was meant to be seen, as well as the fact that the left wall of the apsidal chapel is visible but not the right wall, may imply that the painting was conceived for the left wing of a triptych, to be viewed off-center and to the right.[5] As it is impossible to determine how much the panel has been reduced in width, or whether it was originally enclosed within an engaged frame, it is difficult to estimate the dimensions of the center panel or of the matching wing on the right of this hypothetical triptych. The unique subject of the present panel does imply that the complex must have been devoted to specifically Dominican imagery, and perhaps that its patron was a particularly erudite member of the Dominican order.

One such Dominican triptych painted by Angelico (cat. 21),

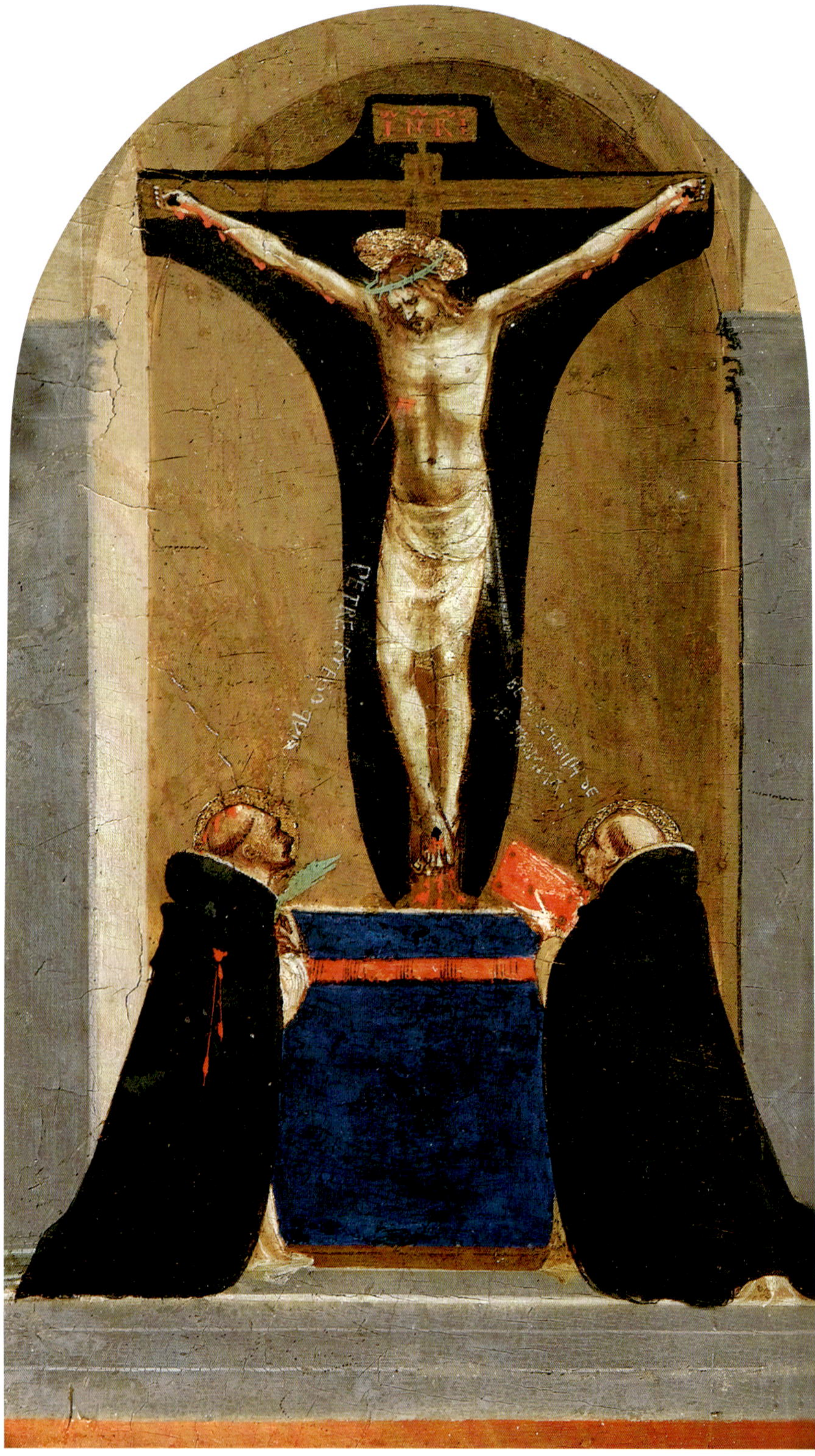

38

probably about 1427, is inappropriately large and too early in style to be associated with the present panel, for which Bellosi proposed a date in the early 1430s, not far removed from what he believed to be its compositional model: Masaccio's *Trinity* fresco in Santa Maria Novella. The clarity, precision, and symmetrical balance of the architecture in this panel, as well as the tangible evocation of atmosphere created by its subtle light effects, preclude so early a date, however, and argue instead for placing it significantly later in the artist's career, after he completed the frescoes in the upper corridor at San Marco and possibly as late as the Annunziata Silver Chest of 1448–50. The attenuated figure types and loose, sketchy handling of paint also suggest a dating toward the end of the artist's activity, if perhaps not as late as the *Christ on the Cross with the Donor, Cardinal Torquemada,* now in the Fogg Art Museum (cat. 39). No other paintings from this stage in Angelico's development can be identified that might be directly associated with this one, but the fact that the present panel has been known to scholars for less than a decade raises hopes that others like it may soon reappear as well. LK

1. Bellosi and Galli 1998.
2. *Acta Sanctorum,* Mar. I, Dies 7, s.v. "S. Thomas Aquinas, Doctor Angelicus Ordinis Praedicatorum," Caput VI, 35.
3. *Acta Sanctorum,* Apr. III, Dies 29, s.v. "S. Petrus Martyr, Ordinis Praedicatorum," Caput I, 6.
4. Vasari (Milanesi ed.) 1878–85, vol. II, p. 513.
5. Similar adjustments to perspective in triptychs by Duccio presuppose an angle of opening for the wings rather than their being read as on the same plane as the center panel. If this were the case here, as well, the present panel would have appeared to the right, not the left, of the center panel.

39.
Christ on the Cross, between the Virgin and Saint John the Evangelist, with the Donor, Cardinal Torquemada

Tempera and gold on panel, 88 x 36 cm (34⅝ x 14⅛ in.)
Fogg Art Museum, Harvard University Art Museums, Cambridge, Massachusetts (1921.34)

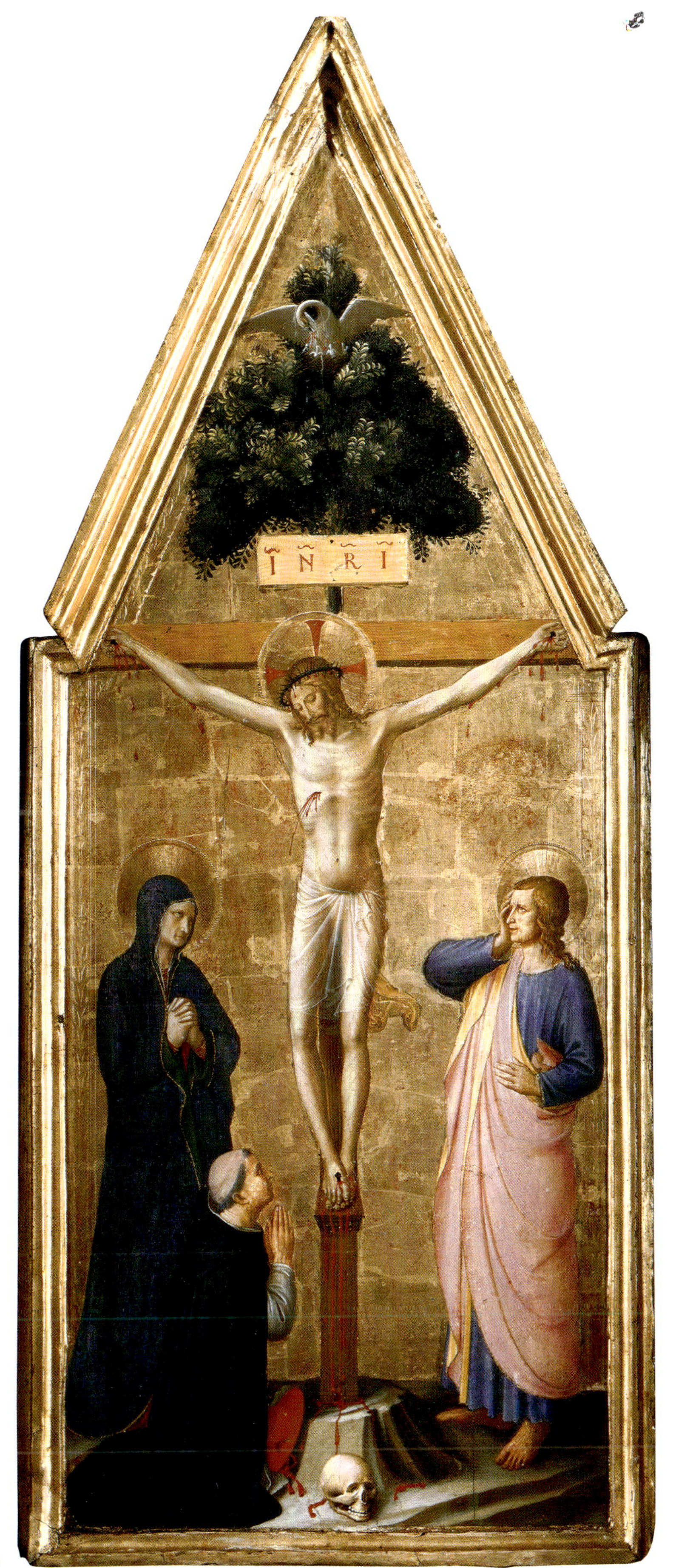

39

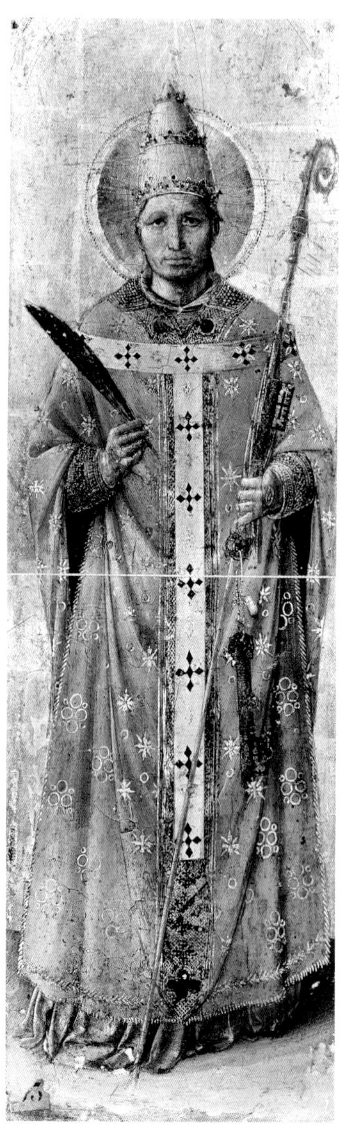

Figure 131. Fra Angelico. *Saint Sixtus*. About 1453–55. Formerly, Collection Deane Johnson, Bel Air, California

Unanimously regarded by scholars as one of the masterpieces of Angelico's late career, this impressive, exceptionally well preserved panel was originally the center of a tabernacle triptych, possibly intended for private devotion. The composition is centered around the monumental figure of the crucified Christ, with the arms of the cross extending the full width of the panel and articulating the division of the picture field into a lower, rectangular zone and a triangular gable above it. Occupying the full space of the painted gable is the motif of the pelican pricking her own breast to feed her young with her blood—a symbol of Christ's sacrifice for humanity. Flanking the cross are the mourning figures of the Virgin and Saint John the Evangelist, and kneeling in adoration below it is the painting's donor, identified as a Dominican cardinal by his dress and the red hat placed prominently next to him.

In 1904, Professor Nöel Valois of Paris, then the owner of this painting, published a lengthy article in which he convincingly established the donor's identity as Cardinal Juan de Torquemada (1388–1468), uncle of the infamous Spanish Inquisitor Tomás de Torquemada (1420–1498).[1] One of the most distinguished theologians of the period, Juan de Torquemada had been called to the court of Eugenius IV in 1435 to fill the position of Master of the Sacred Palace (*Magister Sacri Palatii*), the principal adviser to the pope on all religious matters. In the following years he became an ardent promoter of the pope's cause at the Council of Basel (1436)—where he also argued for the rights of the Dominican Observants of Fiesole in their dispute with the Silvestrines over possession of the convent of San Marco—and he was one of the key speakers at the Council of Ferrara (1438) and of Florence (1439). On December 18, 1439, Eugenius IV, then in residence at Santa Maria Novella in Florence, rewarded Torquemada's efforts by bestowing upon him the title of Cardinal of San Sisto.[2]

In the second edition of his monograph on Angelico, John Pope-Hennessy first associated with the Fogg *Crucifixion* a panel by Fra Angelico formerly on the art market (present location unknown) showing a papal saint identified by the author as Saint Peter (fig. 131).[3] While also recognizing this work as one of the missing lateral panels flanking the *Crucifixion*, Miklós Boskovits suggested more persuasively that this figure was the martyred pope Saint Sixtus II—an obvious reference to Cardinal Torquemada's titular church in Rome.[4] Based on the perception that the saint had been portrayed with the features of Pope Eugenius IV, Boskovits went on to place the painting's execution in the period of the latter's pontificate—specifically, between the end of 1445, when Angelico probably left Florence for Rome, and February 1447, the date of the pope's death.

Boskovits's arguments have been accepted by most subsequent scholars,[5] who include the triptych of the *Crucifixion* among several undocumented panel paintings presumed to have been executed by Fra Angelico during his first Roman period. Among these is the *Last Judgment* triptych (fig. 94) in the Corsini Collection, Rome, which includes, seated to the right of Christ, a figure of Saint Sixtus identified by Strehlke as another portrait of Eugenius IV.[6] Efforts to circumscribe these works within the pontificate of Eugenius IV simply on the basis of the presumed likeness of certain figures to the pope appear forced, however, in light of stylistic considerations and the often-noted similarity of the paintings to Angelico's later production. Pope-Hennessy,[7] followed by Argan[8] and more recently by Mauro Minardi,[9] aptly emphasized the close relationship between the *Crucifixion* and Angelico's last documented work, the panels for the silver chest in Santissima Annunziata, Florence (fig. 132):[10] datable on the basis of documentary and circumstantial evidence between about 1450 and 1452, following the artist's return to Florence and before his second departure for Rome,[11] these scenes provide a firm point of reference for the painting. Common to both, and unique among Angelico's works, is the particular type of Christ—an impossibly slender, pallid figure bathed in a luminous, alabaster glow. It is also in the silver chest panels that one finds the nearest equivalent for the elongated, powerfully statuesque images of the Virgin and the Evangelist, whose sharply delineated, pointed features and gestures express a new depth of emotional intensity not found in the artist's previous production. In no other painting by Angelico is the reality of human suffering more evident than in the face of the Virgin in the Fogg panel, aged by grief into that of an old woman with wrinkles and sunken cheeks; her deeply furrowed brow and downturned mouth, with its clenched lips, belying a dignified effort to restrain an insurmountable grief. Like the silver chest, the *Crucifixion* may be said to mark the final evolution of Angelico's vision toward a monumental religious art imbued with both the nobility and pathos of human existence.

Accepting Pope-Hennessy's late dating of the Fogg picture, William Hood made the interesting suggestion that the *Crucifixion*, an appropriate image for a Dominican cell, may have been executed while both Angelico and Torquemada were in residence in the Dominican monastery of Santa Maria sopra Minerva in Rome in the early 1450s.[12] This important institution was the official headquarters of the order in the city, and it was here that Angelico died and was laid to rest in 1455. According to Vasari, the artist had painted a high altarpiece and an *Annunciation* for the same church, both of which are either lost or unidentified (see cat. 37). In a recent study, Gerardo de Simone has highlighted Juan de Torquemada's extensive participation in the program of rebuilding and reform of the monastery, beginning in the early 1450s, and

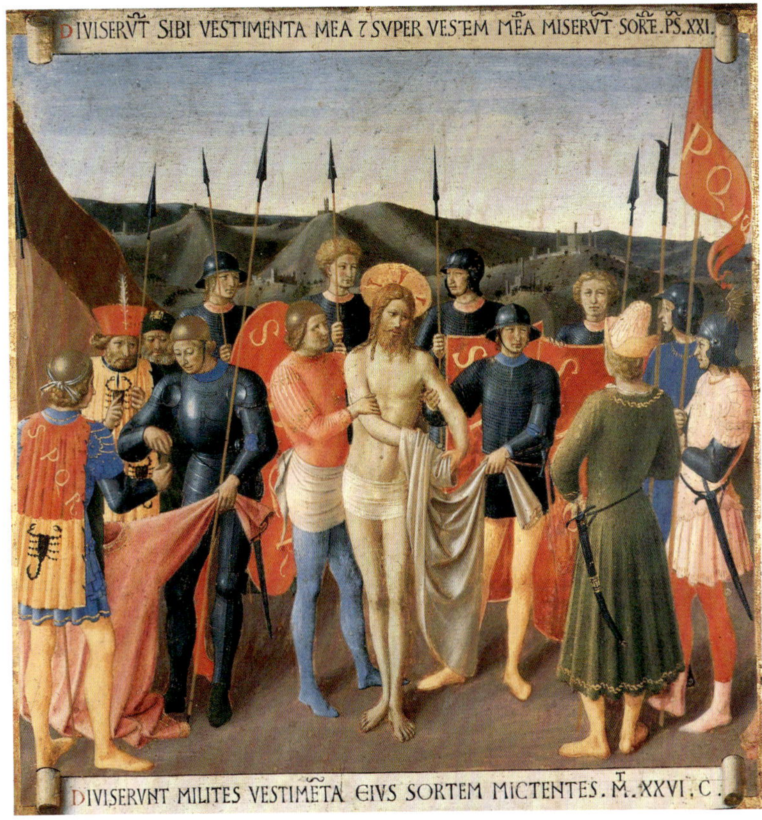

Figure 132. Fra Angelico. *The Spoliation of Christ* (from the Annunziata Silver Chest). About 1450–52. Museo di San Marco, Florence

Angelico's possible role in the design of a (now lost) fresco cycle in the new cloister based on the text of the *Meditationes* composed by the cardinal.[13] One of the scenes in the fresco cycle, reconstructed on the basis of an illustrated manuscript copy of the *Meditationes* in the Vatican Library (Ms. Vat. Lat. 973), contained a portrait of the cardinal kneeling at the feet of Saint Sixtus, which De Simone placed in direct relationship to the portrait in the Fogg *Crucifixion* albeit acknowledging it to have been executed as much as fifteen years later.[14] This lost fresco, it has been argued, served as a model for a third portrait of Torquemada, in which he is shown kneeling in profile beside his cardinal's hat, in an *Annunciation* painted by Antoniazzo Romano for the chapel erected by the cardinal in the same monastery in 1464.[15] It is possible, on the other hand, that the model for both the fresco and the *Annunciation* portrait, in fact, may have been the likeness painted by Angelico in the Fogg triptych, perhaps installed in the cardinal's quarters in Santa Maria sopra Minerva.

A possible clue to the triptych's specific function may be offered by its subject matter and by the unusual prominence given to the motif of the "pelican in her piety," which normally appears as a much smaller, often unnoticed addition above the cross. Based on a report describing how the early-fifteenth-century Neapolitan cardinal Minutolo used to celebrate Mass before a small portable altarpiece of the *Crucifixion*, it has been suggested that such objects may have served a liturgical as well as a devotional purpose.[16] In the case of the Fogg *Crucifixion*, the painting's liturgical use may have been intentionally highlighted by the visual emphasis on the pelican motif, the Eucharistic significance of which had been underscored by Saint Thomas Aquinas in the celebrated hymn "*Adoro te devote*" ("I adore thee devoutly"): "*Pie pellicani, Ihesu domine, / me immundum munda tuo sanguine / Cuius una stilla salvum facere, totum mundum posset omni scelere* . . . ." ("O loving pelican! O Jesu Lord! / Unclean I am. But cleanse me in Thy Blood: / Of which a single drop, for sinners spilt, / Can purge the entire world from all its / guilt . . . ").[17] PP

1. Valois 1904, pp. 461–70.
2. For a summary of the literature on Torquemada, see De Simone 2002, pp. 41–87.
3. The panel was sold at auction at Sotheby's, London, December 6, 1972 (lot 7); Pope-Hennessy 1974, pp. 37, 218.
4. Boskovits 1976b, pp. 43, 45, 53 notes 28, 32. According to Boskovits, this identification would appear to be confirmed by the fragmentary text at the base of the painting: SC . . . STVS.
5. Bowron 1990, p. 97; Spike 1996, p. 195; Bonsanti 1998, p. 146; Strehlke 1998, pp. 51, 119; De Simone 2002, pp. 57–59.
6. Strehlke 1998, pp. 51, 119.
7. Pope-Hennessy 1952, pp. 30, 196; Pope-Hennessy 1974, pp. 37, 219.
8. Argan 1955, p. 111.
9. M. Minardi, in Toscano and Capitelli 2002, p. 179.
10. It is worth noting that, while accepting Boskovits's dating for the *Christ on the Cross*, G. Bonsanti (1998, p. 146) also pointed out that the suggested portrait of Eugenius IV could be a posthumous reference, presumably implying that the image might, in fact, have been executed *after* 1447.
11. Bonsanti 2003, pp. 162–64 (with earlier bibliography).
12. Hood 1993, p. 197.
13. G. De Simone 2002.
14. De Simone (2002, p. 83 n. 116) accepts Boskovits's dating of the Fogg picture before 1447, and he dates the Vatican manuscript to the early 1460s.
15. This portrait was used by Valois (1904) and later authors as the basis for the identification of Torquemada in the Fogg *Crucifixion*.
16. Wilkins 2002, p. 388 n. 19. The author cites the example of the Sienese painter Paolo di Giovanni Fei, whose triptych of the *Trinity and the Crucifixion* in Naples Cathedral was described by eighteenth-century sources as "a little portable altarpiece that folded up, the inseparable companion of Cardinal Enrico Minutolo, who used to celebrate the holy sacrifice of the Mass in front of it wherever he carried it."
17. For a discussion of this hymn, written by Aquinas in praise of the Eucharist and as a statement of faith in its redeeming quality, see Wielockx 1998, pp. 157–74 (with earlier bibliography). The hymn is included in the Roman missal and breviary.

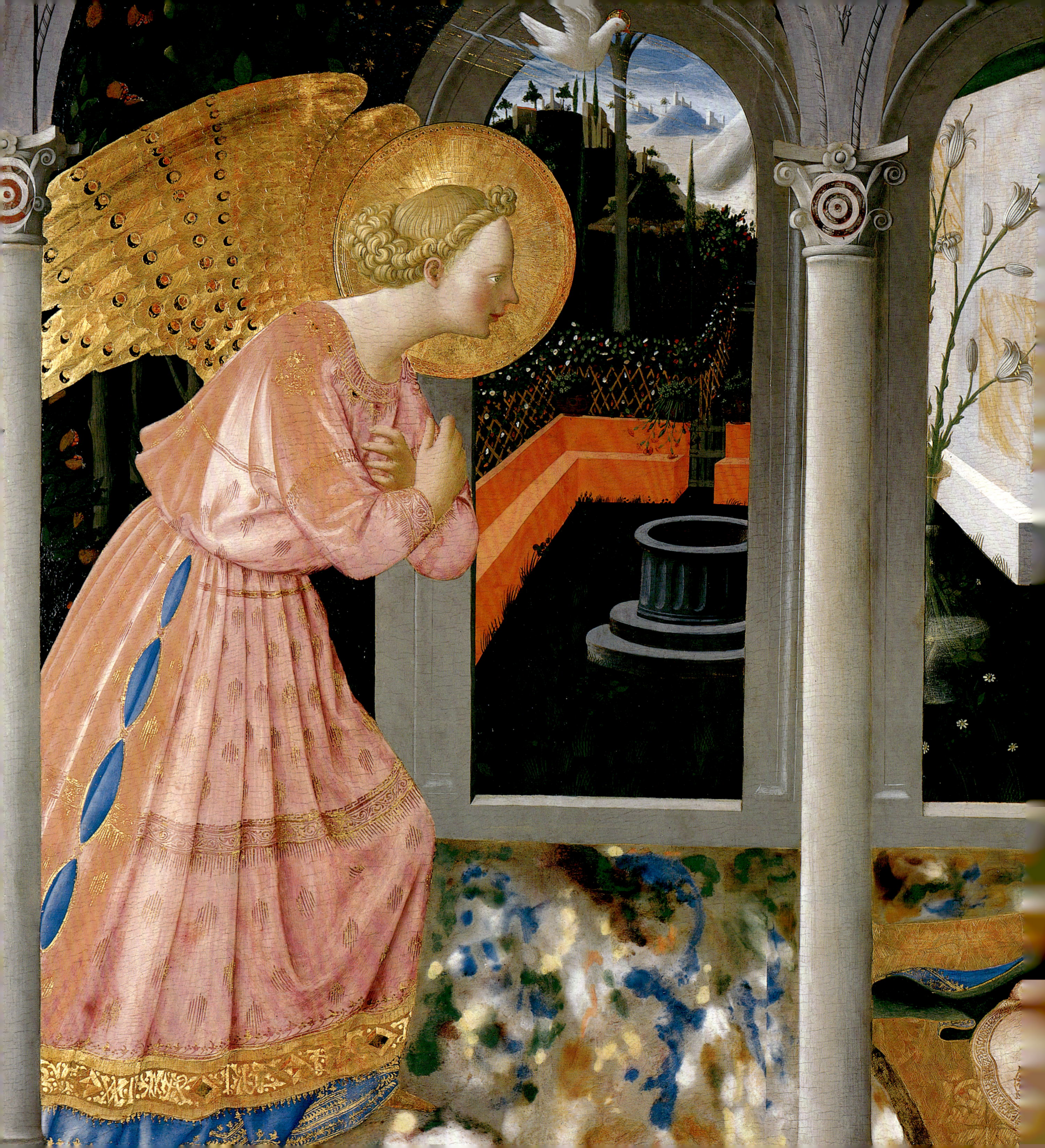

Chapter VIII
Battista di Biagio Sanguigni and Zanobi Strozzi

LAURENCE KANTER

It is impossible to consider the careers of Battista di Biagio Sanguigni and Zanobi Strozzi independently of one another, although the artists are of two distinct generations. Documents reveal that they lived together, with Sanguigni serving as Strozzi's tutor, for at least eight and possibly as many as eleven years, and that Strozzi provided for the aging Sanguigni's financial security for fourteen more years after that, maintaining a house and an annual subvention of grain and wine for the older artist until the latter's death. The records further imply that Strozzi and Sanguigni collaborated regularly on the production of works of art, which has frustrated efforts to identify either of them until relatively recently. In addition, on the basis of circumstantial as well as stylistic evidence, both artists appear to have been actively associated with Fra Angelico's studio at San Domenico, Fiesole, and both can be recognized as the executants of several major works—in whole or in part—issuing from Angelico's workshop.

Battista di Biagio Sanguigni was born in 1393, and while his apprenticeship is undocumented, he was presumably trained in the studio of Lorenzo Monaco. In 1415, signing himself "Battista miniatore," he enrolled in the Compagnia di San Nicola da Bari at the Carmine, and two years later he sponsored the entry of the young Fra Angelico (then Guido di Pietro) into the same confraternity. From at least 1427 to 1433, Sanguigni rented a studio from the Camaldolese monastery of Santa Maria degli Angeli, and sometime within this period he accepted the orphaned Zanobi Strozzi as an apprentice. The two artists are recorded as living together at Palaiuola near San Domenico, Fiesole, until 1438, the year of Strozzi's marriage; Sanguigni continued to live at Palaiuola until his death in 1451.[1]

A first attempt to identify Battista Sanguigni as an illuminator was advanced by Pietro Toesca on the basis of documents of payment to the artist in 1432 for miniatures in a hymnal and in several volumes of an antiphonary for the Augustinian monastery of San Gaggio (fig. 137).[2] The wording of these documents, however, is imprecise, and their relationship to two surviving volumes of choir books from San Gaggio (now in the Museo di San Marco, Florence) has been disputed. Mirella Levi D'Ancona assigned one of the illuminations in the San Gaggio antiphonary to Zanobi Strozzi, and around the others she grouped a heterogeneous body of material, numbering thirty manuscripts, which she identified as the work of Battista Sanguigni.[3] Her grouping was reduced by Kanter,[4] and expanded again by Magnolia Scudieri and Angela Dillon with several convincing new attributions and a questionable suggestion to ascribe to the late career of Battista Sanguigni several books that probably were painted instead by Battista di Niccolò da Padova.[5] In addition to the two volumes of San Gaggio choir books (and a third recently discovered volume), it is now possible to identify Battista Sanguigni as the author of five illuminated manuscripts: a breviary from San Pier Maggiore that has been dated to 1411–14 (Musée Marmottan, Paris); two illuminated copies of Dante's *Divine Comedy* (Biblioteca Nacional, Madrid, Ms. Vit. 23-2; Biblioteca Riccardiana, Florence, Ms. 1008); a book of statutes for the confraternity of the Buca di San Girolamo (see cat. 9); and a missal from San Pier Mercato, Florence. In addition, documents cite several Books of Hours for which Sanguigni was responsible, but if any of these survive they have not yet been identified.

Documents also refer, although somewhat obliquely, to Sanguigni's activity as a panel painter. In his declaration to the *decima al catasto* of 1430, Sanguigni claimed to be unable to recover fifty-two florins owed to him by the estate of Jacopo di Niccolò Corbizzi. This amount suggests that it is likely related to payment for an altarpiece, and, if so, it may possibly be a *Virgin and Child Enthroned, with Saints James the Greater, Maurus, Anthony Abbot, and John the Baptist* (fig. 134, 135, 136), attributed to an artist conventionally known as the Master of 1419 (see pp. 233–34). Such a proposal is supported by stylistic relationships among the group of panels attributed to the Master of 1419[6] and the illuminations in the San Gaggio choir books, as well as to the figures painted in the margins of manuscripts plausibly ascribed to Battista Sanguigni and Zanobi Strozzi in collaboration (see cat. 41). These panels, however, can all be dated earlier than about 1430, prior to or at the beginning of the period of Sanguigni's documented association with Zanobi Strozzi. After this date, Sanguigni's artistic personality appears to have been largely overshadowed by that

Opposite:
Figure 133. Zanobi Strozzi. *The Annunciation* (detail). About 1445–50. National Gallery, London

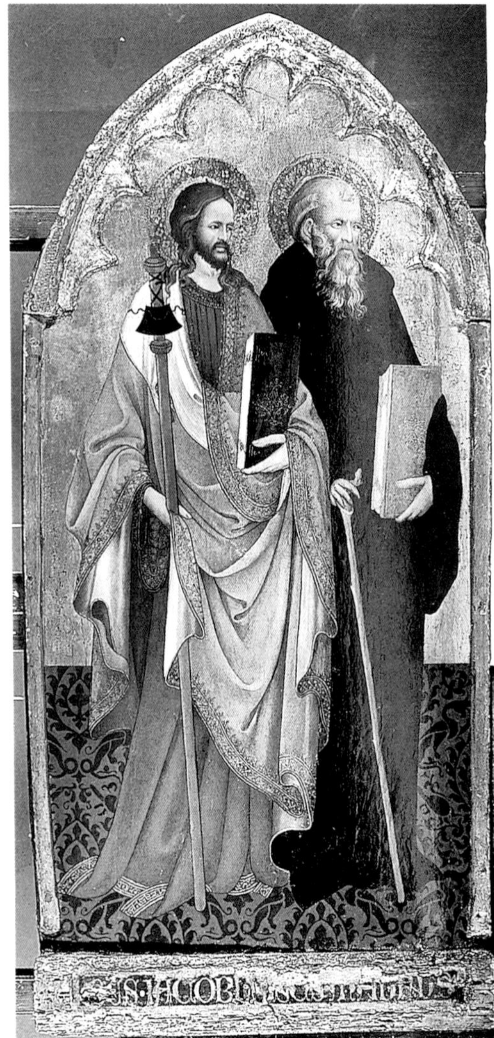

Figure 134. Battista di Biagio Sanguigni. *Saints James the Greater and Maurus.* About 1428–30. Private collection, Switzerland

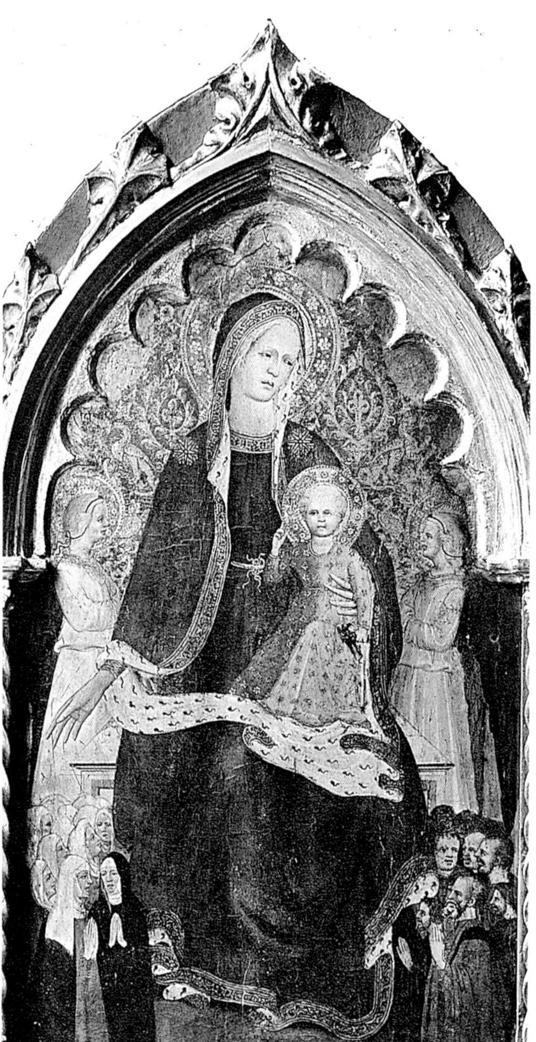

Figure 135. Battista di Biagio Sanguigni. *Virgin and Child Enthroned.* About 1428–30. Private collection, Germany

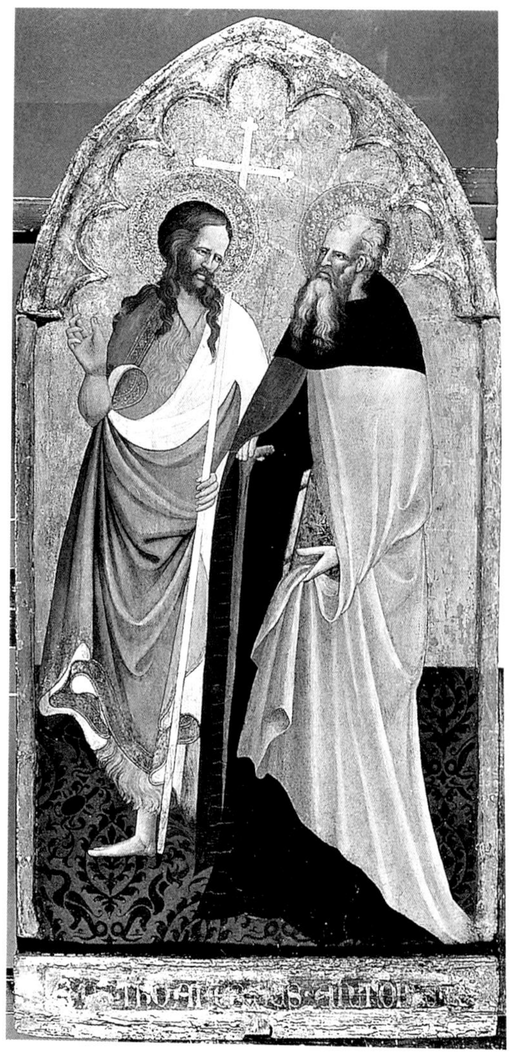

Figure 136. Battista di Biagio Sanguigni. *Saints Anthony Abbot and John the Baptist.* About 1428–30. Private collection, Switzerland

of his pupil Strozzi, and of his friend Angelico. In the last two decades of his life Sanguigni does not seem to have been responsible for the design or conception of any significant body of work, either as an illuminator or as a panel painter, but a hand almost certainly recognizable as his may be detected in a minor capacity in Angelico's workshop productions.

Zanobi di Benedetto di Caroccio degli Strozzi was born on November 17, 1412, to a noble family, one of the largest and wealthiest in Florence. Orphaned before the age of fifteen, he moved sometime after 1427 and before 1430—with his tutor, Battista di Biagio Sanguigni—to a house at Palaiuola near San Domenico, Fiesole. The two artists remained together until 1438 when, following his marriage, Strozzi moved to another residence in the same parish. Very few documents refer to Strozzi in this period, probably as a result of his minority as well as of the fact that he never enrolled in the painters' guild and was therefore unable to accept commissions in Florence under his own name. In 1434 the panels for an altarpiece for the Chapel of Saint Agnes in Santa Maria Nuova were sent to Zanobi Strozzi "*alluogo de frati di San Domenicho di Fiesole,*" suggesting that at least by this date the artist frequented Fra Angelico's studio. The altarpiece in question has been identified, probably correctly, with a *Virgin and Child, with Four Angels,* in the Museo di San Marco, Florence. Although it may be assumed that several other independent commissions received by Zanobi Strozzi probably date from the late 1430s or the early 1440s, much of his activity at the time seems to have been as an assistant or "sub-contractor" to Fra Angelico.

Late in 1445, Angelico moved to Rome, effectively closing the studio at San Domenico, Fiesole. Not coincidentally,

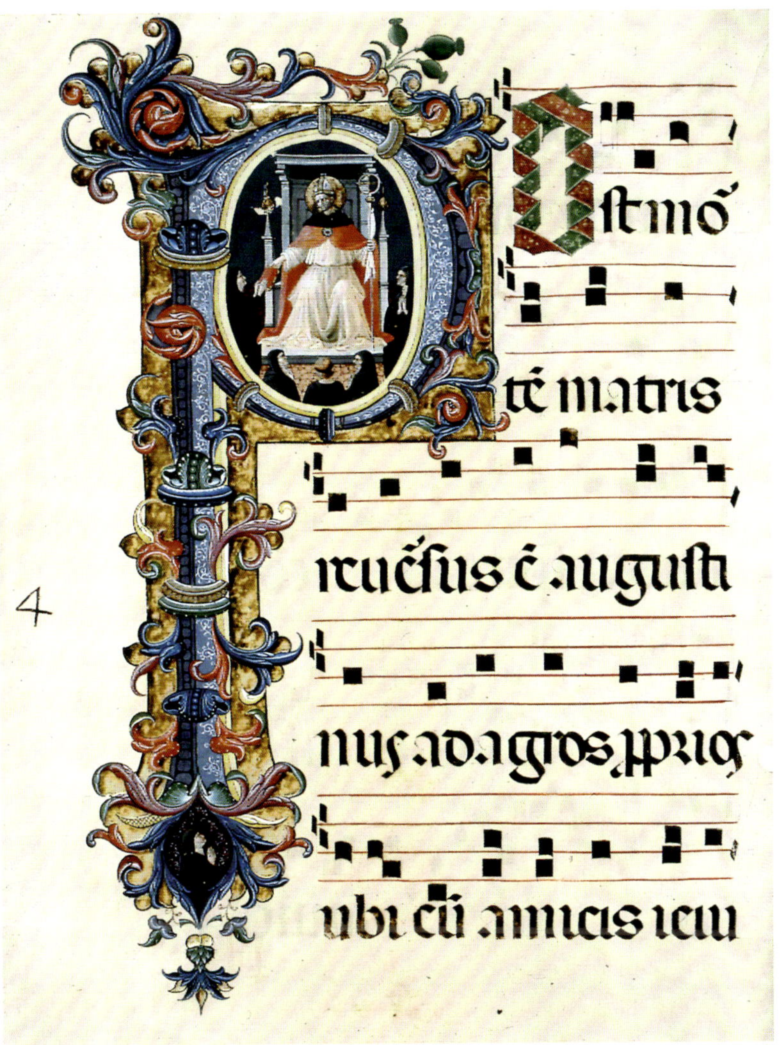

Figure 137. Battista di Biagio Sanguigni. *Saint Augustine Presenting His Rule to the Nuns* (detail, from the San Gaggio antiphonary). After 1432. Museo di San Marco, Florence (Inv. 1890 n. 10073, fol. 19*v.*)

Zanobi Strozzi relocated from Fiesole to Florence in 1446, renting a house in the parish of San Paolo near Santa Maria Novella before buying a house and studio in the parish of San Michele Bertoldi in 1450. It appears that for at least part of this period, Strozzi worked in collaboration with Francesco di Stefano, known as Pesellino, who inherited a studio in the Corso degli Adimari upon the death of his grandfather Giuliano d'Arrigo, on April 1, 1446 (see p. 269). It can also be no coincidence that beginning in 1445 or 1446, Zanobi Strozzi's name occurs with extraordinary frequency in documents of payment for illuminated manuscripts (fig. 138).

Two altarpieces by Zanobi Strozzi can be dated with confidence earlier than 1445—the Santa Maria Nuova altarpiece now in the Museo di San Marco, probably a documented work of 1434–36, and the one reconstructed here in catalogue 44. Both were likely executed in Fra Angelico's studio at San Domenico and possibly, in the case of the latter certainly, with the Dominican master's assistance. More frequently, however, it was Strozzi who aided Angelico, sometimes in a minor capacity, as in adding details to the predella of the Guidalotti altarpiece (cat. 30), and at other times more significantly as an amanuensis. Two major altarpieces undoubtedly commissioned from Fra Angelico, the San Giovanni Valdarno *Annunciation* and the Annalena altarpiece, appear to have been painted almost entirely by Zanobi Strozzi. The *Annunciation* has been dated, on circumstantial grounds, to about 1432, on the assumption that it may be the painting commissioned in that year for the Servite church of Sant'Alessandro in Brescia, for unexplained reasons diverted from its intended destination. This is possible, but if it were commissioned in 1432 it must not have been painted until somewhat later in that decade. Dating the Annalena altarpiece (fig. 79) is more problematic, although a preponderance of recent opinion assumes it also to be a work of the early 1430s. Such a dating is scarcely plausible from a consideration either of the picture's iconography, which seems to allude to the patronage not of Cosimo but of Piero (il Guttoso) or Pierfrancesco de'Medici, or of the vocabulary of its architectural decoration, which alludes to developments in Angelico's style close in date to the Cappella Niccolina frescoes of 1447–48. Furthermore, the narrative structure of its predella necessarily follows rather than precedes the design of the predella of the San Marco high altarpiece (cat. 34) of 1440–42, which it ineffectually copies. Pope-Hennessy's suggestion[7] that the Annalena altarpiece may have been left incomplete by Angelico when he departed for Rome in 1445 is not unpersuasive. It is equally possible, however, that the altarpiece was finished by Zanobi Strozzi following Angelico's final departure for Rome about 1453. In that case, it may have been intended from the start for the convent of Dominican penitent tertiaries at the Annalena—the building of which was begun in 1453—rather than having been transferred there at a later date, as is commonly asserted.

Zanobi Strozzi's later career, in the wake of Angelico's trip to Rome in 1445, can be chronicled more accurately through his work as a manuscript illuminator (fig. 138): he was one of the most important and prolific artists active in mid-century Florence in that field. Of the manuscript commissions he received, no fewer than eighteen fully documented examples survive today (see cat. 46). The majority of these are collaborative enterprises in which the names of Filippo di Matteo Torelli and Francesco d'Antonio del Chierico recur with some frequency. No documents relating to panel paintings by Zanobi Strozzi in these years have yet been unearthed,[8] however, leading in the past to confusion over the separation of his work from that of such artists as Domenico di Michelino, who may again have been one of his collaborators. Nonetheless, Zanobi Strozzi was responsible for painting numerous private devotional panels and at least five altarpieces

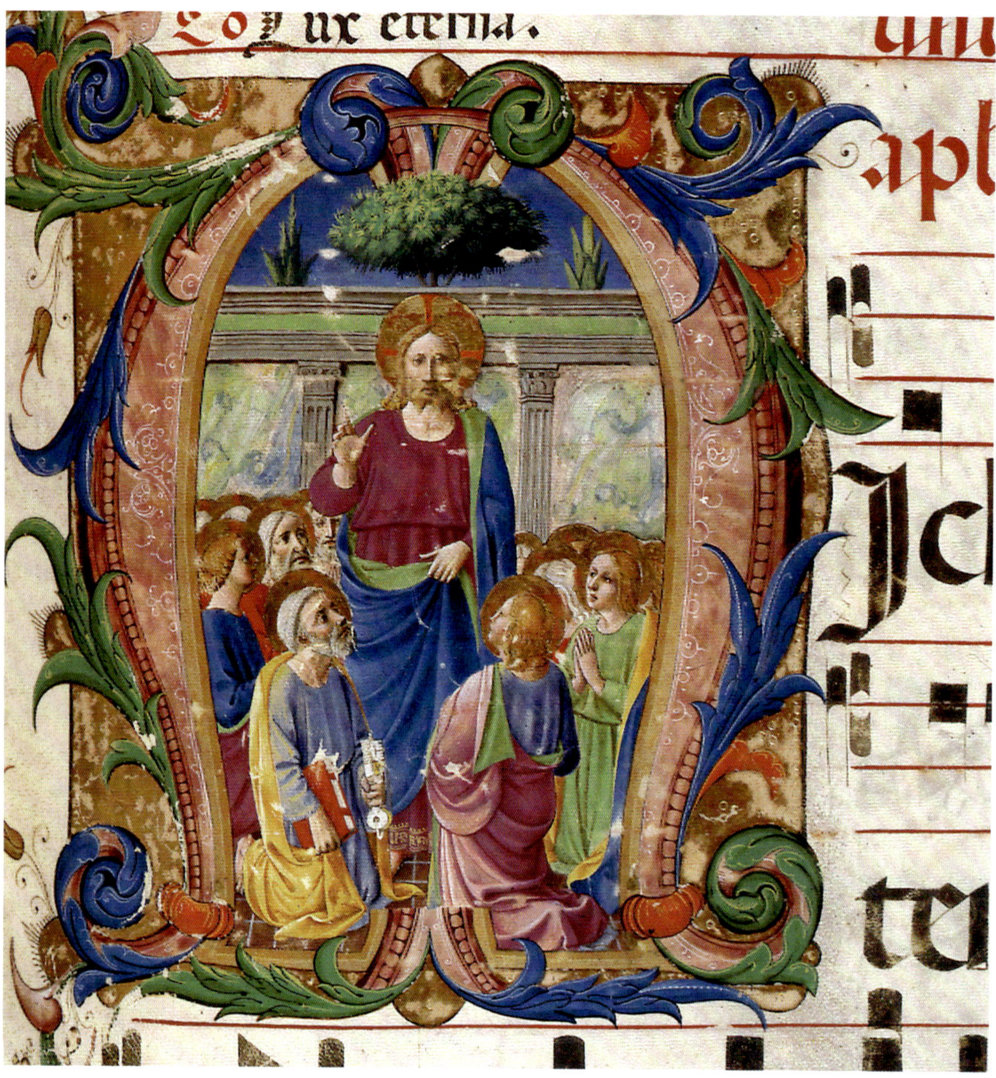

Figure 138. Zanobi Strozzi. *Christ and the Apostles* (from the San Marco graduals). 1448–49. Biblioteca del Convento di San Marco (Cod. 515, fol. 58r.)

(three of them in collaboration with other artists) in this period. The recent discovery of a signature on one of the altarpieces (fig. 133)[9] now makes it possible to outline the course of his mature activity with some precision and to restore him to his proper rank among the minor masters of his generation. Zanobi Strozzi died on December 6, 1468.

1. The fundamental source for the documentation of Sanguigni's life is Cohn 1955, pp. 207–16.
2. Toesca 1917, pp. 126–28.
3. Levi D'Ancona 1962, pp. 54–59; Levi D'Ancona 1970, pp. 1–35.
4. Kanter 2002, pp. 321–31.
5. Scudieri 2003, pp. 33–43; Dillon Bussi 2003, pp. 44–51.
6. A complete list of paintings attributable to the Master of 1419 was published by M. Boskovits (2002a, pp. 332–40).
7. Pope-Hennessy 1974, p. 211.
8. A 1449 payment for a painted "*croce per morti*," registered in the account books of San Marco, has been associated with a much-damaged processional cross now in the Museo Diocesano, Nonantola, brought there from the parish church of San Giovanni Battista at Mocogno (see Ghidiglia Quintavalle 1960, pp. 68–72; A. Di Lorenzo, in Di Lorenzo 2001, pp. 50–55). The iconography of the Mocogno cross, however, suggests that it may have been executed not for San Marco but for San Pier Martire.
9. Gordon 1998, pp. 517–24.

40.

A.
Virgin and Child Enthroned

Tempera on panel: overall, 196.2 x 68.2 cm
(77¼ x 26⅞ in.)
The Cleveland Museum of Art. Gift of the Hanna Fund, 1954 (1954.834)

B.
Saint Julian and Saint James the Greater, with the Annunciatory Angel

Tempera on panel: overall, 173.4 x 70.6 cm
(68¼ x 27¾ in.)
Private collection

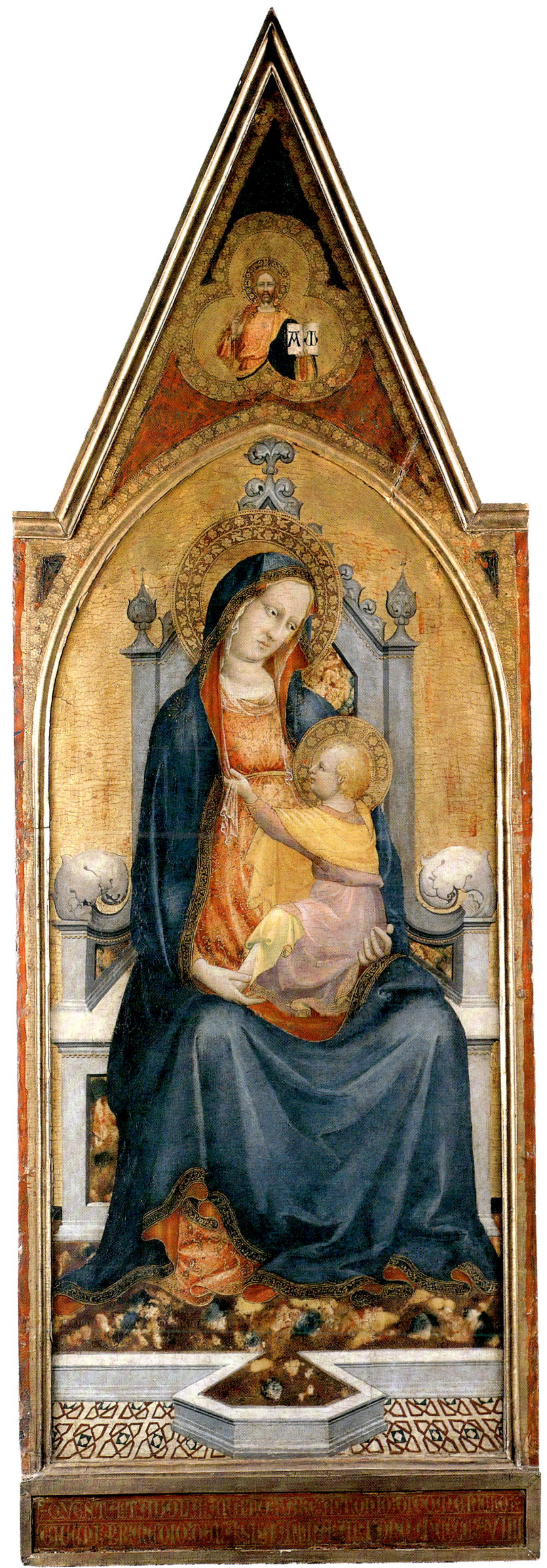

40: A

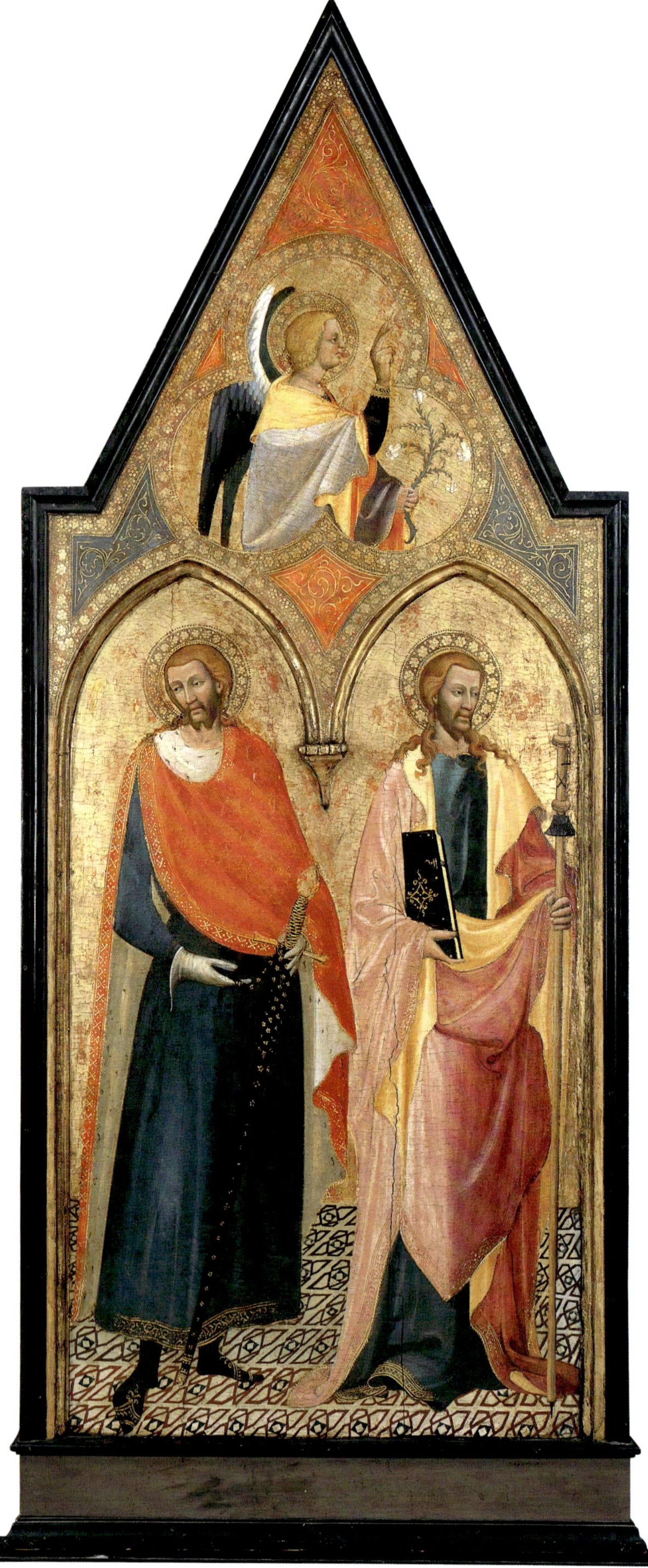

40: B

The *Virgin and Child Enthroned*, flanked on the left by Saints Julian and James the Greater, originally formed part of an altarpiece completed on the right by a third panel (fig. 139) representing Saints John the Baptist and Anthony Abbot.[1] The three panels conform to each other in size, style, marginal decoration, and framing, and they are described together in an eighteenth-century account of the church of San Jacopo alla Cavallina near Barberino in the Mugello: "*l'antica Tavola di detto Oratorio (cioé dei Marchesi Giugni) dietro all'Altar maggiore, coll'Arme de' prefati Signori, sotto della quale vi sono scritte . . . queste parole: S. Julianus. S. Jacobus. S. Maria. S. Joannes Baptista. S. Antonius. E nel mezzo vi é scritto: Questa Tavola a fatto fare Antonio di Domenico Giugni per rimedio dell'anima sua. MCCCCXVIIII*" ("The ancient painting of said Oratorio (belonging to the Marchesi Giugni) behind the high altar, with the arms of the aforesaid gentlemen, under which are written these words: S. Julian, S. James, S. Mary, S. John the

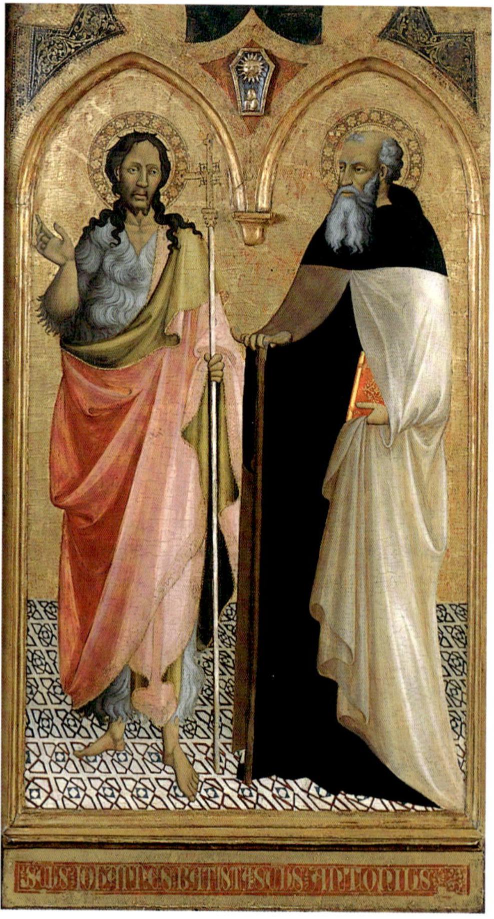

Figure 139. Battista di Biagio Sanguigni. *Saints John the Baptist and Anthony Abbot*. 1419. Estate of Dr. G. Rau, Rielasingen-Worblingen, Germany

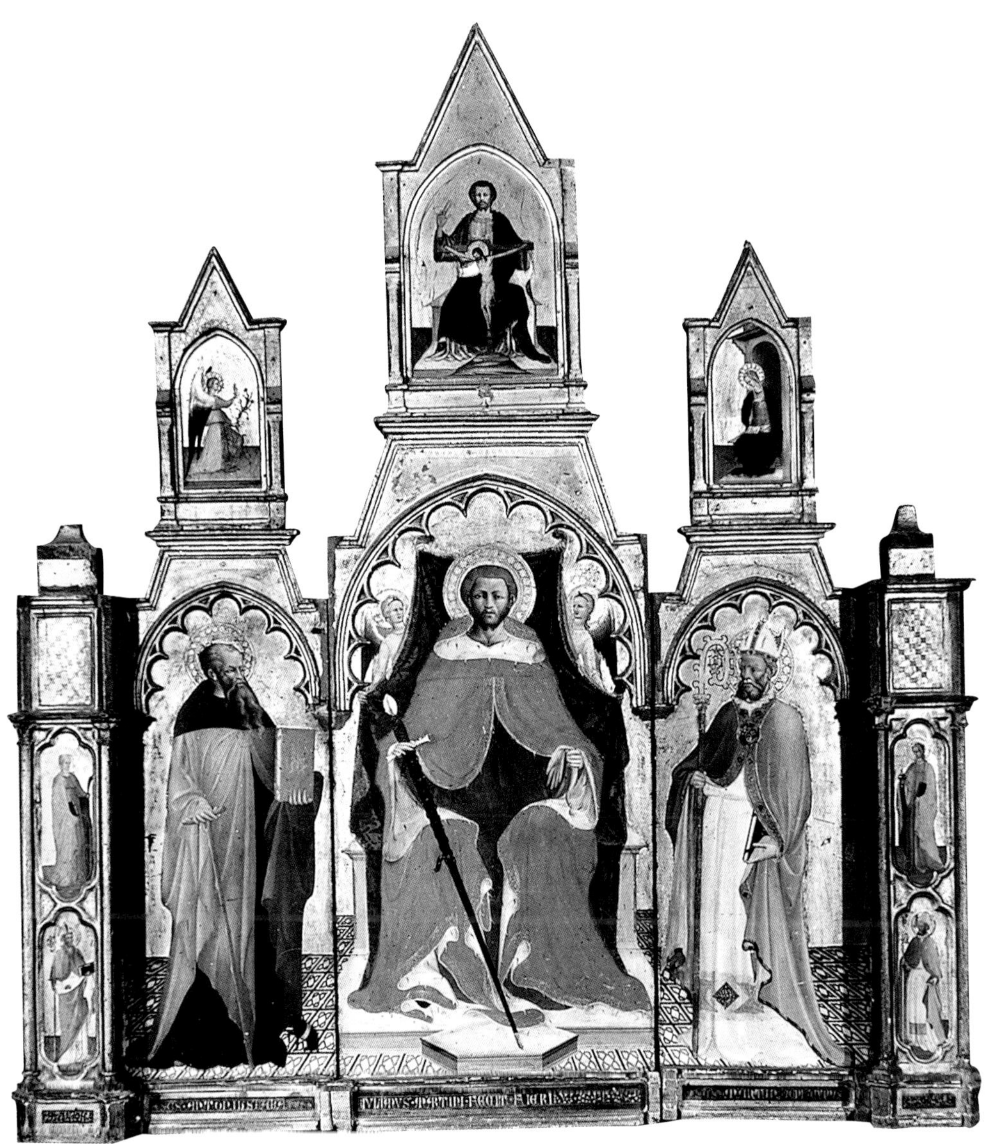

Figure 140. Battista di Biagio Sanguigni. *Saint Julian Enthroned, with Saints Anthony Abbot and Martin.* About 1425. Museo Civico, San Gimignano

Baptist, S. Anthony. And in the middle is written: Antonio di Domenico Giugni had this painting made for the salvation of his soul, 1419").[2] These inscriptions survive intact beneath two of the three panels. The altarpiece was moved to the parish church of San Jacopo alla Cavallina in 1516 from the nearby oratory of Santa Maria a Latera, for which it had been commissioned through a legacy of fifty gold florins included in the will of Antonio di Domenico Giugni in 1414.[3]

The Cleveland *Virgin and Child Enthroned* once bore a false signature of Gentile da Fabriano on the front step of the throne (removed during cleaning in 1954), but has generally been known as the name piece of an anonymous artist called the Master of 1419. First identified by Georg Pudelko in his studies of the minor masters of Late Gothic painting in Florence,[4] the Master of 1419 is only infrequently discussed in the literature. The probable outlines of the career and the extent of the oeuvre of "*questa notevole figura di pittore fiorentino*" ("this notable figure of a Florentine painter") were recently crystallized, however, in a thorough and exemplary study by Miklós Boskovits[5] in which some half dozen altarpieces or altarpiece fragments and an equal number of independent devotional panels were assigned to a period of activity ranging from about 1410 to perhaps 1430. Among these paintings, the present altarpiece assumes an unusual importance not only for being precisely dated (one of the few surviving works by any artist from this period to be so distinguished) but also as a precocious example of the trend in Florence away from the highly expressive Gothicism of Lorenzo Monaco's studio toward a more classicizing and monumental, if equally decorative, formulation as expressed in the art of Masolino and of Fra Angelico early in his career.

John Pope-Hennessy cited the Santa Maria a Latera altarpiece, as well as the Saint Julian altarpiece in San Gimignano (fig. 140) also by the Master of 1419, as a concrete influence on the young Angelico's empirical approach to the problems of the projection of pictorial space in the San Domenico high altarpiece (fig. 28). The importance of the Santa Maria a Latera altarpiece was thrown into even greater relief by the recent identification of the Master of 1419 as Battista di Biagio Sanguigni: its numerous connections to the early work of Fra Angelico now assume a more solid historical foundation, as close connections between the two artists can be documented as early as 1417, although they may be presumed to have known each other long before then and to have remained in contact throughout their lives. It is reasonable to assume that the pictorial structure of the San Domenico high altarpiece is not casually or coincidentally reminiscent of that of the Santa Maria a Latera altarpiece but was developed by Angelico in tandem with, or, at the very least, with a full awareness of, the compositions adopted by Sanguigni in his works of the second decade of the century.

As long as the Santa Maria a Latera altarpiece was the only dated work known by the Master of 1419 (Battista Sanguigni), it was virtually impossible to construct a firm chronology for his development, which appears remarkably static in the approximately one dozen works attributed to him. It is now possible to propose a date for a second altarpiece by the artist, the three panels of which are presently divided between a Swiss and a German private collection (fig. 134, 135, 136).[6] The central panel of this triptych is unusual in showing two groups of devout worshipers—male to the right, and female to the left—kneeling at the feet not of a standing Virgin of Mercy but of an enthroned Virgin and Child. Standing figures of Saint James the Greater and Saint Maurus—who wears a black Benedictine habit—occupy the left wing of the altarpiece, with Saints John the Baptist and Anthony Abbot opposite them on the right. This painting may be related to an entry in

Battista Sanguigni's declaration for the 1430 *catasto,* in which he claims to be owed fifty-two florins (roughly the same price he received for painting the Santa Maria a Latera altarpiece) from the estate of Jacopo di Niccolò Corbizzi, which he is not able to collect as it is being disputed by Corbizzi's heirs: "*i romiti di S. Benedetto e i frati di S. Domenico da Fiesole.*"[7] The coincidence of the patron's name saint, James, standing alongside the Benedictine Maurus in this triptych suggests that it may be the painting cited in this notice, which then would establish that it was completed before 1430, and probably commissioned after 1427.[8]

Given the personal relationship that existed between the two artists, it is interesting to speculate whether Sanguigni's commission to paint the Santa Maria a Latera altarpiece for the heirs of Antonio di Domenico Giugni, received sometime after 1414—plausibly, about 1417 or 1418—may have led the same family to enlist Angelico to paint the *Madonna di Cedri* (fig. 12), now in Pisa,[9] or, conversely, whether Sanguigni's commission may have resulted from their satisfaction with Angelico's work for them. Dating of the Pisa *Madonna* on stylistic grounds could allow for either possibility. The presence of Saint Julian on the left wing of the present altarpiece may, however, imply an alternative source of the commission awarded to Sanguigni. Images of Saint Julian are relatively uncommon in Italian painting in general, but he is included in two altarpieces—this one and one in San Gimignano dedicated specifically to him—and in three panels for private devotion, by Sanguigni: nearly half of his surviving work as a panel painter. The relative popularity of Saint Julian in Florence has been explained by the coincidence of his feast day, August 31, with the suppression of the Ciompi revolt in 1379,[10] but, alternatively, it may be due to the co-dedication to him of one of the principal Florentine confraternities, the Compagnia di San Benedetto Bianco. In 1384, the confraternity moved its quarters to Santa Maria Novella, and in 1428 the Confraternity of San Domenico al Poggio di Fiesole was aggregated with it. By this date, Battista Sanguigni already resided at San Domenico in Fiesole, and it is possible that a number of his commissions were received through connections with this confraternity.

LK

1. G. Pudelko (1938, p. 63) first recognized the association between the *Saints John the Baptist and Anthony Abbot* and the Cleveland *Virgin and Child*, then in the Crawshay collection. The reconstruction was completed by P. Pouncey (1954, pp. 291–92), with the addition of the *Saint Julian and Saint James the Greater*, formerly in the Chalandon collection.
2. Brocchi 1748, p. 179.
3. Cohn 1956b, pp. 49–52.
4. Pudelko 1938, p. 63.
5. Boskovits 2002a, pp. 332–40 (with earlier bibliography).
6. Freuler 1991, pp. 230–31; Boskovits 2002a, pp. 334, 336–38, figures 5–7.
7. Cohn 1955, p. 212.
8. Jacopo di Niccolò Corbizzi makes no claim of an outstanding obligation for such a commission in his *catasto* declaration of 1427.
9. Strehlke 1998, pp. 13–14, 68 n. 6.
10. Joannides 1993, p. 351.

BATTISTA DI BIAGIO SANGUIGNI AND ZANOBI STROZZI

41.
The Ascension of Christ, in an Initial V

Tempera and gold on parchment, mounted on panel, 40.2 x 32.7 cm (15 ⅞ x 12 ⅞ in.)
J. Paul Getty Museum, Los Angeles (2003.104)

The initial *V* begins the Introit to the Mass for the feast of the Ascension: "*Viri Galilaei, quid admiramini aspicientes in caelum?*" ("Men of Galilee, why do you stand looking up to heaven?"). Within the arms of the initial letter, the twelve apostles, some indicated only by their halos, kneel in attitudes of reverence and wonder, looking either upward or quizzically at each other. Two angels standing at the left point out to them the figure of the resurrected Christ, ascending to Heaven on a glory of pale blue clouds. Four half-length angels, two of them bearing olive branches, appear in the curling tendrils of foliate decoration that fill the corners. The composition is surrounded by a painted mosaic border articulated at all four corners and at the centers of each side with eight medallions containing bust- or half-length prophets holding scrolls.

The initial *V* was first identified by Marvin Eisenberg as the missing folio 59 from Cor. 3, in the Biblioteca Medicea Laurenziana, Florence, the third part of a four-volume gradual (temporale) from the famous set of choir books painted for the Camaldolese monastery of Santa Maria degli Angeli.[1] This book, dated 1409 in a colophon (fol. 3*r.*), was provided with eight illuminated initials by Lorenzo Monaco, presumably about or shortly after 1410, all of which show half-length or three-quarter-length images of prophets (folios 35*r.*, 38*v.*, 46*v.*, 65*v.*, 86*v.*, 89*v.*, 93*r.*, 96*v.*). Another illumination, the *Initial* E, *with Saints Peter, John the Evangelist, and Mary Magdalene at the Empty Tomb of Christ* (fol. 27*v.*), is also sometimes attributed to Lorenzo Monaco.[2] The latter seems like a later intervention, however, in a different, more classicizing style, and may be a first attempt to finish the decoration of the volume

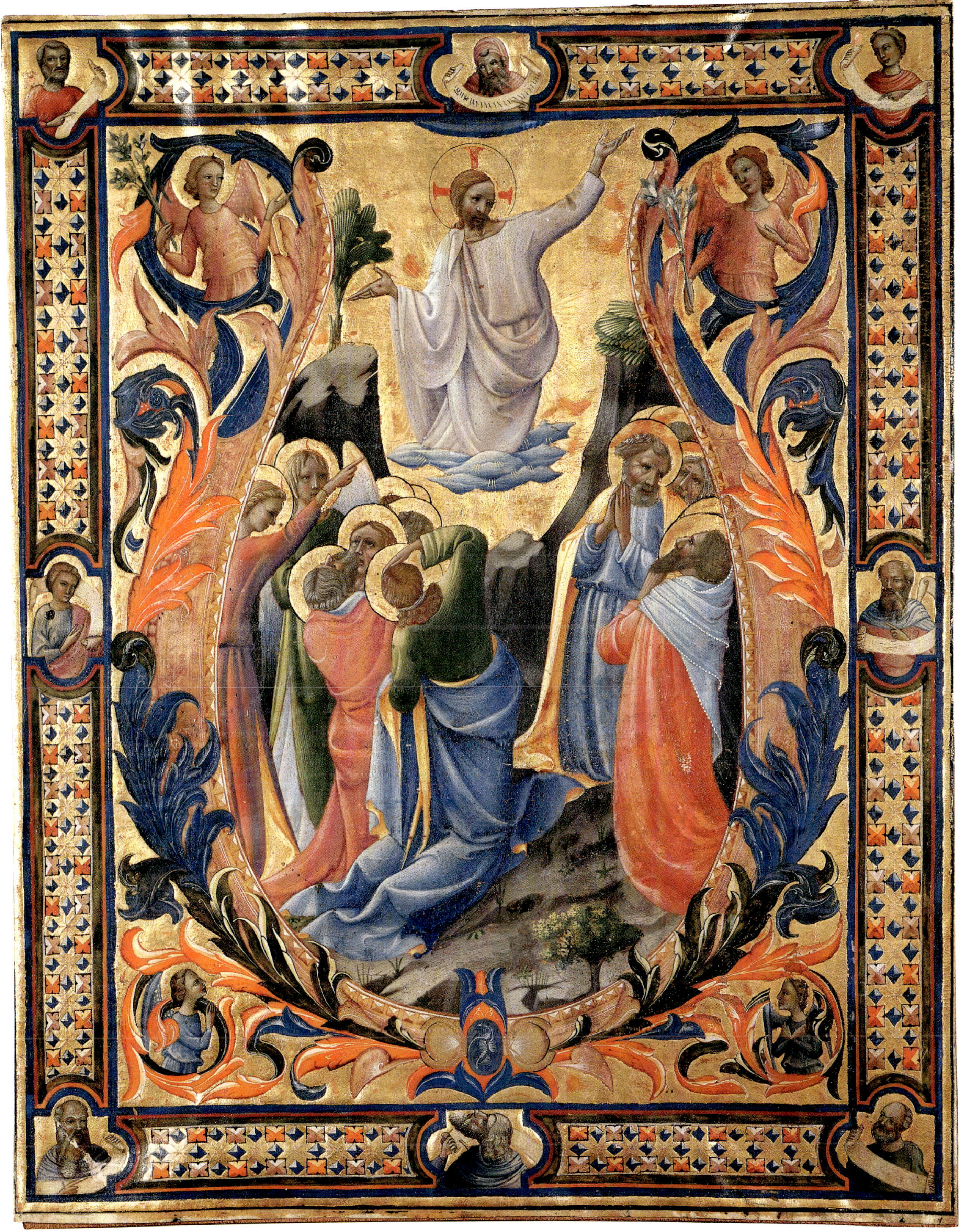

41

after it was abandoned, for unknown reasons, by Lorenzo Monaco. Eleven other narrative illuminations, including the present initial, were provided still later, although some of these may have been advanced by Lorenzo Monaco to the stage of finished underdrawings, as in the first two volumes of the gradual (cat. 1): folio 1*v.*, for example, decorated with a full-page illumination of *The Resurrection, in an Initial* R, was provided with a foliate border and drolleries by Lorenzo Monaco or his studio, while the initial, which looks persuasively like a Lorenzo Monaco design, was clearly painted later.

The authorship of the twelve narrative illuminations in—or subsequently removed from—this volume has been one of the most contentious topics in the study of Early Renaissance manuscript painting in Florence. Attributed early on to Fra Angelico himself,[3] but also to Andrea di Giusto, Battista Sanguigni, Zanobi Strozzi, and a mysterious figure known as Don Niccolò Rosselli, cited in documents of payment in 1454,[4] with the marginal decorations ascribed variously to Bartolommeo di Fruosino, Matteo Torrelli, and the Master of the Codex Squarcialupi,[5] the manuscript has most recently—and prudently—been catalogued as by an unknown master of the fourth decade of the fifteenth century, with an acknowledgment that more than one hand appears to have been involved in completing Lorenzo Monaco's preliminary work.[6] In addition to the difficulty of assessing the heterogeneity of the miniatures in this manuscript, the possibility that some, but not all, of them may be painted directly over designs by Lorenzo Monaco, while others are compositional inventions by one or more artists of a later generation, makes an attributional consensus all but unattainable. It does seem to this writer, however, that sufficiently compelling analogies of figure types and palette permit the assignment of at least a large part of the miniatures in the final decorative campaign on Cor. 3 to Zanobi Strozzi, with the caveat that his work here was not autonomous and that it must be by a considerable margin his earliest efforts as an illuminator.

The identification of Battista di Biagio Sanguigni as the author of the half-length angels and prophets surrounding the scene of the *Assumption* in the Getty initial *V* was based upon an interpretation of documents relating to the biography of Zanobi Strozzi, which suggest that, as the first decade or so of the latter's career evolved under the tutelage of Sanguigni—himself described in other documents as a miniaturist—it was logical to assume that anyone who collaborated with Strozzi on early illuminations might be that elusive master.[7] These angels and prophets, furthermore, bear an incontestable visual relationship both to Sanguigni's documented miniatures of 1432 and to the panel paintings commonly assigned to the Master of 1419, leading to the conclusion that Sanguigni and the Master of 1419 are one and the same. While that identification has been disputed, the attribution of the borders of the Getty leaf to the Master of 1419 has not, and specific analogies between them and the lateral panels of an altarpiece representing Saints James, Maurus, John the Baptist, and Anthony Abbot (fig. 134, 135, 136) have been adduced as confirmation.[8] Now that it is possible to propose that this altarpiece is not the work of an anonymous artist in the second decade of the fifteenth century, as was formerly believed, but may be a documented work by Sanguigni, executed between 1427 and 1430 (see cat. 40), the argument becomes circular.

It remains to disentangle more precisely the nature of the collaboration between Strozzi and Sanguigni on Cor. 3. While the best of his documented work in the San Gaggio hymnal and antiphonary implies that Sanguigni may have been the artist responsible for completing *The Resurrection, in an Initial* R on folio 1*v.*, his intervention elsewhere in the manuscript seems to have been restricted to minor passages within scenes otherwise recognizable as by Zanobi Strozzi or, as in the present instance, to the lavish decorated borders gracing the margins of all the historiated initials. Notwithstanding this apparently subsidiary role, however, the relationship of the two artists as tutor and pupil must be borne in mind, and it remains tempting to identify the completion of Cor. 3 with a document of 1431 in which Sanguigni declares himself in debt to Santa Maria degli Angeli for the purchase of blue pigment. Such a date, or terminus a quo, for Cor. 3 does not conflict with Sanguigni's style in the San Gaggio hymnal—supposedly a documented work of 1432—and it fits in with the completion of the Corbizzi altarpiece sometime between 1427 and 1430. It is also a reasonable date for the hypothetical beginning of Zanobi Strozzi's career. Born in 1412, he is not likely to have been active in so prominent a role much earlier than 1431, and by 1433 he and probably Sanguigni as well were working more consistently in the orbit and in the style of Fra Angelico.

LK

1. Eisenberg 1989, pp. 110–11. The two other initials missing from Cor. 3, folios 19 and 31, were identified, respectively, by M. Bollati (1998, pp. 19–25: *The Children of the World Praising the Lord in an Initial* V; Private collection), and M. Levi D'Ancona (1978, p. 226: *Procession of Children in an Initial* Q, National Gallery of Art, Washington, D.C.).
2. Boskovits 1975, pp. 341–42; Bellosi 1984, p. 307.
3. Ciaranfi 1932, pp. 304, 315 (as "*tendenza dell'Angelico*"); Salmi 1950, pp. 75–77 (as about 1409); Salmi 1954, p. 48 (as about 1420).
4. Berenson 1963, vol. I, p. 6; Longhi 1940, p. 182 n. 15; Levi D'Ancona 1995, pp. 170, 173; M. Boskovits, in Hatvany sale, 1980, p. 13.
5. Salmi 1950, p. 76; Levi D'Ancona 1995, p. 153; Bellosi 1984.
6. M. Scudieri, in Scudieri and Rasario 2003, pp. 115–20.
7. Kanter 2002, pp. 322–23.
8. M. Scudieri, in Scudieri and Rasario 2003, p. 118.

42.

A.

Virgin and Child Enthroned, with Saints Dominic, Thomas Aquinas, Peter Martyr, and John the Baptist, an Angel, and a Soul (?) (center panel); *Christ Carrying the Cross* (left wing); *Christ on the Cross, with Saint Mary Magdalene and a Dominican Beata* (right wing); *The Annunciation* (pinnacles)

Tempera on panel: center panel, 38.3 x 20 cm (15⅛ x 7⅞ in.); left wing, 38.3 x 10.9 cm (15⅛ x 4¼ in.); right wing, 38.3 x 11.4 cm (15⅛ x 4½ in.)
Christ Church Picture Gallery, Oxford. Fox-Strangways Gift (1834 ?)

B.

The Resurrection

Tempera on panel, 26 x 10 cm (10¼ x 3 15/16 in.)
Musée du Louvre, Paris. Bequest of Baron Nathaniel de Rothschild, 1899 (R.F. 1263)

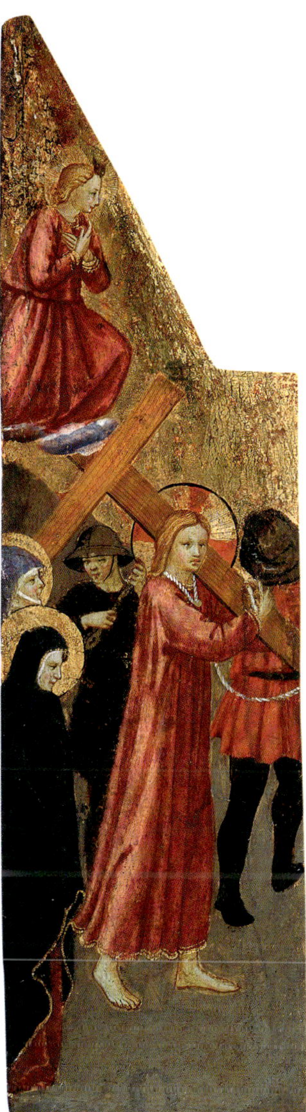
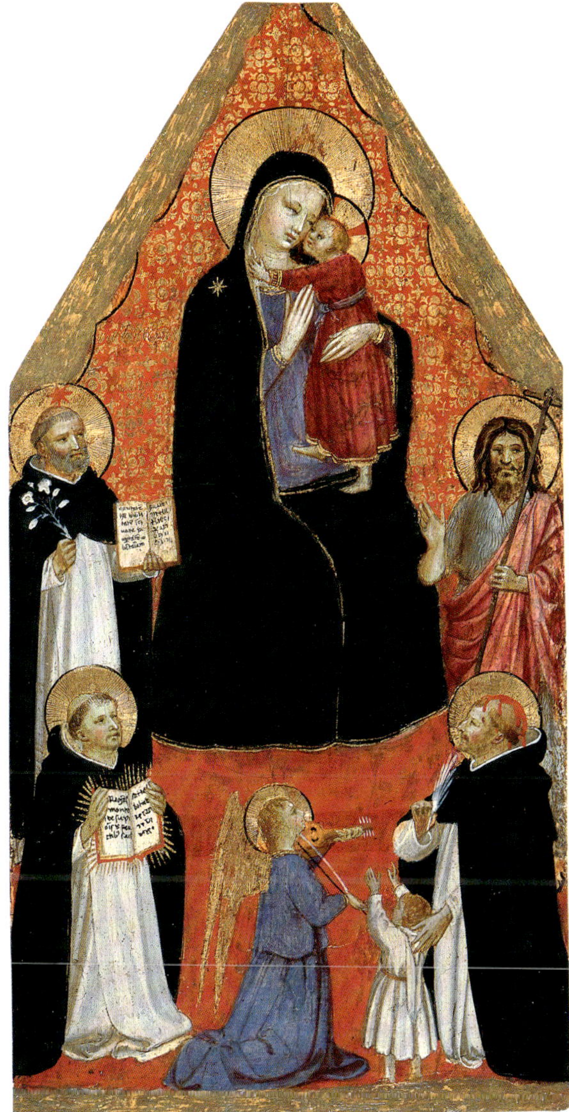
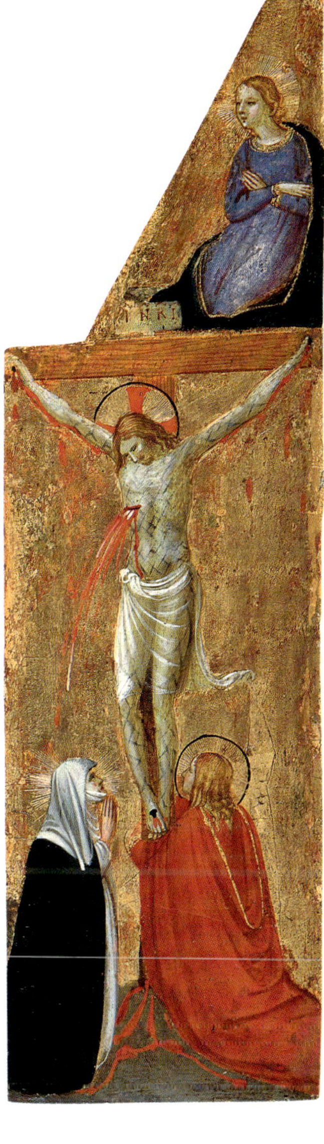

42: A

The Christ Church triptych is largely ignored by students of Fra Angelico and his followers and is little known to art historians in general. Tancred Borenius[1] considered it a forgery or a late imitation, and it was dismissed by Pope-Hennessy with the comment, "the naïve compositions suggest that we have here to do with a pastiche of Angelico's work painted about 1450 by a provincial artist for some local Dominican community."[2] James Byam-Shaw catalogued it more positively as Studio of Fra Angelico, noting a difference in quality between the center panel and the wings, and relating the style of the former to the four reliquaries from Santa Maria Novella (see cat. 28).[3] The notably more accomplished center panel—particularly, the figures of Saints Thomas Aquinas and Peter Martyr kneeling in the foreground—does suggest the possibility that a design by Angelico himself may underlie the conception of this painting, as does the processional arrangement of the figures receding in space on the left wing. Otherwise, Pope-Hennessy's analysis was nearly correct. The relationship of the triptych to the Santa Maria Novella reliquaries is limited to a general borrowing from the *Madonna della Stella* of the interaction between the Virgin and the Christ Child. The facial types of the Virgin and Saint Dominic, and the stiff, elongated figures in the narrative scenes indicate Battista Sanguigni's authorship of the triptych, sometime after 1430. Its closest analogies are to be found in the predella panels executed by Sanguigni for Angelico, such as the *Presentation in the Temple* from the *Annunciation* altarpiece in San Giovanni Valdarno. As this work cannot be precisely dated and as the progress of Sanguigni's late career cannot be anchored to any documents, it is only possible to say of the Christ Church triptych that it is likely to have been painted sometime about 1440.

The *Resurrection* in the Louvre is even less well known than the Christ Church triptych, to which it is self-evidently related in style. Although it had been published by Ricci and Hautecoeur as a work by Fra Angelico,[4] it is not included in any monographic study of the artist. Close examination of the panel on which it is painted reveals that it served as the wing of a triptych. While its sides and bottom edge are original, it has been truncated at the top and thinned down, and damages along its right edge 6.8 centimeters from the bottom and 5.5 centimeters from the top doubtless correspond to the placement of wire hinges that once attached it to the center panel of the complex. Not coincidentally, given the correspondence in style and continuity in subject matter, the Louvre *Resurrection* is almost exactly the same size as the right wing of the Christ Church triptych, which measures 26 centimeters in height without its pinnacle. Cleaning of the triptych in 1965/66 revealed that all three of its component panels, like the Louvre panel, had been thinned, and that engaged moldings on the center panel had been removed from the front surface along the top and bottom edges and cropped off altogether along the sides. Byam Shaw presumed these alterations to have been occasioned by worm damage, but the possibility must be entertained that the wings were double-sided, and were not thinned but sawn in half. Two repaired damages along the left edge of the Christ Church *Crucifixion* probably indicate the removal of hinges at those spots, although the repairs are broader than normal hinge scars. They correspond approximately to the position of the related damages on the right edge of the Louvre *Resurrection,* which may be presumed originally to have been the painted reverse side of the Christ Church *Crucifixion.* The slight difference in width between these two panels implies that their common outer edge was stepped back to form a lip that engaged a similar lip in reverse profile on the left wing when the triptych was closed; such a device is characteristic of fifteenth-century Tuscan triptychs, and its existence is, in any event, implied by the difference in width of the two wings at Christ Church.

A replica or close variant of the Christ Church triptych (fig. 142) is preserved in the John G. Johnson Collection at the Philadelphia Museum of Art (JC Inv. 2034) in which the compositions of the lateral panels are altered slightly to conform to the spatial conventions familiar to artists of a younger generation. The Virgin and Child and the four saints in the center panel are reproduced faithfully, except that Thomas Aquinas and Peter Martyr are shown standing and two additional saints—Francis and Jerome—kneel before them in the foreground. The viol-playing angel of the Christ Church triptych is also reprised in the Philadelphia panel, as is the young boy being presented to the Virgin, although in the later painting he wears secular dress rather than a white habit and

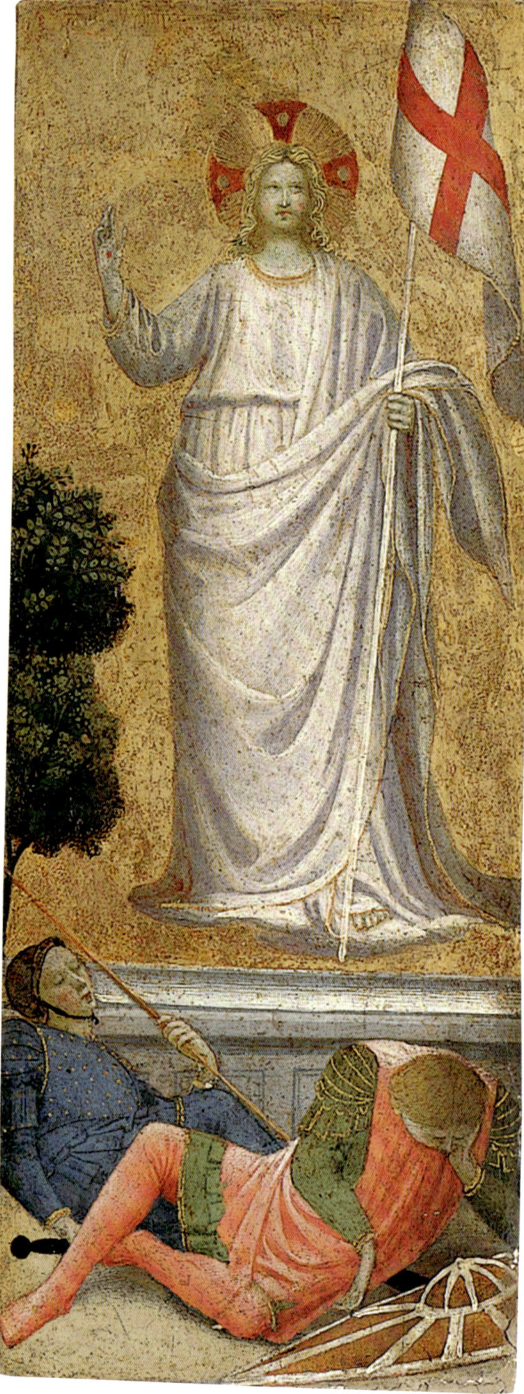

42: B

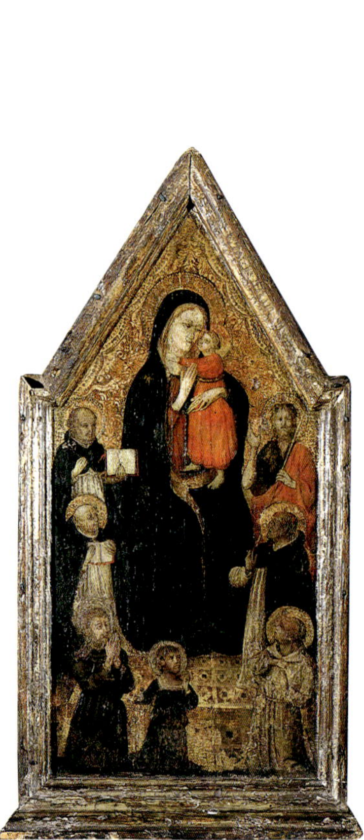

Figure 141. Master of the Johnson Tabernacle. *Virgin and Child Enthroned, with Six Saints.* About 1460. Museo Bagatti Valsecchi, Milan

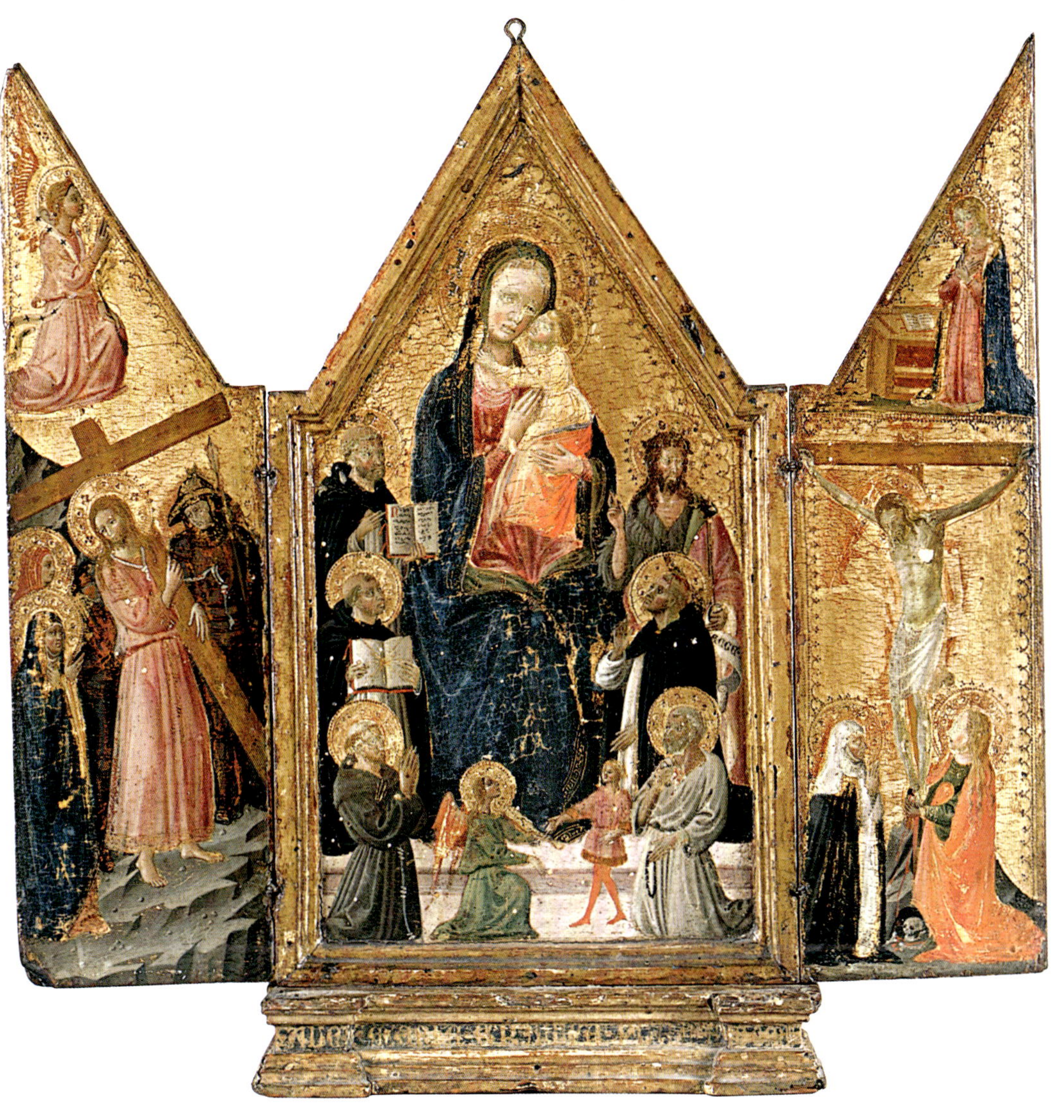

Figure 142. Master of the Johnson Tabernacle. *Virgin and Child Enthroned, with a Music-Making Angel, a Child, and Saints Francis, Thomas Aquinas, Dominic, John the Baptist, Peter Martyr, and Jerome* (center); *Christ Carrying the Cross* (left wing); *Christ on the Cross, with Saints Catherine of Siena and Mary Magdalene* (right wing); *The Annunciation* (pinnacles). About 1460–65. Philadelphia Museum of Art. The John G. Johnson Collection

scapular and he is sponsored by Saint Jerome rather than Peter Martyr. The reverse sides of the wings of the Philadelphia triptych are not painted with narrative scenes but with decorative geometric patterns.

It is argued by Carl Strehlke that the Dominican nun kneeling at the foot of the cross in the right wings of both triptychs is Catherine of Siena—shown, at Christ Church, with the rays of a beata, and with the halo of a saint, following her canonization in 1461, in Philadelphia.[5] This identification is probably correct. Strehlke also suggests that the child in the center panel at Christ Church may have been a novice at a Dominican convent or a new member of one of Florence's confraternities for boys; these children wore white garments during public processions. This is unlikely, however, as the white habit includes a scapular, and the child is too young to have been a Dominican novice. It is possible, instead, that the habit is that of a Dominican tertiary, and it may be that the triptych was not commissioned to celebrate the entrance of the child into either a convent or a confraternity but to commemorate his early death. The boy in both the Christ Church and Philadelphia paintings is shown reaching back to embrace the Virgin and Child rather than in a conventional kneeling posture of reverence or adoration. This is probably to be explained as an expression of his parents' hopes for his reception in Paradise. Furthermore, if the identification of the Louvre *Resurrection* as the original outer face of the right wing of the Christ Church triptych is correct, the Passion and Resurrection iconography of the lateral scenes would refer unmistakably to the salvation of the Christian soul and be more appropriate to a funerary context than to any other.

Two additional replicas of the center panel of the Christ Church triptych were identified by Victor Schmidt. One of these (fig. 141), in the Museo Bagatti Valsecchi in Milan (Inv. no. 984), has been attributed by Everett Fahy to the same artist responsible for the Philadelphia triptych, whom he named the Master of the Johnson Tabernacle.[6] In this painting, as in the Philadelphia version, six saints rather than four flank the enthroned Virgin, but the kneeling angel and the child in the foreground have been replaced by an unidentified figure who may be another saint. The Christ Child is an exact copy of his counterpart in the Christ Church painting—in the Philadelphia version he is shown seated in the crook of his mother's left arm rather than standing on her lap—and the scalloped cloth of honor is reintroduced behind her throne. Another version of the composition, by Bicci di Lorenzo, is in the Heinz Kisters collection in Kreuzlingen, and similarly shows six saints, among them Agnes and Catherine of Alexandria kneeling in the foreground. This last replica incorporates the angel and a child, as at Christ Church and in Philadelphia, but otherwise takes some liberties with poses and figure types entirely characteristic of Bicci di Lorenzo's late painting style. Neither of these two panels is preserved with wings

LK

1. Borenius 1916, no. 47.
2. Pope-Hennessy 1974, p. 230.
3. Byam Shaw 1967, no. 20, pp. 39–40.
4. Ricci 1913, p. 58; Hautecoeur 1926, no. 1294 A.
5. Strehlke 2004, pp. 284–87.
6. Cited in Pavoni 2003, pp. 216–17.

43.
Virgin and Child

Tempera on panel: overall,[1] 77.5 x 44.5 cm (30½ x 17½ in.); picture surface, 77.5 x 41 cm (30½ x 16⅛ in.)
Collection Richard L. Feigen, New York

In this monumental painting, Sanguigni has followed Fra Angelico's example in conflating the imagery of a Virgin and Child Enthroned with that of the Virgin of Humility. From the former are borrowed the motifs of a gilt cloth of honor and a stepped marble pavement, yet the Virgin is clearly seated humbly (on a cushion) on the ground, with her left leg folded beneath her and her right knee drawn up for the Child to stand upon. This composition parallels that of a number of examples of the Virgin of Humility by Fra Angelico, such as those in Berlin (fig. 89), in Amsterdam (cat. 31 B), in a private collection in Switzerland (fig. 61), and, above all, in the Thyssen Collection (cat. 18). In every instance, however, Angelico places the Child to his mother's left—the viewer's right—whereas Sanguigni reverses their arrangement. Several of Fra Angelico's paintings, furthermore, include a pair of small-scale figures in the foreground, either kneeling saints or music-making angels. Sanguigni has replaced these with two vases of flowers set before the face of the marble step and seen implausibly *dal di sotto in su*—a motif that he no doubt borrowed from the center panel of Angelico's Perugia altarpiece of 1437–38 (cat. 30) or its slightly later "replica" in Cortona (fig. 143).

The Feigen *Virgin and Child,* formerly in the Condé collection at Château Biarge (Charente), was first published by Raimond Van Marle in 1928 with an attribution to Domenico di Michelino—to whom it may have been assigned five years earlier by Bernard Berenson.[2] The picture had otherwise been entirely ignored by scholars until it appeared at a public auction in 1999 with an attribution to Zanobi Strozzi (suggested by Everett Fahy).[3] Miklós Boskovits thought that it might be by the young Fra Angelico himself—a suggestion he advanced with some caution due to what he believed (from photographs) to be the poor condition of the painting.[4] However, it is actually in an excellent state of preservation, apart from a split in the panel that extends through the face of the Christ Child but that has resulted in minimal paint loss. The original profile of the composition has been altered by a modern, and fanciful, engaged frame, and the brown color lining the arch of the frame, outside the silhouette of the cloth of honor, is false. The paint surface, however, is unabraded and not affected in any area by repaints. While the elegantly twisting hem of the Virgin's mantle might seem an invention worthy of Fra Angelico, the weaknesses in the foreshortening, especially of

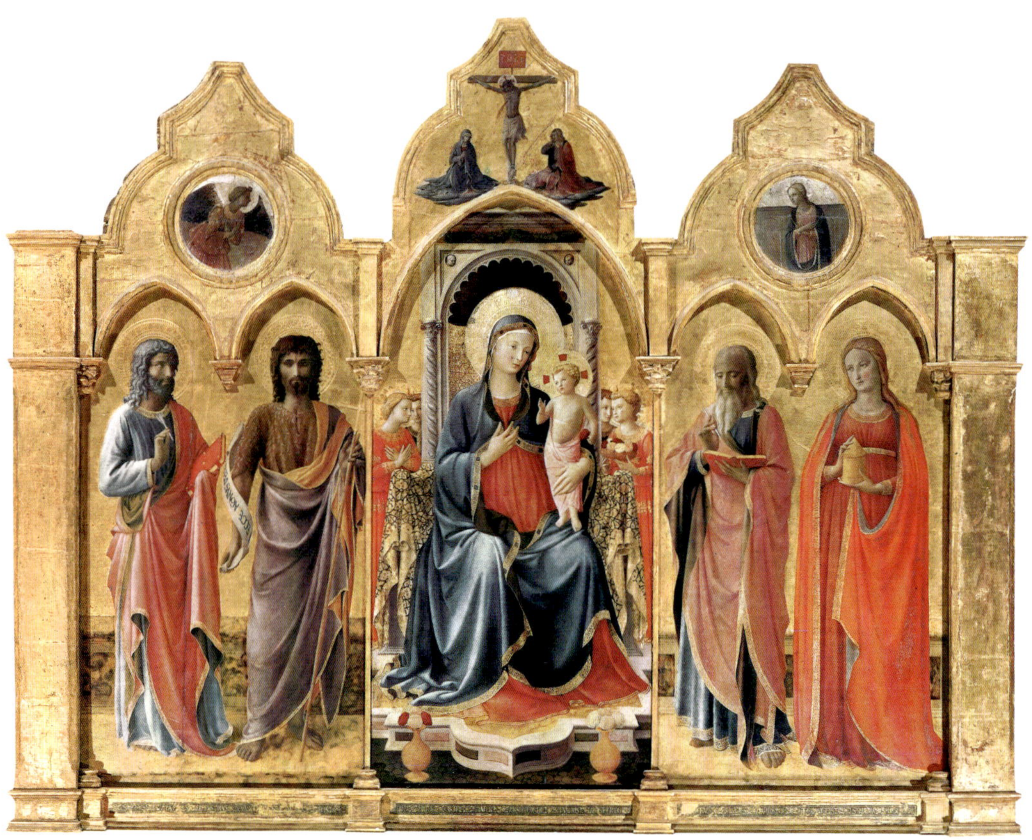

Figure 143. Assistant of Fra Angelico. *Virgin and Child Enthroned, with Four Angels and Saints Mark, John the Baptist, John the Evangelist, and Mary Magdalene* (Cortona Triptych). About 1440–45. Museo Diocesano, Cortona

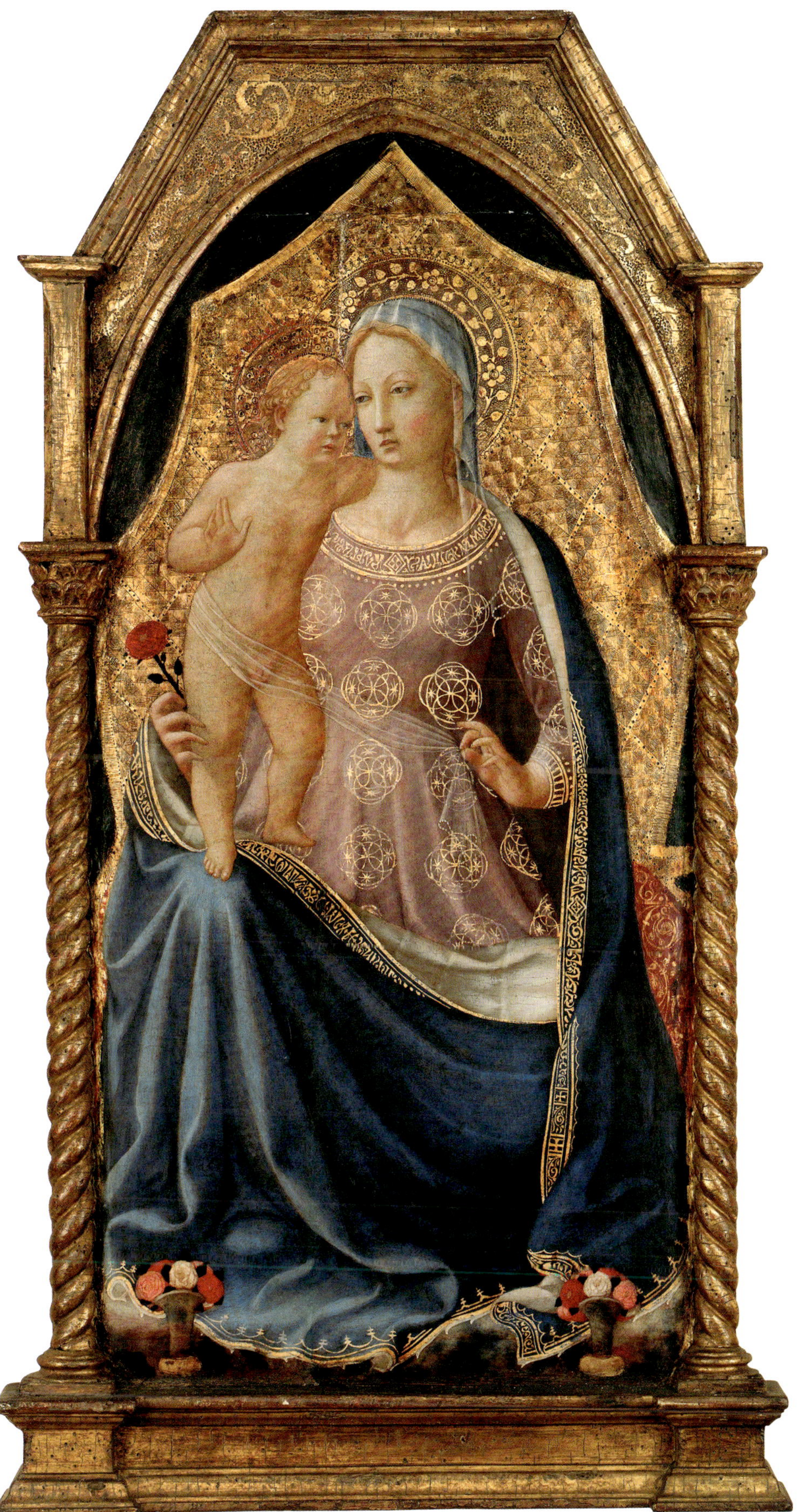

43

the Virgin's hands, and the implausible projection of the vases of flowers from a viewing point radically different from that of the figures unmistakably reveals an execution not by the master but by a follower. That this follower might have been Battista di Biagio Sanguigni is suggested by a comparison of the face of the Virgin with any detail of the Saint Julian altarpiece in San Gimignano (fig. 140) or of the Corbizzi altarpiece (fig. 134, 135, 136): her exaggeratedly high forehead; narrow, slit-like dark eyes, with their unfocused, faraway stare; long, straight nose; and small mouth set impossibly close to the bottom of her chin are all hallmarks of Sanguigni's style.[5]

No documented works by Sanguigni from his last two decades of activity survive to confirm this attribution, although the logic of visual evidence argues strongly in its favor. That Sanguigni's career in the 1430s and, presumably, the 1440s developed directly in the wake of his longtime friend and neighbor, Fra Angelico, as well as in the shadow of his talented pupil, Zanobi Strozzi, is, in any event, implied by those documents of his life that are extant. It is possible to identify some of Sanguigni's collaborations with Strozzi as labors of assistance for Angelico. Such must have been the case, for example, with the San Giovanni Valdarno altarpiece, executed by Zanobi Strozzi over designs by Angelico (who must have been the recipient of the commission), with Sanguigni's participation evident in some of the predella scenes. Work on eight of the ten frescoed scenes from the life of Saint Benedict in the Orange Cloister of the Badia Fiorentina must also have been organized in this fashion, although here Sanguigni's role was considerably greater (see pp. 291–94). This pattern of production inevitably raises the question of whether paintings such as the Feigen *Virgin and Child* were conceived and executed as independent efforts or as the workshop output of the "Fra Angelico studio." Was the painting ordered from Angelico, designed by him, and meant in the first instance to be understood as his work, or was it intended from the start to be recognized as by Battista di Biagio Sanguigni? Unfortunately, no contemporary documentation or commentary exists on which to formulate the answer to such a question. LK

1. Overall dimensions are exclusive of an approximately six-centimeter addition to complete the arch of the panel at the top and of the modern engaged frame. An additional two centimeters of panel may be concealed at the bottom under the molding of the engaged frame.
2. Van Marle 1928, p. 190. A photograph at Villa I Tatti, inscribed "Wildenstein 1923," is filed there under "Domenico di Michelino."
3. Sold at Christie's, New York, May 25, 1999, lot 129.
4. Boskovits 2002a, p. 340.
5. This attribution was first proposed by L. Kanter (2002, pp. 329, 331 n. 22).

44.

A.

Saint John the Baptist, Saint Lawrence, and Saint Nicholas of Bari

Tempera on panel, 76.2 x 47.3 cm (30 x 18⅝ in.)
The Hyde Collection, Glens Falls, New York

B.

Saint Zenobius, Saint Francis, and Saint Anthony of Padua

Tempera on panel, 76.5 x 47 cm (30⅛ x 18½ in.)
Yale University Art Gallery, New Haven.
University Purchase from James Jackson Jarves (1871.31)

C.

The Nativity

Tempera on panel: overall, 20 x 44.1 cm (7⅞ x 17⅜ in.); picture surface, 18.7 x 43.5 cm (7⅜ x 17⅛ in.)
The Metropolitan Museum of Art, New York. Gift of May Dougherty King, 1983 (1983.490)

D.

The Adoration of the Magi

Tempera on panel: overall, 20.3 x 48.2 cm (8 x 19 in.); picture surface, 19 x 47.4 cm (7½ x 18⅝ in.)
National Gallery, London (NG 582)

The evident connection between the Hyde *Saint John the Baptist, Saint Lawrence, and Saint Nicholas of Bari,* formerly in the Sidney collection in Richmond, and the Yale *Saint Zenobius, Saint Francis, and Saint Anthony of Padua* was first noticed by R. Langton Douglas.[1] These paintings clearly served as the lateral panels of an altarpiece, the center panel of which was identified by Pia Palladino with a painting (fig. 144) now in the State Hermitage Museum in Saint Petersburg. Of appropriate format, dimensions, and style to have once belonged to the same complex as the Yale and Hyde panels, the Hermitage panel portrays the enthroned Virgin and the Christ Child, who stands on her lap and holds an orb representing the globe—an image loosely based on the center panel of the Linaiuoli tabernacle of 1433–35 (see cat. 29). Unlike the Linaiuoli Virgin, the Virgin of the Hermitage panel holds a lily in her right hand, and the Christ Child is unclothed and his pose less frontal. The top of the throne is rendered as a shell niche and the back is draped with a cloth of gold that descends over the red cushion on which the Virgin is seated. The corners of the red carpet under the Virgin's feet can be seen cropped at the inner edges of the Yale and Hyde panels, while the reddish brown lining of Saint Zenobius's cope, cropped at the left edge of the Yale panel, encroaches on the right edge of the Hermitage *Virgin and Child.* The head of Saint Zenobius's crosier, which also should appear at the right edge of the Hermitage *Virgin,* has been obscured by black overpaint, which covers the original gold ground of the panel. The same black overpaint is visible in photographs of the Hyde *Saint John the Baptist, Saint Lawrence, and Saint Nicholas of Bari* taken at the time of the sale of the Sidney collection.[2] Finally, the halos of the figures in all three panels are identical in design.

It may be assumed that the Hermitage panel, which measures 89 by 42 centimeters, has been cropped at the bottom by at least seven centimeters, excising the riser of the marble platform on which the lateral saints stand and at least one step of the dais that supports the Virgin's throne. That this riser and step would have been visible at the bottom of the panel below the red carpet is indicated by the latter's trailing ends seen in the lower corners of the side panels, and the additional height they impute to the center panel explains the pronounced upward glances of the lateral saints, which are focused on the faces of the Virgin and Child. Like the Hermitage panel, the tops of the Yale and Hyde panels have been truncated: damages at their upper-left and upper-right corners may indicate the removal of corbels intended to support the spring of an arch, but it is not clear whether the present arched top of the Hermitage picture is original—which would therefore imply a similar shape for the lateral panels as well—or whether it has been altered from an ogival arch. None of the three panels has been altered in width, however, and the coincidence of their relative proportions, coupled with their conformity of style, suggests that the Metropolitan Museum *Nativity* and the National Gallery *Adoration of the Magi* were parts of the predella that once must have been below this altarpiece (fig. 145).

All five panels of this altarpiece represent Zanobi Strozzi's style in the late 1430s or about 1440—the period of his closest dependence on Fra Angelico's example, during which he

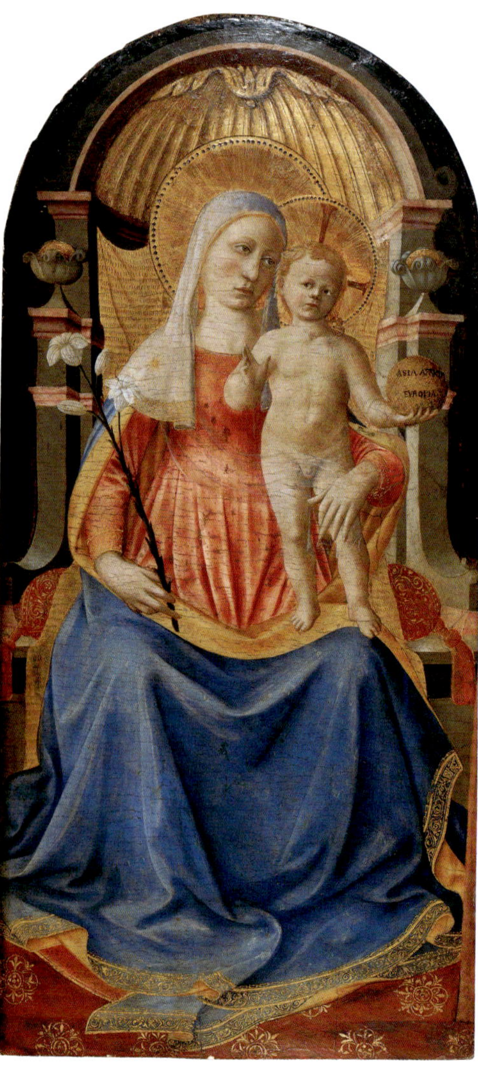

Figure 144. Zanobi Strozzi. *Virgin and Child Enthroned.* About 1435–40. State Hermitage Museum, Saint Petersburg

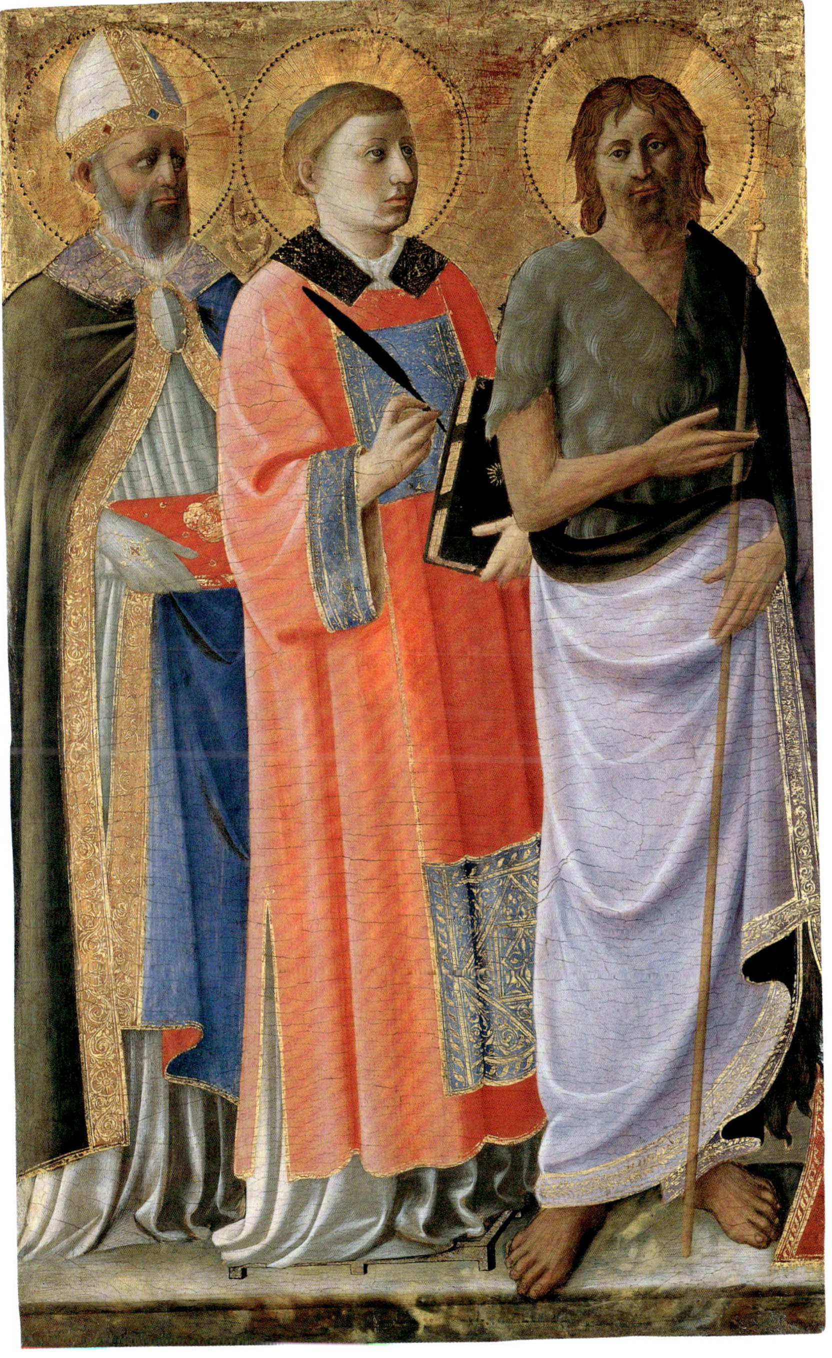

44: A

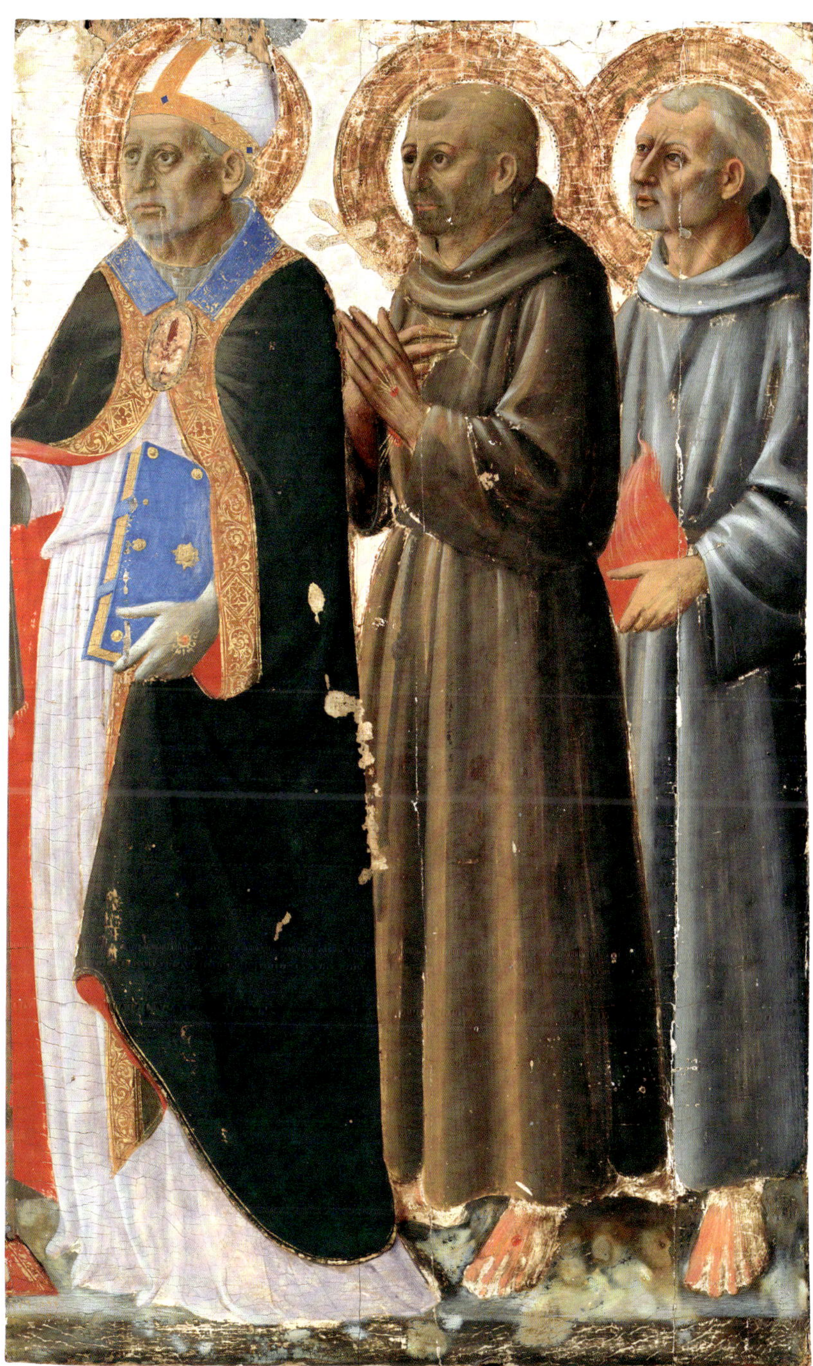

44: B

collaborated on the execution of a number of the Dominican master's commissions. It is, in fact, possible that the present altarpiece was originally a commission awarded to Angelico and "sub-contracted" by him to Strozzi. Keith Christiansen first proposed that a design by Fra Angelico might underlie the rigorous geometry of the centralized composition of the New York *Nativity*.[3] Angelico's intervention in the London *Adoration of the Magi* may have been even more direct and more extensive. There is an evident distinction in quality between Saint Joseph and the kneeling or sitting figures ranged across the foreground of the panel on the one hand and, on the other, the more caricatured, summarily rendered

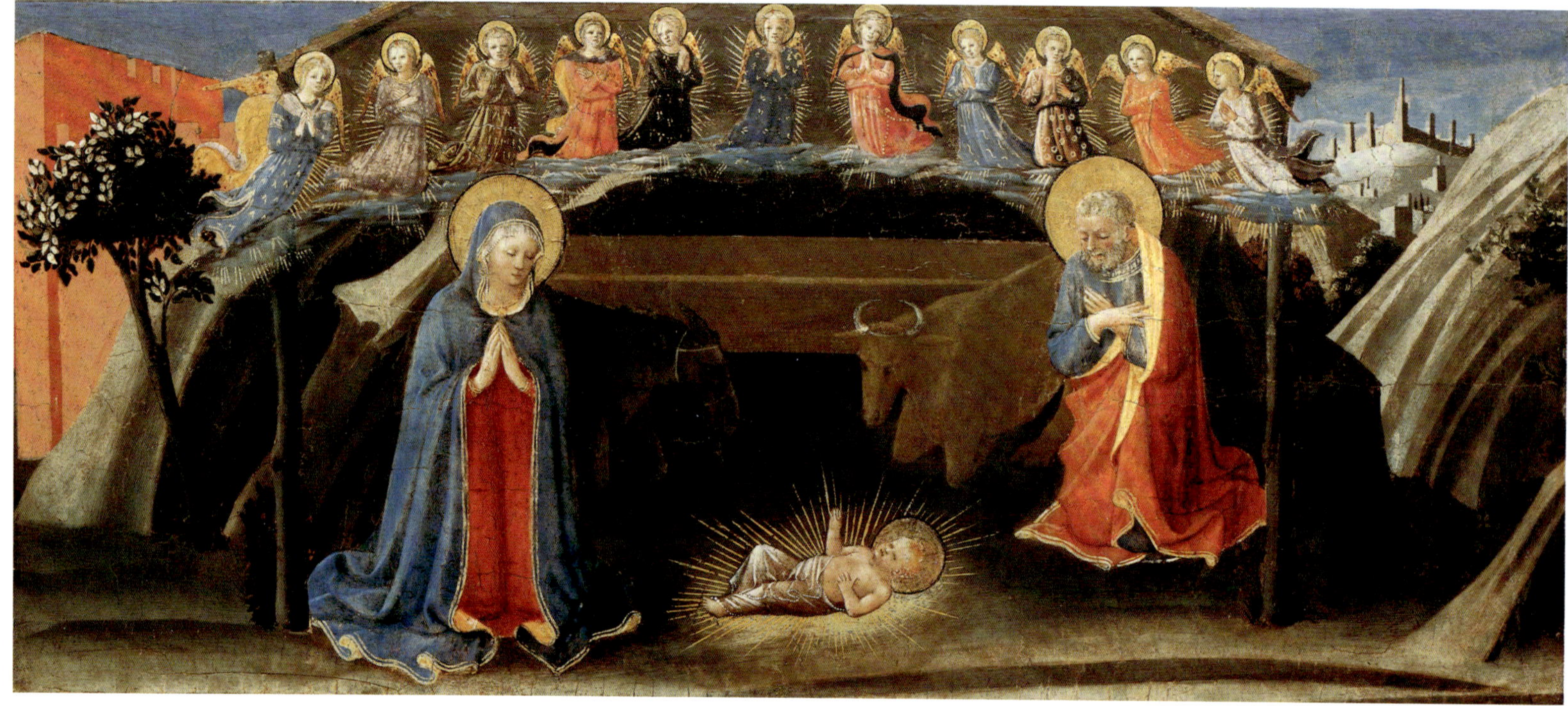

44: C

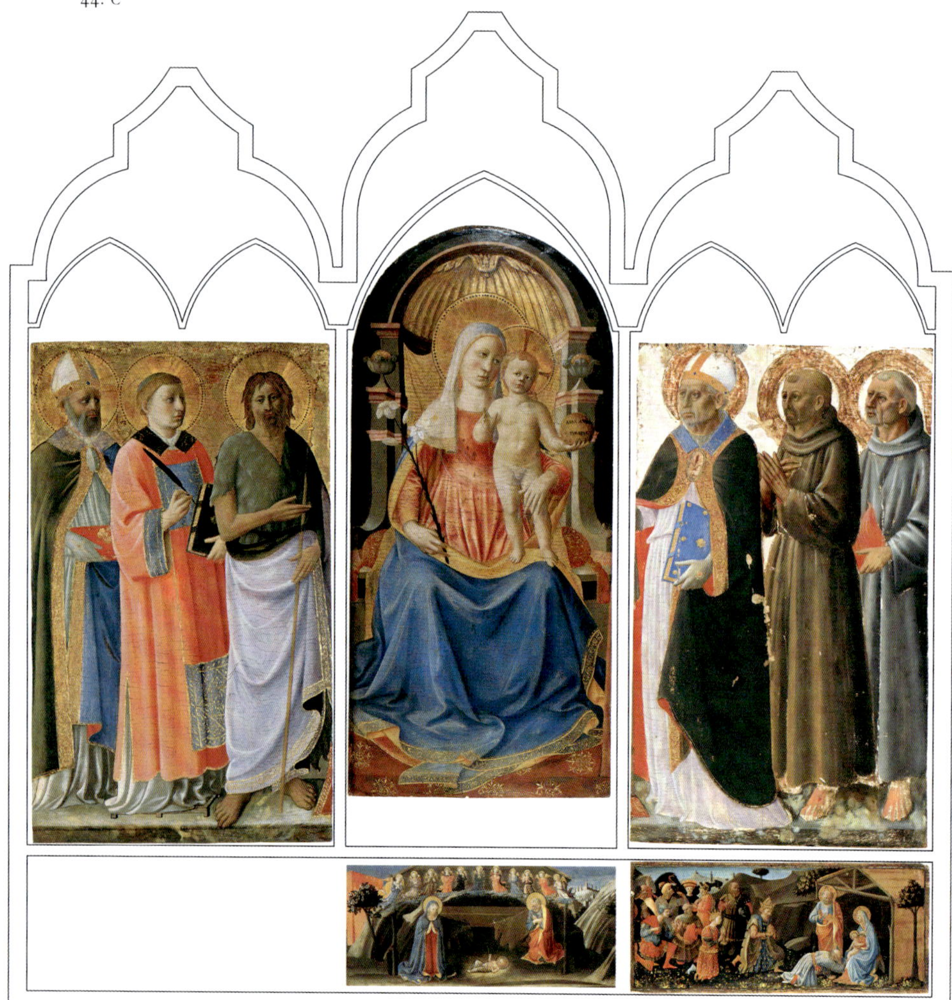

Figure 145. Zanobi Strozzi and Fra Angelico. Franciscan Altarpiece (reconstruction)

line of standing attendants in the background at the left. It might be presumed that the latter represent a typical intrusion by Battista Sanguigni in a composition otherwise painted by Zanobi Strozzi, except that it is precisely the figures of the attendants that most clearly resemble those in Strozzi's small-scale narrative paintings. The foreground figures, instead, are conceived with a meticulous understanding of the fall and textures of drapery fabrics and fur—especially in such gratuitous details as the transparent veils covering the gifts of the two younger Magi or the hat enveloping the hand of the kneeling attendant, second from the left—which is not encountered elsewhere in Zanobi Strozzi's work. These figures are subtly positioned along slight diagonal axes to relieve the planarity of their arrangement, and their poses are enlivened with very sophisticated foreshortenings easily overlooked on so small a scale. It is very likely that Angelico himself painted these eight figures: they are certainly equal in quality to those in his larger and more elaborate scenes in the predella of the Linaiuoli tabernacle (see cat. 29).[4] Angelico's direct intervention might also explain the use of different figure types for Saint Joseph and the Christ Child in the two known panels of this predella, as well as some differences of technique in rendering trees.

Angelico treated the subject of the Adoration of the Magi on numerous occasions throughout his career, varying the poses, attitudes, and positions of the protagonists each time for a different narrative emphasis. In most of his versions of the theme he adopted a circular compositional plan, establishing an empty space in the center of the picture field around which

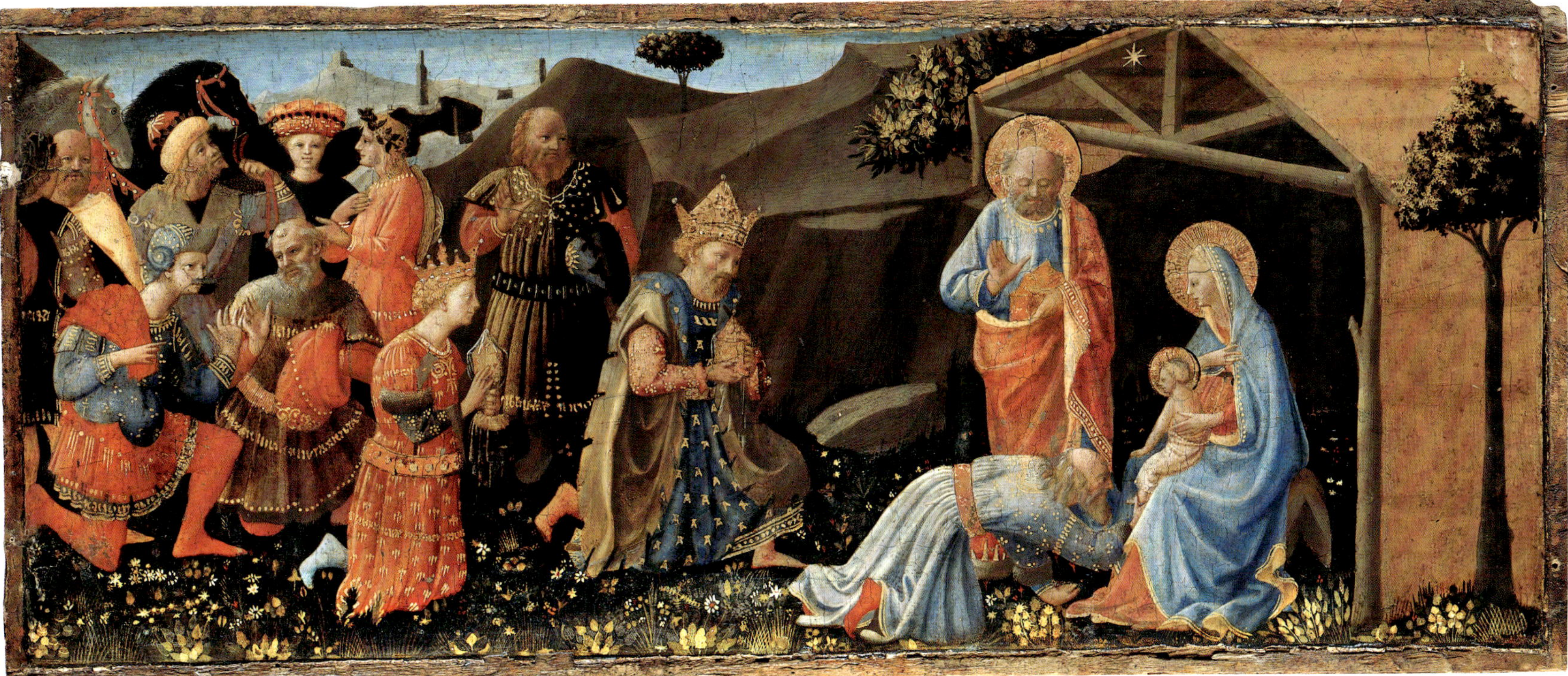

44: D

the figures are arranged that enabled him to augment the feeling of movement within the scene and to add a vertical element to its disposition, thus avoiding the static, frieze-like procession typical of earlier renditions of the subject. The London *Adoration of the Magi* represents a departure from this practice. It borrows the poses of the Holy Family and two of the Magi from the central panel of the Linaiuoli predella (fig. 85) but rotates the figures so that each is more nearly parallel to the picture plane, minimizing the sensation of recession into depth, perhaps in response to the unusually horizontal picture field available to him. This same approach informs the large fresco of *The Adoration of the Magi* (probably 1442; fig. 109) in the dormitory at San Marco, essentially a reprise and expansion of the composition of the London panel save only that the youngest Magus and all the retainers are shown standing rather than kneeling. It is reasonable to date the London panel between these two works, sometime in the last half of the 1430s—a date that also accords well with Zanobi Strozzi's contribution to the predella and to the three main panels of the altarpiece.

The patron and the original location of this reconstructed altarpiece are unknown. Clearly, it was painted for a Franciscan church, based on the presence of Saints Francis and Anthony of Padua in the Yale panel, and this church presumably was in Florence, given the prominence accorded to John the Baptist and Zenobius, patron saints of the city, in positions of honor on either side of the Virgin. It is reasonable to assume, then, that the inclusion of Saints Lawrence and Nicholas of Bari at the left in the Hyde panel refers in some manner either to the name and patronymic of the donor or to the dedication of the chapel in which the altarpiece was installed. The Yale panel was said, in the nineteenth century, to have come from the church of San Salvi in Florence—an Augustinian convent, and therefore not likely to have been the picture's original provenance, but which served as a depot for paintings removed from suppressed ecclesiastical property throughout Florence.[5] Equally possible, however, is that San Salvi was mistakenly recorded instead of San Salvatore, a Franciscan convent on the hill below San Miniato al Monte for which Zanobi Strozzi would later paint his (signed) *Annunciation* altarpiece (fig. 133), now in the National Gallery, London.

LK

1. Cited in Sirén 1916, p. 80. See also Seymour 1970, p. 159.
2. Sold at Christie's, London, April 8, 1938, lot 66; photograph by A. C. Cooper, London, no. 109509. The background of the Yale panel may have been similarly treated, but at some point it was regilded; the new gilding, in turn, was removed in a 1967 cleaning that left the gesso preparation exposed. Removal of the black repaints on the Hyde panel has also exposed what appears to be a later regilding.
3. K. Christiansen, in Metropolitan Museum 1984, pp. 61–62.
4. The kneeling attendant farthest to the left has been damaged and his left hand and the lower part of his face retouched. There is also a large loss, possibly a candle burn, between the middle Magus and Saint Joseph, but this does not affect the painting of any of the figures. The panel is otherwise in an excellent state of preservation.
5. Jarves collection, 1862, p. 11 ("The right wing of an altar-piece, from the suppressed Convent of the Salvi, at Florence"). For the modern history of San Salvi, which, after its appropriation by the state in 1817, was used first as a sanatorium and then as a museum and painting depot, see Padovani and Meloni Trkulja 1982, pp. 2–4.

45.
The Last Judgment

Tempera and gold on panel, 106.5 x 131.5 cm (41⅞ x 51¾ in.)
Private collection

This little-known work is one of two versions of the Last Judgment executed by Zanobi Strozzi in loose imitation of Angelico's paintings now in the Museo di San Marco and in the Gemäldegalerie, Berlin. The second version, dated 1456 and inscribed with the name of the donor, Jacopo di Ludovico Villani, was formerly also located in Berlin (Kaiser-Friedrich-Museum, no. 57; fig. 146), but disappeared during World War II.[1] First attributed by Collobi-Ragghianti to Strozzi, in collaboration with Domenico di Michelino, it was subsequently identified by Cohn with a painting cited by Vasari as having been executed by Strozzi for the Camaldolese church of San Benedetto fuori della Porta a Pinti in Florence.[2]

The present panel may be identified with a *Last Judgment* that first appeared with an attribution to Fra Angelico in the 1854 London sale of the Joly De Bammeville Collection.[3] Its inclusion in that auction was mentioned by Crowe and Cavalcaselle, who referred to the panel as being "much in the style" of the (now missing) Berlin *Last Judgment,* which, in turn, they attributed to a "feeble pupil and imitator of Angelico's manner."[4] The present panel was still listed as a work by Fra Angelico when it reappeared on the art market, in the 1897 sale of the Émile Gavet Collection in Paris.[5] Sometime between this date and 1910, the picture entered the collection of the South African mining baron Sir Joseph B. Robinson (1840–1929), who in 1894 had established his residence at Dudley House in London. When Robinson returned to South Africa in 1910, his entire art collection, including the *Last Judgment,* was put into storage in London, and except for a brief appearance on the art market in 1923, remained virtually inaccessible to scholars until 1958, when it was exhibited at the Royal Academy of Arts.[6] The only author to consider the *Last Judgment* during this time was Berenson, who, in 1932, included the panel in the group of paintings he assigned to Domenico di Michelino[7]—a body of works that, since then, has largely come to be recognized as by Zanobi Strozzi. Berenson's attribution was upheld by Alfred Scharf in a review of the 1958 Royal Academy exhibition, where this same writer also pointed out the compromised state of the *Last Judgment,* presumably the result of later restorations.[8] The various retouches to the original picture surface, especially evident in the heads of the angels and of a few of the apostles to the right of Christ, subsequently prompted Fahy and Pope-Hennessy to question the attribution of the *Last Judgment* to Zanobi Strozzi, tentatively advancing the name of an anonymous painter of a later generation known as the Master of Marradi.[9] This identification was rejected in the most recent discussion of the painting—the catalogue of the 1978 exhibition of the Natale Labia Collection in London, where it was listed as by Fra Angelico, followed by a question mark.[10]

Despite the recent doubts, Berenson's original attribution of the *Last Judgment* to Domenico di Michelino—alias Zanobi Strozzi—is fully confirmed by the comparisons that may be drawn between the greater part of the picture and the artist's documented production from the late 1440s to the early 1450s. The figures' small, doll-like heads with deeply set features and the full, softly cascading draperies bring to mind, in particular, the illuminations executed by Strozzi between 1448 and 1449 in the first volume of a four-part gradual for San Marco (Museo di San Marco, Inv. N. 515; fig. 138)—a commission that was probably entrusted to the artist on the recommendation of Fra Angelico.[11] Especially relevant is the close correpondence between the equally aristocratic Christ of the *Last Judgment* and of the San Marco gradual, or between the bearded figures of apostles and Evangelists in the heavenly court and their counterparts in the miniatures. Similar analogies for the *Last Judgment* may be found in the illuminations painted by Strozzi about 1450 in a psalter for the Badia Fiorentina (cat. 46), suggesting a date for the painting's execution in proximity to both of these commissions: between about 1448 and 1450. Within these chronological parameters it is worth considering whether the pastel tonalities of the painting's palette, and the peculiar rose-tinted sky, unusual in

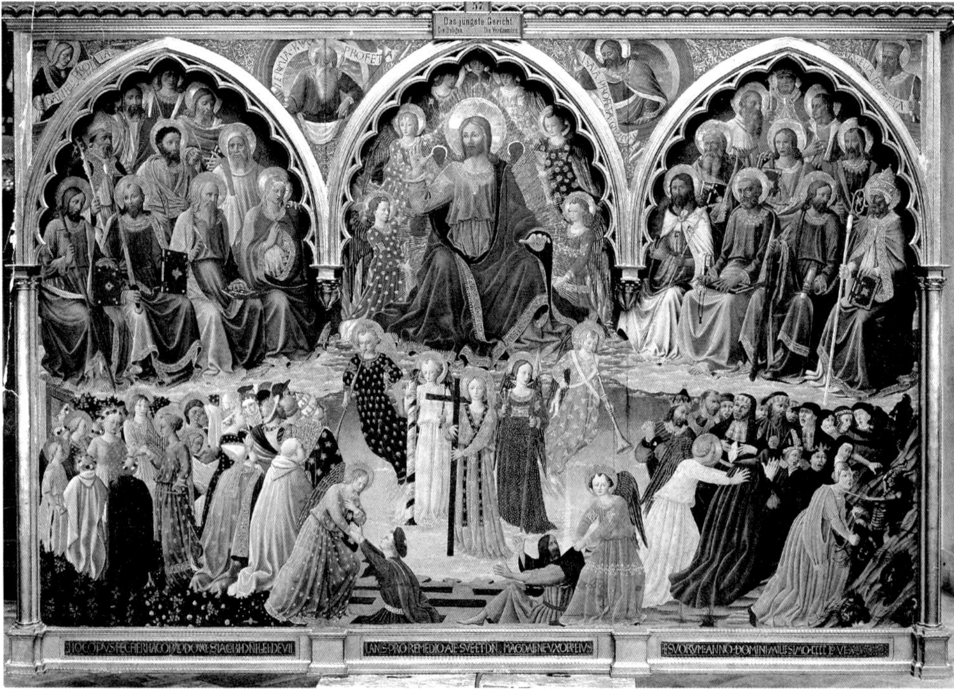

Figure 146. Zanobi Strozzi. *The Last Judgment.* 1456. Formerly, Kaiser-Friedrich-Museum, Berlin

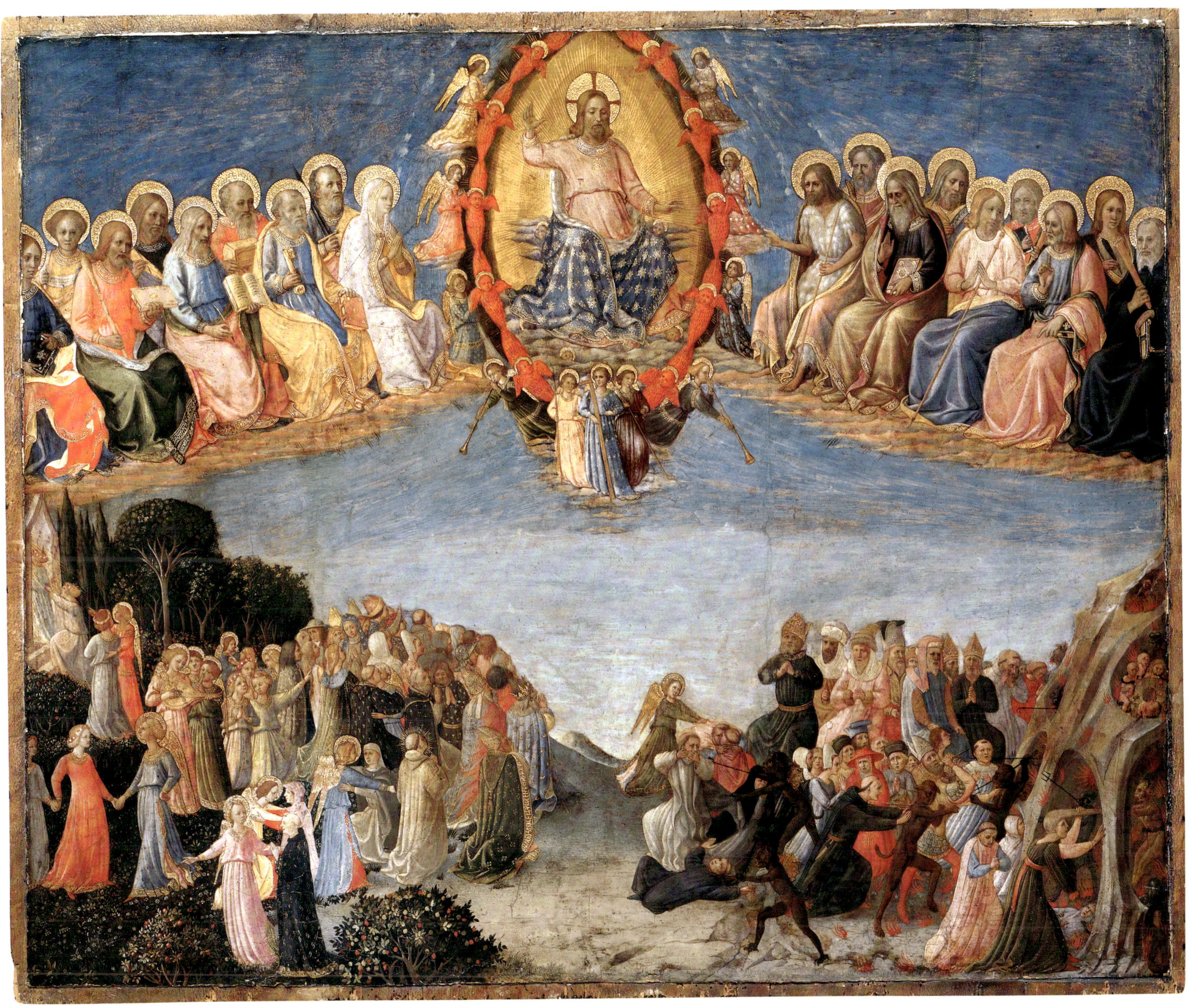

45

Zanobi's production, might have been inspired by the work of the artist's sometime collaborator during these years, Francesco Pesellino (see cat. 54).

The composition of Strozzi's *Last Judgment,* as noted above, reflects the artist's debt to Angelico's famous panel (now in San Marco) for the Camaldolese monastery of Santa Maria degli Angeli, as well as to Angelico's perhaps equally well-known painting now in Berlin (cat. 32), executed in Florence for an unidentified Dominican patron and almost identical in dimensions to the present work. The influence of the Santa Maria degli Angeli panel (fig. 50) is evident in the inclusion of such details as the gates of Paradise along the left edge of the composition, and the cropped treetops at the bottom left. Both works also share a similarity in the placement of Christ in a mandorla of red seraphim surrounded by angels. The present version mirrors the Santa Maria degli Angeli picture, moreover, in the disposition of the double row of seated apostles and Evangelists in an arc that defines the composition, possibly suggesting that this panel originally had a similar, irregularly shaped top. In contrast to the Santa Maria degli Angeli painting, however, the figure of Christ, here, is clearly modeled on the stern judge of the Berlin *Last Judgment,* portrayed at the moment of imparting his verdict to the damned. The Berlin picture is also recalled in the less sharply articulated division between the blessed and the damned, and in the background detail of the angel pushing a soul from one side to the other. It might be presumed that like Angelico's prototype in Berlin, Strozzi's *Last Judgment* also included a single row of empty tombs separating the two realms, which was possibly painted out in later restorations.

Significantly, perhaps, the only iconographic detail that sets Strozzi's depiction of the Last Judgment apart from any other version of the subject by Fra Angelico is the group of bearded figures in exotic headgear, prominently seated with other damned souls, perhaps on a cart, as if awaiting their turn to be judged. The motif, derived from the *Last Judgment* in the Camposanto in Pisa, is also included in Nardo di Cione's frescoes in the Strozzi Chapel in Santa Maria Novella, where five such figures appear in the uppermost row of the damned, directly across from a row of five Old Testament saints, including Adam and Eve. In his study of Nardo's frescoes, Offner proposed that the five figures should be identified, specifically, as the Old Testament sinners Cain, Pharaoh, Korah, Dathan, and Abiram.[12] In the present panel, which does not include a corresponding gathering of Old Testament types among the blessed, and also portrays other contemporary figures, such as the monk in a white (Cistercian ?) habit alongside the more exotic individuals, the seated group may allude more generically to the mixture of all the lamenting "tribes" of the earth; or, more particularly, to the special category of sinners described in *The Golden Legend* as those who "are condemned without being judged," because they are unbelievers.[13] However one chooses to interpret this narrative motif, its reintroduction by Strozzi in the *Last Judgment* should undoubtedly be regarded in terms of the specific wishes of the artist's patron.

A clue to the possibility that this *Last Judgment* may have been a Benedictine commission is perhaps offered by the presence of Saint Benedict, dressed in the traditional black habit, among the apostles and the Evangelists who comprise the entire heavenly court. In the foreground of the composition, moreover, it is a Benedictine monk who is being led to the gates of Paradise by an angel in place of the Dominican monk included in the parallel detail in Angelico's Berlin prototype. Strozzi's employment at the Badia Fiorentina around the time of the painting's execution may not be coincidental and could provide a key to future research. PP

1. The panel was listed as "School of Fra Angelico" in the 1931 catalogue of the Kaiser-Friedrich-Museum (Staatliche Museen zu Berlin 1931, p. 19).
2. Collobi-Ragghianti 1950b, part 2, p. 20; Cohn 1956b, pp. 43–45. See also A. Di Lorenzo, in Di Lorenzo 2001, p. 18.
3. De Bammeville sale, 1854, p. 11, lot 57.
4. Crowe and Cavalcaselle 1864 (1980 ed.), vol. 1, pp. 588–89 n. 3.
5. Gavet sale, 1897, p. 187, lot 728.
6. For the history of the collection, see the preface by Robinson's granddaughter Natale Labia, in South African National Gallery 1975, pp. 1–2. As Labia relates, after putting his collection up for auction in 1923 (sale, Christie's, London, July 6, 1923), Robinson changed his mind, and had most of the pictures, including the *Last Judgment,* bought in and returned to storage.
7. Berenson 1932a, p. 364; the attribution is maintained in Berenson 1963, vol. I, p. 60.
8. Scharf 1958, p. 300.
9. Pope-Hennessy (1974, p. 221) cites the opinion of Everett Fahy.
10. P. Cannon-Brookes, in Wildenstein 1978.
11. Significantly, the payments to Strozzi for the miniatures in this volume were based on estimates provided by Fra Angelico, then prior of the convent of San Domenico in Fiesole. See M. Scudieri, in Scudieri and Rasario 2003, pp. 173–77, and p. 306 n. 10, in the present volume.
12. Offner 1960, p. 52 n. 5.
13. "Secondly, among those to be judged, different ranks or groups will be set apart. According to Gregory there will be four divisions, two among the reprobate, two among the elect. There are some who will be judged and will perish, such as those to whom it is said: 'I was hungry and you gave me no food, etc.' Others are condemned without being judged, such as those of whom it is said: 'He who does not believe is already judged.' They will not hear any word from the Judge, since they were unwilling to receive his word in faith" (Jacopo da Varagine 1993 ed., vol. 1, p. 10).

46.

A.
King David in Prayer in an Initial B

Tempera on parchment, 14.2 x 13.5 cm (5⅝ x 5⅜ in.)
The Metropolitan Museum of Art, New York. Robert Lehman Collection, 1975 (1975.1.2470)

B.
The Trinity in an Initial D

Tempera on parchment, 15 x 10 cm (5⅞ x 3¹⁵⁄₁₆ in.)
Fondazione Giorgio Cini, Venice (No. 2131)

In 1450, Zanobi Strozzi was paid for having painted two frontispieces in a psalter for the principal Benedictine monastery in Florence, the Badia Fiorentina. The two "*principii*" illustrated Psalm 1, introduced with the words *Beatus Vir*, and Psalm 109, which begins *Dixit Dominus*.[1] Several scholars have suggested that the first of these illuminations might be the initial *B* with *King David in Prayer* in the Robert Lehman Collection, which contains cropped, bust-length figures of two Benedictine monks in the corners. This initial was certainly painted as the frontispiece to a psalter: not only is its iconography appropriate to such a function but verses 3–5 of Psalm 1, without musical notation, are inscribed on its reverse side (*[Et omnia quaecumque f]aciet prosperabuntur [non sic inpii, no]n sic: sed tamquam [pulvis quem] proicit ventus [a face terrae ideo non ressurger]unt inpii in iudi[cio necque peccator]es in consilio [iustorum]*). Licia Collobi-Ragghianti first attributed the Lehman initial to Zanobi Strozzi, although she misinterpreted its subject as Christ in Prayer, and made no suggestions for the origin of the cutting.[2] Carl Strehlke suggested that it either might have come from the Badia psalter or from a series of choir books painted by Strozzi in 1456 for the Vallombrosan monastery of San Pancrazio in Florence (the Vallombrosans also wore black habits and followed the Benedictine rule).[3] While Mirella Levi D'Ancona argued for a date close to 1450 for the Lehman initial, she made no mention of the Badia psalter in connection with it, and stated, in 1995, that she knew of no surviving fragments from that commission.[4] Laurence Kanter identified two fragmentary *bas-de-page* miniatures (in a private collection [fig. 147] and in the Wallraf-Richartz-Museum in Cologne [fig. 148]) that might be associated with the Lehman *Initial* B, and proposed—although somewhat tentatively—that they had been included in the Badia psalter.[5]

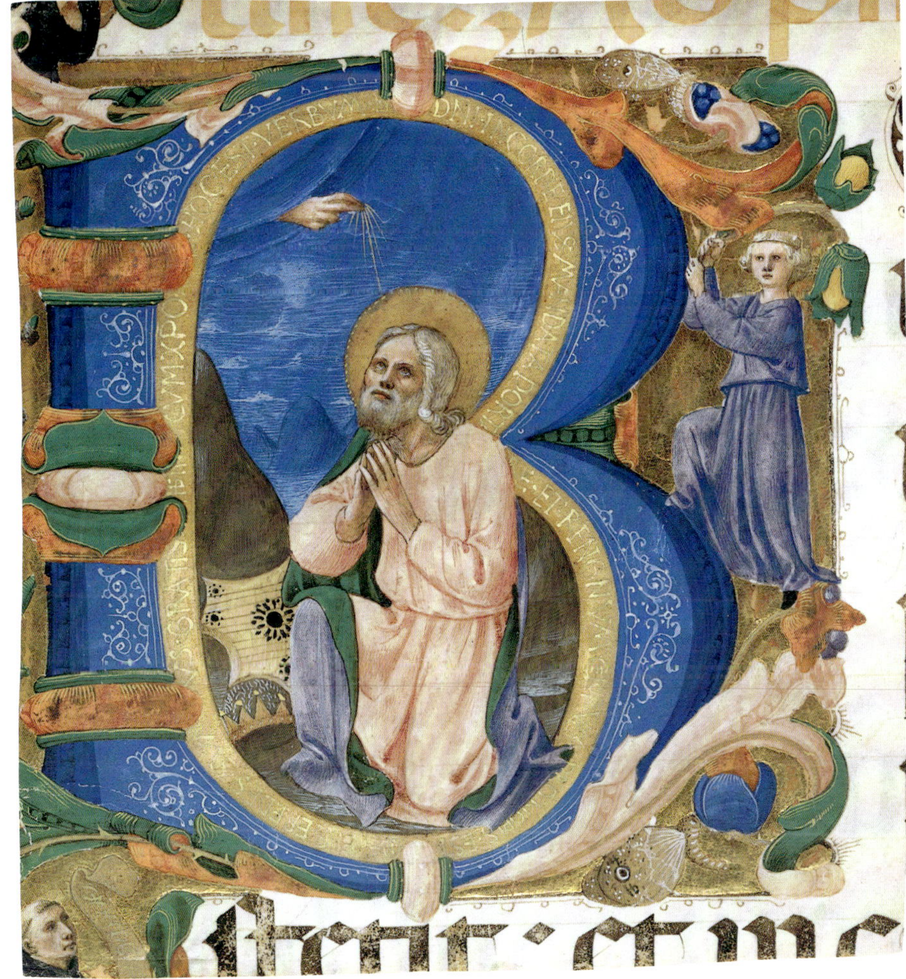

46: A

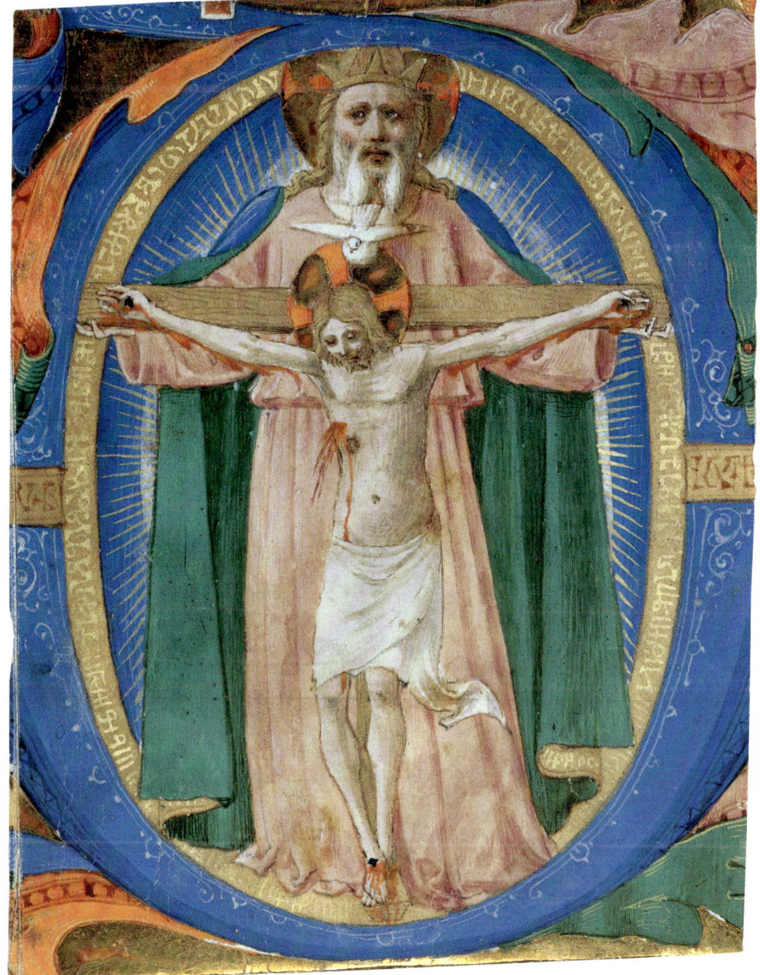

46: B

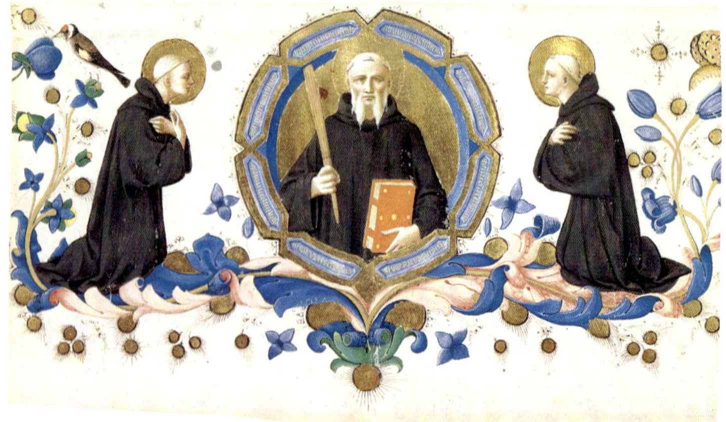

Figure 147 (near right). Zanobi Strozzi. *Bas-de-page* Fragment from a Benedictine Psalter. 1450. Private collection

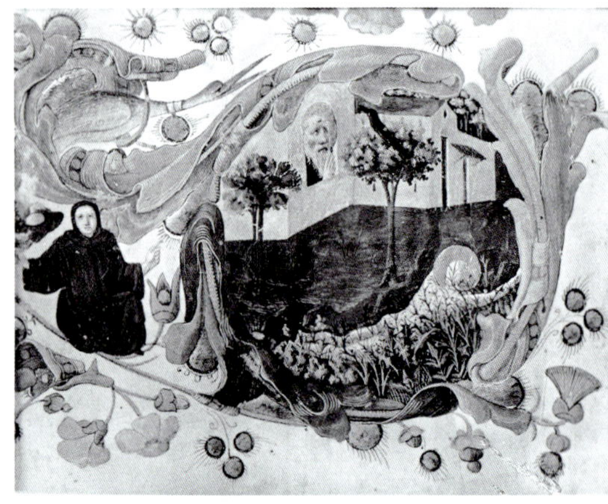

Figure 148 (far right). Zanobi Strozzi. *Bas-de-page* Fragment from a Benedictine Psalter. 1450. Wallraf-Richartz-Museum, Cologne

Francesca Pasut noted that the presence of a scapular over the habit of a Benedictine monk in the Cologne cutting is incompatible with a Vallombrosan provenance.[6] Pasut believed, however, that the *bas-de-page* fragment in a private collection must have come from a separate commission, and she accepted its attribution to Fra Angelico and the date in the 1430s ascribed to the work by Luciano Bellosi,[7] concluding that final proof of the reconstruction of the Badia psalter must await the discovery of additional fragments. Finally, Pia Palladino published the Cini *Trinity in an Initial* D—on the back of which verses 5–6 of Psalm 109 are inscribed, without musical notation ([*Dominus a dextris tui*]*s confregit* [*in die irae suae rege*]*s* [*iudicabit in nationi*]*bus imple*[*bit cadavera conquass*]*abit ca*[*pita in terra multorum* . . .])—as the missing second frontispiece of the Badia psalter, reaffirming the relevance of all four fragments to the document of 1450.[8]

That the Lehman and Cini initials were both removed from a single psalter is clear, and, given the absolute coincidence of their content and style with the document of 1450, their identification as surviving fragments of the psalter for the Badia Fiorentina need not be doubted. At issue only is the relationship to them of the two *bas-de-page* fragments in Cologne and in a private collection, which was proposed initially on the basis of their consonant iconography, style, and palette, as well as on the continuity of motifs in their border decoration. This connection has not been questioned in the case of the Cologne fragment and, indeed, is evident. Equally apparent, however, is the relationship between the Cologne *bas-de-page* fragment and the privately owned example. While an attribution to Fra Angelico of the latter—proposed in the absence of any known related works—is perhaps understandable, it is actually only meaningful as a general indication of the source of its imagery. At no point in his career as a painter, whether on a monumental or a miniaturist scale, did Angelico ever design or execute hands as anatomically imprecise and over sized as those of Saint Benedict in the central roundel of this cutting, nor do any of his saints grasp their attributes as unconvincingly as in the present miniature. These attributes, furthermore, are invariably depicted by Angelico not just realistically but with an aggressive sense of their function in establishing the spatial structure of a scene or image, whereas here they are not especially detailed and they are simply arranged parallel to the picture plane. The thin, deeply shadowed eyes of Saint Benedict are also atypical of Angelico's style, yet they are characteristic of Zanobi Strozzi's, and it is impossible to conclude that this cutting is not part of the same series as the three in New York, Venice, and Cologne. While the face of Saint Benedict appearing at the window of his cell in the Cologne fragment may seem caricatured in its over-scaled relationship to the landscape and architectural details around him, the execution of this cutting and of the initials in New York and in Venice is actually quite refined and worthy of comparison to the privately owned *bas-de-page* illumination. Together, these four fragments reveal Zanobi Strozzi at the zenith of his technical powers, on a par with what is undoubtedly his most distinguished effort as an illuminator: the frontispiece to the 1456 Vallombrosan missal from San Pancrazio now also in the Cini Collection in Venice (cat. 49). LK

1. Archivio di Stato di Firenze, Conventi Soppressi, 78, Badia, Debitori e Creditori (1450–60), published in Levi D'Ancona 1962, p. 265.
2. Collobi-Ragghianti 1950b, part 2, pp. 20, 27, fig. 12.
3. C. B. Strehlke, in Kanter et al. 1994, pp. 350–52.
4. M. Levi D'Ancona, in Hindman et al. 1997, pp. 169–72; Levi D'Ancona 1995, pp. 172–73.
5. Kanter 2001b, pp. 143–47.
6. F. Pasut, in Toscano and Capitelli 2002, pp. 152–53.
7. L. Bellosi, in G. Romano 1990, pp. 39–42; C. B. Strehlke, in Kanter et al. 1994, p. 352; Boskovits 1995, p. 59 n. 23; Bollati 1997, pp. 84–85; Bonsanti 1998, p. 159.
8. Palladino 2003, pp. 158–60.

Nine Drawings for a Reliquary (?)

All: Brush and brown ink, with white gouache and orange wash, incised with a stylus on pink-purple prepared parchment

47.

A.
The Massacre of the Innocents

7.5 x 6 cm (3 x 2⅜ in.)
Museum Boijmans Van Beuningen, Rotterdam
(I-234)

B.
Christ among the Doctors

8 x 6.2 cm (3⅛ x 2⁷⁄₁₆ in.)
Museum Boijmans Van Beuningen, Rotterdam
(I-237)

C.
Christ Washing the Feet of the Apostles

8 x 6 cm (3⅛ x 2⅜ in.)
Museum Boijmans Van Beuningen, Rotterdam
(I-240)

D.
The Last Supper

7.7 x 5.9 cm (3 x 2⅜ in.)
Museum Boijmans Van Beuningen, Rotterdam
(I-236)

E.
Christ in the Garden of Gethsemane

7.5 x 6 cm (3 x 2⅜ in.)
Museum Boijmans Van Beuningen, Rotterdam
(I-235)

F.
The Capture of Christ

7.6 x 6 cm (3 x 2⅜ in.)
Museum Boijmans Van Beuningen, Rotterdam
(I-238)

G.
Christ before Pilate

8 x 6 cm (3⅛ x 2⅜ in.)
Fogg Art Museum, Harvard University Art Museums, Cambridge, Massachusetts (1939.115)

H.
The Crucifixion

8 x 6.2 cm (3⅛ x 2⁷⁄₁₆ in.)
Fogg Art Museum, Harvard University Art Museums, Cambridge, Massachusetts (1939.114)

I.
The Lamentation

7.9 x 6.3 cm (3⅛ x 2½ in.)
Museum Boijmans Van Beuningen, Rotterdam
(I-239)

In his famous treatise on the art of painting, the fifteenth-century artist Cennino Cennini devoted a special chapter to the technique of drawing with a stylus on tinted paper or parchment as a way to introduce tonal variations: "To approach the glory [of the profession] step by step, to start trying to discover the entrance and gateway to painting, you should take up a system of drawing different from the one which we have been discussing up to now. And this is known as drawing on tinted paper; either paper, that is, or parchment. . . . And you may make your tints inclined toward pink, or violet, or green; or bluish, or greenish gray, that is drab colors; or flesh colored, or any you please."[1] These nine small drawings, executed on purple-tinted parchment, now faded to pink in some cases,[2] were probably once included in a larger narrative complex illustrating the life of Christ. When they first appeared on the art market in 1927,[3] they were pasted into an eighteenth-century album bearing "the royal arms," along with a tenth miniature of *The Presentation of Christ in the Temple* (Whereabouts unknown). It has been rightly assumed that additional scenes, such as *The Annunciation, The Nativity,* and *The Adoration of the Magi*—crucial episodes in any medieval and Renaissance Christological cycle—were already missing at the time.[4]

Most authors have recognized the drawings' general dependence on Fra Angelico's large-scale works, focusing in particular on the San Marco frescoes, datable between 1439 and 1443, and on the series of thirty-two scenes from the Infancy and the Passion of Christ, painted by the artist between about 1450 and 1452 for the Armadio degli Argenti (silver chest) in the church of the Santissima Annunziata and now in the Museo di San Marco, Florence. Opinions have varied, however, regarding Angelico's actual involvement in their execution. In the 1927 Mensing sale catalogue the drawings were classified as Florentine, about 1450, and viewed as the product of two different hands influenced by Angelico, one of which was purportedly responsible for the four scenes set against a more faded purple ground (*Christ among the Doctors, Christ before Pilate, The Crucifixion,* and *The Lamentation*). An attribution to the school of Fra Angelico was reiterated by Berenson, who thought the series might be the product of an Umbrian follower of the artist,[5] and by Degenhart and Schmitt,[6] who suggested that, if not intended as book illustrations, the drawings may have served as models for the painters active in Fra Angelico's workshop at San Marco. A specific attribution to Fra Angelico's closest follower and imitator, Zanobi Strozzi, was tentatively advanced by Mongan and Sachs,[7] who, writing specifically about the Fogg drawings (G and H), characterized them as clearly dependent on Fra Angelico in composition and style, but lacking the overall refinement, especially in the execution of the figures, of the artist's autograph production.

Most recent scholarship, on the other hand, has tended to emphasize the close relationship between the drawings' compositional formulas and Fra Angelico's own work over any perceived qualitative differences, leaving open the possibility that the artist himself may have been responsible for them. While also classifying the Fogg drawings as "School of Beato

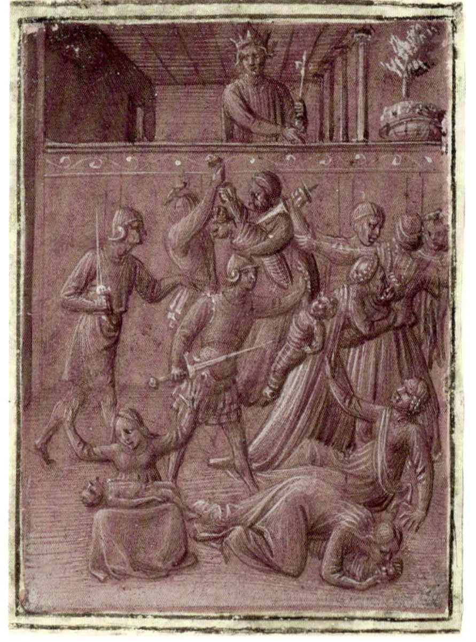
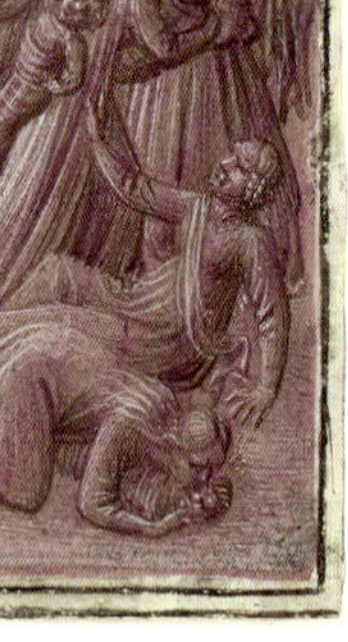

47: A

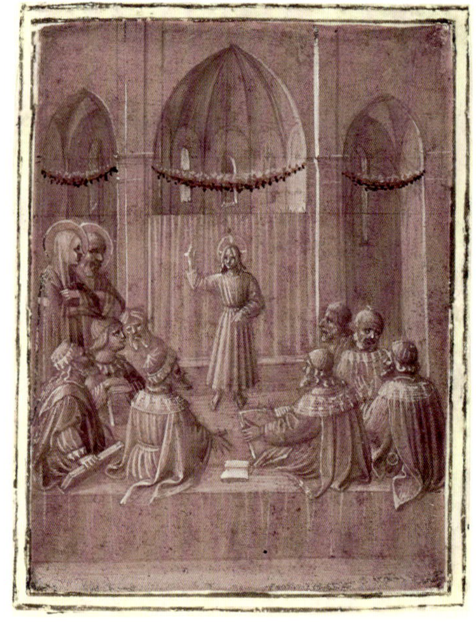

47: B

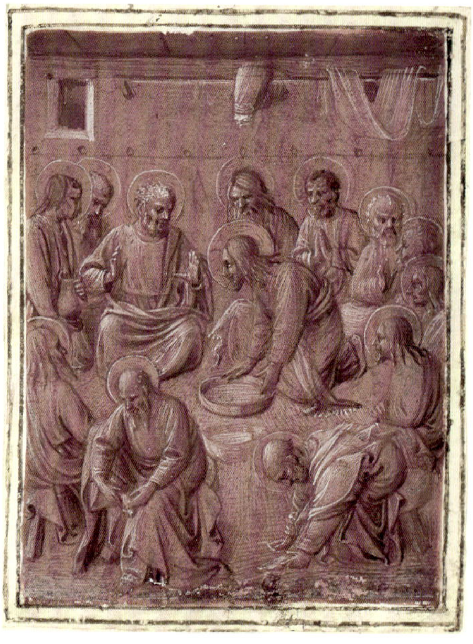

47: C

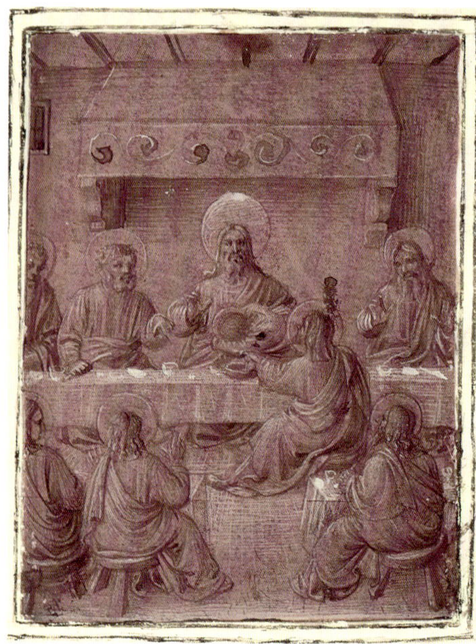

47: D

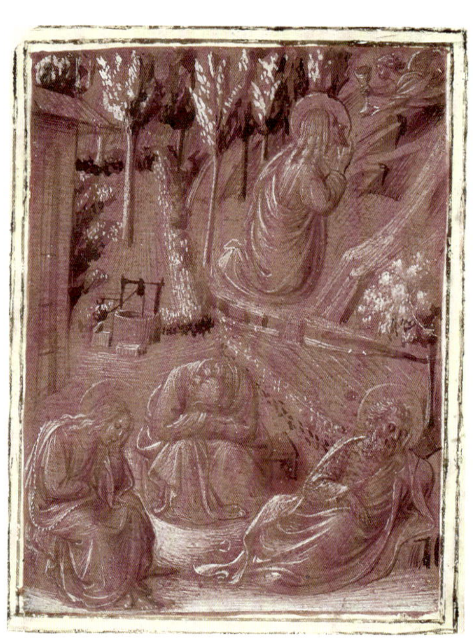

47: E

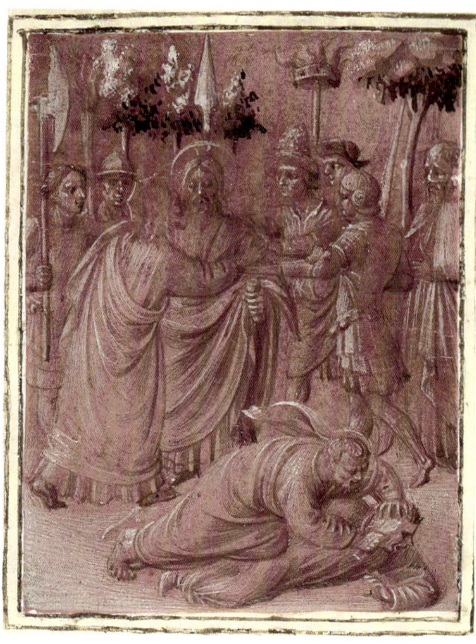

47: F

Angelico," Jonathan Bober[8] has described the entire series as "exceptionally faithful transcriptions of Fra Angelico's style, if not in fact autograph works," proposing that they may have been part of some sort of reproduction or "prefiguration" of the scenes on the Annunziata silver chest. Bober's observations have been further developed by Boskovits,[9] who, in the latest study of the drawings to date, attributes them directly to Fra Angelico, with the suggestion that they may have been executed for Piero de' Medici as presentation models for the Annunziata Silver Chest commission, which Piero had entrusted to the artist in 1448.[10]

As emphasized by all of the above studies, any consideration of the function and authorship of these drawings must depart from a comparison with Fra Angelico's comparable series of scenes for the Annunziata Silver Chest. In this regard it should be pointed out that while some drawings in the series do, in fact, find precise analogies in the Armadio scenes, in the figures' gestures and poses as well as in the compositions, others display equally noticeable differences and are either dependent on works executed by Angelico at earlier stages in his career or they conflate motifs found both in earlier works and on the Annunziata Silver Chest. This aspect of the series

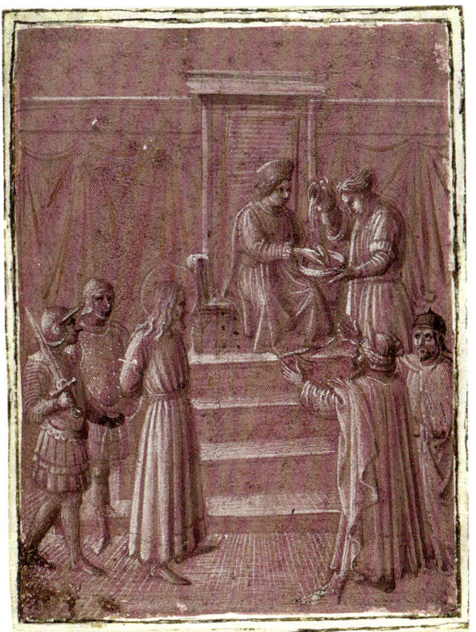

47: G

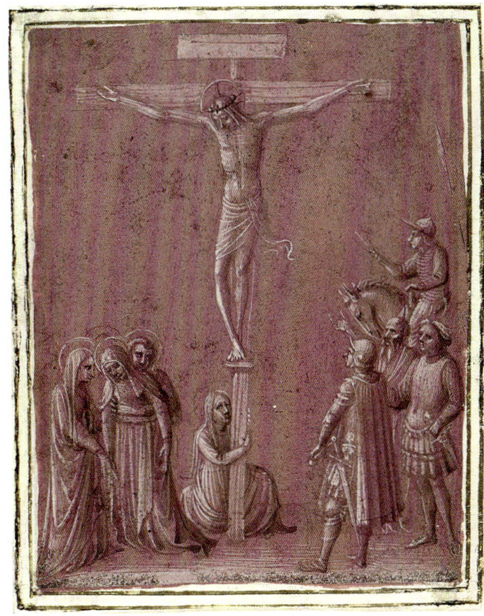
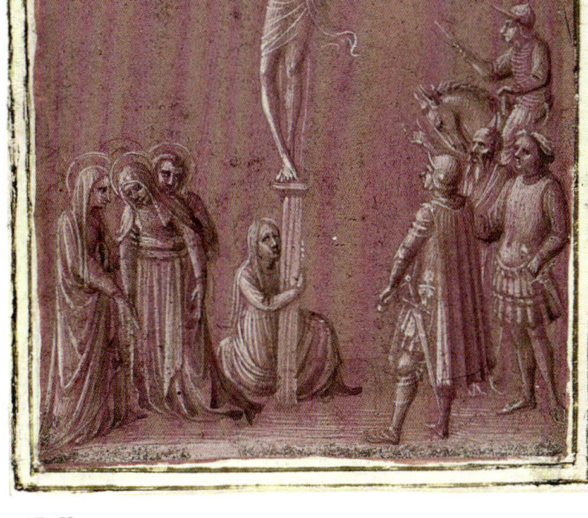

47: H

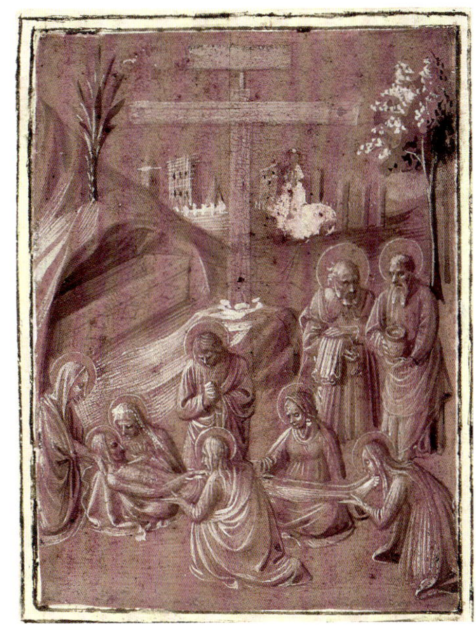

47: I

was also noted by Boskovits, who highlighted the obvious reliance of the missing drawing of the *Presentation* (illustrated in the Mensing sale catalogue of 1927) on the same scene in the predella of Angelico's Cortona *Annunciation,* dated here to about 1430, where the episode is set in an entirely Brunelleschian Renaissance nave in contrast to the Gothic apse in the version on the silver chest. The same author also pointed to the *Lamentation* drawing's debt to the earlier Santa Maria della Croce al Tempio altarpiece (Museo di San Marco, Florence), although in actuality both the setting of the scene and the gestures of the Virgin and of the Evangelist are more clearly derived from the San Marco frescoes (see fig. 149). Such a combination of sources is likewise found in the drawing of *The Capture of Christ,* which integrates the episode of Peter cutting Malchus's ear, as seen on the silver chest (see fig. 150), with that of the Kiss of Judas, as depicted in the San Marco frescoes (fig. 151).

These elements, together with the radical compositional differences between the paintings of certain episodes and the drawings—most noticeable in the versions of *Christ before Pilate* (fig. 152)—cast a strong doubt on the notion of the series as presentation models for the silver chest project. That the latter constituted, in effect, yet another source of inspiration for the drawings rather than the final stage in their evolution is confirmed by the fact that even those scenes most closely related to Angelico's models betray, upon close observation, inaccuracies in the articulation of the space and the architectural structures, as well as in the definition of gestures, which are incompatible with the clarity of vision found throughout the master's body of work. The crooked, slightly askew perspective of the *Christ before Pilate* and the *Last Supper* drawings, or the tilted cross in the *Crucifixion,* provide a marked contrast to Angelico's meticulously laid-out compositions, where all lines disappear toward precise vanishing points. Likewise, it is difficult to explain the discrepancy between a lucidly painted gestural detail such as that of the apostle removing his stocking in the silver chest version of *Christ Washing the Feet of the Apostles* (fig. 153) and the unresolved quality of the same action in the drawing.

If the inconsistencies evident throughout the series, as well as the mixing of compositional elements developed at different moments in Angelico's career rather than their reelaboration, are not in keeping with the master's autograph production, they are, however, not extraneous to the work of Zanobi Strozzi, whose authorship of the series was correctly intuited by Mongan and Sachs.[11] Strozzi's hand is recognizable, above all, in the small, expressively lively figure types that populate these scenes and that are in sharp contrast to the tall, restrained protagonists in the silver chest stories. Typical of Strozzi's style are the charming, caricature-like figures, with their doll-like heads, deeply sunken eyes, and soulful expressions, their profiles defined by a large aquiline nose and a vanishing chin. Their nearest counterparts may be found in Strozzi's small-scale narrative paintings from the mid- to late 1440s, such as the four predella panels in the Pinacoteca Vaticana, or the two remarkable lunettes in the Museo di San Marco of *The School of Albertus Magnus* and *The School of Saint Thomas Aquinas,*[12] as well as in the artist's extensive manuscript production from the same period. Particularly relevant, in terms of their dating, is the close relationship of the drawings to the fragments

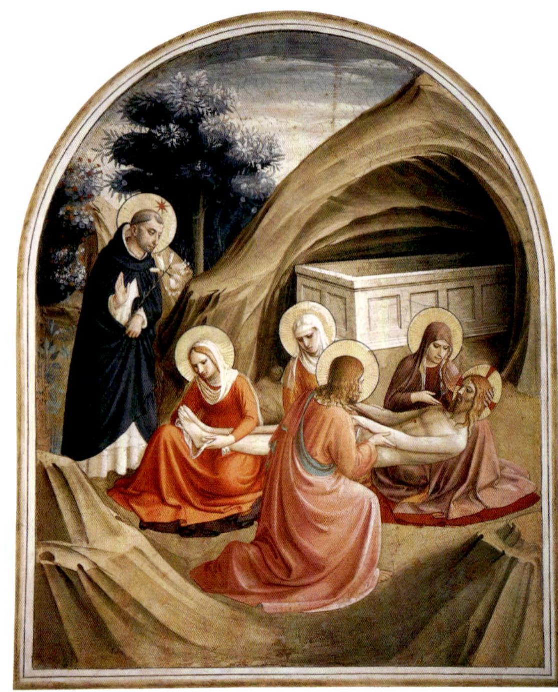

Figure 149. Fra Angelico. *The Lamentation* (cell 2). Convento di San Marco, Florence

of a psalter decorated by Strozzi about 1450 for the Badia Fiorentina (cat. 46), and to the series of graduals illuminated by the artist for San Marco between 1448 and 1454 (fig. 138).[13] The dominant component of these miniatures, like that of the drawings, is their strong adherence to the examples of Fra Angelico, and their carefully realized execution, characterized by the delicacy of modeling and the charming narrative sense that are the hallmark of Strozzi's finest creations.[14]

A clue to the function of these drawings—which, as noted by Bober, approach the character of manuscript illumination by virtue of their exceptionally small size and precious finish—may lie in the painted borders drawn by the artist, in pen and brown ink, around every scene.[15] Such borders are atypical of fifteenth-century Italian model-book drawings but are not uncommon in fourteenth- and fifteenth-century Vulgate manuscripts of the lives of the saints (the so-called *Leggendari* or *Martiriologi*), where they frame drawn and painted vignettes illustrating the salient episodes of the stories. In most of these examples, however, as in the fourteenth-century *Legend of Saint Margaret* (Ashburnam 451) in the Biblioteca Medicea Laurenziana, Florence, or in the *Martiriologio* (Castiglioni 1) in the Biblioteca Nazionale Braidense, Milan, the text accompanying the story is subservient to the illustrations, which take up half or more of the page.[16] In the present case, the size of the drawings and the lack of text on the reverse indicate that, if intended to decorate a manuscript, the scenes would have had to have been arranged in the borders of the page, possibly in a manner resembling that of the recently discovered fourteenth-century Florentine *Passion of Christ* in the Biblioteca Nazionale, Florence.[17]

Another, perhaps more plausible explanation for the lack of text on the reverses of the drawings, as well as for their technique and their minute dimensions, is offered by the interesting suggestion, advanced by Bober, that they may have been conceived as semi-precious, economic versions of the small *verre-églomisé* or enamel inserts that often decorated fifteenth-century reliquaries and processional crosses. This would

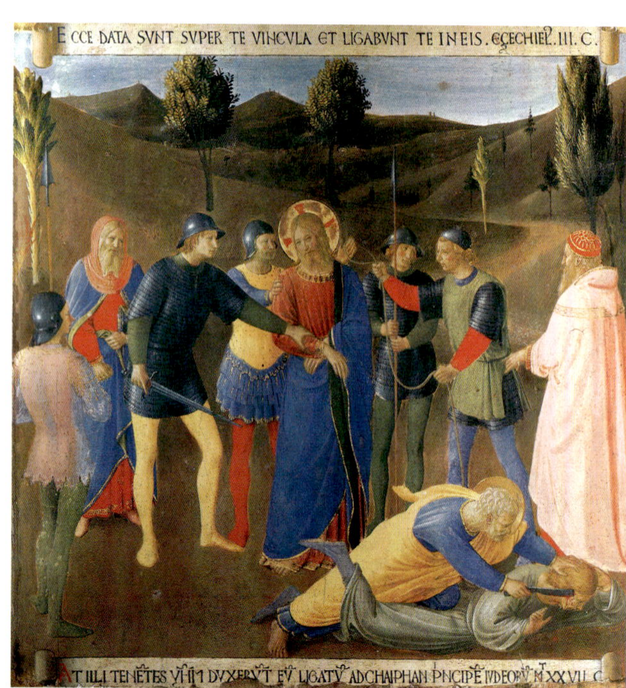

Figure 150 (near right). Fra Angelico. *The Capture of Christ* (from the Annunziata Silver Chest). About 1450–52. Museo di San Marco, Florence

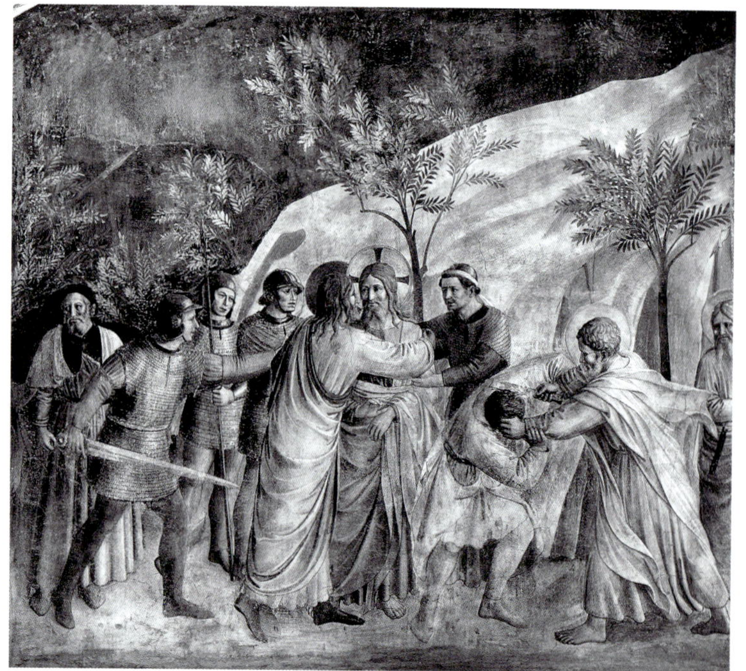

Figure 151 (far right). Fra Angelico. *The Kiss of Judas* (cell 33). Convento di San Marco, Florence

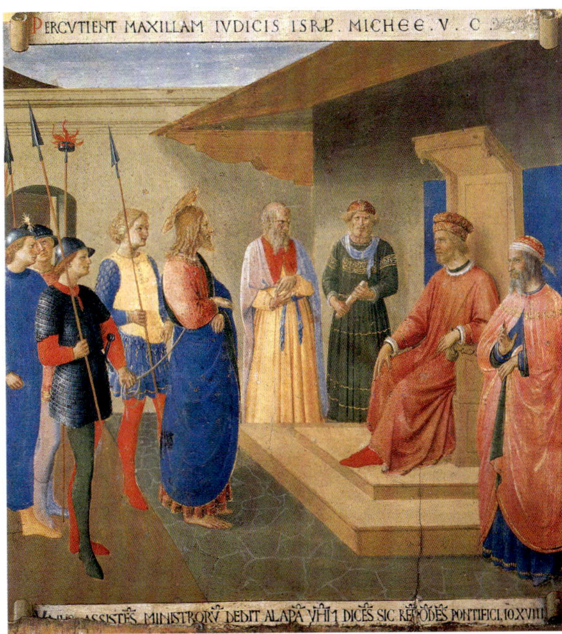

Figure 152 (near right). Fra Angelico. *Christ before Pilate* (from the Annunziata Silver Chest). About 1450–52. Museo di San Marco, Florence

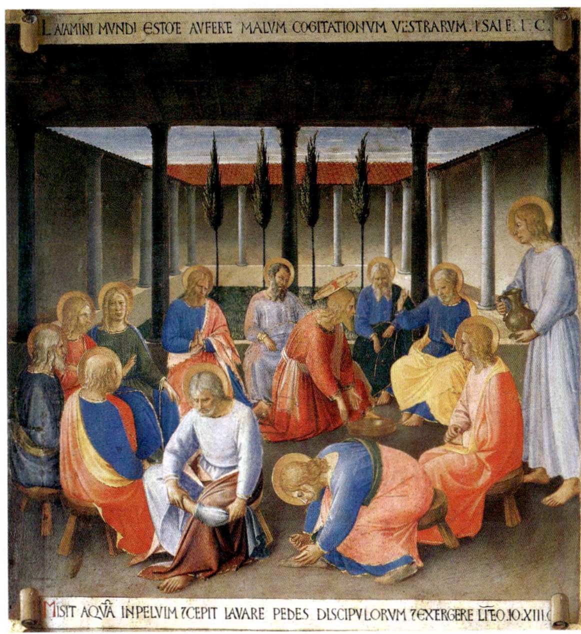

Figure 153 (far right). Fra Angelico. *Christ Washing the Feet of the Apostles* (from the Annunziata Silver Chest). About 1450–52. Museo di San Marco, Florence

account for the high degree of finish of some of the drawings, such as the *Christ Washing the Feet of the Apostles,* where yellow and orange highlights appear to have been introduced to simulate the effects of gold leaf.[18] The most relevant examples of this fusion between goldsmiths' work and miniature painting in Tuscany are found in Sienese territory: witness the illuminations on parchment by the fourteenth-century Sienese painter Niccolò di Ser Sozzo, inserted in round medallions behind glass, on a silver-and-enamel cross formerly in the Museo Civico, Lucignano,[19] or the enameled morse in the Metropolitan Museum containing a miniature of *The Stigmatization of Saint Francis* by Niccolò di Ser Sozzo's contemporary Lippo Vanni.

Although no comparable Florentine examples of this type of object appear to survive, a clue to the drawings' relationship to contemporary goldsmiths' work may be found in their striking similarity in size, format, and compositional formulas to the group of sulfur casts made from a lost series of niello tablets illustrating scenes from the Creation and the Passion of Christ, which are presently divided between the British Museum in London (fig. 154) and the Musée du Louvre in Paris.[20] The casts, related by most modern scholars to the early production of Maso Finiguerra (1426–1464), the fifteenth-century Florentine goldsmith renowned as a master of niello work,[21] appear originally to have decorated a small portable altarpiece in the Camaldolese monastery of Santa Maria degli Angeli, Florence. They were seen there by the eighteenth-century historian Luigi Lanzi,[22] who referred to them as follows:

> *Le prove del primo genere fatte dal Finiguerra sono perite in gran parte. Quelle che ne hanno in Firenze i PP. Camaldolesi gli si ascrivono ma senza certezza.* [In note] *Veggionsi in un altarino portatile; e dovean esser prove di qualche niellatore che avesse fatte in argento quelle storie, per ornare qualche simile altarino o stipo di sacre reliquie, se male non congetturo. Prima d'introdurvi il niello ne fece la prova in questi zolfi, incastrati poi con bella simmetria nel predetto mobile. Son di varie forme e grandezze, e secondano l'architettura dell'altarino, adattati al timpano, a sodi, a pilastrini, ec. Molti ne son periti; molti ne esistono; i più piccioli rappresentano per lo più i fatti della Bibbia, i più grandi istorie evangeliche in numero di 14, alte quasi un sesto di braccio.*[23]

A tentative reconstruction of the "altarino" described by Lanzi, incorporating the seven scenes from the Creation, in the British Museum, and the fourteen scenes from the Passion, divided between the British Museum and the Louvre, was attempted by Blum;[24] however, his Venetian-inspired Renaissance triptych contrasts with Lanzi's references to a tympanum and to small pilasters, which suggest, rather, a form more in keeping with a traditional Tuscan altarpiece. A closer reflection of the design of the original structure might be found in the famous fourteenth-century Sienese Reliquary of the Holy Corporal in the Duomo in Orvieto, an imposing multi-tiered silver tabernacle decorated with thirty-two rectangular, enamel vignettes illustrating the life of Christ and the Miracle of the Holy Corporal at Bolsena (fig. 155).[25]

The enticing possibility that the drawings may have been inserted into a structure similar to the one that contained the sulfur casts, and that they may have provided a model for Maso Finiguerra's niello designs, is suggested by the hitherto unnoticed relationship between several of the same compositions

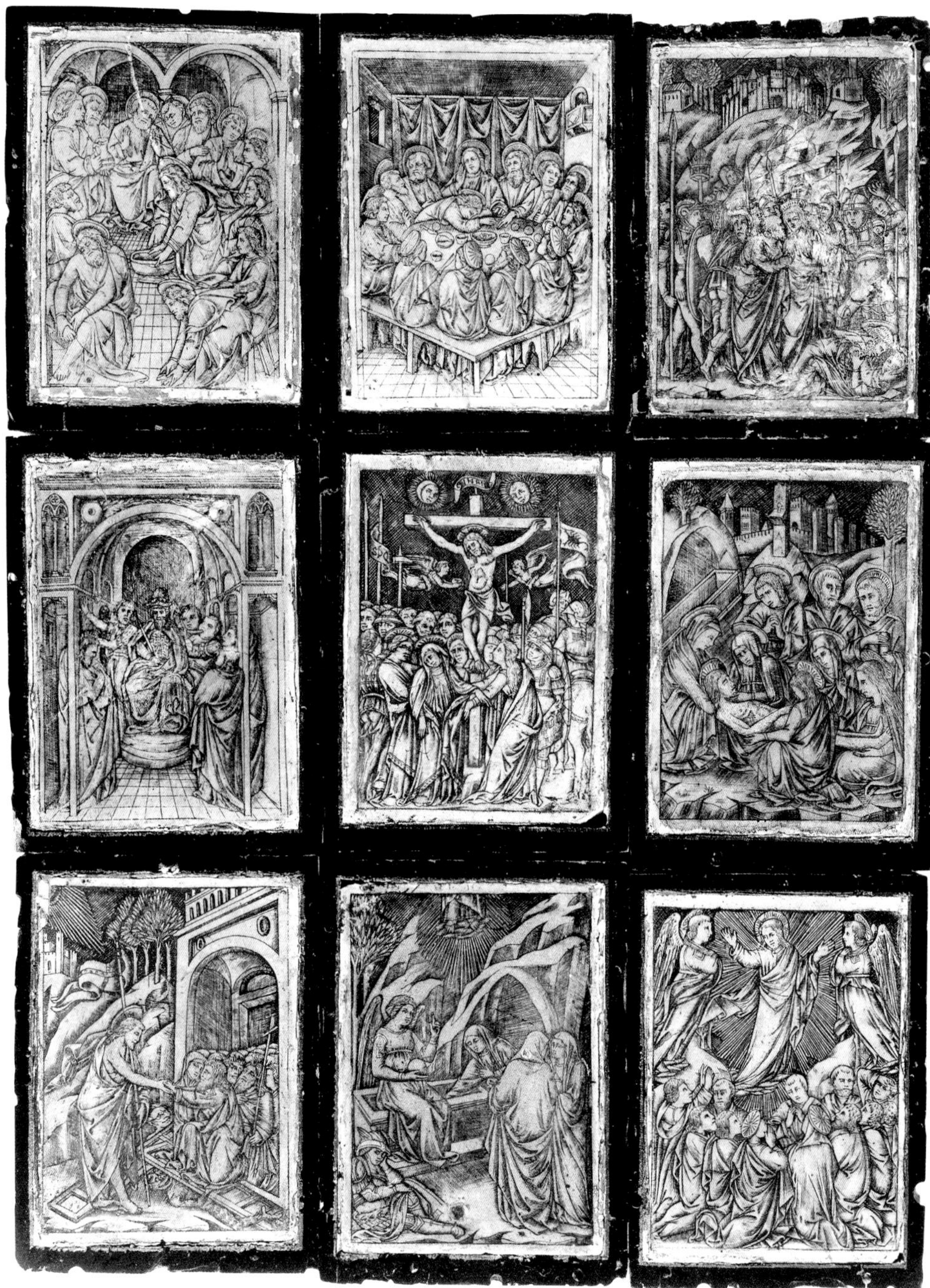

Figure 154. Maso Finiguerra. Nine Scenes from the Passion. Niello sulphur casts. After 1452. British Museum, London

in the two series. In the most extensive study of the casts to date, John Goldsmith Phillips[26] noted the close dependence of the Creation scenes on Ghiberti's bronze doors for the Florentine Baptistery, installed in 1452, thus establishing a probable terminus post quem for the dating of the series. The same author had more difficulties, however, in finding iconographic precedents for the Passion scenes, ultimately suggesting not entirely convincing comparisons with German engravings and the work of Filippo Lippi. A more persuasive argument was made by Konrad Oberhuber,[27] who traced their possible derivations to fifteenth-century book illumination, isolating a specific source for the composition of the Louvre *Pentecost* in a miniature painted by a collaborator of Zanobi Strozzi, between 1447 and 1449, in a lectionary for Florence Cathedral (Biblioteca Medicea Laurenziana, Florence, ms. Edili 146, f. 65*r*.).[28] Given the coarse nature of the miniature in question, and the fact that the casts are not related to any other illuminations in that volume, it is possible that both works may have been based on a lost prototype. Nevertheless, Zanobi Strozzi's involvement in the decoration of the same lectionary acquires a particular significance in consideration of the fact that no less than three of the artist's compositions in the series of drawings—*Christ Washing the Feet of the Apostles, The Capture of Christ,* and *The Lamentation*—appear to have provided models for other niello designs. Despite the insertion of the figures in a more clearly articulated Renaissance interior in the London *Christ Washing the Feet of the Apostles*, or the addition of figures and a townscape in the London *Capture of Christ*, the reliance of these scenes on Strozzi's compositions—from which they derive the disposition of the figures, as well as their individual gestures and expressions—is unmistakable.

The full extent to which the niellist may have been influenced by the drawings remains unclear, given the unknown number of missing scenes from each of the two series. The radical compositional variations in other episodes common to both suggest, however, that the goldsmith drew his inspiration from a variety of sources, beyond Ghiberti and Zanobi Strozzi, and possibly including Fra Angelico, whose various depictions of *The Agony in the Garden* appear conflated in the British Museum cast of the same subject.[29] What may be safely surmised is that the complete Passion cycle executed by Strozzi, whether inserted into a structure comparable to the one that contained the sulfur casts or into another type of reliquary object, was on public display in a Florentine convent or church and available as a model to be copied by others.[30] Possibly part of a commission entrusted to Zanobi Strozzi in the early 1450s, when the artist was most in demand as an illuminator for some of the principal churches in the city, it may be among the rare surviving examples of a once-common type of object, entailing collaborations between the best miniaturists and goldsmiths of the period.

PP

1. Cennini 1960 ed., pp. 9–11.
2. In her examination of the Fogg drawings, Penley Knipe (1997–98) noted that it is often difficult to identify red organic dyes, but she advanced the possibility that the ground used here may very well be the color described by Cennini as "*morella*" or "*turnsole*"—a plant-derived dye common in the medieval period.
3. The drawings were sold by M. Ant. W. M. Mensing, Amsterdam, July 5–6, 1927, lot 149.
4. M. Boskovits, in Toscano and Capitelli 2002, pp. 156–59.
5. Berenson 1938, vol. II, p. 18.
6. Degenhart and Schmitt 1968, pp. 451–52.
7. Mongan and Sachs 1940, p. 6.
8. J. Bober, in Mongan, Oberhuber, and Bober 1988, no. 4a.

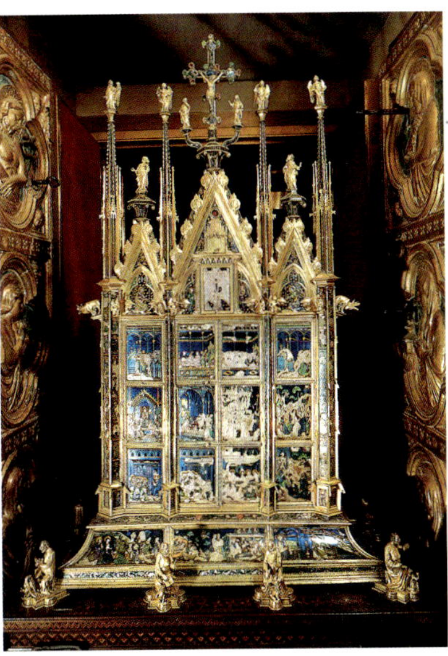

Figure 155. *Reliquary of the Holy Corporal.* Orvieto Cathedral

9. M. Boskovits, in Toscano and Capitelli 2002, pp. 156–59.
10. It is generally assumed that since Fra Angelico was in Rome working for Nicholas V in 1448 and 1449, he did not begin actual work on the silver chest series until about 1450, when he is again recorded in Florence (G. Bonsanti, in Scudieri and Rasario 2003, pp. 162–64, with earlier bibliography).
11. Mongan and Sachs 1940.
12. M. Scudieri, in Scudieri and Rasario 2003, pp. 201–7.
13. For the San Marco graduals, see ibid., pp. 173–84.
14. It is worth noting that the close resemblance of these illuminations to the style of Fra Angelico has led in some instances to the same attributional debate surrounding the drawings. Most recently, F. Pasut (in Toscano and Capitelli 2002, pp. 152–53) reiterated Bellosi's attribution of the *Saint Benedict between Maurus and Placidus* fragment from the Badia psalter to Fra Angelico, while accepting Zanobi Strozzi's authorship of the remaining miniatures from the same volume; see catalogue 46.
15. According to Albert Elen, who kindly examined the Rotterdam drawings for me, the purple ground is applied on the flesh side of the parchment, just within the painted borders. In some cases (for example, in *The Last Supper*), however, the ground overlaps the border lines, allowing one to conclude, as Elen notes (written comunication), that it was applied after the border had already been delineated. As a result, the framing device must be considered an integral part of the original composition.
16. For these and other related manuscripts, see Gentile 1998, pp. 296–311.
17. Ceccanti 2001–2, pp. 171–80.
18. In light of this hypothesis, the technical observation made by Knipe (1997–98), that "The surface [of the Fogg drawings] was possibly burnished, though it is more likely that the areas of gloss are due to pressure from prolonged contact with an object," acquires a particular relevance. The drawings' placement behind glass in a reliquary might, in fact, also account for the uneven fading of the purple ground, depending on the different levels of light exposure of the various parts of the object. Such a conclusion must, of course, remain speculative.
19. The cross was stolen from the museum in 1914 and has never been found. See C. De Benedictis, in Labriola, De Benedictis, and Freuler 2002, pp. 126–27, figures 45–46, p. 311, figures 230–245.
20. Hind 1936, nos. 134–152, pp. 38–40,; Blum 1950, nos. 2–6, p. 11.
21. Blum 1950; Phillips 1955, pp. 9–11; K. Oberhuber, in Levenson, Oberhuber, and Sheehan 1973, p. 4.
22. Lanzi 1792–96 (1837–39 ed.), vol. I, pp. 132–33.
23. "The first proofs of this kind made by Finiguerra have perished for the most part. Those which are in the possession of the fathers of Camaldoli, in Florence, are ascribed to him but without certainty. [In note] They are to be seen in a small portable altarpiece; and, if I am not mistaken, they must have been the casts of some niello worker who had executed those histories in silver, to decorate a similar small altarpiece or small reliquary cupboard. Before introducing the niello, he had these casts made in sulfur, which were then set with beautiful symmetry in the aforementioned furnishing. They are of various form and size, and accommodate the architecture of the small altar, adapted to the tympanum, the bases, the small pilasters, etc. Many have perished; many survive; the tiniest represent mostly the events of the Old Testament; the largest, 14 in number and almost a sixth of a *braccio* high, stories from the New Testament." It should be noted that Hind (1936, p. 39) mistakenly cited the convent mentioned by Lanzi as that of the Carmelites. The same error appears later in Phillips (1955, p. 9) and in K. Oberhuber (in Levenson, Oberhuber, and Sheehan 1973, p. 4 n. 18), both of whom, it is to be presumed, based their information on Hind. The critical history and dating of these casts—objects that were often used as decorations themselves (Hind 1936, p. 9)—is tied to that of two niello paxes with the *Crucifixion* in the Museo Nazionale del Bargello, Florence. The latter have been variously associated with "certain paxes" by Finiguerra, "with minute histories of the Passion of Christ," which were seen by Vasari ([Milanesi ed.] 1878–85, vol. III, p. 287) in the Florentine Baptistery, and with records of payment, dated between 1452 and 1455, to Finiguerra and to the goldsmith Matteo Dei, for each executing a silver-and-niello pax (Collareta and Capitanio 1990, nos. 38–40, pp. 133–48, with earlier bibliography). Following Hind (1936, pp. 9–11), some authors (Phillips 1955, p. 11; K. Oberhuber, in Levenson, Oberhuber, and Sheehan 1973) have sought to associate the lost niellos with this commission, citing Vasari's allusion to Passion scenes, as well as the formal relationships between the niello designs and these paxes. Considering that Vasari's description applied to more than one pax, however, the mention of small "stories" of the Passion cannot be taken to refer specifically to a single cycle, but rather, more generically, to the sizes and subject matter of all the various paxes together. Beyond this, the presence of a *Crucifixion* in the niello series would seem to preclude the possibility of this scene also being the main subject of the structure to which the niello series belonged. This would exclude the possibility of the Bargello paxes being associated with the niello series purely on iconographic grounds. In the final assessment, any association of the lost niello series with Florence Cathedral must remain entirely speculative.
24. Blum 1933, p. 221, fig. 13.
25. For this masterpiece of Sienese goldsmiths' work, see Carli 1964, and, most recently, Cioni 1998, pp. 468–621.
26. Phillips 1955, p. 10.
27. K. Oberhuber, in Levenson, Oberhuber, and Sheehan 1973, p. 21 n. 18.
28. Edili 146 is the third part of a four-volume lectionary (Biblioteca Medicea Laurenziana, Florence, ms. Edili 144–147), which was included in a large series of choir books commissioned for the newly built cathedral of Florence in 1438 (Dillon Bussi 1997, pp. 79–96). According to documents, the decoration of the lectionary volumes was entrusted to the Florentine illuminators Bartolomeo and Giovanni Varnucci, and to the Paduan-born illuminator Battista di Niccolò da Padova, although Zanobi Strozzi, who was responsible for the decoration of other volumes in the same series, appears to have intervened in the execution of the largest miniature in ms. Edili 146 (folio 11*r*.). While Zanobi's authorship of that illumination has been unanimously recognized by scholars, the attribution of the remaining miniatures in Edili 146, including the *Pentecost*, continues to be the subject of speculation. After being associated with Battista di Niccolò da Padova by M. Levi D'Ancona (1962, pl. 8), they were tentatively, although more persuasively, identified as the work of Giovanni Varnucci by A. Dillon Bussi (1997, pp. 79–80); the same author, however, recently amended her previous opinion (in Scudieri and Rasario 2003, pp. 44–51), suggesting instead a less plausible and visually unconvincing attribution to Battista di Biagio Sanguigni, whose participation in this commission is otherwise undocumented.
29. In this regard it is worth noting that the composition of the Louvre cast of *The Last Judgment* is repeated in a drawing in The Metropolitan Museum of Art (Robert Lehman Collection, 1975.1.562), attributed to the Umbrian painter Ottaviano Nelli (Forlani Tempesti 1991, no. 63, pp. 174–77) . The drawing, measuring 28.2 x 18.8 centimeters, and thus considerably larger than those under consideration here, is in brush and brown ink, with brown wash heightened with white, on greenish blue paper. Nothing is known of its original provenance, although, based on an old notation now almost illegible, it is presumed to have been included in Vasari's *Libro de' disegni*. As was first noted by Degenhart and Schmitt (1968, no. 256, pp. 331–32) the stylistic and formal discrepancies between the drawing and the niello design suggest, again (as in the case of the *Pentecost* cast and the Laurenziana miniature), that both works are based on a lost prototype.
30. That it was not uncommon for goldsmiths to be asked to copy works in another medium is indicated by a document dated November 19, 1454, recording the Arte della Lana's commission to the goldsmith Giovanni Poggi for a silver-and-enamel pax for Florence Cathedral, to be executed in the same manner and form as a niello pax in the hospital church of Santa Maria Nuova (Poggi 1988 ed., vol. II, p. 91).

48.

Virgin and Child (Madonna of Humility)

Tempera on panel: overall, 66.7 x 45.6 cm (26¼ x 18 in.); picture surface, 66 x 44.2 cm (26 x 17⅜ in.)
Worcester Art Museum, Massachusetts. Theodore T. and Mary G. Ellis Collection, 1940 (1940.40)

In addition to his numerous commissions for illuminated manuscripts (at least eighteen documented examples survive today), and his collaborations with Fra Angelico in the 1430s and 1440s on panel paintings and frescoes, Zanobi Strozzi sporadically pursued a career as a monumental painter in his own right. Six altarpieces (see cat. 44) and an equal number of independent compositions of the *Virgin and Child* have been identified as by his hand. Three of the altarpieces appear to have been collaborative works, possibly reflecting the strictures of Florentine guild regulations that constrained Strozzi to secure many of his commissions through the agency of another artist. This is not the case with the *Virgin and Child* compositions: five of them represent the Madonna of Humility and all appear to have been designed and executed by Strozzi alone. These, and a handful of smaller narrative panels, more miniature-like in scale (see cat. 51), must constitute what remains of the "*quadri e tavole per tutta Fiorenza, per le case de' cittadini,*" ascribed by Vasari to Zanobi Strozzi in his Life of Fra Angelico.[1]

The Worcester *Virgin and Child* was part of the famous collection of Early Italian paintings formed by Samuel Woodburn in London early in the nineteenth century. At that time it was framed together with two wings (also then attributed to Fra Angelico) representing *The Expulsion of the Damned* and *The Reception of the Blessed*—fragments of a *Last Judgment*—now on loan to the Museum of Fine Arts, Houston, although there is no evidence that the three panels belonged together originally.[2] Berenson assigned the painting to Domenico di Michelino, and Licia Collobi-Ragghianti and Mario Salmi isolated it from that larger group of pictures, recognizing it as the work of

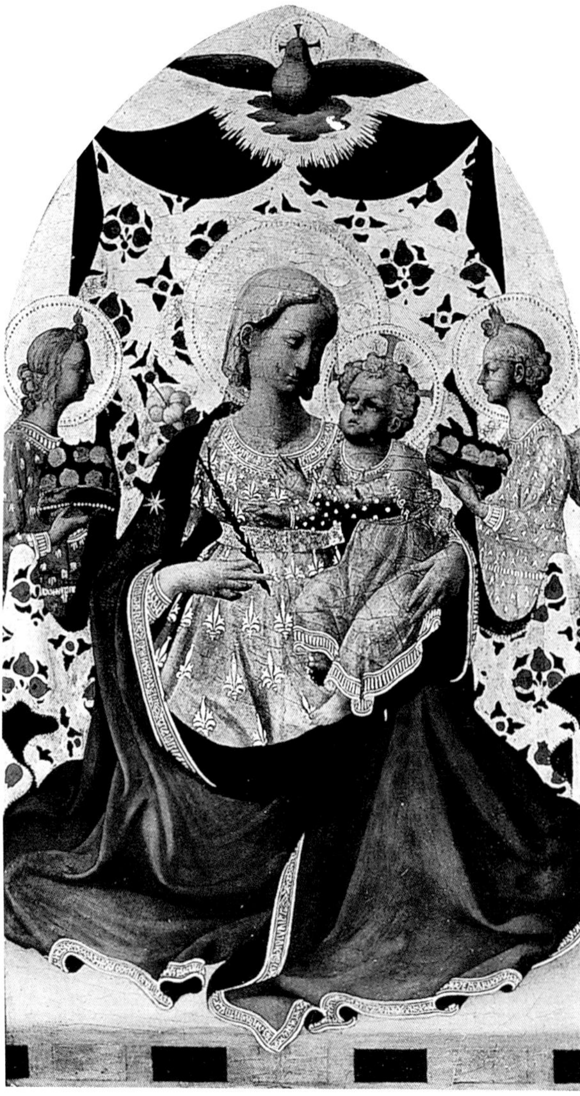

Figure 156 (near right). Zanobi Strozzi. *Madonna of Humility* (Buckingham Palace Madonna). About 1430–35. Her Majesty Queen Elizabeth II

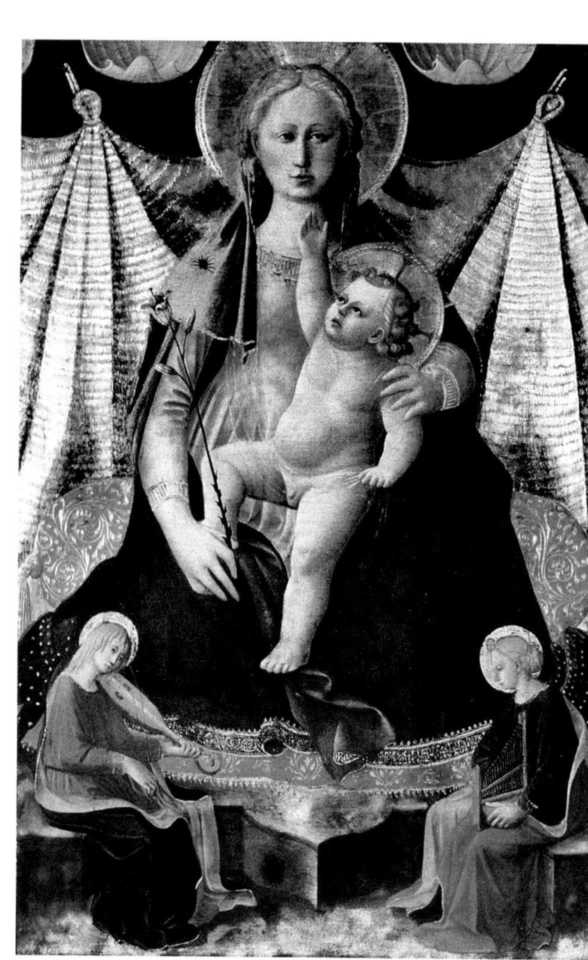

Figure 157 (far right). Zanobi Strozzi. *Madonna of Humility*. About 1440–42. Museo Poldi Pezzoli, Milan

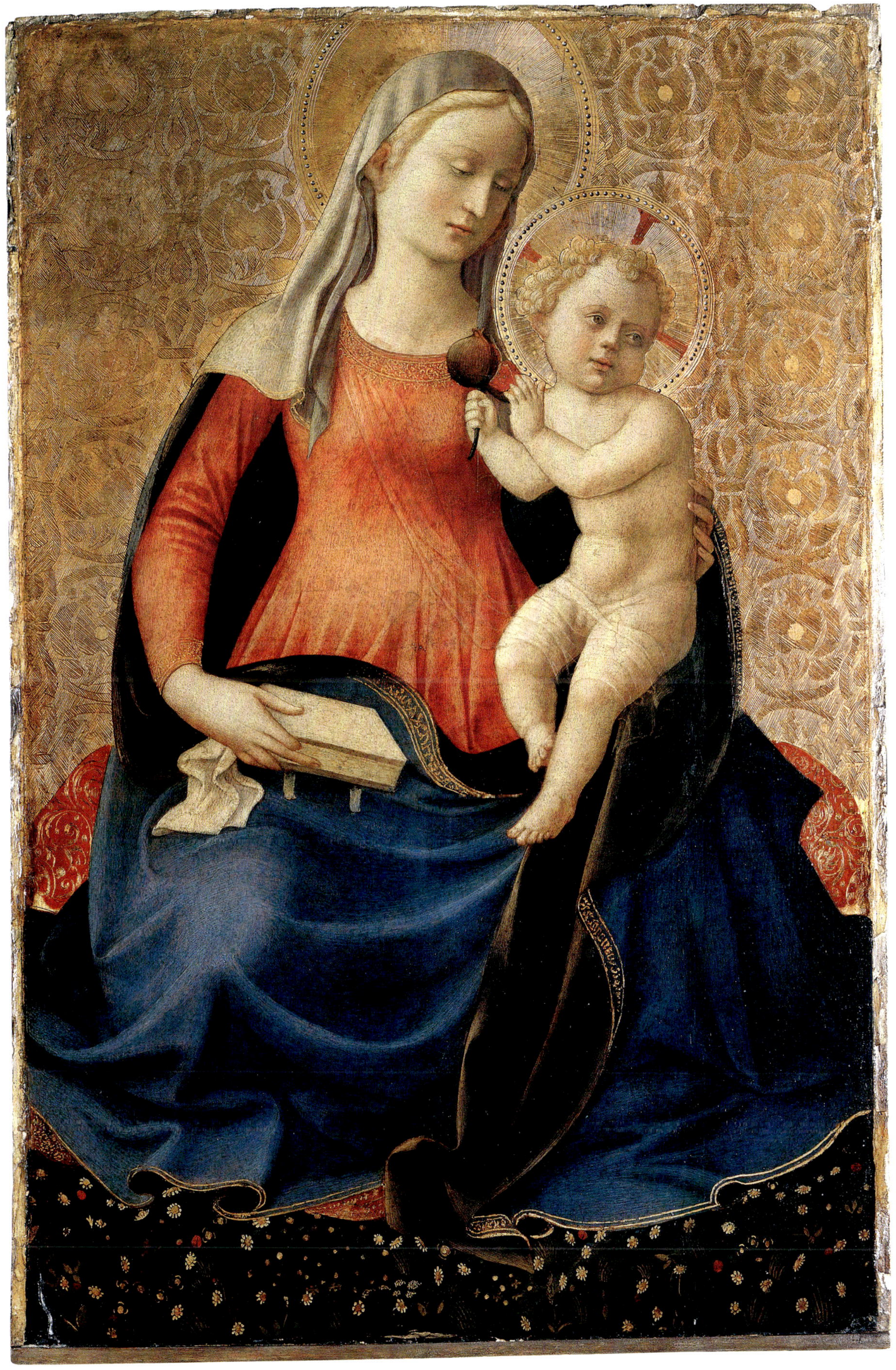

48

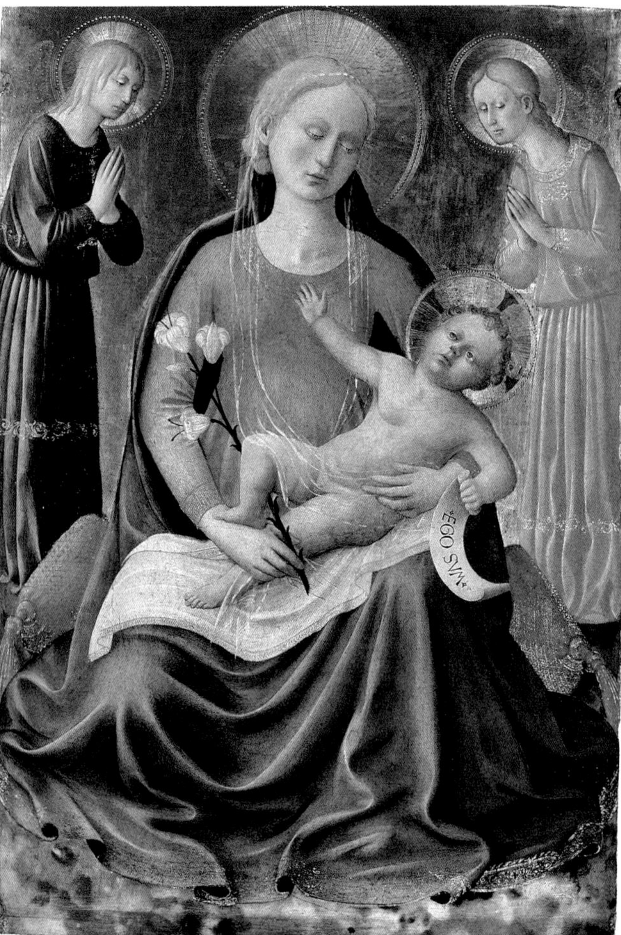

Figure 158. Zanobi Strozzi. *Madonna of Humility*. About 1445–46. Private collection, Turin

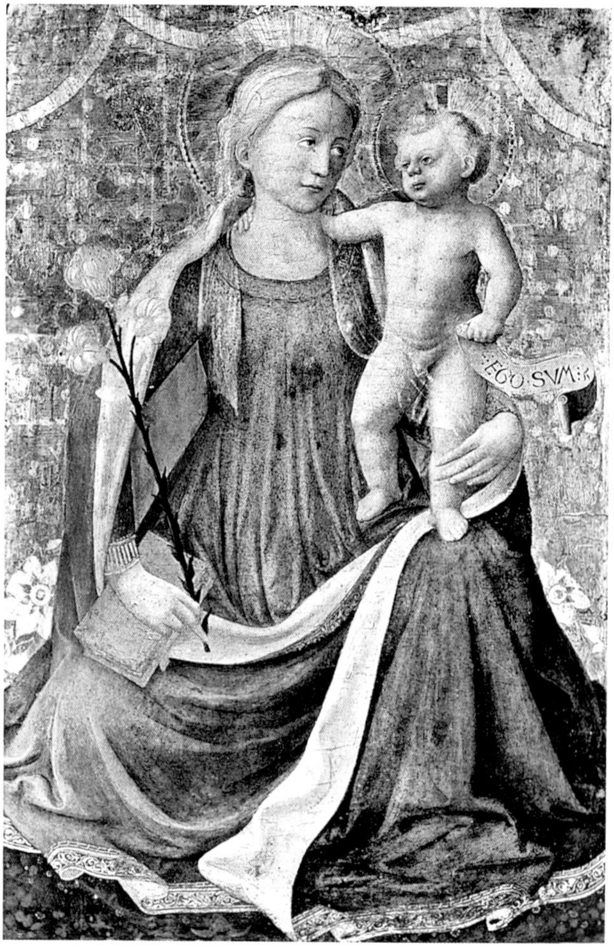

Figure 159. Zanobi Strozzi. *Madonna of Humility*. About 1446–48. The University of Arizona Museum of Art, Tucson

Zanobi Strozzi.[3] While discussions of Zanobi Strozzi as an artist have been much confused since then by numerous misattributions, there can be no doubt that this composition and four others of the *Madonna of Humility* are indeed, by Strozzi. The earliest of these paintings (fig. 156)—the picture in the English Royal Collection, which gave rise to the epithet by which Strozzi was briefly known: the Master of the Buckingham Palace Madonna—was probably painted in the first half of the 1430s, before the documented altarpiece for Santa Maria Nuova now in the Museo di San Marco and possibly not long after Strozzi's contribution to Cor. 3 from Santa Maria degli Angeli (see cat. 41). This painting is distinguished from the others in the series both by its significantly earlier date and by its compromised condition, both of which account for attempts to attribute it to a different artist.

Following the Buckingham Palace *Madonna of Humility* by perhaps as few as five—and certainly less than ten—years is an eccentric composition (fig. 157), formerly in the Mario Crespi collection and now in the Museo Poldi Pezzoli in Milan, which reasonably can be dated to about or shortly after 1440.[4] Strozzi's three other paintings of the same subject must be grouped close together at the end of that decade or in the first years of the 1450s—the period during which he was engaged on the illumination of the San Marco choir books (1446–54; fig. 138). The earliest of these (fig. 158), formerly in the Achilito Chiesa collection and now in a private collection in Turin,[5] recalls the London *Annunciation* altarpiece (fig. 133) in its figure types and, like that work, it was presumably painted about the time of Angelico's departure from Fiesole in 1445. The temperature of its palette and its introspective, classicizing calm reflect the atmospheric warmth and mood of Angelico's Florentine paintings of the Madonna from the mid-1440s, such as those in Bern (cat. 35) and in Turin (fig. 173). Equally classicizing but slightly less brooding and more monumental is a *Virgin and Child* (fig. 159) in the Kress Collection at the University of Arizona, Tucson. An experimental image, it is apparently contemporary with the Strasbourg *Journey of the Magi* (cat. 54 B) or the Dublin *Assumption of the Virgin* altarpiece (fig. 162), both of about 1446–48. The shortcomings of its composition—notably, the awkward arrangement of the Virgin's right leg and arm parallel to the picture plane and the Christ Child's impossibly long right arm stretching behind his mother's neck—are corrected in the Worcester *Virgin and Child,* the last and most understated in the series. For Berenson, this was the "most important remaining achievement" of the artist he believed to be Domenico di Michelino—more gracious, more winning, and livelier than the other Madonnas to which it relates.[6] Its figure types and palette are closest to the illuminations in the last of the San Marco graduals, and it is possible that it may have been executed as late as 1452–54. LK

1. Vasari (Milanesi ed.) 1878–85, vol. II, p. 520.
2. The Samuel Woodburn collection was sold at Christie's, London, June 9–11, 1860; see Woodburn sale, 1860, lot 83. See also M. Davies, in Worcester Art Museum 1974, pp. 311–12. The wings were published by F. Todini, in Walpole Gallery 1995, pp. 12–15, where it is mistakenly assumed that Padre Vincenzo Marchesi's 1852 citation of them as in an English private collection referred to that of Sir John Ramsden, Bart., who, in fact, purchased them at the Woodburn sale. It is possible that these wings originally may have formed part of a Last *Judgment* composition with another fragment, preserved in the Musée du Petit Palais, Avignon (MI 468), showing Christ in Judgment with the twelve apostles.
3. Berenson 1932b, p. 524; reprinted in Berenson 1970, p. 160. Collobi-Ragghianti 1950b, part 2, p. 18; Salmi 1950, p. 151.
4. A. Di Lorenzo, in Di Lorenzo 2001, pp. 22–27.
5. Ibid., pp. 46–49.
6. Berenson 1932b, p. 524; reprinted in Berenson 1970, p. 160.

ZANOBI STROZZI AND FILIPPO DI MATTEO TORELLI

49.
Saint John Gualbert in Glory in an Initial G

Tempera and gold, on parchment, 73.8 x 52.5 cm (29 x 20⅝ in.)
Fondazione Giorgio Cini, Venice

As indicated by the dated inscription inside the yellow border of the initial *G,* this leaf was removed from a volume belonging to the Vallombrosan monastery of San Pancrazio in Florence: "HOC OPVS FECIT BENEDICTVS ABBAS S[AN]C[T]I PRANCHATII AN[N]O D[OMI]NI · MCCCCL·V·I·I · REGNANTE KALISTO PAPA · TERZO" ("Benedict, Abbot of San Pancrazio, made this work in the year 1457, under the pontificate of Callixtus III"). Illustrating the text "*Gaudeam et letemur*" ("Rejoice and be glad") is the assumption into Heaven of Saint John Gualbert, the order's founder, witnessed by twelve black-clad Vallombrosan monks, gathered in prayer below him. The scene, which recalls the iconography of the Assumption of the Virgin, shows the standing saint, his hands joined in prayer, surrounded by golden rays. Interestingly, slight losses in this portion of the miniature, revealing a blue ground, might indicate that he was originally set against a celestial backdrop subsequently covered with gold leaf.[1] A feeling of spaciousness in the landscape below the saint is conveyed by the pronounced recession in depth of the semi-circle of monks, with the minute towers of a distant city visible between the hills behind them.

The *Saint John Gualbert in Glory* was first published by Nino Barbantini in 1940, when it was still in the Cini castle at Monselice, near Padua.[2] Listed as "Tuscan, 1457," it was mentioned by Barbantini among the fifty or so works complementing the famous ex-Hoepli miniatures acquired by Vittorio Cini in 1939. In 1950 Licia Collobi-Ragghianti attributed the illumination to Zanobi Strozzi, and associated it with a volume decorated by the artist for San Pancrazio, which had been cited by Milanesi in 1878: "In 1457 he [Zanobi] executed in the book of Saint John Gualbert for San Pancrazio the figure of that saint seated on a throne."[3] Although unable to identify the miniature recorded by Milanesi, Collobi-Ragghianti convincingly proposed that the same codex (now lost) may also have included, in addition to the Cini leaf, a second fragment with *The Assumption of the Virgin,* formerly in the Holford Collection in London (fig. 160).[4] This illumination, first identified by Van Marle as the work of Zanobi Strozzi,[5] was inscribed on the lower border "TEMPORE DOMINI BENEDICTI ABBATIS" ("At the time of Abbot Benedict"), confirming its likely association with the same commission as the Cini page, if not the same volume.

Collobi-Ragghianti's attribution was not accepted by Toesca in his 1958 catalogue of the Cini Collection, although the author identified the hand of Strozzi's collaborator in the San Marco choir books, Filippo di Matteo Torelli, in the execution of the leaf's border.[6] In 1959, however, Mirella Levi d'Ancona published a series of documents from San Pancrazio that firmly established Zanobi Strozzi's participation in the decoration of this missal and outlined the circumstances of its commission.[7] Among the sources cited by Levi D'Ancona was a book of memoirs written between 1452 and 1456 by Fra Benedetto Toschi, the abbot of San Pancrazio named in the Cini and ex-Holford illuminations.[8] Toschi records that between October 1456 and May 1457, Zanobi Strozzi and the illuminator Filippo di Matteo Torelli were paid for the decoration of a new missal that had been commissioned by Toschi's predecessor, "messer Ricciardo." This volume apparently included the legend of Saint Pancras (San Pancrazio) together with five of the principal Masses of the year (not specified), and it was not illuminated. In addition to taking over the decoration of the new missal, Toschi decided to add three more Masses: those of Saint John Gualbert, of the Apostles, and of the Dead. These were written by Frate Antonio Cavoni, a monk at San Pancrazio who, according to Levi d'Ancona, is also recorded as a scribe at San Marco, and therefore may have had a role in the hiring of Strozzi and Torelli.

As Toschi reports, the missal was completed and bound by the end of July 1457. On May 4, 1457, Zanobi Strozzi had been paid for the "figures in the illumination to the Mass of Saint John Gualbert," and on May 17, for the "figures in the illumination to the Mass of Saint Pancras." In the second instance it is specified that Torelli received payment for the foliation and all the other decorative elements on the same page. Based on these documents Levi D'Ancona identified the Cini leaf as the one that illustrated the Mass of Saint John Gualbert, in which Strozzi had intervened in the execution of the narrative scene, while Torelli, as in the San Marco choir books, was responsible for the foliated initial and border. The same author acknowledged that the ex-Holford miniature of the *Assumption* might come from San Pancrazio, based on its inscription alone, but since the subjects of the five Masses cited by Toschi are not known, she considered this hypothesis purely speculative. Such a conclusion seems overly cautious, however, as the *Assumption* is typically always included in the sanctoral part of the missal, where the Mass of Saint John Gualbert would have appeared. No other miniatures have been identified that might illustrate any of the other seven Masses cited by Toschi (the four additional unnamed ones, plus those of Saint Pancras, of the Apostles, and of the Dead). It is not clear from Milanesi's description of the miniature in this volume whether the saint "seated on a throne" was John Gualbert or Pancras. In the first eventuality, that illumination could have illustrated the Mass for the Feast of Saint John Gualbert, celebrated July 12, while the Cini page would have illustrated the Mass for the Translation of the saint's body, celebrated October 10. If, however, the miniature in question showed Saint Pancras, it would undoubtedly have been the illustration for the Mass of that saint, cited in the May 17 payment to Strozzi.

The commission for the decoration of the new missal may be viewed in light of Fra Benedetto Toschi's wider program of renovation for San Pancrazio. In about the same period, between 1454 and 1456, the abbot had commissioned the Florentine artist Neri di Bicci to execute various paintings for the monastery, including an elaborate fresco dedicated to Saint John Gualbert in the cloister (now in the church of Santa Trinita, Florence).[9] This work shows John Gualbert enthroned, surrounded by Vallombrosan saints and blessed, with Toschi himself kneeling in prayer at his feet. The abbot's profile, perhaps not coincidentally, recalls that of the Vallombrosan monk painted by Torelli in the upper border of the Cini leaf; seen looking upward, beyond the pages of the volume, he appears to be leading his monks in pious contemplation of their founder's ascent to Heaven.

PP

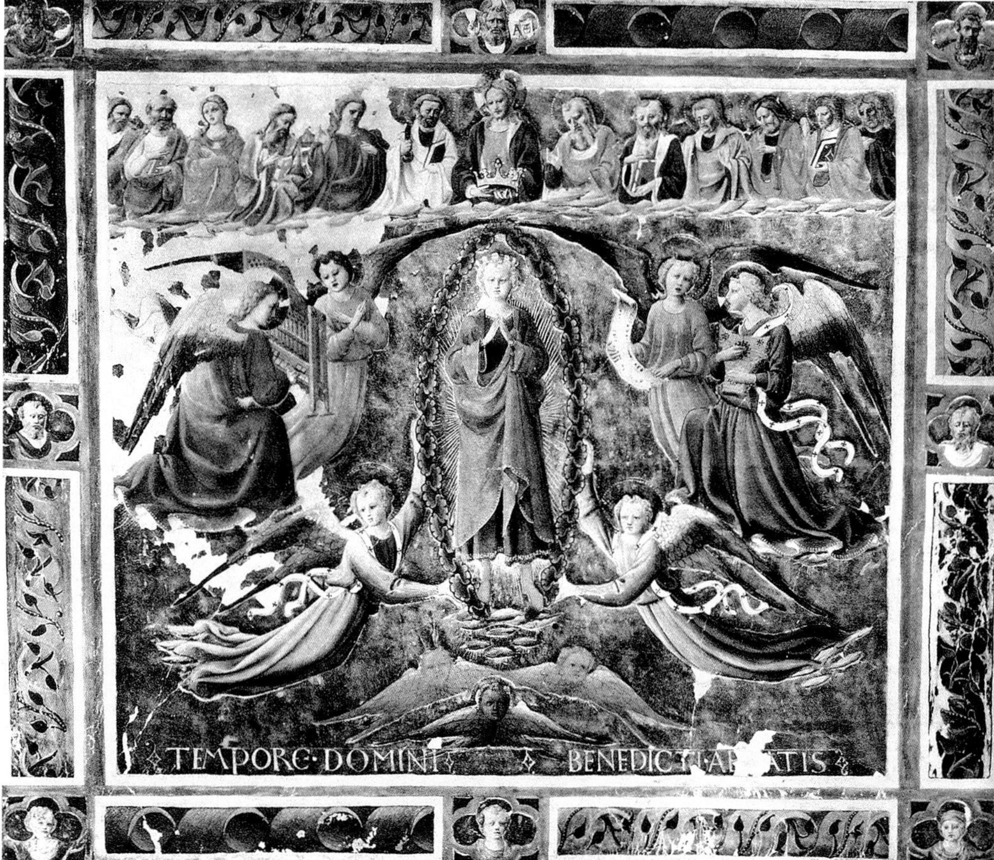

Figure 160. Zanobi Strozzi. *The Assumption of the Virgin*. 1456–57. Formerly, Holford Collection, London

1. This observation was kindly confirmed (in writing) by Giampaolo Chinellato and Marina Nahabed in the course of their examination of the leaf.
2. Barbantini 1940, pp. 290, 319, fig. 399.
3. Collobi-Ragghianti 1950b, part 2, p. 20; Vasari (Milanesi ed.) 1878–85, vol. II, p. 521 n. 1: "*Nel 1457 fece nel libro di San Giovanni Gualberto per San Pancrazio la figura di quel santo seduta in trono*."
4. Benson 1927, vol. I, pp. 18–19, pl. XIII; Holford sale, 1927, lot 1.
5. Van Marle 1928, p. 169.
6. Toesca 1958, p. 50, pl. O (as "Florence: XV century").
7. Levi D'Ancona 1959, pp. 6, 17–18; Levi D'Ancona 1962, pp. 266–67.
8. I have not been able to consult this document firsthand. My references to it are based on the full transcription of the relevant sections in Levi D'Ancona 1962, p. 266. M. Salmi (1955, p. 33) had already identified Toschi as the abbot mentioned in the Cini inscription, but believed him to be the author of the miniature.
9. Neri di Bicci 1976 ed., pp. 22–23, 26–27, 58–59; Padoa Rizzo 2002a, pp. 112–13 (for the fresco, in particular).

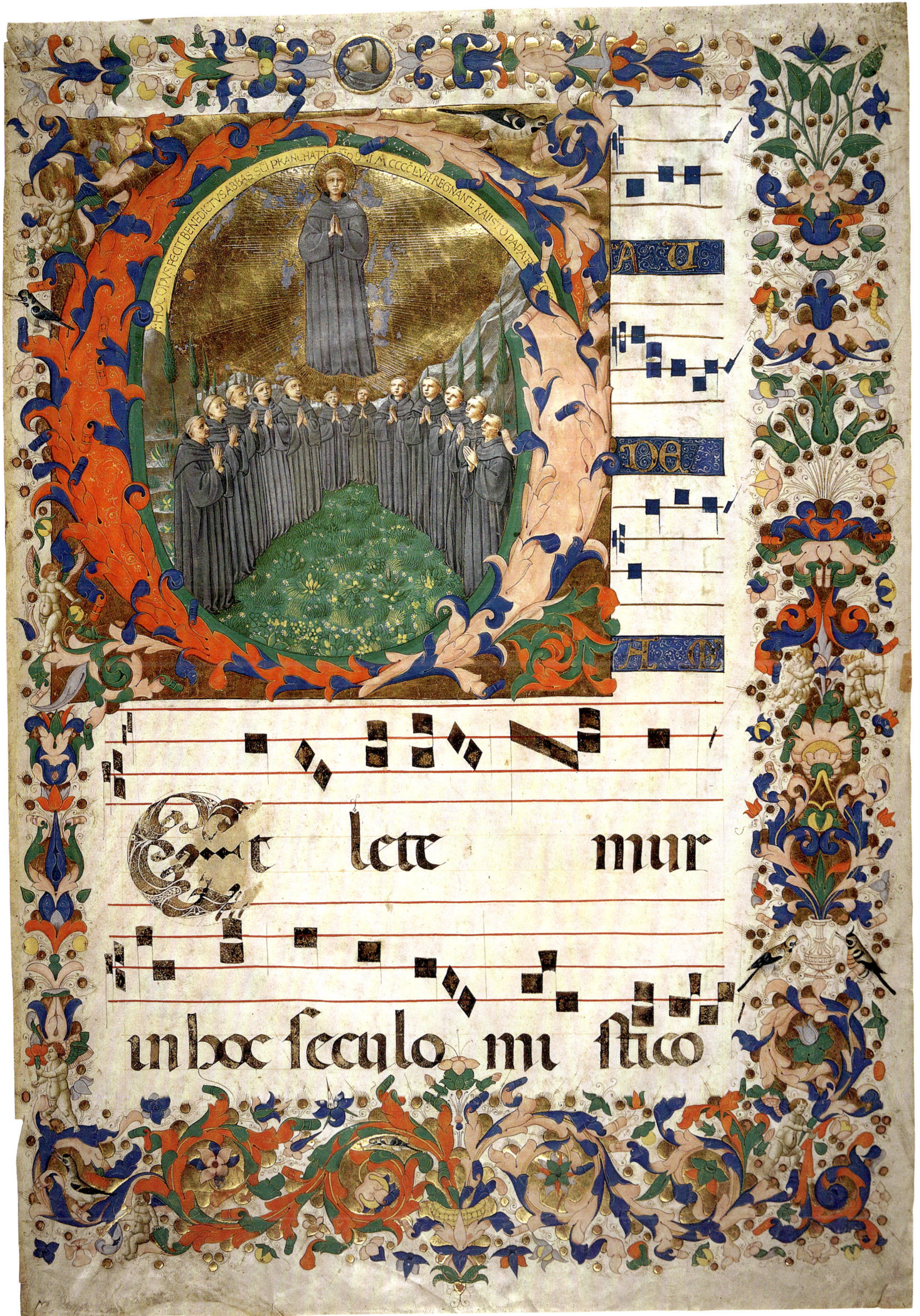
HOC OPUS FECIT BENEDICTUS ABBAS SCI PRANCHATII
DNI M CCCCLVII REGNANTE KALISTO PAPA
Et lete mur
in hoc seculo mi stico

49

50.
Virgin and Child Enthroned, with Four Angels

Tempera on panel: overall, including original frame, 150.5 x 92.7 cm (59¼ x 36½ in.); picture surface, 76.8 x 48.9 cm (30¼ x 19¼ in.)
Brooklyn Museum, New York. Gift of Mrs. Arthur Lehman (53.189)

The last in sequence of Zanobi Strozzi's *Virgin and Child* compositions, the Brooklyn *Madonna* is also the least like the artist's other efforts in this genre. It is the only one of six surviving images by Strozzi that does not portray the Virgin as the Madonna of Humility, and, conversely, it is the artist's only portrayal of an enthroned Madonna that is not part of a larger altarpiece complex. It is also unusual in not owing its primary debt of inspiration to Fra Angelico. The four angels arrayed in receding pairs on either side of the Virgin's throne reflect a convention that became popular in Florence in the second half of the fifteenth century, while the aggressive, twisting pose of the Christ Child, whose body stretches across the full width of his mother's lap, derives from Donatello's late experiments in relief sculptures of the Virgin and Child. In only one earlier painting, the Worcester *Madonna of Humility* (cat. 48), did Zanobi Strozzi break the psychological link between mother and child by showing the Infant Christ looking to one side and out of the composition. However, in that painting the Child does not interrupt the silhouette of the Virgin's sheltering body, but, instead, turns his chest, arms, and legs back toward her, whereas in the Brooklyn painting his active pose conveys a determination to escape her protecting embrace.

The evidence of figure style and composition places the Brooklyn panel at the end of Zanobi Strozzi's career. The closest parallels for the thin, tense angels and for the proportionately smaller heads of all the figures are to be found in the Hieronymite altarpiece from Fiesole, now in the Musée du Petit Palais, Avignon, often thought to date to about (or after) 1460.[1] The same figures and a like tendency away from Fra Angelico's dominating influence appear in the illuminations to three volumes of an antiphonary in the Biblioteca Medicea Laurenziana, Florence (ms. Edili 149, 150, 151), one of which is dated by inscription to 1467.[2] The ideation and execution of the Brooklyn *Virgin and Child* must be presumed to have occurred sometime within that decade as well.

The frame that surrounds the Brooklyn *Madonna* is original to it[3]—a rare, surviving example from this date of an elaborate Tuscan tabernacle frame conceived for a painting rather than for a stucco or terracotta relief. Although few such frames are preserved intact, they must have been fairly common, if costly, at the time. It is interesting to note that Filippo Baldinucci cited a document of 1470, two years after Zanobi Strozzi's death, according to which a certain Benedetto d'Aldobrandino di Giorgio presented his son Francesco with a "*colmo,*" or tabernacle, painted by Strozzi, valued at fifteen florins, as a wedding present.[4] The object in question could well have been the Brooklyn panel, but it should be kept in mind that at least four of Zanobi Strozzi's five compositions of the *Madonna of Humility* (the exception being the Buckingham Palace version) could have been framed in this way, and that it is quite probable that he painted other images of this type that either do not survive or have yet to be identified.

LK

1. M. Davies (1951, pp. 120–21) and M. Laclotte (1956, p. 69) place this altarpiece after 1460 on the basis of Saint Jerome's gray habit and leather belt, supposedly not adopted by the Hieronymites of Fiesole until that date. M. Meiss (1974, p. 136) later pointed out that the gray habit and leather belt were in use by the Hieronymites earlier, but a date of about or after 1460 was nonetheless defended by A. De Marchi (in Di Lorenzo 2001, p. 49 n. 20), correctly, on stylistic grounds.
2. Levi D'Ancona 1962, p. 261.
3. The painting is executed on a panel that originally served as the backing board for the entire frame; it was cut out—four drill holes to begin the saw cuts remain visible at the corners of the composition on the back—possibly not long before it was sold to Arthur and Adele Lehman in the first half of the last century. This was presumably done to allow for the thinning and cradling of the painted image, compensating for the excessive worm damage still noticeable in large parts of the frame. The cradle, unfortunately, has caused a number of vertical splits to form in the panel, with minor paint losses resulting along the largest of them, through the Virgin's face and body. These losses have been minimally retouched, and the painting overall is in an excellent state of preservation. However, the figure of God the Father blessing, in the tympanum of the frame, is considerably damaged.
4. Baldinucci 1681 (1845 ed.), pl. 502; A. Di Lorenzo, in Di Lorenzo 2001, pp. 17, 21 n. 24.

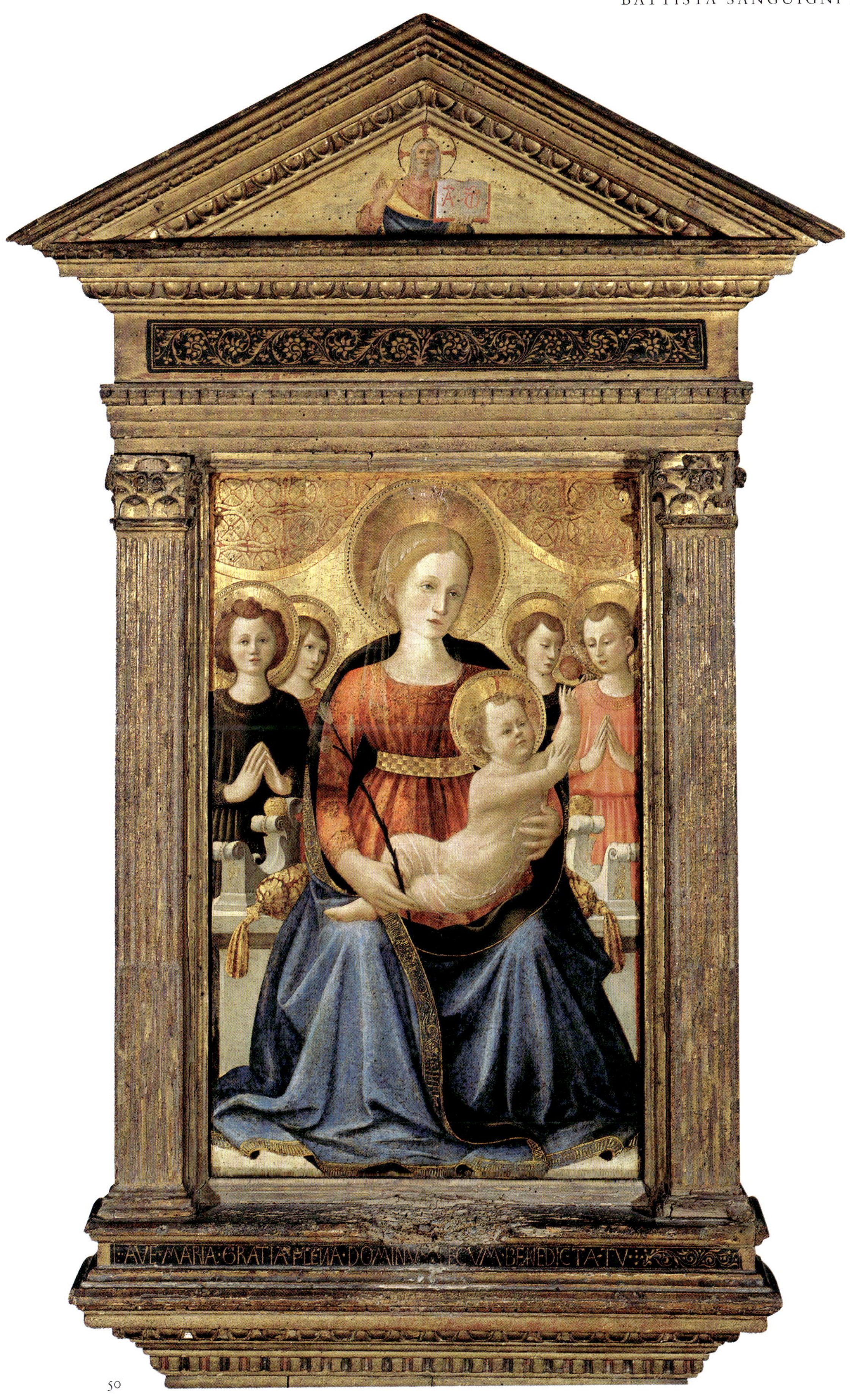

50

51.
The Nativity (The Adoration of the Christ Child)

Tempera on panel: overall, 38.7 x 29.2 cm (15¼ x 11½ in.); picture surface, 33 x 23.2 cm (13 x 9⅛ in.)
The Metropolitan Museum of Art, New York. Rogers Fund, 1924 (24.22)

Acquired by the Metropolitan Museum as a work by Fra Angelico, the *Nativity* has been recognized by most scholars, and subsequently by the Museum itself, as a workshop production. Zeri's tentative attribution to Zanobi Strozzi, although not acknowledged in any other study of the artist, is certainly correct, as a consideration of the figure types of the Virgin and the Child alone suffice to demonstrate.[1] The composition loosely derives from a painting of a similar subject and format in The Minneapolis Institute of Arts (cat. 17)—an early work by Fra Angelico—and more directly from the *Nativity* scene on the Annunziata Silver Chest of about 1448–50 (fig. 58); the latter may be accepted as a terminus post quem for dating the Metropolitan Museum panel. The painting's somber palette and restrained figure style would seem to argue for a date at the end of the 1450s, after the miniatures in Gradual B at San Marco (1453–54) if not, in fact, in the early 1460s.

The *Nativity* is one of only three independent, small-format narrative panels by Zanobi Strozzi known to survive. Along with an *Annunciation* in the Philadelphia Museum of Art (picture surface, 30.5 x 28 centimeters)[2] and a *God the Father Enthroned* in the Musée Jacquemart-André, Paris (picture surface, 25 x 19.5 centimeters),[3] these paintings originally must have been part of a more numerous class of object for which Zanobi Strozzi was well known—those that Vasari described him as having made "*per tutta Fiorenza, per le case de' cittadini*." Any additional function served by these three paintings, other than as images of private devotion, is not apparent. They are usually assumed to have been wings of diptychs or triptychs, but the present painting retains its original engaged frame and imitation-porphyry painted back,[4] and there is no physical evidence that it was ever attached to another panel. It is possible that the three pictures are early examples of an object not originally intended for an explicitly functional purpose in devotional ritual but as a pious form of domestic decoration. While images of the Virgin and Child are commonly encountered in this context from the mid-fourteenth century onward, narrative scenes are rare before the last quarter of the fifteenth century. It is interesting to speculate whether Vasari's characterization of Zanobi Strozzi was meant as an acknowledgment of his role in the inception of this new market for works of art.

LK

1. Zeri and Gardner 1971, pp. 79–80 (with earlier bibliography). Pope-Hennessy (1974, p. 230, fig. 92 [whereabouts incorrectly given as The Minneapolis Institute of Arts]) rejected this attribution, and the Metropolitan Museum retains the more generic description as "Workshop of Fra Angelico" (see Baetjer 1995, p. 15).
2. C. B. Strehlke, in Kanter et al. 1994, pp. 358–61.
3. C. B. Strehlke, in Di Lorenzo 2001, pp. 44–45.
4. The imitation porphyry and its painted white surround on the back of this panel are usually assumed to be original, but evidence to substantiate this is inconclusive. There is no gesso layer beneath this paint, and in some areas it does not continue beneath two vertical battens that were certainly added to the panel at a later date and that have recently been removed by George Bisacca, Conservator in the Department of Paintings Conservation at The Metropolitan Museum of Art. The horizontal wood grain of the panel is somewhat anomalous but does not indicate that it was once part of a predella: the profile and carpentry of the engaged frame and the presence of what appears to be a gesso drip along the right edge argue against such a reconstruction. Any evidence of an original hanging device at the top edge of the panel, if one existed, was lost when a two-inch-wide strip of walnut was inserted into the back of the panel across the top edge to replace damaged wood in that area.

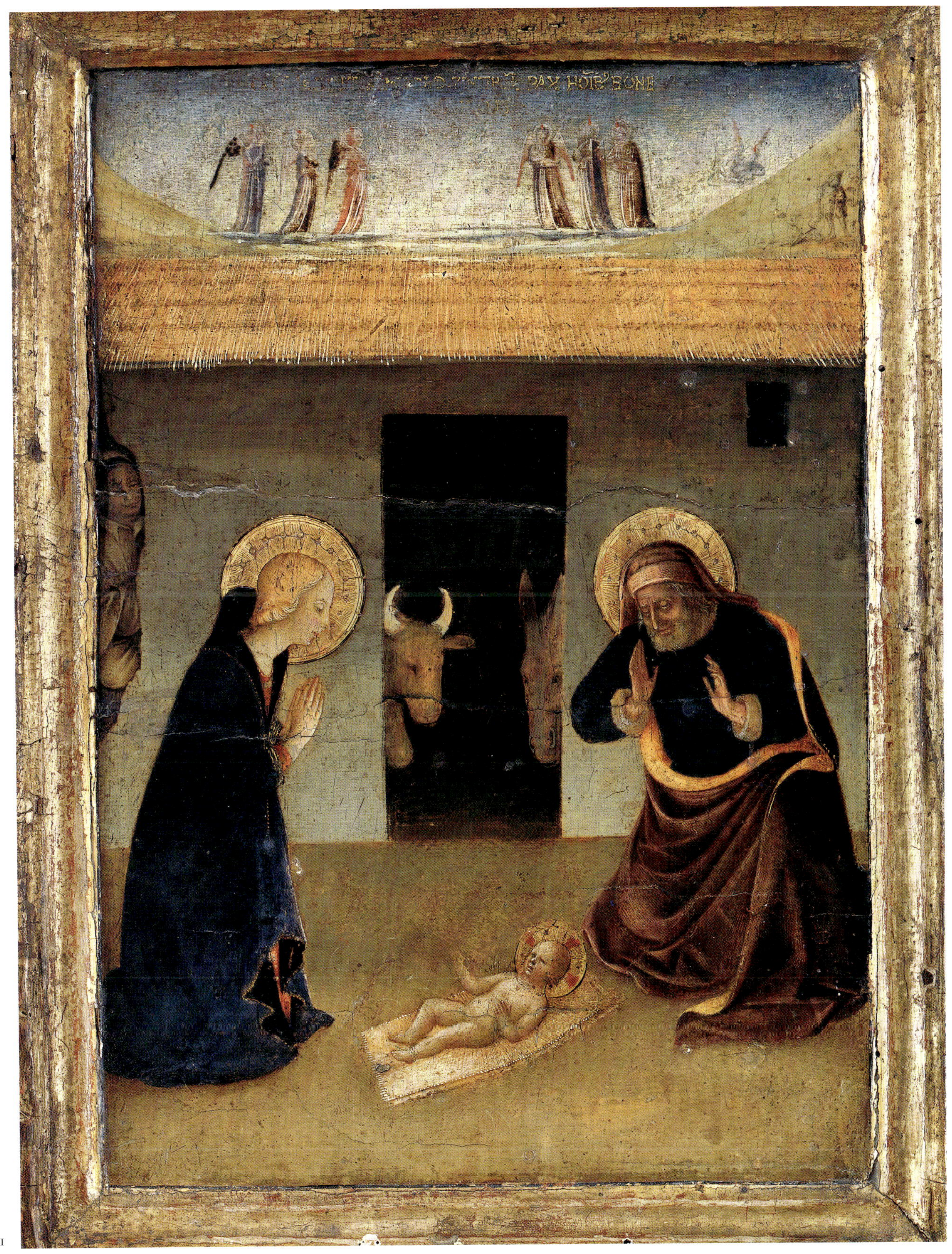

51

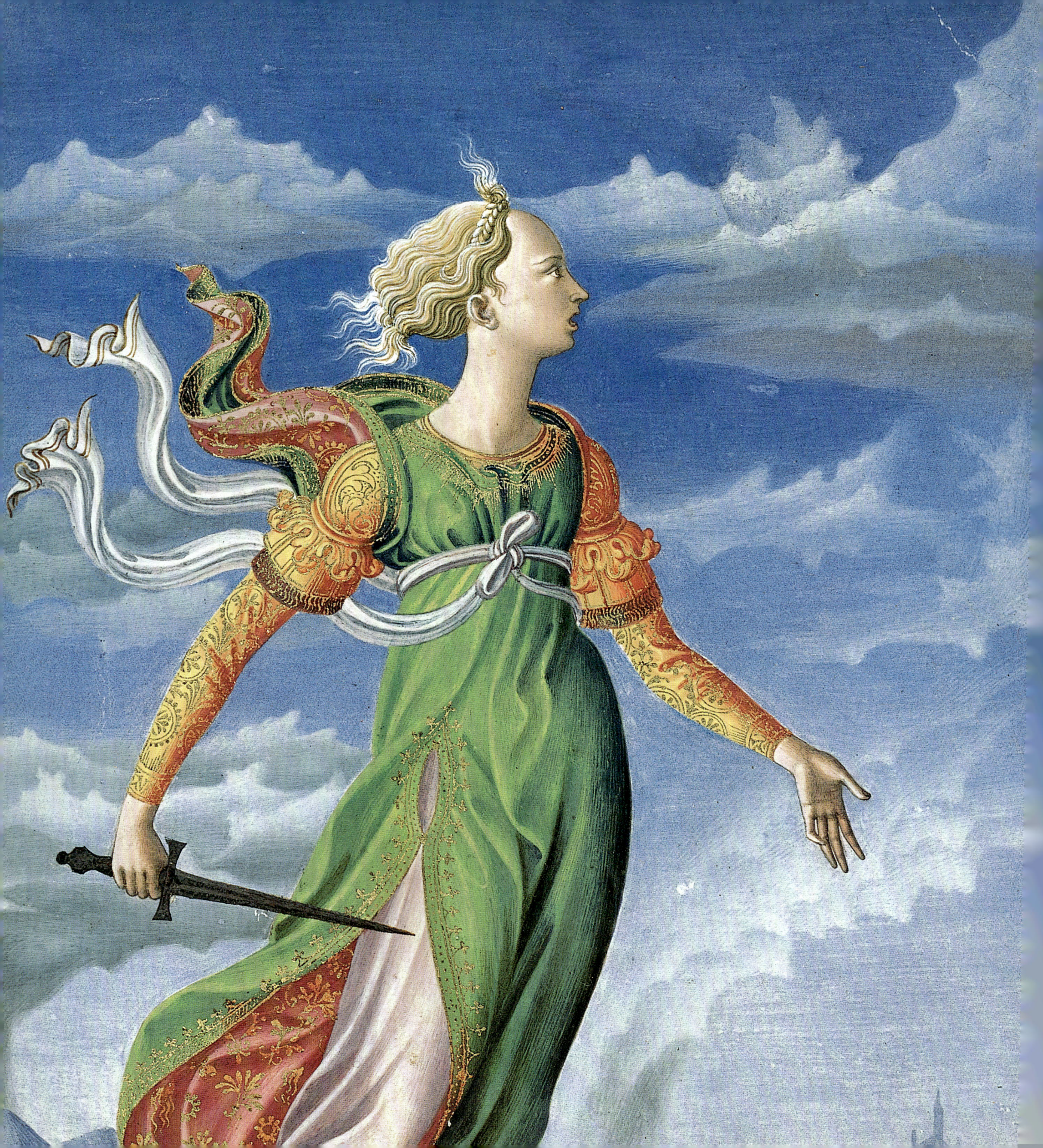

Chapter IX
Francesco di Stefano, called Pesellino

LAURENCE KANTER

Opposite:
Figure 161. Pesellino. *Carthage* (detail), from *De Bellum Poenicum.* About 1447–48. State Hermitage Museum, Saint Petersburg

Francesco di Stefano was born in Florence in 1422. Following the death of his father, before 1427, he was raised by—and later apprenticed to—his maternal grandfather, the painter Giuliano d'Arrigo, called Il Pesello, from whose name the diminutive, Pesellino, is derived. In 1442 he married, and in 1447 he is recorded as working in the studio in the Corso degli Adimari formerly operated by his grandfather, who had died on April 1, 1446. On August 1, 1453, Pesellino formed a commercial alliance with the painters Piero di Lorenzo di Pratese and Zanobi del Migliore, whereby all three masters shared the proceeds from whatever work was produced in their joint studio, no matter who painted it. In September 1455 Pesellino accepted the commission to paint an altarpiece for the Compagnia dei Preti della Trinità in Pistoia; now in the National Gallery, London, the *Trinity* altarpiece is the only fully documented painting by the artist. Unfortunately, it was left little more than half finished upon Pesellino's death, at the age of thirty-five, on July 29, 1457.[1] Domenico Veneziano and Fra Filippo Lippi were hired to appraise its state, and a year later Lippi was commissioned to complete the work, which he did by 1460. The recent and entirely persuasive study by Dillian Gordon[2] of the division of labor on the *Trinity* altarpiece now establishes a definitive standard for attributions to Pesellino, and allows for a clearer analysis of his relationship to the several artists with whom he collaborated or by whom he was most influenced.

The death of Giuliano d'Arrigo (Pesello) in 1446, the date at which Pesellino may be presumed to have inherited his grandfather's studio, coincided with Zanobi Strozzi's relocation from Fiesole to Florence (see pp. 228–29). Strozzi is not documented as having bought his own studio until several years later, and it appears that in the interim he may have been a tenant in Pesellino's shop or may have entered into a formal partnership with the young painter. Strozzi and Pesellino collaborated on at least three commissions (see cat. 54), all of which may be dated on the basis of style to approximately this period, and, therefore, on circumstantial grounds can be more precisely situated between 1446 and, probably, 1448. The most ambitious of these works comprises an altarpiece, the main panel of which, representing *The Assumption of the Virgin* (fig. 162), is in the National Gallery of Ireland, Dublin, and the predella, depicting *The Penitence of Saint Jerome* (fig. 163), *The Dormition of the Virgin* (fig. 164), and *The Stigmatization of Saint Francis* (fig. 165), is in the Museo Comunale, Prato.

The Dublin *Assumption* was first attributed to Zanobi Strozzi by Paolo D'Ancona nearly a century ago—an opinion largely accepted by subsequent scholars.[3] Even those who assigned it, instead, to Domenico di Michelino did so believing that artist to have been responsible for most of the panel paintings now recognized as by Zanobi Strozzi.[4] More recently, Anna Padoa Rizzo proposed an alternative attribution for the main panel of the altarpiece to Giovanni di Consalvo, the putative author of a cycle of frescoes in the Orange Cloister at the Badia Fiorentina (see pp. 291–94), in collaboration with Domenico di Michelino, to whom she assigned the execution of the predella.[5] For Andrea De Marchi and Andrea Di Lorenzo, only the two outer scenes of the predella, the *Saint Jerome in Penitence* and the *Stigmatization of Saint Francis,* could be accepted as the work of Domenico di Michelino, while the central scene of the predella—the *Dormition of the Virgin*—and the entire main panel of the altarpiece were clearly by Zanobi Strozzi.[6] Finally, and perceptively, Magnolia Scudieri noticed that the main panel was itself a collaborative effort that must be assigned to at least two different hands, although her proposal to identify them as Giovanni di Consalvo and Domenico di Michelino, as well as to divide the three scenes of the predella among these two painters and Zanobi Strozzi,[7] is not convincing.

The two artists involved in painting the main panel of the *Assumption* altarpiece divided their responsibilities roughly in half. The upper part of the composition, with the Virgin in a mandorla supported by six angels, together with the central *Dormition of the Virgin* from the predella, is recognizably the work of Zanobi Strozzi, as was maintained by Di Lorenzo and De Marchi. At the same time, the comparisons made by Anna Padoa Rizzo and Magnolia Scudieri between these figures and those in the Orange Cloister frescoes are entirely valid; they serve, however, not to discredit this attribution but to

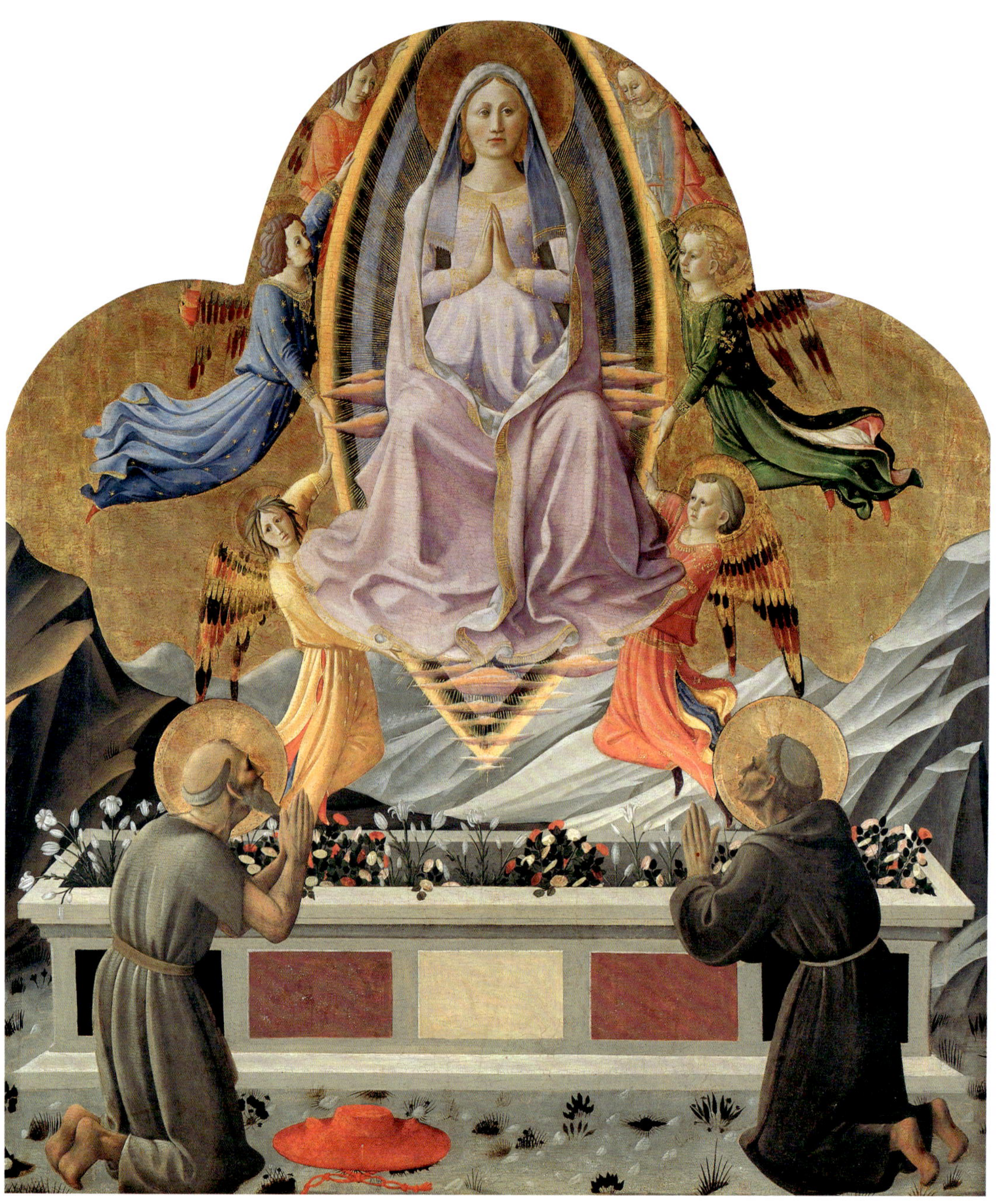

Figure 162. Zanobi Strozzi and Pesellino. *The Assumption of the Virgin*. About 1446–48. National Gallery of Ireland, Dublin

demonstrate that it was Strozzi and not the still enigmatic Giovanni di Consalvo who was partly responsible for the decorations at the Badia Fiorentina. The two foreground saints, by contrast, are different in conception, drawing, and palette. They are shown convincingly foreshortened in three-quarter lost profile; their hair and beards, the rims of their ears (seen audaciously from behind), and the veins in their necks are rendered in meticulous detail; and they kneel convincingly on a stony ground enlivened by small clumps of grasses and weeds, some of them crushed flat by stones into ellipses carefully foreshortened in space. The moldings on the left of the Virgin's tomb (those on the right side of the tomb were damaged and repainted and cannot be judged in this regard) are conceived with an architectonic accuracy of design and modeling well beyond the capacities or interests of Zanobi Strozzi, while the lighting and coloration of the rocky landscape corresponds to that in the two lateral panels of the altarpiece predella but not to the backgrounds of any of Strozzi's securely attributed works. These same qualities, however, which are also shared by the kneeling or sitting figures in the outer scenes of the predella, effectively eliminate the pedestrian Domenico di Michelino as the possible author of these parts of the altarpiece. Only the young Pesellino painted in this style and at this level of assurance in mid-century Florence, and a comparison with

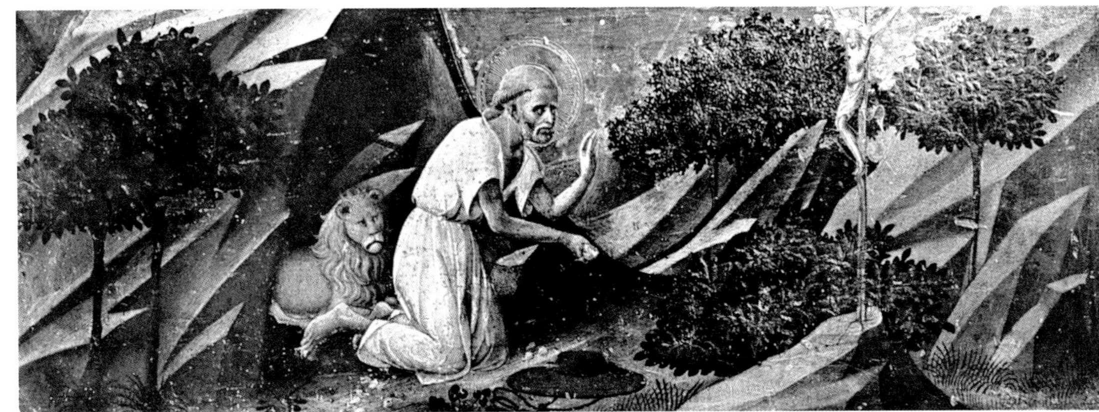

Figure 163. Pesellino. *The Penitence of Saint Jerome*. About 1446–48. Museo Comunale, Prato

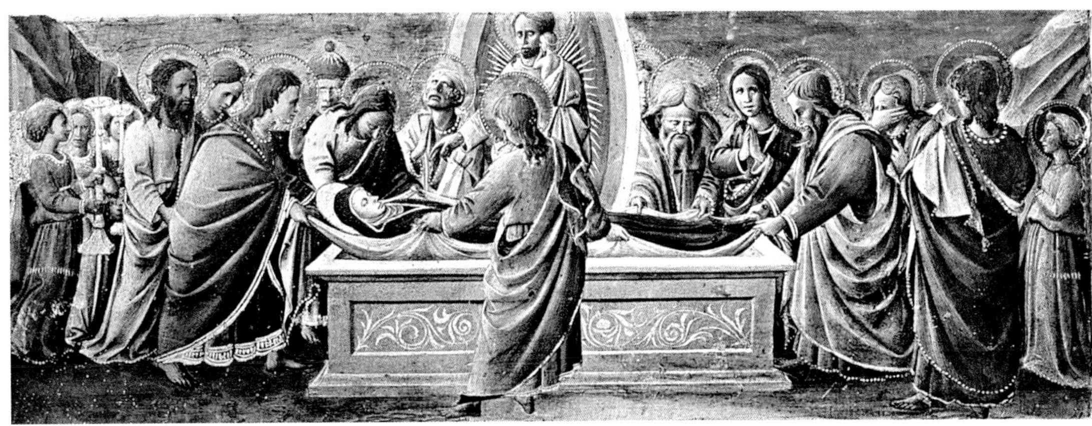

Figure 164. Zanobi Strozzi. *The Dormition of the Virgin*. About 1446–48. Museo Comunale, Prato

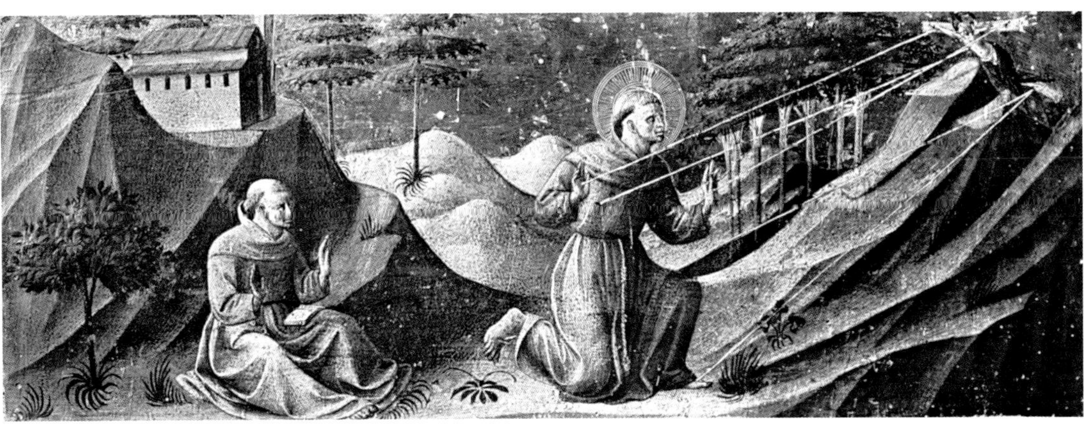

Figure 165. Pesellino. *The Stigmatization of Saint Francis*. About 1446–48. Museo Comunale, Prato

his panel of *The Journey of the Magi* in Williamstown, also included in this exhibition (cat. 54 A), makes his identification as Zanobi Strozzi's collaborator on the Dublin altarpiece a certainty.

The division of labor between Zanobi Strozzi and Pesellino on the Dublin/Prato altarpiece appears to have been all but equal. The same is not true, however, of the illuminated *De Bellum Poenicum* by Silius Italicus from 1447 or 1448: Pesellino assumed the lion's share of responsibility for the manuscript's decoration, supplying seven full-page miniatures (see fig. 161, 166, 167, 168, 169, 170), while Strozzi, apparently aided by his long-time companion Battista Sanguigni, provided only a painted frontispiece.[8] By about 1448, the inferential date of two cassone panels in the Isabella Stewart Gardner Museum, Boston, representing *The Triumphs of Petrarch,* Pesellino was painting independently and in a style easily identifiable with his mature works. He is not known to have collaborated again with Zanobi Strozzi after this date, and the influence of Fra Angelico gradually ceded over the next few years to that of Fra Filippo Lippi. Sometime about 1450, Pesellino provided the predella to Lippi's altarpiece for the Cappella del Noviziato in Santa Croce (the altarpiece is in the Galleria degli Uffizi, Florence, and the predella is divided between the Uffizi and the Musée du Louvre, Paris), indicating that he enjoyed, at least briefly, a formal relationship with the Carmelite master.

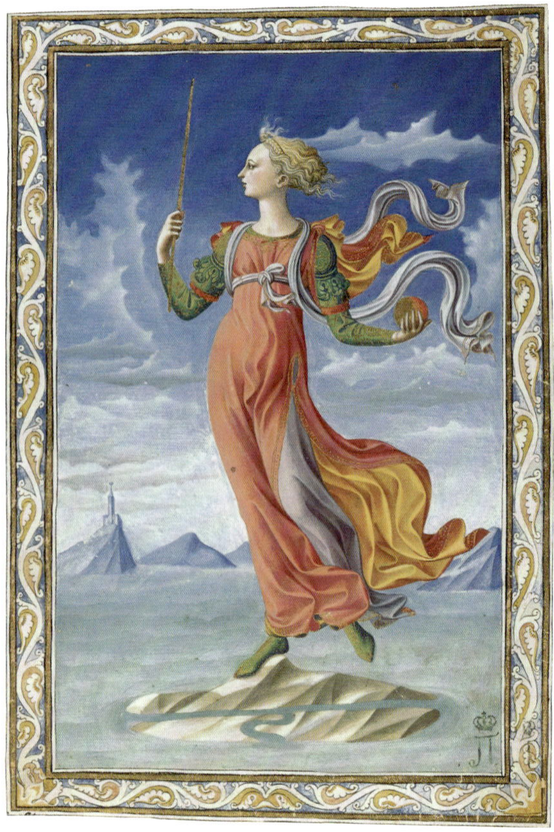

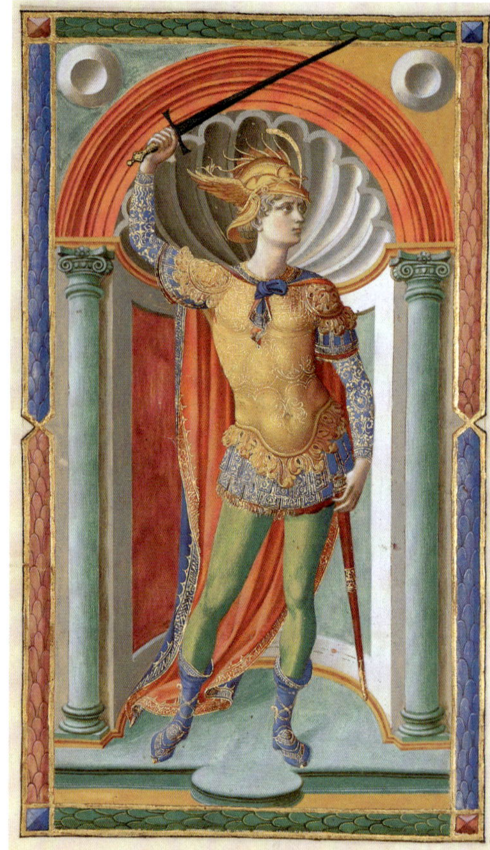

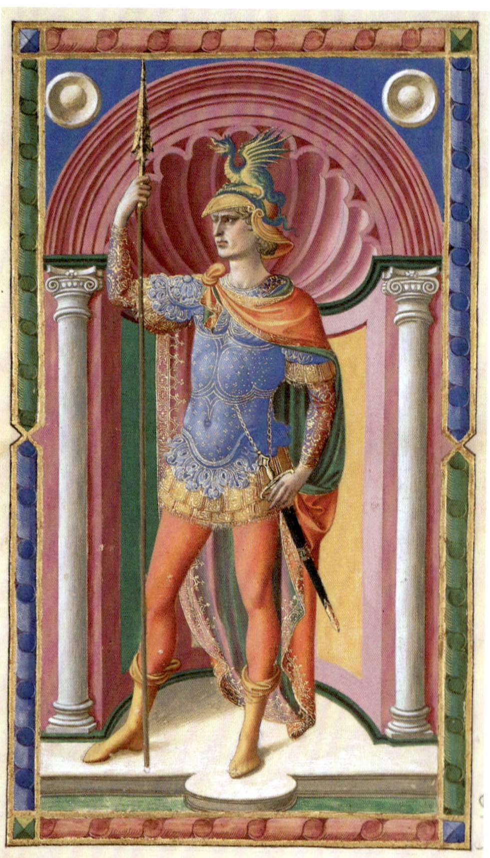

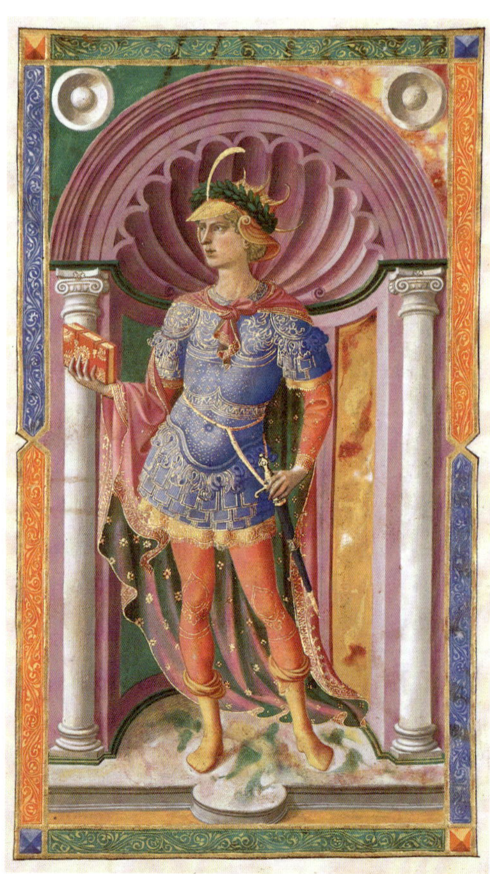

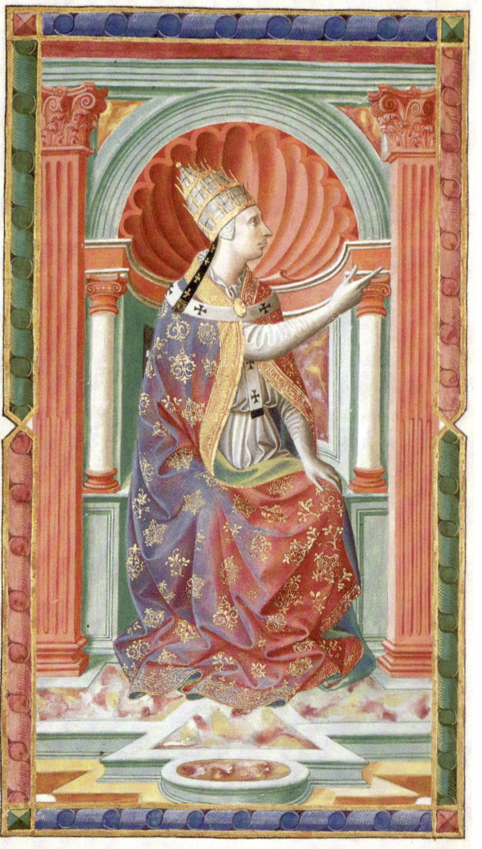

Figure 166 (above left). Pesellino. *Allegory of Rome*, from *De Bellum Poenicum*. About 1447–48. State Hermitage Museum, Saint Petersburg

Figure 167 (above center). Pesellino. *Scipio Africanus*, from *De Bellum Poenicum*. About 1447–48. State Hermitage Museum, Saint Petersburg

Figure 168 (above right). Pesellino. *Hannibal Kartaginensis*, from *De Bellum Poenicum*. About 1447–48. State Hermitage Museum, Saint Petersburg

Figure 169 (near right). Pesellino. *Silius Italicus, auctor*, from *De Bellum Poenicum*. About 1447–48. State Hermitage Museum, Saint Petersburg

Figure 170 (far right). Pesellino. *Nicholaus V, Pontifex-Maximus*, from *De Bellum Poenicum*. About 1447–48. State Hermitage Museum, Saint Petersburg

The intelligent admixture of two powerful but unrelated and seemingly antithetical strains in Florentine painting—the incisive naturalism and classical restraint of Angelico and the Masacciesque monumentality and coloristic exuberance of Filippo Lippi—characterizes Pesellino's mature style. This was clearly a self-conscious effort on Pesellino's part, and the idiomatic results, although developed over a tragically short period of less than ten years, captivated an entire generation of painters following in his wake. While the number of paintings that can be attributed unequivocally to Pesellino in this period is small—these include only two altarpieces, three predellas, two sets of *spalliera* panels, one pair of cassone panels, and a handful of works for private devotion—their influence was immense—disseminated, in part, by copies executed during his lifetime, presumably by his commercial partners Piero di Lorenzo and Zanobi del Migliore. This important aspect of Florentine culture in general, and of Pesellino's activity in particular—the reproduction of celebrated images for a wide consumer audience—has as yet been only inadequately investigated.

LK

1. See Gronau 1938, pp. 123–46, for a summary of documents relating to Pesellino.
2. Gordon 2003, pp. 260–87.
3. D'Ancona 1914, p. 53; Collobi-Ragghianti 1950b, part 2, p. 17; L. Berti, in Florence 1955, p. 111; Marchini 1958, pp. 25–26.
4. Van Marle 1928, p. 196; Berenson 1932a, p. 365; Berenson 1963, vol. I, p. 61. This dichotomy was recognized by F. Zeri (1974, p. 92) when he grouped the Dublin altarpiece with the paintings he assigned to "Pseudo-Domenico di Michelino" or "Master of the Buckingham Palace Madonna," now identified as Zanobi Strozzi.
5. Padoa Rizzo 1997b, p. 106. A. Padoa Rizzo cited A. Bernacchioni as the source of her attribution of the predella, and in addition proposed a provenance for the altarpiece from the Cappella dell'Assunta in Prato Cathedral. Such a provenance argued circumstantially for dating the altarpiece after 1441, even though Giovanni di Consalvo is last recorded in Florentine documents in 1438. A provenance for this altarpiece from the cathedral of Prato was contested by A. Di Lorenzo (in Di Lorenzo 2001, p. 21 n. 28), who plausibly argued, instead, that it came from a Hieronymite church.
6. A. Di Lorenzo, in Di Lorenzo 2001, p. 21 n. 28; A. De Marchi, in Di Lorenzo 2001, p. 49 n. 19.
7. M. Scudieri, in Scudieri and Rasario 2003, pp. 185–87. See also Kanter 2003, pp. 605–8.
8. For this manuscript, see M. Ferro, in Bellosi 1990a, pp. 128–33; Franci and Ceccanti 1993–96, pp. 83–88.

52.
The Annunciation

Tempera on panel, 25.4 x 33.3 cm (10 x 13⅛ in.)
The Fine Arts Museums of San Francisco. Gift of The de Young Museum Society (54.3)

The Lanckorónski *Annunciation,* so-named after the Polish count in whose distinguished collection in Vienna it long resided, is famous as one of the most enigmatic paintings of the Florentine Early Renaissance. Set in a sweeping architectural space of haunting simplicity—seemingly, an interior at the left and an exterior at the right—the scene combines the emotional clarity and muted pathos of Fra Angelico's renditions of the subject with the structural solidity and atmospheric weight of paintings by Domenico Veneziano. Attributions have generally waivered between the immediate circles of these two masters, with an occasional perceptive reference to the early style of Francesco Pesellino.[1] The recent, convincing identification of Pesellino's work in the studio of his grandfather Giuliano d'Arrigo (known as Pesello),[2] as well as of his early collaborations with Zanobi Strozzi, make this attribution a certainty. The *Annunciation* reveals the same command of naturalistic devices and of the principles of linear perspective, and the same tactile sense of modeling, as may be discerned in the lateral panels of the Prato predella or the lower half of the Dublin *Assumption* altarpiece. Its figure style closely relates to those panels, as well as to the Williamstown *Journey of the Magi* (cat. 54 A). The *Annunciation* represents a transitional phase in Pesellino's development, bridging the gap between these "independent" works and several paintings from Pesello's workshop plausibly executed by Pesellino in his grandfather's name or as part of commissions to the older artist, such as the zodiacal frescoes in the cupola of the Old Sacristy at San Lorenzo or the *desco* with the *Rape of Helen* formerly in the Cook collection at Richmond. Pesellino must have been actively engaged as his grandfather's assistant from about 1440 until the latter's death in 1446. It is reasonable to assume that the *Annunciation* was painted toward the end of this period, immediately prior to the young artist's collaborations with Zanobi Strozzi.

The *Annunciation* presumably was designed as part of a narrative predella, the usual context in which panels of this size, format, and subject are encountered. If this were so, however, no other fragments of this predella, or of the altarpiece from which it came, are known to survive, unless the complex was, like much of Pesellino's early work, a collaborative enterprise, and another artist was responsible for the remainder of the project. A *Nativity* in the Clowes Collection at the Indianapolis Museum of Art, by an unknown imitator of Fra Angelico,[3] is of approximately the same date as the Lanckorónski *Annunciation* and of an appropriate size (26 x 52 centimeters) to have occupied the center of the same predella, but it is a work of art of significantly more modest aesthetic ambition, and the association of these two panels in a single commission would be entirely conjectural. A more attractive hypothesis might be to link the *Annunciation* to a mysterious panel in the Strossmayer Gallery in Zagreb representing *The Stigmatization of Saint Francis* and *The Death of Saint Peter Martyr* (24.3 x 43.8 centimeters)—a painting comparable in quality to the Lanckorónski picture and equally difficult to characterize stylistically.[4] There is no intrinsic reason to assume, however, that the Lanckorónski *Annunciation* must have been part of a joint undertaking, nor—if that were so—that Pesellino's collaborator was necessarily an artist from the circle of Fra Angelico: for now, the question must remain open. LK

1. Longhi (1928b, p. 35 n. 2) notes the influence of Domenico Veneziano; M. Salmi (1928–29, p. 13) described it as similar to the style of Fra Angelico and of Pesellino; G. Pudelko (1935, p. 76 n. 11) called it Pesellinesque; and Berenson (1963, vol. I, p. 220) placed it between Fra Angelico and Domenico Veneziano.
2. Neri Lusanna 1989, p. 421.
3. Fraser 1973, p. 8.
4. Strossmayer Gallery 1939, p. 9; Zlamalik 1982, pp. 90–91. The Zagreb panel relates to the five fragments of a *Thebaid* discussed on page 105 note 3.

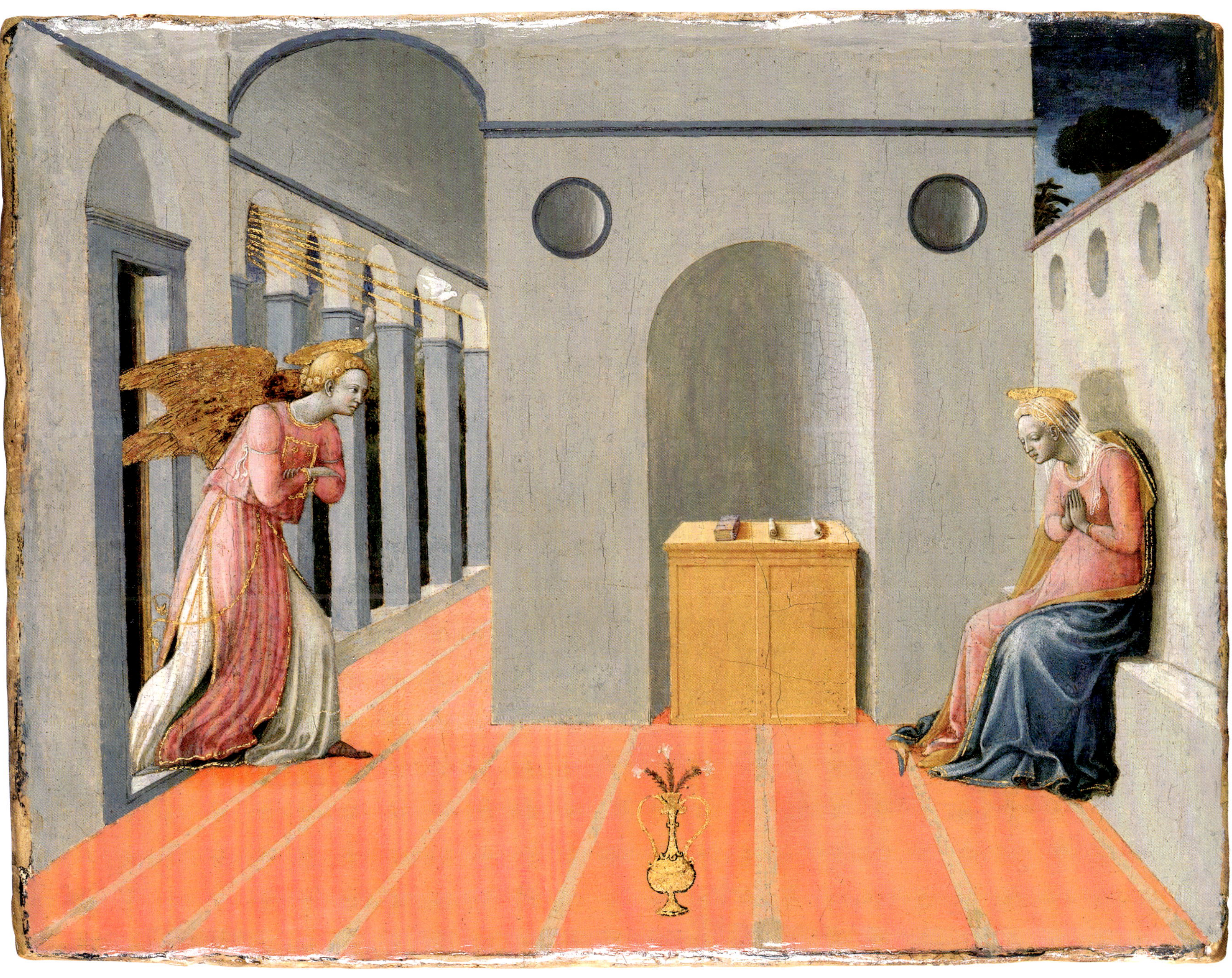

52

53.
Virgin and Child

Tempera on panel, 75.2 x 56.5 cm (29⅝ x 22¼ in.)
The Metropolitan Museum of Art, New York. Theodore M. Davis Collection, Bequest of Theodore M. Davis, 1915 (30.95.254)

When it first entered The Metropolitan Museum of Art, as part of the bequest of Theodore Davis, this haunting image of the Madonna was ascribed to Masolino—an attribution of convenience for many early-fifteenth-century Florentine paintings that did not conform entirely to the known parameters of the major masters of the period. It was recognized by Mario Salmi as a work by the artist responsible for the Lanckorónski *Annunciation* (cat. 52)[1]—an association that has been widely acknowledged since then.[2] Aside from their divergence in scale, the only material differences between the Davis *Virgin and Child* and the Lanckorónski *Annunciation* are a function of their contrasting states of preservation—exceptionally fine in the case of the *Annunciation,* and evenly abraded in the case of the Madonna. The flat, gilded halos in the latter panel are, apparently, the result of a later intervention, replacing the originals, which were painted in perspectival recession like those in the Lanckorónski *Annunciation.*

Roberto Longhi, who generally took exception to any suggestion introduced by Salmi, has been the only scholar to reject an attribution to the "Master of the Lanckorónski Annunciation" for the Davis Madonna.[3] However, he perceptively related the painting to the late works of the artist he knew as the Master of the Bargello Judgment of Paris, now identified as Pesellino's grandfather, Giuliano d'Arrigo (Pesello). Longhi ascribed the "luminous elegance" of the Davis Madonna to the hypothetical influence of Domenico Veneziano on the elderly Master of the Bargello Judgment of Paris/Giuliano d'Arrigo, but it is now possible to recognize this influence instead as an indication of the activity within the latter's workshop of his gifted grandson Francesco di Stefano, called Pesellino, who was openly receptive to the innovations of both Domenico Veneziano and Fra Angelico. Francesco's clear-sighted amalgamation of these divergent stylistic sources, so evident in the Lanckorónski *Annunciation,* is typical of the chameleon-like blending of influences that characterizes his entire career, culminating in the reappraisal of models by Fra Filippo Lippi apparent in his late works, which form the basis of his very considerable posthumous reputation.

There has been some discussion of the origin of the compositional type adopted in this painting, showing the Virgin in half-length behind a parapet, in front of a shell niche. A feature common to several works from Pesellino's maturity and reproduced endlessly by his many followers and assistants—now known collectively by the epithets "Pseudo-Pier Francesco Fiorentino" or "Lippi-Pesellino Imitators"—the invention of the motif is sometimes traced back to paintings by Fra Filippo Lippi or to the sculptural reliefs of Luca della Robbia.[4] Lippi experimented with this compositional form on several occasions, and in each instance he seems to be alluding to a sculptural prototype. The reliance of the present painting on the inspiration of a sculptural example is less obvious; while it is possible that a relief such as Luca della Robbia's "*Bliss Madonna*" in The Metropolitan Museum of Art (fig. 171) may underlie the genesis of Pesellino's Davis Madonna, the dating of the latter, which is unlikely to have been painted after 1445 or perhaps 1446, makes the issue of precedence difficult to resolve.

LK

1. Salmi 1928–29, p. 13.
2. Pudelko 1935, p. 76 n. 11; Berenson 1963, vol. I, p. 219; Neumeyer 1965, pp. 7–8; Zeri and Gardner 1971, pp. 94–95.
3. Longhi 1928b, p. 35.
4. See J. Draper, in Christiansen 2005, p. 196.

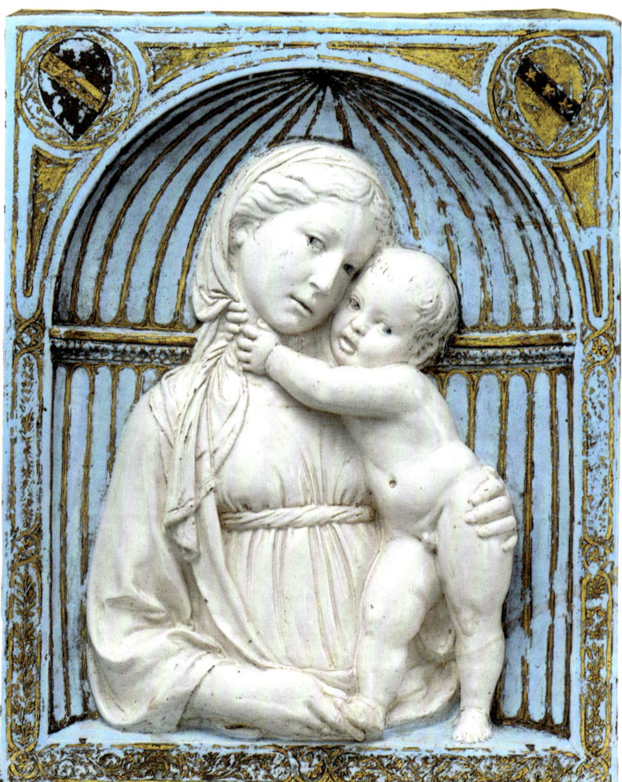

Figure 171. Luca della Robbia. *Virgin and Child in a Niche* ("*Bliss Madonna*"). About 1445–50. The Metropolitan Museum of Art, New York. Bequest of Susan Dwight Bliss, 1966 (67.55.98)

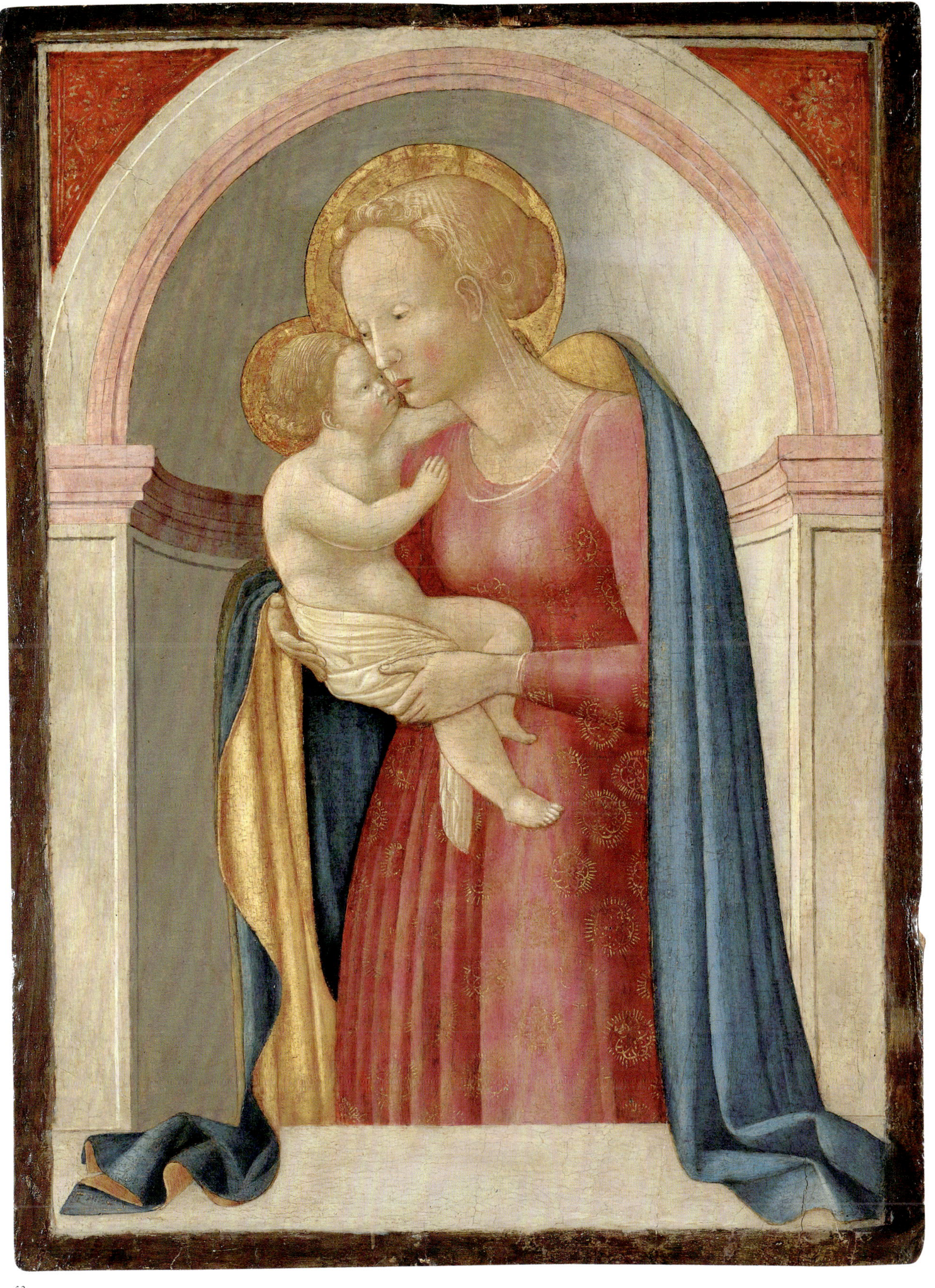

53

PESELLINO

54.

A.

The Journey of the Magi: Melchior Crossing the Red Sea

Tempera on panel, 65.1 x 70 cm (25⅝ x 27½ in.)
The Sterling and Francine Clark Art Institute, Williamstown, Massachusetts (1955.940)

ZANOBI STROZZI

B.

The Journey of the Magi: Jasper Riding from the Kingdom of Tharsis

Tempera on panel, 66 x 72 cm (26 x 28⅜ in.)
Musée des Beaux-Arts, Strasbourg (Inv. No. 261)

The visit of three kings from the Orient to adore the newborn Christ Child, alluded to briefly in Scripture (Matthew 2: 1–12), enjoyed great prominence in the later Middle Ages both as a liturgical commemoration (the feast of Epiphany, celebrated on January 6), and as a political metaphor in the perennially shifting balance of power between secular rulers and the Church.[1] Although widely embraced for special veneration at princely courts from an early date, the story of the Three Kings, who are also known as the Three Wise Men or the Magi, assumed a particular civic importance in republican Florence. Beginning in 1390, a procession of elaborate opulence, including a cavalcade of citizens dressed as the kings and their extensive retinue, reenacted the event on January 6, parading from the Baptistery (later, from the Palazzo della Signoria) to a crèche erected at the church of San Marco. This procession, paid for both through taxation and private funds, soon became one of the city's principal public spectacles. Its organization was the responsibility of the Compagnia de' Magi—perhaps the most socially conspicuous of Florence's confraternities before its dissolution in the 1490s—whose headquarters were established at San Marco. The popular and political prestige of the event were consolidated after 1434, with the return of Cosimo de' Medici from exile and his personal patronage of the procession (and of San Marco). On January 6, 1443, at the formal consecration of the newly rebuilt San Marco, Pope Eugenius IV granted (in perpetuity) seven years' indulgence from Purgatory to anyone attending the procession and subsequent Mass at the church on the feast of Epiphany.[2]

In Italian painting, the journey of the Magi from their separate realms is usually encountered as a series of subsidiary vignettes in the background of an image of the Epiphany or Adoration of the Kings. Independent representations of the travels of each king, of their convergence upon Jerusalem to speak with Herod before proceeding to Bethlehem, or of their departure together to return by a different route to the Orient (thereby avoiding betraying the Holy Family to Herod) are exceedingly rare. One key instance is to be found in the chapel in the Medici palace in Florence, where, in 1459, Benozzo Gozzoli decorated three walls with frescoes depicting the journey of the Magi; their goal is the subject of Filippo Lippi's altarpiece of the *Adoration of the Christ Child* (now in the Gemäldegalerie, Berlin), which originally stood against the fourth wall. The two panels discussed here seem to be the only other surviving Florentine examples that portray this theme. Clearly, they are incomplete in their present form: not only does each panel show figures incongruously cropped at the outer edges but they include only two of the three Magi. In the Williamstown panel, Melchior, the eldest of the kings, balances a casket of gold, his gift to the Christ Child, in his lap; in the Strasbourg panel, Jasper, the youngest of the kings, holds his gift, a monstrance filled with myrrh, before him.[3] Missing is the second Magus, Balthasar, and possibly other panels representing the audience of the kings with Herod, the Adoration of the Christ Child, or the return of the kings to the Orient.

It is difficult to state with certainty what function these panels originally might have fulfilled since none like them can be adduced for comparison. Fahy observed that they are too tall to have been part of an altarpiece predella, and that their subjects are inappropriate for the decoration of nuptial cassoni;[4] instead, he suggested that they might have been intended to decorate the walls of a confraternal oratory, such as that of the Compagnia de' Magi at San Marco, and that a clue to their provenance may lie in the prominent bright yellow and red stripes decorating the boats in the Williamstown panel. These colors, repeated in the livery of two of the boatmen in that scene, may well bear a heraldic significance (as gules and or), and, if so, Carl Strehlke's proposal (see p. 206) to associate them with Alfonso of Aragon, King of Naples, is worthy of consideration. That the cycle might have been commissioned for King Alfonso or for a Neapolitan retainer is debatable, since the colors of Aragon do not recur in the Strasbourg panel, but that the Magus Melchior is meant to be a conscious, topical evocation of Alfonso as the wise king who came from over the sea is highly persuasive. It is also possible, however, that in addition to their connection with the house of Aragon, yellow and red could have been introduced in the Williamstown panel as a fanciful heraldic device elaborated from the description of King Melchior contained in the most widely disseminated version of the story of the Magi, John of Hildesheim's *Liber trium Regum* of about 1370. In that text, Melchior is said to be King of Nubia and Arabia, and it is reported that "all the earth in the land of Arabia is red; and also stones and trees and all other things that grow in that land for the most part are red. And in that land is found gold wonderfully red, and that gold is the best gold that is in all the world."[5]

Another hint of the panels' provenance may be gleaned from a consideration of their authorship. Although both have been assigned to the standard range of artists within Fra

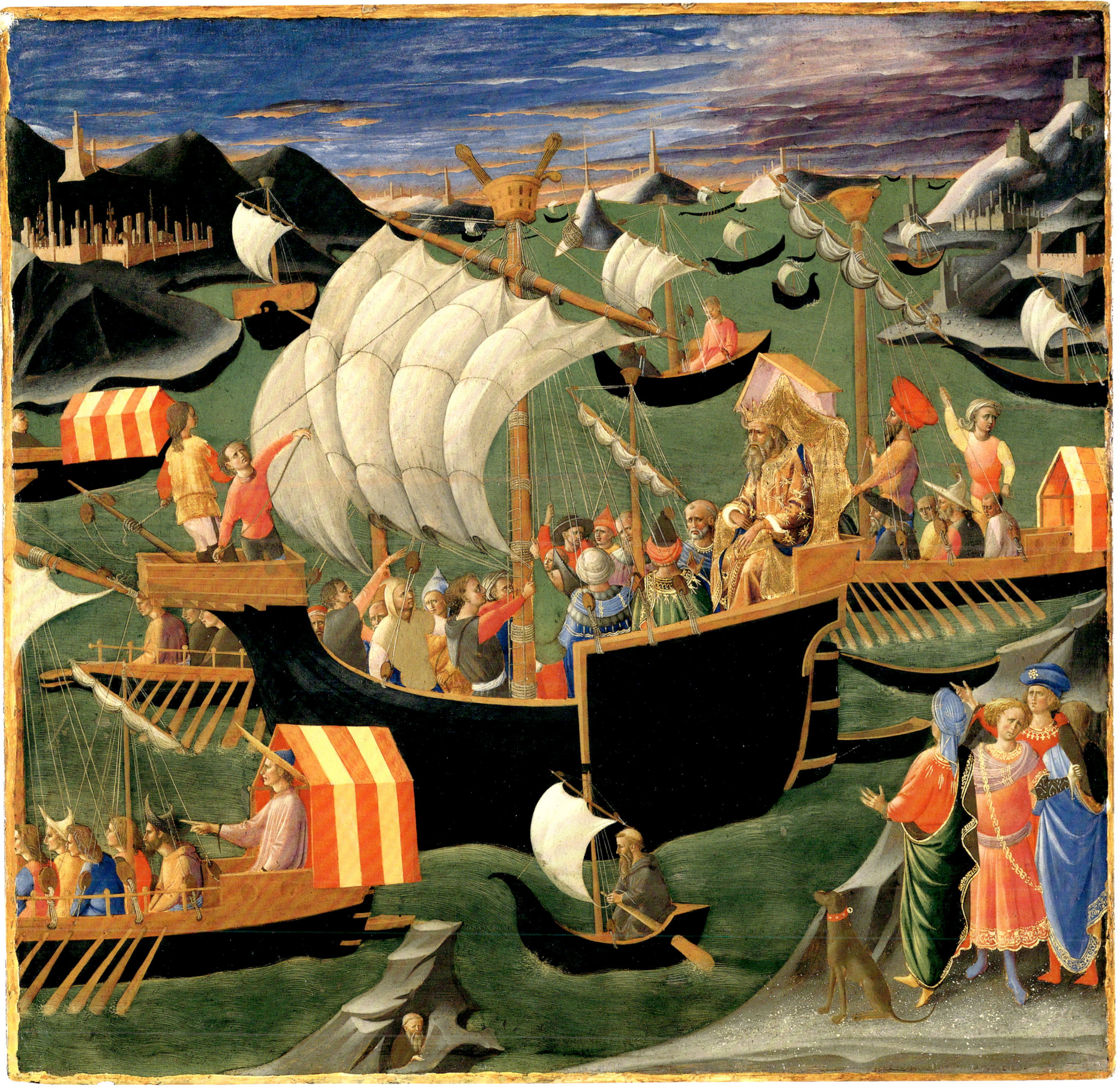

54: A

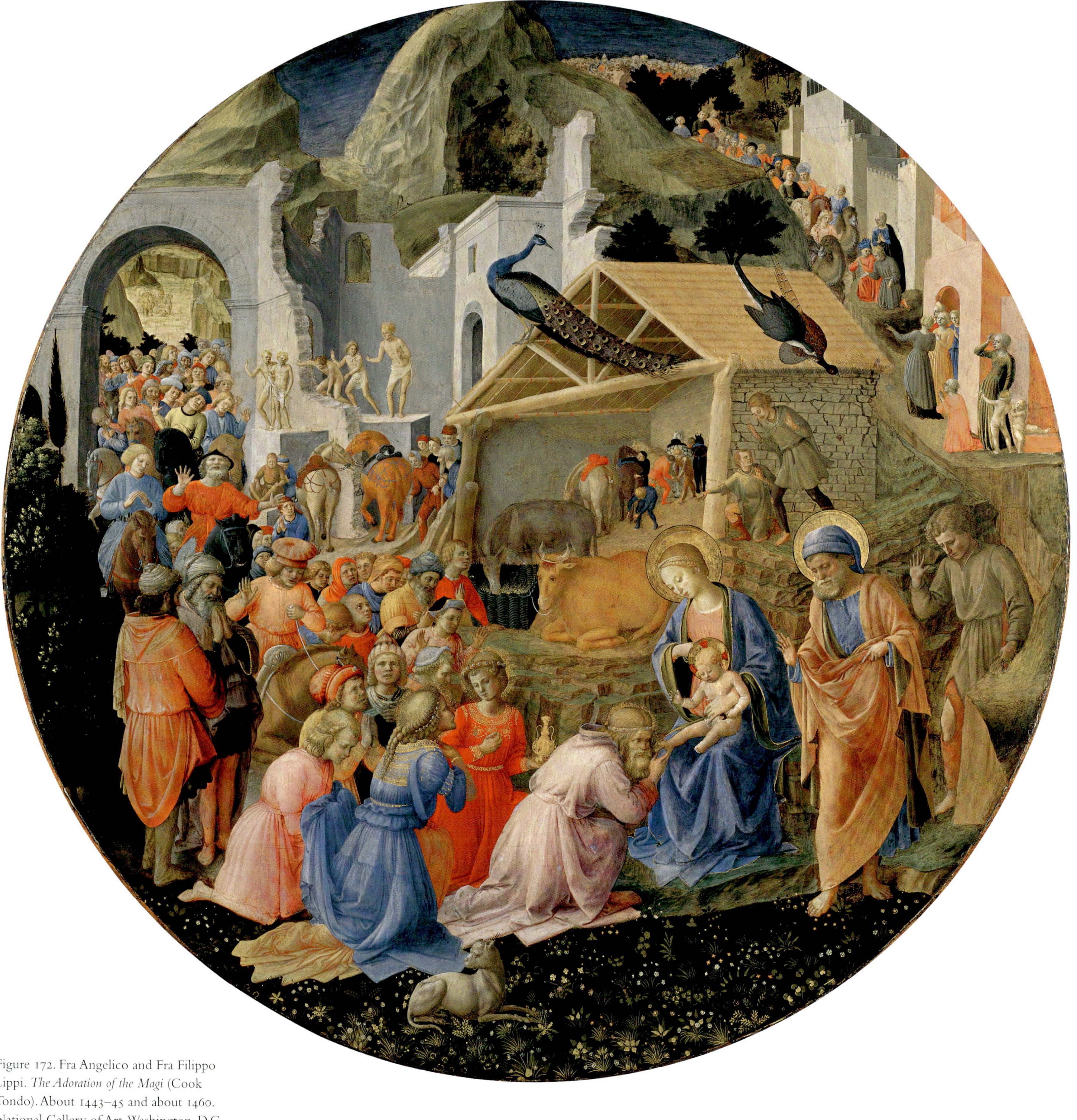

Figure 172. Fra Angelico and Fra Filippo Lippi. *The Adoration of the Magi* (Cook Tondo). About 1443–45 and about 1460. National Gallery of Art, Washington, D.C.

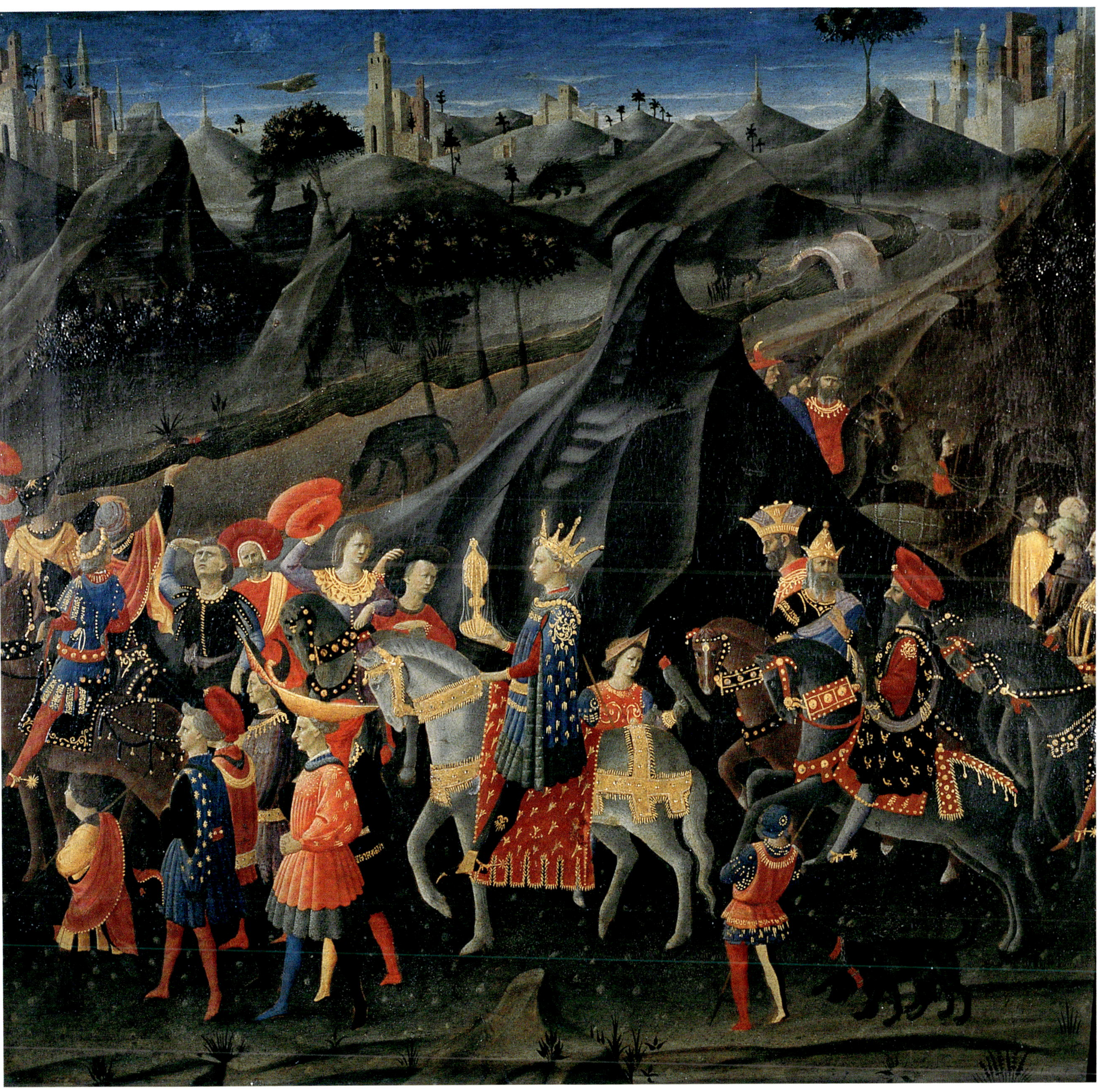

54: B

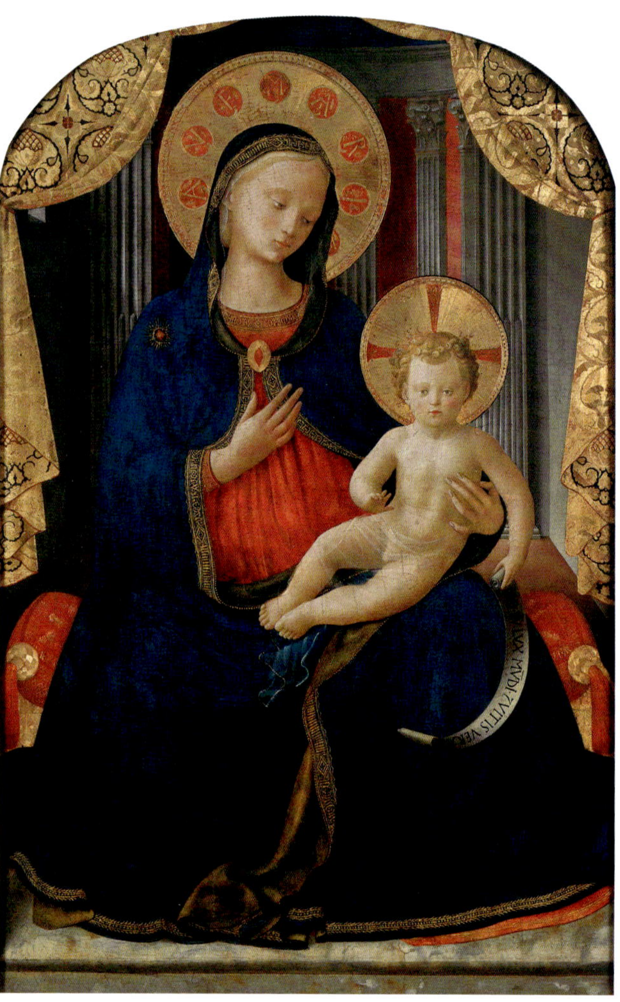

Figure 173. Fra Angelico. *Virgin and Child* (*Madonna of Humility*). About 1445. Galleria Sabauda, Turin

Angelico's sphere of influence, Fahy correctly recognized the panels as the work of Pesellino (Williamstown) and Zanobi Strozzi (Strasbourg), and associated them with the illuminated *De Bellum Poenicum* of Silius Italicus of about 1447 as a second instance of active collaboration between these two masters. Adding to this small group of works the Dublin *Assumption of the Virgin* altarpiece and its predella in Prato (see pp. 269–71) reinforces the probability that these collaborations were not ad hoc but, instead, indicate a period of formal association, possibly in the studio that Pesellino had inherited from his grandfather in 1446. Proposing a date of about 1446–47 for the panels on circumstantial as well as stylistic grounds helps narrow the search for the missing panel of the third Magus or for the *Adoration* that undoubtedly completed the series, which could have been painted by Pesellino, Zanobi Strozzi, or, conceivably, by another artist altogether.

One painting of the *Adoration of the Magi*—now in the National Gallery of Art in Washington and commonly known as the Cook Tondo after one of its previous owners (fig. 172)—is a compelling candidate for the missing climax of this series. The unusual prominence accorded to the procession of the Magi in this painting—specifically, to their travels together from Jerusalem to Bethlehem, after having met at the palace of Herod—encourages speculation that it might have been complemented by independent scenes of the journeys of each of the Three Kings. Consideration of the authorship of the tondo, furthermore, suggests a date close to 1445 for its commission and probably before 1448 for its completion, a coincidence that reinforces the plausibility of its association with Pesellino's and Strozzi's panels in Williamstown and in Strasbourg.

The earliest reference to the Cook Tondo, in an inventory of the Palazzo Medici drawn up in 1492, following the death of Lorenzo il Magnifico, situates it in the large ground-floor room in the palace known as the "*camera di Lorenzo*."[6] Also recorded in that room were Paolo Uccello's three monumental paintings of the Battle of San Romano and three others that have never been successfully identified. These last are described in the inventory as "*uno di battaglie e draghi et lioni et uno della storia di Paris, di mano di Pagolo Ucello e uno di mano di Francesco di Pesello, entrovi una chaccia*" ("one with battles and dragons and lions and one with the story of Paris, by the hand of Paolo Uccello, and one by the hand of Francesco di Pesello, within it a hunt"). Uccello's battle pictures were moved into the Palazzo Medici from the Palazzo Bartolini-Salimbeni, probably in 1484,[7] and therefore were not part of a series either with the *Adoration of the Magi* tondo or with the other three paintings listed as in the room. Indeed, the summary descriptions of those three paintings suggest either that they did not form a coherent group even among themselves or else that their subjects were unusual enough not to have been recognized correctly by the compiler of the 1492 inventory. It would not require a significant leap of imagination to interpret the subject of the Strasbourg panel as a hunt, with its cavalcade of courtly figures, a falconer standing beside the king's horse, a pair of hounds in the foreground, and a stag and other game in the background. Similarly, the flotilla of galleys and boats sailing away from the gesticulating figures in the foreground of the Williamstown painting might be interpreted as a "*storia di Paris*" if that were understood to refer not to the shepherd's judgment of the three goddesses but to the rape of Helen by the prince of Troy. Nor is it difficult to imagine the third Magus, Balthasar, King of Gondolia and Saba, symbolized or even accompanied by lions (and dragons) in the missing third panel of the series.[8]

The attribution and dating of the Cook Tondo have been much disputed, although most scholars now agree that both Fra Angelico and Fra Filippo Lippi were involved to some degree in its execution.[9] Proposals to allocate areas of the paint surface to each of these two masters are uniformly unsatisfactory, however, and all proceed from the assumption that the composition was left unfinished by one and later brought to completion by the other. An alternative possibility that the painting had been substantially—perhaps entirely—completed by Angelico before being altered for as yet unexplained reasons by Filippo Lippi[10] is suggested both by a comparison with Angelico's other versions of the subject and by attentive examination of the still visible portions of the hypothetical first painting campaign, all of which were brought to a high degree of finish. Thus, for example, the women and children emerging from the city gate in the middle ground at the extreme right in the tondo are kneeling and looking across at an area now occupied by the roof of the manger that is demonstrably an awkward later addition; originally, they must have been admiring the cortege of the Magi as it wound across the center of the panel. Most of the spectators crowded at the left are looking either above the Virgin's head or in front of and below her, perhaps implying that the painting once portrayed not the Adoration of the Magi but the Nativity or the Adoration of the Shepherds, with the Christ Child lying on the ground and the star of Bethlehem or an angelic choir above. The full extent of such adaptations is not yet evident, but it is possible to state with some assurance that whatever its original appearance, Fra Angelico's work on this painting must date on stylistic grounds to the years between completion of the San Marco high altarpiece (about 1442) and his departure for Rome late in 1445, approximately contemporary with such paintings as the Turin *Madonna of Humility* (fig. 173) or the Bern *Virgin and Child* (cat. 35)—a period in which he was regularly assisted by Benozzo Gozzoli, whose hand appears in a minor capacity in the Cook Tondo as well.[11]

Based only on the circumstantial connection between the dates of the three paintings in Williamstown, Strasbourg, and Washington, it is interesting to speculate on the possibility that they might, in the first instance have been commissioned—perhaps by Cosimo de' Medici—to decorate the oratory of the Compagnia de' Magi at San Marco shortly after the rededication of the church in the presence of Eugenius IV on January 6, 1443. The reasons for their subsequent removal and the "modernization" of the tondo by Filippo Lippi, probably about 1460, are not fully apparent, but could have been occasioned by a desire to reinstall the pictures in the new Palazzo Medici in the via Larga. For now, any explanations—indeed, the scenario itself—must remain purely hypothetical.

LK

1. See Trexler 1997, *passim*, for a discussion of the lengthy evolution of the theme and its representation in Western art.
2. Hatfield 1970, pp. 107–61.
3. The third Magus, Jasper (or Caspar), is usually represented in Northern painting as a black king; in Italian art, he is generally portrayed as white and as conspicuously younger than the other two kings.
4. E. Fahy, in Di Lorenzo 2001, pp. 71–75.
5. John of Hildesheim 1955 ed., p. 12.
6. Muntz 1888, p. 60; Spallanzani and Gaeta Bertelà 1992, p. 12.
7. See Cagliotti 2001, pp. 37–54; Gordon 2003, pp. 378–97.
8. In the nineteenth century, the Williamstown panel and the Cook Tondo were both in the collection of William Coningham (1815–1884) in London. It has not been possible, however, to establish that they remained together continuously after leaving the Palazzo Medici. A painting plausibly identifiable with the Cook Tondo is listed in an inventory of the Palazzo Guicciardini in Florence in 1643 (Fallani 1992, pp. 177–78), but no paintings clearly identifiable with the Williamstown or the Strasbourg *Journey of the Magi* are recorded there. However, there is listed "*un quadretto entrovi un paesino con due lioni et un serpente*" (ibid., p. 181) that might be a fragment of the missing third painting from the Palazzo Medici.
9. See Boskovits and Brown 2003, pp. 21–30, for a thorough summary of published opinions regarding this picture.
10. All of the authors who have discussed the sequence of work on this panel agree that it was begun by Angelico and finished by Lippi, except Jeffrey Ruda (1975, pp. 6–39). Ruda's contrary opinion is based on the observation that the landscape foreground, which he believes to be typical of Angelico, overlaps the robes of the kneeling Magi, which were painted by Lippi. The observation is accurate but the conclusion does not follow, as the foreground in its present state was certainly not painted by Angelico.
11. See Angelini 1986, p. 22; Bellosi 1990b, pp. 44–45. Gozzoli's intervention in this tondo provides a terminus ante quem of 1448—the last date at which he is known to have been in Florence during Fra Angelico's lifetime—for the initial phase of its execution, and provides an additional circumstantial argument for its having been completed and later altered rather than abandoned incomplete and later finished. It is difficult to imagine a situation in which the panel might have been removed from Angelico's workshop and handed over to Lippi if both Gozzoli and Zanobi Strozzi were available to complete the work, over their master's design.

55.
A Miracle of Saint Sylvester

Tempera on panel: overall, 31 x 78.5 cm (12 3/16 x 30 7/8 in.); picture surface, 29.6 x 77.9 cm (11 5/8 x 30 5/8 in.)
Worcester Art Museum, Massachusetts (1916.12)

The episode from the legend of Pope Saint Sylvester (r. 314–35) portrayed in this panel is the event that confirmed the emperor Constantine's conversion to Christianity and secured the conversion of his mother, Helena, as well. According to *The Golden Legend,* Helena approved of her son's rejection of paganism but deplored his choice of Christianity over Judaism. At the emperor's instigation, she called together in Rome the most learned doctors of both faiths to dispute the merits of their beliefs, and appointed two philosophers, Cato and Zenophilus, to arbitrate the discussion. Saint Sylvester refuted all the Jewish arguments from Scripture until the chief of the Jews, Zambri, challenged him to match words with deeds. Zambri claimed that he would prove that his God was the one true God by repeating the secret name of the Almighty: after hearing it no creature could remain alive. A wild bull was brought into the hall; Zambri whispered the secret name into its ear, and instantly the bull fell dead. Sylvester countered that a name with the power to slay could only be that of the devil, and he, in turn, challenged Zambri to restore the bull to life. Zambri could not do so; Sylvester prayed and ordered the bull to rise in the name of Christ and to depart in peace, and immediately the animal did as he was commanded. Upon witnessing this, Helena, the philosophers Cato and Zenophilus, and all the Jewish doctors including Zambri were converted to Christianity. In the painting, Saint Sylvester kneels in prayer as the bull staggers to its feet. Zambri, behind the bull, is visibly astonished by the miracle, while Helena (at the far right), her counselors, the Jewish doctors, and members of the emperor's court are shown in various attitudes of wonder and perplexity.

Two panels in the Galleria Doria Pamphilj in Rome (measuring 30.5 x 58 centimeters each), which recount further episodes from the legend of Saint Sylvester, are approximately the same height as the Worcester panel, although not as wide, and undoubtedly once were situated on either side of it, in a single predella. In the first of these panels (fig. 174), at the left, Sylvester is brought before the prefect Tarquinius, who orders him to sacrifice to idols or suffer cruel torture and death. Sylvester prophesied that it would be Tarquinius, not himself, who would die that very night, and suffer eternal torment for his lack of faith. As shown in the center of the panel, Sylvester, looking on from his prison window, observes the prefect at dinner that evening swallowing a fish bone, which lodged in his throat; at midnight the prefect died, and Sylvester, as seen at the right, was freed from prison. The second panel (fig. 175) illustrates the final episode from the legend of Saint Sylvester, in which the emperor Constantine asked him to rid the city of Rome of a dragon whose poisonous breath had been killing three hundred people a day. Sylvester bound the dragon's mouth, sealed the bonds with the sign of the cross, and revived two pagan priests who had been overcome by the noxious fumes, whereupon a great number of their following were converted to Christianity.

There can be no reasonable doubt that the Worcester and Doria Pamphilj panels originally belonged together in a single

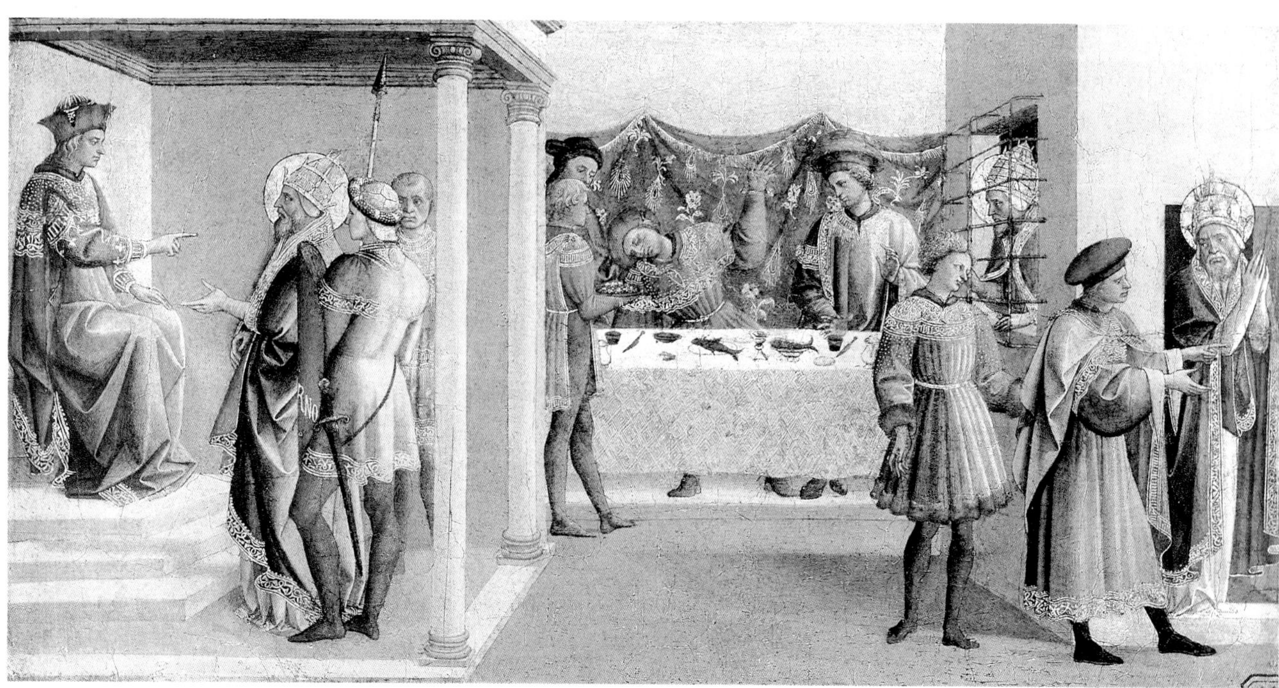

Figure 174. Pesellino. *Saint Sylvester before Tarquinius.* About 1453–55. Galleria Doria Pamphilj, Rome

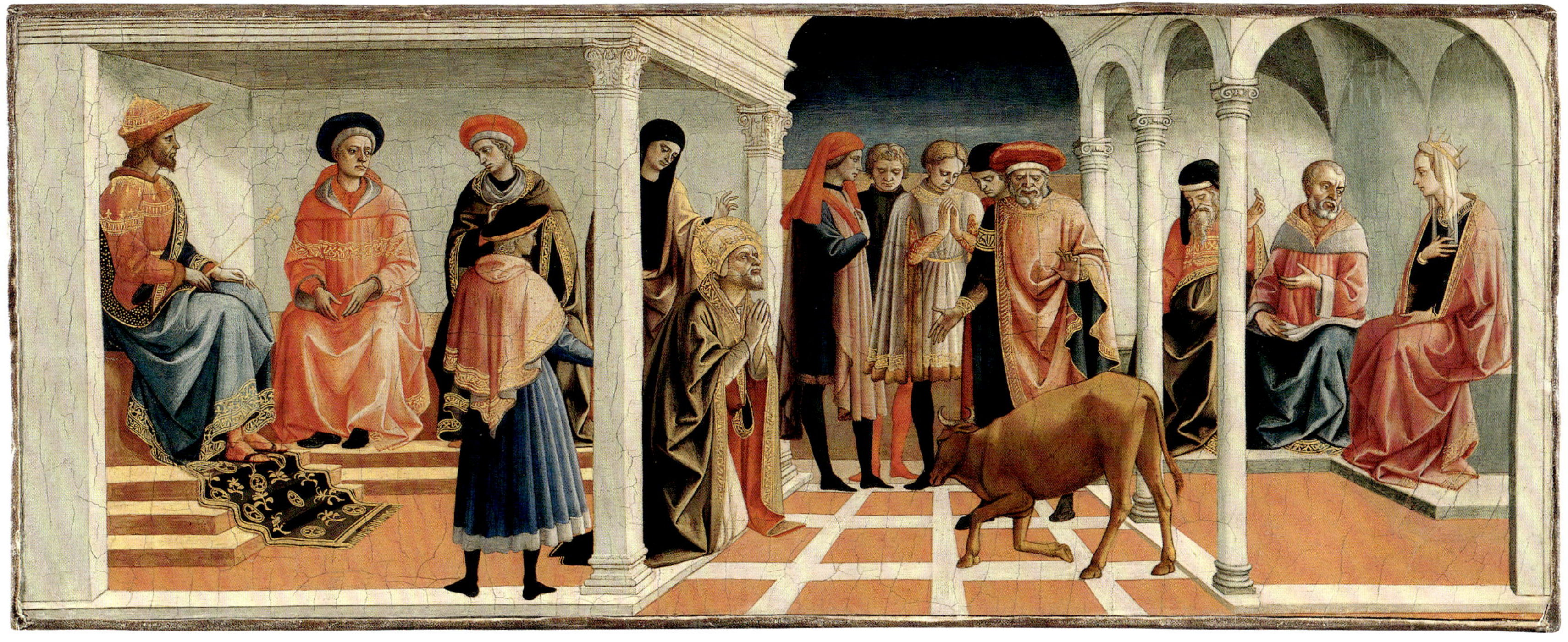

55

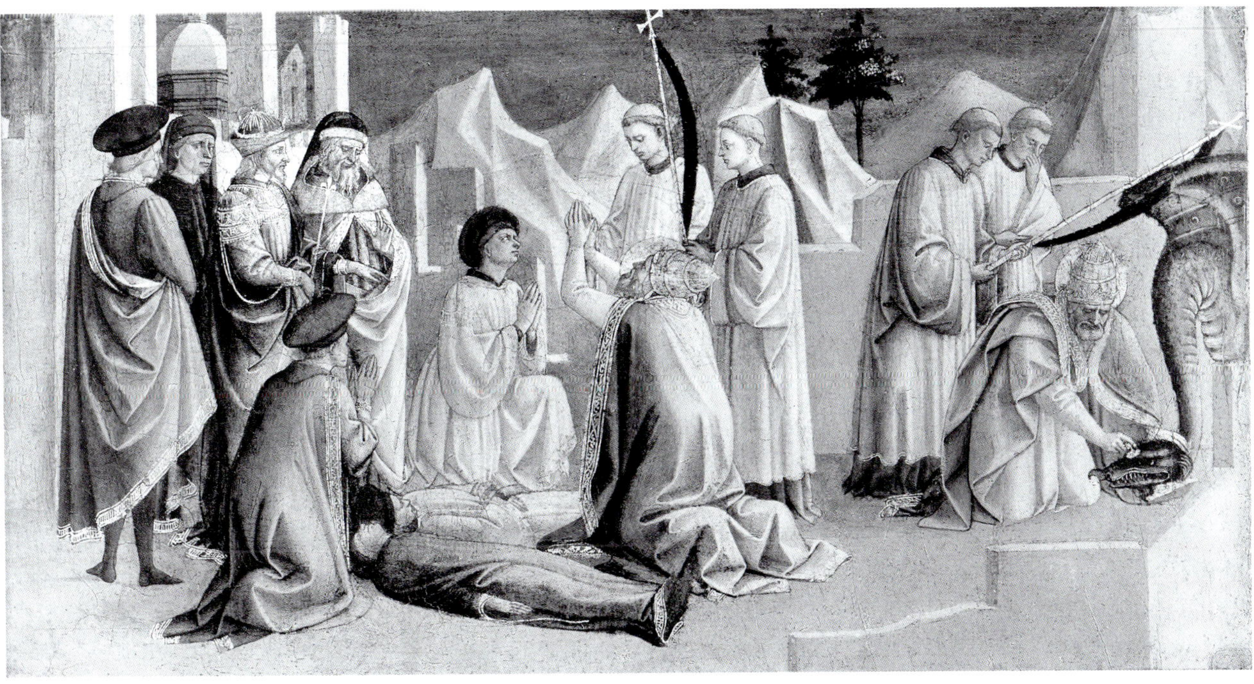

Figure 175. Pesellino. *Saint Sylvester Binding the Dragon's Mouth*. About 1453–55. Galleria Doria Pamphilj, Rome

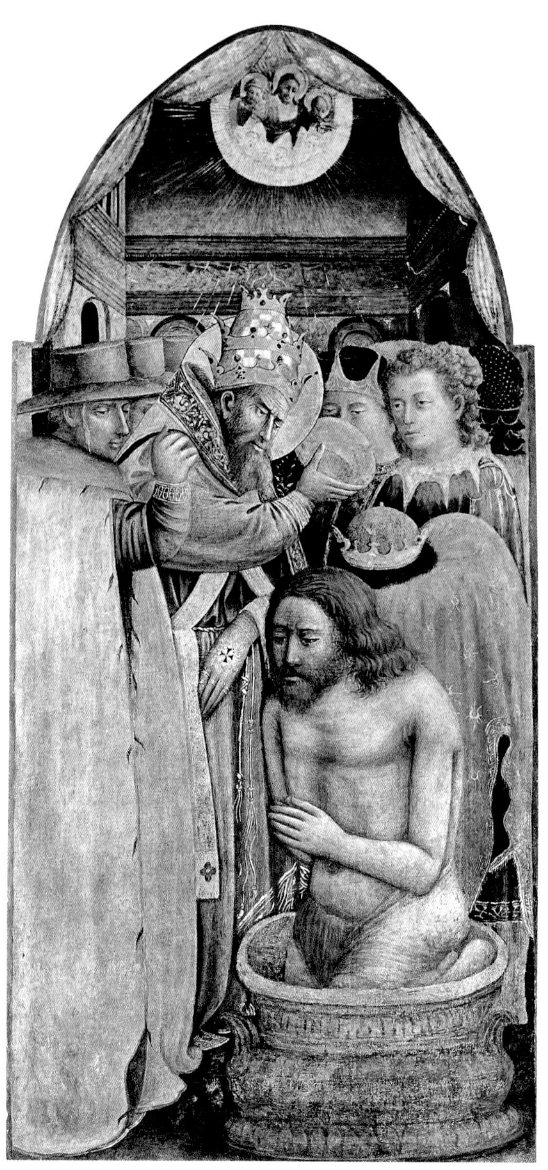

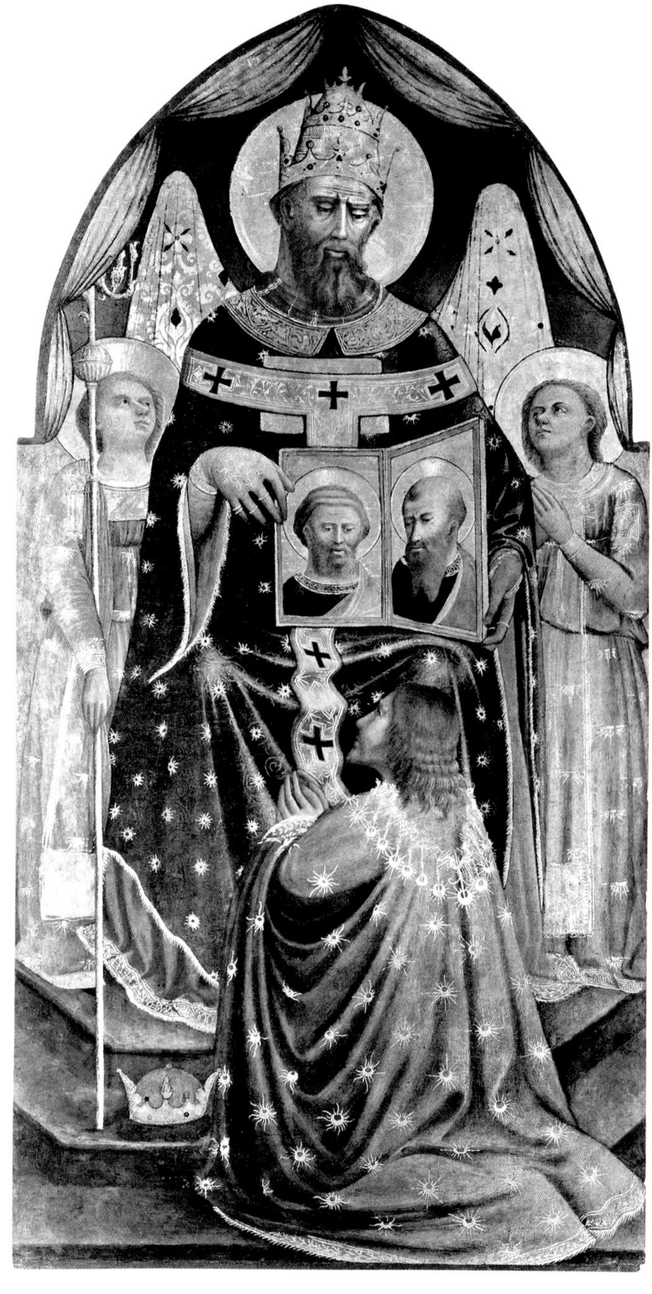

Figure 176 (above left). Master of the Castello Nativity (?). *The Baptism of Constantine.* About 1453–55. State Hermitage Museum, Saint Petersburg

Figure 177 (above right). Master of the Castello Nativity (?). *Saint Sylvester Enthroned, Displaying Images of Saints Peter and Paul.* About 1453–55. State Hermitage Museum, Saint Petersburg

complex; it is possible that they remained together until about 1850, when Mrs. Jameson described having seen three panels in the collection of Prince Doria depicting episodes from the legend of Saint Sylvester, which, she believed, were by Fra Angelico.[1] Two, not three, panels are listed in the catalogue of paintings in the Doria palace in 1851,[2] however, and the Worcester panel is first recorded separately only in 1915, in the sale catalogue of Lord Northesk's collection.[3] That all three panels are by the same artist—Pesellino—has never been questioned: of exceptional quality, they are typical examples of the accomplished architectural perspective, figural foreshortenings, psychological penetration, and proliferation of naturalistic detail that he achieved in his mature works. The bright, saturate palette of the Worcester picture is also characteristic of Pesellino's mature style, although in this case it may be slightly exaggerated by early cleanings to which the painting was subjected, which appear to have removed the cast shadows and some of the subtle atmospheric effects still visible in the Doria Pamphilj panels.

No proposal has yet been advanced for identifying the altarpiece to which this predella might have belonged, yet a clue may be offered by a consideration of the narrative sequence of the Worcester and Doria Pamphilj panels: while they seem to comprise a complete predella, they omit several key episodes from the legend of Saint Sylvester—above all, the climactic event of the Baptism of Constantine. A painting of this subject, now in the Hermitage in Saint Petersburg (fig. 176), incorrectly attributed to Andrea di Giusto, was evidently once the wing of an altarpiece roughly contemporary with the Worcester/Doria Pamphilj predella. The central panel of this altarpiece, now also in the Hermitage (fig. 177), represents Saint Sylvester enthroned, displaying images of Saints Peter and Paul to the kneeling emperor Constantine.[4] The emperor had been instructed by Saints Peter and Paul in a dream to appeal to Pope Sylvester for a remedy for his leprosy. Sylvester showed Constantine portraits of the saints to confirm that it was they who had appeared to him; then he cured the emperor, who by this act was converted to Christianity. The subject and whereabouts of the other side panel of this altarpiece are unknown. It undoubtedly represented another episode from the legend of Saint Sylvester, possibly the saint ordering Constantine to build the basilica of Saint Peter's at the Vatican. Given the complementary nature of the narratives of the Hermitage altarpiece and the Worcester/Doria Pamphilj predella—narratives otherwise rarely encountered in Florentine painting—and the reasonable correspondence in dimensions among them, it is not difficult to imagine that they were originally all part of a single complex.

An inscription formerly on the reverse of the Hermitage panels recorded the donor's given name (*Hoc opvs fieri* [*fecit*] *Andreas* ["Andrea had this work (made)"]) and the votive nature of his commission (*Qvale Constantinvs mvdatvs fvi Alepra* ["Like Constantine I was cured of leprosy"]). The inscription on the missing third panel probably contained the donor's patronymic and a date. The attribution to Andrea di Giusto, first proposed by Crowe and Cavalcaselle,[5] proceeded from the mistaken assumption that the "Andrea" memorialized in this inscription was the artist rather than the donor. Although a number of scholars still support this attribution, Liphart, instead, recognized the style of the panels as derivative of the School of Fra Filippo Lippi.[6] The Hermitage pictures are unequivocally by the same hand as a *Crucifixion* now in the Musée du Petit Palais, Avignon (Inv. 20199),[7] and all three panels demonstrate striking analogies with works by two artists associated with Pesellino's shop: the Master of the Castello Nativity and Zanobi Machiavelli. Both of these painters are known primarily for paintings from the 1460s and 1470s. Their early careers have been the subject of speculation and debate fueled by documents specifying that in 1453 Pesellino entered into a commercial alliance with the artists Zanobi del Migliore and Piero di Lorenzo di Pratese, who might be identifiable with either the Master of the Castello Nativity, or Machiavelli, or with both of them.[8] The reconstruction here of an altarpiece that clearly resulted from the collaboration of Pesellino and another, unknown painter might indicate that the latter could have been either the Zanobi or Piero mentioned in the document of 1453, and conversely that 1453 should be considered a terminus post quem for the execution of the Worcester and Doria Pamphilj predella panels. LK

1. Jameson 1850, p. 408.
2. Galleria Doria Pamphilj 1851, nos. 319, 330. M. Davies (1974, p. 421 n. 2) refutes the claim that all three panels might once have been together in the Doria collection since the panel now in Worcester does not appear in the 1851 Doria catalogue. Mrs. Jameson's reference, however, published in 1850, implies that she saw the panels together prior to that date, and R. Henniker-Heaton (1926, p. 155) states that at the time of its sale from Lord Northesk's collection (1915), the center panel was reported to have been purchased in Italy "some fifty or sixty years previously."
3. Sold, Sotheby's, London, June 30, 1915, lot 117 (as School of Perugino).
4. Kustodieva 1994, pp. 51–53 (Inv. nos. 2442 [174 x 87 cm], 2443 [157 x 73 cm]).
5. Crowe and Cavalcaselle 1903–14, vol. IV (1911), p. 64 n. 2; Berenson 1932a, p. 12; Berenson 1963, vol. I, p. 6.
6. Liphart 1912, no. 1650; Kaftal 1952, col. 936, nos. 6–7.
7. M. Laclotte and É. Mognetti (1976, no. 15) identify the artist as Andrea di Giusto, an attribution first proposed, but later doubted, by Berenson, based on the painting's relationship to the Hermitage panels.
8. C. Lachi (1995, pp. 21–24) identified the Master of the Castello Nativity with Piero di Lorenzo di Pratese, on the basis of her attribution to the latter of parts of Filippo Lippi's *Coronation of the Virgin* altarpiece from Sant'Ambrogio (Uffizi, Florence), the documents of payment for which mention a certain Piero di Lorenzo *dipintore*. Lachi's attributions to the early career of the Master of the Castello Nativity are wildly heterogeneous among themselves, however, and Annamaria Bernacchioni (oral communication, cited by Di Lorenzo 2005, pp. 290–93) demonstrated that the Piero di Lorenzo documented in Lippi's shop was a gilder and not the same person as Piero di Lorenzo di Pratese. K. Christiansen, A. De Marchi, and A. Di Lorenzo (in Christiansen 2005, pp. 39–65, 67–95, 290–93) all acknowledge this discrepancy but leave open the possibility of identifying the Master of the Castello Nativity with Piero di Lorenzo di Pratese. A. Bernacchioni (1992, pp. 171–80) and M. Holmes (1999, p. 270 n. 135) have also suggested the more persuasive likelihood that some works among the group formerly assigned to "Pseudo-Pier Francesco Fiorentino" may be the work of Piero di Lorenzo di Pratese. Assuming that Zanobi Macchiavelli and Zanobi del Migliore might be the same artist, M. Salmi (1916–18, pp. 49–56) attempted to conflate the so-called "Compagno di Pesellino" (see Logan Berenson 1901, pp. 18–34, 333–43) with the early career of Zanobi Macchiavelli, but this effort was based on the misattribution to Zanobi of several paintings now recognized as autograph works by Pesellino.

56.
Virgin and Child, with Six Saints

Tempera on panel: overall, 26.4 x 23.8 cm (10⅜ x 9⅜ in.); picture surface, 22.6 x 20.3 cm (8⅞ x 8 in.)
The Metropolitan Museum of Art, New York. Bequest of Mary Stillman Harkness, 1950 (50.145.30)

Part of the celebrated collection formed by the Englishman William Beckford in the early nineteenth century, this jewel-like panel traditionally was attributed to Fra Angelico until Crowe and Cavalcaselle recognized it as a work by Pesellino.[1] After a brief attempt to reassign it to the young Benozzo Gozzoli,[2] the attribution to Pesellino was reiterated by Bernard Berenson and has been accepted by all critics since.[3] Indeed, not only is this painting a typical example of Pesellino's mature efforts but it also should be regarded as among the very finest of his rare surviving works. It is painted with an unparalleled delicacy and is even more refined than his early illuminations in the *De Bellum Poenicum* of Silius Italicus in the Hermitage (fig. 161, 166, 167, 168, 169, 170), with a precision in rendering the effects of directed light more sophisticated than that mastered by any other painter active in mid-century Florence, with the possible exception of Fra Angelico. It was perhaps this recollection of Angelico's accomplishments that led Federico Zeri to suggest a date for the painting in the second half of the 1440s, when the influence of the Dominican master could still be detected in Pesellino's work alongside that of Fra Filippo Lippi.[4] However, the obsessive attention to minute naturalistic detail evident in the foreground of the painting and in the saints' armor and robes, and the intense psychological penetration of the expressions and gestures of all the figures can only meaningfully be compared with the artist's last works: the cassone panels with scenes from the story of David, now in the National Gallery, London, and the *Trinity* altarpiece also in London. A date for the present painting after 1455 seems likely.

The size, format, and composition of the Metropolitan Museum panel make it a virtually unique object within the tradition of Florentine fifteenth-century painting. Pesellino has adopted the standard devotional subject of the Virgin and Child with saints, commonly encountered on independent tabernacles and on the center panels of triptychs, to a novel, square format and unusually intimate size. He has, furthermore, arranged his figures not in the typical "stacked" manner of a devotional tabernacle but in the carefully rationalized spatial configuration of an altarpiece of the type popularized by Fra Angelico's high altarpiece for San Marco (cat. 34) or Domenico Veneziano's *Saint Lucy* altarpiece. Although he has suppressed all architectural references other than the complicated and beautifully foreshortened marble dais below the Virgin's (invisible) throne, he has taken great pains to establish orthogonals of recession along which the figures are situated, and to calibrate their reduction in size as a function of their distance behind the notional front plane of the picture. The only concessions to tradition admitted in this regard are the incongruously large size of the Virgin and the Christ Child, who, while seated, tower over the doll-like saints around them. It is a tribute to the artist's pictorial genius that this archaic device of hieratic propriety does not notably disrupt the visual unity of the image.

There has been some dispute over the identity of the six saints in this panel, only one of whom—Saint Jerome in cardinal's robes, second from the left—is portrayed with unambiguous attributes. The elderly saint at the far left is generally identified as Anthony Abbot, although he does not carry a tau-shaped staff and is not accompanied by a pig or wild boar, uncharacteristically is shown reading a book, and does wear a highly particularized habit, including a scapular, which might indicate a specific monastic order. The two female saints at the rear are presently catalogued by the Metropolitan Museum as Cecilia (?) and Catherine of Alexandria (?), but, again, neither bears a clearly recognizable attribute and only one (on the right) holds a martyr's palm. The warrior saint at the far right is invariably recognized as George, which may be correct but cannot be demonstrated with certainty. The bishop saint next to him has in the past been believed to be Louis of Toulouse or Bonaventure, both Franciscans; however, he wears white robes, not brown, beneath his cope, no knotted rope is visible at his waist, and his cowl is dark gray. It is more likely that his present identification as Augustine is correct. A drawing in the Louvre of this figure often is thought to be an autograph preparatory study by Pesellino, and equally often is dismissed as a copy after the painting.[5] The fact that the right side of the figure is left blank exactly where he is overlapped in the painting by the saint alongside him suggests that the latter possibility is the more likely.

LK

1. Crowe and Cavalcaselle 1869–76, vol. III, p. 103.
2. Richter 1894, p. 240; Ffoulkes 1894, p. 156.
3. Berenson 1896, p. 124; see Zeri and Gardner 1971, pp. 96–98, for a complete annotated bibliography.
4. Zeri and Gardner 1971, pp. 96–98.
5. Degenhart and Schmitt 1968, vol. II, no. 528; vol. IV, pl. 364 b.

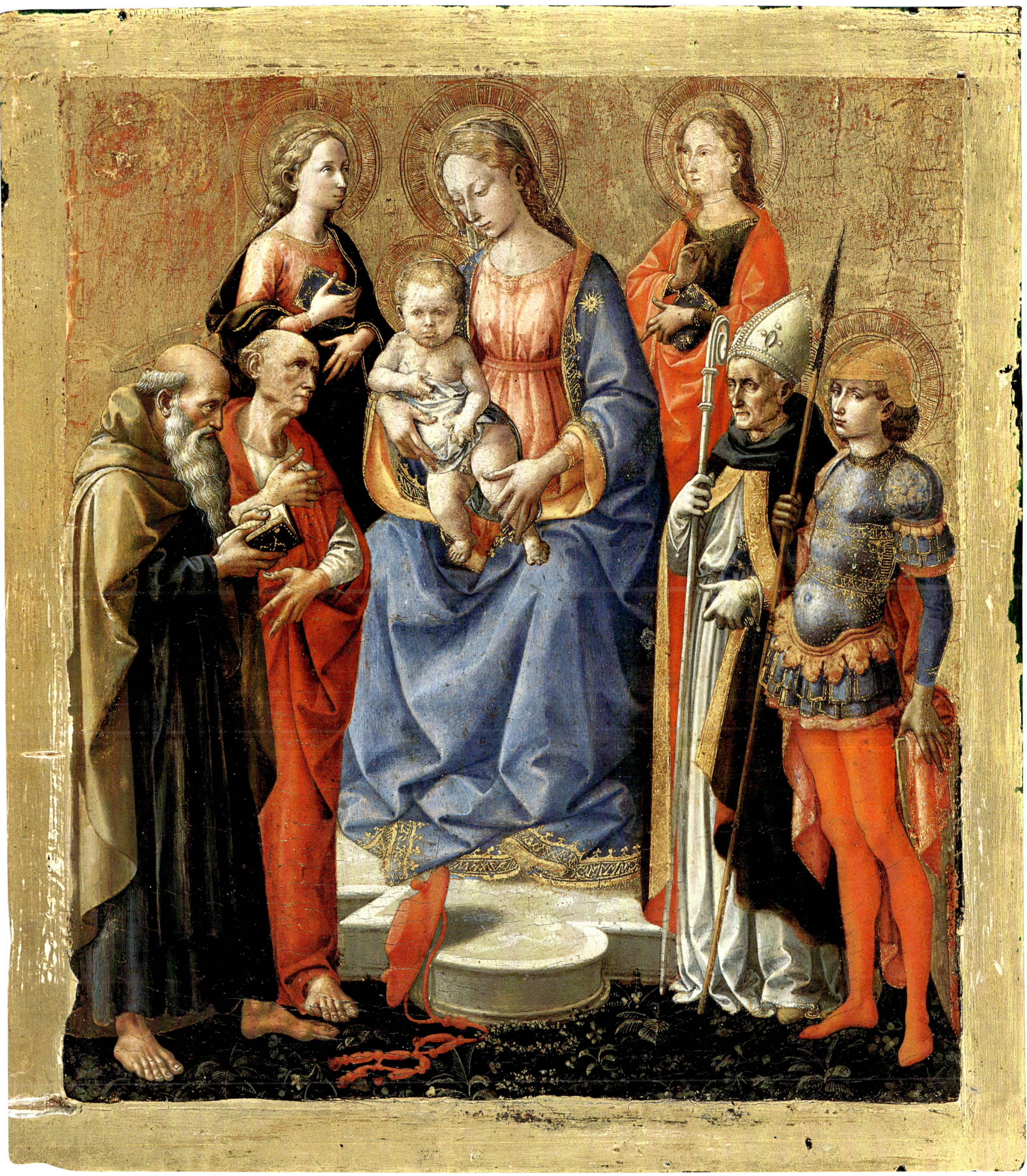

56

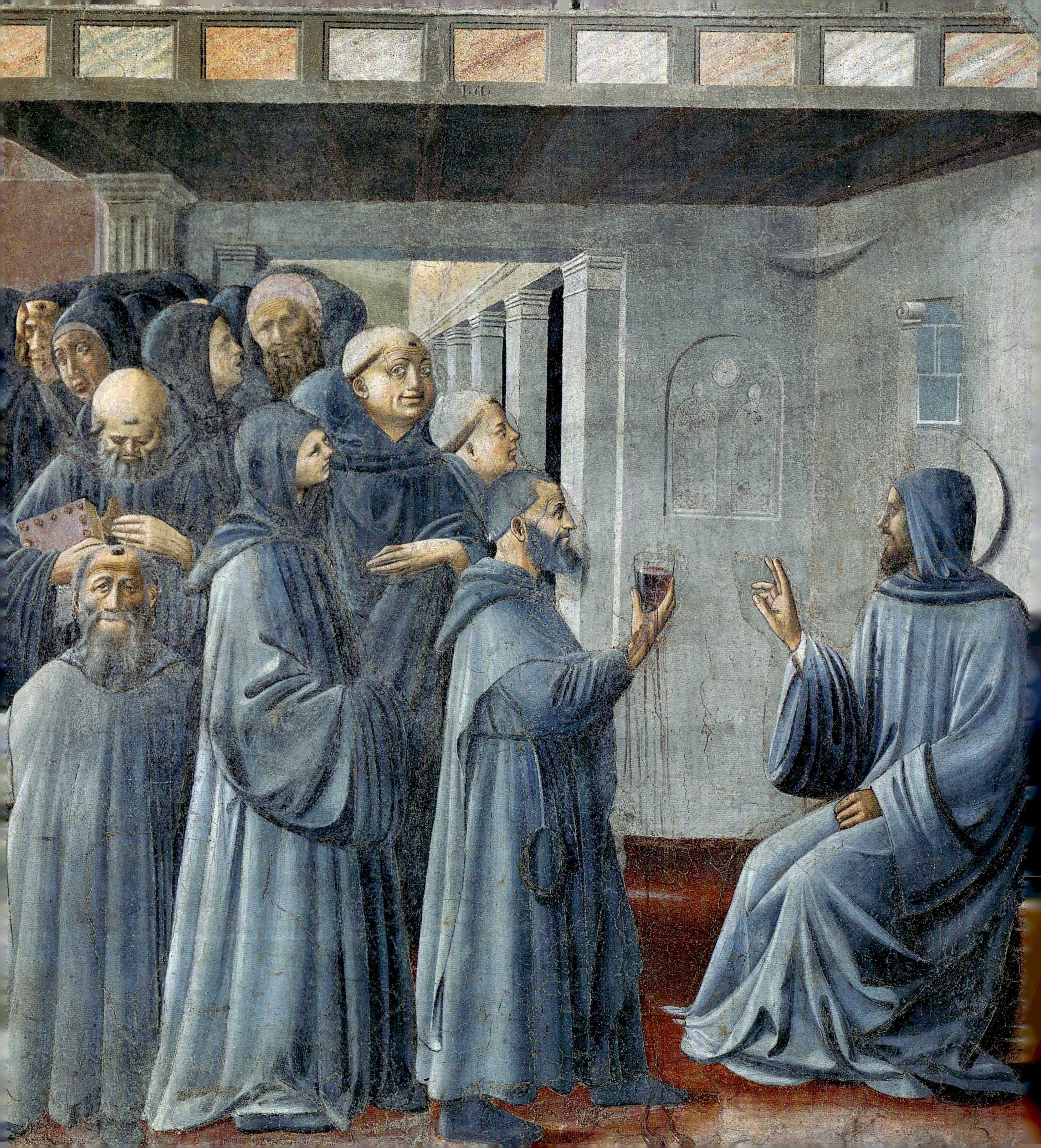

Chapter X
Giovanni di Consalvo and the Master of the Sherman Predella

LAURENCE KANTER

One of the thorniest issues addressed by students of the work of Fra Angelico and his followers has been the problem of Giovanni di Consalvo—or, as he is sometimes named in documents, Giovanni da Portogallo. This mysterious personality is first cited as a witness in two notarial acts drawn up in the chapter house of San Domenico in Fiesole, in January and May 1435, on the first occasion in the company of Zanobi Strozzi. His name next appears, between May 18, 1436, and July 8, 1438, in the ledgers of the Badia Fiorentina as the recipient of modest payments for pigments associated with the fresco decoration of the Orange Cloister there, and for miscellaneous artistic projects such as manuscript illuminations. Based on these documents, Giovanni di Consalvo is widely assumed to be the author of at least ten of the eccentric and exotic frescoes in the Orange Cloister illustrating the legend of Saint Benedict, although the payments to him cover only a minimal fraction of the actual expenses of this work. Futhermore, Giovanni di Consalvo is not called *Maestro* in any document that refers to him, and several scholars have argued that he was probably an assistant or *garzone* in the workshop of another artist, who delegated him to purchase pigments and relay payments. This argument may be supported by the fact that Giovanni di Consalvo left Florence for Portugal, apparently in the summer of 1438, and is not mentioned again in any Florentine records after that date, yet payments to "*lo dipintore che dipigne il chiostro*" reappear in the Badia account books between September 23 and December 16, 1439.[1]

The Orange Cloister frescoes have long eluded firm attribution to any known artist, notwithstanding their singular distinction of being at least partially documented and precisely datable. They have fascinated art historians for their sophisticated organization of narrative, coupled with a relatively naïve figure style; for their distinctive palette; and for their idiosyncratic treatment of pictorial space, alternately progressive and *retardataire*. Debate has focused on whether this peculiar blend of qualities is to be ascribed to the influence of Fra Angelico, Paolo Uccello, or Domenico Veneziano, and whether their author might have been a member of the workshop of one of these three masters. It has been argued that the specific peculiarities of these frescoes may be adduced as proof that they are by Giovanni di Consalvo, as his presumed Iberian (that is, extra-Florentine) training would be one possible explanation for their eccentricities. Conversely, it is also claimed that such arguments are purely inductive, since nothing whatever is known of the painting style of Giovanni di Consalvo. Despite such uncertainties, and the undeniable difficulty of interpreting the documentary evidence relating to him, Giovanni di Consalvo has been adopted by a majority of scholars as the probable "Master of the Orange Cloister."

The thirteen surviving scenes from the legend of Saint Benedict painted on the north and west walls of the Orange Cloister (one occupies the west corner of the south wall) are clearly only a part of what must originally have been a complete narrative cycle. The subjects of the surviving frescoes are drawn from the first fifteen books of the life of Saint Benedict attributed to Saint Gregory the Great, the final twenty-three chapters of which would have provided more than sufficient material to fill the remaining eleven bays of the cloister. When, in the early sixteenth century, Bronzino was called upon to repair or replace the damaged fourth scene in the series, he was not requested to complete anything else, which implies that the remainder of the cycle was intact at that time. It is, therefore, important to recognize that attempts to associate payments registered in the account books with individual frescoes that survive today are compromised by the loss of nearly half of the complete cycle. This is especially significant in that the two final surviving scenes, the *Discovery of the Fiction of Totila* (fig. 181) and the *Reception of Totila* (fig. 182) in the southwest corner of the cloister, are universally recognized to be by a different artist than the other eleven (the fourth of which, *The Temptation of Saint Benedict,* is also by another hand, as it is the fresco repainted by Bronzino). While it is possible that these two frescoes were added to the series later and that they represent the work of an artist who intervened after Giovanni di Consalvo's departure for Portugal in 1438, it is not necessary to assume that this was the case. It is, in fact, likely, given the placement of these two frescoes in the cloister, that many—and perhaps all—of the missing scenes on the south

Opposite:
Figure 178. Fra Angelico and Zanobi Strozzi. *The Miracle of the Poisoned Wine* (detail). 1436–39. Orange Cloister, Badia, Florence

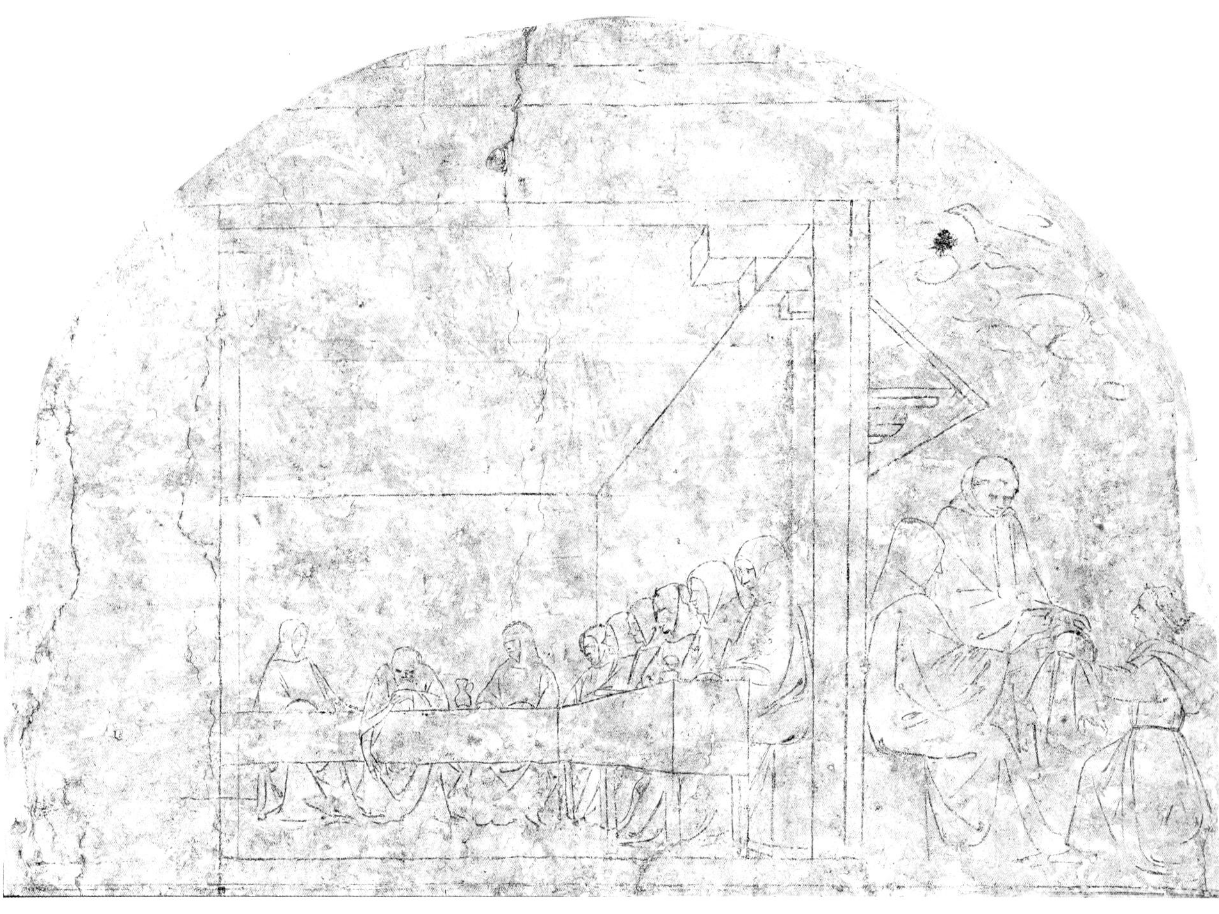

Figure 179. Fra Angelico. *The Miracle of the Poisoned Bread* (*sinopia*). 1436–39. Orange Cloister, Badia, Florence

and east walls were painted by this second artist. Furthermore, it is impossible to be certain that his work followed that of the principal "Master of the Orange Cloister": there is no evidence to show that his frescoes did not precede or were not executed contemporaneously with work on the north and west walls.

Beyond the problem of characterizing the work of this second painter, who might for convenience be labeled here the "Totila Master," close study of the other ten Orange Cloister frescoes, and of their *sinopia* underdrawings revealed in a cleaning campaign in the 1970s, indicates that at least three artists working together were involved in their design and execution. The first of these was a painter of exceptional talent who, on the basis of circumstantial evidence alone, might be identified as Fra Angelico. Vasari ascribed another fresco in the lower cloister of the Badia to Fra Angelico—an image in the lunette over the refectory door of Saint Benedict enjoining silence—and the only individual named in documents in connection with work on the Orange Cloister frescoes, Giovanni di Consalvo, is otherwise known to have frequented the studio at San Domenico in Fiesole. Above all, the spatial and figural sophistication of the *sinopie,* especially that of the ninth scene, which recounts the Miracle of the Poisoned Bread (fig. 179), unmistakably points to Angelico's authorship.

The Miracle of the Poisoned Bread is set in a deeply receding interior space, viewed obliquely from the center left, so that the viewer is made to realize that part of the refectory table and, presumably, several more monks are hidden from his sight behind the left framing pilaster of the doorway—a remarkable conceit for this date, which is only paralleled in Florentine painting in the predella scenes to Angelico's Louvre *Coronation* and in his Perugia altarpiece (cat 30). The integrity of the spatial illusion is maintained by the carefully calibrated diminution in size of the monks seated along the right side of the table, even though this results in the protagonist of the scene, Saint Benedict, being the smallest figure in the fresco. Saint Benedict appears a second time in this same fresco, outside the refectory, at the right, seated in lost profile on a low bench beneath a projecting awning that scrupulously follows the perspectival scheme of the main scene, disappearing quickly "around the corner" of the exterior right wall. The artist who was assigned the task of realizing this design in paint (fig. 180), however, was utterly incapable of following the subtlety of Angelico's lead. The exterior awning was suppressed altogether, and the unarticulated upper surface of the lintel above the doorway was rendered as an implausibly arcaded second story pierced by diminutive Gothic bifora. The engaging

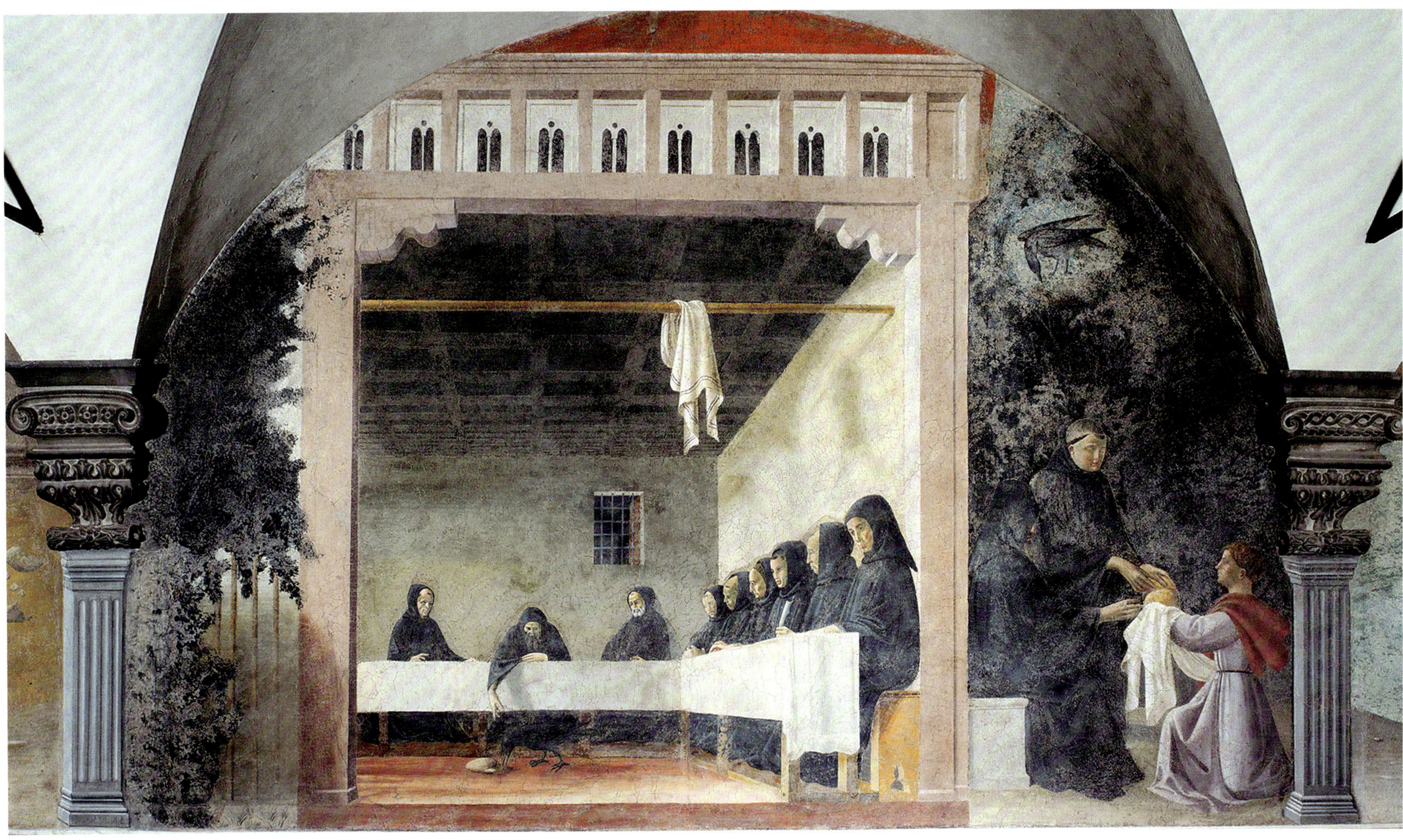

Figure 180. Battista di Biagio Sanguigni (?). *The Miracle of the Poisoned Bread*. 1436–39. Orange Cloister, Badia, Florence

variety of poses among the monks was reduced to inexpressive repetition, with blank faces protruding unpersuasively from stiff cowls, and the brilliant gesture of Saint Benedict in the *sinopia*, pulling back his right sleeve as he rises slightly from his seat to reach over the table toward the loaf of bread on the floor before him, was entirely dissipated in the fresco by painting his hand at rest, flat on the table.

Not only do the ambitious spatial conceits of this *sinopia* and the clarity with which it conveys the human drama of the narrative indicate the mind of Fra Angelico but the elegance and economy of its line betray his hand as well. The same may be suggested for the two scenes that follow this one and for most of those that precede it in the cloister, although the first—showing the departure of Saint Benedict from Norcia—is stiffer and clumsier in its execution than the others and may be a copy or tracing of a design on paper by Fra Angelico. None approaches in its final painted form the promise of the underlying drawing, but neither do they all diverge in the same way or to the same degree as *The Miracle of the Poisoned Bread*. One, *The Miracle of the Poisoned Wine* (fig. 178), the last fresco on the north wall and the fifth in narrative sequence, disappoints significantly less than the others. It is much closer in detail and spirit to its drawing than is any other fresco, and the introduction of decorative architectural details not specified in the *sinopia* does not compromise the meaning or spatial structure of the scene. Furthermore, one figure in the fresco as it was finally painted—the monk holding the glass of wine before Saint Benedict—is rendered with a breathtaking accuracy of naturalistic detail: the weight of the fabric of his robes and the fall of light across their pleats is skillfully conveyed, and the minute observation of his facial features (perhaps this is a portrait of the abbott Gomezio, who commissioned the frescoes ?) lends the painting a realism that is not repeated, or even approximated, in any other fresco in the cloister. Indeed, taking into account all of Florentine mural painting in this period, only the portrait-like heads in the monumental *Crucifixion* in the chapter house at San Marco are equal in accomplishment, and it is reasonable to propose that Angelico himself supplied the two *giornate* of labor that this figure required.[2]

While far more incisive and of a higher quality than most of the figures in the frescoes elsewhere in the cloister, the other depictions of monks in *The Miracle of the Poisoned Wine* are too caricatured in facial type and effect to be attributed to Fra Angelico. Instead, they recall the figures in the early predella panels of Zanobi Strozzi—a connection that was intuited by

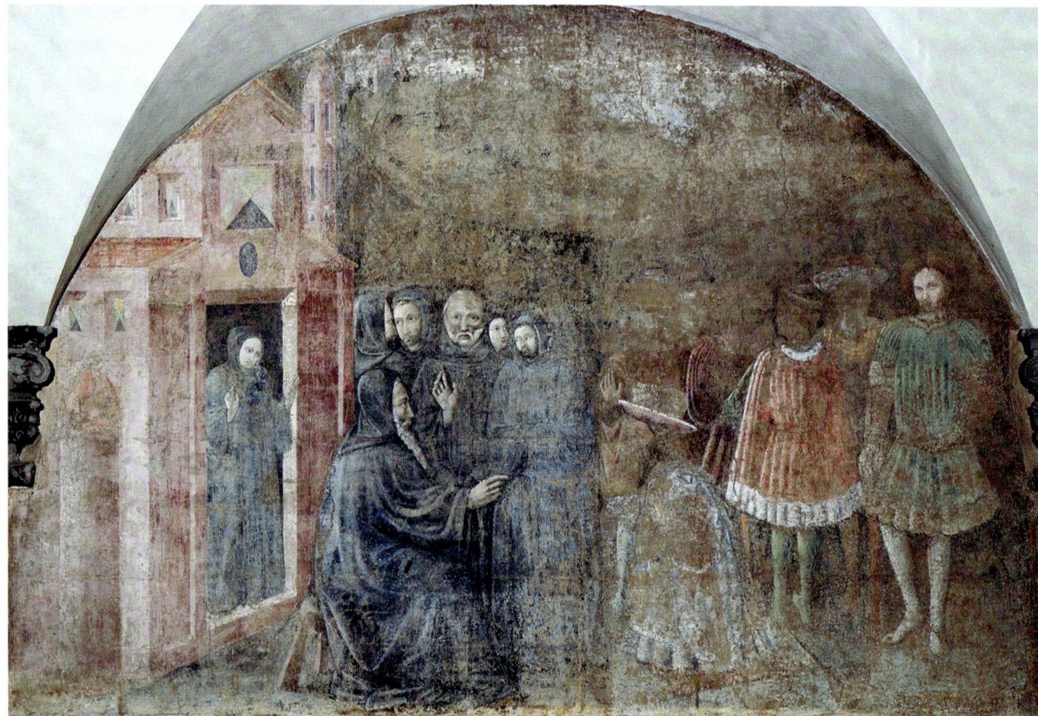

Figure 181. Master of the Sherman Predella (?). *The Discovery of the Fiction of Totila.* 1436–38. Orange Cloister, Badia, Florence

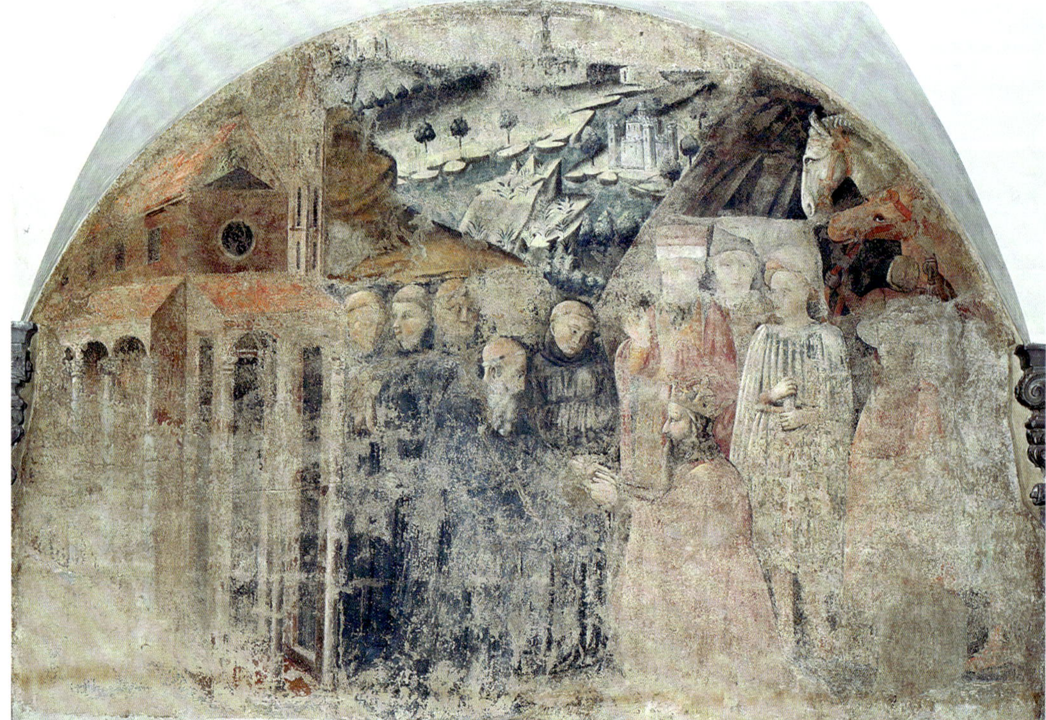

Figure 182. Master of the Sherman Predella (?). *The Reception of Totila.* 1436–38. Orange Cloister, Badia, Florence

Anna Padoa Rizzo when she assigned the Dublin *Assumption of the Virgin* altarpiece (fig. 162) and the *Dormition of the Virgin,* the center panel of its predella (fig. 164), to the artist she designated as the "Master of the Orange Cloister," Giovanni di Consalvo;[3] both of these paintings are characteristic works by Zanobi Strozzi. It appears that Strozzi participated actively in the decoration of the Orange Cloister only in a limited capacity, as his distinctive manner of painting is not easily recognized outside of the scene of *The Miracle of the Poisoned Wine.* It may have been Strozzi who painted the preceding fresco in the cycle, the *Investiture of Saint Benedict and the Miracle of the Bell,* as well as four figures of attendant Benedictine monks in the *Miracle of the Bell Hook* on the west wall, the seventh fresco in narrative sequence, but little else can be ascribed to him with confidence. Generally, Zanobi Strozzi was a more intelligent and faithful translator of Fra Angelico's designs in those works on which they collaborated than was the idiosyncratic painter of the remainder of the Orange Cloister frescoes.

Who was this painter? It is impossible to say with certainty that he cannot have been Giovanni di Consalvo, especially as that mysterious figure is named together with Zanobi Strozzi in documents nearly contemporary with payments for the Orange Cloister frescoes. It is more tempting, however, to propose that he might have been another artist known to have worked with Zanobi Strozzi and who is mentioned in documents along with him with much greater frequency: Battista di Biagio Sanguigni. In addition to manuscript illuminations, Sanguigni was responsible for a small number of altarpieces whose curiously blank, expressionless quality does, in fact, echo the emotional tenor of the Orange Cloister frescoes. These paintings also exploit a figural canon related to that of the frescoes; both are populated by individuals with spindly, elongated bodies, small heads, and large hands, in generally stiff poses. It would require a leap of faith to claim unequivocally that the Orange Cloister frescoes represent Sanguigni's style as a monumental painter in this medium, but it is not unreasonable to advance such a hypothesis in anticipation of further discoveries that might help to substantiate it.

Identifying this third "Master of the Orange Cloister" as either Battista Sanguigni or Giovanni di Consalvo may never be a matter of consensus, but in any event it remains to determine who the "Totila Master," the fourth painter, was, and the possibility that he might have been Giovanni di Consalvo cannot be dismissed. Indeed, if it is legitimate to search for extra-Florentine cultural influences anywhere among the Orange Cloister frescoes, and to explain them as a function of the painter's Iberian origins, it is primarily in the two *Totila* scenes (fig. 181, 182) that they are to be found—as was previously recognized by Licia Collobi-Ragghianti and others.[4] Neither the compositional organization of these frescoes, nor the

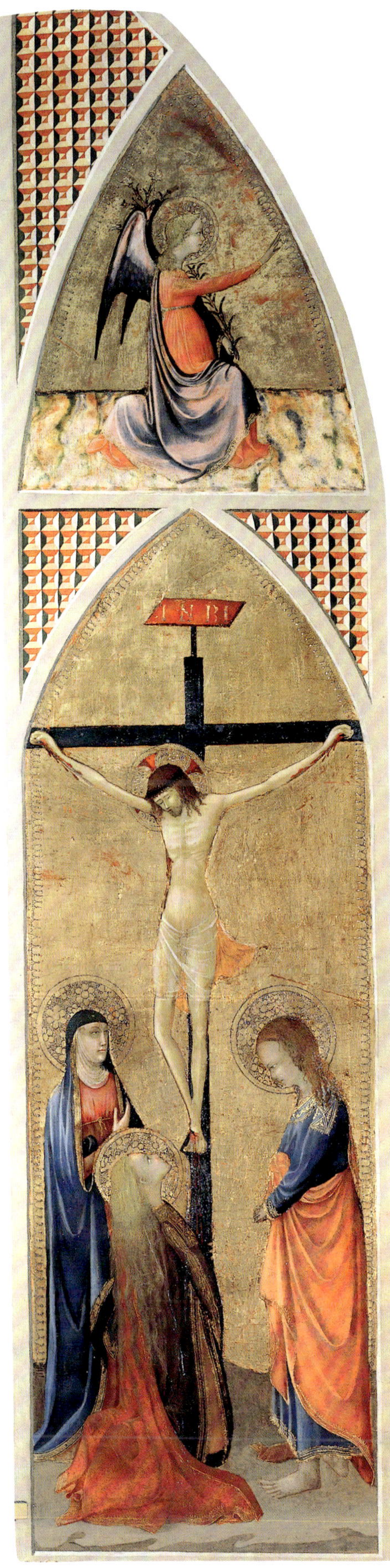

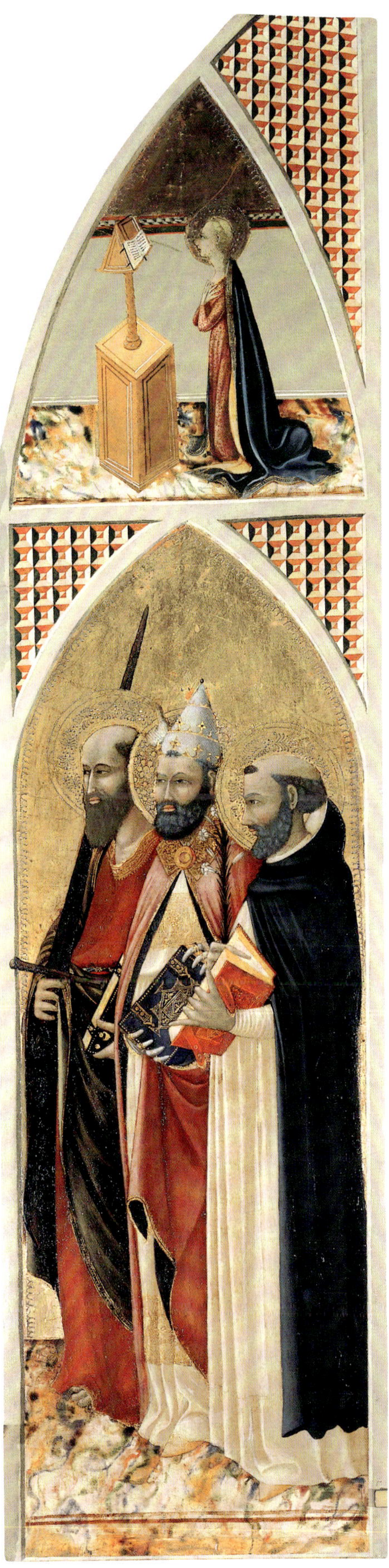

painted architecture or landscape settings, nor such details as the costumes worn by Totila's retinue may be traced to Florentine sources. Proposing an attribution of the scenes to Giovanni di Consalvo assumes both that he was, in fact, an independent painter, and that it is possible to deduce something of his probable style from logical inference alone, yet neither of these contentions is susceptible to proof. In the absence of any more substantial comparative material, such observations can only contribute circumstantial support to a hypothesis. However, expanding the inquiry to include a small number of panel paintings that might also be works by the "Totila Master" may possibly shed further light on the problem of resolving his identity.

The works in question are grouped in modern art-historical literature under the rubric "Master of the Sherman Predella." This painter was first isolated by John Pope-Hennessy in a discussion of the so-called Sherman predella in the Museum of Fine Arts, Boston (cat. 57), when he challenged its traditional attribution to the great Sienese master Sassetta.[5] For Pope-Hennessy, the Master of the Sherman Predella was a follower of Fra Angelico, active primarily in the 1440s, who had absorbed influences from the current generation of Sienese painters. Roberto Longhi expanded the list of works for which the Sherman Master was responsible, arguing that they were the product of a more precocious mentality than that suggested by Pope-Hennessy. For Longhi, the Sherman Master was a follower of Lorenzo Monaco and a contemporary of Masolino, active in the second and third decades of the fifteenth century.[6] Angelo Tartuferi—in an important study that introduced two large tabernacle wings (fig. 183) into the small oeuvre of the Sherman Master—concurred with Longhi's vision of the artist as a follower of Lorenzo Monaco, and restricted the probable period of his activity to the 1420s and 1430s.[7] Tartuferi must be correct in recognizing the termination of the Sherman Master's career at the end of the 1430s. It may also be appropriate to emphasize the affinity of his paintings to Lorenzo Monaco's late works, although whether this is a matter of direct influence or of a comparable Gothic training is unclear.

Attribution to the Sherman Master of the tabernacle wings now in the Galleria Nazionale dell'Accademia in Florence raises the question of his identity in an entirely different manner than has previously been considered. Not only are the six

Figure 183. Master of the Sherman Predella. *The Crucifixion; Saints Paul, Gregory the Great, and Dominic;* and *The Annunciation* (tabernacle wings). About 1435–38. Galleria dell'Accademia, Florence

figures in these two panels painted on a significantly larger scale than anything else known by this master but, in addition, they are markedly more eccentric in style, and suggestively similar to the exotic figures populating the two *Totila* scenes in the Orange Cloister fresco cycle. These similarities range from such basic morphological connections as the simplified and oversized oval shapes of the heads; the small, sharply cut almond-shaped eyes; or the short, straight arms and large, claw-like hands; to the hesitant and unconvincing manner in which heads issue from drapery collars, or limbs are extended in a simulation of movement. Once again, such analogies may be a matter of coincidence rather than a basis for secure attribution, but the possibility that the Master of the Sherman Predella might be identifiable with Giovanni di Consalvo da Portogallo does add some plausible biographical elements to the visual evidence of the artist's career. Not least of these are his documented association with the studio of Fra Angelico in the mid-1430s and his departure from Florence to return to Portugal in 1438—which would explain both the source of his imagery and the extreme scarcity of his surviving works. Short of the fortuitous recovery of a signature or document, however, this hypothetical identification must remain little more than tantalizing.

1. For an excellent résumé of the documents and critical literature concerning Giovanni di Consalvo and the problem of the Orange Cloister frescoes, see Leader 2000, esp. pp. 21–98, 206–32.
2. It therefore may not be a coincidence that *The Miracle of the Poisoned Wine* is the only fresco in the Orange Cloister distinguished by an inscription: the initials "I.M." are painted as though engraved, in Roman majuscule letters, near the center of the lintel above the crowd of monks in the foreground. Although this inscription has defied interpretation thus far, it is perhaps not idle to speculate whether it might be meant to indicate frater "Iohannes Mugellensis."
3. Padoa Rizzo 1997b, p. 106.
4. Collobi-Ragghianti 1950a, p. 374 n. 21; Collobi-Ragghianti 1955a, p. 391; L. Berti, in Baldini and Berti 1957, pp. 68–70; Procacci 1960b, p. 66.
5. Pope-Hennessy 1939, p. 184.
6. Longhi 1940, p. 185 n. 22; Longhi 1948, pp. 161–62; Longhi 1967, pp. 38–40.
7. A. Tartuferi, in Scudieri and Rasario 2003, pp. 78–81.

MASTER OF THE SHERMAN PREDELLA (GIOVANNI DI CONSALVO DA PORTOGALLO ?)

57.

The Martyrdom of Saint Agnes (?), The Flagellation of Christ, and Saint Jerome in the Wilderness

Tempera on panel: overall, 28.6 x 52.5 cm (11¼ x 20⅝ in.)
Museum of Fine Arts, Boston. Gift of Zoe Oliver Sherman in Memory of Samuel Parkman Oliver (22.635)

The female martyr in the left-hand scene lacks any traditional attributes that might identify her. Traditionally believed to be Saint Catherine, she was described by Roberto Longhi as Saint Agnes, instead, which is likely to be correct. It was Agnes who was ordered by the prefect Sempronius in fourth-century Rome to be burned at the stake after she refused either to renounce Christianity or to marry the prefect's son. When the flames of her martyrdom left her unharmed, she was stabbed in the neck. In the painting, the saint kneels in profile between two piles of burning faggots, praying to an angel who is flying down from the right while an executioner at the left, behind her, raises his dagger. In the right-hand scene, Saint Jerome, beating his breast with a stone and holding a rosary, kneels in a barren landscape, his eyes raised to the left and heavenward. The principal episode, in the center panel, shows the flagellation of Christ, before the arcaded gallery of a classical building, attended by the swooning Virgin and four holy figures at the right. This unprecedented scene, placing equivalent emphasis on the sufferings of Christ and of the Virgin, has been explained as an evocation of Thomas à Kempis's *Meditationes vitae Christi* and, possibly, as an illustration of one of the five sorrowful Mysteries of the Rosary.[1]

Despite the fact that this work has always been known as the Sherman predella, the title should be understood in a generic sense only, as it is not clear what its original function might have been. Although of a size and shape often associated with predella panels, the painting presents a number of unusual features in the arrangement of the events and in its structure—including its relatively thin support and the presence of a continuous gilt band, of uniform width, dividing the scenes and surrounding the entire composition—which are not typical of such objects. It is possible, instead, that it decorated some liturgical furnishing or that it was mounted on the wall of an oratory or confraternal chapel. A number of panels from the studio of Bicci di Lorenzo and Neri di Bicci, related in format and composition to this one, seem to have fulfilled a similar

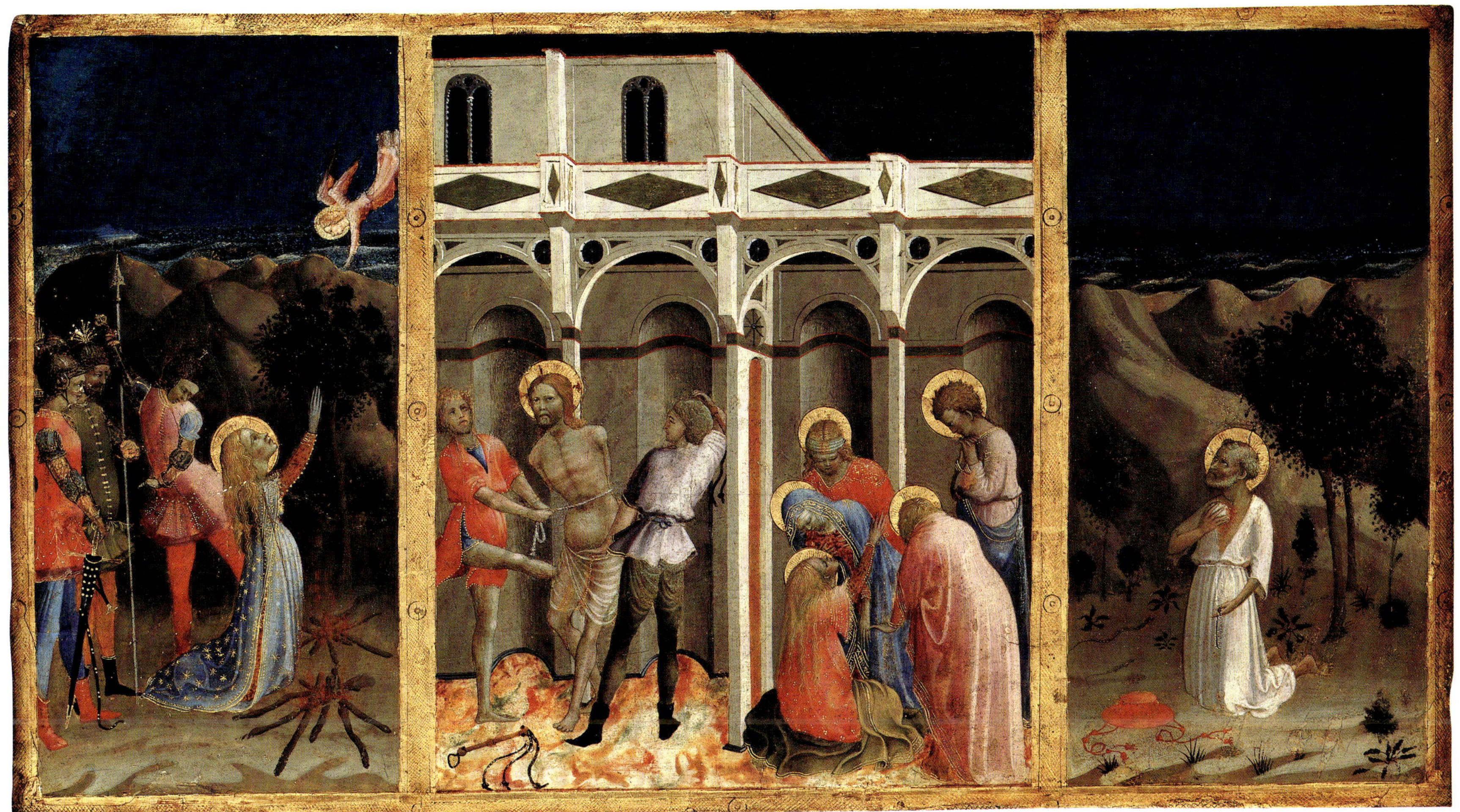

57

function, but no examples intact and in situ survive to confirm the proposal. If this painting were a confraternal commission, it is likely either that the confraternity was dedicated to celebrating the Mysteries of the Rosary or that it was consecrated to the patronage of Saints Agnes and Jerome. One obvious possibility would be the Compagnia di Sant'Agnese at the Carmine in Florence, for, like the Dominicans, the Carmelites figured prominently in promoting devotions to the rosary.

The Sherman predella was known to scholars, following its discovery in the 1920s and for nearly two decades afterward, as a probable early work by Sassetta. It was dismissed both from that artist's catalogue of works and from the context of Sienese Quattrocento painting in 1939, when John Pope-Hennessy noted its predominant influence as that of Fra Angelico in the 1430s. For Pope-Hennessy, the Sherman predella was a unicum, but Roberto Longhi subsequently added three more works to the Sherman Master's oeuvre, and shifted his profile as an artist to an earlier generation. A mistaken attempt by Kanter to characterize the Master of the Sherman Predella as active in provincial centers in eastern Tuscany was corrected by Tartuferi who, however, preferred Longhi's precocious estimate of the dates of the Sherman Master's activity and his elevated opinion of the painter's stature within the Florentine tradition to Pope-Hennessy's more realistic assessment both of the master's merits and his chronology. Whether or not one accepts the identification (proposed above) of the Master of the Sherman Predella with Giovanni di Consalvo, the known range of the latter's activity, restricted to little more than the years between 1435 and 1438, coincides reasonably well both with the stylistic character and the extreme scarcity of works by this engaging but minor master.

LK

1. Kanter 1994, p. 143.

58.
The Intercession of Christ and the Virgin

Tempera on panel, 22.5 x 40.5 cm (8 7/8 x 16 in.)
Collection Richard L. Feigen, New York

The *Intercession of Christ and the Virgin* represents a distinctive formulation of an unusual subject. It is the first, and smallest, of a series of fifteenth-century replicas of an altarpiece (fig. 184) originally mounted, sometime before 1409, on the inner façade of Florence Cathedral and now in The Cloisters Collection at The Metropolitan Museum of Art in New York.[1] The altarpiece, unusual for the period in having been painted on canvas rather than panel, is a work by Lorenzo Monaco of the 1390s.[2] Its composition is derived from a twelfth-century text composed by Ernaldus of Chartres, but ascribed in the fourteenth century to Saint Bernard of Clairvaux: "O man, you have a secure access to God when the Mother is before her Son, and the Son before His Father. The Mother showed her breast to her Son, the Son showed His wounds to His Father. There where the proofs of love are so many no one can be denied." This text was widely disseminated as chapter 39 of the popular fourteenth-century treatise the *Speculum humanae salvationis*. Lorenzo Monaco interpreted the imagery of this text literally, providing inscriptions on his painting elucidating the gestures of Christ and the Virgin. Christ, touching the wound in his side with his right hand, looks upward as he says, "My Father, let them be saved for whom you wished that I suffer the Passion." The Virgin, baring her breast with her left hand and with her right hand indicating a group of supplicants, says, "Dearest Son, have mercy on them for the milk that I gave you." These gestures, although not the inscriptions, have been retained exactly by the Master of the Sherman Predella, except that the Virgin reaches modestly toward her chest rather than baring her breast. Also derived closely from its model are the details of God the Father in a starry mandorla and the dove of the Holy Spirit that links him to Christ, the three together forming the Trinity.

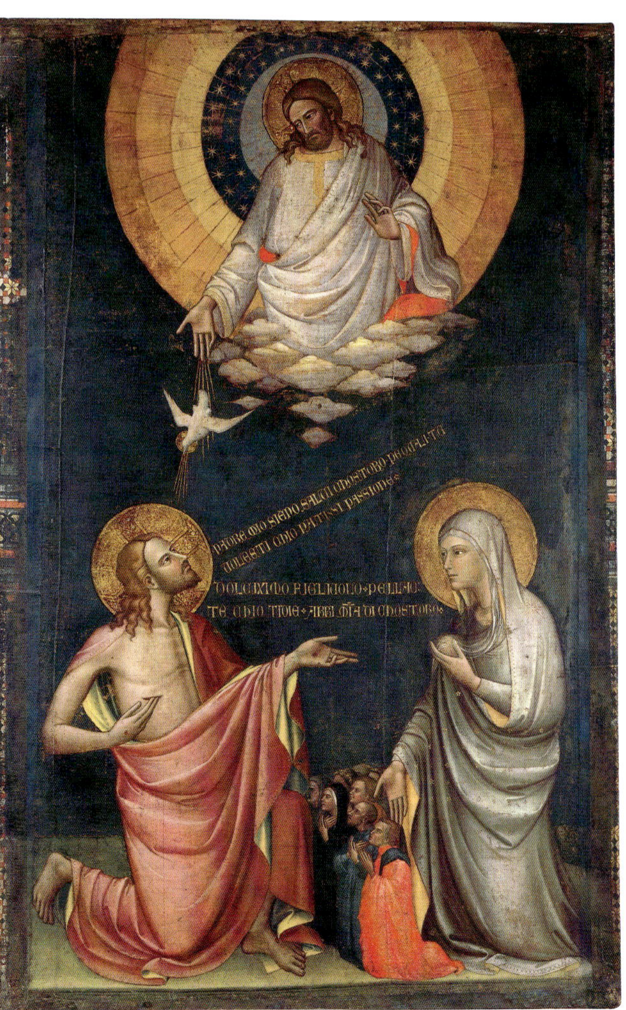

Figure 184. Lorenzo Monaco. *The Intercession of Christ and the Virgin*. About 1395–1400. The Metropolitan Museum of Art, New York. The Cloisters Collection, 1953 (53.37)

This beautifully preserved panel was in a private Florentine collection when, in 1948, it was recognized by Roberto Longhi as by the same hand as the so-called Sherman Predella in the Museum of Fine Arts, Boston (cat. 57).[3] Only the second work to be added to the artist's corpus, it nonetheless permitted Longhi to reiterate his opinion of this master as a progressive painter of the 1420s and 1430s, rather than as the derivative one Pope-Hennessy envisioned when he first isolated this artistic personality ten years earlier. Longhi later[4] suggested that certain archaisms in the master's style might be explained by training received in Lorenzo Monaco's studio in the years preceding Masaccio's revolution of Florentine visual culture, making him a contemporary of Francesco d'Antonio and Paolo Schiavo. While Longhi's date of the 1430s for the *Intercession* and the Sherman Predella may be correct, it seems preferable to discuss the eccentricities of the artist's style in other terms, and to reject attempts to advance the beginnings of his career into the second and third decades of the fifteenth century. It is specifically with Fra Angelico's paintings of the early 1430s, and with Zanobi Strozzi's parallel efforts in the same years, that the *Intercession* and the Sherman Predella have the strongest affinities. If the identification of the Master of the Sherman Predella with Giovanni di Consalvo is correct, these affinities could actually be the fruits of a collaboration in Angelico's workshop in the years between 1435 and 1438.

The shape and size of the *Intercession of Christ and the Virgin* suggest that it originally served as the pinnacle of a small devo-

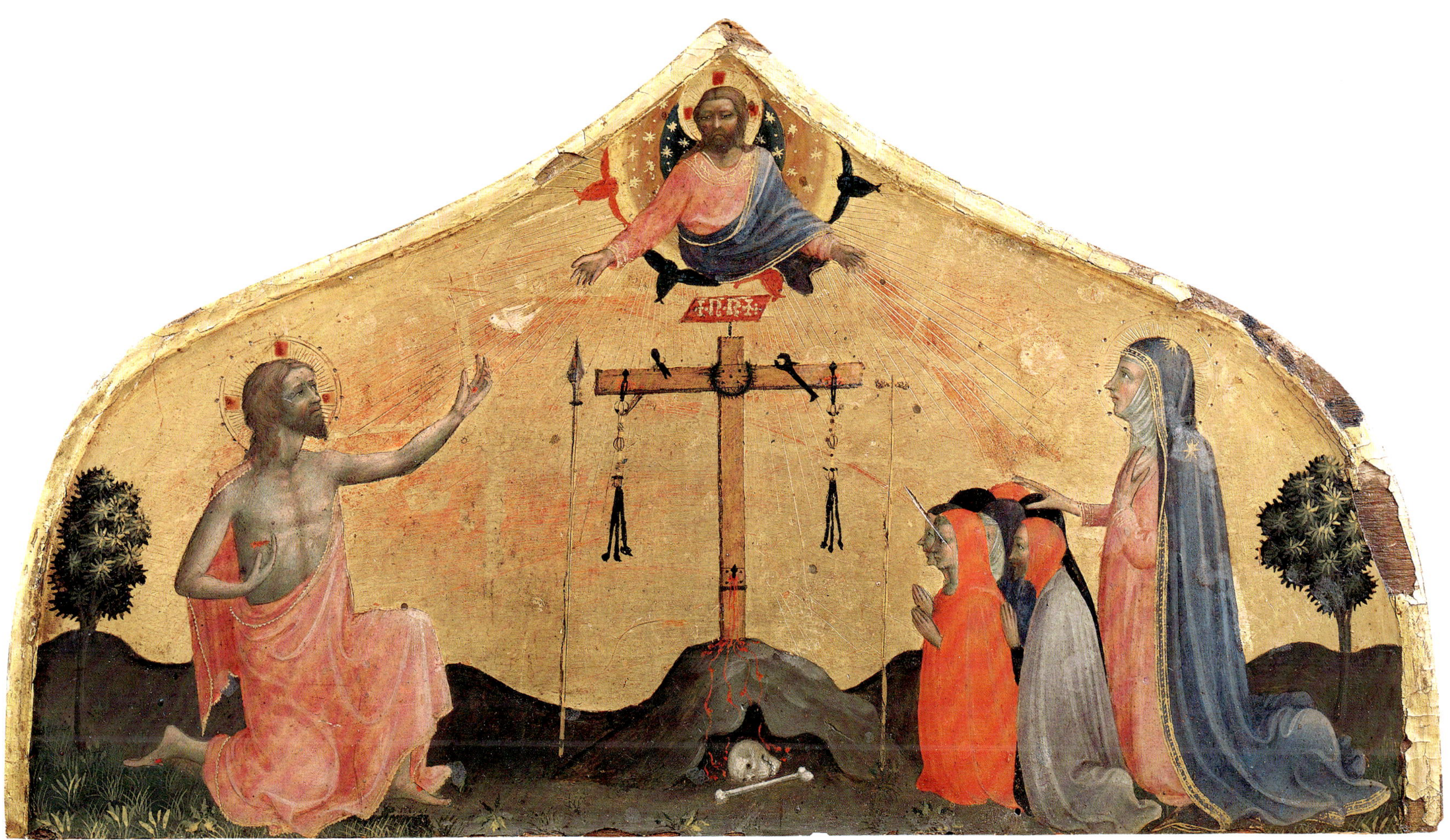

58

tional tabernacle. As the grain of its wood support is horizontal, it is likely that the painting was glued onto the front of the main panel of the tabernacle and projected forward from the painted surface of the image below it. Such a structure implies that the tabernacle was a triptych whose wings folded flush below this panel, leaving the image of the *Intercession* exposed when the triptych was closed. A parallel for the shape of the complete center panel is represented by a *Virgin and Child Enthroned* by the Master of the Judgment of Paris (Giuliano d'Arrigo) in the Fogg Art Museum in Cambridge.[5] As this shape is relatively unusual, one might presume that the Fogg panel was prepared in the same carpenter's shop as the *Intercession of Christ and the Virgin*—with which it is, in any event, approximately contemporary. Unfortunately, no further panels or fragments have yet been identified that seem logical candidates for completing the triptych by the Master of the Sherman Predella.

LK

1. Meiss 1954, pp. 302–17.
2. This painting has been attributed to a wide range of artists active in the last decade of the fourteenth century, including Niccolò di Pietro Gerini (Borenius 1922, pp. 156 ff.; Panofsky 1927, pp. 293 ff., 305ff. n. 106; Oertel 1960, p. 24; Boskovits 1975, pp. 105–6, 386, 412), an assistant of Niccolò di Pietro Gerini (Offner 1927, p. 94), Mariotto di Nardo (Berenson 1936, p. 295), Lorenzo di Niccolò (Fahy 1978, pp. 380–81), and, most recently, the Master of Santa Verdiana, alias Tommaso del Mazza (S. Pasquinucci and B. Deimling, in Offner/Boskovits 2000, pp. 352–63). The correct attribution was proposed in the first instance by E. Fahy (cited in Baetjer 1995, p. 13), and is adopted in an excellent technical study of the painting by Hale (2000, pp. 31–41).
3. Longhi 1948, pp. 161–62.
4. Longhi 1967, pp. 38–40.
5. Bowron 1990, p. 118 (as by the Master of the Carrand Tondo).

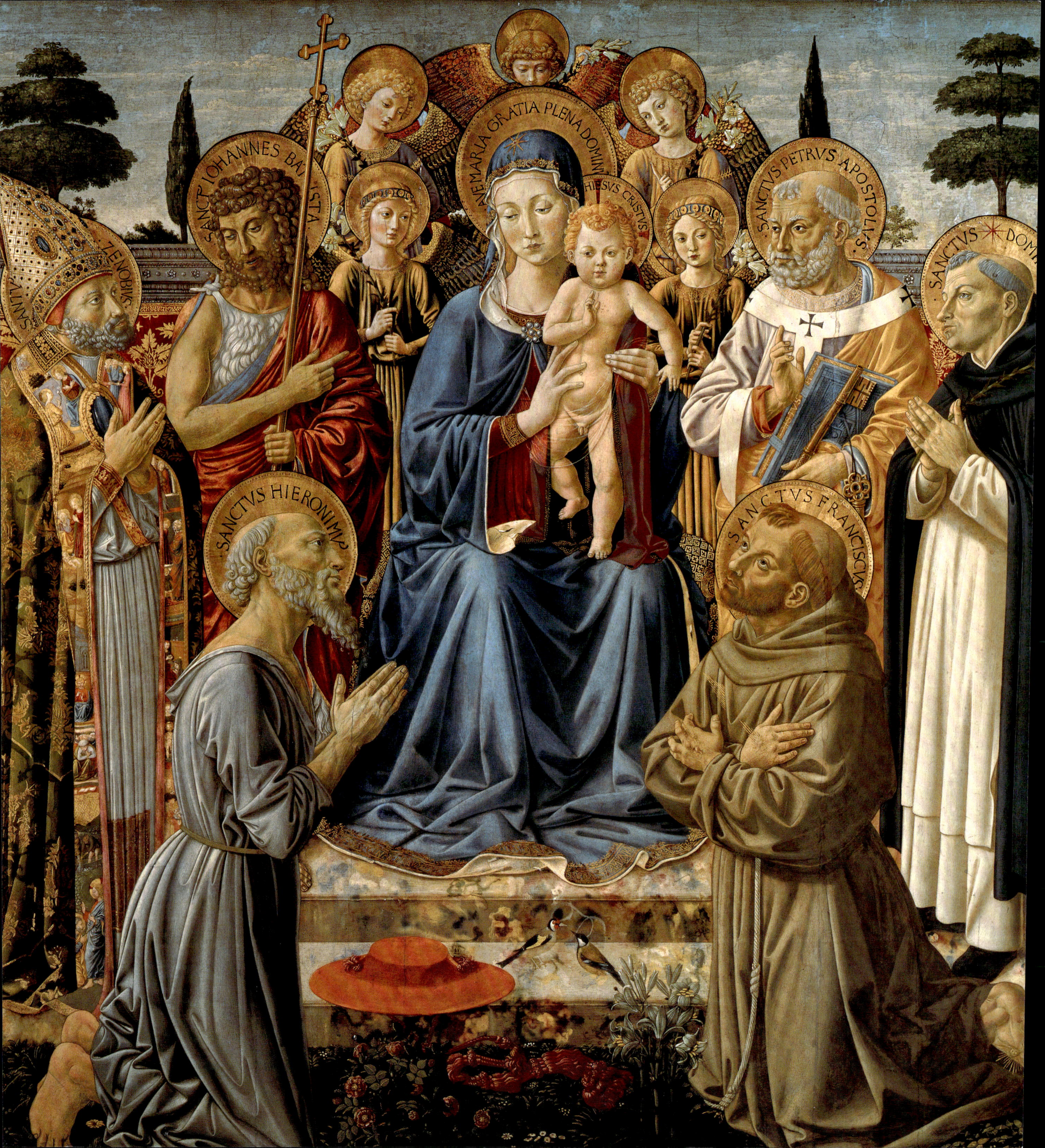
AVEMARIA GRATIA PLENA DOMIN
IHESVS CRISTVS
SANCTVS PETRVS APOSTOLVS
ZENOBIVS
SANCTVS FRANCISCVS

Chapter XI
Benozzo Gozzoli (Benozzo di Lese di Sandro)

PIA PALLADINO

Generally regarded as Fra Angelico's closest follower and collaborator, Benozzo Gozzoli was born in Florence sometime between 1420 and 1421. Baptized Benozzo di Lese di Sandro, he is referred to in documents as Benozzo di Lese or Benozzo da Firenze. The surname, Gozzoli, by which he is commonly known, was assigned to the artist by Vasari, who took it from a branch of the family that had settled outside of Florence. Benozzo's grandfather, Sandro di Lese, was a "*scardassiere,*" or wool comber, and his father, Lese, a "*farsettaio,*" or tailor.[1]

Nothing is known of Benozzo's artistic formation, and his name does not appear in any of the registers of the Florentine painters' guild. The earliest records of the artist's activity, dated 1439 and 1441, are in the form of payments made to him by the Florentine confraternity of Santa Maria delle Laudi e di Sant'Agnese in the church of Santa Maria del Carmine: the first payment is for painting the figure of the risen Christ on a shroud for the dead and the second, for a "*compasso,*" or small processional panel, commissioned by Giovanni del Pugliese. The decorative character of these minor works, both now lost, has led Anna Padoa Rizzo to speculate that Benozzo may have carried out his apprenticeship in one of the large and busy workshops engaged in artisanal production, such as painted banners, chests, and other domestic furnishings, as well as more important commissions for altarpieces and frescoes.[2] Significantly, while the 1439 document refers to the artist as "*Benozzo di Lese dipintore*" ("Benozzo di Lese painter"), the 1442 property declaration of his grandfather states that "he is learning to paint"; this reference is crossed out and replaced with "is a painter" in the next property declaration of 1446. Although the 1442 document might be colored by the grandfather's wish to claim Benozzo as a dependent for tax purposes, it could imply that at this date the artist was working in another master's studio, whereas by 1446 he was unquestionably on his own.

The next record of Benozzo's activity following the confraternity's commissions is a contract dated January 1444 between the artist and Lorenzo and Vittorio Ghiberti, in which Benozzo, described as "painter," pledges to work for three years on the east doors of the Florentine Baptistery—the famous "Gates of Paradise"—promising to labor "in good faith and without fraud as required by Lorenzo." While the specific nature of Benozzo's involvement is not mentioned in the document, the fairly high wage he received suggests that he was engaged in work of some responsibility, beyond the task of chasing usually assigned to minor assistants.[3]

The Ghiberti contract is the last record of the artist's presence in Florence prior to his engagement, along with Fra Angelico, on the (now lost) frescoes for the Chapel of Saint Peter in the Vatican, for which he was paid in May 1447, and on the decoration of the Chapel of San Brizio in Orvieto Cathedral, which occupied him and Angelico in the summer of that same year. The Orvieto frescoes, for which Benozzo is recorded as having served as the "*consotio,*" or associate of Angelico, represent the earliest documented works by the artist to have come down to us, although opinions remain sharply divided as to the extent of his participation.[4] The same debate has affected the evaluation of Benozzo's role in the decoration of the Cappella Niccolina in the Vatican, on which Angelico was at work, possibly at intervals, between the end of 1447 and 1449. Although Benozzo's name is not mentioned in documents relating to this work, stylistic and circumstantial evidence suggest that he accompanied Angelico from Orvieto back to Rome to assist him in this endeavor as well as in the completion of the frescoes in the Chapel of Saint Peter. During this period Benozzo appears to have also executed a fresco cycle referred to by Vasari as in the Observant church of Santa Maria in Aracoeli in Rome, of which all that remains is an image of Saint Anthony of Padua with angels and two kneeling donors.[5]

In the summer of 1449 Benozzo petitioned the *Opera* of Orvieto Cathedral to be allowed to complete the frescoes in the Chapel of San Brizio left unfinished by Angelico. While it is generally assumed that the artist went to Orvieto directly from Rome, it is possible that he may have been in Florence before this date, having followed Angelico there, if only temporarily, at the end of the previous year (see cat. 60). Failing to obtain the commission for the Orvieto Cathedral frescoes

Opposite:
Figure 185. Benozzo Gozzoli. *Virgin and Child Enthroned, with Five Angels and Saints Jerome, Zenobius, John the Baptist, Peter, Dominic, and Francis* (Alterpiece of the Purification). 1461. National Gallery, London

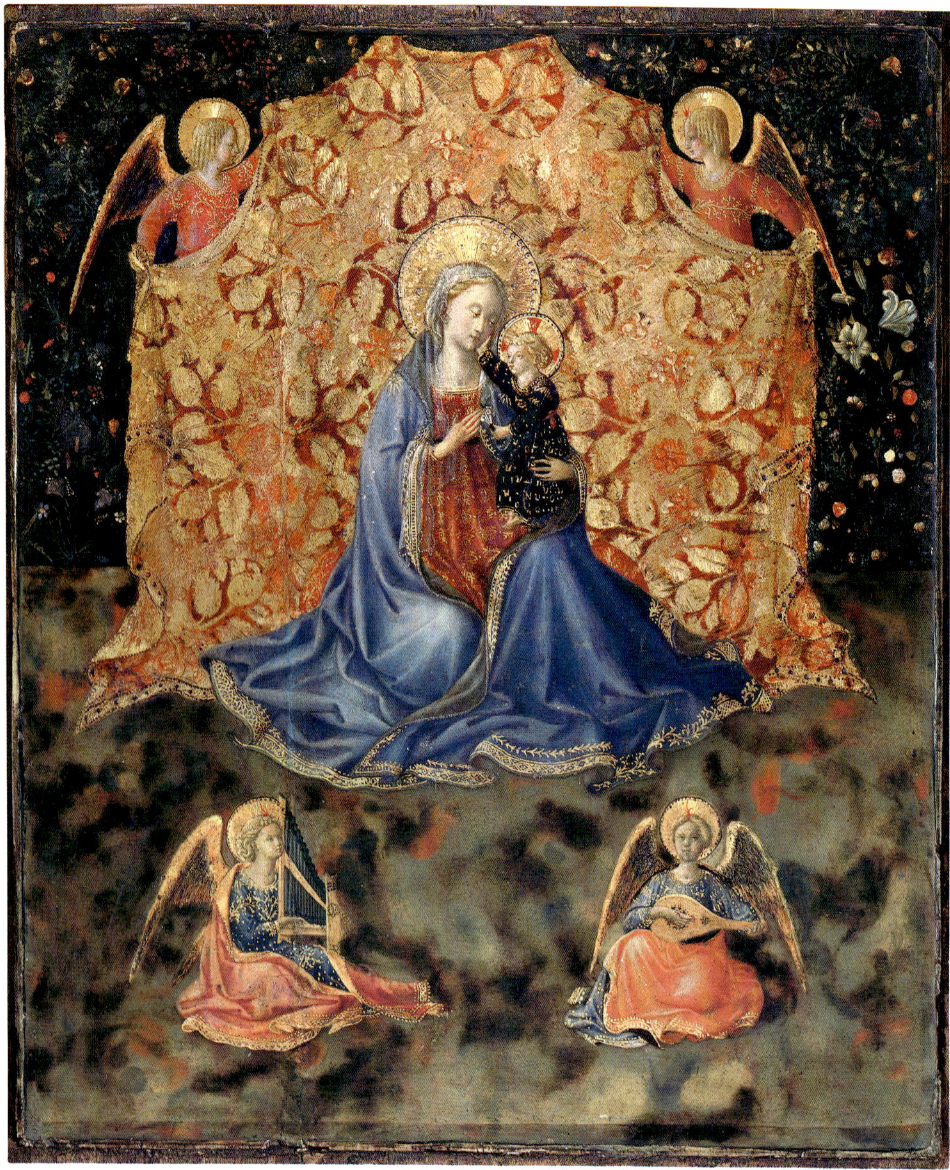

Figure 186. Benozzo Gozzoli. *Virgin and Child, with Angels* (*Madonna of Humility*). About 1440–45. Accademia Carrara, Bergamo

(which remained incomplete until the intervention of Luca Signorelli fifty years later) or, more probably, because of the outbreak of revolution in the city, Benozzo left Orvieto for Montefalco, another Umbrian town located not far from Assisi. Between 1450 and 1452 the artist was busy with the fresco decoration of the Franciscan churches of San Fortunato and San Francesco in Montefalco; for San Fortunato he also painted a large altarpiece of *The Assumption of the Virgin,* now in the Pinacoteca Vaticana. The Montefalco paintings, the artist's earliest signed-and-dated production and his first major independent commissions, are of paramount importance in the evaluation of Benozzo's style and artistic formation.

Between 1453 and 1458 Benozzo received commissions for frescoes and altarpieces in various other locations in Umbria and the Latium region. The artist is recorded in Rome once more in September 1458, when he and the Spanish painter Salvador de Valencia were paid for various objects and church furnishings, such as banners and cardinals' seats, which they had painted for the coronation of the new pope, Pius II (r. 1458–64). Benozzo's involvement in the production of these (now lost) works may signal an appreciation for and recognition of his decorative and technical skills, beyond the formal qualities of his art. The extent of the artist's reputation by this date is attested by the prestigious commission awarded to him by the Medici in 1459 to paint an elaborate fresco cycle, depicting the procession of the Magi, in the chapel of their Florentine palace in the via Larga. Two years later, possibly on the recommendation of the Medici, Benozzo was asked to paint a large altarpiece for the Confraternity of the Purification of the Virgin and of Saint Zenobius, located in San Marco. The imposing structure, which, according to the contract, was to be modeled on the one painted by Angelico for the high altar of the same convent, is now divided between the National Gallery, London (fig. 185), and various other European and American collections.[6] Remarkable for its brilliant coloristic effects and elaborately decorated surfaces, it possesses little of the spatial and formal sophistication of Angelico's prototype, but fully testifies to Benozzo's consummate craftsmanship.

From 1464 to 1467 Benozzo was in San Gimignano, where he executed a large fresco cycle with scenes from the life of Saint Augustine for the church dedicated to the saint, as well as other works in the surrounding area. During this period, Benozzo continued to be supported by the Medici, as testified by a letter addressed to Lorenzo de' Medici in July 1467, in which the artist thanks him for intervening on behalf of one of his workshop assistants accused of theft.[7]

Between 1468 and 1485 Benozzo was in Pisa, entrusted with the prestigious commission to decorate the north wall of the city's famous civic cemetery, the Camposanto, with scenes from the Old and the New Testament. The artist continued to work in Pisa, on other commissions, until 1495, when he was forced to leave the city following its revolt against Florence and expulsion of all Florentines in residence there. Benozzo died two years later in Pistoia. His last recorded works are two paintings on canvas of *The Crucifixion* and *The Resurrection,* possibly executed with the collaboration of his sons Francesco and Alesso, for the Florentine bishop of Pistoia.

While the course of Benozzo's stylistic development following the signed-and-dated frescoes of 1450 in Montefalco is well documented, the parameters of his activity prior to this date, and the nature of his early relationship with Fra Angelico, remain the object of speculation. Based on Vasari's assertion that Benozzo was a "pupil" ("*discepolo*") of Angelico, and on the documented association of the two artists at the Vatican and in Orvieto, scholars have variously sought to discern the

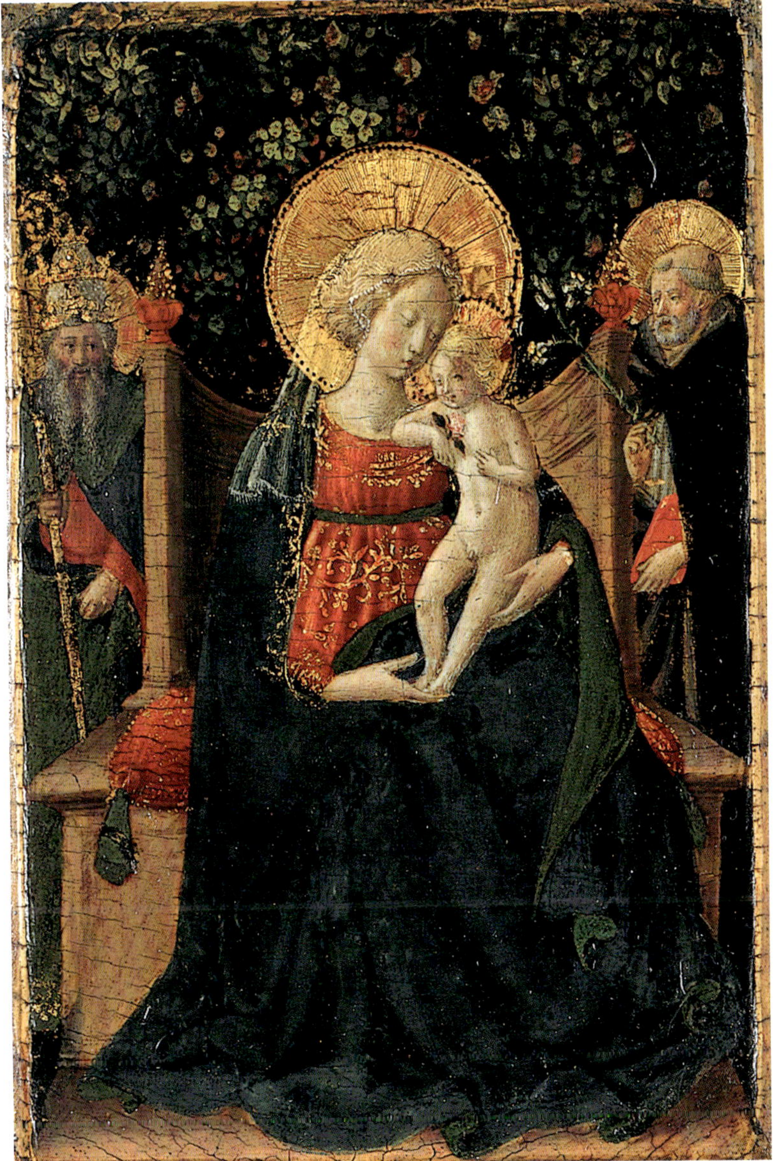

Figure 187. Benozzo Gozzoli. *Virgin and Child Enthroned, with Saints Dominic and Sixtus* (?). About 1440–45. Courtauld Institute of Art Gallery, London

artist's hand in Angelico's workshop production at San Marco, and in other paintings from the same period. Most recently, Boskovits[8] has discounted Gozzoli's participation in the San Marco frescoes, suggesting that the artist's connection to Angelico was less that of an apprentice than of an occasional collaborator strongly influenced by the older master. The extent of Angelico's impact on the young Benozzo is clearly discernible in a handful of small-scale works, convincingly regarded by Boskovits as the artist's first independent efforts in the early 1440s, such as the precious *Madonna of Humility* (fig. 186) in the Accademia Carrara, Bergamo, which appears closely inspired by Angelico's equally refined *Virgin and Child* (fig. 91) in the Pinacoteca Vaticana (recently dated between 1440 and 1445,[9] but possibly painted half a decade earlier). Executed in the same years is the *Virgin and Child Enthroned* (fig. 187) in the Courtauld Institute of Art Gallery, London, with which Boskovits rightly associated, as part of the same diptych, a much-ruined *Man of Sorrows, with a Kneeling Donor,* formerly in the Haas Collection, Detroit. Less convincing is the inclusion among this nucleus of early works of the small *Crucifixion* formerly in a private collection in Paris, first published by Longhi as the work of Benozzo, and of the illuminations in the *Vaticinia Pontificia* in the British Library, London (Ms. Harley 1340), for which the closest point of reference are the Montefalco frescoes of about 1450.[10] Still problematic, moreover, is the attribution to the young Benozzo of the *Virgin and Child Enthroned, with Angels,* in the National Gallery, London—a work not unreasonably associated in the past with Domenico Veneziano, and recently regarded by Kanter as the product of an Umbrian follower of Angelico.[11]

1. The trade of the *farsettaio* was specifically concerned with the making of *farsetti,* the close-fitting wool or linen doublets worn by men over an undergarment.
2. Padoa Rizzo 1991, pp. 207–9; A. Padoa Rizzo, in Toscano and Capitelli 2002, pp. 18–19. This hypothesis is taken up by Cole Ahl 1996, p. 6.
3. Most recently, A. Padoa Rizzo (in Toscano and Capitelli 2002, p. 18) reiterated the possibility, first advanced by Ciardi Dupré Dal Poggetto (1967, pp. 60–73; M. G. Ciardi Dupré Dal Poggetto, in Florence 1978, pp. 397–98) that Benozzo actually intervened in the execution of some of the reliefs. The claim was categorically refuted by Middeldorf and other authors (cited by M. G. Ciardi Dupré Dal Poggetto, in Florence 1978).
4. See M. Boskovits (in Toscano and Capitelli 2002, pp. 42–43) and G. Testa (1996, pp. 80–81) for the full range of opinions.
5. Cole Ahl 1996, pp. 251–52.
6. Boskovits and Brown 2003, pp. 346–51; Strehlke 2004, pp. 194–201 (with earlier bibliography).
7. Cole Ahl 1996, pp. 153, 279.
8. M. Boskovits, in Toscano and Capitelli 2002, pp. 41–55, 133–41.
9. A. Galli, in Di Lorenzo 2001, pp. 38–39.
10. A date for the *Crucifixion* formerly in Paris, close to that of the Montefalco frescoes, was persuasively suggested by Longhi (1960a [1975 ed.], pp. 123–27). An actual provenance for this painting in the church of San Fortunato in Montefalco was first suggested by S. Nessi (1980, p. 95; 1997, pp. 44–46). This association has been disputed by E. Lunghi (1997, pp. 29–30), who nevertheless proposes an even later date for the painting, about 1460. Despite the recent dating by M. Boskovits and by F. Pasut of the British Library miniatures as early as 1440–45 (in Toscano and Capitelli 2002, pp. 142–45), other scholars have pointed out their close relationship to both the Paris *Crucifixion* and the Montefalco frescoes (Dalli Regoli and Landolfi 1992, pp. 416–17; Cole Ahl 1996, p. 22).
11. Gordon 2003, pp. 44–49 (with earlier bibliography); Kanter 2004, p. 107.

59.
The Crucifixion, with Saint Jerome and Saint Dominic

Tempera and gold on panel, 30.5 x 17.8 cm (12 x 7 in.)
Collection Richard L. Feigen, New York

This small panel, probably intended for private devotion, shows Christ on the cross, flanked by Saint Dominic and the penitent Saint Jerome, dressed in a sackcloth and about to beat his chest with a stone. In the background, situated in a valley surrounded by cultivated green hills, is a walled city that may be tentatively identified as Florence, with the Duomo on the right, the crenellated towers of the Palazzo Vecchio in the center, and the river Arno flowing from the mountains behind it. The presence of Saint Dominic and Saint Jerome kneeling in adoration before the cross, rather than the traditional standing figures of the Virgin and Saint John the Evangelist, suggests that the image may have been produced either for a confraternity dedicated to Saint Jerome within the Dominican establishment or, as an object of prayer and meditation on the ascetic ideal, for someone affiliated with the Dominican Observants. In both function and iconography this work may be compared with a *Crucifixion* by Pesellino (National Gallery of Art, Washington, D.C.), which shows the penitent Saint Jerome and Saint Francis, rather than Saint Dominic, kneeling at the foot of the cross. That image has been dated by Boskovits to between 1445 and 1450, and is presumed to have served as an object of private devotion within the circle of Observant Franciscans.[1]

The Feigen *Crucifixion* has been universally accepted as a work by Benozzo Gozzoli since it was first published with this attribution in J. P. Richter's 1901 catalogue of paintings then in the Drury-Lowe Collection at Locko Park, England.[2]

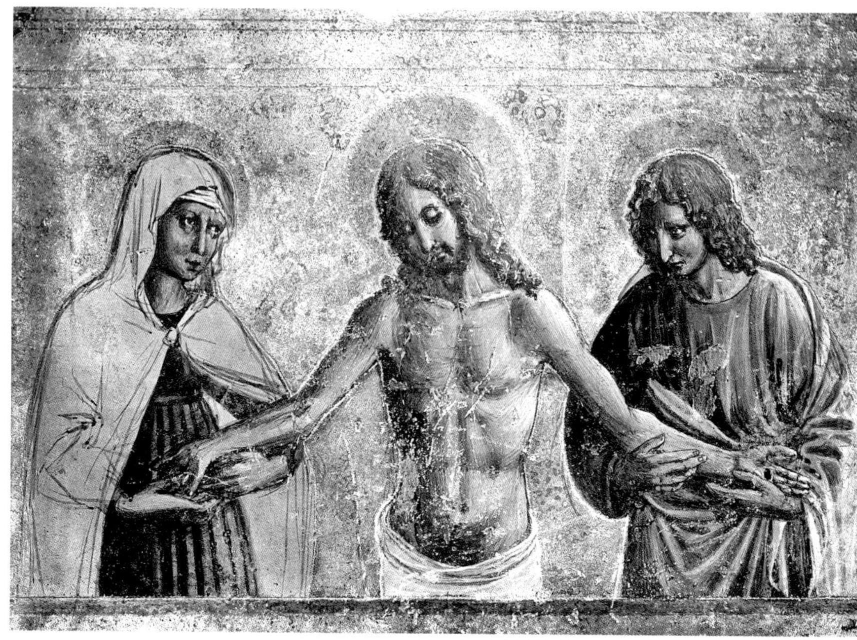

Figure 188. Benozzo Gozzoli. *Pietà*. 1452. San Francesco, Montefalco

Opinions on its dating, however, have diverged widely between those who have considered it a product of the artist's early career and others who have viewed it as a mature effort, possibly executed as late as 1466–67.[3] Following Anna Padoa Rizzo, most recent authors have concurred in assigning the painting to Benozzo's Florentine sojourn, between 1459 and 1463/64.[4] According to Cole Ahl, the image should be situated in close proximity to the 1461 altarpiece for the Compagnia della Purificazione, in San Marco; the same confraternity, the author argues, which may also have been responsible for commissioning the present work.

A careful examination of the Feigen *Crucifixion* next to the small predella scenes of the Purification altarpiece, or next to the Detroit *Virgin and Child* (cat. 60) included here and dated between 1462 and 1463/64, makes it very difficult to accept these works as the product of the same moment in the artist's development. The soft modeling and delicately proportioned figure types in the *Crucifixion*, and its naturalistic atmospheric effects, such as the rose-tinted, sunset sky above the distant landscape, are in marked contrast to the robust, incisively delineated forms, and the crystalline, almost metallic, surfaces, of Benozzo's Florentine paintings. Above all, the slender, loosely defined anatomy of Christ in the Feigen picture is incompatible with the more muscular, crisply drawn Christ of the Florentine works, and is, instead, more closely related to the artist's earliest models, such as the *Crucifixion*, formerly in a private collection in Paris, first discovered by Longhi,[5] or the *Pietà* below the frescoed altarpiece, dated 1452, in the apse of the church of San Francesco in Montefalco (fig. 188). Other points of comparison may be drawn between the Feigen *Crucifixion* and the small *Madonna and Child, with Saint Francis, Saint Bernardino, and a Donor,* in Vienna (Gemäldegalerie der Akademie der Bildenden Künste; Inv. 221), which is generally assigned to the same period as the Montefalco frescoes, between 1450 and 1452.[6] This last work shares with the *Crucifixion* the same distinctive low-keyed palette and twilit atmospheric effects, as well as the loose handling of the paint surface.

A date for the Feigen *Crucifixion* just before Gozzoli's activity in Montefalco is suggested by the close correspondence between the kneeling figures of Dominic and Jerome and those in Benozzo's fresco of *Saint Anthony of Padua* in the Albertoni Chapel in Santa Maria in Aracoeli, Rome. The stylistic relationship between this work and the *Crucifixion* was already noted by Van Marle, who, however, dated the fresco between 1453 and 1458.[7] It has subsequently been argued, on circumstantial evidence, that the decoration of the Albertoni Chapel was actually undertaken by Benozzo between 1446

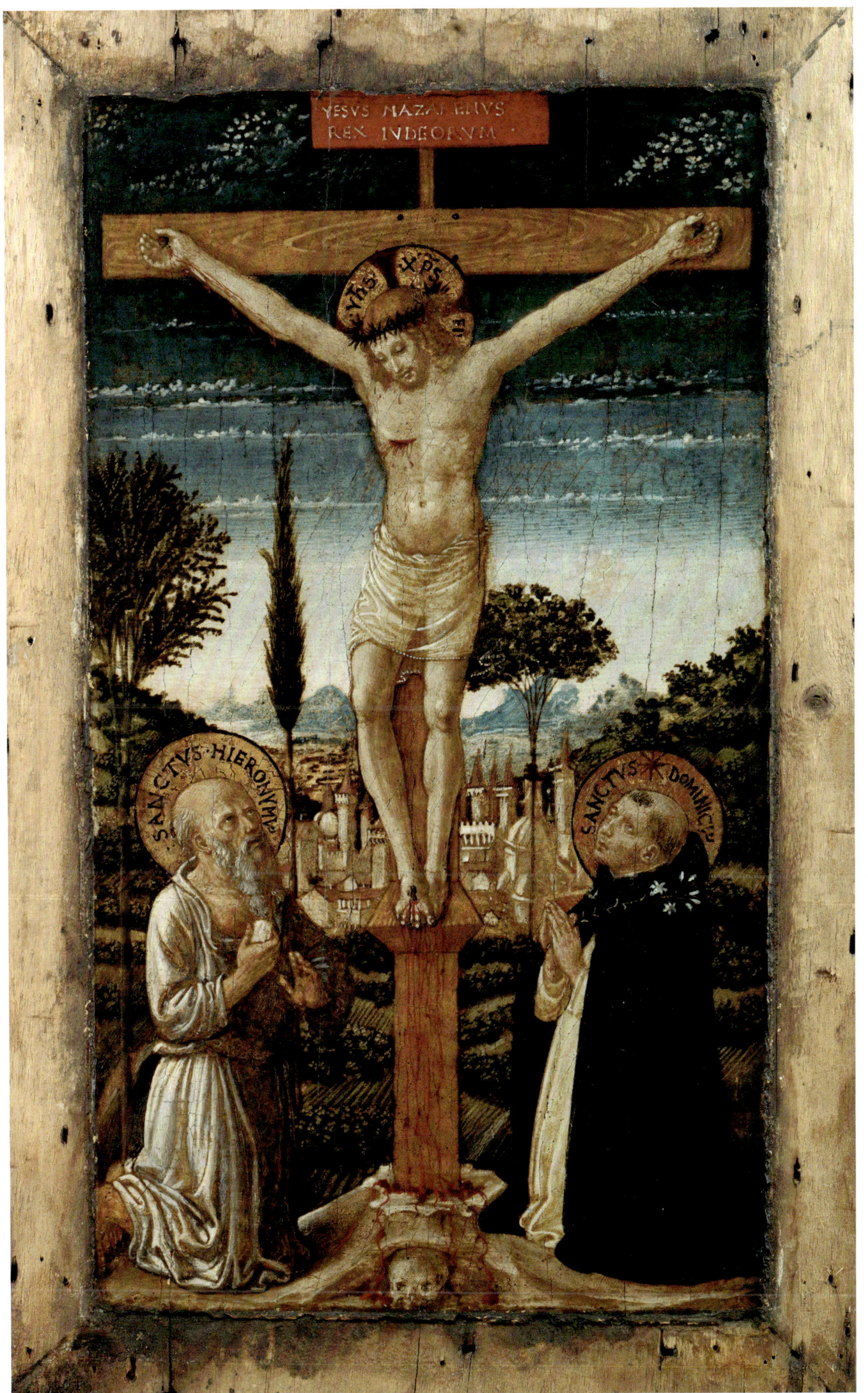

59

and 1449, during the years of his collaboration with Angelico in Rome and in Orvieto.[8] Typical of the artist's work at this date, and equally discernible in the Feigen *Crucifixion,* is the overall spontaneity of execution and the attention accorded to the characterization of the figures and the play of light on their hair and individual features.

As noted above, the view of Florence in the background suggests that this painting was a Florentine commission, perhaps awarded to the artist by someone affiliated with the popular Confraternity of Saint Jerome, whose earliest history is interwoven with that of the Dominican Observants of Fiesole. The confraternity, established in 1410, originally met in the Hieronymite monastery in the hills of Fiesole founded by the Florentine nobleman Carlo Guidi of Montegranelli in 1405 (see cat. 9). A strong supporter of Guidi's cause was the famous Dominican Giovanni Dominici, who later went on to found the Observant Convent in Fiesole on a site not far from that of the Hieronymites. The ties between the two institutions, both supported by the highest ranks of Florentine nobility, are reflected in the fact that in processions in Fiesole and in Florence the monks of the Monastery of Saint Jerome followed behind the processional cross of the Dominicans. Moreover, when, about 1412, the Confraternity of Saint Jerome moved into its final headquarters in the hospital of San Matteo in Florence, located across from the monastery of San Marco, it was a Dominican brother who was appointed to the official role of *correttore,* or spiritual guide, to its members.[9]

Gozzoli's relationship to Fra Angelico in the late 1440s, and his introduction into Dominican circles specifically affiliated with the Confraternity of Saint Jerome, may explain the circumstances leading to the commission for the Feigen *Crucifixion.* Although clear documentary evidence for the artist's presence in Florence during this period is lacking, there is no reason to preclude the possibility that he may have followed Angelico back to the city toward the end of 1448 or the beginning of 1449, executing this work before his final departure for Orvieto in the summer of 1449.[10]

PP

1. Boskovits and Brown 2003, pp. 569–70.
2. Richter 1901, no. 74, pp. 29–30.
3. Cole Ahl 1996, p. 223 (with earlier bibliography).
4. Padoa Rizzo 1992, p. 81; Acidini Luchinat 1994, p. 41; Cole Ahl 1996, p. 223; Boskovits and Brown 2003, p. 345 n. 14.
5. Longhi 1960a, pp. 3–7. See also M. Boskovits, in Toscano and Capitelli 2002, pp. 47–48.
6. M. Minardi, in Toscano and Capitelli 2002, pp. 208–11.
7. Van Marle 1929, pp. 142–43.
8. Cole Ahl 1996, pp. 251–52; M. Boskovits, in Toscano and Capitelli 2002, p. 46; B. Cirulli, in Toscano and Capitelli 2002, p. 230; Boskovits and Brown 2003, p. 344.
9. Ridderbos 1984, pp. 73–84; Artusi and Patruno 1994, pp. 189–92; Strehlke 2003b, pp. 8–9.
10. The first record of Benozzo's activity following his collaboration on the Cappella Niccolina is a document dated July 3, 1449, petitioning the Opera del Duomo in Orvieto to complete the Cappella Nova frescoes. The next document, dated July 12, 1449, is a reimbursement to the artist, from the Opera, "for two ounces of ultramarine blue brought from Florence." The possibility that Benozzo may have arrived in Orvieto from Florence is raised by S. Nessi (in Toscano and Capitelli 2002, p. 83), who, however, eventually dismisses this hypothesis in favor of the unlikely supposition that the artist, instead, made a quick trip to Florence between July 3 and 12, specifically to acquire the rare color. That Angelico may have been in Florence before the end of 1448 is suggested by a notation in the *Libro di Ricordanze* of San Marco, in which it is stated that "*frate Giovanni dipintore,*" prior of San Domenico, had provided appraisals for the value of the miniatures executed between September 20, 1448, and March 1449 by Zanobi Strozzi in a gradual for San Marco (Orlandi 1964, pp. 194–95; M. Scudieri, in Scudieri and Rasario 2003, pp. 173–77). According to the notation, Zanobi was to be paid five lire per miniature, based on Angelico's estimate. The same records show that payments were made to the artist in four installments, each at the appraised five-lire rate, beginning on November 13, 1448. This would seem to confirm that Angelico was in Florence at least by this date.

BENOZZO GOZZOLI

60. *Virgin and Child, with Seraphim and Cherubim*

Tempera and gold on panel, transferred to a new panel support, 65.4 x 50.5 cm (25¾ x 19⅞ in.)
The Detroit Institute of Arts (77.2)

This panel has often been rightly cited as among the best preserved and most striking images from Benozzo Gozzoli's maturity, reflecting to the fullest the artist's decorative sensibility and technical virtuosity. Dazzling in its coloristic effects, the painting reads as a carefully orchestrated harmony of alternating red, blue, and gold surfaces, made all the more vivid by meticulously painted highlights. The powerfully monumental figure of the standing Virgin, wearing a richly embroidered gold dress and a blue cloak lined with ermine, appears against a shimmering background of alternating red seraphim and blue cherubim, their wings stippled in gold and with gold highlights on their faces and hair. The Christ Child, dressed in a yellow tunic with blue highlights and a deep-red cloak, is being supported by his mother in a seated position; his right hand is raised in blessing and his left hand clasps a goldfinch, a symbol of the Passion. Increasing the visual impact of the image is the hard, incisive modeling of the figures and the draperies, as if chiseled in relief, and the intensely observed decorative details, such as the shiny row of pearls decorating the Virgin's dress or the delicately painted hairs of the ermine lining.

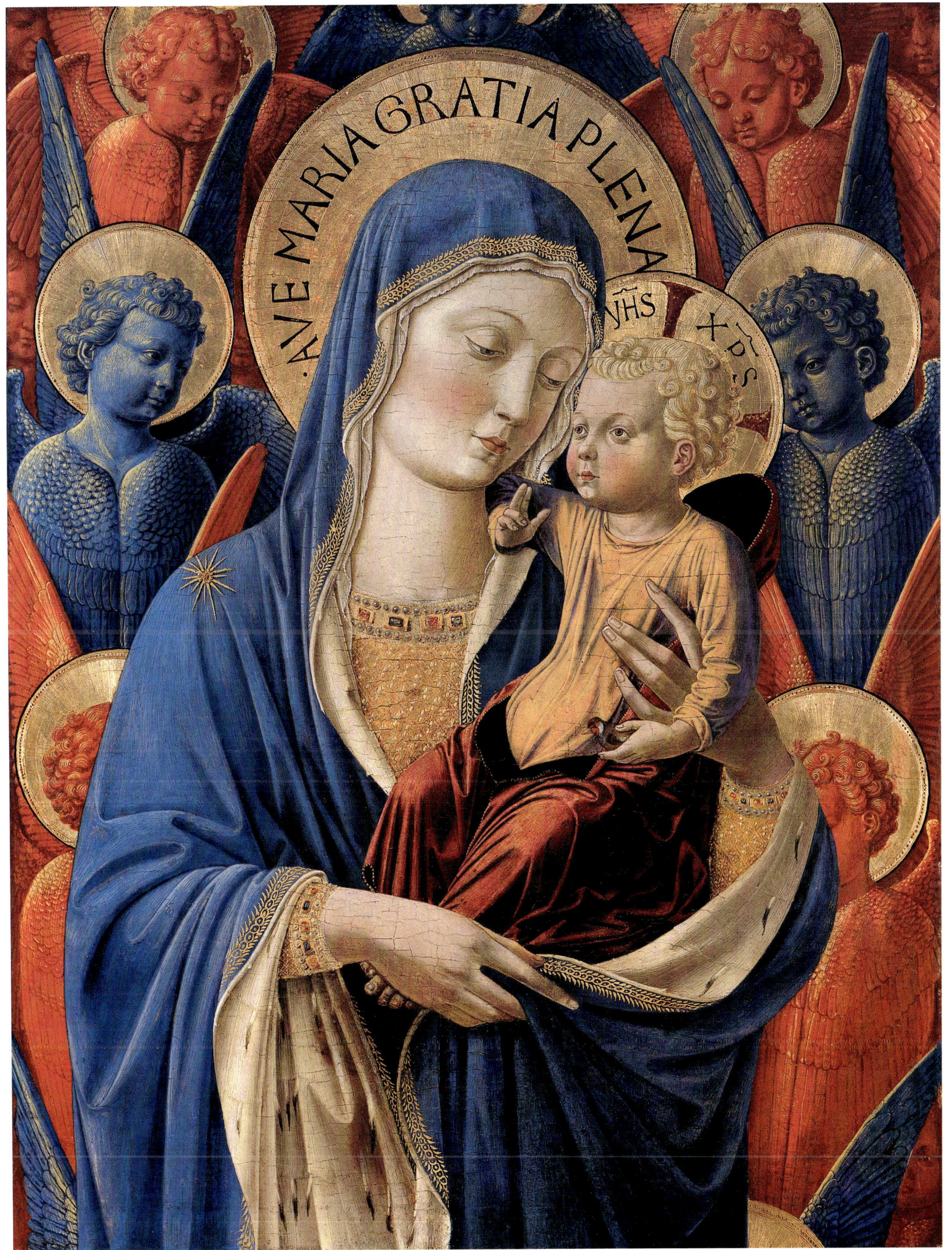

60

As indicated by the cropped wings and halos of the angels, the panel was reduced on all sides at an unknown date, suggesting—as recently noted by Cristina Acidini Luchinat—that the original painting may have been significantly larger and the Madonna possibly enclosed in a mandorla.[1] The picture was already in its present form in 1908, when Franz Wickhoff first published it as a work by Benozzo Gozzoli, listing it among those then in the collection of Baron H. von Tucher in Vienna.[2]

Although dated by Wickhoff to the artist's Pisan period, in the 1480s, and by Cole Ahl to his Umbrian period, between 1452 and 1456, the Detroit *Madonna* has been convincingly viewed by most scholars as a product of Benozzo's Florentine sojourn, from 1459 to 1464.[3] Within the parameter of these dates, however, opinions have varied regarding whether the painting was executed before or after the artist's activity in the Medici palace. Focusing on the high quality of the work, Acidini Luchinat advanced the interesting suggestion that the Detroit painting might have been made as a presentation piece for Cosimo de' Medici, leading to the commission to decorate the Chapel of the Magi. Citing the cluster of seraphim and cherubim surrounding the Virgin as an iconographic device inspired specifically by the example of Donatello in the Old Sacristy of San Lorenzo or in the design for the Duomo window with the Coronation of the Virgin, Acidini Luchinat viewed the Detroit picture as a conscious reelaboration by the artist of some of the most prestigious, groundbreaking examples of Florentine art that would have struck a particular chord with the older Medici.

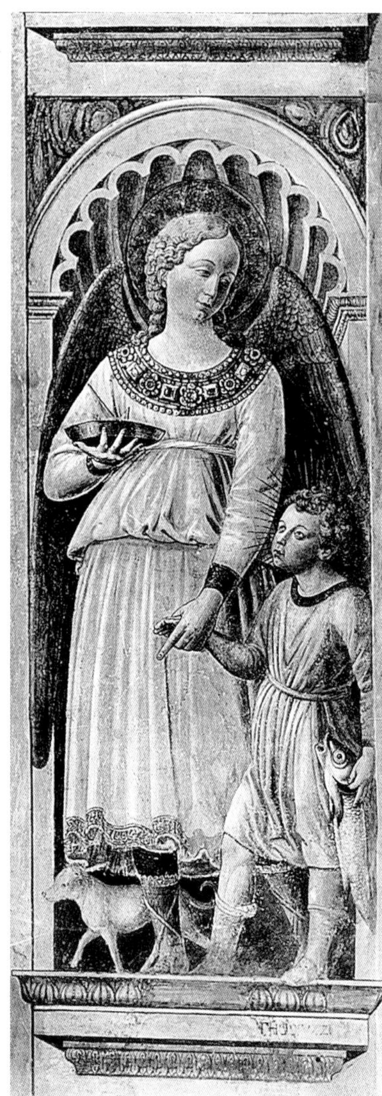

Figure 189. Benozzo Gozzoli. *The Archangel Raphael and Tobias*. 1464–65. Sant'Agostino, San Gimignano

While it is tempting to speculate on the possibility of Medici involvement in the commissioning of the Detroit *Madonna*, stylistic evidence supports a date for its execution following the Chapel of the Magi frescoes and, as first proposed by Pope-Hennessy and most recently by Rosaria Mencarelli and Marco Bussagli,[4] in close proximity to the Altarpiece of the Purification (fig. 185) in the National Gallery, London. Completed between 1461 and 1462 for the Compagnia della Purificazione in San Marco, this ambitious, large-scale complex was the second most important Florentine commission entrusted to Benozzo after the Medici Chapel. It is here that one finds the nearest equivalent not only for the bright palette and robust, incisively modeled figures of the Detroit picture but also for the exceptionally refined handling of the paint and the glistening quality of the intensely lit, plastically rendered surfaces. Although Pope-Hennessy dated the Detroit panel about 1460, further comparisons with the artist's later, documented production suggest that it may be possible to advance the period of its execution into the last years of Benozzo's Florentine stay, preceding his departure for San Gimignano in 1463–64. The relief-like, stony monumentality of the Detroit *Virgin and Child* and its obsessively described decorative details foreshadow, in fact, the salient qualities of the artist's San Gimignano frescoes. The rounded proportions of the Virgin anticipate the powerful female figures painted by Benozzo between 1464 and 1465 in the choir of the church of Sant'Agostino, and the stunning border of precious stones along the neckline of her dress is but a reduced version of the identical ornamentation prominently displayed on the tunic of the archangel Raphael in the same cycle (fig. 189). The almost dizzying, tapestry-like arrangement of seraphim and cherubim behind and around the Virgin, moreover, would appear to look forward to the decorative solutions adopted by the artist in the 1466 fresco of *Saint Sebastian* in the Collegiata in San Gimignano, where a similar, heavenly niche is provided for the bust-length figures of Christ and the Virgin.

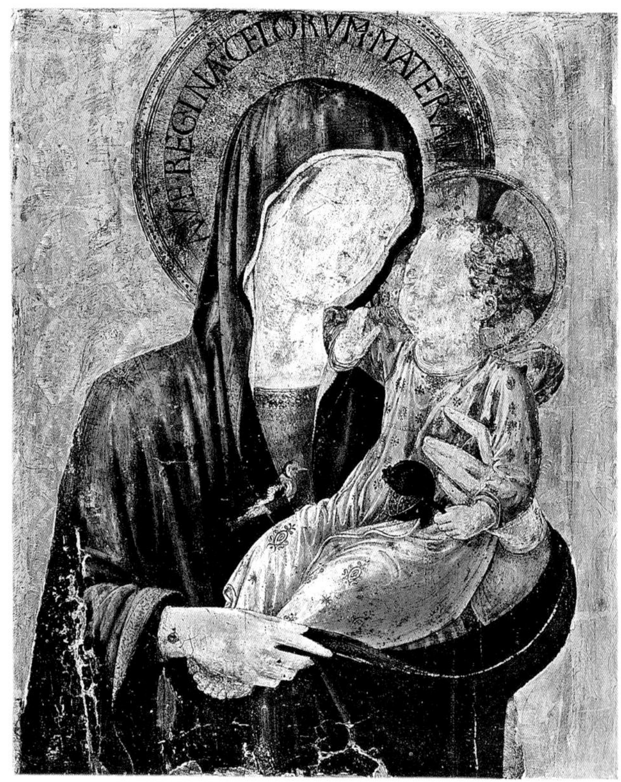

Figure 190. Benozzo Gozzoli. *Virgin and Child*. Fogg Art Museum, Harvard University Art Museums, Cambridge, Massachusetts

The circumstances of the commissioning of the present picture may never be known, but the presence of a second, much-damaged version, in the Fogg Art Museum in Cambridge, Massachusetts (fig. 190), would seem to suggest that it was a work of some importance.[5] Coincidentally, this second painting was also owned by Baron von Tucher, and before entering the Fogg museum in 1907 its appearance was identical to that of the Detroit picture in every detail except for its engraved gold background and the pomegranate held by the Christ Child. Restorations undertaken in 1922 revealed, however, that the work had been extensively repainted and that the gilt background was entirely modern. Although difficult to evaluate in its present state, the Fogg painting is still regarded by most scholars as closely related to the Detroit panel, and is attributed to the hand of Benozzo, working over the same cartoon.[6]

While the Fogg picture would seem to conform, in both format and iconography, to standard images of the Madonna and Child for private devotion, the fragmentary nature of the Detroit panel raises some questions as to its original function. Acidini Luchinat's hypothesis that the pattern of cherubim and seraphim formed a mandorla around the Virgin would imply that the panel was once much taller and could possibly have been the center of an altarpiece. While images of the Virgin in a mandorla are usually associated with the Assumption, a fourteenth-century panel attributed to the Florentine painter Puccio di Simone and presumed to have been the center of a larger structure indicates the existence of another, less common iconographic type of the standing Virgin and Child "in glory" surrounded by a heavenly entourage of seraphim and angels.[7] Equally relevant, however, is a comparison of the Detroit panel in its present form with several variants of the same iconographic type produced in the workshops of later Umbrian painters, such as Antonio da Viterbo and other followers of Pinturicchio and of Perugino.[8] Reduced versions of fully developed compositions of the *Assumption,* these paintings show the standing Madonna in three-quarter length, with the blessing Child in her arms, in an almost completed mandorla of cherubim heads. Whether or not they were originally included in larger complexes, such images may point to the existence of an Umbrian prototype for the Detroit *Madonna,* reinterpreted by Benozzo through his experience of Donatello's example.

PP

1. C. Acidini Luchinat, in Toscano and Capitelli 2002, p. 110.
2. Wickhoff 1908, p. 22. The painting, which was in the Ford collection in Detroit in 1932, was bequeathed to The Detroit Institute of Arts in 1977. By that date it had already been transferred from its original poplar support to a new panel. According to notes by the restorer who made the transfer in 1956 (kindly communicated to me by Serena Urry), the original panel was composed of two vertical members, with the joint 2½ to 3 inches from the left edge. The back was covered with a thin layer of gesso. X-radiographs of the painted surface after its transfer appear to show flaking along all four edges, possibly confirming that the panel had, indeed, been reduced on all sides.
3. Cole Ahl 1996, pp. 214–15 (with earlier bibliography).
4. Pope-Hennessy 1979, pp. 18–19; R. Mencarelli, in Garibaldi 1998, p. 78; M. Bussagli, in Toscano and Capitelli 2002, p. 253.
5. Cole Ahl 1996, pp. 210–11.
6. Despite D. Cole Ahl's effort to date the painting "in the early to mid-1450s," its present condition makes any judgment of dating or quality highly questionable.
7. Offner/Boskovits 2001, pp. 442–45.
8. For these works, see F. Todini (1989, vol. I, pp. 258–59, vol. II, figures 1241–1243, 1252), who describes them as typical of the many versions of the Madonna and Child in a mandorla of seraphim by Umbro-Roman followers of Pinturicchio and of Perugino.

BENOZZO GOZZOLI

61.
The Adoration of the Christ Child

Tempera on panel, 50.8 x 33 cm (20 x 13 in.)
Collection Richard L. Feigen, New York

This panel, whose early provenance is unknown, first appeared on the art market in 2001 with an attribution to Benozzo Gozzoli's youngest son and later collaborator, Alesso di Benozzo.[1] It was subsequently reassigned to Benozzo Gozzoli by Laurence Kanter, followed by Diane Cole Ahl, who published it as a product of the artist's last years, about 1495.[2]

In both format and iconography the painting is typical of a type of devotional image of the Virgin in Adoration that was developed in Florence and throughout Tuscany by Filippo Lippi and his followers, beginning in the second half of the fifteenth century. The subject itself was derived from the Brigittine vision of the Nativity popularized in the previous century, which described the birth of Christ in terms of his sudden appearance on the ground, naked and enveloped in a glow of light, before the Virgin kneeling in prayer. In the course of the fourteenth century, and into the fifteenth, as reflected by Angelico's own work (see cat. 17, 27A), this version of the event often replaced traditional Nativity scenes with the Child in a manger, emphasizing the mystical quality of the birth. The theme was further developed by Filippo Lippi in the *Adoration* painted about 1459 for the altar of the Medici Chapel (now in the Gemäldegalerie, Berlin), situated below Gozzoli's frescoes. This work, which transferred the focus of the composition to the Virgin worshiping the Child, became the prototype for countless versions of the subject made for private devotion by artists in Lippi's immediate circle, such as the Master of the Castello Nativity, and in the workshops of a later generation of Florentine painters such as the Master of the Johnson Nativity.[3] In these images, which provide the closest prototype for the composition of the Feigen *Adoration,* the vertical compositional format is taken up almost entirely by the figure of the Virgin, with the Child lying naked on the hem of her dress. Directed at the Child from the sky are a series of divine rays, symbolic of God's intervention; in the present case, these are replaced by a single dotted white line emanating from a tiny star, only partially visible above the roof of the shed. Whereas many versions omit the figure of Joseph altogether, some, as here, still include him in the background along with other traditional components of Nativity scenes such as the ass and the ox, the shed, and the shepherd in the distance.

Stylistically, the Feigen *Adoration* may be compared with works by Benozzo from the last decade of his activity, following the frescoes in the Camposanto in Pisa, completed in 1484, and leading up to his death in Pistoia in 1497. While the obliquely foreshortened roof at the entrance to a cave most resembles that found in the Pisan fresco of the *Adoration of the Magi,* the massively proportioned figure types and loose compositional structure find their nearest equivalent in the 1491 tabernacle of the *Visitation* in Castelfiorentino. At the same time, the thinly applied, dry brushstrokes, and muted earth tones with white highlights, recall the two extraordinary canvases painted by the artist at the end of his life, perhaps for the Bishop's Palace in Pistoia, and now divided between the National Gallery of Art in Washington, D.C., and the Museo Horne in Florence.

Although these works are normally catalogued as by Benozzo, it is generally recognized that evaluation of the artist's output during this last phase of his activity must take into account the intervention of assistants in what must have become by this date a large workshop, as well as the documented collaboration of his two sons, Francesco (b. 1469) and Alesso (1473–1528). Confirming the visual evidence of a disparity in execution among the various parts of the Castelfiorentino frescoes, Anna Padoa Rizzo first published a seventeeth-century source recording the existence of a now-lost inscription around the scene of the *Visitation,* with the names of Benozzo and his two sons, along with the date 1491.[4] Based on this evidence, Padoa Rizzo proceeded to credit Alesso as the author of specific passages in these frescoes—most notably, that of the standing angel above the *Visitation,* which, in turn, she convincingly related to a stylistically homogeneous group of works formerly assembled by scholars under the name "Maestro Esiguo" or "Alunno di Benozzo"; she then proposed that they all be viewed as independent products of Alesso's activity.[5] Following Padoa Rizzo's studies, most authors have gone on to identify Alesso's involvement, and to a lesser extent that of his brother, in the Washington and Horne paintings.[6]

While considering the possibility of workshop participation in the execution of the present panel, it should be stated that the solid, rounded proportions of the Virgin are inconsistent with the elongated, gracile figures with sharp, pointed features that distinguish Alesso's hand in the Castelfiorentino *Visitation* or in the body of works ascribed to Alesso / "Alunno di Benozzo," precluding an attribution to that artist. The shadowy figure of Alesso's older brother, Francesco, is more difficult to isolate. The vocabulary of the present painting, however, appears compatible with the evolution of Benozzo's own stylistic idiom from the San Gimignano frescoes, suggesting that the intervention of another hand in its execution is unlikely.

PP

1. Sold, Sotheby's, London, July 12, 2001, lot 60.
2. Laurence Kanter (verbal opinion, recorded in the Feigen files); D. Cole Ahl, in Toscano and Capitelli 2002, p. 187. On the back of the painting is an inscription indicating that, at an unspecified date, it was on the French art market with an attribution to Benozzo: "Benozzo Gozzoli 1446 / no. 135 École Lombard. Fin du XV siècle / Vaux 200 fcs."
3. For these two artists, see Strehlke 2004, pp. 121–23, 271–75 (with earlier bibliography).
4. A. Padoa Rizzo, in Proto Pisani and Padoa Rizzo 1987, p. 22.
5. Padoa Rizzo 1989, pp. 22–25.
6. A. Padoa Rizzo and A. Bernacchioni, in Gregori et al. 1992, pp. 94–95, 116–17; Cole Ahl 1996, pp. 195–99; N. Pons, in Padoa Rizzo 1997a, pp. 156–57. M. Boskovits (in Boskovits and Brown 2003, pp. 352–54) appears to be the only author to categorically deny the intervention of assistants in the Washington *Raising of Lazarus.*

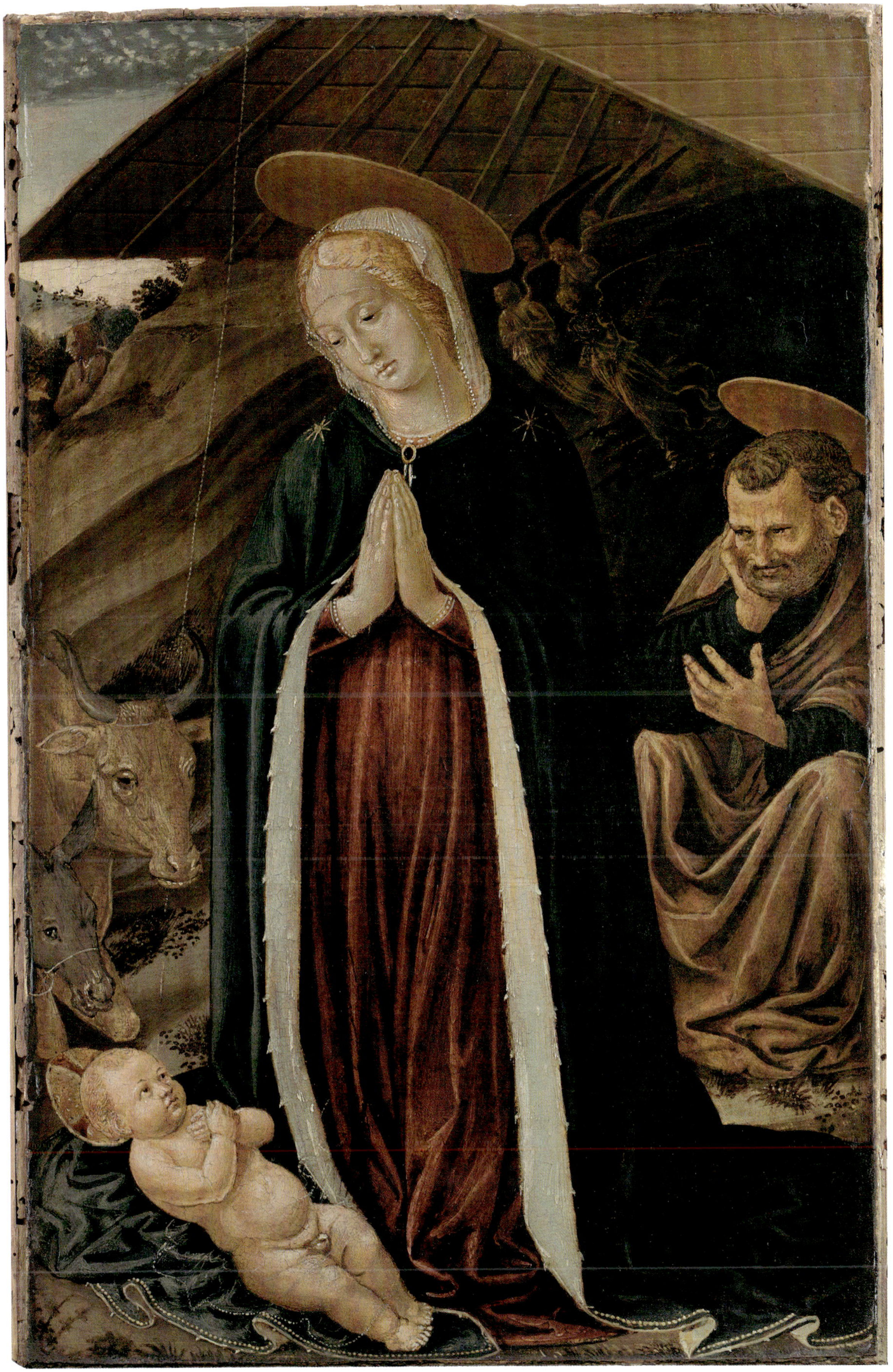

61

Appendix

"Itinerary of Petrus de Cruce" (see cat. 5 A)

[rub.] *Infrascripte sunt peregrinationes totius terre sancte que a / modernis peregrinis visitantur. Et est sciendum quod in / illis locis in quibus est signum crucis ibi est indulgen / tia a pena et a culpa. In aliis vero locis in quibus non est signum / crucis sunt VII. annorum. et VII. Quadragenarum dierum de in/dulgentia. Predicte autem indulgentie concesse fuerunt a/sancto Silvestro papa ad preces sancti et magni Constantini imperatoris / et sancte Helene matris eius. / Primo peregrinationes Jopen usque / Jerusalem.* / In civitate Jopen idest Jaffa et locus ut sanctus Petrus a/postolus resuscitavit Thabitam servitricem appostolorum. Et ibi / prope est locus in quo sanctus Petrus stabat ad piscandum. / Item civitas Lidie in qua est eccelsia sancti Georgii ubi ipse fuit / decollatus. Et etiam ibi locus in quo sanctus Petrus sanavit / Eneam paraliticum. Item civitatis Ramula. Item castrum Emaus / in quo est ecclesia ubi duo discipuli cognoverunt Christum in fractione / panis. Est etiam ibi sepulchrum Cleophe qui fuit unus de duobus / discipulis. Item civitas Ramatha in qua natus fuit sanctus Io/seph qui Christum deposuit de cruce. Item ecclesia et sepulchrum Samu / elis prophete. Item Cesarea Philippi in qua Christum interogabat discipulos / suos dicens "Quid dicunt homines est Filium hominis." [rub.] *Iste sunt peregrinationes ci/vitatis sancta Ierusalem. /* In primis introitu civitatis porte Ierusalem et in/dulgentia a pena et a culpa + Item introitu ecclesie / sancti Sepulchri oriti + Item modicum infra ecclesiam est lapis / nigri coloris supra que Yhesus Christus fuit unctus et aromatizatus / postquam fuit depositus de cruce + Item in sacro loco montis Calvarie ubi Christus fuit crucifixus et mortuus + Item / in sepulchro Domini Nostri Yhesu Christi filii dei vivi + Item sub Monte Calvarie est capella ubi fuit inuentum caput Ade. / Item iuxta Montem Calvarie est columna supra quam Christus fuit co/ronatus et consputus. Item ubi sancta Crux fuit inventa et / etiam due cruces latronii et clavi Christi + Item capella sancte / Helene matris illustrissimi Constantini imperatoris. Item alia / capella ubi milites miserunt fortem supra vestimenta Christi. / Item quam locus que dicitur Carcer Christi. Item alius ubi Christus apparuit beate Marie Magdalene in die Resurrectionis in forma / ortolani. Item capella in qua est columna alia ad quam Christus fu/it ligatus, flagellatus, collaficatus, et in facie consputus. / Item una parva capella propre seu iuxta ad honorem Magdalene. / Item locus ubi beata Virgo Maria Mater Dei et sanctus Iohannes Evangelista / stabant tempore passionis Christi. [rub.] *Omnia suprascripta loca contineritum in / ecclesiam Sancti Sepulchrum. Infrascripta vero sunt extra ecclesiam.* / In primis sunt quatuorum capelle quarum prima est Virginis Marie et beati Iohannis Evan/geliste. Secunda est sancti Michaelis et Angelorum. Tertia est sancti Iohannis Baptiste. / Quarta est sancte Marie Magdalene. Item in medio platee ante portam sepulchri Domini Nostri est lapis ubi Christus requievit paululum baiularis crucem / in sanctissimis humeris + item schola Virginis Marie matris Dei. / Item locus quem dicitur Licostratos ubi sedit pro tribunali Pilatus qui iudica/vit Christum ad mortem. Item domus Pilati in qua Christus fuit ligatus et flage/llatus et de spinis coronatus + Item domus Anne que fuit soces Cayphe ubi / servus pontificis dedit alapam Iesu dicens "Sic respondes pontifici." / Item domus Herodis ubi Christus fuit inductus veste alba et eum Herodes / sputavit cum exercitu suo et remisit ad Pilatum. Item domus Cayphe qui erat princeps sacerdotum ubi Christus fuit facie vellatus, consputus, co/laphyzatus, et tota nocte vexatus. Item domus Symonis leprosi ubi / Christus remisit Marie Magdalene peccata sua dicens "Remittuntur tibi / peccata multa quia dilexisti multum." Item ecclesia seu domus beate Anne in qua fuit nata beata Virgo Maria + Item probatica piscina ubi Christus / sanavit languidum triginta octo annos gentem in infirmitate sua. / Item in muro civitatis sancte Ierusalem sunt porte auree per quas Dominus / intravit in ramis palmarum sedendo supra asinam. Item est templum / Domini in quo beata Virgo Maria presentavit filium suum et Symeon ac/cepit eum in ulnas suas et benedixit Deum et dixit "Nunc di/mittis Domine servus tuum in pace" + Item in torrente Cedron est locus / ubi sanctus Stephanus fuit lapidatus. Item est vallis Iosephat / ubi erit generale iudicium. Et in medio vallis est sepulchrum / beate Marie Virgine + [rub.] *Iste sunt peregrinationes Vallis Iosephat.* / Item est locus in quo sanctus Stephani fuit lapidatus. Item torrens / Cedron de quo legitur in Vangelio et dicitur quo lignum sancte cru/cis stetit ibi pro ponte per multa tempora. Item locus in quo Christus / ter oravit ad patrem. [rub.] *Peregrinationes montis Oliveti.* / In monte Oliveti est ortus ubi Christus fuit captus et ligatus. / Item locus ubi Christus duxit tres apostolos dicens eis "Sed/ete hic donec vadam illuc et orem." / Item est locus ubi sanctus / Petrus abscidit auriculam Malchi Servi Pontificis. Item locus / ubi sanctus Thomas recepit zonam a Virginie Maria ascendente / in celum. Item locus ubi Christus conflevit supra civitatem. Item locus / ubi angelus presentavit palmam Virgini Marie dicens ei " Tali / die eris assumpta in celum cum filio tuo." Item locus que dicitur / Gallilea ubi Christus apparuit undecim apostolis. Item ecclesia et locus / de quo Christus ascendit in celum. Item ecclesia et sepulchrum sancte / Pelagie. Item locus que dixit Bethpage. Item ecclesia sancti Marci / Evangeliste in qua apostolis composuerunt Credo. Item ecclesia in qua / Christus docuit apostolos orare dicens "Pater Noster." Item locus ubi vir/go Maria sedit fatigada, visitando omni die loca ista sancta. / Item ecclesia Icobi Minoris in qua Christus sibi apparuit in / die Pasce. Et in ipsa sancti postmodus fuit ille sepultus. Et ibi est etiam / sepulchrum propheta quondam nomine Zacharias. [rub.] *Peregrinationes vallis Syloe.* / In vallis Siloe est fons in qua beata Virgo Maria lavit paniculos / Yhesu Christi quando ipsum presentavit in templum. / Item fons Siloe in / quo cecus fuit illuminatus. Item locus ubi fuit sectus ab Iudeis / Ysayas propheta et ibi prope est sepulchrum eius. Item grota ubi absconde/runt se apostoli quando Christus fuit captus in orto. / Item campus sanctus / qui emptus triginta argenteis. [rub.] *Peregrinationes sacri montis Syon.* / In monte Syon est locus ubi Iudei rapere voluerunt corpus / Beate Virginis quando ab apostolis portabatur ad sepulchrum. Item locus / ubi sanctus Petrus flevit amare denegationem Christi. Item ecclesia / Sancti Angeli ipsa est domus Anne Pontificis ad quam Christus primo fuit exa/minatus et a lapis cesus. Item ecclesia Sancti Salvatoris; ipsa est domus / Cayphe Pontificis ad quam Christus fuit contemptus examinatus, spu/to sedatus, velatus et in capite percussus, et a Petro ter negatus. / Item ecclesia sancte Marie in qua est locus ubi ipsa stetit per quattordecim an/nos post Ascensionem Christi filii sui et inter modicum ibidem / migravit de hoc seculo + Item locus ubi beatus Johannes Evangeli/sta dicebat missam beate Marie Virgini. Item locus ubi sanctus Ma/thias fuit electus in ordine apostolorum. Item oratorium Virginis Marie / in quo stabat in oratione ante ecclesiam vel cenaculum. Item locus / ubi fuit sepultus secunda vice sanctus Stephanus cum Gama/liele et Abibon. Item locus ubi Christus aliquando predicabat po/pulis. Item locus ubi beata Virgo Maria sedebat in predicatione / filii sui. Item sepulchrum David, Solomonis et aliorum regum. Item / locus ubi fuit assatus agnus pascalis. Item cenaculum ubi Christus / comedit cum discipulis agnum pascalem et instituit altissimum sacra/mentum sui Corporis et Sanguinis + Item locus ubi Christus lavit pe/des discipulorum. Item in die Ascentionis exprobravit incredulita/tem eorum et duritiam cordis. Item locus ut apostoli receperunt spiritum / sanctum in die Pentecostes + Item locus ubi Christus apparuit sancto Thome / et apostolis clausis ianuis. Item locus ubi fuit decollatus sanctus / Iacobus Maior. Item locus ubi Christus apparuit tribus Mariis in die pa/sce dicens eis "Ave te." Item iuxta montem est locus ut Abraam vo/luit ymolare filium suum Ysaach domino. [rub.] *Peregrinationes Bethleem /* Primo ubi hospitati fuerunt tres magi. Item / ubi stella reapparuit tribus magis. Item ecclesia ubi natus fuit Helias propheta. Item sepulchrum Rachelis. Item ecclesia vir/ginis Marie in qua est locus ubi Yhesus Christus est natus + Item pre/sepui domini + item locus ubi puer Yhesus fuit circumcisus + / Item locus ubi stella disparuit magis. / Idem capella sancti Iero/nimi. Item sepulchrum eiusdem. Item capella sanctorum Innocentium et / sepulchrum eorum. Item ecclesia sancte Marie Virginis in qua an/gelus docuit sibi et Joseph viam Egipti. Item ecclesia angelorum / in qua angelus dixit pastoribus Christi nativitatem. Item ecclesia / sive sepulchrum duodecimo prophetarum. Item monasterium sancti Sabbe abbatis / [rub.] *Peregrinationes Bethanie.* / In Bethania est / sepulchrum sancti Lazari de quo Christus eum vocavit + Item / domus Symonis Leprosi in qua Maria Magdalena fracto / alabastro unxit pedes Yhesu et impleta est domus ex odore unguenti. / Item locus ubi Martha dixit Christo "Domine si fuisses hic frater meus non fuisset mor/tuus." Item domus Marthe. Item domus Marie Magdalene in qua ipsa tunc stabat quando Martha dixit ei "Magister adest et vocat te." [rub.] *Peregrinationes fluminis Iordanis.* / Primo monasterium / sancti Joachim patris Virginis Marie. Item Mons Quarantene radix / in quo Christus ieiunavit quadraginta diebus + Item in sumitate istius / montis est locus ubi diabolus portavit Christum dicens "Hic omnia tibi da/bo si cadens" etcetera. Item civitas Jericho in qua Christus fuit hospitatus / in domo Zacharie. / Item ubi Christus illuminavit cecum. / Item monaste/rium sancti Johannis Baptiste. Item flumen Iordanus + Item / monasterium sancti Ieronimi in vasta solitudine. Item Mare Mor/tuum in quo submerse fuerunt quinque civitates. Item ultra flumen / Iordanum est desertum Marie Egiptiache ubi ipsa fecis penitentiam. / [rub.] *Peregrinationes in montana Iudee* / In montana Iudee est monasterium Sancte Crucis in quo crevit / unum de lignis sancte crucis. Item domus Symeonis qui Christum recepit in ulnis qundo fuit presentatus in templo. Item ecclesia sancti Io/hanis Baptiste in qua Virgo Maria salutavit Elisabeth et dixit / "Magnificat anima mea dominum." Item locus ubi sanctus Johannes Baptista fu/it natus. Item domus Zacharie in qua accepit pugilarem etcetera / et dixit "Benedictus Dominus Deus Israel." [rub.] *Peregrinationes vallis Mambre.* / In valle Mambre est locus ubi Habraam tres vidit et unum ado/ravit. Item civitas Ebron in qua sepulti sunt Adam, Habra/am, Ysaach et Jacob et uxores eorum. Item locus ubi Adam fuit forma/tus. Item desertum in quo sanctus Johannes Baptista fecit penitentiam. [In the margins] [rub.] *Pere/grinationes Na/zareth* / Primo ubi fuit sepultus prima vice sanctus Stephanus. / Item Abbreiam castrum in quo est ecclesia in qua Beata Virgo Maria recognovit perdidisse filium suum puerum Yhesum. / Item Puteus samaritane. Item civitas Napulosa vel Sichar in qua sepulta sunt ossa Joseph qui fuit venditus in Egyptum. / Item civitas Sebastem in qua fuit incarceratus et decollatus sanctus Jo/hannes Baptista. Item castrum Iehennym in quo Christus mundavit / decem leprosos. Item in civitate Naym Christus resuscitavit a mor/tuis filium vidue. Item in Nazareth est ecclesia in qua Virgo Maria / fuit ab angelo salutata + Item fons de quo puer Yhesus porta/bat aquam matri sue. Item locus ubi Iudei voluerunt precipi/tare Yhesum. Yhesus autem transiens per medium illorum ibat. Item mons / Thabor in quo Christus fuit transfiguratus + Item civitas Caphar/naum in qua Christus fecit multa miracula. Item mare Galilee in quo / Christus fecit multa signa. Item in civitate Tyberiadis est locus ubi / Christus vocavit Matheum a Thelonio. Item locus ubi Christus resusci/tavit a morte filiam Archisinagogi. Item locus ubi Christus come / dit cum Matheo. Item mons in quo Christus satiavit quinque milia hominum / de quinque panibus. Item alius mons in quo Christus satiavit quattor millia / hominum de septem panibus. Item civitas Sydon in qua mulier dixit Christo "Beatus / venter qui te portavit" / Item civitas in qua Christus sanavit filiam / Cananee etcetera. Sunt et alia loca que non visitantur. [rub.] *Peregrinationes Damasci* / Prope Damascus est locus ubi Christus dixit sancto Paulo "Saule Sau/le cur me persequeris." Item in muro Damasci est adhuc / fenestra per quam sanctus Paulus exivit. Item infra civitatem / est domus in qua sanctus Paulus fuit baptizatus. Item domus / Ananie Christi discipuli que dictum Paulum recepit et baptizavit. / [rub.] *Peregrinationes Monty / Synay* / Primo civitas Gazara in qua sanctus Samson fuit mortu/us. Item in monte Synay est monasterium sive ecclesia / sancte Marie de Rubo in qua requiescit corpus sancte Katerine / virginis. Item post tribunam istius ecclesia est locus ubi Deus appa/ruit Moysy in medio rubi. Item in medio montis est locus ubi / Helias fecis penitentiam. Item in sumitate montis Deus de/dit tabulas legis Moysy. + Item viridarium in quo est locus / ubi sanctus Honofrius fecit penitentiam. Item alius mons sancte Katerine / in cuius sumitate angeli posuerunt corpus eiusdem virginis. Item / Mare Rubrum. [rub.] *Peregrinationes terre Egipti* / In civitate Massare vel Alchaire sunt multe ecclesie christianorum / inter quas est ecclesia sancte Marie de Columpna in qua est corpus / sancte Barbare. Item quattor flumina ultra civitatem hanc in Caldea que / egrediuntur de Paradiso Terrestri. Videlicet, Eufrates, Nilo, Gior., et Tigris. / Item in orto soldani est vinea balsami et in eo sunt diversa animalia / videlicet dromedarii, cucudrili, patami, camelli, et multa alia. Item / monasterium sanctorum Antonii monachi et Pauli primi here/mite et alia multa. Item prope civitate sunt hornea Ioseph, que / fecit tempore famis. Item a predicta civitate Massare per tres / dies in terra Egipti est quedam patria nomine Mepheluto in qua / est monasterium Iacobitarum nomine El Marach, ubi est capella in qua beata virgo Maria stetit per septem annos cum filio suo / Yhesus, et Ioseph. Et celebratur ibidem festum ad omnibus Christianis terra / Egipti in die ramis palmarum. Item ultra flumina predicta ex al/tera parte est maxima turrem Babel ubi facta est con [. . .]linguarum, etcetera. / Ex altera parte sunt montes Armenie in quibus requievit archa Noe / tempore diluviis. Item in civitate Alexandrie est locus in quo sancta / Katerina fuit decollata. Item ubi defunctus est sanctus Iohannes Ele/mosinarum et Patriarcha. / Item locus ubi fuit martirizatus sanctus / Marchus Evangelista, et postea ibidem sepultus. /

[rub.] *Expliciunt peregrinationes terre sanctae.*

In primis in insula cipri crucem sanctam que pendet miraculose in / aere in quondam monte ubi habitant viri religiosi. Item corpus sancti / Barnabe. Item in insula Pathmos est locus ubi stetit Iohannes Evangelista / et ubi sepultus est. Item in Rodo in ecclesia sancti Iohannis in qua sunt relique / sanctorum innumerabiles vidi digitum sancti Iohannis Baptiste / cum quo ostendit Christum / dicens "Ecce agnus Dei." Item in insula Crete corpus beati Titi discipuli beati Pau/li apostoli. Item in civitate Candie corpus beati Alexandri Archiepiscopi ordinis pre/dicatorum. Item Mothone corpus beati Leonis. Item in Corphu ecclesiam / sancte Marie de Casopoli ubi cotidie coruscat miraculis. Item in / provincia Dalmatie in Ragusi corpus sancti Blasii. Item in Spalato corpus / sancti Donini. Item in Traguno corpus sancti Augustini ordinis predicatorum. / Item in Iadra corpus sancti Prati et corpi sancti Symeonis et sancti Grisogoni et / sancte Anastasie. Item in Nona corpus sancti Anselmi. Item in Arbe corpus sancte Tecle. Item / in Ytalia in civitate Rovignio corpus sancte Eufemie. Item Iustino corpora sanctorum Mauri /et Basilii. Item in Trieste corpus sancti Iusti. / Item in Aquileia corpus sancti Hermacore di/scipuli sancti Marci Evangeliste et corpus sancti Raimundi Regis cuius sepulchrum est elevatum a terra, / et corpus sancte Doratee et allia quam plura corpora sanctorum. Item Utini corpora sancti Beltrami et sancti / Duvici. Item in Fusio corpora sancti Librari et sancte Tabite. In Venetia corpora sanctorum et sanctarum Marci, Desideri, Viti, Lucie, Marine, Cristine, Barbare, Maximi, / et costam Christofori, et inter sui pluries indulgentis in Ascensione Domini.+ Item Pa/due corpora sanctorum hic infrascripta, Mathie, Lucie, Prosdocimi, Antonii ordinis minorum, Iu/stine et alias plures reliquias. In Vicentia corpora sanctorum Cosme e Damia/ni. In Verona corpora sancti Zini et multa alia. In Mantua corpus sancti Longi/ni. In Mutina corpus sancti Geminiani. In Regio corpora sanctorum Grisanti, Prosperi / et Darie. In Parma corpus sancti Orlandini. In Bononia corpus beatissimi / patris Dominici fundatoris ordinis predicatorum cuius pretioso capiti largitus fui / unam crucem pretii viginti ducati in qua est lignum crucis et reliquie beate Lucie / et sancti Christofori. Item in eadem civitate corpora sanctorum Petronii, Florianii, Vitalis et / Agricole et Iuliane et sancti Proculi atquem plurima alia. In Ymola corpora / sancti Cassiani, Gismondi, et Petri Venali. In Faventia corpus beati Da/miani. Item in Forlivio corpora sanctorum Marculini et Iacobi ordinis predicatorum. / In Cesena corpus sancti Martiniani. In Ravena corpora sanctorum Apolinaris / Vitalis et undecim Archiepiscoporum et multa alia. In Arimino corpora sanctorum Iuliani / Johannis, Thome et Symonis conversi ordinis predicatorum et sancte Innocentie et sancti Gau/dentii in cuius ecclesia sunt alia corpora sanctorum. In Pesauro corpus beate Mitline. / In Fano corpus sancti Paterniani. In Urbino corpus sancte Piligetis et Crigenti/ni. In Senegania brachium sancte Marie Magdalene. In Ancona corpus / corpus [*sic*] sancti Ciriachi. / In Firmo corpus sancti Sanini. In Sancto Severino corpus sancti / Severini et Melani et Illuminati. / In Camerino corpus sancti Venantii / et Tuodini. In provincia Regium in civitate Barensi corpus sancti Nicolai et in rever/sione in quaedam silva agressus fui a quinque serpentibus venenonsi et invocato / nomine sancti Nicolai recesserunt me dimisso incolume. In Monte Gar/gano ecclesiam et locum Archangeli Michaelis et in reverssione similiter / tres lupi rapaces agresi fuerunt me post quos venerunt alii / duo et invocatis nominibus sancti Michaelis et Nicholai me dimiserunt in pace. / In Neapoli corpus sancte Clare. In Benevento corpus sancti Bartholomei apostoli. / In insula Malfi corpus sancti Andree apostoli. / In Aquileia corpus sancti Petri Confesso/ris.+ In Caieta corpora sanctorum Erasmi, Probi, et Marcii. In Monte / Cassino corpora sancti Benedicti et Scolastice. In Tuscia in Luca corpus sancti Frigii et sancti / Romani et sancte Cite et crucem Nichodemi. / In Pisis corpus sancti Rainerii. / In Prato coronam zona sancte Marie Virginis. In Florentia corpus sancti Zanobii et Iu/liane. In Senis corpus sancti Galgani et beati Ambrosii et beate Katerine / ordinis predicatorum. In Aretio corpus sancti Donati. In Castello corpus beate Marga/rite ordinis predicatorum. In Agubio corpus sancti Baldi. In Perusio corpus sancti Herculani et Pape Benedicti ordinis predicatorum in quoque domo est indulgentia a pe/na et a culpa + In Asisio corpus sancti Francisci ordinis minorum ubi est ecclesia / sancte Marie de Angelis et est ibi indulgentia. + In Fuligno corpus sancti Feli/ciani. In Spoleto corpus sancti Pontiani. In Narni corpus sancti Iovenalis. In / Reate corpus sancte Barbare. / In Roma corpora apostolorum Petri et Pauli + et sanctorum Laurentii et Stephanii et caput sancti Johannis Baptiste et corpus sancte Agnetis et multa alia. In Lumbardia in civitate Cumana corpus sancti Pelegrini. In Me/diolano corpus sancti Petri Martiris ordinis predicatorum et sancti Ambrosii et Storgui. In Papia corpus sancti Augustini. Placentie corpus sancti Antonini. In Lodio corpora sanctorum Danielis Gualteri et beati Petri. In Ianua corpus sancti Desiderii et catinum cene domini in quo comedit cum discipulis Pasca et caudam / asine supra quam Christus equitavit in ramis palmarum. In Alemania in / civitate Pragenum corpora sanctorum Ladislai, Wenceslai et Sigismundi regum. / In Trevis corpora sanctorum Helene matris Constantini et Marthe hospite Christi. / In Colonia corpora Trium Magorum et decem millia virginum et multa plura alia. In Aquisgrani interulam virginis Marie et est indulgentia + In Traiecto / corpus sancti Gervasii. / In Britania corpus sancti Gidotii / In Francia civi/tate Bononia Minori corona gloriose Virginis Marie. In Parisio / corpora sanctorum Dionisii et Germani. Item crucem et coronam et duos clavos Christi. / in Tholosa corporora apostolorum Symonis et Iude, Jacobi, Philippi, et linte / amen cum quo Christo fuit involutus in sepulchro. Item corpus eximii doc/toris sancti Thome de Aquino ordinis predicatorum. In Avinione corpus sancti Petri / Liciburgi. In Viena corpus sancti Antonii Abbatis. + In Marsilia corpora sanctorum Lazarii Maximini. In castro Sancti Maximini corpus sancte Marie / Magdalene. In Galitia provincie Hispanie corpus sancti Iacobi Apostoli + Et ibidem / est finis terre. In Lisbona corpus sancti Vicentii quod est in domo fratrum pre/dicatorum.

Bibliography

Acidini Luchinat 1994
Cristina Acidini Luchinat. *Benozzo Gozzoli*. Milan, 1994.

Agati 2003
Maria Luisa Agati. *Il libro manoscritto: Introduzione alla codicologia*. Rome, 2003.

B. Agosti et al. 1998
Barbara Agosti et al. *Quattro pezzi Lombardi (per Maria Teresa Binaghi)*. Brescia, 1998.

G. Agosti and Hirst 1996
Giovanni Agosti and Michael Hirst. "Michelangelo, Piero d'Argenta and the *Stigmatisation of St. Francis*." *The Burlington Magazine* 138 (October 1996), pp. 683–84.

Ainsworth 1994
Maryan Wynn Ainsworth. *Petrus Christus: Renaissance Master of Bruges*. Contributions by Maximiliaan P. J. Martens. Exhib. cat., The Metropolitan Museum of Art, New York. New York, 1994.

Ainsworth and Christiansen 1998
Maryan Wynn Ainsworth and Keith Christiansen, eds. *From Van Eyck to Bruegel: Early Netherlandish Painting in The Metropolitan Museum of Art*. Exhib. cat., The Metropolitan Museum of Art, New York. New York, 1998.

Alberti 1972 ed.
Leon Battista Alberti. *On Painting and On Sculpture: The Latin Texts of "De Pictura" and "De Statua."* Edited with translations, introduction, and notes by Cecil Grayson. London, 1972.

Alberti 1988 ed.
Leon Battista Alberti. *On the Art of Building in Ten Books*. Translated by Joseph Rykwert, Neil Leach, and Robert Tavernor. Cambridge, Massachusetts, 1988.

Albertini 1510 (1863 ed.)
Francesco Albertini. *Memoriale di molte statue e pitture della città di Firenze* [1510]. Florence, 1863.

Alexander 1970
Jonathan J. G. Alexander. "A Manuscript of Petrarch's *Rime* and *Trionfi*." *Victoria and Albert Museum Yearbook* 2 (1970), pp. 27–40.

Alexander 1994
Jonathan J. G. Alexander, ed. *The Painted Page: Italian Renaissance Book Illumination, 1450–1550*. London and New York, 1994.

Angelini 1986
Alessandro Angelini. *Disegni italiani del tempo di Donatello*. Florence, 1986.

Argan 1955
Giulio Carlo Argan. *Fra Angelico: Biographical and Critical Study*. Translated by James Emmons. Geneva, 1955.

Artusi and Patruno 1994
Luciano Artusi and Antonio Patruno. *Deo gratias: Storia, tradizioni, culti e personaggi delle antiche confraternite fiorentine*. Rome, 1994.

Attwood 1989
Philip Attwood. "A Medal of Nicholas V by Paladino." *The Medal*, no. 14 (1989), pp. 24–27.

Aurigema 2000
Maria Giulia Aurigema. "Committenze non romane di Niccolò V." In *Niccolò V nel sesto centenario della nascita: Atti del convegno internazionale di studi, Sarzana, 8–10 ottobre 1998*, edited by Franco Bonatti and Antonio Manfredi, pp. 415–24. Vatican City, 2000.

Baetjer 1995
Katherine Baetjer. *European Paintings in The Metropolitan Museum of Art by Artists Born before 1865: A Summary Catalogue*. New York, 1995.

Baldini 1956
Umberto Baldini. "Contributi all'Angelico: La predella della pala di San Marco e l'armadio per gli argenti della SS. Annunziata." *Commentari* 7 (1956), pp. 78–85.

Baldini 1970
Umberto Baldini. *L'opera completa dell'Angelico*. Milan, 1970.

Baldini 1977
Umberto Baldini. "Contributi all'Angelico: Il Trittico di San Domenico di Fiesole e qualche altra aggiunta." In *Scritti di storia dell'arte in onore di Ugo Procacci*, vol. I, pp. 236–46. Milan and Florence, 1977.

Baldini 1986
Umberto Baldini. *Beato Angelico*. Florence, 1986.

Baldini and Berti 1957
Umberto Baldini and Luciano Berti. *Mostra di affreschi staccati*. Exhib. cat., Forte di Belvedere, Florence. Florence, 1957.

Baldini and Dal Poggetto 1972
Umberto Baldini and Paolo Dal Poggetto, eds. *Firenze restaura: Il laboratorio nel suo quarantennio*. Exhib. cat., Fortezza da Basso, Florence. Florence, 1972.

Baldinucci 1681 (1845 ed.)
Filippo Baldinucci. *Notizie dei professori di disegno*. Vol. I. Florence, 1681. Reprint ed., Florence, 1845.

Baldinucci 1768
Filippo Baldinucci. *Notizie de' professori del disegno da Cimabue in quà*. Vol. III. Florence, 1768.

De Bammeville sale, 1854
Catalogue of the Very Choice Collection of Pictures of E. J. De Bammeville, Esq.; Comprising Most Rare and Interesting Works of the Great Italian Masters of the Thirteenth, Fourteenth, Fifteenth, and Sixteenth Centuries, Several of the Early German and Flemish Schools, and a Few of the Later Dutch and French Masters; also, a Beautiful Work of Luca Della Robbia. Sale cat. London: Christie and Manson, June 12, 1854.

Barbantini 1940
Nino Barbantini. *Il Castello di Monselice*. Venice, 1940.

Barstow 1990
Kurt Barstow. "The Education of the Imagination: Cardinal Juan de Torquemada's *Meditationes* and Dominican Reform in the Fifteenth Century." M.A. thesis, University of California, Berkeley, 1990.

Baschet 1993
Jérôme Baschet. *Les Justices de l'Au-Delà: Les représentations de l'enfer en France et en Italie (XIIe–XVe siècle)*. Rome, 1993.

Bazin 1949
Germain Bazin. *Fra Angelico*. London, 1949.

Becattini 1990
Ivo Becattini. "Il territorio di San Giovenale ed il Trittico di Masaccio: Ricerche ed ipotesi." In "*Masaccio 1422/1989," dal trittico di San Giovenale al restauro della cappella Brancacci: Atti del convegno del 22 aprile 1989, Pieve di San Pietro a Cascia, Reggello*, pp. 17–26. Figline Valdarno, 1990.

Bellosi 1966
Luciano Bellosi. "Il Maestro della Crocifissione Griggs: Giovanni Toscani." *Paragone*, n.s. 17, no. 193 (1966), pp. 44–58.

Bellosi 1984
Luciano Bellosi. "Due note in margine a Lorenzo Monaco miniatore: Il 'Maestro del Codice Squarcialupi' e il poco probabile Matteo Torelli." In *Studi di storia dell'arte in memoria di Mario Rotili*, vol. I, pp. 307–13. Naples, 1984.

Bellosi 1988
Luciano Bellosi. "Giovanni di Francesco Toscani." In *Arte in Lombardia: Tra Gotico e Rinascimento*, edited by Miklós Boskovits, pp. 196–97. Milan, 1988.

Bellosi 1989
Luciano Bellosi. "Donatello e il recupero della scultura in terracotta." In *Donatello-Studien*, pp. 130–45. Munich, 1989.

Bellosi 1990a
Luciano Bellosi, ed. *Pittura di Luce: Giovanni di Francesco e l'arte fiorentina di metà Quattrocento.* Exhib. cat., Casa Buonarroti, Florence. Milan, 1990.

Bellosi 1990b
Luciano Bellosi. "Giovanni di Francesco e l'arte fiorentina di metà Quattrocento." In Bellosi 1990a, pp. 17–54.

Bellosi 1996
Luciano Bellosi. "Una testimonianza su Dino Dini e sull'Angelico a San Marco." In *Gli affreschi del Beato Angelico nel convento di San Marco a Firenze: Rilettura di un capolavoro attraverso un memorabile restauro,* edited by Daniela Dini, pp. 22, 26–28. Turin, 1996.

Bellosi 2002
Luciano Bellosi, ed. *Masaccio e le origini del Rinascimento.* With the collaboration of Laura Cavazzini and Aldo Galli. Exhib. cat., Casa Masaccio, San Giovanni Valdarno. Milan, 2002.

Bellosi and Galli 1998
Luciano Bellosi and Aldo Galli. *Un nuovo dipinto dell'Angelico.* Turin, 1998.

Benesch 1967
Otto Benesch. *Master Drawings in the Albertina: European Drawings from the 15th to the 18th Century.* With the collaboration of Eva Benesch; translated by R. Rickett and M. Schön, revised by Felice Stampfle and Ruth Kramer. Greenwich, Connecticut.

Benson 1927
Robert Benson, ed. *The Holford Collection, Dorchester House; with 200 Illustrations from the Twelfth to the End of the Nineteenth Century.* 2 vols. Oxford, 1927.

Bent 1984
George Bent. *Santa Maria degli Angeli and the Arts: Patronage, Production, and Practice in a Trecento Florentine Monastery.* 2 vols. Ph.D. diss., Stanford University, Palo Alto, California.

Bent 2000
George Bent. "A Patron for Lorenzo Monaco's Uffizi Coronation of the Virgin." *The Art Bulletin* 82 (June 2000), pp. 348–54.

Berenson 1896
Bernard Berenson. *The Florentine Painters of the Renaissance.* London, 1896.

Berenson 1903
Bernard Berenson. *The Drawings of the Florentine Painters: Classified, Criticised and Studied as Documents in the History and Appreciation of Tuscan Art; with a Copious Catalogue Raisonné.* 2 vols. New York.

Berenson 1904
Bernard Berenson. *The Florentine Painters of the Renaissance.* 2nd ed. New York, 1904.

Berenson 1909
Bernard Berenson. *The Florentine Painters of the Renaissance.* 3rd ed. New York, 1909.

Berenson 1929–30
Bernard Berenson. "Quadri senza casa." *Dedalo* 10 (1929–30), pp. 133–42.

Berenson 1932a
Bernard Berenson. *Italian Pictures of the Renaissance: A List of the Principal Artists and Their Works with an Index of Places.* 3 vols. Oxford, 1932.

Berenson 1932b
Bernard Berenson. "Quadri senza casa—Il Quattrocento fiorentino, I." *Dedalo* 12 (1932), pp. 512–41.

Berenson 1936
Bernard Berenson. *I pittori italiani del Rinascimento: Catalogo dei principali artisti e delle loro opere con un indice dei luoghi.* Milan, 1936.

Berenson 1938
Bernard Berenson. *The Drawings of the Florentine Painters.* 3 vols. Chicago, 1938.

Berenson 1961
Bernard Berenson. *I disegni dei pittori fiorentini.* 3 vols. Translated by Luisa Vertova Nicolson. Milan, 1961.

Berenson 1963
Bernard Berenson. *Italian Pictures of the Renaissance: A List of the Principal Artists and Their Works with an Index of Places. Florentine School.* 2 vols. London, 1963.

Berenson 1970
Bernard Berenson. *Homeless Paintings of the Renaissance.* Edited by Hanna Kiel. Bloomington, 1970.

Bern 1936
Führer durch die Sammlungsausstellung: Gemälde und Plastik. Exhib. cat., Kunstmuseum, Bern. Bern, 1936.

Bernacchioni 1992
Annamaria Bernacchioni. "Le forme della tradizione: pittori fra continuità e innovazioni." In *Maestri e botteghe: Pittura a Firenze alla fine del Quattrocento,* pp. 171–80. Milan, 1992.

Bernacchioni 2003
Annamaria Bernacchioni. "Arcangelo di Cola per i banchieri Esaù Martellini e Ilarione de' Bardi." In *I Da Varano e le arti: Atti del Convegno internazionale, Camerino, Palazzo Ducale, 4–6 ottobre 2001,* edited by Andrea De Marchi and Pier Luigi Falaschi, vol. I, pp. 233–44. Ripatransone, 2003.

Berti 1963
Luciano Berti. "Miniature dell'Angelico (e altro)," part 2. *Acropoli* 3, no. 1 (1963), pp. 1–38.

Berti 1967
Luciano Berti. *Angelico.* Florence, 1967.

Berti, Bellardoni, and Battisti 1965
Luciano Berti, Bianca Bellardoni, and Eugenio Battisti. *Angelico a San Marco.* Naples, 1965.

Berti and Paolucci 1990
Luciano Berti and Antonio Paolucci, eds. *L'età di Masaccio: Il primo Quattrocento a Firenze.* Exhib. cat., Palazzo Vecchio, Florence. Milan, 1990.

Bietti Favi 1990
Monica Bietti Favi. "Indizi documentari su Lippo di Benivieni." *Studi di storia dell'arte* 1 (1990), pp. 243–52.

Biganti 1998
Tiziana Biganti. "Un prestigio da riconquistare: La famiglia Guidalotti nella prima metà del XV secolo." In Garibaldi 1998, pp. 102–19.

Birke and Kertész 1995
Veronika Birke and Janine Kertész. *Die italianischen Zeichnungen der Albertina: Generalverzeichnis.* Vol. III. Vienna, 1995.

Birmingham 1955
Exhibition of Italian Art from the 13th Century to the 17th Century. Exhib. cat., Museum and Art Gallery, Birmingham. Birmingham, England [1955].

Blum 1933
André Blum. "Les nielleurs du Quattrocento et Maso Finiguerra." *Gazette des Beaux-Arts,* ser. 6, 9 (1933), pp. 214–30.

Blum 1950
André Blum. *Les nielles du Quattrocento.* Paris, 1950.

Boccaccio 1960 ed.
Giovanni Boccaccio. *The Nymph of Fiesole (Il ninfale fiesolano).* Translation by Daniel J. Donno based on the Italian text of Vincenzo Pernicone. New York, 1960.

Bode 1888
Wilhelm von Bode. "La Renaissance au Musée de Berlin, IV: Les peintres florentins du XVe siècle." *Gazette des Beaux-Arts,* ser. 2, 37 (1888), pp. 472–89.

Bollati 1997
Milvia Bollati. "Una nota per Beato Angelico miniatore e un Messale ritrovato." In *Scritti per l'Istituto Germanico di Storia dell'Arte di Firenze,* pp. 81–86. Florence, 1997.

Bollati 1998
Milvia Bollati. "Battista di Biagio Sanguigni." In *Ridono le carte: Medieval and Renaissance Illuminations,* pp. 19–25. BEL catalogue 2. London, 1998.

Bombe 1912
Walter Bombe. *Geschichte der Peruginer Malerei bis zu Perugino und Pinturicchio.* Berlin, 1912.

Bona 1909
Vincenzo Bona. *Catalogo della Regia Pinacoteca di Torino.* Turin, 1909.

Bonaventure 1977 ed.
Saint Bonaventure. *Meditations on the Life of Christ: An Illustrated Manuscript of the Fourteenth Century. Paris, Bibliothèque Nationale, Ms. Ital., 115.* Translated by Isa Ragusa; completed and edited by Isa Ragusa and Rosalie B. Green. Princeton Monographs in Art and Archaeology, 35. Princeton.

Bonsanti 1983
Giorgio Bonsanti. "Preliminari per l'Angelico restaurato." *Arte cristiana* 71, no. 694 (1983), pp. 25–34.

Bonsanti 1990
Giorgio Bonsanti. "Gli affreschi del Beato Angelico." In *La Chiesa e il Convento di San Marco a Firenze* 1989–90, vol. II, pp. 165–72.

Bonsanti 1998
Giorgio Bonsanti. *Beato Angelico: Catalogo completo.* Florence, 1998.

Bonsanti 2003
Giorgio Bonsanti. "Beato Angelico e gli inizi di Benozzo." In

Benozzo Gozzoli: Viaggio attraverso un secolo; Convegno internazionale di studi (Firenze–Pisa, 8–10 gennaio 1998), edited by Enrico Castelnuovo and Alessandra Malquori, pp. 47–62. Pisa, 2003.

Borenius 1916
Tancred Borenius. *Pictures by the Old Masters in the Library of Christ Church, Oxford: A Brief Catalogue with Historical and Critical Notes on the Pictures in the Collection.* London, 1916.

Borenius 1922
Tancred Borenius. "A Florentine Mystical Picture." *The Burlington Magazine* 41 (October 1922), pp. 156–58.

Borsook 1980
Eve Borsook. *The Mural Painters of Tuscany, from Cimabue to Andrea del Sarto.* 2nd ed. Oxford, 1980.

Boskovits 1968
Miklós Boskovits. "Sull'attività giovanile di Mariotto di Nardo." *Antichità viva* 7, no. 5 (1968), pp. 3–13.

Boskovits 1975
Miklós Boskovits. *Pittura fiorentina alla vigilia del Rinascimento.* Florence, 1975.

Boskovits 1976a
Miklós Boskovits. *Un "Adorazione dei Magi" e gli inizi dell'Angelico.* Bern, 1976.

Boskovits 1976b
Miklós Boskovits. "Appunti sull'Angelico." *Paragone*, n.s., 27, no. 313 (1976), pp. 30–54.

Boskovits 1983
Miklós Boskovits. "La fase tarda del Beato Angelico: Una proposta di interpretazione." *Arte cristiana*, 71, no. 694 (1983), pp. 11–23.

Boskovits 1990
Miklós Boskovits. *Early Italian Painting, 1290–1470: The Thyssen-Bornemisza Collection.* With the collaboration of Serena Padovani; translated by Françoise Pouncey Chiarini. London, 1990.

Boskovits 1991
Miklós Boskovits. "Il Maestro di Incisa Scapaccino e alcuni problemi di pittura tardogotica in Italia." *Paragone*, n.s., 47, no. 501 (1991), pp. 35–53.

Boskovits 1994
Miklós Boskovits. *Immagini da meditare: Richerche su dipinti di tema religioso nei secoli XII–XV.* Milan, 1994.

Boskovits 1995
Miklós Boskovits. "Attorno al *Tondo Cook*: Precisazioni sul Beato Angelico, su Filippo Lippi e altri." *Mitteilungen des Kunsthistorisches Institutes in Florenz* 39, no. 1 (1995), pp. 32–68.

Boskovits 2002a
Miklós Boskovits. "Ancora sul Maestro del 1419." *Arte cristiana* 90, no. 812 (2002), pp. 332–40.

Boskovits 2002b
Miklós Boskovits. "Il Beato Angelico e Benozzo Gozzoli: Problemi ancora aperti." In Toscano and Capitelli 2002, pp. 41–56.

Boskovits 2005
Miklós Boskovits, with Daniela Parenti. *Da Bernardo Daddi al Beato Angelico a Botticelli: Dipinti fiorentini del Lindenau-Museum di Altenberg.* Exhib. cat., Museo di San Marco, Florence. Florence, 2005.

Boskovits and Brown 2003
Miklós Boskovits and David Alan Brown. *Italian Paintings of the Fifteenth Century.* The Collections of the National Gallery of Art, Systematic Catalogue. Washington, D.C., 2003.

Bowron 1990
Edgar Peters Bowron. *European Paintings before 1900 in the Fogg Art Museum: A Summary Catalogue Including Paintings in the Busch-Reisinger Museum.* Cambridge, Massachusetts, 1990.

Braunfels 1949
Wolfgang Braunfels. *Die Verkundigung.* Düsseldorf, 1949.

Brefeld 1994
Josephie Brefeld. *A Guidebook for the Jerusalem Pilgrimage in the Late Middle Ages: A Case for Computer-Aided Textual Criticism.* Hilversum, 1994.

Brière 2002
Michel Brière. *L'Image de Dieu: Petite méditation avec une oeuvre du bienheureux Fra Angelico.* Paris, 2002.

Brigstocke 1976
Hugh Brigstocke. "Panels Showing the Death of St. Ephrain." *The Burlington Magazine* 118 (August 1976), pp. 585–89.

Brocchi 1748
Giuseppe Maria Brocchi. *Descrizione della provincia del Mugello. . . .* Florence, 1748.

Brunetti 1977
Giulia Brunetti. "Una vacchetta segnata A." In *Scritti di storia dell'arte in onore di Ugo Procacci*, vol. I, pp. 228–35. Milan, 1977.

Budge 1934
Ernest A. Wallis Budge, ed. and trans. *Stories of the Holy Fathers, Being Histories of the Anchorites, Recluses, Monks, Coenobites and Ascetic Fathers of the Deserts of Egypt, between A.D. 250 and A.D. 400 Circiter.* Compiled by Athanasius, Palladius, Saint Jerome, and others. London, 1934.

Buonanni 1699
Filippo Buonanni. *Numismata pontificum romanorum quae a tempore Martini V usque ad annum MDCXCIX vel authoritate publica, vel privato genio, in lucem prodiere.* 2 vols. Rome, 1699.

Buranelli 2001
Francesco Buranelli, ed. *Il Beato Angelico e la Cappella Niccolina: Storia e restauro.* Novara, 2001.

Burke 2004
Jill Burke. *Changing Patrons: Social Identity and the Visual Arts in Renaissance Florence.* University Park, Pennsylvania, 2004.

Burroughs 1990
Charles Burroughs. *From Signs to Design: Environmental Process and Reform in Early Renaissance Rome.* Cambridge, Massachusetts, 1990.

Butkovich 1969
Anthony Butkovich. *Iconography: St. Birgitta of Sweden.* Los Angeles, 1969.

Butterfield 2000
Andrew Butterfield. *Masterpieces of Renaissance Sculpture: An Exhibition of Sculpture from the Collection of Michael Hall, Esq.* Exhib. cat., Salander-O'Reilly Galleries, New York. New York, 2000.

Byam Shaw 1967
J. Byam-Shaw. *Paintings by Old Masters at Christ Church Oxford.* London, 1967.

Cadogan 1991
Jean K. Cadogan, ed. *Wadsworth Atheneum Paintings.* Vol. II, *Italy and Spain, Fourteenth through Nineteenth Centuries.* Hartford, 1991.

Cagliotti 2001
Francesco Cagliotti. "Nouveautés sur la *Bataille de San Romano* de Paolo Uccello." *Revue du Louvre* 4 (2001), pp. 37–54.

Callmann 1975
Ellen Callmann. "Thebaid Studies." *Antichità viva* 14, no. 3 (1975), pp. 3–22.

Callmann 1979
Ellen Callmann. "The Growing Threat to Marital Bliss as Seen in Fifteenth-Century Florentine Painting." *Studies in Iconography* 5 (1979), pp. 73–92.

Callmann 1995
Ellen Callmann. "Subjects from Boccaccio in Italian Painting, 1375–1525." *Studi sul Boccaccio* 23 (1995), pp. 19–78.

Calzolari et al. 1975
Silvio Calzolari et al. *Viaggiatori e pellegrini italiani in Terrasanta fra Trecento e Quattrocento: Atti del Seminario di Storia Medievale, Università degli Studi di Firenze, Anno Accademico, 1974–75.* 2 vols. Florence, 1975.

Caneva 2001
Caterina Caneva, ed. *Masaccio: Il trittico di San Giovenale e il primo '400 fiorentino.* Milan, 2001.

Cannon 1998
Joanna Cannon. "Dominic *alter Christus*?: Representations of the Founder in and after the *Arca di San Domenico*." In *Christ among the Medieval Dominicans: Representations of Christ in the Texts and Images of the Order of Preachers,* edited by Kent Emery, Jr., and Joseph Wawrykow, pp. 26–48. Notre Dame, Indiana, 1998.

Cantatore 2000
Flavia Cantatore. "Niccolò V e il Palazzo Vaticano." In *Niccolò V nel sesto centenario della nascita,* edited by Franco Bonatti and Antonio Manfredi, pp. 399–410. Proceedings of a conference in Sarzana, Italy, October 8–10, 1998. Vatican City, 2000.

Cardile 1976
Paul Julius Cardile. "Fra Angelico and His Workshop at San Domenico (1420–1435): The Development of His Style and the Formation of His Workshop." Ph.D. diss., Yale University, 1976.

Cardini 1982
Franco Cardini, ed. *Toscana e Terrasanta nel Medioevo.* Florence, 1982.

Cardini 2000
Franco Cardini. "Francesco in Oriente." In *In Terrasanta: Dalla crociata alla custodia dei luoghi santi,* edited by Michele Piccirillo, pp. 138–39. Exhib. cat., Palazzo Reale, Milan. Florence, 2000.

Cardini 2002
Franco Cardini. *In Terrasanta: Pellegrini italiani tra medioevo e prima età moderna.* Bologna, 2002.

Carli 1964
Enzo Carli. *Il Reliquiario del Corporale ad Orvieto.* Milan, 1964.

Cartier 1857
Ernest Cartier. *Vie de Fra Angelico da Fiesole de l'Ordre des Frères Prêcheurs.* Paris, 1857.

Casalini et al. 1987
Eugenio Casalini et al., eds. *Tesori d'arte dell'Annunziata di Firenze.* Exhib. cat., Santissima Annunziata, Florence. Florence, 1987.

Castelfranchi Vegas 1983
Liana Castelfranchi Vegas. *Italia e Fiandra nella pittura del Quattrocento.* Milan, 1983.

Castelfranchi Vegas 1989
Liana Castelfranchi Vegas. *L'Angelico e l'Umanesimo.* Milan, 1989.

Cavalca 1858 ed.
Domenico Cavalca. *Vite de' Santi Padri di Frate Domenico Cavalca: Colle vite di alcuni altri santi.* Edited by Bartolommeo Sorio and A. Racheli. Trieste, 1858.

Ceccanti 2001–2
Melania Ceccanti. "Immagini per una (ri)trovata Passione di Cristo trecentesca in volgare." *Rivista di storia della miniatura,* nos. 6–7 (2001–2), pp. 171–80.

Cennini 1960 ed.
Cennino Cennini. *The Craftsman's Handbook: "Il libro dell'arte."* Translated by Daniel V. Thompson, Jr. New York, 1960.

Centi 1989
Tito S. Centi. "La Chiesa e il convento di San Marco a Firenze." In *La Chiesa e il Convento di San Marco a Firenze* 1989–90, vol. I, pp. 13–78.

Chiarini 1960
Marco Chiarini. "Nota sull'Angelico." *Arte antica e moderna,* no. 11 (1960), pp. 278–81.

***La Chiesa e il Convento di San Marco* 1989–90**
La Chiesa e il Convento di San Marco a Firenze. 2 vols. Florence, 1989–90.

Christiansen 1984
Keith Christiansen. "Workshop of Fra Angelico [Guido di Pietro] . . . *The Nativity.*" In Metropolitan Museum of Art 1984, pp. 61–62.

Christiansen 2005
Keith Christiansen, ed. *From Filippo Lippi to Piero della Francesca: Fra Carnevale and the Making of a Renaissance Master.* Exhib. cat., The Metropolitan Museum of Art, New York. New York, 2005.

Ciabani 1992
Roberto Ciabani. *Le famiglie di Firenze.* Vol. I. With the collaboration of Beatrix Elliker; contributions by Enrico Nistri et al. Florence, 1992.

Ciaranfi 1932
Anna-Maria Ciaranfi. "Lorenzo Monaco miniatore." *L'arte* 35 (1932), pp. 285–317.

Ciardi Dupré Dal Poggetto 1967
Maria Grazia Ciardi Dupré Dal Poggetto. "Sulla collaborazione di Benozzo Gozzoli alla porta del Paradiso." *Antichità viva* 6, no. 6 (1967), pp. 60–73.

Ciardi Dupré Dal Poggetto 1980
Maria Grazia Ciardi Dupré Dal Poggetto, ed. *Il tesoro della Basilica di San Francesco ad Assisi.* Catalogue by Rosalia Bonito Fanelli et al. Assisi, 1980.

Ciardi Dupré Dal Poggetto 1996
Maria Grazia Ciardi Dupré Dal Poggetto. "I dipinti di Palazzo Medici nell'inventario di Simone di Stagio delle Pozze: Problemi di committenza e di arredo." In *La Toscana al tempo di Lorenzo il Magnifico: Politica, economia, cultura, arte,* vol. I, pp. 131–64. Pisa, 1996.

Cioni 1998
Elisabetta Cioni. *Scultura e smalto nell'Oreficeria senese dei secoli XIII e XIV.* Florence, 1998.

Clark 1930
Kenneth Clark. "Italian Drawings at Burlington House." *The Burlington Magazine* 56 (April 1930), pp. 175–87.

Cleveland Museum of Art 1974
The Cleveland Museum of Art. *Catalogue of Paintings.* Part 1, *European Paintings before 1500.* Cleveland, 1974.

***Il codice magliabechiano* 1536–46 (1892 ed.)**
Il codice magliabechiano, cl. XVII. 17, contenente notizie sopra l'arte degli antichi e quella de' Fiorentini da Cimabue a Michelangelo Buonarroti, scritte da anonimo fiorentino [1536–46]. Edited by Carl Frey. Berlin, 1892.

Cohn 1955
Werner Cohn. "Il Beato Angelico e Battista di Biagio Sanguigni." *Rivista d'arte* 30, ser. 3, 5 (1955), pp. 207–16.

Cohn 1956a
Werner Cohn. "Nuovi documenti per il B. Angelico." *Memorie domenicane* 73, n.s. 32 (1956), pp. 218–20.

Cohn 1956b
Werner Cohn. "Notizie storiche intorno ad alcune tavole fiorentine del '300 e '400." *Rivista d'arte* 31, ser. 3, 6 (1956), pp. 41–72.

Colasanti 1921–22
Arduino Colasanti. "Nuovi dipinti di Arcangelo di Cola da Camerino." *Bollettino d'arte,* ser. 2, 1 (1921–22), pp. 538–45.

Cole 1977
Diane Cole. "Fra Angelico: His Role in Quattrocento Painting and Problems of Chronology." 2 vols. Ph.D. diss., University of Virginia, 1977.

Cole Ahl 1980
Diane Cole Ahl. "Fra Angelico: A New Chronology for the 1420s." *Zeitschrift für Kunstgeschichte* 43 (1980), pp. 360–81.

Cole Ahl 1984
Diane Cole Ahl. "Il 'Dio Padre' del Beato Angelico al Louvre: Analisi di un'opera giovanile." *Antichità viva* 23, no. 3 (1984), pp. 19–20.

Cole Ahl 1996
Diane Cole Ahl. *Benozzo Gozzoli.* New Haven, 1996.

Collareta and Capitanio 1990
Marco Collareta and Antonella Capitanio. *Oreficeria sacra italiana.* Florence, 1990.

Collobi-Ragghianti 1950a
Licia Collobi-Ragghianti. "Domenico di Michelino." *Critica d'arte,* ser. 3, 8, no. 5 (January 1950), pp. 363–78.

Collobi-Ragghianti 1950b
Licia Collobi-Ragghianti. "Zanobi Strozzi pittore," parts 1–2. *Critica d'arte,* ser. 3, 8, no. 6 (March 1950), pp. 454–73; 9, no. 1 (May 1950), pp. 17–27.

Collobi-Ragghianti 1955a
Licia Collobi-Ragghianti. "Una mostra dell'Angelico." *Critica d'arte,* n.s., 2, no. 10 (1955), pp. 389–94.

Collobi-Ragghianti 1955b
Licia Collobi-Ragghianti. "Studi angelichiani." *Critica d'arte,* n.s., 2, no. 7 (1955), pp. 22–47.

Collobi-Ragghianti 1974
Licia Collobi-Ragghianti. *Il libro de' disegni del Vasari.* 2 vols. Florence, 1974.

Contorni 1991–92
Gabriella Contorni. "La villa di Careggi al tempo di Lorenzo il Magnifico." *Quasar* 6–7 (1991–92), pp. 9–18.

Corrigan 1996
Kathleen Corrigan. "Early Medieval Psalter Illustration in Byzantium and the West." In *The Utrecht Psalter in Medieval Art: Picturing the Psalms of David,* edited by Koert van der Horst, William Noel, and Wilhelmina C. M. Wüstefeld, pp. 85–103. 't Goy, The Netherlands, 1996.

Corsini 1984
Italian Old Master Paintings, Fourteenth to Eighteenth Century. Exhib. cat., Piero Corsini Gallery, New York. New York, 1984.

Cracco 1963
Giorgio Cracco. "Banchini, Giovanni di Domenico." In *Dizionario biografico degli Italiani,* vol. V (1963), pp. 657–64. Rome, 1963.

Crowe and Cavalcaselle 1864
Joseph Archer Crowe and Giovanni Battista Cavalcaselle. *A New History of Painting in Italy.* 3 vols. London, 1864. Reprint ed., New York, 1980.

Crowe and Cavalcaselle 1869–76
Joseph Archer Crowe and Giovanni Battista Cavalcaselle. *Geschichte der Italienischen Malerei.* 6 vols. Leipzig, 1869–76.

Crowe and Cavalcaselle 1883
Joseph Archer Crowe and Giovanni Battista Cavalcaselle. *Storia della pittura in Italia dal secolo II al secolo XVI.* Vol. II, *L'arte dopo la morte di Giotto.* 2nd ed. Florence, 1883.

Crowe and Cavalcaselle 1903–14
Joseph Archer Crowe and Giovanni Battista Cavalcaselle. *A History of Painting in Italy: Umbria, Florence, and Siena, from the Second to the Sixteenth Century.* 6 vols. London, 1903–14.

D'Addario 1960
Arnaldo D'Addario. "Agli, Antonio." In *Dizionario biografico degli italiani,* vol. I, pp. 400–401. Rome, 1960.

Dalli Regoli and Landolfi 1992
Giggetta Dalli Regoli and Gemma Landolfi. "Un testo profetico medievale in un codice quattrocentesco: I *Vaticinia Pontificum* e il

m.s. Harley 1340 della British Library." In *Il codice miniato: Rapporti tra codice, testo e figurazione; Atti del III congresso di storia della miniatura,* pp. 405–23. Florence, 1992.

Damiani, Marchetti, and Scudieri 1995
Giovanna Damiani, Luciano Marchetti, and Magnolia Scudieri, eds. *Rinvenimenti e restauri nel complesso monumentale di San Marco,* Florence, n.d. [1995], pp. 13–22.

D'Ancona 1908
Paolo D'Ancona. "Un ignoto collaboratore del Beato Angelico (Zanobi Strozzi)." *L'arte* 11, no. 1 (1908), pp. 1–15.

D'Ancona 1914
Paolo D'Ancona. *La miniatura fiorentina (secoli XI–XVI)*. Vol. I. Florence, 1914.

D'Arienzo 2003
Michele D'Arienzo. "Il Pellegrinaggio al Gargano tra XI e XVI secolo." In *Culte et pèlerinages à Saint Michel en Occident: Les trois monts dédiés à L'Archange,* edited by Pierre Bouet, Giorgio Otranto, and André Vauchez, pp. 219–44. Rome, 2003.

Datini 1972
Giulio Datini, ed. *Musei di Prato. Galleria di Palazzo Pretorio, Opera del Duomo, Quadreria communale.* Bologna, 1972.

Davies 1951
Martin Davies. *National Gallery Catalogues: The Earlier Italian Schools.* London, 1951.

Davies 1961
Martin Davies. *National Gallery Catalogues: The Earlier Italian Schools.* 2nd ed. London, 1961.

Davies 1974
Martin Davies. *European Paintings in the Collection of the Worcester Art Museum.* Worcester, 1974.

Degenhart and Schmitt 1968
Bernhard Degenhart and Annegrit Schmitt. *Corpus der italienischen Zeichnungen, 1300–1450.* Part 1, 4 vols. Berlin, 1968.

Delcorno 1998
Carlo Delcorno. "Produzione e circolazione dei volgarizzamenti religiosi tra medioevo e rinascimento." In *La Bibbia in italiano tra Medioevo e Rinascimento: Atti del Convegno internazionale, Firenze, Certosa del Galluzzo, 8–9 novembre 1996,* edited by Lino Leonardi, pp. 3–22. Florence, 1998.

Delfiol 1982
Renato Delfiol. "Su alcuni problemi codicologico-testuali concernenti le relazioni di pellegrinaggio fiorentine del 1384." In Cardini 1982, pp. 141–76.

De Marchi 1985
Andrea De Marchi. "Per la cronologia dell'Angelico: Il trittico di Perugia." *Prospettiva* 42 (1985), pp. 53–57.

De Marchi 1992
Andrea De Marchi. "Una fonte senese per Ghiberti e per il giovane Angelico." *Artista: Critica dell'arte in Toscana,* 1992, pp. 130–51.

De Roover 1963
Raymond De Roover. *The Rise and Decline of the Medici Bank, 1397–1494.* New York, 1963.

De Simone 2002
Gerardo De Simone. "L'ultimo Angelico: Le *Meditationes* del cardinale Torquemada e il ciclo perduto nel chiostro di S. Maria sopra Minerva." In "Presenze cancellate: Capolavori perduti della pittura romana di metà '400," *Ricerche di storia dell'arte* 76 (2002), pp. 41–87.

Dillon Bussi 1997
Angela Dillon Bussi. "La miniatura quattrocentesca per il Duomo di Firenze: Prime indagini e alcune novità." In Lorenzo Fabbri and Marica Tacconi, *I libri del Duomo di Firenze,* pp. 79–96. Florence, 1997.

Dillon Bussi 2003
Angela Dillon Bussi. "Battista miniature." In Scudieri and Rasario 2003, pp. 44–51.

Di Lorenzo 2001
Andrea Di Lorenzo, ed. *Omaggio a Beato Angelico: Un dipinto per il Museo Poldi Pezzoli.* Exhib. cat., Museo Poldi Pezzoli, Milan. Cinisello Balsamo, Italy, 2001.

Di Lorenzo 2005
Andrea Di Lorenzo. "Documents in the Florentine Archives." In Christiansen 2005, pp. 290–93.

Douglas 1900
R. Langton Douglas. *Fra Angelico.* London, 1900.

Draper 1992
James David Draper. *Bertoldo di Giovanni: Sculptor of the Medici Household.* Columbia, Missouri, 1992.

Dunkerton and Gordon 2002
Jill Dunkerton and Dillian Gordon. "The Pisa Altarpiece." In *The Panel Paintings of Masolino and Masaccio: The Role of Technique,* edited by Carl Brandon Strehlke and Cecilia Frosinini, pp. 89–109. Milan, 2002.

Eisenberg 1976
Marvin Eisenberg. "'The Penitent St. Jerome' by Giovanni Toscani." *The Burlington Magazine* 118 (May 1976), pp. 274–83.

Eisenberg 1984
Marvin Eisenberg. "Some Monastic and Liturgical Allusions in an Early Work of Lorenzo Monaco." In *Monasticism and the Arts,* edited by Timothy Verdon, pp. 271–89. Syracuse, New York, 1984.

Eisenberg 1989
Marvin Eisenberg. *Lorenzo Monaco.* Princeton, 1989.

Elen 1989
Albert J. Elen. *Missing Old Master Drawings from the Franz Koenigs Collection Claimed by the State of The Netherlands.* The Hague, 1989.

Elen 1995
Albert J. Elen. *Italian Late-Medieval and Renaissance Drawing-Books: From Giovannino de Grassi to Palma Giovane.* Leiden, 1995.

Eubel 1901
Conrad Eubel. *Hierarchia Catholica Medii Aevi.* Vol. II, *Ab anno 1431 usque ad annum 1503 perducta.* Regensburg, 1901.

Eubel 1960
Conrad Eubel. *Hierarchia Catholica Medii Aevi.* Reprint of 2nd ed. Vols. I–II. Pavia, 1960.

Fahy 1978
Everett Fahy. "On Lorenzo di Niccolo." *Apollo* 108 (1978), pp. 374–81.

Fahy 1987
Everett Fahy. "The Kimbell Fra Angelico." *Apollo* 125 (March 1987), pp. 178–83.

Fahy 1994
Everett Fahy. "Florence and Naples: A Cassone Panel in The Metropolitan Museum of Art." In *Hommage à Michel Laclotte,* pp. 231–93. Paris, 1994.

Fallani 1992
Valentina Fallani. "Piero Guicciardini e la sua quadreria fidecommissaria nella Firenze medicea del Seicento." Ph.D. diss., University of Florence, 1992.

Fehlmann and Freuler 2001
Marc Fehlmann and Gaudenz Freuler. *Die Sammlung Adolf von Stürler.* Exhib. cat., Kunstmuseum Bern. Bern, 2001.

Fesch collection, 1841
Catalogue des tableaux composant la galerie de feu son Éminence le Cardinal Fesch. Rome, 1841.

Ffoulkes 1894
Costanza Jocelyn Ffoulkes. "Le Esposizioni d'Arte italiana a Londra." *Archivio storico dell'arte* 7 (1894), pp. 151–76.

Ficarra 1968
Annamaria Ficarra, ed. *L'anonimo magliabecchiano.* Naples, 1968.

Florence 1955
Mostra delle opere del Beato Angelico: Nel quinto centenario della morte, 1455–1955. Exhib. cat., Museo di San Marco, Florence. Florence, 1955.

Florence 1978
Lorenzo Ghiberti: Materia e ragionament. Texts by Mina Bacci, Luciano Bellosi et al. Exhib. cat., Museo dell'Accademia and Museo di San Marco, Florence. Florence, 1978.

Florence 1986
Andrea del Sarto, 1486–1530: Dipinti e disegni a Firenze. Exhib. cat., Palazzo Pitti, Florence. Florence, 1986.

Forlani Tempesti 1991
Anna Forlani Tempesti. *The Robert Lehman Collection, V, Italian Fifteenth- to Seventeenth-Century Drawings.* New York, 1991.

Fornari Schianchi 1997
Lucia Fornari Schianchi, ed. *Catalogo delle opere dall'Antico al Cinquecento. Galleria Nazionale di Parma.* Vol. I. Milan, 1997.

Franci and Ceccanti 1993–96
Andrea Franci and Melania Ceccanti. "Le miniature del Silio Italico e la formazione di Pesellino." *Miniatura* 5–6 (1993–96), pp. 83–88.

Francini Ciaranfi n.d.
Anna Maria Francini Ciaranfi. *Beato Angelico: Gli affreschi di San Marco a Firenze.* Milan n.d. [1951].

Fraser 1973
A. Ian Fraser. *A Catalogue of the Clowes Collection.* Indianapolis, 1973.

Fremantle 1970
Richard Fremantle. "Masaccio e l'Angelico." *Antichità viva* 9, no. 6 (1970), pp. 39–49.

Freuler 1991
Gaudenz Freuler, ed. "*Manifestatori delle cose miracolose*": *Arte italiana del '300 e '400 da collezioni in Svizzera e nel Liechtenstein.* Exhib. cat., Villa Favorita, Fondazione Thyssen-Bornemisza, Lugano-Castagnola. Lugano-Castagnola and Einsiedeln, Switzerland, 1991.

Freuler 2001
Gaudenz Freuler. "Fra Angelico." In Fehlmann and Freuler 2001, pp. 118–23.

Frommel 1997
Christoph Luitpold Frommel. "Il San Pietro di Niccolò V." In *L'architettura della Basilica di San Pietro: Storia e costruzione. Atti del convegno internazionale di studi, Roma, Castel S. Angelo, 7–10 novembre 1995,* edited by Gianfranco Spagnesi, pp. 103–10. Quaderni dell'Istituto di Storia dell'Architettura 25, no. 30 (1995–97). Rome, 1997.

Frommel 2004
Christoph Luitpold Frommel. "I programmi di Niccolò V e di Giulio II per il palazzo del Vaticano." In *Domus et splendida palatia: residenze papali e cardinalizie a Roma fra XII e XV secolo,* edited by Alessio Monciatti, pp. 144–68. Pisa, 2004.

Frosinini 1986
Cecilia Frosinini. "Il passaggio di gestione in una bottega pittorica fiorentina del primo rinascimento: Lorenzo di Bicci e Bicci di Lorenzo." *Antichità viva* 25, no. 1 (1986), pp. 5–15.

Frosinini 1998
Cecilia Frosinini. "Considerazioni su Lorenzo Monaco: Problemi di documentazione e di tecnica." In *Lorenzo Monaco, tecnica e restauro: L'Incoronazione della Vergine degli Uffizi, l'Annunciazione di Santa Trinita a Firenze,* edited by Marco Ciatti and Cecelia Frosinini, pp. 15–20. Florence, 1998.

Frugoni 1988
Chiara Frugoni. "Altri luoghi, cercando il Paradiso (Il ciclo di Buffalmacco nel Camposanto di Pisa e la committenza Domenicana)." *Annali della Scuola Normale Superiore di Pisa,* ser. 3, 18, no. 4 (1988), pp. 1557–1643.

Fusetti and Virilli 1998
Sergio Fusetti and Paolo Virilli. "Il Polittico Guidalotti: Osservazioni e considerazioni durante il restauro." In Garibaldi 1998, pp. 126–35.

Galleria Doria Pamphilj 1851
Catalogo dei quadri esistenti nella Galleria del Principe Doria Pamphili. Rome, 1851.

Galli 2002
Aldo Galli. "Nanni di Bartolo." In Bellosi 2002, pp. 124–26.

Gamba 1936
Carlo Gamba. *Botticelli.* Milan, 1936.

Gardner 1998
Elizabeth E. Gardner. *A Bibliographical Repertory of Italian Private Collections.* Vol. I. Vicenza, 1998.

Gardner von Teuffel 1997
Christa Gardner von Teuffel. "Fra Angelico's Bishop Saints from the High Altar of S. Domenico, Fiesole." *The Burlington Magazine* 139 (July 1997), pp. 463–65.

Garibaldi 1998
Vittoria Garibaldi, ed. *Beato Angelico e Benozzo Gozzoli: Artisti del Rinascimento a Perugia; itinerari d'arte in Umbria.* Exhib. cat., Galleria Nazionale dell'Umbria, Perugia. Cinisello Balsamo, Italy, 1998.

Gavet sale, 1897
Catalogue des objets d'art et de haute curiosité de la Renaissance; tableaux, tapisseries, composant la collection de M. Émile Gavet. Sale cat. Paris: Galerie Georges Petit, May 31–June 9, 1897.

Gengaro 1944
Maria Luisa Gengaro. *Il Beato Angelico a San Marco.* Bergamo, 1944.

Gentile 1998
Sebastiano Gentile, ed. *Oriente Cristiano e Santità: Figure e storie di santi tra bisanzio e l'Occidente.* Exhib. cat., Biblioteca Nazionale Marciana, Venice. Milan, 1998.

Ghiberti 1998 ed.
Lorenzo Ghiberti. *I Commentari; Biblioteca Nazionale Centrale di Firenze, II, I, 333.* Edited by Lorenzo Bartoli. Florence, 1998.

Ghidiglia Quintavalle 1960
A. Ghidiglia Quintavalle. "La 'croce per morti' di Zanobi Strozzi." *Bollettino d'arte,* ser. 4, no. 45 (1960), pp. 68–72.

Giantomassi and Zari 2001
C. Giantomassi and D. Zari. "La tecnica pittorica." In *Il Beato Angelico e la Cappella Niccolina. Storia e restauro,* pp. 99–109. Novara, 2001.

Gilbert 1975
Creighton Gilbert. "Fra Angelico's Fresco Cycles in Rome: Their Number and Dates." *Zeitschrift für Kunstgeschichte* 38 (1975), pp. 245–65.

Gilbert 1984
Creighton Gilbert. "The Conversion of Fra Angelico." In *Scritti di storia dell'arte in onore di Roberto Salvini,* pp. 281–87. Florence, 1984.

Gilbert 2003
Creighton Gilbert. *How Fra Angelico and Signorelli Saw the End of the World.* University Park, Pennsylvania, 2003.

Giurescu Heller 2002
E. Giurescu Heller, ed. *Icons or Portraits?: Images of Jesus and Mary from the Collection of Michael Hall.* Exhib. cat., The Gallery at the American Bible Society, New York. New York, 2002.

Gómez-Moreno 1957
Carmen Gómez-Moreno. "A Reconstructed Panel by Fra Angelico and Some New Evidence for the Chronology of His Work." *The Art Bulletin* 39 (1957), pp. 183–93.

Gordon 1998
Dillian Gordon. "Zanobi Strozzi's 'Annunciation' in the National Gallery." *The Burlington Magazine* 140 (August 1998), pp. 517–24.

Gordon 2003
Dillian Gordon. *The Fifteenth Century: Italian Paintings.* Vol. I. National Gallery Catalogues. London, 2003.

Grabski 1990
Józef Grabski, ed. *Opus Sacrum: Catalogue of the Exhibition from the Collection of Barbara Piasecka Johnson.* Exhib. cat., Royal Castle, Warsaw. Vienna, 1990.

Gregori et al. 1992
Mina Gregori, Antonio Paolucci, and Cristina Acidini Luchinat. *Maestri e botteghe. pittura a Firenze alla fine del Quattrocento.* Milan, 1992.

Gronau 1938
Giorgio Gronau. "In margine a Francesco Pesellino." *Rivista d'arte* 20 (1938), pp. 123–46.

Gualandi 1843
Michelangelo Gualandi. *Memorie originali italiane risguardanti le Belle Arti.* Ser. IV. Bologna, 1843.

Guasti 1857
Cesare Guasti, ed. *La cupola di Santa Maria del Fiore; illustrata con i documenti dell'archivio dell'opera secolare. Saggio di una compiuta illustrazione dell'opera secolare e del tempio di Santa Maria del Fiore.* Florence, 1857.

Gucci 1990 ed.
Giorgio Gucci. *Viaggio ai luoghi santi,* edited by Marcellina Troncarelli. In Lanza and Troncarelli 1990.

Habig 1979
Marion A. Habig, ed. *St. Francis of Assisi: Writings and Early Biographies. English Omnibus of the Sources for the Life of St. Francis.* 3rd rev. ed. London, 1979.

Haines 1983
Margaret Haines. *The "Sacrestia delle Messe" of the Florentine Cathedral.* Florence, 1983.

Hale 2000
Charlotte Hale. "The Technique and Materials of the Intercession of Christ and the Virgin Attributed to Lorenzo Monaco." In *The Fabric of Images: European Paintings on Textile Supports in the Fourteenth and Fifteenth Centuries,* pp. 31–41. London, 2000.

Hamburger 1998
Jeffrey F. Hamburger. "'Frequentant Memoriam Visionis Faciei Meae': Image and Imitation in the Devotions to the Veronica Attributed to Gertrude of Helfta." In Kessler and Wolf 1998, pp. 229–46.

Hannema 1952
Daniel George Hannema. *Chefs-d'oeuvre de la collection D. G. van Beuningen.* Exhib. cat., Musée du Petit Palais, Paris. Paris, 1952.

Hatfield 1970
Rab Hatfield. "The Compagnia de' Magi." *Journal of the Warburg and Courtauld Institutes* 33 (1970), pp. 107–61.

Hatvany sale, 1980
The Hatvany Collection: Highly Important Old Master Drawings. Sale cat. London: Christie, Manson, and Woods, June 24, 1980.

Hautecoeur 1926
Louis Hautecoeur. *Musée National du Louvre: Catalogue des peintures exposées dans les galeries. Vol. II, École italienne et école espagnole.* Paris, 1926.

Henderson and Joannides 1991
J. Henderson and Paul Joannides. "A Franciscan Triptych by Fra Angelico." *Arte cristiana* 79, no. 42 (1991), pp. 3–6.

Henniker-Heaton 1926
Raymond Henniker-Heaton. "A Predella by Pesellino." *The Burlington Magazine* 49 (October 1926), pp. 155–61.

Herlihy et al. 2002
D. Herlihy, C. Klapisch-Zuber, R. Burr Litchfield, and A. Molho, eds. "Florentine Renaissance Resources: Online *Catasto* of 1427." www.stg.Brown.edu/projects/catasto. Providence, 2002.

Hiller von Gaertringen 2004
Rudolf Hiller von Gaertringen. *Italienische Gemälde im Städel, 1300–1550: Toskana und Umbrien.* Mainz, 2004.

Hind 1936
Arthur Mayger Hind. *Nielli, Chiefly Italian of the XV Century: Plates, Sulphur Casts and Prints Preserved in the British Museum.* London, 1936.

Hind 1938
Arthur M. Hind. *Early Italian Engraving: A Critical Catalogue with Complete Reproduction of All the Prints Described.* Part 1, 2 vols. London and New York, 1938.

Hindman et al. 1997
Sandra Hindman, Mirella Levi D'Ancona, Pia Palladino, and Maria Francesca Saffiotti. *The Robert Lehman Collection, IV, Illuminations.* New York, 1997.

Holford sale, 1927
Pictures of the Italian School: First Portion of the Collection of the Late Sir George Lindsay Holford. Sale cat. London: Christie, Manson, and Woods, July 15, 1927.

Holmes 1999
Megan Holmes. *Fra Filippo Lippi: The Carmelite Painter.* New Haven, 1999.

Hood 1993
William Hood. *Fra Angelico at San Marco.* New Haven, 1993.

Israëls 2003
Machtelt Israëls. "Sassetta, Fra Angelico and Their Patrons at S. Domenico, Cortona." *The Burlington Magazine* 145 (November 2003), pp. 760–76.

Jacopo da Varagine 1993 ed.
Jacopo da Varagine. *The Golden Legend: Readings on the Saints.* Translated by William Granger Ryan. 2 vols. Princeton, 1993.

Jameson 1850
Mrs. A. Jameson. *Sacred and Legendary Art.* 2nd ed. London, 1850.

Jarves collection, 1862
Descriptive Catalogue of "Old Masters," Collected by James J. Jarves to Illustrate the History of Painting from A.D. 1200 to the Best Periods of Italian Art. Cambridge, 1862.

Jerome 1893 ed.
Saint Jerome. *The Principal Works of Saint Jerome.* Edited by Philip Schaff; translated by W. H. Fremantle, with the assistance of G. Lewis and W. G. Martley. Grand Rapids, 1893.

Joannides 1993
Paul Joannides. *Masaccio and Masolino: A Complete Catalogue.* London, 1993.

John of Hildesheim 1955 ed.
John of Hildesheim. *The Story of the Three Kings, Which Originally Was Written by John of Hildesheim in the Fourteenth Century and Now Is Retold by Margaret B. Freeman.* New York, 1955.

Jones 1984
Roger Jones. "Palla Strozzi e la sagrestia di Santa Trinita." *Rivista d'arte* 37 (1984), pp. 9–106.

Kaftal 1952
George Kaftal. *Saints in Italian Art: Iconography of Saints in Tuscan Paintings.* Florence, 1952.

Kanter 1994
Laurence B. Kanter. *Italian Paintings in the Museum of Fine Arts Boston.* Vol. I, *13th–15th Century.* Boston, 1994.

Kanter 2000
Laurence B. Kanter. "A Rediscovered Panel by Fra Angelico." *Paragone* 51, ser. 3, no. 29 (2000), pp. 3–13.

Kanter 2001a
Laurence B. Kanter. "An Annunciation by Fra Angelico." In *Rediscovering Fra Angelico: A Fragmentary History,* edited by Clay Dean, pp. 13–39. New Haven, 2001.

Kanter 2001b
Laurence B. Kanter. "Florentine Illuminations in the Wallraf-Richartz-Museum: Zanobi Strozzi and a Proposal for Matteo di Pacino." *Wallraf-Richartz-Jahrbuch* 62 (2001), pp. 143–54.

Kanter 2002
Laurence B. Kanter. "Zanobi Strozzi miniatore and Battista di Biagio Sanguigni." *Arte cristiana* 90, no. 812 (2002), pp. 321–31.

Kanter 2003
Laurence B. Kanter. "The School of S. Marco" (exhibition review). *The Burlington Magazine* 145 (August 2003), pp. 605–8.

Kanter 2004
Laurence B. Kanter. Review of Boskovits and Brown 2003. *The Burlington Magazine* 146 (February 2004), pp. 105–8.

Kanter et al. 1994
Laurence B. Kanter et al. *Painting and Illumination in Early Renaissance Florence, 1300–1450.* Exhib. cat., The Metropolitan Museum of Art, New York. New York, 1994.

Kelly 1996
Thomas Forrest Kelly. *The Exultet in Southern Italy.* New York, 1996.

Kent 1981
F. W. Kent. "The Making of a Renaissance Patron." In *Giovanni Rucellai ed il suo Zibaldone,* vol. II, *A Florentine Patrician and His Palace,* by F. W. Kent et al., pp. 9–87. London, 1981.

Kessler and Wolf 1998
Herbert L. Kessler and Gerhard Wolf, eds. *The Holy Face and the Paradox of Representation: Papers from a Colloquium Held at the Bibliotheca Hertziana, Rome, and the Villa Spelman, Florence, 1996.* Bologna, 1998.

Kleeman and Willner 1993
Eva C. Kleeman and Saskia G. Willner. *Museum Boymans-Van Beuningen Rotterdam. Italiaanse schilderijen, 1300–1500: Eigen collectie / Italian Paintings, 1300–1500: Own Collection.* Rotterdam, 1993.

Klesse 1967
Brigitte Klesse. *Seidenstoffe in der italienischen Malerei des 14. Jahrhunderts.* Bern, 1967.

Knipe 1997–98
Penley Knipe. "Grounds on Paper: An Examination of Eight Early Drawings." Fogg Art Museum files, 1997–98.

Königliche Museen zu Berlin 1898
Königliche Museen zu Berlin. *Beschreibendes Verzeichnis der Gemälde.* Berlin, 1898.

Koschatzky, Oberhuber, and Knab 1971
Walter Koschatzky, Konrad Oberhuber, and Eckhart Knab, eds. *Italian Drawings in the Albertina.* Greenwich, Connecticut, 1971.

Kugler 1847
Franz Kugler. *Handbuch der Geschichte der Malerei seit Constantin dem Grossen.* 2 vols. 2nd ed. Berlin, 1847.

Kustodieva 1994
Tatyana K. Kustodieva. *The Hermitage Catalogue of Western Painting: Italian Painting, Thirteenth to Sixteenth Centuries.* Moscow, 1994.

Labriola, De Benedictis, and Freuler 2002
Ada Labriola, Cristina De Benedictis, and Gaudenz Freuler. *La miniatura senese, 1270–1420.* Milan, 2002.

Lachi 1995
Chiara Lachi. *Il Maestro della Natività di Castello.* Florence, 1995.

Laclotte 1956
Michel Laclotte. *De Giotto à Bellini: Les primitifs italiens dans les musées de France.* Paris, 1956.

Laclotte and Mognetti 1976
Michel Laclotte and Élisabeth Mognetti. *Peinture italienne, Avignon—Musée du Petit Palais.* Paris, 1976.

Laclotte and Mognetti 1987
Michel Laclotte and Élisabeth Mognetti. *Avignon, Musée du Petit Palais. Peinture italienne.* 3rd ed. Paris, 1987.

Ladis 1981
Andrew T. Ladis. "Fra Angelico: Newly Discovered Documents from the 1420s." *Mitteilungen des Kunsthistorischen Institutes in Florenz* 25 (1981), pp. 378–79.

Lanza and Troncarelli 1990
Antonio Lanza and Marcellina Troncarelli, eds. *Pellegrini scrittori: Viaggiatori toscani del Trecento in Terrasanta.* Florence, 1990.

Lanzi 1792–96 (1837–39 ed.)
Luigi Lanzi. *Storia pittorica dell'Italia.* 14 vols. in 5. Venice, 1792–96. Reprint ed., Venice, 1837–39.

Lawson 2001
James Lawson. "Alberti's Prologue to Practice as a Church Architect." *Albertiana* 4 (2001), pp. 45–68.

Leader 2000
Anne Leader. "The Florentine Badia: Monastic Reform in Mural and Cloister." Ph.D. diss., New York University, Institute of Fine Arts, 2000.

Levenson, Oberhuber, and Sheehan 1973
Jay A. Levenson, Konrad Oberhuber, and Jacquelyn L. Sheehan.

Early Italian Engravings from the National Gallery of Art. Washington, D.C., 1973.

Levi D'Ancona 1959
Mirella Levi D'Ancona. "Zanobi Strozzi Reconsidered." *La Bibliofilia* 61 (1959), pp. 1–38.

Levi D'Ancona 1962
Mirella Levi D'Ancona. *Miniatura e miniatori a Firenze dal XIV al XVI secolo: Documenti per la storia della miniatura*. Florence, 1962.

Levi D'Ancona 1970
Mirella Levi D'Ancona. "Battista di Biagio Sanguigni (1392/3–1451)." *La Bibliofilia* 72 (1970), pp. 1–35.

Levi D'Ancona 1978
Mirella Levi D'Ancona. "I corali di S. Maria degli Angeli ora nella Biblioteca Laurenziana e le miniature da essi asportate." In *Miscellanea di studi in memoria di Anna Saitta Revignas*, pp. 213–35. Florence, 1978.

Levi D'Ancona 1993–94
Mirella Levi D'Ancona. *The Choir Books of Santa Maria degli Angeli in Florence*. 2 vols. Florence, 1993–94.

Levi D'Ancona 1995
Mirella Levi D'Ancona. *I corali del monastero di Santa Maria degli Angeli*. Florence, 1995.

***Il libro di Antonio Billi* 1516– (1991 ed.)**
Il libro di Antonio Billi [1516–]. Edited by Fabio Benedetucci. Rome, 1991.

Liebrich 1997
Julia Liebrich. *Die Verkündigung an Maria: Die Ikonographie der italienischen Darstellungen von den Anfangen bis 1500*. Cologne, 1997.

Lightbown 1978
Ronald Lightbown. *Sandro Botticelli*. 2 vols. Berkeley and Los Angeles, 1978.

Lillie 1986
Amanda Rhoda Lillie. "Florentine Villas in the Fifteenth Century: A Study of the Strozzi and Sassetti Country Properties." Ph.D. diss., Courtauld Institute of Art, University of London, 1986.

Liphart 1912
E. Liphart. *The Imperial Hermitage. Catalogue of the Picture Gallery*. Part 1, *Italian and Spanish Painting*. Saint Petersburg, 1912.

Loenertz 1937
Raymond Joseph Loenertz. *La Société des Frères Pérégrinants: Étude sur l'Orient Dominicain*. Rome, 1937.

Loenertz 1975
Raymond Loenertz. "La Société des Frères Pérégrinants de 1374 à 1475. Étude sur l'Orient Dominicain, II." *Archivum Fratrum Praedicatorum* 45 (1975), pp. 107–45.

Logan Berenson 1901
Mary Logan [Berenson]. "Compagno di Pesellino et quelques peintures de l'école," parts 1–2. *Gazette des Beaux-Arts*, ser. 3, 26 (1901), pp. 18–34, 333–43.

Longhi 1928a
Roberto Longhi. "Un dipinto dell'Angelico a Livorno." *Pinacotheca* 1, no. 3 (1928), pp. 153–59.

Longhi 1928a (1968 ed.)
Roberto Longhi. "Un dipinto dell'Angelico a Livorno [1928]." In Longhi 1968, pp. 37–45.

Longhi 1928b
Roberto Longhi. "Ricerche su Giovanni di Francesco." *Pinacotheca* 1 (1928), pp 34–48.

Longhi 1940
Roberto Longhi. "Fatti di Masolino e di Masaccio." *Critica d'arte* 5, no. 3–4, fasc. 25–26 (1940), pp. 145–91. Reprinted in Longhi 1975.

Longhi 1948
Roberto Longhi. "Il Maestro della predella Sherman." *Proporzioni* 2 (1948), pp. 161–62.

Longhi 1960a
Roberto Longhi "Una crocifissione di Benozzo Giovine." *Paragone* 123 (1960), pp. 3–7. Reprinted in Longhi 1975, pp. 123–27.

Longhi 1960b
Roberto Longhi. "Uno squardo alle fotografie della mostra: 'Italian Art and Britain' alla Royal Academy di Londra." *Paragone* 11, no. 125 (1960), pp. 59–61.

Longhi 1967
Roberto Longhi. "Un nuovo numero del 'Maestro della Predella Sherman.'" *Paragone*, n.s. 31, no. 211 (1967), pp. 38–40.

Longhi 1968
Roberto Longhi. *Me pinxit e quesiti caravaggeschi, 1928–1934*. Vol. IV of *Opere complete di Roberto Longhi*. Florence, 1968.

Longhi 1975
Roberto Longhi. *"Fatti di Masolino e di Masaccio" e altri studi sul Quattrocento, 1910–1967*. Florence, 1975.

Lowe 1934–66
E. A. Lowe, ed. *Codices latini antiquiores: A Palaeological Guide to Latin Manuscripts Prior to the Ninth Century*. 12 vols. Oxford, 1934–66.

Lunghi 1997
Elvio Lunghi. *Benozzo Gozzoli a Montefalco*. Assisi, 1997.

Mack 1982
Charles Randall Mack. "Bernardo Rossellino: L. B. Alberti and the Rome of Pope Nicholas V." *Southeastern College of Art Conference Review* 10, no. 2 (1982), pp. 60–69.

Mack 1987
Charles Randall Mack. "Nicholas the Fifth and the Rebuilding of Rome: Reality and Legacy." In *Light on the Eternal City: Observations and Discoveries in the Art and Architecture of Rome*, edited by Hellmut Hager and Susan Scott Munshower, pp. 31–56. Papers in Art History from The Pennsylvania State University, 2. State College, Pennsylvania, 1987.

Magnanimi 1980
Giuseppina Magnanimi. "Inventari della collezione romana dei principi Corsini," parts 1–2. *Bollettino d'arte*, ser. 6, 65, no. 7 (July–September 1980), pp. 91–126; no. 8 (October–December 1980), pp. 73–114.

Malquori 1993
Alessandra Malquori. *"Tempo d'Aversità": Gli affreschi dell'altana di Palazzo Rucellai*. Rome, 1993.

Malquori 1996
Alessandra Malquori. "Storie dei Padri del deserto nel Convento di Santa Maria Novella a Firenze." *Annali della Scuola Normale Superiore di Pisa, Classe di lettere e filosofia*, ser. 4, *Quaderni* 1–2 (1996), pp. 79–93.

Malquori 2001
Alessandra Malquori. "La 'Tebaide' degli Uffizi—Tradizioni letterarie e figurative per l'interpretazione di un tema iconografico." *I Tatti Studies: Essays in the Renaissance* 9 (2001), pp. 119–37.

Van Mander 1603–4 (1994 ed.)
Karel van Mander. *The Lives of the Illustrious Netherlandish and German Painters, from the First Edition of the Schilder-boeck (1603–1604)*. Translated and edited by Hessel Miedema. Vol. I: *The Text*. Doornspijk, 1994.

A. Manetti 1490? (1887 ed.)
Antonio Manetti. *Operette istoriche edite ed inedite* [1490?]. Compiled and edited by Gaetano Milanesi. Florence, 1887.

G. Manetti 1999 ed.
Giannozzo Manetti. *Vita di Nicolò V.* Translation and commentary by Anna Modigliani; introduction by Massimo Miglio. Rome, 1999.

Marchese 1845–46
Vincenzo Marchese. *Memorie dei più insigni pittori, scultori e architetti domenicani*. 2 vols. Florence, 1845–46.

Marchi 2002
Alessandro Marchi. "Arcangelo di Cola." In *Pittori a Camerino nel Quattrocento*, edited by Andrea De Marchi, pp. 160–69. Jesi, Italy, 2002.

Marchini 1958
Giuseppe Marchini. *La Galleria Comunale di Prato*. Florence, 1958.

Mariani Canova 1998
Giordana Mariani Canova. "La porpora nei manoscritti rinascimentali e l'attività di Bartolomeo Sanvito." In *La porpora: Realtà e immaginario di un colore simbolico*, edited by Oddone Longo, pp. 339–71. Proceedings of a conference in Venice, October 24–25, 1996. Venice, 1998.

Marino 2000
Eugenio Marino. "Il Beato Angelico: Saggio sul rapporto personaopere visive ed opere visive-persona." *Memorie domenicane* 31 (2000), pp. 135–338.

Van Marle 1928
Raimond van Marle. *The Development of the Italian Schools of Painting*. Vol. X, *The Renaissance Painters of Florence in the 15th century; the First Generation*. The Hague, 1928.

Van Marle 1929
Raimond van Marle. *The Development of the Italian Schools of Painting*. Vol. XI, *The Renaissance Painters of Florence in the 15th Century; the Second Generation*. The Hague, 1929.

Meiss 1951
Millard Meiss. *Painting in Florence and Siena after the Black Death*. Princeton, 1951.

Meiss 1954
Millard Meiss. "An Early Altarpiece from the Cathedral of Florence." *The Metropolitan Museum of Art Bulletin*, n.s., 12, no. 10 (1954), pp. 302–17.

Meiss 1961
Millard Meiss. "Contributions to Two Elusive Masters." *The Burlington Magazine* 103 (February 1961), pp. 57–66.

Meiss 1974
Millard Meiss. "Scholarship and Penitence in the Early Renaissance: The Image of St. Jerome." *Pantheon* 32 (1974), pp. 134–40.

Melli 2002
Lorenza Melli. "Il disegno per Benozzo." In Toscano and Capitelli 2002, pp. 117–29.

Metropolitan Museum 1984
Notable Acquisitions, 1983–1984: The Metropolitan Museum of Art. New York, 1984.

Micheletti 1959
Emma Micheletti. *Masolino da Panicale.* Milan, 1959.

Middeldorf 1955
Ulrich Middeldorf. "L'Angelico e la scultura." *Rinascimento* 6, no. 2 (1955), pp. 179–94.

Miglio 1975
Massimo Miglio. "Canensi, Michele." In *Dizionario biografico degli italiani,* vol. 18, pp. 10–12. Rome, 1975.

Modesti 1988
Adolfo Modesti. "La serie papale di restituzione di Girolamo Paladino." *Medaglia,* no. 23 (1988), pp. 7–57.

Momigliano Lepschy 1966
Anna Laura Momigliano Lepschy, ed. *Viaggio in Terrasanta di Santo Brasca con l'Itinerario di Gabriele Capodilista, 1458.* Milan, 1966.

Mongan and Sachs 1940
Agnes Mongan and Paul J. Sachs. *Drawings in the Fogg Museum of Art.* Cambridge, Massachusetts, 1940.

Mongan, Oberhuber, and Bober 1988
Agnes Mongan, Konrad Oberhuber, and Jonathan Bober. *I grandi disegni italiani del Fogg Art Museum di Cambridge.* Milan, 1988.

Morachiello 1995
Paolo Morachiello. *Beato Angelico: Gli affreschi di San Marco.* Milan, 1995.

Morçay 1913
Raoul Morçay. "La cronaca del convento fiorentino di San Marco: La parte più antica, dettata da Giuliano Lapaccini." *Archivio storico italiano* 71 (1913), pp. 3–31.

Morello and Kanter 1999
Giovanni Morello and Laurence B. Kanter, eds. *The Treasury of Saint Francis of Assisi.* Exhib. cat., The Metropolitan Museum of Art, New York. Milan, 1999.

Morello and Wolf 2000
Giovanni Morello and Gerhard Wolf, eds., with Herbert L. Kessler. *Il volto di Cristo.* Exhib. cat., Palazzo delle Esposizioni, Rome. Milan, 2000.

Moroni 1840–61
Gaetano Moroni, comp. *Dizionario di erudizione storico-ecclesiastica da S. Pietro sino ai nostri giorni.* 103 vols. Venice, 1840–61.

Muller 2003
Norman Muller. "Technical Note." *Record, The Art Museum, Princeton University* 62 (2003 [2004]), pp. 28–31.

Muntz 1888
Eugène Muntz. *Les collections des Médicis au XVe siècle: Le musée, la bibliothèque, le mobilier (appendice aux précurseurs de la Renaissance).* Paris, 1888.

Muratoff 1930
Pavel Pavlovich Muratoff. *Fra Angelico.* Translated from the Russian by E. Law-Gisiko. London, 1930.

Neri di Bicci 1976 ed.
Neri di Bicci. *Le ricordanze (10 marzo 1453–24 aprile 1475).* Edited by Bruno Santi. Pisa, 1976.

Neri Lusanna 1989
Enrica Neri Lusanna. "Aspetti della cultura tardo-gotica a Firenze: Il 'Maestro del Giudizio di Paride.'" *Arte cristiana* 77, no. 735 (1989), pp. 409–26.

Nessi 1980
Silvestro Nessi. *Montefalco e il suo territorio.* Spoleto, 1980.

Nessi 1997
Silvestro Nessi. *Benozzo Gozzoli a Montefalco.* Assisi, 1997.

Neumeyer 1965
Alfred Neumeyer. "The Lanckorónski Annunciation in the M. H. de Young Memorial Museum." *The Art Quarterly* 28 (1965), pp. 5–17.

Niccolò da Poggibonsi 1945 ed.
Fra Niccolò da Poggibonsi. *Libro d'Oltramare.* Edited by Alberto Bacchi della Lega; revised by P. B. Bagatti. Jerusalem, 1945.

Nuttall 2004
Paula Nuttall. *From Flanders to Florence: The Impact of Netherlandish Painting, 1400–1500.* New Haven, 2004.

Oertel 1960
Robert Oertel. *Italienische Malerei bis zum Ausgang der Renaissance.* Munich, 1960.

Oertel 1961
Robert Oertel. *Frühe italienische Malerei in Altenburg: Beschreibender Katalog der Gemälde des 13. bis 16. Jahrhunderts im Staatlichen Lindenau-Museum.* Berlin, 1961.

Offner 1920
Richard Offner. "A St. Jerome by Masolino." *Art in America* 8, no. 2 (1920), pp. 68–76.

Offner 1927
Richard Offner. *Studies in Florentine Painting: The Fourteenth Century.* New York, 1927.

Offner 1933
Richard Offner. "The Mostra del Tesoro di Firenze Sacra, II." *The Burlington Magazine* 63 (1933), pp. 166–78.

Offner 1945
Richard Offner. "The Straus Collection Goes to Texas." *Art News* 44, no. 7 (May 15–31, 1945), pp. 16–23.

Offner 1960
A Critical and Historical Corpus of Florentine Painting. Section 4, *The Fourteenth Century.* Vol. II, *Nardo di Cione.* New York, 1960.

Offner/Boskovits 2000
Richard Offner. *A Critical and Historical Corpus of Florentine Painting.* Sec. 4, vol. VIII, *Tradition and Innovation in Florentine Painting, Giovanni Bonsi—Tommaso del Mazza.* Edited by Miklós Boskovits. Florence, 2000.

Offner/Boskovits 2001
Richard Offner. *A Critical and Historical Corpus of Florentine Painting.* Sec. 3, vol. V, *Bernardo Daddi and His Circle.* Edited by Miklós Boskovits. Florence, 2001.

Oppenheimer sale, 1936
Catalogue of the Famous Collection of Old Master Drawings Formed by the Late Henry Oppenheimer, Esq., F.S.A. Sale cat. London: Christie, Manson, and Woods, July 10–14, 1936.

Orlandi 1954a
Stefano Orlandi. "Il Beato Angelico." *Rivista d'arte,* ser. 3, 4 (1954), pp. 161–97.

Orlandi 1954b
Stefano Orlandi. "Su una tavola dipinta da Fra Filippo Lippi per Antonio del Branca nel febbraio 1451." *Rivista d'arte,* ser. 3, 4 (1954), pp. 199–201.

Orlandi 1955a
Stefano Orlandi. "Beato Angelico: Note cronologiche." *Memorie domenicane* 72 (1955), pp. 3–37.

Orlandi 1955b
Stefano Orlandi. *"Necrologio" di Santa Maria Novella.* 2 vols. Florence, 1955.

Orlandi 1964
Stefano Orlandi. *Beato Angelico. Monografia storica della vita e delle opere con appendice di nuovi documenti inediti.* Florence, 1964.

Van Os and Prakken 1974
H. W. van Os and Marian Prakken, eds. *The Florentine Paintings in Holland, 1300–1500.* Amsterdam and Maarssen, 1974.

W. Paatz and E. Paatz 1952
Walter Paatz and Elizabeth Paatz. *Die Kirchen von Florenz, ein Kunstgeschichtliches Handbuch.* Vol. IV. Frankfurt, 1952.

Padoa Rizzo 1969a
Anna Padoa Rizzo. "Benozzo ante 1450." *Commentari* 20 (1969), pp. 52–62.

Padoa Rizzo 1969b
Anna Padoa Rizzo. "Una precisazione sulla collaborazione di Benozzo agli affreschi del convento di San Marco." *Antichità viva* 7 (1969), pp. 9–13.

Padoa Rizzo 1972
Anna Padoa Rizzo. *Benozzo Gozzoli, pittore fiorentino.* Florence, 1972.

Padoa Rizzo 1981
Anna Padoa Rizzo. "Nota breve su Colantonio, van der Weyden e l'Angelico." *Antichità viva* 20, no. 5 (1981), pp. 15–17.

Padoa Rizzo 1989
Anna Padoa Rizzo. *Arte e committenza a Pistoia alla fine del XV secolo: Benozzo Gozzoli e i figli Francesco e Alesso. Nuove ricerche.* Pistoia, 1989.

Padoa Rizzo 1991
Anna Padoa Rizzo. "L'attività di Benozzo Gozzoli per la Compagnia di Santa Maria delle Laudi e di Sant'Agnese (1439–1441)." *Rivista d'arte,* ser. 4, 43 (1991), pp. 203–9.

Padoa Rizzo 1992
Anna Padoa Rizzo. *Benozzo Gozzoli. Catalogo completo dei dipinti.* Florence, 1992.

Padoa Rizzo 1997a
Anna Padoa Rizzo, with Annamaria Bernacchioni, Nicoletta Pons, and Lisa Venturi. *Benozzo Gozzoli in Toscana.* Florence, 1997.

Padoa Rizzo 1997b
Anna Padoa Rizzo. *La Cappella dell'Assunta nel Duomo di Prato.* Florence, 1997.

Padoa Rizzo 2001
Anna Padoa Rizzo. "Gli esordi di Masaccio: Committenti e fruitori." In *Masaccio: Il trittico di San Giovenale e il primo '400 fiorentino,* edited by Caterina Caneva, pp. 155–59. Milan, 2001.

Padoa Rizzo 2002a
Anna Padoa Rizzo. *Iconografia di San Giovanni Gualberto: La pittura in Toscana.* Pisa, 2002.

Padoa Rizzo 2002b
Anna Padoa Rizzo. "Una lunga vita operosa." In Toscano and Capitelli 2002, pp. 15–39.

Padoa Rizzo 2003
Anna Padoa Rizzo. *Benozzo Gozzoli: Un pittore insigne, "pratico di grandissima invenzione."* Milan, 2003.

Padovani and Meloni Trkulja 1982
Serena Padovani and Silvia Meloni Trkulja. *Il Cenacolo di Andrea del Sarto a San Salvi: Guida del museo.* Florence, 1982.

Palladino 2003
Pia Palladino. *Treasures of a Lost Art: Italian Manuscript Painting of the Middle Ages and Renaissance.* Exhib. cat., The Metropolitan Museum of Art, New York. New York, 2003.

Pandimiglio 1987
Leonida Pandimiglio. *Felice di Michele vir clarissimus e una consorteria: I Brancacci di Firenze.* [Ivrea, Italy], 1987.

Panofsky 1927
Erwin Panofsky. "'Imago Pietatis': Ein Beitrag zur Typengeschichte des 'Schmerzensmanns' und der 'Maria Mediatrix.'" In *Festschrift für Max J. Friedländer zum 60. Geburtstage,* pp. 261–308. Leipzig, 1927.

Panofsky 1956
Erwin Panofsky. "Jean Hey's 'Ecce Homo': Speculations about Its Author, Its Donor, and Its Iconography." *Bulletin des Musées Royaux des Beaux-Arts,* nos. 3–4 (1956), pp. 95–138.

Paoli 1996
Emore Paoli. "Il programma teologico-spirituale del Giudizio Universale di Orvieto." In *La Cappella Nova o di San Brizio nel Duomo di Orvieto,* edited by Giusi Testa, pp. 65–77. Milan, 1996.

Paolozzi Strozzi 2000
Beatrice Paolozzi Strozzi, ed. *Il parato di Niccolò V per il Giubileo del 1450.* Exhib. cat., Museo Nazionale del Bargello, Florence. Florence, 2000.

Papi 1982
Massimo Papi. "Santa Maria Novella di Firenze e l'Outremer Domenicano." In Cardini 1982, pp. 87–107.

Pasculli Ferrara 2000
Mimma Pasculli Ferrara, ed. *Itinerari in Pugli: Tra arte e spiritualità.* Rome, 2000.

Pasquinucci 1998
Simona Pasquinucci. "Note sulla cultura figurativa a San Miniato fra Trecento e Quattrocento." In *Sumptuosa tabula picta: Pittori a Lucca tra gotico e rinascimento,* edited by Maria Teresa Filieri, pp. 112–19. Lucca, 1998.

Pastor 1938–61
Ludwig Pastor. *The History of the Popes from the Close of the Middle Ages.* Edited by Frederick Ignatius Antrobus. Various editions and editors. 40 vols. London, 1938–61.

Pavoni 2003
Rosanna Pavoni, ed. *Museo Bagatti Valsecchi.* Vol. I. Milan, 2003.

Penndorf 1998
Jutta Penndorf, ed. *Frühe italienische Malerei im Lindenau-Museum Altenburg.* Leipzig, 1998.

Perosa 1960
Alessandro Perosa, ed. *Il Zibaldone Quaresimale.* Vol. I of F. W. Kent et al., *Giovanni Rucellai ed il suo Zibaldone.* London, 1960.

Phillips 1955
John Goldsmith Phillips. *Early Florentine Designers and Engravers: Maso Finiguerra, Baccio Baldini, Antonio Pollaiuolo, Sandro Botticelli [and] Francesco Rosselli.* Cambridge, Massachusetts, 1955.

Piccolomini 1918 ed.
Aeneas Sylvius Piccolomini. *Der Briefwechsel, III. Abteilung: Briefe als Bischof von Siena.* Edited by Rudolf Wolkan. Fontes rerum austriacarum, ser. 2, Diplomataria et acta, vol. 68. Vienna, 1918.

Piero della Francesca 1995 ed.
Piero della Francesca. *Libellus de quinque corporibus regularibus.* Facsimile ed. 3 vols. Florence, 1995.

Pietrangeli 1993
Carlo Pietrangeli. *La Biblioteca Casanatense.* Edited by Angela Adriana Cavarra. Florence, 1993.

Poggi 1988 ed.
Giovanni Poggi. *Il Duomo di Firenze.* Edited by Margaret Haines. 2 vols. Florence, 1988.

Pope-Hennessy 1939
John Pope-Hennessy. *Sassetta.* London, 1939.

Pope-Hennessy 1952
John Pope-Hennessy. *Fra Angelico.* London, 1952.

Pope-Hennessy 1964
John Pope-Hennessy. *Catalogue of Italian Sculpture in the Victoria and Albert Museum.* Vol. I. London, 1964.

Pope-Hennessy 1974
John Pope-Hennessy. *Fra Angelico.* 2nd ed. London, 1974.

Pope-Hennessy 1979
John Pope-Hennessy. "The Ford Italian Paintings." *Bulletin of The Detroit Institute of Arts* 57, no. 1 (1979), pp. 15–23.

Pope-Hennessy 1984
John Pope-Hennessy. "Roger Fry and The Metropolitan Museum of Art." In *Oxford, China, and Italy: Writings in Honour of Sir Harold Acton on His Eightieth Birthday,* edited by Edward Chaney and Neil Ritchie, pp. 229–40. New York, 1984.

Popham 1930
[A. E. Popham.] Drawings entries. In Royal Academy of Arts 1930.

Popham 1931
A. E. Popham. *Italian Drawings Exhibited at the Royal Academy, Burlington House, London 1930.* London, 1931.

Popham and Pouncey 1950
A. E. Popham and Philip Pouncey. *Italian Drawings in the Department of Prints and Drawings in the British Museum.* Vol. 1, *The Fourteenth and Fifteenth Centuries.* 2 vols. London, 1950.

Pouncey 1954
Philip Pouncey. "A New Panel by the Master of 1419." *The Burlington Magazine* 96 (September 1954), pp. 291–92.

Procacci 1929
Ugo Procacci. "Il Soggiorno fiorentino di Arcangelo di Cola." *Rivista d'arte* 11 (1929), pp. 119–27.

Procacci 1960a
Ugo Procacci. "Di Jacopo d'Antonio e delle compagnie di dipintori del corso degli Adimari nel XV secolo." *Rivista d'arte* 20 (1960), pp. 3–70.

Procacci 1960b
Ugo Procacci. *Sinopie e affreschi.* [Milan, 1960.]

Proto Pisani and Padoa Rizzo 1987
Rosanna Caterina Proto Pisani and Anna Padoa Rizzo. *Gli affreschi di Benozzo Gozzoli a Castelfiorentino (1484–1490).* Pisa, 1987.

Pudelko 1935
Georg Pudelko. "The Minor Masters of the Chiostro Verde." *The Art Bulletin* 17 (1935), pp. 71–89.

Pudelko 1938
Georg Pudelko. "The Maestro del Bambino Vispo." *Art in America* 26 (1938), pp. 47–63.

Pushkin State Museum 1995
Five Centuries of European Drawings: The Former Collection of Franz Koenigs. Exhib. cat., State Pushkin Museum, Moscow. Milan, 1995.

Ricci 1913
Seymour de Ricci. *Description raisonnée des peintures du Louvre.* Vol. I, *Italie et Espagne.* Paris, 1913.

Rice 1985
E. F. Rice, Jr. *Saint Jerome in the Renaissance.* Baltimore, 1985.

Richa 1755
Giuseppe Richa. *Notizie istoriche delle chiese fiorentine.* Vol. III. Florence, 1755.

Richa 1762
Giuseppe Richa. *Notizie istoriche delle chiese fiorentine, divise ne' suoi quartieri.* Vols. IX–X, *Del quartiere di S. Spirito.* Florence, 1762.

Richard 1984
Jean Richard. "Les relations de pèlerinages au Moyen Âge et les motivations de leurs auteurs." In *Wallfahrt kennt keine Grenzen: Themen zu einer Ausstellung des Bayerischen Nationalmuseums und des Adalbert Stifter Vereins, München,* edited by Lenz Kriss-Rettenbeck and Gerda Möhler, pp. 143–54. Munich, 1984.

Richardson 1955–56
E. P. Richardson. "A Fra Angelico Madonna." *Bulletin of The Detroit Institute of Arts* 35, no. 4 (1955–56), pp. 86–88. Reprinted in *The Art Quarterly* 19, no. 3 (1956), pp. 318–20.

Richter 1894
Jean Paul Richter. "Die Ausstellung italienischer Renaissancewerke in der New Gallery in London." *Repertorium für Kunstwissenschaft* 17 (1894), pp. 235–42.

Richter 1901
Jean Paul Richter. *Catalogue of Pictures at Locko Park.* London, 1901.

Ridderbos 1984
Bernhard Ridderbos. *Saint and Symbol: Images of Saint Jerome in Early Italian Art.* Groningen, 1984.

Roberts 1993
Perri Lee Roberts. *Masolino da Panicale.* Oxford, 1993.

Robinson sale, 1923
Well-known Collection of Pictures by Old Masters. Sale cat. London: Christie, Manson, and Woods, July 6, 1923.

Röhricht 1963
Reinhold Röhricht. *Bibliotheca Geographica Palaestinae.* Jerusalem, 1963.

G. Romano 1990
Giovanni Romano, ed. *Da Biduino ad Algardi: Pittura e scultura a confronto.* Turin, 1990.

S. Romano 1992
Serena Romano. *Eclissi di Roma: Pittura murale a Roma e nel Lazio da Bonifacio VIII a Martino V (1295–1431).* Rome, 1992.

S. Romano 2000
Serena Romano. "L'acheropita lateranense: Storia e funzione." In Morello and Wolf 2000, pp. 39–41.

Rosenthal 1928
Jacques Rosenthal. *Bibliotheca Medii Aevi Manuscripta, Pars Altera.* Catalogue, no. 90. Munich, 1928.

Rossi 1876
Adamo Rossi. "Documenti sulle requisizioni dei quadri fatte a Perugia dalla Francia ai tempi della Repubblica dell'Impero." *Giornale di erudizione artistica* 5 (1876), fasc. 9–10, pp. 225–56, 288–303, 321–52.

Rossi 1877
Adamo Rossi. "Documenti sulle requisizioni dei quadri fatte a Perugia dalla Francia ai tempi della Repubblica dell'Impero." *Giornale di erudizione artistica* 6 (1877), fasc. 1–2, pp. 3–25; fasc. 3–4, pp. 65–110.

Royal Academy of Arts 1930
Exhibition of Italian Art, 1200–1900. Exhib. cat., Royal Academy of Arts, London. London, 1930.

Ruda 1975
Jeffrey Ruda. "The National Gallery Tondo of the Adoration of the Magi and the Early Style of Filippo Lippi." *Studies in the History of Art* 7 (1975), pp. 6–39.

Russell 1996
F. Russell. "An Early Crucifixion by Fra Angelico." *The Burlington Magazine* 138 (May 1996), pp. 315–17.

Rykwert and Engel 1994
Joseph Rykwert and Anne Engel, eds. *Leon Battista Alberti.* Exhib. cat., Palazzo del Tè, Mantua. Milan, 1994.

Saalman 1959
Howard Saalman. "Giovanni di Gherardo da Prato's Designs Concerning the Cupola of Santa Maria del Fiore in Florence." *Journal of the Society of Architectural Historians* 18, no. 1 (March 1959), pp. 11–20.

Salatino 1992
Kevin Salatino. "The Frescoes of Fra Angelico for the Chapel of Nicholas V: Art and Ideology in Renaissance Rome." Ph.D. diss., University of Pennsylvania, 1992.

Salmi 1916–18
Mario Salmi. "Zanobi Machiavelli e il 'Compagno del Pesellino.'" *Rivista d'arte* 9 (1916–18), pp. 49–56.

Salmi 1928–29
Mario Salmi. "Gli affreschi nella Collegiata di Castiglione Olona—II." *Dedalo* 9 (1928–29), pp. 3–29.

Salmi 1948
Mario Salmi. *Masaccio.* Milan, 1948.

Salmi 1950
Mario Salmi. "Problemi dell'Angelico." *Commentari* 1 (1950), pp. 75–81, 146–56.

Salmi 1954
Mario Salmi. *Italian Miniatures.* Translated by Elisabeth Borgese. New York, 1954.

Salmi 1955
Mario Salmi. *La miniatura italiana.* Milan, 1955.

Salmi 1958
Mario Salmi. *Il Beato Angelico.* Spoleto, 1958.

Sanford collection, 1847
Catalogue of Paintings Belonging to the Rev. J. Sanford; Collected in Italy, from 1815 to 1837. London, 1847.

Santagostino Barbone 1989
Anna Santagostino Barbone. "Il Giudizio Universale del Beato Angelico per la chiesa del monastero camaldolese di S. Maria degli Angeli a Firenze." *Memorie domenicane,* no. 20 (1989), pp. 255–78.

Scardeone 1560
Bernardino Scardeone. *De antiquitate urbis Patavii.* Basel, 1560.

Scharf 1958
Alfred Scharf. "The Robinson Collection." *The Burlington Magazine* 100 (September 1958), pp. 299–304.

Scheller 1995
Robert Walter Hans Peter Scheller. *Exemplum: Model-Book Drawings and the Practice of Artistic Transmission in the Middle Ages (ca. 900–ca. 1470).* Tranlated by Michael Hoyle. Amsterdam, 1995.

Scherrer 1875
Gustav Scherrer. *Verzeichniss der Handschriften der Stiftsbibliothek von St. Gallen.* Halle, 1875. Facsimile reprint, Hildesheim and New York, 1975.

Schmarsow 1897
August Schmarsow. "Meister des XIV. und XV. Jahrhunderts im Lindenau-Museum zu Altenburg." In *Festschrift zu Ehren des Kunsthistorischen Institutes in Florenz,* pp. 143–96. Leipzig, 1897.

Schmidt 1995
Victor M. Schmidt. "Vroege Italiaanse schilderijen in Museum Boymans-van Beuningen." *Incontri* 10 (1995), pp. 87–91.

Schmidt 2002
Victor M. Schmidt. "Portable Polyptych with Narrative Scenes: Fourteenth-Century De Luxe Objects between Italian Panel Painting and French *Arts somptuaires.*" In *Italian Panel Painting of the Duecento and Trecento,* edited by Victor M. Schmidt, pp. 395–419. Studies in the History of Art, 61. Washington, D.C., 2002. Proceedings of a symposium held June 5–6, 1998, in Florence, and October 16, 1998, in Washington, D.C.

Schönbrunner and Meder 1896–1908
Josef Schönbrunner and Josef Meder, eds. *Handzeichnungen alter Meister aus der Albertina und anderen Sammlungen.* 12 vols. Vienna.

Schottmüller 1911
Frida Schottmüller. *Fra Angelico da Fiesole: Des Meisters Gemälde.* Stuttgart, 1911.

Schottmüller 1924
Frida Schottmüller. *Fra Angelico da Fiesole: Des Meisters Gemälde.* 2nd ed. Stuttgart, 1924.

Scudieri 1998
Magnolia Scudieri. "Michelozzo a San Marco e il convento preesistente." In *Michelozzo, scultore e architetto (1396–1472),* edited by Gabriele Morolli, pp. 107–13. Florence, 1998. Paper presented at a 1996 conference.

Scudieri 2000
Magnolia Scudieri. "La Biblioteca di San Marco dalle origini a oggi." In *La Biblioteca di Michelozzo a San Marco tra recupero e scoperta,* pp. 9–43. Florence, 2000.

Scudieri 2003
Magnolia Scudieri. "Sanguigni, Beato Angelico, Zanobi Strozzi: Attività parallele o intersecanti?" In Scudieri and Rasario 2003, pp. 33–43.

Scudieri 2004
Magnolia Scudieri. *The Frescoes by Angelico at San Marco.* Florence and Milan, 2004.

Scudieri and Rasario 2000
Magnolia Scudieri and Giovanna Rasario, eds. *La Biblioteca di Michelozzo a San Marco tra recupero e scoperta.* Florence, 2000.

Scudieri and Rasario 2003
Magnolia Scudieri and Giovanna Rasario, eds. *Miniatura del '400 a*

San Marco: Dalle suggestioni avignonesi all'ambiente dell'Angelico. Exhib. cat., Museo di San Marco, Florence. Florence, 2003.

Sebregondi 1991
Ludovica Sebregondi. *Tre Confraternite fiorentine: Santa Maria della Pietà, detta "Buca" di San Girolamo, San Filippo Benizi, San Francesco Poverino.* Florence, 1991.

Sensi 2003
Mario Sensi. *Santuari, pellegrini, eremiti nell'Italia Centrale.* 3 vols. Spoleto, 2003.

Serra 1934
Luigi Serra. *L'arte nelle Marche.* Vol. II, *Il periodo del Rinascimento.* Rome, 1934.

Seymour 1970
Charles Seymour, Jr. *Early Italian Paintings in the Yale University Art Gallery: A Catalogue.* New Haven, 1970.

Shapley 1966
Fern Rusk Shapley. *Paintings from the Samuel H. Kress Collection.* Vol. I, *Italian Schools XIII–XV Century.* London, 1966.

Shell 1972
Curtis Shell. "Two Triptychs by Giovanni dal Ponte." *The Art Bulletin* 54 (March 1972), pp. 41–46.

Sirén 1916
Osvald Sirén. *A Descriptive Catalogue of the Pictures in the Jarves Collection Belonging to Yale University.* New Haven, 1916.

Skemer 2001
D. C. Skemer. "Amulet Rolls and Female Devotion in the Late Middle Ages." *Scriptorium* 55, part 2 (2001), pp. 197–227.

South African National Gallery 1975
South African National Gallery, Cape Town. *Natale Labia Collection on Loan to the South African National Gallery, Cape Town.* Cape Town, n.d. [1975].

Spallanzani and Gaeta Bertelà 1992
Marco Spallanzani and Giovanna Gaeta Bertelà, eds. *Libro d'inventario dei beni di Lorenzo il Magnifico.* Florence, 1992.

Spencer 1957
John R. Spencer. "*Ut rhetorica pictura*: A Study in Quattrocento Theory of Painting." *Journal of the Warburg and Courtauld Institutes* 20 (1957), pp. 26–44.

Spike 1996
John T. Spike. *Fra Angelico.* New York, 1996.

Spinelli 1988
Riccardo Spinelli. "Sull'antica collocazione del trittico di Mariotto di Nardo di Santa Margherita a Tosina." *Paragone,* n.s., 455, no. 7 (1988), pp. 44–51.

Sricchia Santoro 2003
Fiorella Sricchia Santoro. "Jean Fouquet en Italie." In *Jean Fouquet: Peintre et enlumineur du XVe siècle,* edited by François Avril, pp. 50–63. Exhib. cat., Bibliothèque Nationale de France. Paris, 2003.

Staatliche Museen Preussischer Kulturbesitz 1978
Staatliche Museen Preussischer Kulturbesitz, Gemäldegalerie, Berlin. *Catalogue of Paintings, 13th–18th Century.* Translated by Linda B. Parchall. 2nd rev. ed. Berlin-Dahlem, 1978.

Staatliche Museen zu Berlin 1931
Staatliche Museen zu Berlin, Gemäldegalerie, Berlin. *Beschreibendes Verzeichnis der Gemälde im Kaiser-Friedrich-Museum und Deutschen Museum.* 9th ed. Berlin, 1931.

Stinger 1985
Charles L. Stinger. *The Renaissance in Rome.* Bloomington, 1985.

Strehlke 1994
Carl Brandon Strehlke. "Fra Angelico Studies." In Kanter et al. 1994, pp. 25–42.

Strehlke 1998
Carl Brandon Strehlke. *Angelico.* Milan, 1998.

Strehlke 1999
Carl Brandon Strehlke. Review of Garibaldi 1998. *The Burlington Magazine* 141 (August 1999), pp. 477–79.

Strehlke 2003a
Carl Brandon Strehlke. "Pedro Berruguete, Paredes de Nava (Palencia)." *The Burlington Magazine* 145 (July 2003), pp. 539–41.

Strehlke 2003b
Carl Brandon Strehlke. "The Princeton *Penitent Saint Jerome,* the Gaddi Family, and Early Fra Angelico." *Record: The Art Museum, Princeton University* 62 (2003 [2004]), pp. 4–27.

Strehlke 2004
Carl Brandon Strehlke. *Italian Paintings, 1250–1450, in the John G. Johnson Collection and the Philadelphia Museum of Art.* Philadelphia, 2004.

Strehlke and Frosinini 2002
Carl Brandon Strehlke and Cecilia Frosinini, with contributions by Roberto Bellucci et al. *The Panel Paintings of Masolino and Masaccio: The Role of Technique.* Milan, 2002.

Strossmayer Gallery 1939
Jugoslavenska Akademija Znanosti i Umjetnosti. *Katalog Strossmayerove Galerije.* Vol. I, *Talijanske slikarski skole.* Zagreb, 1939.

Stubblebine et al. 1980
James H. Stubblebine, with Mary Gibbons, Frank Cossa, Sharon Sitt, and George Chapman. "Early Masaccio: A Hypothetical, Lost *Madonna* and a Disattribution." *The Art Bulletin* 62 (March 1980), pp. 217–25.

Stuttgarter Galerieverein 1950
Frühe italienische Tafelmalerei. Exhib. cat., Stuttgarter Galerieverein, Stuttgart. Stuttgart, 1950.

Sumption 1975
Jonathan Sumption. *Pilgrimage: An Image of Mediaeval Religion.* Totowa, New Jersey, 1975.

Testa 1996
Giusi Testa. "*Et vocatur dictus . . . .*" In *La Cappella Nova o di San Brizio nel Duomo di Orvieto,* edited by Giusi Testa, pp. 26–31. Milan, 1996.

Todini 1989
Filippo Todini. *La pittura umbra: Dal Duecento al primo Cinquecento.* 2 vols. Milan, 1989.

Toesca 1917
Pietro Toesca. "Manoscritti miniati della Biblioteca del Principe Corsini a Firenze." *Rassegna d'arte antica e moderna* 17, 4, part 1 (1917), pp. 117–28.

Toesca 1930
Pietro Toesca. *Monumenti e studi per la storia della miniatura italiana: La collezione di Ulrico Hoepli.* Milan, 1930.

Toesca 1958
Pietro Toesca. *Miniature di una collezione veneziana.* Venice, 1958.

Toscano 2002
Bruno Toscano. "Maestri e compagni tra Orvieto e Montefalco." In Toscano and Capitelli 2002, pp. 57–77.

Toscano and Capitelli 2002
Bruno Toscano and Giovanna Capitelli, eds. *Benozzo Gozzoli: Allievo a Roma, maestro in Umbria.* Exhib. cat., Chiesa-Museo di San Francesco, Montefalco. Milan, 2002.

Trexler 1997
Richard Trexler. *The Journey of the Magi: Meanings in History of a Christian Story.* Princeton, 1997.

Valois 1904
Noël Valois. "Fra Angelico et le Cardinal Juan de Torquemada." In *Société Nationale des Antiquaires de France, Centenaire, 1804–1904: Recueil de mémoires publ. par les membres de la Société,* pp. 461–70. Paris, 1904.

Vasari (Milanesi ed.) 1878–85
Giorgio Vasari. *Le vite de più eccellenti pittori scultori ed architettori.* Edited by Gaetano Milanesi. 9 vols. Florence, 1878–85. Based on 2nd ed. of Vasari of 1568.

Vasari 1911 ed.
Giorgio Vasari. *Lives of Seventy of the Most Eminent Painters, Sculptors, and Architects.* 4 vols. Edited by E. H. Blashfield, E. W. Blashfield, and A. A. Hopkins; translated by Mrs. Jonathan Foster. New York, 1911.

Venchi et al. 1999
Innocenzo Venchi et al. *Fra Angelico and the Chapel of Nicholas V.* Recent Restorations of the Vatican Museums, vol. III. Vatican City, 1999.

Venturi 1911
Adolfo Venturi. *Storia dell'arte italiana.* Vol. VII, *La pittura del Quattrocento.* Milan, 1911.

Venturi 1924
Adolfo Venturi. *L'arte a San Girolamo.* Milan, 1924.

Vespasiano da Bisticci 1963 ed.
Vespasiano da Bisticci. *Renaissance Princes, Popes, and Prelates: The Vespasiano Memoirs, Lives of Illustrious Men of the XVth Century.* Translated by William George and Emily Waters; introduction by Myron P. Gilmore. New York, 1963.

Virch 1962
Claus Virch. *Master Drawings in the Collection of Walter C. Baker.* New York: The Metropolitan Museum of Art, 1962.

Viroli 1980
Giordano Viroli. *La Pinacoteca Civica di Forlì.* Forlì, 1980.

Vitalini Sacconi 1968
Giuseppe Vitalini Sacconi. *Pittura marchigiana: La scuola camerinese.* Trieste, 1968.

Vos and Van Os 1989
Rik Vos and Henk van Os, eds. *Aan de oorsprong van de schilderkunst. Vroege Italiaanse schilderijen in Nederlands bezit. The Birth of Panel Painting. Early Italian Paintings in Dutch Collections.* The Hague, 1989.

Wagner 1974
Hugo Wagner. *Kunstmuseum Bern: Italienische Malerei 13. bis 16. Jahrhundert.* Bern, 1974.

Walpole Gallery 1995
Treasures of Italian Art: Works from the Fifteenth to the Eighteenth Century. Exhib. cat., Walpole Gallery, London. London, 1995.

Warr 2002
Cordelia Warr. "Religious Habit and Visual Propaganda: The Vision of the Blessed Reginald of Orléans." *Journal of Medieval History* 28 (2002), pp. 43–72.

Watson 1971
Paul F. Watson. "Boccaccio's *Ninfale Fiesolano* in Early Florentine Cassone Painting." *Journal of the Warburg and Courtauld Institutes* 34 (1971), pp. 331–33.

Watson 1985–86
Paul F. Watson. "A Preliminary List of Subjects from Boccaccio in Italian Painting, 1400–1550." *Studi sul Boccaccio* 15 (1985–86), pp. 149–66.

Wattenbach 1958
Wilhelm Wattenbach. *Das Schriftwesen in Mittelalter.* 4th ed. Graz, 1958.

Whitman 1991
Nathan T. Whitman. "The First Papal Medal: Sources and Meaning." *The Burlington Magazine* 133 (December 1991), pp. 820–24.

Wickhoff 1892
Franz Wickhoff. "Die italianischen Handzeichnungen der Albertina. Part II: Die römische Schule." *Jahrbuch der Kunsthistorischen Sammlungen der Allerhöchsten Kaiserhauses* 13 (1892), pp. CLXXV–CCLXXXIII.

Wickhoff 1908
Franz Wickhoff. "Die Sammlung Tucher." *Münchner Jahrbuch der Bildenden Kunst* 3 (1908), pp. 21–29.

Wielockx 1998
Robert Wielockx. "Poetry and Theology in the *Adoro te devote:* Thomas Aquinas on the Eucharist and Christ's Uniqueness." In *Christ among the Medieval Dominicans: Representations of Christ in the Texts and Images of the Order of Preachers,* edited by Kent Emery, Jr., and Joseph Wawrykow, pp. 157–74. Notre Dame, Indiana, 1998.

Wildenstein 1978
Twenty Masterpieces from the Natale Labia Collection: A Loan Exhibition in Aid of the City of Birmingham Museums and Art Gallery Appeal Fund. Exhib. cat., Wildenstein & Co., London. London, 1978.

Wilkins 2002
David G. Wilkins. "Opening the Doors to Devotion: Trecento Triptychs and Suggestions Concerning Images and Domestic Practice in Florence." In *Italian Panel Paintings of the Duecento and Trecento,* edited by Victor M. Schmidt, pp. 371–93. Studies in the History of Art, 61. Washington, D.C.: National Gallery of Art, 2002. Proceedings of a symposium held June 5–6, 1998, in Florence, and October 16, 1998, in Washington, D.C.

Wilson 1995
Carolyn C. Wilson. "Fra Angelico: New Light on a Lost Work." *The Burlington Magazine* 137 (November 1995), pp. 737–40.

Wilson 1996
Carolyn C. Wilson. *Italian Paintings, XIV–XVI Centuries, in the Museum of Fine Arts, Houston.* Houston, 1996.

Wolf 1998
Gerhard Wolf. "From Mandylion to Veronica: Picturing the 'Disembodied' Face and Disseminating the True Image of Christ in the Latin West." In Kessler and Wolf 1998, pp. 153–79.

Wolf 2000
Gerhard Wolf. "'Or fu sì fatta la sembianza vostra?': Sguardi alla 'vera icono' e alle sue copie artistiche." In Morello and Wolf 2000, pp. 103–14.

Woodburn sale, 1860
Pictures by the Greatest Early Italian Masters: Comprises Chefs-d'oeuvre of Nearly All the Great Italian Luminaries of Art, from Giotto to Perugino; also, the Reserved Pictures from Mr. [Samuel] *Woodburn's Late Residence in Park Lane.* Sale cat. London: Christie, Manson, and Woods, June 9–11, 1860.

Worcester Art Museum 1974
Worcester Art Museum. *European Paintings in the Collection of the Worcester Art Museum.* Worcester, Massachusetts, 1974.

Wright 2000
Rosemary Muir Wright. "Introduction to the Psalter." In *Studies in the Illustration of the Psalter,* edited by Brendan Cassidy and Rosemary Muir Wright. Stamford, Lincolnshire, 2000.

Wurm 1907
Alois Wurm. *Meister- und Schülerarbeit in Fra Angelicos Werk.* Strasbourg, 1907.

Zampetti 1971
Pietro Zampetti. *Paintings from the Marches: Gentile to Raphael.* London, 1971.

Zangheri 1989
Luigi Zangheri. *Ville della provincia di Firenze: La città.* Milan, 1989.

Zeri 1950
Federico Zeri. "Arcangelo di Cola da Camerino: Due tempere." *Paragone* 1, no. 7 (1950), pp. 33–38.

Zeri 1969
Federico Zeri. "Opere maggiori di Arcangelo di Cola." *Antichità viva* 8, no. 6 (1969), pp. 5–15.

Zeri 1974
Federico Zeri. "Major and Minor Italian Artists at Dublin." *Apollo* 99 (February 1974), pp. 88–103.

Zeri and Gardner 1971
Federico Zeri and Elizabeth E. Gardner. *Italian Paintings. A Catalogue of the Collection of The Metropolitan Museum of Art: Florentine School.* New York, 1971.

Zlamalik 1982
Vinko Zlamalik. *Strossmayerova Galerija Starih Majstora Jugoslavenske Akademije Znanosti i Umjetnosti.* Zagreb, 1982.

Zucker 1975
Mark J. Zucker. "Parri Spinelli's Lost Annunciation to the Virgin and Other Aretine Annunciations of the Fourteenth and Fifteenth Centuries." *The Art Bulletin* 57 (1975), pp. 186–95.

Index

Page numbers in *italic* type refer to illustrations; page numbers in **boldface** type refer to the main entry for a catalogue item, including its illustrations.

Photograph Credits

Abegg-Stiftung, Riggisberg (Christoph von Viràg): fig. 27
Accademia Carrara, Bergamo, Archivio Fotografico : fig. 186
AFS BAPSAE, Pisa: fig. 12
Albright-Knox Art Gallery, Buffalo: cat. 5 D
Alinari / Art Resource, New York: fig. 17, 19, 25
Foto Amoretti / Fondazione Magnani-Rocca, Corte di Mamiano, Parma: fig. 69
Jörg P. Anders / Staatliche Museen zu Berlin, Gemäldegalerie: cat. 32
Ashmolean Museum, Oxford: fig. 77
Museo Bagatti Valsecchi, Milan: fig. 141
Nicolo Orsi Battaglini / Art Resource, New York: cat. 29; fig. 86, 132
Bayer & Mitko, Artothek: cat. 21 C, 21 D; fig. 115–18
Biblioteca Apostolica Vaticana, Vatican City: fig. 13, 14
Benjamin Blackwell: cat. 19
Courtesy, Miklós Boskovits, Florence: fig. 20
Brooklyn Museum: cat. 50
Christ Church Picture Gallery / The Governing Body, Christ Church, Oxford: cat. 42 A
The Cleveland Museum of Art: cat. 15, 40 A
Courtauld Institute of Art Gallery, London: cat. 13 A–C
The Samuel Courtauld Trust, Courtauld Institute of Art Gallery, London: fig. 187
The Detroit Institute of Arts: cat. 20, 25 F, 25 G, 60
Courtesy, Everett Fahy, New York: fig. 21, 22
Foto Matteo de Fina / Fondazione Giorgio Cini, Venice: cat. 34 B, 46 B, 49
The Fine Arts Museums of San Francisco: cat. 25 E, cat. 52
Finnish National Gallery / Central Art Archives: fig. 37
Isabella Stewart Gardner Museum, Boston: cat. 28
The J. Paul Getty Museum, Los Angeles: cat. 16 A, 16 B, 41
Graphische Sammlung Albertina: cat. 22
Hamilton Kerr Institute: fig. 34
Houghton Library, Harvard College: cat. 5 A–C; fig. 18
The Barbara Piasecka Johnson Collection Foundation: cat. 11
Katya Kallsen / President and Fellows of Harvard College: fig. 190
Copyright Kimbell Art Museum, Fort Worth: cat. 25 A
Kunstmuseum, Bern: cat. 7, 35
Erich Lessing / Art Resource, New York: fig. 76
Joseph Levy: cat. 44 A
Lindenau-Museum, Altenburg: cat. 24 A, 24 D, 24 E, 34 F
Allan Macintyre / President and Fellows of Harvard College: cat. 14, 47 H, 47 G
Aldo Mela, Pisa: cat. 33
The Metropolitan Museum of Art, New York, The Photograph Studio: cat. 1 B, 4, 5 E, 8, 10 A, 12 A, 12 B, 23, 25 D, 37 B, 43, 44 C, 46 A, 51, 53, 56, 58, 59, 61; fig 22, 122, 171, 184
The Minneapolis Institute of Arts: cat. 17, 34 A
Musée des Beaux-Arts, Nice/Musée Jules Chéret: fig. 8
Musée des Beaux-Arts, Strasbourg: cat. 54 B
Museo Nacional del Prado, Madrid: fig. 51, 57
Museum Boijmans Van Beuningen, Rotterdam: cat. 6, 47 A–F, 47 I
Museum of Fine Arts, Boston: cat. 36 A, 57
Museum of Fine Arts, Houston: fig. 62
Copyright National Gallery, London: cat. 10 B, 10 C, 21 B, 44 D; fig. 7, 38, 43–45, 133, 185.
National Gallery of Art, Board of Trustees, Washington, D.C.: cat. 34 G; fig. 90, 123, 172
National Gallery of Ireland, Dublin: cat. 34 H; fig. 162
Joshua Nefsky: cat. 2
New York University, Institute of Fine Arts: fig. 16, 32, 33, 35, 36, 60, 131, 135, 140, 146, 148, 156–159, 163–165, 174, 175, 188, 189
Ernani Orcorte / Ministero per i Beni e le Attività Culturali, Soprintendenza per il Patrimonio Storico, Artistico ed Etnoantropologico del Piemonte: cat. 25 I; fig. 92, 173
Philadelphia Museum of Art: cat. 25 C; fig. 142
Preussischer Kulturbesitz, Bildarchiv, Berlin / Art Resource, New York: fig. 65–67, 89, 96
Quattrone Snc: fig. 97–110, 127, 149, 151
Réunion des Musées Nationaux / Art Resource, New York: cat. 30 C, 34 I, 42 B; fig. 39, 40, 74, 129, 130
Copyright Rijksmuseum, Amsterdam: cat. 31 B
The Royal Collection Enterprises: cat. 25 H
San Diego Museum of Art: fig. 10
Scala / Art Resource, New York: cat. 25 B; fig. 1–6, 28, 52, 54, 75, 79, 85, 93, 94, 143, 155
Schweizerisches Institut für Kunstwissenschaft, Zürich: fig. 134, 136
SMK Foto: cat. 1 A, 1 C
Courtesy, Soprintendenza BAPPSAD dell'Umbria–Perugia: cat. 30 B; fig. 87
Soprintendenza PSAE di Parma e Piacenza, Archivio Fotografico, Foto Galloni e Medioli, su Concessione del Ministero per i Beni e le Attività Culturali: cat. 21 A
Soprintendenza Speciale per il Polo Museale Fiorentino, Gabinetto Fotografico: fig. 47–50, 53, 58, 68, 70, 73, 78, 80–84, 95, 111–114, 119, 120, 137, 138, 150, 152, 153, 178–183
Nazario Spadoni, Forlì: cat. 27 A, 27 B
Staatsgalerie, Stuttgart: fig. 37 C
Städelsches Kunstinstitut, Frankfurt / Ursula Edelmann-Artothek: fig. 55
Rick Stafford / President and Fellows of Harvard College: cat. 39
State Hermitage Museum, Saint Petersburg: fig. 11, 144, 161, 166–170, 176, 177
The Sterling and Francine Clark Art Institute, Williamstown, Massachusetts: cat. 54 A
SVO Art, Versailles / Peter Schälchli, Zürich: fig. 41, 42, 139
Thyssen-Bornemisza Collection, on deposit in the Museu Nacional d'Art de Catalunya, Barcelona: cat. 18
Copyright Trustees of the British Museum, London: cat. 26; fig. 72, 154
Vatican Museums, Vatican City: cat. 24 B, 30 A; fig. 9, 88, 91, 121, 124–126
The Wadsworth Atheneum Museum of Art, Hartford: cat. 31 A
Bruce M. White: cat. 9, 45
Courtesy, Wildenstein and Co., Inc.: cat. 40 B; fig. 61
Greg Williams / The Art Institute of Chicago: cat. 34 C
Worcester Art Museum, Massachusetts: cat. 48, 55
Yale University Art Gallery, Digital Media Department: cat. 16 C, 16 D, 37 A, 44 B